NIETZSCHE AND THE
PHILOLOGY OF THE FUTURE

A. T.

2.

3.

27

A page from Nietzsche's notebooks (GSA 71/63, Bl 21 Vs = P I 7, 43). The first paragraph reads: "Aristoxenus erzählt, daß Plato die Schriften des [unleserlich] habe verbrennen wollen. Es gelang ihm nicht. Aber die Zeit, bewältigt vom Christenthum, vernichtete sie. Dies die größte Bosheit des Supranaturalismus" (BAW 3:363). ("Aristoxenus relates that Plato wanted to burn the writings of [illegible]. He did not succeed. But time, overwhelmed by Christianity, destroyed them. This [was] the greatest malice of supernaturalism.")

JAMES I. PORTER

Nietzsche and the
Philology of the Future

STANFORD UNIVERSITY PRESS

STANFORD, CALIFORNIA 2000

Stanford University Press
Stanford, California
© 2000 by the Board of Trustees
of the Leland Stanford Junior University
Printed in the United States of America

Library of Congress Cataloging-in-Publication Data
Porter, James I.
   Nietzsche and the philology of the future / James I. Porter.
       p.   cm.
   Includes bibliographical references and index.
   ISBN 0-8047-3667-7 (alk. paper)—ISBN 0-8047-3698-7 (paper : alk. paper)
   1. Nietzsche, Friedrich Wihem 1844–1900—Contributons in classicism.
   2. Classicism—History and criticism. I. Title.
   B3318.C56 P67 2000
   193—dc21   00-041055

∞ This book is printed on acid-free, archival quality paper.

Original printing 2000
Last figure below indicates year of this printing:
09 08 07 06 05 04 03 02 01 00

Typeset by Robert C. Ehle in 10/14 Janson.

Contents

Preface

This book began its life as a dyslexic reading of Nietzsche (which all readings of him in some sense are). While working on a graduate dissertation on the possible connections between atomism and the development of aesthetic theory in Greek and Roman antiquity, I was dismayed to discover that Nietzsche, in a dissertation of his own, had not only entertained some of the ideas I was experimenting with at the time but had also mistakenly rejected them as impossible (for instance, the idea, which is in fact recorded in antiquity, that Democritus had composed several works on poetry and poetics). It was doubtless this initial irritation that brought me back to Nietzsche's philological notebooks a few years later: I was unwilling to let Nietzsche off the hook. It was only then that I realized that the mistake was mine, not his: Nietzsche *had* accepted these titles as authentic; I had simply read the wrong pages of his notebooks and not those in which he presented his change of mind. Needless to say, it was a great relief to find that Nietzsche's instincts, so sure in so many other instances, had not failed him here after all. And so too, when I finally got round to drafting the pages that led to this book, there was a double pleasure in reliving the discoveries I had felt I was making in my dissertation and in finding them confirmed again in Nietzsche.

The specific idea for the present study arose in a quip I made in passing to Helen Tartar one day and then as a wager that I wonder if I would ever have the daring to make again (though I hope I would). The study, originally written in a white heat of six months, subsequently underwent a number of incarnations and radical face-lifts until reaching its present—and to me still provisional—form. I can well sympathize with Nietzsche's heartfelt plaint and virtual motto, which reverberated in my head from start to finish: "und doch kann ich die schöne Form nicht finden, nach der ich suche." The plan of my original study was to cover the full span of Nietzsche's career, and that is what resulted at the time. It later grew apparent to me, in the course of revisions, that covering the earliest philological stretches alone was enough to try any reader's patience—not to speak of the looming editorial nightmare I was starting to foresee. The project subsequently divided into two, and then into three, now fully autonomous parts whose unity exists only in memory (and in a pilot version of the larger-scale study, an article solicited by Dan Conway in 1990 and published in 1992). Consequently, I have accumulated a number of debts over the years, and I wish to acknowledge some of these here. Recording them now reminds me how friendships established or reaffirmed in the course of one's studies are by far the most important side benefit of scholarship, and possibly its secret raison d'être.

Alina Clej, Eric Downing, and Dalia Judovitz read and reread parts or all of the manuscript as it evolved from the very start, and they provided priceless and unfailing support throughout. These three were my intellectual touchstones and my personal morale-building choir. I am forever in their debt. Alan Code read an early version of the complete manuscript, and his reactions at the time were invaluable to me, as had been Ingo Seidler's before that. Andrew Barker and Thomas Cole generously read the chapter on rhythm in one of its earlier incarnations. Their comments, in addition to saving me from technical errors, reassured me that ancient rhythm is not an area where agreement is likely to be found in the near future. Tony Grafton kindly fielded queries about F. A. Wolf lobbed at him via e-mail. As the manuscript reached its very last stage, Sally Humphreys and Albert Henrichs shared their knowledge of nineteenth-century scholarship with me on specific historical questions, and I was lucky enough to meet Hildegard and Hubert Cancik and to profit from their learning and friendship. Bernd Seidensticker, a gracious host while I spent a year in Berlin as I made the final revisions for this book (and its companion piece on *The Birth of Tragedy*), helped me puzzle out obscurities in Nietzsche's and Wilamowitz's language, to the extent that this was possible. Prior to that, Ernst Behler and Christiaan Hart Nibbrig had lent me not only friendly support but also key advice at a critical juncture, at a time when I was wondering whether to cut the philological material loose from the rest of the manuscript and to publish each part separately. Their advice, which came in unison and which I trusted implicitly, was decisive. Josué Harrari, who refereed the original manuscript along with Ernst Behler, had made a similar suggestion at the time, which later proved right. I deeply regret that Ernst Behler did not survive to be able to see the results. Finally, to Helen Tartar I owe an incalculable debt. Over the course of our acquaintance she showed herself to be the Platonic Form of an editor in addition to a real friend. Initially and always welcoming, she was also the only acquisitions editor I had ever met who had an intellectual theory about her editorial praxis. Her steady encouragement and advice, and her painstakingly detailed comments on portions of the manuscript, were a source of great inspiration to me, for which I cannot sufficiently thank her. Other debts to other individuals, of which there are several, are either mentioned in the notes or tacitly acknowledged by the very existence of this book.

Parts of this study were presented before audiences in Atlanta, Berkeley, Chicago, San Diego, Lille, Heidelberg, Bristol, and Tübingen. I gained immensely from each of these occasions, and am especially grateful to those individuals whose invitations made it possible for these exchanges to take place. Ever since arriving at the University of Michigan I have inflicted my raw ideas about Nietzsche on countless graduate students in comparative literature and classical studies, to whom I owe both thanks and apologies. For generous support, financial and other, I am grateful to the University of Michigan, the Stanford Humanities Center, and the Alexander von Humboldt-Stiftung. My colleagues at Michigan helped to provide an ideal context in which to carry out my work, even when it led me away from classical studies and comparative literature narrowly conceived, above all my program and departmental chairs, Stuart McDougal, Ludwig Koenen, Sharon Herbert, and Deans John D'Arms and Edie Goldenberg. A special word of thanks goes to Chris Powell and the staff of the Humanities Text Initiative and to members of the Interlibrary Loan and Reference Services of Hatcher Library at the University of Michigan, as well as to the staff of the Goethe- und Schiller-Archiv in Weimar, especially Wolfgang Ritschl, Erdmann von Wilamowitz-Moellendorff, and Roswitha Wollkopf, for facilitating my research; and to Elizabeth Berg, Martin Hanft, and others at Stanford University Press, for their editorial assistance. Chris Luebbe and Camilla MacKay helped correct the final page proofs, and Chris prepared the index. I am grateful to both for their meticulous efforts.

Lastly, to Alina Clej I owe the divine inspiration that I should write my second book first. Without her shrewd counsel and, later on, firm prodding, I might never have written this book at all.

I wish to dedicate this study to my family, and especially to the memory of my father, for their nurturing support throughout. Books might get written without families standing squarely behind them, but this one certainly did not.

Abbreviations

German Editions

    KGW *Kritische Gesamtausgabe. Werke*

    KGB *Kritische Gesamtausgabe. Briefwechsel*

    KSA *Kritische Studienausgabe. Sämtliche Werke*

    KSB *Kritische Studienausgabe. Sämtliche Briefe*

    GA *Großoktavausgabe*

  MusA *Musarion Ausgabe*

  BAW *Historisch-kritische Gesamtausgabe. Werke*

  BAB *Historisch-kritische Gesamtausgabe. Briefe*

See Bibliography for further details and for conventions used in citations.

Early Essays and Lectures

    "DW" "The Dionysian Worldview" (1870) *KSA*, 1:553–77

    "ECP" "Encyclopedia of Classical Philology" (1871/1873-74[?]) *KGW* 2.3: 341–437

    "GrS" "The Greek State" (1872) *KSA*, 1:764–77

    "HC" "Homer's Contest" (1872) *KSA*, 1:783–92

  "HCP" "Homer and Classical Philology" (1869) *KGW*, 2.1:248–69

    "IST" "Introduction to Sophoclean Tragedy" (1870) *KGW*, 2.3:7–57

    "OF" "On the Future of Our Educational Institutions" (1872) *KSA*, 1:643–752

    "OS" "On Schopenhauer" (1867/68) *BAW*, 3:352–61

    "OT" "On Teleology" (1867/68) *BAW*, 3:370–71

"PP"   "The Preplatonic Philosophers" (1869/70[?]–76) *KGW*, 2.4:211–362

"PTG"   "Philosophy in the Tragic Age of the Greeks" (1873) *KSA*, 1:801–72

"R"   "Description of Ancient Rhetoric" (1874) *KGW*, 2.4:415–502

"Rückblick"   "Retrospective View of My Two Years at Leipzig" (1867/68) *BAW*, 3:291–315

"SWB"   "Science and Wisdom in Battle" (1875) *KSA*, 8:97–120

"TL"   "On Truth and Lying in an Extra-Moral Sense" (1872/73) *KSA*, 1:875–90 (trans. C. Blaire, in Gilman et al. 1989, 246–57)

"TSK"   "Teleology Since Kant" (1867/68) *BAW*, 3:372–94

"WPh"   "We Philologists" (1875) *KSA*, 8:1–96, 121–27

Works in Translation*

A   *The Antichrist*

"Attempt"   *"Attempt at a Self-Criticism"* (second preface to *BT* [1886])

BGE   *Beyond Good and Evil*

BT   *The Birth of Tragedy*

CW   *The Case of Wagner*

D   *Daybreak*

EH   *Ecce Homo*

GM   *On the Genealogy of Morals*

GS   *The Gay Science*

HA   *Human, All Too Human*

NCW   *Nietzsche Contra Wagner*

TI   *Twilight of the Idols*

UM   *Untimely Meditations*

WP**   *The Will to Power*

Z   *Thus Spake Zarathustra*

---

*Cited by section numbers ("Pref." = Preface; "F" = Foreword).

**Note on *WP*: This posthumous edition of the late fragments is used only for the sake of its convenience of reference for nonspecialists. Incomplete and by no means authoritative (its organization was contrived by its editors), *WP* remains for now the only existing translation of the later Nachlass. Cross-references to the German editions will be found in *Nietzsche-Studien* 9 (1980): 446–90 (a concordance compiled by Marie-Luise Haase and Jörg Salaquarda).

KANT

CJ   *Critique of Judgment*
CR   *Critique of Pure Reason*

SCHOPENHAUER

W   *Die Welt als Wille und Vorstellung*

OTHER

DK   Diels-Kranz, *Die Fragmente der Vorsokratiker*. 6th rev. ed.
DL   Diogenes Laertius, *Lives of the Philosophers*

NIETZSCHE AND THE
PHILOLOGY OF THE FUTURE

Introduction

Friedrich Nietzsche (1844–1900), who was once a classicist before he declared himself to be a philosopher, fits uncomfortably into either disciplinary paradigm. Studied in the past from two exclusive points of view, he has in fact suffered from two forms of inattention. Classicists have for the most part shunned his philology in the wake of his fall into disrepute. As a consequence his early philological writings, preserved mainly in note form (but available in every major edition of his corpus), go largely unnoticed and unread, while readers of his later writings who ignore the earlier materials unwittingly reproduce the prejudice that has clouded Nietzsche's afterlife from within classical studies. Caught in between, and in fact appearing at the chronological midpoint of his life (1872), stands Nietzsche's first and most sensational book, *The Birth of Tragedy*. That book occupies a troubling because uncertain middle ground, with its residues of philological obsession and its questionable philosophical commitments (the allegiances to Schopenhauer and Wagner), all of which are soon, it is either hoped or feared, to be abandoned in favor of a way of thinking that is more original, and in any case more recognizably "Nietzschean." A picture of Nietzsche has in this way formed around the external facts of his career—those of his curriculum vitae—and around the fate of his reception, all built upon a series of exclusions. Classicists who do not get beyond *The Birth of Tragedy* (and even those who occasionally do) and readers of Nietzsche who do not look at the writings prior to 1872 are at least this much in agreement: Nietzsche's first book is almost without exception seen as a departure from his early philological and classical ways. The divided reception of Nietzsche has created a barrier to understanding his thought on both sides of his readership.

My intention in this study is to begin to challenge this polarized picture by retracing the contours of Nietzsche's earliest philological thinking and by opening the way to a fresh view of his later thinking. I hope, in the process, to displace the developmental logic that has been a controlling factor in Nietzsche's reception and to decenter the view that fastens onto *The Birth of Tragedy* as a dramatic turning point in Nietzsche's thought. Stylistically, Nietzsche's first book was a breakthrough of sorts. It is also a unique work, as much so as any other that Nietzsche wrote. Professionally speaking, it was a suicidal work, being a fantastic piece of imagining dressed up in scholarly garb (and self-evidently so). But *The Birth of Tragedy* does not mark a break in Nietzsche's thinking, whether away from his philological understanding of antiquity or toward a gradual emancipation from metaphysics. The view that it does is in fact a mere assumption, given that the work of interpretation needed to unearth and evaluate his early thinking remains a glaring lacuna in Nietzsche scholarship. On the other hand, the very idea of reclaiming Nietzsche for philosophy has problems of its own, given his never-ending polemic with the conventional projects of philosophy. Nietzsche's ways of thinking ultimately exceed both designations. And yet his writings, throughout the entirety of his corpus, remain essentially contaminated by the discourses that he regularly opposes. Nietzsche's writing and thinking are stranger, and more consistent, than they have been credited with being in the past.

It is indisputable that Greek and Roman antiquity remains as central to Nietzsche's thinking in 1888 as it was in 1868. What is less well recognized is that in his later writings Nietzsche continues to treat the same problems that he had treated in his earlier writings, and often in the same ways. Questions about the religion, art, and culture of the classical world are from first to last bound up for Nietzsche with questions about knowledge, culture, history, and the subject. And the reverse is true as well. Nietzsche finds it difficult to separate questions about modernity from those about antiquity at any point in his career. Nor, surprisingly, are the problems of classical philology ever far from his mind, even toward the end of his career, as the second preface to the reissue, in 1886, of *The Birth of Tragedy* shows: "After all, even today practically everything in this field"—the field of philology—"remains to be discovered and dug up by philologists!"[1] What is more (and this is less well known), Nietzsche frequently plunders his philological notebooks from the 1860s and 1870s for ideas that he then carries over, sometimes verbatim, into his later notebooks, or into his later correspondence, or into his published writings, whether to defend or develop them. (The remark just quoted is itself one instance.)[2] Surely if Nietzsche felt he needed to consult his own philological notebooks in later life, so should we.

Few things, in fact, are as illuminating about Nietzsche's mind or as fascinating to read as the prolific early notebooks and correspondence, the many sketches and plans, the unfinished dissertations and studies (for example, on the atomist philosopher Democritus), the essay drafts on Homer and Hesiod, the lecture notes on classical literature and religion, on rhythm and meter, the scattered but ubiquitous reflections on method and pedagogy, and even the proposed title pages and tables of contents (in multiple and varied forms) of never-written works or lectures, all of which were recorded before 1872, let alone those philological notebooks that he continued to fill up, often resuming the earlier notes and sketches, even as he prepared his next two books for publication, *Untimely Meditations* (1873–76) and *Human, All Too Human*, Part I (1878). (Nietzsche resigned from his teaching post in 1879.) Anyone who has read and studied closely any of these earlier documents, or even just one of them—for instance, the essay on "Homer and Classical Philology" (1869)—will never again be able to view *The Birth of Tragedy* as the only key to grasping Nietzsche's troubled relation to the classical heritage and its disciplined study. Anyone who has perused Friedrich Albert Lange's stinging and very much Lucretian critique of classical mythology, religion, and metaphysical beliefs in the opening pages of his *Geschichte des Materialismus und Kritik seiner Bedeutung in der Gegenwart* (1866), a work that Nietzsche knew by heart and adored, will never again feel confident that Nietzsche ever meant his first book, *The Birth of Tragedy*, to be anything other than a mythology that is not to be believed in, any more than the Kantian thing in itself, which Nietzsche problematizes early on, likewise with the help of Langean arguments. These are the materials that will be the subject of the present study. *The Birth of Tragedy*, a work that needs to be confronted in its own complexity, will be touched on only indirectly in this study and directly elsewhere.[3] A subsequent study will take up the later writings and will work out some of the implications that a revised image of the early Nietzsche holds for our understanding of the later Nietzsche.[4] Even so, anyone attuned to the later writings should be able to glimpse in the present book some of the trademark features of the more familiar Nietzsche of the last decade of his career. In fact, it is my hope that the frequent appearance of the "later" Nietzsche in the early writings will be sufficiently disorienting to provoke reflection on the adequacy of our current characterizations of Nietzsche, and not just about the way we continue to periodize his writings.

To read Nietzsche at any point in his career is to plunge into the world of the nineteenth century, of which Nietzsche is both a critic and a specimen. One of his central concerns throughout his career, and one that will be central to this study, was to determine the ways in which philosophy and philology are symptomatic of modern cultural habits, ideologies, and imaginings. Nietzsche may well have outlined the most trenchant model still available for exhuming the ghostly specters of Western society, in the form of a cultural anthropology. An incessant preoccupation with the symptomatology of the modern "subject"—its ailments, its illusions, and the signs of its irrepressible presence—is, I believe, what unifies Nietzsche's oeuvre more than any other single question. But he arrived at this inquiry through a philological perspective, according to which subjective identity is viewed as part of a historical process. Embodied in practices, habits, and institutions, these inheritances, of which classical antiquity is a crucial part, undergo, much like any historical object or text, the vicissitudes of transmission, decipherment, reconstruction, reception, and especially falsification (whether through unwilled or willful misunderstanding):[5] all of these factors are integrally bound up with the ways in which subjects form themselves and are formed in turn. Philology, in other words, gives Nietzsche a deeper sense of the historically contingent nature of inherited conceptions, prejudices, and assumptions and of the cultural contexts in which these flourish. By the same token, philology can be used to expose some of the ahistorical and naturalized assumptions in contemporary culture. Philology, on this view, is the apprehension of a cultural error, or more precisely of a mode of cultural mystification. This would seem to imply a startling fact. Not only is Nietzsche's later so-called philosophical critique of culture an extension of his philology; his later cultural criticism is in ways a form of philology—a form of reading, deciphering, and interpreting, but especially a form of detecting the self-betraying signs of a subject, wherever these may appear, and especially when they seem least of all to be in evidence.

Nietzsche's critiques are no less interesting for first taking shape in the field of classical studies. On the contrary, philology gave Nietzsche an immediate view onto the condition of modernity and especially of the modern German cultural imaginary, which inevitably will be the ultimate topic of this study—that is, the ways in which Nietzsche's contemporary modernity imagined itself, its identity, and its history. Nietzsche's philological writings acquire a different look when they are read as inquiries into a cultural condition that is all the more salient given the stark contrasts that are involved whenever the present is faced with the problems of its own history, of its modernity, and of meaning and mythology in the largest and most vital sense of these words. Nietzsche obtained the insights he did in part simply by observing the habits of classical philologists, his most immediately available "case study" of paradigmatically modern subjects of knowledge, belief, and deception. In a word, Nietzsche practices, and virtually wages, philology as a form of cultural criticism in the years leading up to *The Birth of Tragedy*. Indeed, through philology Nietzsche successfully mounts a ranging (and at times unsparing) critique of his own culture with a profundity that rivals, and even preempts, his later writings. His earliest writings contain the most compelling critique to date of the role of antiquity in the modern world. He has never been more relevant and needed—or more underexploited.

Thus, one of the aims of the present study, beyond offering a reading of Nietzsche's philological thinking, is to reevaluate the traditions within and against which Nietzsche's earliest activity must in any case be understood, the primary interest being not so much the debates that run through his century as the various currents and especially maneuvers that underlie them all (most notably idealism and disavowals of different kinds). Doing so will entail offering a critique of the German cultural imaginary in the spirit of Nietzsche, and not simply contenting ourselves with Nietzsche's explicit statements about these traditions. Hence, this study will feature discussions of his predecessors and successors in philology and in the German tradition of Hellenism, such as J. J. Winckelmann, Wilhelm von Humboldt, F. A. Wolf, August Boeckh, G. Bernhardy, K. O. Müller, F. G. Welcker, U. von Wilamowitz-Moellendorff, and W. Schadewaldt—their wrestlings with the competing impulses of classicism, humanism, and historicism and, above all, with their own location as classicists in the modern world.

My discussions follow the premises of Nietzsche's various critiques of philology. His philology is critical of contemporary culture for the same reasons that it is critical of contemporary philology: the one phenomenon is reflected in the other. Philology, like the objects it would embrace, is seen by Nietzsche to be in the first instance a symptom of modernity; and so too, he finds, philology can be used to diagnose the cultural assumptions of the historical present. This is an insight that is worth preserving even to this day. It reaches beyond the (Nietzschean) commonplace that philology invents for itself an antiquity it can then go on to "discover." What is of even greater interest than the game of "find and seek" familiar from the essay "On Truth and Lying in an Extra-Moral Sense" (1872/73) are the less familiar and far more disturbing mechanisms that facilitate this kind of invention: "*Only insofar as man forgets himself as a subject*," Nietzsche writes there, "indeed as an *artistically creative* subject, does he live with some calm, security, and consistency."[6] This self-forgetting—which is to say, this disavowal—is the actual truth of the lie that defines and even constitutes a subject. Philologists are not only individually submitted to this unconscious agency. Fraught with the memory of the past, which they do not so much remember as *misremember*, their agency is, as it were, the unconscious activity of their culture at large.[7]

Still, one may wonder how classical philology, that hallowed instrument of pure and timeless learning, can become an instrument of cultural critique. Nietzsche thought it could for a number of reasons. Constantly flirting with anachronism, not just in the ways in which philology is practiced but in the very practice of the discipline and in its stubborn attachment to the past, the activity of philology cannot help but be, in Nietzsche's famous phrase, "untimely," standing as it does athwart the present.[8] Philology is thus uniquely situated to throw a strange and estranging light on the present. Second, however untimely it may be, philology is simultaneously a product of the present, which for Nietzsche means the bourgeois present of the post-Enlightenment, or, in less kindly terms, "the culture of philistinism."[9] And so, not only does philology stand in contradiction to the present; it represents the contradictions of the present in their purest form, and in a form that lends itself immediately to critique. Finally, in fulfilling a compensatory function in the ahistorical present (ahistoricity being, Nietzsche will hold, the form in which the present experiences its historicity), philology is an active agent in the construction of modern ideologies—which is to say, the constitutive illusions of modern cultural life. It is in these respects that classical study is quintessentially modern and that its ideology is closely bound up with the ideology of modernity. Modernity, in turn, actually requires the cultivation of antiquity for its own self-definition: only so can it misrecognize itself in its own image of the past, that of a so-called classical antiquity. To sum up, modernity can in effect afford to be ahistorical so long as philology, with its false memory of the past and of its actual place in the present, does the work of historical remembrance for it.[10] A critical philology can undo some of this work.

That said, it is not principally by becoming more historically accurate that philology can work against itself (for merely to approximate to the past would be to disavow the modernity of philology all over again), but rather by turning the intrinsic untimeliness of the discipline to critical advantage. This position, which represents Nietzsche's view from the start, is nowhere more eloquently set out than in the foreword to the second of his *Untimely Meditations* (1874):

> It is only to the extent that I am a pupil of earlier times, especially the Hellenic, that though a child of the present time I was able to acquire such untimely experiences. That much, however, I must concede to myself on account of my profession as a classicist: for I do not know what meaning classical philology could have for our time if it was not untimely—that is to say, acting counter to our time and thereby acting on our time and, let us hope, for the benefit of a time to come.
> (*UM*, II, F)

Standing in a critical relation to both the past and the present, the philologist of the future—foreshadowed in the first instance by Nietzsche himself—can begin to undertake the project of cultural criticism by underscoring philology's conditions of possibility. It can do this by foregrounding what it means to be untimely in the way that philology necessarily is, but also by exposing something of the *impossibility* of philology and its self-appointed tasks (this is its "antinomy"). The program is a decidedly uncomfortable one to assume, for there seems to be no safe place for a practicing critic to stand: "These few [who are entitled to the critical distance afforded by philology] measure our present against antiquity, as critics of the present, and they measure antiquity against their own [modern] ideals, and so are critics of antiquity."[11]

The aim of philology, critically conceived, is not to substitute a more adequate picture of the ancients but to bring out the inadequacies of the one we already have. The criteria of inadequacy here are not objective, as they are in the case of conventional philology. Instead, they are internal and symptomatic. Inconsistencies of argument, traces of projective reasoning, anachronistic touches, motives that are unexpressed and possibly not even understood—such are the telltale signs of an inauthentic and self-deceived image of the past. The critique is in the first instance cultural and psychological, not epistemological in nature, and this focus upon the subject rather than the object of knowledge is likewise a constant in Nietzsche even beyond his Basel days. Throughout his philology, Nietzsche criticizes a doubting subject that claims in fact to know (doubtfulness being both the condition of philology from its inception and a symptom of the contemporary present age). But as with his interest in the transmission of philological errors and illusions, so too here Nietzsche's critique is implicitly, and sometimes outspokenly, directed at the institutions of society through which subjectivity is powerfully mediated. His critique thus has unexpected implications for any analysis of the material production of knowledge and subjects and of modern ideology generally. Consequently, the Nietzsche who emerges from philological writings, very like (I would argue) the Nietzsche of the later writings, is not a philosopher but a critic of culture and its institutions; he is not a free spirit but highly conscious of the delusion that any such freedom can only be; he is not emancipated from cultural forms but reminds his readers of their position as cultural subjects, and of his own as well. Undoubtedly, the question about Nietzsche's calling as a critic of culture needs to be reformulated, starting with the concept of critique itself, which in the light of Nietzsche's practice is far less glamorous than it often seems today. Nietzsche, who inspired so much of contemporary thought, can be summoned once again in order to help revise it.

A closer look at Nietzsche's practice of philology can be revealing, and it can lead to a reappraisal of his later critiques. Philology as practiced by Nietzsche can be broken down into three related activities that shade off into one another. In the first instance, it is Nietzsche's way of submitting the self-assured practices of nineteenth-century classicists (which is to say, classical philology in its institutionalized form) to a withering critique. He was by no means the first to challenge the discipline. Throughout the nineteenth century the legitimacy of the discipline of classics was challenged from beyond its own walls, and it was itself up in arms, debating its own mission and character. Nietzsche was merely entering the fray. The debate is familiar even today. Do classical studies have a future? Can they be sufficiently objective? Is philosophy (today we say "theory") relevant to philology? These issues take an interesting turn in Nietzsche's case, however, because he can be critical of all the parties concerned: he migrates freely among the various sides in the debate, ultimately giving quarter to none.

Gottfried Hermann (1772–1848) is a case in point. Pitting himself against speculative and anachronistic tendencies in philology, Hermann had written in the early part of the century that pseudo-philology of this kind is based on empty "perceptions [*Anschauungen*]," not on what ancient sources say: "To be sure, [the pseudo-philologist] conceives in his mind's eye an antiquity—if not the real one, then at least an imaginary one; if not the old one, then at least a new one"; and if anyone should wish to discover where these "perceptions" really come from, "let him read the moderns, not the ancients."[12] In revenge, Nietzsche would reiterate and also invert Hermann's damning criticism (which was openly directed against August Boeckh). Not only would he recommend that philologists read the moderns in order to appreciate the ancients; it is the philologist who is dreaming and imagining antiquity, with his cherished historical positivism, his naive faith in the ability to reconstruct and grasp the past in its original condition, his hubristic claim to be able to separate the spurious from the authentic with any certainty.[13] Nietzsche's assault touches nothing less than the conditions of possibility that define classical philology. Characteristically, he would make the point not through pamphlets and polemics but through his own practice of philology, which is a vivid illustration of the fact that what makes philological reconstruction possible is (as with Kant's postulate of a thing in itself) the mere possibility of its possibility; it has no other ground than itself.[14] Nietzsche's philology serves to foreground its own conditions of possibility, laying them radically bare, and demonstrating in the process that philology is nothing other than the result of what might be called a "will to philology." It is true that not all of Nietzsche's philology is as radically subversive as this, or at least not always (or visibly) so. And so his more radical philology has an added function: it is self-critical. "I know the philologists, I am myself one."[15]

Second, and this flows from Nietzsche's attack on the philological estab-lishment, philology is a critique of modernity and its self-assurances. For to the extent that philology gives itself its own grounds (of truth, evidence, and validity) it is a fundamentally modern activity. The antiquity it "discovers" is one that it in fact projects. Antiquity is never really known as such; what can be known—and perhaps only known, but not directly acted on—are the projected ideals of a modernity that imagines for itself an antiquity. This projection is what Nietzsche calls an "aestheticization" or "idealization" of the historical past, and he takes it to be a fact about modernity that it can know itself and its past only in this mode of oblivion. Classical antiquity exists for us moderns today in the form of a disavowal. And if completely avowing disavowal lies beyond the reach of possibility, provoking reflection about this very impossibility does not. Hence, cultural critique not only flows directly from a reflection about classical philology construed as a prob-lem. It leads to a generalized disquiet. The goal is not "overcoming" classi-cal antiquity or breeding "hatred" toward it, although Nietzsche occasion-ally maintains the opposite.[16] These attitudes, too, are hopelessly out of reach, for what has to be overcome is idealization itself, and that appears in the end to be as inevitable as culture and indeed synonymous with it.

Instead, Nietzsche directs attention to the compulsive charms of a neces-sary delusion, at the very least with the hope of spoiling some of the easy pleasures of contemplating a remote antiquity. He thus helps us locate some of the precise coordinates of our contemporary idealizations. Or else he points out the greatest delusion of all: the modern myth of its emancipation from its determinants, from the past, and from inherited ideals. To imagine that one has "overcome" antiquity is to engage in a characteristically mod-ern gesture of triumphal self-affirmation: "A completely furious and unbri-dled hatred for philology flourishes wherever the ideal as such is feared, wherever the modern subject falls down in happy wonderment before him-self, wherever ancient Greece is looked upon as a point of view that has been overcome and is therefore entirely irrelevant."[17] This criticism of Nietzsche's from 1869 is tricky. Affecting to defend the idealism of classical philology, he is attacking the idealism of another, more disguised kind, the premise of modernity's emancipation from ideals. Here too, as before, Nietzsche is his own object-lesson, and theatrically so. Irretrievably a creature of modernity, he constructs an antiquity that shares the very same flaws as the antiquity he critiques (classical antiquity as an ideal). Looking ahead, we can see that the taint of being modern is something he will never deny about himself. In his more exhibitionistic moments he will even flaunt it: "I have a subtler sense for signs of ascent and decline than any man has ever had. . . . I know both, I am both" (*EH*, II:1). The early philologist and the later philosopher, both of them shrewd critics of culture and frank assessors of the risks of cultural belonging, are on this score indistinguishable.

Finally, philology comes down to a theory and practice of reading and understanding, a hermeneutics (and in this, Nietzsche is fully in line with nineteenth-century German thinking). Nietzsche does not, as I mentioned, explicitly devote himself to a polemical defense of his view. Instead, he chooses a far more radical path (and in this he is thoroughly innovative): he embodies the theory directly in his writing. This aspect of Nietzsche's philology, which anticipates the way in which his texts will be read (as it were, the philology *of* Nietzsche) is the most difficult to describe and to pin down.[18] It touches the very style of his thinking, which is paradoxical to the core. Some of this paradoxicalness derives from Nietzsche's equation of aesthetic judgment, the only kind available to ourselves, with the act of deception and self-deception (aesthetic values being mere illusions that are unwilled but unavoidable). Some of it derives from the ways in which Nietzsche performatively implicates himself in what he sets out to describe, not always in the ostensible mode of critique. His critique can be avowedly Kantian and post-Enlightenment in style, or it can be concealed by the adoption of the language of the German Hellenists and neoclassicists. Or else it can hide itself in the accepted practice of wild hypothetical speculation mingled in among the tangle of textual critical maneuvers. His critique is addressed, in other words, in the same language as its objects. In each case, deciding on the source of the critique, distinguishing between simulated and "authentic" voices in Nietzsche, can be difficult and sometimes exasperating. To a far greater extent than the things Nietzsche actually says, it is the elusive positionality of his writing, the uncertain location of his voice and his viewpoint, and the possibilities of identification that he opens up, that account for the danger that his writing poses to a reader. Here, the only reliable criteria one can have are a sense of the limits of Nietzsche's daring, of the reach of his self-contradictions, and a faith in his seemingly unlimited critical capacities.

This last criterion is perhaps the most important of all. I believe that no ideas were ever sacrosanct or beyond suspicion for Nietzsche, who embodied a thoroughly critical and (it is too often forgotten) self-critical attitude of mind throughout his career. Critique for Nietzsche is no simple affair. It is complex, conflicted, and ambivalent; it involves the subject of the critique in the object of its critique; and it is layered over with unwanted identifications. In Nietzsche's hands, critique requires first and foremost strategies of posturing and positioning, of staging and voicing. Nietzsche's favorite form of criticism and self-criticism is an effective, if bizarre, compromising of his ideas with their nemeses (whether, say, Plato or Schopenhauer). Nor is this tactic always signaled as such. This, too, is a steady, if overlooked, feature of his writing, from beginning to end. His early writings thus share with his later writings two general features: the substance of his critiques, which can be devastating, and the elusiveness of what they leave in their wake. The early writings also point ahead to another hallmark of his later writings: his theatrical, improvisational talents, his ability to launch himself into a role even when he has arguments against the tenability of the position he adopts. It is this combination that makes Nietzsche so exhilarating to read and so difficult to understand. He is elusive, but no more so than the targets of his critique. To read Nietzsche is to be confronted above all with a problem of identification. It is to engage in a profound crisis of identity.

This crisis of identities is not one that Nietzsche invents. He finds it ready-made in his culture. And it festers in the rhetorical complexities of his writings, which pass into wayward contradiction. Nietzsche's early writings offer an articulation of the unarticulated inheritance of classical philology, and it should not cause much surprise if his way of staging the problems, as in a theater, are as contorted as the dilemmas he sets out to expose. Appearances notwithstanding, his critiques are not directed first and foremost against particular ideals, such as those of Hellenism (whether the ideals of classicism and humanism or of their romantic counterclassical excesses), nor those of the positivistic model of historicism (for example, its concealed humanism and classicism). Rather, they are directed against the gestures that maintain these illusions: the acts of self-deception, disavowal, and self-delusion that actually constitute the ideals in question. Thus, Nietzsche's target in his philological writings is not philology per se but the all-too-human subject of philology, the beholder of antiquity today. And so too, wherever

Nietzsche exposes the incoherencies in the classical philological enter-prise—its inability to project a coherent image of the ancient past, its shun-ning of modernity, and even its contradictory racism and nationalism—Nietzsche is drawing to the surface the fundamental antagonisms, the insoluble foundational logics, and the perplexities of the objects of his cri-tique—which is to say, of the subjects who embody these incoherencies and then vanish into them in the guise of timeless and objective truth. Thus, what emerges from an analysis of Nietzsche's early writings is not only a practice of critique but a theory of subjective identity. Nietzsche's philology, I want to claim, inevitably contains such a theory. It highlights the role that collective agency plays in the construction of cultural fantasies and in the fashioning of identifications (rather than of identities, pure and simple). Of these cultural fantasies, morality is one, history is another—and the truths of classical philology are a third. Nietzsche had these insights from the very beginning of his career, and he recognized, likewise from the beginning, why to have one is to have them all.

Needless to say, Nietzsche has from the start been something of a chal-lenge to the classical philologist. "*Ich bin ein Verhängniss*," he would later pro-claim about himself: not a philologist, let alone a philosopher, but a *fate*.[19] The strange, if divided, fascination that Nietzsche has exercised upon philol-ogists—ranging from repulsion and repression to lingering curiosity (not to speak of unacknowledged appropriation)—seems only to establish the valid-ity of this immodestly premature assertion about himself.[20] A particularly apt example is to be found in one of Wilamowitz's most brilliant pupils, Rudolf Pfeiffer (1889–1979), whose name is virtually synonymous with classical philology in its most rigorous form today. Like most classicists, Pfeiffer is aware of Nietzsche's presence, which is strangely compelling even in its defi-ciency: "I cannot refrain—*pace* Wilamowitz—from mentioning Friedrich Nietzsche, Ritschl's favourite pupil." These words come from the preface to his magisterial handbook, the *History of Classical Scholarship from the Begin-nings to the End of the Hellenistic Age* (1968). Specifically, Pfeiffer cannot refrain from mentioning Nietzsche's earliest plan to write "A History of Lit-erary Studies in Antiquity and Modernity." In Pfeiffer's words, Nietzsche "wanted to find out the general ideas that had influenced the study of antiq-uity and to demonstrate the links between classical scholarship and the dom-inant philosophy of every age."[21]

As we shall see, Pfeiffer's one-line summary barely grazes the mark. How could it do any better than this when Nietzsche goes on in the same set of notes to compare the history of ideas to a "history of drives [*Triebe*]" and to talk about the "imaginary" consistency of all identities and equivalences?[22] But let that pass. Conceding Nietzsche's notes from 1867 to 1871 to be "remarkable" (1872 being the fatal turning point in Nietzsche's career), Pfeiffer dismisses Nietzsche's planned project, which was in its own way a history of classical scholarship rivaling Pfeiffer's, as never fully "worked out" and then abandoned in the name of much darker and more desperate undertakings ("his own fatal philosophy").[23] Nietzsche, evidently, does not fit into Pfeiffer's scheme of *philologia perennis*, or "philology everlasting" and "eternal," namely the view that the undying mission of philology is to encounter "the text as such, its purity, truth, and authenticity."[24] The phrase is a pointed inversion of Leibniz's *philosophia perennis* ("everlasting philosophy"). For Pfeiffer, philosophy and philology are each other's antitheses, and so his inversion is meant to affirm their eternal separation. Whether he can successfully carry out this separation is another question.[25]

Nietzsche's early motto, which he coined in 1869, is likewise an inversion of a phrase borrowed from a philosopher (Seneca), and it likewise addresses the relation of philosophy to philology. Only, now the inversion goes the other way: *philosophia facta est quae philologia fuit* ("what was once philology has now been made into philosophy"). Nietzsche in effect counters Pfeiffer's claim about *philologia perennis* by conceding that philology is indeed "everlasting," but in an exactly opposite sense. If the substance of philology is finite ("The object of the philology of antiquity is in no way endless"—so a note from 1867/68), its task is "inexhaustible."[26] Philology does not uncover the past. It discovers the present in the light of the past's endless futurity. As he writes seven years later in "We Philologists," completing his earlier thought,

> Philology as a science of antiquity is naturally not of an eternal duration; its material can be exhausted. What is inexhaustible is the ever new accommodation of each age to antiquity, the measuring of the present against the past. Give the philologist the job to understand *his* age by means of antiquity and his job will be an eternal one.[27]

Hence the comment, which anticipates by eleven years his remark from the second preface to *The Birth of Tragedy* quoted earlier: "Some think that philology is finished—and I believe it hasn't yet begun."[28]

Nietzsche's philological writings, while they gaze upon the past, are in fact faced toward the present and the future. In his own phrase, which would prove to be fateful but which would also unwittingly preempt his future critics once again, he is constantly in search of "a philology of the future." A letter from 2 June 1868 to his lifelong friend Paul Deussen gives us the phrase for the first time as well as a valuable glimpse into Nietzsche's early attitude toward his discipline:

> You generally will find that most philologists are somehow morally eccentric creatures. This is partly to be explained physiologically, inasmuch as they are compelled to lead a life that goes against nature, to overfeed their minds with a supply of nonsense, to neglect their spiritual development at the cost of their memory and judgment. The rarest commodity among philologists today is precisely a fine capacity for enthusiasm: its sorry surrogate is self-overestimation and vanity. I was pained to hear this about [Jacob] Bernays, whom I am accustomed to consider all in all the most brilliant representative of a philology of the future (i.e., the next generation after Ritschl, Haupt, Lehrs, Bergk, Mommsen, etc.).

Nietzsche will later adopt the etiquette for himself. In his notebooks on rhythm he projects a work that is to begin: "Introduction: The Philologist of the Future."[29] Whatever else Nietzsche meant by the phrase, a philology of the future will entail inquiry into the past as it affects the present. The note from "We Philologists" set off above resumes: "This is the antinomy of philology: *antiquity* has in fact always been understood *from the perspective of the present*—and should the *present* now be understood *from the perspective of antiquity?*"

The notes from "We Philologists" are remarkable not only for what they say but also given the time when they say it. They appear a short three years after the scandal of *The Birth of Tragedy*, which left Nietzsche professionally ostracized, surrounded by a wall of mute hostility, and with a meager handful of students.[30] The myth that Nietzsche more or less abandoned philology with the publication of *The Birth of Tragedy* is plainly wrong, not only in the light of a statement like this but also given the complexity of his views toward antiquity both early and late in his career. And because he could never abandon these early views, Nietzsche could never abandon philology either. On the contrary, the view that he did bears all the marks of an institutional wish-fulfillment. Wilamowitz, after all, believed to the last that he had single-handedly driven Nietzsche out of the profession after publicly pleading with him to do so in 1872 in his pamphlet *Zukunftsphilologie! (Philology of the Future!).*[31] And in 1941, another of Wilamowitz's pupils, Karl Reinhardt, would write, "The history of philology has no place for Nietzsche; his positive achievements are far too few for that."[32] In making the claim come true, and in abandoning Nietzsche, philologists have lost a unique opportunity to enter into a critical reflection on their own profession. The question today is whether philology can ever again reclaim Nietzsche and his most valuable insights.

True, the occasional ally has risen to Nietzsche's defense among classicists, if only to defend Nietzsche against himself, whether by certifying his scholarly talents or, more grandly, by praising his insight into notions such as "the Greek mind" or "Greek thought."[33] The polemical reply to Wilamowitz by Erwin Rohde, a pamphlet facetiously titled *Afterphilologie*, hardly counts. The event and the argument were both orchestrated by Nietzsche himself, and not even the title, which is untranslatable, is Rohde's. (The prefix *"after-"* combines the meanings of "false," "anal," and "post-"; "rearguard" brings out some of the dimensions of the word here.[34]) But even apologies on Nietzsche's behalf fail to keep at bay the reality of his complete apostasy from the projects of classical philology, as these are conventionally conceived. It is doubtful that Nietzsche can be rescued as an acceptable classicist, or even as an acceptable instance of German Hellenism, let alone Graecomania, any more than he can be freed from the charge, first leveled by Wilamowitz, of his eventually repudiating historicism and of willfully misreading his classical sources.[35] Nor can Nietzsche's philology be reduced, approvingly or disapprovingly, to a purely imaginative exercise or a mere deconstructive fantasy.[36] The principal object of Nietzsche's philology at every stage of his professional career was not the Greek mind. It was the modern mind—emblematically, the contemporary German mind—that he wanted, above all, to illuminate. And the same holds, mutatis mutandis, for Nietzsche's more recognizably philosophical writings, however we date their first beginnings, but in any case right down to the last glimmerings of his career, as a separate set of arguments could show and as the present book will suggest in passing.[37]

That said, my purpose in this study is not, or not primarily, to begin to redress the inattention that has plagued Nietzsche's philology. Even if I do believe that Nietzsche's *philologica* can be shown to contain a wealth of insights into the traditional objects of classical philology, I do not mean here to vindicate those insights. I will not be offering an appreciation, in this sense, of Nietzsche's contributions to the study of the classics. What is of interest to me in this book are the wayward aspects of Nietzsche's philology, his departure from conventional philology in the course of his very practice of the discipline—his *Afterphilologie*, if you like, waged in the name of *Zukunftsphilologie*. Boldness and extremity, not regretful conformity, are what most characterize his stance as a philologist, and that is his trademark later on as well. Skeptical of philology and its methods from the very beginning, Nietzsche puts into practice what might be called a skeptical counterphilology. Whatever else it accomplishes, such a counterphilology does not step outside and beyond philology. It is not an emancipation from the discipline, nor is it the enactment of sheer contumacy. On the contrary, what Nietzsche carries out is a far more insidious form of critique. To all appearances assuming the posture of professional committedness, Nietzsche traces in silhouette the ways in which conventional philology erodes its own foundations from within. Thus, Nietzsche's philology, even at its most perverse, is not irreducible to philology in the conventional style. It presents itself rather as a mirror of philology's least wanted features. Above all, Nietzsche's philology brings to light the underlying fantasies of the modern historical imagination, of which the shimmering image of antiquity is merely one of the most attractive and prominent examples.

Given the dilemmas of Nietzsche's position, as he stands within and without his discipline, the most effective way to bring out the inadequacies of philology, he finds, is to repeat them in a visible form. Hence Nietzsche's dissimulated strategies for eliciting, rather than merely naming, contradictions of the sort described above: he literally enacts the dilemmas of contemporary attitudes to the classical past, repeating prejudices, methods, assumptions, and contradictions, often in the guise of proposing alternatives to them, or else (just as deceptively) in place of criticizing them. This makes for tricky reading, but that is part of the point. Nietzsche's critique is, we might say, performatively enacted; it dramatically represents what it critiques, and so makes the problem of philology into an acutely actual one. Philology here suddenly becomes a problem of reading and discerning, of finding one's way through a maze of assumptions, and of finding oneself complicitly in their midst. The sheer positional difficulties that such counterphilology entails, the noncoincidence of voice, meaning, and intention that marks it, are immense, and they have a direct bearing on Nietzsche's general conception of meaning itself—philology in the broadest sense of the word. At the end of the day, he can claim with all due innocence to have done no more than repeat the gestures of his contemporaries, albeit with a certain, telltale hyperbole: their movements are simply better concealed (chiefly, by the norms they incarnate). Antiquity on this approach is not exactly "overcome." The subject is conditioned by history and culture and ineliminable as such. The illusions surrounding classical antiquity are intimately bound up with what a modern subject is. Historically entrenched and culturally reinforced, they cannot be erased but at best can be qualified, remarked on, disqualified, and perhaps made a little less seductive than they otherwise tend to be.

Peering into the antique Greek past, to the extent that we willingly accept (say) Nietzsche's surface narrative of a fifth-century decline, which he did not invent but only adopted and made even more problematic than it already was, we are trapped (or lured) into reading into that past the very features of our own desire: we see ourselves. And yet, the truth of these myths, the myths that Nietzsche retells, is all but imperceptible to the modern reader, due to the inverted form in which modernity appears to itself in them. Nietzsche does model his noble ideal after this airbrushed portrait of the Greeks. And he does represent the archaic aristocratic ideal as permanently lost to history, a loss that can be dated to the movements toward democracy in fifth-century Athens (exemplarily, under the tutelage of Euripides and Socrates). But here, too, Nietzsche is a most unreliable witness to his own meaning: archaic blissfulness is nothing but the confection of the neoclassical and romanticizing view of the aristocratic Greek spirit. It is an assemblage of clichés familiar from Goethe, Schiller, and other eighteenth-century thinkers, as well as from more contemporary sources. To take *The Birth of Tragedy* or any of Nietzsche's models of antiquity at face value is not to misread them (there being no correct and proper way to read Nietzsche's multiply overdetermined writings): it is to fatally misrecognize oneself in them. Antiquity is an imaginative displacement of the present, disguised as not being one. In this way Nietzsche implicates his audience in the displacement all over again. And, between the lines, he offers a shrewd comment on the motives and the mechanisms of the illusionism whereby "classical antiquity" is produced.

The argument I have just sketched out holds consistently across all of Nietzsche's earliest philological writings, from the late 1860s down to *The Birth of Tragedy* and beyond. What it shows is that modernity, on Nietzsche's view, is bound up with a specific set of ideologies, many of which serve to obscure the precisely locatable historical determinants of modernity itself. The blindnesses of modernity express themselves in a presumption of freedom, not only from the past, but from time itself. As Nietzsche is at pains to show, modernity may appear to have invented an antiquity ("so-called classical antiquity"), but modernity did not invent itself. It is in its own way as syncretistic a phenomenon as are the evolving conceptions of the ancient gods traced by Nietzsche in his 1871 lecture on Greek religion. On the contrary, modernity is part of a long chain of effects, stemming from antiquity, that are no less historically determinate or "real" for being retroactively produced or else just retroactively visible.

Modernity—at least on this story about it—is thus as much written by the past as it writes the past that it imagines for itself. The denial of both of these features, of this complex overdetermination, is crucial to the mythologies of modernity. Nietzsche would fully agree with the following remark by Roland Barthes:

> *Now it is when History is denied that it is most unmistakably at work.* . . . The teleology common to the Novel and to narrated History is the alienation of the facts: the preterite is the very act by which society affirms its possession of the past and its possibility. . . . It involves giving to the imaginary the formal guarantee of the real, but while pre-

serving in the sign the ambiguity of a double object, at once believable and false.[38]

The study of the "classics" is the disciplinary equivalent of Barthes's "preterite." It is, or would like to be, the "zero degree" of historical distance, eliminating from sight the very act of historical representation, leaving only the residue, the universal essence of "classical antiquity." Nietzsche's goal in his counterphilology is to remind us of the way in which that residue comes to be produced, of the sheer effort (and denial) that goes into the making of a transparent relation to the past:

> Historical understanding is nothing other than the grasping of certain facts based on philosophical presuppositions. The level of the presupposition determines the value of the historical understanding. For a fact is something that is endless, never fully reproducible.[39] There are only degrees of historical understanding. ("ECP," 344)

To this Nietzsche would also add that grasping facts includes grasping prior historical understandings and the tacitly held philosophical assumptions behind them. An endless regress of facts and their evaluation is inescapable. Nietzsche's philology has something of the same endlessness about it.

As a consequence, Nietzsche's writings are no less easy to characterize before 1872 than they are after that date. One argument implied by this book is that Nietzsche's frames of reference remain constant from 1867 down to his last jottings in 1889. Not only are his themes more or less identical, but his style of positionality is as well. If this is right, then Nietzsche cannot be assumed to have passed from a philosophical naïveté (as if in a "precritical" period) to some emancipated, free-spirited thinking that definitively outgrew the theoretical problems (and not just the philological materials) that he had encountered early on. I doubt that Nietzsche believed in grand emancipatory possibilities at any point in his career. His readings of the Presocratics (Heraclitus, Parmenides, or Democritus) put this beyond doubt for the early period: what these reflections show is something about the inescapability, not just of the category of the subject, but of its idealism—which is always bound up, for Nietzsche, with the subject's infinite capacity for delusion. What we learn is that Nietzsche's inquiries into ancient philosophy do not reveal a premetaphysical thinking that points to a region beyond metaphysics, as is frequently held. On the contrary, Nietzsche's early writings reveal the *inescapability* of metaphysical thinking. Here, one of the few attempts to construe Nietzsche's writings from his "philological" period (in this case, the Presocratics) is paradoxically clouded by the doubtful habits of reading his later writings as (allegedly) antimetaphysical tracts. But as Nietzsche says quite plainly in both phases, early and late, "It is absolutely impossible for the subject to want [and hence, to be able] to see and know something beyond itself: knowledge and being are the most contradictory spheres there are." The "subjective concept" is "eternal": we can never accede to a region "beyond the wall of relations" by which we are conditioned, for beyond these lies merely "a mythical primordial ground of things."[40]

This sense of subjective limits is a constant element of Nietzsche's writing that profoundly conditions and qualifies them all. This is, I realize, bound to be a controversial claim. And although I cannot argue the point out here, I believe that the most basic ingredients of his thinking are all in place well before *The Birth of Tragedy*. It is even arguable that by 1870 Nietzsche had already exhausted the limits of his critical attitudes toward many of the classical problems of philosophy and culture, and that the subsequent writings add little in the way of substance to that criticism, but merely expatiate upon it in new ways. This is not to deny that changes occur in the style and focus of Nietzsche's thought. It is to suggest, however, that these changes never reflect anything more than momentary kinds of requirement, which are always local and strategic. Nietzsche's thought does not evolve; it is ceaselessly *restless*. As a result, and at the very least, his early analyses of philosophy, culture, knowledge, and the subject present us with a tough problem: through his philology Nietzsche arrives at positions that put into doubt his later positions, many of them central. But to establish this would require a study of a much greater scope than can be offered here; it would require a revised view of what is commonly taken to be Nietzsche's philosophy from the later period. At best, I hope to lay the groundwork for such a larger assessment.

Retracing the steps by which Nietzsche acquired this apprehension of philology will be the subject of the first two chapters, which take up Nietzsche's changing attachment to philology as a method of reclaiming historical materials, and the infusion of a special brand of Kantianism that he absorbed from a reading of Friedrich Albert Lange's critical *History of Materialism*. As it happens, Nietzsche acquired these lessons in the course of researching and sketching out a never finished "dissertation" on Democritus, the Greek atomist of the fifth century B.C.E. It is through the unlikely marriage, in 1867, of materialism and a "skeptical" philology, a story that remains mostly untold, that Nietzsche discovered how both could be used as tools for critically interrogating the metaphysical tradition from Parmenides to Plato, Kant, Schopenhauer, and beyond: how they might overturn the "hatred for physicists and physicians" (the materialists) that had been cultivated for centuries in the West. Democritus himself provides a model for such a critique. Reconstructing Democritus philologically is a complex and critical act of negation and affirmation that allows Nietzsche to keep the moves of atomism afloat as a strategic counter to the metaphysical, silent reading of Democritus, even after Nietzsche has refuted the assumptions of atomism on logical grounds but validated them as a heuristic strategy. Nietzsche's skeptical philology and his rescue of Democritus from the philosophical tradition are of a piece. Together they stamp his outlook for years to come.

This story about the two faces of his philology, his skeptical doubting of certainty and his reinvestment of doubts with a poeticizing belief, furnishes the complementary topics of chapters 1 and 2, respectively. On the one hand, Nietzsche's turning of his own brand of philology against itself is an instance of (as it were) the "will to philology." It has roots in the "Pyrrhonism" that lies at the origins of the philological tradition, which was involved from the very first in the difficult activity of authenticating texts without ever jettisoning the precious and scarce commodity of the past, and thus took the form of a tradition composed of first- and second-order doubts—of doubts, and of doubts about doubts. In its modern form, philological doubt develops into a disciplinary habit and a sign of professional prestige, into what has been called "negative criticism," which designates the unrelenting focus on errors, on inconsistencies, and on weaknesses in the evidence—into "a preference for error over truth."[41] Nietzsche's philology as a rule is a demonstration of these excesses within conventional philology and of the tenuousness of its results. His writings are conscious provocations that bring themselves to the brink of credibility. He "exhausts" traditional philology by identifying with its inner perversity. But Nietzsche's practice of a doubting and self-doubting philology has a further paradigmatic value: it is proof of his identity with his age. Philologists are prototypes of the modern soul, whose current disease is to be doubtful of itself. Nietzsche never changed his view about this larger cultural diagnosis. If in 1867/68 he could hold that "doubt now seems as morally correct as belief formerly did," in 1872 he could give an account of "today's" recipient of *Bildung* as one who is thrown into a chaos of emotional states, among which figure skepticism and doubt, alternating with elation, hope, and despair, all of these concealed by "that sublime illusion of ["academic"] freedom." A decade on, he will resume his ambivalent analysis of the "diseased" and "self-doubting present,"[42] and then, characteristically, will enjoin "a *duty* to suspicion today" upon anyone who would transcend the limitations of her culture (so as to move "beyond the bourgeois world") and would combat its most basic malaise.[43] Is critique a cure or a symptom? That is the uncertainty that plagues the later works, and it colors Nietzsche's earliest philology as well. The logic of philology entails that philology must work against itself; the critical act is caught in its own self-reflection; positive knowledge is forever banished. Skepticism directed finally against itself thus has an air of desperation about it: it points to the limits of cultural and critical possibilities. Nietzsche's writing, in both phases, performs these acts of desperation theatrically.[44]

Nietzsche's encounter with the atomist philosopher Democritus is of capital importance, not only to Nietzsche's evolving stance toward the claims of philology or philosophy, but to his very style of thinking. Nietzsche trades heavily on the critical potentials of atomism. To recuperate the doctrine from its fragmentary remains is inevitably to recuperate some of its critical force, but what will be of interest to us here is not so much the extent to which Nietzsche annotates the critical potentials of atomism during these early years as the way in which his own approach to antiquity tacitly comes to assimilate the traits of atomism conceived as a model of intellectual subversion and, more broadly, of cultural critique. In a word, Nietzsche's philology transforms itself into an instrument of demystification that can be directed, in the spirit of Democritus, at contemporary myths, starting with those that enshroud the philological discipline itself. Indeed, it is through the very form of his philology (in the first instance, his choosing to concentrate—with a certain abandon—on the atomistic hypothesis) that Nietzsche accomplishes one of his major goals: destruction of the classical ideal. Starry-eyed notions as to what is "classical" about classical antiquity can hardly withstand the rebarbative spectacle of atoms jostling one another in the void, which Nietzsche is more than glad to put in the full view of his imagined readers and occasional lecture students. "What," he asks at one point, as if addressing the objection to himself, "does Greek corpuscular theory have to do with the meaning of life?"[45] There is nothing here to justify the classicizing vision of "'Greek harmony,' 'Greek beauty,' 'Greek cheerfulness,'" that "ineffectual rhetoric of beauty" that had ruled Germany since the generation of Winckelmann and Humboldt in the previous century and even during the more recent surge of historicism. Nietzsche castigates this latter, together with his contemporary culture, as "our present cultured historiography," finding neither to be cultured or historically minded, but merely presentist in disguise.[46]

Nietzsche's philology, by contrast, is frequently motivated by a distaste for all forms of classicism, indeed by a wish to challenge its pernicious hold over the modern imagination.[47] And while it is true that his desire to confront his contemporaries with the spectacle of atomism was exceptional in his day (atomism hardly being the staple of German Hellenism, let alone of classical philology), what is of even greater significance are the anticlassical methods he acquires along the way. Through his contact with Democritus, Nietzsche schools himself in the nature of imaginative investments and disinvestments, in the exposure of such identifications, in the rhetoric of shock, and in the construction of conceptual systems and especially scenarios that collapse within and upon those who construct and behold them. These are the very techniques and strategies that arguably will come to typify Nietzsche's later critiques of the commonplaces of modern German and European culture; but they are the all-too-neglected hallmark of his philological writings as well. And since classical philology is the medium through which the youthful Nietzsche finds those commonplaces distilled, it is only natural that he should set about combating them where he finds them, and in philological ways. That, at least, is how things go until the mid-1870s, his last scholarly publication appearing in 1873 (the second installment of an article that had appeared three years earlier).[48] At that point he finally broke free of the constraints of philology and began his search for a more expressive and more public medium, a need that the *Untimely Meditations* (1873–76) and then the aphoristic collection *Human, All Too Human* (1878–1880) would begin to fulfill.[49] But it should be stressed that this shift, which is from one set of constraints to another, is primarily a shift in genre and style rather than of method and object.[50] Nietzsche's evolution is in the first instance of a writerly kind, or perhaps more accurately, it is one of decibel: his writings merely get shriller, while their ironies become harder to overhear. And yet his target, at every stage of his career, remains constant: it is the various fascinations that afflict the contemporary German mind.

The story of Nietzsche's involvement with Democritus has been a matter of near total neglect.[51] This is to be explained, in part, by the inaccessibility of the relevant materials, which remain incompletely edited, not to say untranslated (like all of Nietzsche's juvenilia, a new edition has been promised).[52] These problems notwithstanding, there has long been a mass of material ready to evaluate, and its neglect is astonishing. One should have thought, for instance, that the bare fact of Nietzsche's involvement with Greek Presocratic philosophy, and especially Democritus, would be sufficient to have at least aroused some interest in the possible relevance of that culminator of the Presocratics, Democritus, to Nietzsche's later philosophical outlook ("Our current way of thinking is to a high degree Heraclitean, Democritean and Protagorean" [1888][53]). As for his earlier outlook, no argument is needed: "Democritus," Nietzsche once proclaimed, "is the only philosopher who is still alive today" (1867/68).[54] This neglect by scholars is all the more surprising given the intense interest that Nietzsche consistently showed throughout his career in the problems of materialism—problems concerning the body, the senses, materiality, and the issue of efficient causality, not to mention atomism proper. The latter is not only an explicit topic in the last writings on the will to power. Nietzsche's later theory can in fact be shown to have encompassed some form of atomism in its own formulation—most centrally, in the notion of *Kraftatomen*, or atoms of force, will, and power, which are the notional constituents and agents of the will to power.

Nietzsche's fascination with materialism is, however, deeply ambivalent. The world for Nietzsche is at no point in his writings reducible to anything, let alone to its material substance or shape. On the contrary, the world is irreducibly complex, fraught with meaning, and a battleground of conflicting and irreconcilable understandings. Matter is a deeply problematic category, one of reality's many questionable reductions. Reality may or may not be constituted by matter, but the very category of matter (substance), like that of reality, is bound to be contaminated by our experience of the world.

And so, although partial to the atomistic cause, Nietzsche is not a material-ist; he is at best a strategic materialist (when it suits him to adopt the pose). His inquiry into ancient materialism is thus not about the body but about *the body lost* and yet forever disturbingly proximate.[55] The project is undertaken without a hint of romanticism or nostalgia. Democritus is for Nietzsche the paradigmatic instance of the *problem* of materialism, both philosophically and culturally.

Atomism tends to be remembered by Nietzsche chiefly in the form that Democritus gave it: Epicurus, the epigone and heir to atomism, is "naiver, idyllic, grateful," less representative of physical atomism and more repre-sentative of a softer, moralizing demystification ("Democritus lived a fabu-lously simple life; Epicurus' life appears to be an imitation"[56]). A harsh critic of his atomist predecessor, Epicurus receives little notice in the early notes and tends to be assimilated to the Christian scourging of Democritus' pagan ideas, both early and late in Nietzsche's corpus. Democritus is not assimil-able in any form to Christian ideology, though Epicurus plainly is (*"Epicure-anism* in *Christianity"*[57]). In contrast, Epicurus' contemporary Pyrrho, the full-blooded skeptic, "harks back to Democritus *via* Protagoras" and leans toward "nihilism."[58] But the relationship between Democritus and Epicurus is complex (they can be assimilated to one another as well), and it will be touched upon in several places below. Atomism, in any case, is not a mar-ginal phenomenon in Nietzsche's thought; it is one of his enduring and defining obsessions. That, however, is another story. Our interest here is with his early obsessions.

Nietzsche takes away from his studies on Democritus much more than an insight into a largely lost philosophical system, let alone a determination of the authenticity of Democritus' titles (which was the initial impetus of his project). He discovers how philology can function as a form of cultural crit-icism in the modern age. Detailing some of the ways in which Nietzsche begins to realize this project of criticism on the heels of his *Democritea* is the focus of the next two chapters. Chapter 3 discusses Nietzsche's lectures and notebooks on classical rhythm and meter (1870–72). The premise and con-clusion of these rarely analyzed notes is the incommensurability of ancient and modern sensibilities to time. It was Nietzsche's original intention to include in *The Birth of Tragedy* a section devoted to rhythm. In its place we find a few stray comments on rhythm (mainly in connection with Apollo), but also implicitly a wholesale and covert adaptation of Nietzsche's thesis from the lecture notes, which throws into profound doubt any straightforward reading of the later work, and in particular any reading that wishes to view the Dionysian as a valorized physiological or metaphysical condition, and not as an allegory for a dubious idealism retrojected from the present onto antiquity. This is hardly the only instance in which Nietzsche's early notes undermine the narrative premises of *The Birth of Tragedy*. Tracing some of the ways in which his notebooks challenge the surface design of this later work will be a secondary motif of the present study.

What the notebooks on rhythm purport to give is "a history of sensations," and especially of the sense of time. This history Nietzsche finds to be irrecuperable, inasmuch as the modern sensibility to dynamic rhythm, based on accentual measures, is incapable of appreciating the ancient sense of time, which is quantitative and proportional in its architectonics. Again, Nietzsche is exploring the paradoxes of classical philology, and so his theory is as much a metacritical one as it is a positive (albeit skeptical) contribution to the history of an ancient field. At stake in the background to these early essays and sketches are theoretical reflections on temporality, history, and sensation, as well as the relation between force and force's limits. These inquiries flow directly into *The Birth of Tragedy*, into Nietzsche's general conceptions of historiographical and recuperative writing (evident most prominently in a text like the famous second essay of *Untimely Meditations*, "On the Uses and Disadvantages of History"), and eventually into the late doctrine of "the will to power."

Chapter 4 treats another lecture course, the "Encyclopedia of Classical Philology," which was first offered in 1871 and possibly again in 1873. If the notes on rhythm seem to fulfill Nietzsche's later momentary musing upon the idea that "it would be *a task*: to characterize Greek culture as irretrievable"—that is, as "unrepeatable [*unwiederbringlich*]"[59]—a task that squares rather badly with the ostensible aim of *The Birth of Tragedy out of the Spirit of Music*—the lecture course on classical philology goes to the other extreme. Intended as a protreptic to the study of philology, the "Encyclopedia" is a passionate plea for complete immersion in the past: "We want to grasp the [classical] phenomenon at its highest level and to grow with it." For this reason, "*Hineinleben* is the goal." The "Encyclopedia" lectures do not merely stand diametrically opposed to the lectures on rhythm from the previous semester. In their advocacy of German classicism they make a jarring contrast with *The Birth of Tragedy*, the anticlassicist biases of which are obvious, despite the qualified praise showered there by Nietzsche upon his classicist predecessors, Winckelmann and Goethe.[60] In the lectures, heavy doses of Winckelmann, Lessing, Schiller, Goethe, and Kant are recommended to aspiring philologists as a prerequisite to the study of antiquity. How immersing oneself in modern German classicism is supposed to square with the goal of immersion in classical antiquity is a central interpretive problem posed by the "Encyclopedia," and this will be at the heart of the discussion in chapter 4.

Clearly, if one were to consider just these materials alone, one would be hard-pressed to give a rational explanation for Nietzsche's zigzags between 1871 and 1875. Classicism and anticlassicism, statements about the recuperability and the irrecuperability of antiquity, anachronism and antiquarianism all sit side by side, with little hope of resolution. How can we make sense of Nietzsche's contradictions? How consistent, indeed, is his project of envisioning antiquity? And given the surrounding lecture materials and notebooks, how definitive a statement is his *Birth of Tragedy*? Nietzsche's posture in his "Encyclopedia" is anything but straightforward, any more than are the contradictions native to classicism itself. Nietzsche is constantly pressing the question of philology's precarious commensurability to its objects. ("I fear that we do not understand these Greeks in a sufficiently 'Greek' way.")[61] Demonstrating this is the aim of chapters 1 through 4, the purpose of which is to lay the groundwork for an assessment of Nietzsche's overall views toward antiquity, both early and late, in chapter 5.

Chapter 5 confronts the question that the vacillations toward antiquity exposed in the foregoing chapters collectively raise. I argue against the widely held assumption that Nietzsche's vision of classical antiquity is more or less consistent, starting with *The Birth of Tragedy* if not before—the assumption that Nietzsche's antiquity is consistently anticlassical, steeped in images of terror and horror (in contrast to the ossified Greek "serenity" of classicism), and committed to a preclassical, archaic focus (Greece of the sixth and early fifth centuries). Against this consensus view, I believe that Nietzsche's stances toward antiquity are more like postures than fixed positions. They are provisional. They shift according to the occasion and in response to changing materials and problems. They are provocative and paradoxical. And they in no way lend themselves to a reduction either to one

another or even to themselves. Quite the contrary, his positions are constitutively and profoundly evasive.

To illustrate the point, a broader spectrum of the early writings is sur-
veyed in this final chapter. Materials from Nietzsche's earliest philology are
revisited (his writings on Homer, Hesiod, and the Presocratics, or rather
"Preplatonics" as he prefers to call them), while other contemporary materials are adduced for discussion for the first time (for example, his studies on
Theognis of Megara). The range of materials discussed also widens.
Included now are philological materials postdating *The Birth of Tragedy* (the
essays on contest culture in ancient Greece, "Homer's Contest" and "Science and Wisdom in Battle"; the critique of the profession, "We Philologists"); section 9 of *The Birth of Tragedy* itself (on Prometheus and the
Aryan/Semitic myths of mankind's fall or ascent into its own condition); and
later forays into Dionysianism, Apollinianism, and Epicurus (who, significantly, can represent either tendency, Aryanism or Semitism, pagan virtue or
decadence and Christianity). This selective reading attempts to show how
highly contestable the assumption is that Nietzsche's vision of antiquity, at
any point in his writings, is either consistent or coherent.

Nietzsche's vacillations are meaningful, even sought-after by him. He
makes them into an intellectual trait that will imprint itself on his writings
for years to come. "Only certainty is terrible," he once wrote to Deussen (4
April 1867). And nothing is more uncertain than the polychromatic and
shifting perspectives of Nietzsche's writings at every phase of his career. But
in order to understand how his vacillations are meaningful and not merely
idiosyncratic, one has to take into account the background from which
Nietzsche's various versions of antiquity in fact emerge: the nineteenth-
century German debates over classicism and historicism, which in turn need
to be viewed in relation to their origins in the later eighteenth century and
their subsequent developments in our own century. The most concealed
aspect of this tradition—and it is one tradition, in dialogue with itself—is the
commitment to the classical ideal that is incarnate in the "classical" object of
philology itself. It is true that in the century after Winckelmann and Humboldt the desire on the part of classicists to be philological issues in a flight
into historical *realia* and away from an earlier humanism and idealism. And
yet this trend toward so-called historicism notwithstanding, the problematic
pursuit of "the idea of antiquity *an sich*," viewed as a self-contained totality,

gets perpetuated in another form.[62] "The Germanic love affair with the South," as Nietzsche calls the desirability of the classical past, is in no way impaired during the phase of philology's industrialization in the nineteenth century. Nietzsche's philology, from first to last, often seems designed to elicit and then to embarrass the inconsistency of these postures and practices within philology.

Much more could and should be said. This study does not pretend to give a complete reckoning of Nietzsche's philology, or of its extensions, or even of Democritus as he appears in Nietzsche's later writings. It is not my intention to exhaust the topics at hand. I have not touched on his lectures on Plato, or the remaining Presocratics, or his treatments of the fifth-century sophists or the later Cynics, except in passing and as seemed relevant.[63] Nor do I discuss his lectures on Greek religion or literary history or on Latin grammar, not to speak of his theory of language and rhetoric that he develops in 1874, which is one of the relatively few aspects of his philology to have drawn any appreciable notice from students of his later writings. (In return, Nietzsche's earlier theory of language, which he develops in connection with atomistic physiology and then in connection with Greek rhythm, *is* discussed in this study.)[64] Any of these topics would make a suitable point of entry into Nietzsche's philological thinking. I have merely taken up a few of the connecting threads of Nietzsche's early philology, many of which happen to have a long afterlife in his subsequent writings. Particularly to be regretted is the exclusion of the fascinating note material from 1869/70, which brings about a collision of Schopenhauer and atomism, or the notes on temporal atomism from 1873, which will be briefly alluded to in chapter 3 and discussed in greater detail elsewhere. Nietzsche's philology develops in tandem with his philosophical thinking, as is illustrated by the notes on Kantian teleology to be discussed in chapter 2. But what is even more significant (and still less understood), his philological and philosophical thinking develops in the form of highly speculative scenarios that expose their various subject matters alongside the modalities of their postulation (whether the starkly reduced settings of Democritean atoms or the primary antagonisms of forces and quantitative barriers in the lectures on rhythm). It is these scenarios, the staging of conceptual possibilities in a quasi-allegorical way, that matter more in the end to Nietzsche's thinking than either philology or philosophy. This construction of arguments by way of staged *Ur-*

settings is essential to understanding Nietzsche's purported "genealogical" narratives of births and declines in the later writings. I hope at least to provide a glimmering of this potential here.

Looking ahead, I believe we can say that Nietzsche's late writings substitute for the myths of philology an even more transparent set of myths—those of his own making (his theoretical fictions of the Overman, the will to power, the idea of an uncontaminated genealogical analysis, self-overcoming, and so on). Nietzsche's later writings not only convey an explicit critique of culture. They also perform a subliminal critique, along the lines described in this Introduction. Subtly repeating the very errors of logic they attack, his writings are fashioned as a trap, luring readers, performatively and demonstratively (in part through Nietzsche's own example), into the hidden recesses of their own subjectivities, their culture, and their conceptions of history. This is what any philology of the future will require. Nietzsche's relevance will continue to be guaranteed, it is fair to say, so long as his works continue to "work" upon readers, luring them into construing his positive meanings—which is to say, so long as they lure readers into producing misreadings of his texts and of themselves. Judging from the way in which they continue to be read, it is doubtful that his writings have outlived their usefulness. Nietzsche's writings thus become more than a matter of textuality; they become a mirror of the reader. *Ich bin ein Verhängniss*, he could justifiably claim about himself—not a philologist or a philosopher, but a fate: our fate.

CHAPTER I

Skeptical Philology

So far as concerns the authority of the tradition, I implore you to be as free with your thoughts as you can be.

—NIETZSCHE TO DEUSSEN, APRIL/MAY 1868

In the summer of 1867, Nietzsche embarked on a project that in many ways would prove to be a decisive turning point in his career. This was his first extended, but by no means final, engagement with the shadowy Greek philosopher from the fifth century B.C.E., Democritus of Abdera (ca. 460–380 B.C.E.).[1] From one perspective, it might appear as if all his philological training and prior studies at the Naumburg Gymnasium, Schulpforte (1858–64), then at the universities of Bonn (1864–65) and Leipzig (1865–69, with the interruption of a brief spell of military service and a subsequent convalescence), had led up to this moment, which was virtually one of conversion. Nietzsche's mind was always of a speculative cast, as some of his first and astonishingly precocious outpourings from the early 1860s testify. But despite the fact that classical philology in Germany was suffused with philosophical speculation (inspired variously by Kant, Friedrich Schlegel, Schleiermacher, Schelling, and Hegel), philosophy and philology were not traditionally part of the same pedagogical matrix in the German curriculum, and so the two pursuits tended to remain separate ingredients of Nietzsche's initial formation[2]—that is, until the moment of their sudden convergence, in the form of his encounter with the atomist Democritus.

Nietzsche's earliest scholarly passion was not philosophy but the sixth-century moralist and elegiast Theognis of Megara, a Greek aristocrat whom Nietzsche could occasionally liken to a Junker and berate as "mindless."[3] The study, begun at Pforte and completed in Leipzig, earned him favorable recognition from the eminent classicist Friedrich Wilhelm Ritschl (1806–1876), who quickly took the promising young talent under his wing and encouraged him to complete the essay for publication in *Rheinisches Museum für Philologie*, which at the time was edited by Ritschl (the article appeared in 1867). Looking back in 1868 upon his initial interview with the learned scholar and his eventual mentor from Bonn (and later Leipzig), Nietzsche would see it as "the moment of my birth as a philologist" ("Rückblick," 300). This was also the way it looked to him two decades later: "one day I was suddenly a philologist" (*EH*, III:9).

Subsequent studies brought Nietzsche's conception of philology to a swift maturation. As his interests in contemporary philosophy deepened (chiefly in Schopenhauer and Kant), the focus of his philological research shifted accordingly. Alongside his forays into Aeschylus, the Greek lyric poets, Homer, Hesiod, and the Suda (a Byzantine lexicographical source, and a mine of information for all Greek literature), Nietzsche developed an interest in the third-century C.E. epitomizer of Greek philosophers and their lives, Diogenes Laertius. The three studies on Diogenes that resulted and were published in 1868/69 and 1870 are often held to be Nietzsche's most substantial and lasting contributions to philology.[4] But his mind was ambitiously racing toward larger goals. There was, for instance, a plan to survey comprehensively the history of Greek literature (in the widest sense of the term) from a fresh perspective and with a new method. This became more or less the guiding ambition of Nietzsche's philological enterprises until his final departure from university life in 1879. More immediately and concretely, Nietzsche's hope was to produce a complete reappraisal of the history of ancient philosophy, based on its transmission by the ancients ("Diogenes Laertius, Stobaeus, ps.-Plutarch, etc.," letter to Rohde of 16 June 1869). The work was to have included critical editions of texts with commentary and was to have been coauthored by Hermann Usener, who later went on to edit the corpus of Epicurus, and who would observe publicly about the author of *The Birth of Tragedy* that he was *wissenschaftlich todt*, "finished as a scholar."[5] Privately, Nietzsche could deprecate Usener for being "a well-intentioned Biedermann with no special talent."[6] Needless to say, nothing came of the plan, like so many of Nietzsche's projects during these years. Strangely, Nietzsche's early career, brilliant in its ambitiousness, is marked more by what he did not achieve than by what he did. That career is, however, best viewed as dotted not by false starts but by false endings. In a real sense, Nietzsche never decisively renounced any of his plans. He simply found other ways to give them expression.

Meanwhile, closely linked to the studies on Diogenes Laertius, another project was fermenting in Nietzsche's mind and in his notebooks, focused for the first time around an ancient philosopher and involving nothing less than the wholesale reconstruction of a single philosophical system: the atomism of Democritus. The incentive was doubtless Nietzsche's discovery of Friedrich Albert Lange's just-published *History of Materialism* (1866), in which Democritus is featured as a cornerstone of the Western philosophical tradition down to Kant and into the nineteenth century. Nietzsche was enchanted with the book and its complex thesis (it expounded a revision of Kantianism that rendered Kant compatible with a version of physical materialism). Evangelical letters were penned to friends over the next two years, urging them to convert to Lange. Nietzsche rated the *History* "the most significant philosophical work of the last decades," and claimed an intellectual self-sufficiency on the basis of Kant, Schopenhauer, and "this book by Lange" alone: "I need nothing else" (letter to Mushacke, November 1866). As a token of his gratitude, Nietzsche intended to send Lange a copy of his dissertation on Democritus once it was finished. It never was. Even so, the *Democritea* project fills a fair proportion of Nietzsche's notebooks for the next two years, from the late summer of 1867 (already a first stab at an essay) to the spring of 1869, and (evidently) again in 1870, although the overlap with the study of Diogenes Laertius and his sources, which was an ongoing project during these years, can at times be so complete that either set of notes can count as evidence for the other.[7] A study on Kant's notion of teleology, begun in April 1868, came on the heels of the *Democritea* project, only to be abandoned soon afterward. Nietzsche could not be bothered with Kantian finalities.[8] He was following the dictates of another teleology, one that was obscure even to himself, though it was his own: "I am noticing how my philosophical, moral, and scholarly strivings are tending toward *one* goal; and that I—perhaps as the first of all philologists—am achieving wholeness" (letter to Deussen, February 1870).

The same thought is used to close his fascinating inaugural speech from May of 1869, "On Homer's Personality." The speech, later privately published as "Homer and Classical Philology," was delivered at Basel, where he assumed his first university post. But on this ceremonial occasion Nietzsche seems to have been announcing a program that would lead not to an *Antritt* but to an *Austritt* from philology, that is, to a complete departure from the discipline. In a moment of what he called a "confession of faith," Nietzsche made public "the goal of a philologist's striving"—the philologist exemplarily in question being himself. The gist he disclosed in a brief and deliberately memorable credo (reversing a saying of Seneca's, and thus inverting his relation to at least some of his audience—it was, to his elation, a full house): *philosophia facta est quae philologia fuit*, "What was once philology has now been made into philosophy."[9] The reduction is indicative but problematic, as is the program at which it aims—namely, the encompassing of philology within a philosophical Weltanschauung, "whereby everything separate and individual vanishes into thin air, a thing to be rejected, while only what is whole and unitary remains" ("HCP," 268–69).[10] It is an odd conclusion, especially in view of the body of the essay, by which it is utterly betrayed. One cannot help but imagine Nietzsche reveling in the stir his confession must have caused in his audience (in a letter to his friend and fellow classicist Erwin Rohde he says only that its medley of "philosophical and aesthetic viewpoints" created a "lively impression"). It must surely have made him appear something of the *Fremdling* he had expressly hoped it would not ("HCP," 269), but which he increasingly came, nonetheless, to feel (letter of 16 June to Rohde)—however "convinced" he could represent his audience to have been by his performance (letter to his mother from mid-June). Its pitiful epigraph, a fourteen-line epigram attached to the privately printed version (1869), tells another story: "I stand there in Basel, undaunted / Yet lonely—O woe is me! / And I shout out loud: 'Homer! Homer!' / Everyone takes offense. / They go to church and then back home, / And they laugh at the loudly shouting man," etc. ("HCP," 248).[11]

The appeal to a new kind of philology, with its immanent paradoxes, was the fruit of lessons learned in the course of Nietzsche's effort to come to grips with the elusive and decidedly antiteleological thinking of Democritus—an odd starting point for any "goal," but then Nietzsche's progress was hardly a linear one.[12] The *Democritea* had been left in an unfinished state earlier that year in Leipzig (1869). Work on *The Birth of Tragedy* would be undertaken in earnest in the fall (although preparations had been underway since the winter of 1868).[13] Hence, Usener's damning verdict on Nietzsche—that with this book he was "dead as a scholar [*wissenschaftlich todt*]"—is twice wrong. It is based on a misconception about Nietzsche's first book; and it comes too late, as the Homer essay amply shows, and as a note contemporary with the studies on Democritus already foretells and forestalls: "Scholarship has something dead about it [*Die Wissenschaft hat etwas Todtes*]."[14]

It would be wrong, in any case, to suppose that the *Democritea*, an ambitious work announced by Nietzsche for the first time in September 1867 (in a letter to Ritschl, his mentor), and intended for a dedicatory volume in honor of the same, was never brought to completion. The volume in which it was to have appeared never materialized, though not through any fault of Nietzsche's. This did not hold Nietzsche back. He kept working toward a new collection of Democritus' fragments, envisioned as the continuation of the initial project (as he disclosed to Rohde in early December of 1868). This latter project, too, came to naught. Even so, the atomists are a permanent feature of Nietzsche's lecture courses down to the summer semester of 1876, while traces of the original project persist in the notebooks into 1877.[15] Atomism continues, moreover, to loom large in his other, more speculative writings from the same period.[16] But by then, and indeed already by around 1870, Democritus and atomism had transformed entirely in Nietzsche's mind. Nietzsche never really abandoned his *Democritea* project. Rather, its parameters were gradually redefined, and then they assumed an entirely inexhaustible character.

Valentin Rose and Skeptical Philology

The directions that Nietzsche's project took can be suggested briefly. Originally, the plan was to reopen the issue of the authenticity of the writings attributed to Democritus, numbering (on Nietzsche's first reckoning) as many as three hundred. These were preserved in the Callimachean *Pinakes*, the largely lost Alexandrian catalogues of all Greek literature available at the time of their making in the third century B.C.E. The Democritean portion was further redacted three hundred years later in the catalogue of titles arranged in quartets by Tiberius' royal astrologer, the Egyptian Platonist and apparently neo-Pythagorean Thrasyllus. (This list, totaling somewhere between fifty-two and seventy titles, depending upon how you count them, is preserved in Diogenes Laertius' *Lives of the Philosophers*.) Other scattered sources played into the figures as well. The numbers seem fantastic, and the more so for being as discrepant as they are.[17] Indeed, part of the intention was to determine the outer limits of Democritus' long-lost production, which even after its disappearance was known in antiquity to have been prodigious, although its size (Nietzsche reasoned) may have been exaggerated. Some falsifications were patent. How much of what passed for tradition was genuine? And how was this transmission in its vicissitudes to be explained? For obvious reasons, coming to grips with worries like these would have been a prerequisite to any new collection of the fragments, a project that Nietzsche envisaged as a culmination to his study. His aim was to arrive at an estimation comparable in rigor to Valentin Rose's newly appeared *Aristoteles Pseudepigraphus* (1863), a dry, generally blinkered (and today, discredited) sourcebook that contested the attribution of a great many works by Aristotle. Nietzsche admired the study, even as he justifiably complained of its stiff-necked, often misguided conclusions and its unpalatable style: Rose's "cynicism" toward his public is plain to see in his refusal to give complete citations (giving and not giving these is something of a minor obsession with Nietzsche),[18] and "even in his lack of punctuation" (another obsession of the writer Nietzsche).[19] Rose's style, Nietzsche surmised, was deliberately fashioned after Aristotle's own crabbed prose.

Nietzsche's choice to make Rose into an object of his fixations and to translate him into the pantheon of great philologists is simply bizarre. A recent scholar notes that Rose's opinions "bordered on paranoia."[20] Possibly, Rose was the bitter pill of philology that Nietzsche was forcing himself to swallow, but as we shall see he would eventually outbid even Rose in his skepticism toward the classical sources. There is in fact far more to Nietzsche's fixation on Rose than a passing obsession. In essence, the hope was to do for Democritus what Rose had attempted but failed to do for Aristotle— namely, to expose in systematic fashion the falsely ascribed writings (the extant titles and fragments) of the Democritean corpus. Nietzsche himself contributed to the refutation of Rose's thesis about Aristotle in a lecture (in January of 1867) to the student philological society he had helped to found.[21] But this does not seem to have lessened his interest in Rose's method, or to have deterred him from trying it out with the hope of greater success in another arena—one, in fact, that Rose had himself already touched on in 1854, when in a few short pages he made a sweeping rejection of the greater part of the titles ascribed to Democritus.[22] Nietzsche could feel himself to be the continuator of Rose's method, which he was taking to new heights. Indeed, Nietzsche at first toyed with the idea that the writings of Democritus could be reduced to a trim *two* titles, the only two deemed genuine in the Byzantine Suda (*The Great Diacosmos* and *On the Nature of the Cosmos*).[23] At the very least, this would have undermined the modern edition of Democritus by Friedrich Wilhelm August Mullach (1843; 2d ed., 1860), which Nietzsche regarded as hopelessly deficient. "Mullach is a negligent [*nachlässiges*] blockhead," he would write to Rohde in 1868, possibly making a tart pun on the imprecisions of Mullach's "old-fashioned" *Nachlass*-philology.[24] Nietzsche was riding the crest of current fashion, or whatever he took that to be. In any case, the title that Nietzsche gives to his work in his correspondence at this early stage of his project is *On the Spurious Writings of Democritus*.

Rose's hard-nosed skepticism toward the sources of classical literature may not have been the vogue so much as it represented an extreme within the discipline. In fact, the tendency to skepticism (or "Pyrrhonism"[25])—broadly speaking, a hermeneutics of suspicion—was more or less a fixed feature of classical philology from its inception. Evaluation (*krisis*), the highest critical art recognized by the Alexandrians in the age of Callimachus, after all involved the capacity to distinguish spurious from authentic texts.[26] Still, methodological skepticism took on a new symbolic value from the eighteenth century onward, as classical philology strove to wrest for itself the status of a full-fledged science (*Wissenschaft*) amid the emerging and competing academic disciplines in Germany.[27] The brazen philology of Friedrich August Wolf (1759–1824) was exemplary in this regard, and Wolf gladly assumed the role of spokesperson for his generation:

> If our forefathers had heard that serious doubts were raised as to
> whether Homer, the greatest of writers, used the art of writing, they

would have cried out that the lovers of paradoxes no longer had any shame. Now we have begun to examine the natures of ancient monuments more profoundly and to judge each event by the mental and moral habits of its time and place, while keeping the strictest law of history—that we do not call into doubt things which are true and supported by honest witnesses, and that we do not take as established things which are passed down in any way whatever or adorned with the name of some author or other. (*Prolegomena to Homer*, chap. 12, p. 71)

Wolf was reacting in part to the dreamy vision of the classical past that had pervaded learned culture from the Renaissance to the late eighteenth century, in France and in Germany, but he was also flexing his muscles in a familiar way that signified the latest modernity.[28] Half a century later, Valentin Rose would carry on the same tradition, with all the zeal of a technician. And Nietzsche was extending this lineage, though, as we shall see, in anything but a mechanical way. Skepticism à la Rose embodied (at least to Nietzsche's mind) the state of the art of philology, and Nietzsche wore it proudly like a badge.[29]

Suspicions of forgery in the case of Democritus were by no means unwarranted, given the general state of affairs in the so-called "doxographical" world of later antiquity, the world that literally digested classical authors (in the form of philosophical histories, accounts, and retellings that were particularly vulnerable to distortion) before passing them on to a grateful and often unsuspecting posterity.[30] The sibling traditions of falsified scholarship and genuine scholarship had developed side by side in antiquity (and beyond), to the point of near indistinguishability, and even the most honest of postclassical epitomizers and compendiasts could be counted on to grind their own theoretical axioms, often at the expense of their sources.[31] And so, Nietzsche suspects at one point, the ancient fabrications about Democritus' wide-ranging interests, inflating the dimensions of his corpus, were designed to take away some of the luster that Aristotle and the later Peripatetic tradition had always enjoyed.[32] Thrasyllus, Democritus' later redactor, a Neoplatonist with Pythagorean leanings, is no more reliable than (say) Bolus, a Hellenistic forger and impostor with medical and magical interests of a weird Pythagorean bent (see *BAW*, 3:259–70, "Bolus and His Factory," that is, of forgery). But Thrasyllus' sins were, in contrast, those of an overheated philologist and a philosophical enthusiast of "a Faustian nature" who was well out of his depth, and so he is more sympathetically drawn by Nietzsche, only to be roundly condemned in the last analysis.[33] But these cautions aside, a new attitude toward antiquity was crying out for adoption. Rose had laid bare a whole new genre of literary history, one that pointed toward its falsification and its need for radical revision. And Nietzsche felt himself to be a part of the next wave of scholarship.

A Volte-face: Skepticism Turned Against Itself

In the initial essay-draft of the *Democritea* (July–September 1867), Rose's method is said to raise questions that are so pressing they will become the source for a "movement" that "gradually will take hold of the whole of ancient Greek literature."[34] Half a year later (between October 1867 and April 1868), this movement has at least taken hold of Nietzsche. No longer submitting unquestioningly to the traditions of antiquity, to its statements about itself or to the "naive trust" that its authority instantly inspired, philology must now give itself over to the "unsteady tides of skepticism," amid the shards and fragments of the classical heritage, which up to now had offered only an illusory foothold. Hyperbolically taking Rose's program to new limits, Nietzsche was also broaching new unknowns: "Distrustfulness is as boundless now as trust was heretofore, while doubt now seems as morally correct as belief formerly did."[35] *Quellenforschung*, or source criticism, must be obedient to the sober realities of its evidence, as well as dig deeper, more energetically, and more searchingly—to unknown lengths, and at unpredictable costs.[36] And if new limits were to be broached, Nietzsche had found his man. Perhaps few authors of antiquity are as seductive, as doubtfully attested in his *ipsissima verba*, and as talked about in the classical sources, as Democritus.[37]

The task became a mission. It swelled into "a larger project," and Nietzsche carried this burden about himself for the better part of eight months. On 13 February 1868, he wrote to his friend Mushacke that the Democritean study had become an obsession: "It has been rankling in my mind for the past three months"; he was, he confessed, unable to find a firm contour or frame for the project.[38] Increasingly possessive of "my *Democritea*"[39] and forecasting his many later "intellectual pregnancies," Nietzsche would suffer sharp laboring pains and "pangs of conscience" come April. "As a consequence," he wrote to Rohde, his colleague and confidant, "since that day [when he embarked upon his *Democritea*] I have been dragging myself and my Democritus about, like an expecting woman, though without any immediate prospect of birth" (letter of 3 April 1868).

The "pangs of conscience" that Nietzsche feels are the symptom of a progressive disease with multiple complications (one of which was materializing in the form of "my Democritus"). Briefly, these involve the betrayal of philology by philosophy; a feeling, contaminated with guilt, of sharing a conspiratorial complicity with Plato against Democritus; a growing, uncontrollable obsession with atomism; and a curiously compounded skepticism. Nietzsche was in fact learning to adjust Rose's skeptical philology to the new epistemology and the historical outlook of Lange's book on materialism. But at the same time he was learning to make adjustments in "his Democritus"; for there is no question that Nietzsche was consciously appropriating an image of Democritus to suit his own evolving thought, in the nurturing shade of Lange. Meanwhile the lessons came hard. "The whole affair has become rather dubious," Nietzsche writes in the same letter to Rohde. Nietzsche's doubts here stem, significantly, from a twofold skepticism. They continue to be directed against a naiver form of philology and its oversubmissiveness to historical authority. (This is a recurrent theme for Nietzsche during this period; his papers are riddled with detectivelike "suspicion" and "doubt.") And now, suddenly, he begins to put in doubt his own initial intuitions about the received tradition on Democritus and its dubious authority. Nietzsche's skepticism is, in other words, one that is turned inward—against Rose, against skepticism, and consequently against himself.[40]

The notebooks reveal a Nietzsche increasingly doubtful of his earlier judgments. Works previously taken away from Democritus are restored to him; arguments against attribution are overturned one by one and field by field. The grounds for these revised opinions are illuminating. Titles and even entire areas of inquiry which earlier were dismissed as "unlikely" and "hardly plausible" later gain readmittance for the reverse reasons: they are suddenly "likely," "plausible," "not unworthy" of the philosopher; certain works in principle "agree with Democritus' character," they "must" be genuine, are the kind of thing that "any" materialist thinker would wish to write about; they flow from the logic of Democritus' system as its "necessary consequences," and so on.[41]

Nietzsche certainly had his work cut out for him with this project of reclamation. Democritus is reputed (and is still believed today) to have written on a dazzling range of subjects rivaled only by Aristotle, whose own universality of reach is seemingly boundless.[42] Framed on either side by the origins of the universe and its proliferation into other worlds, Democritus' titles cover virtually everything in between, from the hidden physical constituents of reality (the nature and shapes of atoms) to their effects on the phenomenal world (sensation, vision, and epistemology). Linking these two extremes, and filling in much of the ground intervening, are investigations into more discrete forms of science (medicine, physiology, biology, and mathematics) and into cultural phenomena (religion, ethics, language, and the arts). Thus, in question at a given moment may be writings as odd as those apparently devoted to agriculture. Earlier rejected by Nietzsche as irrelevant to the typical concerns of a philosopher, the georgic writings are now characteristic of Democritus' ranging method and interests (Rose had deemed unlikely the same title attested for Aristotle, and had doubts about the Democritean title as well).[43] And so the work, preserved in title only (*On Agriculture*) "can be genuine": "For horticulture and agriculture agree with his character."[44] Similar reversals of judgment occur in other areas. Testimonia previously taken at face value are now read more critically, which means, paradoxically, that they are read more charitably. So, for example, the failure of Aristotle's disciple, Eudemus of Rhodes, to mention Democritus among the Presocratic mathematicians is to be explained by the fact that Eudemus' list comprised "innovators": Democritus may therefore be assumed to have been, if not an innovator, then at least "well versed in mathematics."[45]

This last is a crucial piece of deduction, because it must brave against the combined evidence of Epicurus' own rejection of mathematics (a troubling fact, since Epicurus often mirrors Democritean thinking), the doxography of an ancient source (the damning silence of Eudemus' testimony), and finally Lange's own disparaging view of mathematical pursuits (for their tendency toward idealism).[46] Against all odds Nietzsche nonetheless comes down in favor of the slim but unimpeachable evidence of Democritus' activity in mathematical controversies. One such piece of evidence is the famous "cone fragment" (fr. 155 DK), a geometrical puzzle; and there is Cicero's corroborating testimony that Democritus was "an educated man and an accomplished mathematician."[47] Another example of the way Nietzsche could turn the tables on doubt, this time with reference to the origins of philology itself: Democritus came after Protagoras, therefore "we can also credit Democritus with the grammatical writings [attributed to him], since Protagoras had already dealt with *orthoepeia*," the science that regards the correctness of names and diction.[48] This relatively late and hard-won concession to Democritus' interest in the theory of language is all-important, and we shall come back to it in the next chapter. Music, grammar, and ethics are one by one returned to the fold. Eventually, Democritus is even vindicated on several points. He was "right" on the question of the formation of the universe, and his thinking about its origins was likewise "enlightened."[49] Nietzsche has traveled some distance, indeed.

Crucial to understanding this gradual volte-face is the following entry, which graphically conveys its own content:

> Aristoxenus relates that Plato wanted to burn the writings of [illegible]. He did not succeed. But time, overwhelmed by Christianity, destroyed them. This [was] the greatest malice of supernaturalism. (*BAW*, 3:363)

The name whose illegibility may nonetheless be read in this remark is none other than that of Democritus. The information comes from the ancient author of philosophers' lives, Diogenes Laertius (9.40), and Nietzsche makes reference to it on at least half a dozen other occasions. Initially, Nietzsche treats the story as apocryphal: it must have been invented by the Peripatetics out of malice toward Plato, and conceivably was one way of accounting for the odd fact that Plato is utterly silent on the subject of Democritus or atomism, an omission that was noticed in antiquity (Diogenes is a case in point).[50] Democritus is nowhere so much as named in the whole of the extant Platonic corpus, whereas Aristotle makes the atomist's views into a constant point of reference (and polemics), and he even devoted a (now lost) work, possibly in two books, to his doctrines (*On Democritus* or *Problems Taken [or Arising] from the Works of Democritus*).[51] Plato's silence may be telling, but Nietzsche is more interested in what Democritus wrote than in what Plato did not.[52] And so, like a literary detective, Nietzsche deduces from the anecdote that "Aristoxenus is to be believed. There couldn't have been too many writings. Otherwise, Plato's idea would have been stark mad" (4:38)—an odd conclusion to draw, but one that is anyhow reversed later on. Elsewhere, the same testimony is taken to argue the voluminousness of Democritus' corpus (4:84).[53] The apparent discrepancy is most likely an example of Nietzsche rehearsing a rhetorical—that is, dialectical—strategy for his projected work (to be discussed in a moment). He is also shadow-boxing with Rose, who had adduced the anecdote as evidence of the slender proportions of Democritus' corpus.[54] Ultimately, Nietzsche will decide that the features of the anecdote point to a fabrication by a sympathetic biographer of the atomist, Diocles of Magnesia (4:98), a late Epicurean whom we will meet again at the end of the following chapter. Democritus may or may not, then, have been miraculously rescued from the fate of Plato's "private auto-da-fé," but the bulk of his writing was lamentably lost, in the aftermath of Plato's silence and over the centuries.

Lamentably, but not irretrievably. Previous talk about "spurious works" gives way to talk about "*lost* works."[55] Nietzsche declares his intention to "reconstruct" Democritus' portrait and thereby to counteract the tides of history, but especially of "supernaturalism"—not least of all the Christian variety, which in Platonic fashion denies the validity of matter and the relevance of its philosophical exponents alike. Nietzsche's historical reassessment of Platonism, his skeptical philology, and his reinvention of Democritus are closely bound up together, conceptually and in their mutual discovery. Wholly absorbed in his project, Nietzsche feels himself to be driven by an invisible engine, impelled into never before dreamt-of philosophical depths, toward an unforeseen but now increasingly visible end: "[My essay] has *attained a philosophical background, something that none of my previous projects ever achieved.* . . . All my projects . . . point like telegraph poles toward the goal of my studies."[56]

Valentin Rose's view now becomes the departure point for a critical reassessment of the ancient traditions about Democritus, the impetus for which is a "growing *certainty*" and a riven methodology—increasingly directed "*against Rose.*"[57] Nietzsche's dividedness of mind is perhaps nowhere more palpable than in the desperation of an entry from late 1867 to early 1868, which reads:

> *Rose's judgment* is somewhat *precipitous.*
>
> He can be right on the question of the ethical writings.—No.

to which the thought is quickly appended:

It is a matter of presenting, in all clarity, the tangle of reasons and arguments and truth's hovering on a knife's edge. (4:80)

The notebooks are at times an ambiguous source of evidence. In some cases, where they appear to reflect a growing conviction, they can be shown merely to reflect the rhetorical structure of the planned work (with arguments enacted as "moves" within a dialectical strategy aimed at stimulating doubts, only to remove them in light of further considerations). In other cases, one can only make guesses. So, for instance, the ethical fragments appear as spurious a few pages after they were admitted as authentic (4:47, 42). Here, Nietzsche is rehearsing an argument from the commonplace assumption about the premises of physical atomism (wherein speculations on ethics, language, or art have no obvious place), only to reject it summarily. Yet one further example of Nietzsche's coming round to an acceptance, albeit in a dialectical context (constructed as a phase of his argumentation "against Rose," here barely sketched in), of testimony discredited by Rose and others. Rehearsals of the strategy occasionally add to the confusing appearance of the notebooks, which are themselves as fragmentary as any collection of ancient testimonia and texts. Autopsy of the manuscripts would perhaps verify their exact collation and the precise unfolding of Nietzsche's methods. But it appears certain that Nietzsche is often working out argumentative transitions in a pro and con fashion so as to demonstrate the assumptions and implications of a narrower view of atomism and to replace them with a wider, more accommodating vision.[58] According to a letter to Gersdorff,[59] Nietzsche's stated aim is to "awaken" in the reader the same sequence of steps that he himself took, from the initial stumbling blocks of doubt ("which pressed down on me unsought for and powerfully") to a final conversion of sorts—illustrating, along the way, not only prior philological errors but also his own. This tactic, Nietzsche writes, broaching a tension that will run through all of his philological undertakings, "requires discipline and a fresh haleness of thought and poetic invention [*Denken und Dichten*]."[60]

In the passage above concerning Rose's judgment, it seems likely that Nietzsche's own convictions are indeed wavering on the knife's edge of a jagged conscience. But on the question of physics and ethics, his doubts are not about the place of the ethical writings (he had already convinced himself of their authenticity, and he was now running through a simulation of doubt), but about the venture as a whole, which was leaving him with a skepticism of a deeper kind. It is understandable that Nietzsche should feel torn, given his increasingly partisan view of things and the critical watershed in method he has reached. "The whole affair has become rather dubious, and is crumbling apart before my passably rigorous philological conscience" (letter to Rohde, 3 April 1868). Philology provided both the bane and the cure. Doubting doubtfulness itself, Nietzsche arrives at a point of double negation, and a qualifiedly positive return. Hence the proud affirmation that Democritus, formerly viewed askance, now occupies a different frame. His individual characteristics—his "personality" taken as a whole—are suddenly richer and more revealing:

> In the end, however, when my skepticism could get a grip on all the inferences, the picture turned itself around in my hands; I gained a new comprehensive image [*Gesammtbild*] of the outstanding personality of Democritus, and from this superior vantage point the tradition regained its rightful due. (Letter to Gersdorff, 16 February 1868)

This process is described by Nietzsche, in consciously affected Hegelian argot, as "the redemption of the negation through its negation" (ibid.). It was this process in particular that Nietzsche had hoped to illustrate by reproducing it in his reader's mind. So refashioned, his project now is to fill in the parentheses of Plato's erasure, to "reconstruct" Democritus or rather a counter-Democritus, even if this means always within the brackets of a hostile tradition: "I have reconstructed him entirely afresh."[61] After all, it was *Nietzsche himself* who in effect had blotted out the name of Democritus in his notes, a complex gesture that rendered the ground fertile for Democritus' eventual restoration. Plato would not succeed.[62]

The Matter of History: F. A. Lange's 'Geschichte des Materialismus'

The idol must be shattered into fragments.

— F. A. LANGE[63]

If in the spring of 1869 Nietzsche could relish, with conspiratorial glee, the thought that he was "infecting" his pupils in Basel with philosophy (he was teaching Plato's *Phaedo* at the time),[64] he had already infected himself with a new sense of potency and health. Philology was crumbling before itself; method had turned into skepticism; and skepticism was turning into a self-consuming skepticism of another kind. After all, to doubt requires a belief ("even skepticism contains in itself a belief") that can easily be turned into another doubt—or another belief.[65] "There is nothing alarming about this condition; it is not a symptom of the illness of our field," Nietzsche would assure himself and his reader, in a draft of a never-finished disquisition on philological method from the winter semester of 1867/68, presumably meant as a preamble to the study on Democritus. A Saturnine image captures the point, and all the more prophetically, inasmuch as it is an image that recurs in Nietzsche's subsequent writing:

> One should not forget that skepticism, by dint of its peculiar nature, bites into its very own children; and that it is wont to strike a limit—at which point it performs a somersault, and travels back along the same path that it just now abandoned. (3:342)[66]

Philology, driven forward by doubt, must at once achieve and demolish its own results: in this way, tradition is both "undermined" and—"perhaps," once truth is chased from out of its places of concealment—"confirmed," even though the tradition will have been shown in either case "to have stood on feet of clay."[67] A Hegelian would say that truth so sought is discovered "through the negation of the negation," and is therefore no self-standing truth at all. "But for anyone displeased with that variety of truth, there is always a nonnegligible bonus. For no one shall leave this table unfed, provided he doesn't bring to it an overfastidious palate" (ibid.).

Nietzsche's peculiar, unfinicky, and reflexive, self-devouring skepticism is first and foremost an attack on the piety of dogmatism ("Every trace of dogmatism has now withered away"). It is aimed against the reification of method, and undertaken above all in the name of engaging what he calls *"the problem of thinking"* (3:338–40). Thought, moved by "that so-called faculty of common sense," Nietzsche has come to see, is a *"perpetuum mobile*, an ungraspable thing,*"* at most a relative measure of mind in its cultural refraction. Clearly, Nietzsche has not merely been struck with a sudden illumination about Democritus. When he excitedly reported that his essay had "attained a philosophical background. . . . All my projects . . . point like telegraph poles toward the goal of my studies," he was not thinking primarily of his newly gained insights into atomism. He was thinking, in the first instance, of his insight into a new kind of philology, a philology based on the only valid premise that can be entertained about classical sources. This was not Rose's brand of philological skepticism, which is ultimately premised on the certainty of (ascertainable) foundations and factual bases, but a radical doubting of every foundational appeal, coupled with a reaffirmed belief in philological appearances that, paradoxically, never ceases to be detached from itself. "Only certainty is horrifying," he would write to Deussen on 4 April of 1867. Philological certainty rests on the quicksands of doubt; nothing is certain unless we make it so. A critical philology must accordingly reflect its own instabilities and embrace them, in a way that surpasses the uncritical and naively positivistic method used by Rose, in relation to whom Nietzsche is now both heir and corruptor.

Again, Nietzsche was able to reach these conclusions only through a fortuitous combination of events, which included his happening upon Rose's "uncovering" of the pseudepigrapha of Aristotle, upon Lange's own skeptical epistemology and critical history, and upon a materialist philosopher with skeptical tendencies like Democritus. On the latter Nietzsche could not only try out his new methodological instruments but also confirm them twice over, as it were, in their very application: in the successful recovery of Democritus, and in the recovery of Democritus' own methodological skepticism, which increasingly bears an uncanny resemblance to Nietzsche's own. Needless to say, there is something troubling about this convergence of method and object, which in a way ought to be radically self-defeating. Hovering uncertainly between rediscovery and self-confirming hypothesis, Nietzsche's study on Democritus might appear to be a perversion of philological method, little more than an exercise in futility, or, worse still, a spectral *Schreckbild* of philology and its fragile hold on the past. (Recall that as he envisages it at one point, his book will be a vivid and deliberate illustration of a philological error—his own.) But this verdict, while in ways true, is hardly the whole story, since Nietzsche is in fact redefining what can be viewed from the perspective of philology. What is more, he is being propelled on to larger horizons.

By running together philology and philosophy, Nietzsche is taking himself significantly beyond Lange—not to mention Rose, who, as is characteristic of philologists of his day, offers virtually no account of his method.[68]

This is the case even if Lange may have supplied Nietzsche with the suggestion that philology was in its own way a kind of skeptical critique, or with the
notion that Democritus' single greatest contribution lay in his discovery of
"a clear, methodical [and "scientific"] view of things."[69] "Metaphysics as a
critique of concepts," writes Lange, "must go about its business more acutely
and carefully than the philological critique of a transmitted text, the historical critique of the sources of a narrative, [or] the mathematical-physical critique of a hypothesis of natural science."[70] Nietzsche would accept the
underlying premise of this remark but contest the way in which Lange
divides up his categories. Conceptual critique is necessarily philological, historical, and so on; at some point, these three areas cannot even be distinguished any longer, so closely are they intertwined. What the notes to the
Democritea present, then, is a unique synthesis of Nietzsche's three inspira-
tions: philosophy, history, and philology, all of which fall, in Nietzsche's eyes,
within a broader cultural matrix and (as it happens) within a matrix of
broadly aimed cultural criticism, the outlines of which will emerge as we
proceed. In order to see more clearly just how Nietzsche has fused Lange's
philosophy with Rose's philology—thereby producing a *novum* of his own
making—it will be helpful to take up some of the main features of Lange's
influential *History of Materialism and Critique of Its Significance in the Present*,
not least as these pertain to the style and spirit of the work. A strong taste for
ambivalence and contradiction pervades Lange's *History*. This sense of irreducible complexity is in many ways the prime mover of his argument, and it
informs his view of matter and materialism as much as it enlivens his philosophical style. None of this would be lost on Nietzsche.[71]

The book opens with a striking yet simple observation: "Materialism is as
old as philosophy, but no older." Ostensibly, Lange's central narrative traces
the gradual modification of materialism, and especially Democritean materialism, over the centuries: from its atomistic origins in Leucippus, Democritus' predecessor earlier in the fifth century, to its elaboration and defense
in Epicurus and Lucretius (in the fourth and first centuries B.C.E.), and to the
Renaissance revival of science; to Bacon, Gassendi, Hobbes, and De la Met-
trie in the sixteenth, seventeenth, and eighteenth centuries; and finally past
Kant and into the newer materialisms of the nineteenth century (the positivistic natural sciences, and especially the budding sciences of experimental
psychology, physiology, and chemistry in Germany and all of Europe).[72] But
in another way, even though this is not one of the work's overt claims, Lange

traces the history of these changes in the form of their pervasive repetition. At the origins of culture lies a naturalistic conception of things, clouded by "the contradictions of dualism"—unspecified, these are left to our imagination—and by a belief in "the phantasy-images of personification" (p. 3). Presumably, Lange has in mind some proto-distinction between empirical reality and whatever lies metaphysically beyond it, foreshadowing (and encumbering) the history of philosophy to come. There is no evidence that human understanding ever surmounts this archaic dilemma and its blind figural mechanisms, and every evidence that personification is the very modality in which thought, forever caught in the conflicting toils of materialism and idealism, goes about its daily business (pp. 373–74, 489).

Philosophy, it is hinted, whether materialist or other, is at its origins a rebaptism of the very dualisms it strives to overcome. "The first attempts to get free of these contradictions, to conceive the world in a unitary way, and to rise above the common ground of sensory appearances, are already pathways into the field of philosophy" (p. 3). Throughout, Lange is attentive to the paradoxes of philosophy, to its inner dissensions (dissensions rooted, it would seem, in this primordial indeterminacy), and to its fruitless squabblings. "Even the concept of matter," he reminds the reader at one point (p. 86), "is and remains an object of metaphysics," however much metaphysics may be opposed to materialism—and however much materialism may strive to shake itself free of metaphysics. This explains, at least in part, why the history of philosophy has to be written not only from the perspective of the history of materialism but also against that materialistic perspective, in the form of its critique.[73] The conflict within philosophy is as deeply rooted as consciousness itself. Small wonder, then, that the history of philosophy cannot avoid being in its own way philosophical, critical, and internally dissonant all at once.

The repeated attempts and failures of philosophy to lift itself above the constraints of sensation, but most of all above its own contradictions, provide the micro-rhythms of Lange's critical history of philosophy. There is an unmistakable density of references back to the first stirrings of philosophy in Greece, to the atomists, the sophists, to Aristotle and others, matched by an equal density of anticipations forward from the account of ancient philosophy to its modern parallels and fulfillments. (An example is the Democritean principle of "the equivalence of all being," which the nineteenth century, wrestling with it still, has not succeeded in proving scientifically.) These glances forward and back serve as constant reminders that ancient dramas

SKEPTICAL PHILOLOGY **51**

are being replayed in newer settings; and that philosophy has yet to elevate itself above the most basic contradictions that lay at its origins. Perhaps the single most salient rhythm in Lange's narrative, however, is the passage from Democritean materialism to Protagorean sensualism (phenomenalism) and nominalism. This development is presented almost as a dialectical move-ment, although Lange never uses the term, and there is very little that is Hegelian in his account. It is a movement that asserts itself at critical junc-tures, chiefly in the advances, which Lange takes to be genuine, within the evolution of philosophy and science. Tracing this movement briefly will be essential to gaining an insight into Nietzsche's fluid understanding of the many roles and guises of materialism.

"Sensualism," Lange writes, is "a natural extension of materialism" (p. 13). It is a reconciled and relaxed, virtually indifferent stance toward the world of appearances, frankly subjectivist (though premised on materialist principles—e.g., the belief in the reducibility of reality to matter) and com-fortably relativist and conventionalist. "Protagoras made himself at home in this world of appearances" (p. 236). His sophistic credo was *homo mensura*, man is the measure; but the credo might as well be Lange's. Protagoras fur-nishes a much-needed supplement to Democritean objectivism. His soph-istry adds a critical tension to both stances, and it deepens the contradictions inherent on either side (for instance, the latent tendencies to skepticism and dogmatism detectable in both).[74] The larger drama between materialism and idealism is played out in subsequent centuries, but with innumerable varia-tions and by players who themselves represent more than one consistent view—whether between Berkeley and d'Alembert, Hume and Kant, or Kant and Lange. There are empirical materialists, skeptical and dogmatic materi-alists. Materialists are, unbeknownst to themselves, idealists of a sort; and idealists cannot seem to get along without some postulates of materialism (leaving aside the question of "material idealists," who are not to be con-fused with "formal idealists" such as Kant). It is not a story with a single, simple plot. But neither is Lange's exposition, for all its idiosyncrasy and beguiling richness, a paradigm of lucidity.

Kant is a climactic moment in the history retailed by Lange, and I discuss Lange's fascinating view of Kant in my study of *The Birth of Tragedy*. Suffice it to say here that Kant's thing in itself has approximately the same status as the inner "physical-psychical" organization of our own bodies: both have a doubtful, but ineliminable, existence; they are necessary fictions and never simply real. Fusing Kant and materialism, Lange ends up with a position that is deeply critical of both. The fact that materialism is "no older" than philosophy suggests that materialism has no prior, let alone a priori, grounding in the world: it exists by virtue of being a philosophical perception, no more and no less. Lange's final and most extreme criticism of materialism is perfectly consistent with this: materialism, too, *dichtet*, or condenses realities out of poetic vapor. The "impulse" or "drive [*Trieb*]" to poetic invention that is "lodged in our breasts" is the actual source of the contradictions that interminably arise between the testimony of both our senses and our faculty of understanding on the one hand and the products of philosophy, art, and religion on the other (p. 346). In Lange's view (as it will be for Nietzsche), the danger lies not in the drive per se but in its stilling by belief. Thus, "*soul, world*, and *god*," as products of the ideas of reason, are only expressions of an internal "striving for unity"; "ascribe to them an external existence and you land in the shoreless sea of metaphysical error" (p. 272). The materialist, Lange believes, is susceptible to another kind of stilling: he suffers from an excess of satisfaction and a complacency toward appearances. Lacking the "drive" to go beyond the deliverances of the senses, most blatantly of all in picturing through sensuous language what lies beyond them, the materialist is too ready to allow sense-impressions and theory to "blend" into an "indissoluble whole." He is too placid to loosen the grip of these structures by means of "paradoxical questions" posed in an entirely new language, or through experiments which, "in place of aiming at a mere extension in the particulars [of knowledge], *plunge received ways of thinking into ruin*, and bring in their train entirely new insights into the field of the sciences" (pp. 345–46; emphasis added). There is more to Lange's vision than just thinking and creation (*Denken und Schaffen*). He is pleading for the actuation of what he calls the "revolutionary" potentials of knowledge. Sotto voce, the thinker he is vigilantly prompting toward and beyond new forms of materialism is in fact not Kant, whom he has already displaced, but himself.

"Philology as Critique"

Kant had only spelled "the beginning of the end" of materialism. Lange writes the end of that beginning. And Nietzsche follows hard on his heels.

Lange's vision of things, in which metaphysics, the history of philosophical discourse, and a sense of their constitutively divided anthropology are brought together in a radical, self-resisting mix, will profoundly impress itself upon Nietzsche, not just in his early encounter with Democritus and with classical philology but over the decades to come, in the stages leading up to *The Birth of Tragedy* and then on to the later and indeed the very last writings. From the beginning, Nietzsche was an ecstatic and, as we shall see, clear-minded recipient of Lange's ideas. Here he could find, for instance, a satisfying confirmation of his ambivalent reading of Schopenhauer and of his own view that philosophy is a form of art. To quote from Lange, whom Nietzsche quotes in his correspondence, metaphysics is the "edifying art of joining concepts," which so recognized can now enjoy unhampered, free rein in the "wide-open field of its world-historical playground" (p. 268). "Art," he continues, "is free, even in the field of concepts. Who would refute a phrase of Beethoven, and who would accuse Raphael's *Madonna* of error?" (p. 269).[75] For the moment, we need only retain a few of the basic insights that Nietzsche could borrow from Lange, for example the concept of "critique"—that is, "skepticism tamed and made methodical" (p. 276). Nietzsche would find a way to turn this dialectical skepticism into a method of philology, or rather into a program for such a method ("philology as critique").[76] For the most part, no actual philology would result from this method except incidentally, and it is unclear whether any really could—certainly not within the framework of philology as it was practiced in the nineteenth century, or today for that matter. But a new conception of culture and criticism could emerge out of a new critical philology, though this would require a further unleashing of the radical potentials of Lange's insight.

Three major consequences flow immediately from the unlikely confrontation of Lange, Rose, and Democritus, the first being a reappraisal of Rose. In a sense, Lange faced Nietzsche with a compounded dilemma. Rose's results, applied to Democritus, would demolish part of the historical foundations of Lange's critical history. Yet on the face of it, Lange's endorsement of critical skepticism might be thought to underwrite this demolition. On the other hand, reading Lange, Nietzsche could perceive that Rose's skepticism was at most an extension of philological positivism, a surrender to positive fact. Strangely, Rose had shown as blind a faith in the "phenomena" of his material as any naive materialism might require: whatever failed to meet certain empirical criteria and rules for evidence (rules that originate in the mind of the philologist, not in the evidence) simply could no longer be entrusted with a solid existence. To Rose's faint-hearted skepticism Nietzsche would oppose a more radical and bracing methodological skepticism, whereby the facts of classical phenomena could be redeemed only as revived and reconstructed, and as a matter of conscious assumption. It is only once they are forsworn of certainty, having been passed through the sieve of "unlimited skepticism" (which itself must be submitted to doubt), that the now re-created facts about antiquity may be accredited with another certainty, that of the philologist's "literary judgment" (3:339). Redemption like this yields a most uncertain brand of certainty: the durability of whatever survives inspection is offset by the provisional and poetic embrace of its continued existence; a fact can be affirmed only in its negation, as a twice-negated thing, if it is to be at all ("the redemption of the negation through its negation"). Nietzsche's is in this sense a philology founded on discipline and a fresh "haleness" of thought and invention, *Denken und Dichten*. In Lange's terms, philology is a disciplining of knowledge through doubt, and it accords equal weight to "knowing" and to "creating," with revolutionary potential for both. Some of this is captured by Nietzsche's explicit intention to "exhaust," by intellectual rigor and even by intellectual violence, the strengths of Rose's method and the limits of literary history (3:336).

A second consequence for Nietzsche's view of philology flows from one of Lange's central discoveries: namely, that "our categories," around which our sensations are arranged, "play the same role as our senses." In other words, the forms of sensation are themselves sensations or the product of sensations.[77] The same mechanism that produces sensation also produces our idea of matter; at one level, there is no way to distinguish the one from the other; at another, there is no need to: both are equally "products" of the way we are and of "our organization" (this somewhat vague refrain is tirelessly repeated by Lange). Transferred to classical philology, Lange's point can be taken to mean that the objects of the philologist's gaze (which is to say, texts and their relations) are the matter of his method, which itself obeys the same rules as its matter, although this kind of philological materialism (positivism and an obsession with the data of *realia*) was the developing trend in philology during the nineteenth century anyway.[78] In the case of Democritus, the convergence is all the more intense, and the analogies penetrate down and up the grand edifice of philological understanding. Here, the texts are themselves about the constitution of matter, and philological method must reach beyond philology in order to confront the problems of natural science knowledgeably.[79] Convergence becomes reflection, and as a consequence Nietzsche's philology begins to emulate Democritean physiology itself. It might not be an exaggeration to claim that, consciously or unconsciously, Nietzsche has in fact adopted a Democritean style of philology (in pointed contrast with Rose's "Aristotelian" style of philology [4:71]). Charged with a certain *Schwung* ("abandon") and a strong dose of "poetic sense," traits he found to be completely missing from traditional scholarship (3:338, 343), Nietzsche's philology is based on heurism, analogy, and "combination"—all characteristic of Democritus' own methods of hypothesis and inference. But it is equally based on a doubtfulness that, like Democritus' skeptical strain, undermines these logical instruments: "In the canonics [that is, those works devoted to establishing the "criterion of truth"], Democritus contradicts the possibility of carrying out proofs" (4:77). The absolutes of knowledge thus become in one respect precisely that: absolute, whether absolutely unknowable or subject to absolute doubt. At the point of their common affliction, in their gravitation toward the abysses of knowledge and doubt, idealism and atomistic materialism are one.

This convergence of method and object, which in ways can be inimical to both, is touched on in only a few places in Nietzsche's published notebooks, but it is implicit throughout.[80] So, for instance, in contemplating the alternatives to a philology based on isolated details, he can write:

> My method consists in turning a cold shoulder on a single fact as soon as a wider horizon reveals itself, etc. Thus, our striving is a wandering into the unknown, with the *wavering* hope of eventually finding a goal, whereupon one can [at last] come to rest.

Lange had called the thing in itself a much "yearned for" but impossible "resting point" for thought.[81] Nietzsche is in effect abandoning the philological thing in itself, though with much broader consequences than Lange, ever bent on a positive reconstruction of philosophy, would allow. Nietzsche continues,

Such goals are, however, insights with a critical impact only upon ourselves. The results of an inquiry stirs our understanding, but the core of our being remains cold. But finally one stumbles upon views, *analogies*, etc., which powerfully set us in motion.

It is no different in the case of inquiry in the natural sciences. (3:336–37; emphases added)[82]

Literary study (*philologia*) and the study of nature (*physiologia*) can be compared, to the embarrassment of both. A page earlier, Nietzsche was critical of the "laxness" of literary scholarship, which operates according to few laws but with a multitude of analogies for every "appearance" that it encounters.[83] Inquiry by analogy is tantamount to a kind of poetry. This being the case, "the best that one can do is [opt for] a *conscious* poetic minting of minds, events, characters, etc." As for the question whether a truthful correspondence with past realities is attainable, Nietzsche's reply is both skeptical and equivocal, as might be expected: "doubtful, but possible" (3:336). But these concessions, rather than removing philology from natural science, instead draw it closer. Here, too, Lange's sanctioning influence is to be felt, for Lange had already reached the conclusion that philosophy, science, art, and religion all have in common with any human enterprise an inventive "poetry of concepts," or a fictionalization of their respective objects and limits.[84] Correspondence, for instance between theory and reality, is in particular something to be eschewed: an unobtainable and unverifiable desideratum, it is ultimately dispensable too.[85] Henceforth, knowledge of fact is either unreachable or irrelevant (viz., relevant in ways we cannot imagine and can barely conceive); either way, a doubtful skepticism "made methodical" rules.

It needs to be underscored that this rejection of philological positivism goes beyond epistemological doubt. Nietzsche is fully prepared to concede a possible knowledge of facts if pressed to do so. What he denies is that such knowledge constitutes knowledge in a meaningful sense, in a sense that corresponds to the way knowledge is actually used. This is part of his argument against positivism in philology. Thus, "knowledge of a given influence"— say, between ancient authors or ideas—"proves nothing," and the same holds for knowledge of any "single fact" (3:369). They prove nothing, because the criterion of what matters in philology is not proof but, quite the contrary, *whatever fascinates and compels.* Hence, determining a philological fact, say the authenticity of a title attributed to Democritus, "is a psychological problem. The tradition cannot prove it [one way or another]" (4:48). And in any case, "it is always only the relation to the present that attracts us" to the objects of our knowledge (3:370; cf. 2:255 [1863]), and that relation is an imaginary one. Clearly, knowledge is meaningful only as an active appropriation carried out in the name of larger, often unexpressed, cultural agencies; and these fulfill powerful needs and desires that, emanating from the present (the "needs of one's age"), exceed any one individual's control or knowledge (3:320–21). Nietzsche's accounts of the classical traditions in antiquity and into the present are nothing if not an illustration of this axiom. They trace the history of a compulsion.

Now, if applying skepticism to what can be known about the antique past is one way of exhibiting, virtually of dramatizing, the peculiar contingency of culturally informed knowledge and the limits of what can be known, it is also a way of depicting the peculiar contingencies of knowledge in the modern world.[86] For in Nietzsche's eyes, the modern present is marked above all by skepticism: it is literally racked by doubt.[87] Philology is merely one of the more public arenas in which culture at large can be seen performing a violent operation upon itself—upon its cultural heritage, its history, and its reservoir of self-images—in the effort to attain some degree of sovereignty over itself. The effects of this wide-scale effort are at once destructive and recuperative, yet ultimately self-defeating: the authority of the past, scandalized by a superior knowledge, eventually reasserts itself in a purified form, whether in the form of a classical ideal or in its apparent antithesis, philological positivism and historicism.

It is here that the real significance of a figure like Valentin Rose finally emerges: he represents the tendency of an entire age. "The naive confidence in classical antiquity and its statements about itself has vanished" in the modern world, as has every outward show of piety toward the past as well (3:341). And yet, since doubtfulness is now taken for a sign of unflinching moral rectitude (*Sittlichkeit*), skepticism, tamed by the duties of conscience, has a lulling effect on the modern mind. Hence the naive positivism of Rose, which Nietzsche chooses to combat with a radical image of itself. Philology may have grown "unlimitedly skeptical" of late, at least in appearance, but it has yet to draw out the last consequences of skepticism (3:339–40). Nietzsche appeals to a contemporary parallel: Auguste Comte's belief "that scientific thought appears on the scene the moment metaphysical and mythical conceptions are swept aside" is utterly mistaken. For never before did a more metaphysical and mythical thought appear to mankind; the idea is itself pure poetry (3:340, 349). This theme and its complications, the fitful conspiratorial relation between doubtfulness and the claims of knowledge in the modern age, has a long afterlife in Nietzsche. For now, we need only note how the desire to bring skepticism to its logical conclusion in the interests of "critical" rigor involves applying skepticism to itself. Only so can the negation be negated. Thus, if what Nietzsche's philology ultimately brings to light is the self-contradicting knowledge of a doubting subject, this is a way of putting on show the—to his mind insufficiently acknowledged—methods of conventional philology, of a doubting subject that claims in fact to know. Nietzsche's philology thus reveals a form of knowledge that is peculiarly modern. It is this capacity and willingness to look uncertainty in the face and to assume the burden of being a modern subject that typifies his new and radical philology, the slogan for which might as well be "Subjectivity Prevails" (3:369). Nietzsche's slogan in *The Antichrist*, "Philology as *ephexis* in interpretation"—a skeptical withholding of belief and judgment as to truth and falsehood, and an infinite patience in interpretation—is the direct heir to the solutions he lights upon in these early years at Leipzig and Basel.[88] In the course of this dramatic revision in Nietzsche's concept of philology, a revised image of Democritus emerges as well.

It becomes increasingly difficult to draw a neat division between the Democritus of the sources and Nietzsche's Democritus. This is because Nietzsche changes the object of philology—even at the cost of making philology a self-consuming activity in the process: henceforth, that object is the philologist as subject. The insight is crucial, and it is directly bound up with Nietzsche's newfound appreciation for what he calls the "personality" of Democritus. For at issue in philological questions, Nietzsche reasons, is first and foremost the philologist's subjective attachments to his objects. And so it happens that the turning point in his inquiries into Democritus comes with his revelation about the philosopher's "character" and personal stamp. In fact, Nietzsche's relation to Democritus at this point becomes very much a personal affair, as much a matter of intimate attachment and affinity as of objective and considered distance. Writing against the grain of philosophical tradition and even against Epicurus, Nietzsche must find a point of entry that he can call his own: "I personally like the figure of Democritus immensely; to be sure, I have reconstructed him entirely afresh, as our historians of philosophy never do either him or Epicurus justice, since they are too pious and like Jews before their Lord."[89] "Piety" here has nothing to do with respect for Democritean physiology. On the contrary, "piety" can only refer to the spiritualism and dogmatism of scholarship (Nietzsche names Schleiermacher as an example) that work to blunt the radical and doubtful edge of atomism. Nietzsche normally reserves this kind of critique for Epicurus himself, objecting to the latter's ideals of quietism, realism, and voluntarism, all of which are betrayals of atomism as it was originally conceived by its founders, and all of which—to Nietzsche's mind, at least—have obvious scholarly equivalents. (Epicurus was in fact anything but a dogmatic disciple: he could be irreverent and at times hostile toward his atomist forebears, as shown by his bizarre denial that Leucippus ever existed, or by his more serious claim in his study *On Nature* that Democritus' physical determinism was self-refuting, and which Epicurus' introduction of the swerve, the incalculable leap of atoms from their compulsory itineraries, was designed to undo, so as to salvage the possibility of free will and a subject's self-determination.[90]) Thus, although Epicureanism is, in Nietzsche's eyes, in its own way a kind of spiritualization of the atomistic hypothesis, here Nietzsche is siding with the atomists en bloc.[91] Over against all these distortions, Nietzsche could claim finally to have "won a new comprehensive image of the outstanding *personality* of Democritus."

This is the third and last consequence of Nietzsche's fusion of Lange and Rose. For here, too, Nietzsche is not only working in Lange's spirit; he seems be following some of Lange's express indications. There is, for instance, Lange's repeated claim that the only reliable guide to the history of materialism is "*the whole person [der ganze Mensch]*": what counts is the powerful, and as it were material, impression cast by a singular mind in the course of its discoveries, the totality of its signature, rather than the vaporous diffusion of its ideas. In fact, Lange openly recommends a "biographical" and frankly materialist approach to the history of thought (pp. 346, 349); and his own work is for the most part organized around stellar figures and their ideas, viewed as embodied in systems of thought, virtually in styles of thought, rather than as pale, disembodied concepts. For "the history of philosophical doctrines is not just a pure evolution of ideas; rather, the personality of the bearers of ideas constantly impinges on those ideas." It does so with an intensity that implies, at some level, a physiological investment, a working of drives and instincts, and an approach that is manifestly "interested," and never disinterested (p. 16). As Nietzsche would later write, "In the philosopher . . . there is nothing whatever that is impersonal; and above all, his morality bears decided and decisive witness to *who he is*—that is, in what order of rank the innermost drives of his nature stand in relation to each other" (*BGE*, §6).[92] The first instance of this phenomenon to be mentioned by Lange in his history is, of course, "the magnificent personality of Democritus" (ibid.).

Nietzsche's sudden and personal appreciation for Democritus is a further index of the distance he has traveled: it marks a complete reversal from his position at the outset of his inquiry, which is astonishingly dispassionate about the Democritean question. In particular, it is around the concept of "personality," or the character of the full-bodied person, that the change has taken place. Nietzsche's initial view was not just that Democritus' writings could be shown to be spurious, following Rose's methods. It was that the task of disqualifying these titles was entirely secondary to the more pressing problem concerning the authenticity of Aristotle's works, as this was raised by Rose. The question mark that troubles the Democritean titles, Nietzsche writes early on, is a mere "pendant," while the issue of Aristotle's corpus of writings takes precedence not only over Democritus' writings but over "Democritus himself, whose portrait has to be done over again here in only a few of its features" (3:248 [July–September 1867]). Even so, the individuality of Democritus (once it is attained) is for Nietzsche inseparable from larger concerns that threaten to dissolve the very ground of his attachments. The first of these, oddly enough, has to do with the very reasons why Nietzsche wishes so passionately to embrace "his" Democritus—an act that is decidedly problematical, as we shall see.

Addressing himself to the question concerning the goals of philology, Nietzsche transcends the issue of capturing the past as it really was by taking on the larger issue of what it is that motivates, psychologically, the desire to do so. Gazing beyond his study on Democritus, which he predicts will contain nothing but "bitter truths" for philologists,[93] he envisions a vast, second project: "It will be a history of literary studies in antiquity and in the modern period. I am initially unconcerned with details; what lures me on is *das*

Allgemein-Menschliche" (letter to Rohde of 1–3 February 1868). This universality shorn of all detail is not Goethean and romantic: it is an anthropological constant, strangely (and almost physiologically) defined as the "felt *need* for a literary history." The history of this history would cover, first, the way in which the need for a literary history initially takes form (say, in the early reception of Homer). Then it would show how this need is shaped at the hands of "the philosophers" (presumably, Plato, then Aristotle and the later Peripatetic schools) and by subsequent generations of scholars—all of whom stand in the shadow of great geniuses, like Homer or Democritus, who are themselves no more than the expression of "typical" ideas. The point is that these individual geniuses are but the embodiment of projected and generalized needs and drives, the invention of a culture. Nietzsche's thinking is both circular and paradoxical. To have defined literary history as the response to some need, some essential requirement, and (as it turns out) some essential lack (a lack of genius) is already to step well beyond the comfortable frames of academic reference, and to ready "bitter" truths for philology indeed.[94]

The allusion, in the same letter, to Schopenhauer's influence notwithstanding (it is heavily ironic),[95] Schopenhauer is conspicuous for his absence in Nietzsche's philological speculations, and no doubt this is deliberate. At the time, Nietzsche identifies the worst of philology's tendencies—specialization, pessimism, rejection of life and art—with Schopenhauer's Weltanschauungen.[96] Nietzsche himself seems to connect the foregoing reflections with atomistic teaching: "Epicurus' theory of human need already stems from Democritus," he observes at one point (4:55). If so, then we have perhaps another indication of Nietzsche's "atomistic" philology. As he writes in a series of notes that parallel the project on the "history of literary studies" announced in his letter to Rohde, in place of a "history of ideas" Nietzsche envisions a "history of drives"; once reduced in this way, history finds a common denominator "with the natural sciences."[97] It is only by recovering the logic, or rather the illogic, of need that the logic of history, forever inaccessible, may be rendered intelligible. This is the best that can be hoped for, a mere *Gesetzmäßigkeit*, or "lawlike correspondence," between subject and object, of the sort that is revealed in natural inquiry. For the "chain" of history is governed by no sublime necessity, no natural reason, but at most by a "smaller" necessity. Its parts are minima, virtually atomistic and chaotic ("above all, the smallness of the chain's pieces has to be stressed"), and most of all, dissimilar.[98] It is only through "combinations" and analogies that an image of the historical process can be generated. Nevertheless, Nietzsche insists, all identities and equivalencies remain purely "imaginary"; and so too any grand view one might have of history, written in majescule, is an "illusion." By his own admission, this theory amounts to a kind of skepticism.[99] The point is summed up in brilliant fashion, though with generous help from Lange: we have enough to do, even far more than it is possible to do, whenever we go about trying to strip away the layers of subjectivity that cloak our own appearances (that is, the way we appear to ourselves) and those of our historical and philological sources. The attempt yields only the appearance of objectivity, which is in fact "nothing but 'subjectivity' on another level."[100] And that is a fact that a scholar like Valentin Rose would never admit to.[101]

In what way could Nietzsche's personalized Democritus elude the very (and seemingly inevitable) constraints on his reconstruction, from within a literary history—the constraints posed by our need for venerable geniuses to enshrine in some history? Nietzsche's point, I think, is that Democritus does not elude these constraints at all. He exists in Nietzsche's philology precisely to illustrate them. Democritus is the paradox of Nietzsche's philology, and inseparable from his conception of him. It is therefore exceedingly difficult to separate Nietzsche's reconstruction of Democritus from his desire and willingness to reconstitute him as a whole figure. Yet, in what way is Democritus' "personality," so won, "typical"? And of what?

"Homer and Classical Philology"

Clarification of a sort is to be found in the published version of Nietzsche's inaugural speech at Basel, "Homer and Classical Philology." Originally imagined as an essay "On Homer's Personality," the piece is a brilliant display of Nietzsche's subtly congested and self-eroding thought, what he elsewhere refers to as "my Homeric *paradoxa*."[102] Besides carrying through an implicit extension and problematizing of Lange's views of *Persönlichkeit*, which gives the essay its "philosophical and aesthetic" content, the essay also represents a radicalization, and consequently a critique, of existing philological assumptions, especially those of Friedrich August Wolf, who revolutionized the field at the end of the previous century.[103] Nietzsche's essay deserves close analysis, but only a rapid glance will be possible in what follows, set briefly against the background of Wolfian philology, which is central to Nietzsche's essay.

At issue in the essay is how one is to locate and define what is Homeric in the Homeric poems. The question, racking eighteenth- and nineteenth-century European philologists with academic doubt, was whether the poems spring from a common source ("Homer") or from a multiple and centuries-long tradition of oral recitation; whether they are integrally unified or mere compilations—in a word, whether "Homer" was the author of the *Iliad* and the *Odyssey*. The issue, which continues to burn today, is still known as it was in Nietzsche's day as "the Homeric question."[104] Nietzsche's solution is strategic rather than final. In ways, it anticipates Foucault's complex answer to the question "What is an Author?": "We believe in the one great poet of the *Iliad* and the *Odyssey—just not in Homer as this poet*" (p. 266).[105] Nietzsche is not simplifying the issue by isolating Homer from the poems' "great author" (the last of the arrangers to put the finishing touches on them, and thus the heir to Homer's name). He is complicating the meaning of Homer's name by forcefully sundering the questions of text, authorship, and attribution at the level of their theoretical construction. The issue is not one that can be solved empirically. No papyrus or shard of pottery could ever prove the necessary oneness of the identities held apart in Nietzsche's declaration, or ever falsify his point: Homer is and is not, and will always (never) be, the author of the *Iliad* and *Odyssey*. He exists at the level of theoretical fiction that lies embedded in an ancient and ongoing practice of reading—and at the nebulous vanishing point of an authorial instance.[106] "Homer" is thus divided within. The name stands for an institutionalized function—one implied by a sequence of cultural developments into the present, which Nietzsche equates with "Alexandrianism"—as opposed to a purely literary function.[107] And quite daringly, given the facts of posthumous meaning (and here Nietzsche takes a rather un-Foucauldian psychological turn), "Homer" stands for an "aesthetic judgment" (p. 264), an image of unity and originality that was produced over the centuries by readers who sought, with varying success, to locate the presiding *Ur*-genius in these monumentalized and culturally consecrated works. This, despite the fact that such an "origin" is as much a mere "phantom" and projection as is the "original and perfect design [*Plan*]," the guiding intentionality that was as precious as Homer's supposed identity, and sought for just as hard among generations of readers, from Aristotle to the Alexandrian commentators to Wolf and beyond (p. 265).[108]

"Homer" is not only the product of an aesthetic judgment. He is also an imagination, covering over what is in fact, Nietzsche reasons, an impossibility—which is to say a factual impossibility made real through imaginary means (p. 264). "Homer," conceived as unique and as endowed with an individualized "personality," is as fragile and inaccessible a unity as are each of the two poems, whose very physical dimensions and repleteness of singular scenes and images preclude their ever being grasped, respectively and individually, in a single, synoptic, and totalizing glimpse (*Gesammtblick*) that is impossible in reality: "The plan of an epic such as the *Iliad* is not a whole, not an organism, but a sequence of pieces strung together, a product of a reflection that proceeds by aesthetic rules" (p. 264). This is not to say that a unifying glimpse of the *Iliad* or *Odyssey* is not possible in theory, but only that the artist who most succeeds poetically, through conscious organization, will be one who most *deceives* the reader into imagining the epic "as if the whole hovered before him [that is, the artist, himself a prototype for the reader] in a powerful instantaneity, as a vivid whole" (p. 265).[109] Such an image of unified wholeness may exist, but it will do so only as an illusion. Nietzsche had made the same point in his unfinished essay on "Teleology Since Kant": "The 'whole' is itself only a representation" ("TSK," 381). In both cases, Nietzsche is forcefully challenging the basic assumptions of the teleology of representation, although here the question is linked to a presumed teleology of reading (where, moreover, Aristotle is invoked as an authority for such a conception).[110] The alternative, which is a matter of perhaps even greater desperation, is to attempt to "think out" the whole by subsuming it (also in Kantian fashion) under a notional and conceptual "schema"—if this is actually a distinct alternative at all. In fact, the central, nagging question behind Nietzsche's essay is whether Homer—the figure of Homer embodied by his poems—is not actually one such conceptual schema standing for a totality (the aesthetic unity of his poems); that is, whether in Homer "a concept has been made out of a person or a person out of a concept" (p. 257).

Nietzsche leaves his listeners with a deliberately unsatisfying and slightly unfocused answer to this most urgent "'Homeric question.'" The lack of focus stems not from a lack of resolve, but from the visualizing apparatus that Nietzsche's supple reasoning requires: "Homer" can be had, but not Homer; the illusion is there for one's enjoyment, but only on condition of its being an illusion, in at least two senses. Homer's unity as a person and the unity of his poems are the illusory product of an artistic epigone who, at some unspecified historical moment, endowed the poems with a conscious order and unity, but only through vastly inferior artistic capacities.[111] In contrast with this later artist, Nietzsche postulates the instinctive, unconscious, and "real" poet, a figure who recedes facelessly and irrecoverably into his tradition, only to reappear at the other end as an invention of the Alexandrian critics in the third century B.C.E. "Homer" as the author of the two epics is something that we owe to these earliest philologists, whom Nietzsche admires for their having whittled down to size the legendary *Wundermann*. In this way, Homer, the supernaturally gifted and thus "inaccessible" prototype of all poetry to come, a mere myth, is made into a *"possible* poet"— that is to say, a historical poet endowed with a "tangible personality" (pp. 264, 256).[112] But if the Alexandrians gave rise to "the psychological possibility of *a* Homer"—and Nietzsche here crucially fails to specify whose psychology he means, the critics' or Homer's—that possibility was elaborated in the form of a "hypothesis" only (p. 256). Thus, what we term and celebrate as Homer's "unity" is but a relatively recent reading of the Homeric epics and the projection of an illusory plan into them, while "Homer" is a mere by-product of this illusion, an aesthetic judgment.[113] Readers of the poems are thus victims of the twofold illusion that Homer is the poems' author and that those poems have a recognizable unity. In both cases, what the reader "grasps" is the mere illusion of a *possibility*. Illusion or delusion? The problem is whether the poems can even be taken in at all without the minimal assumption of their unifying instance—that is to say, whether their perception can ever be anything other than aesthetic. In themselves, they are "nothing more than a succession of especially fine and impressive *loci*, chosen in accordance with a subjective standard of taste" (p. 263), a fragile will o' the wisp. At their heart lies an "empty name," a void, that is capable of posing simultaneously as innermost "kernel" and outermost "husk" (pp. 258, 261). The illusion at the heart of Homer is as necessary and unavoidable as it is false and irretrievable. That is what has proved so valuable about the hypothesis, or question, of Homer's identity (*die Persönlichkeitsfrage*): it is "the fruitful kernel of an entire cycle of questions [*Fragencyklus*]," even if these spin, in the end, around an empty place (p. 254).[114]

Oddly, while the question of "the real poet" is blurred more or less to the point of being dismissed, that of "personality" is quietly and disturbingly dropped from consideration, but only after it has been made utterly indistinctive. At one point, Nietzsche remarkably suggests the complete convergence of the "personalities" of the synthetic epigone and his poetic precursor, as if their poetic intentions were fundamentally identical in the end, merely the instinctual and conscious faces, respectively, of one and the same poetic need: "The relative imperfection [!] of the design of the epics should not be grounds for seeing in the maker of that design *a different personality* from the actual poet" (p. 265; emphasis added).[115] With this, Nietzsche's essay attains a spectacular level of contradiction. The later artist is elevated to a stature and even a degree of "instinctual creativity" rivaling Homer's (p. 266). But then again, how could we ever tell these apart? "Homer," after all, is the deceptive appearance that the poems give as part of their effect; he is their imaginary unifying instance. Homer's epigone is in a way Homer's impostor. At this point, the question of "personality" might appear to have been voided of significance, but in fact the question is not dropped at all. Rather, it is transferred to the domain of philology and the question of *its* identity. Homer, it appears, can no longer be separated from his reception, from his being positioned within a philological operation. (A question not directly asked but only hinted at in the essay is whether Homer's artistic epigone, being the first to focus the image of Homer's identity, doesn't have a claim to being the first philologist.) And yet if we turn our gaze away from Homer and toward philology, the situation is scarcely any more assuring, or any less blurry.

The first part of the essay, which turns exclusively on the definition not of "Homer" but of "philology," is in fact ridden with doubts, anxieties, and divisions, and not the wholeness toward which the essay strives and finally claims to celebrate. Indeed, with the very first mention of philology, which is to say from the opening sentence, the essay plunges into the midst of confusion: "There is no clear and coherent view of classical philology on offer in this day and age." The thought frames and colors everything that follows. No matter where one looks, Nietzsche continues, whether among disciplinary insiders or among the educated lay public, what one finds is a lack of consensus and a clash of perspectives regarding the nature and purpose of classical studies. Small wonder that agreement over Homer's identity has proven so hard to reach: philology is hardly in control of its own doubtful identity, which is betrayed by its multiple strata of disciplinary elements, its inherent "lack of any conceptual unity," and its splintered and often conflictual character. Whatever semblance of unity it enjoys is thanks to "the impetus of philological personalities," who take philology wherever they lead, imparting to the discipline a momentary, if illusory, focus.[116] Nietzsche is not inventing or exaggerating. Doubts and divisions were very much alive in the contemporary classical world, and Nietzsche, true to form, is echoing them with a certain affirmative vehemence, all the while affecting to rally to the defense of his discipline in its time of distress. Attacked from various quarters from without, classics had been made to feel like an untimely pursuit ever since its professionalization around the turn of the nineteenth century, and the same pressures could wreak havoc from within the discipline.[117]

The most famous of the divisions within classical studies was that between Gottfried Hermann (1772–1848) and August Boeckh (1785–1867), two powerful "philological personalities" if ever there were any (although Nietzsche does not mention them by name). During the early half of the nineteenth century their antagonism nearly split the profession into two warring camps, the one narrowly textual and linguistic, the other broadly historical and antiquarian, though this characterization is too rough and ready: the fissures were often of a subtler kind, while fundamental points of agreement could be disguised by overheated polemics. A generation earlier, Wolf had stirred up a whirlwind of controversy of his own with his analysis of Homer. Specialization and fragmentation were increasingly taking their toll as well. Coursing through all of these conflicts, and afflicting everyone on all sides of the debates, was a deeper tension between classicism (or humanism) and modernism, troubling the study of antiquity with the question of its "untimeliness." Nietzsche has all of this in mind—not only the jagged fault lines but also the labyrinthine connections that join together again the disparate faces of the classical world and its study.[118]

Standing back from the fray, Nietzsche can declare that philology, in its concept and in its traditions, "is as much part history as it is part natural science and part aesthetics" (p. 249). Strangely "centauric," philology is at most in an inorganic *Aggregatzustand*: it exists in the condition of an aggregate, but unstably (the analogy, interestingly enough, is to atomic aggregates).[119] As with Homer's poems, all that binds this farrago of scholarly activities together is but "*the name* 'philology'" itself (ibid.; emphasis added). Still worse, philology suffers from an insurmountable obstacle, which it nonetheless struggles to overcome (although positing and overcoming this obstacle is what in fact defines philology): the unbridgeable "gap [*Kluft*] between the ideal antiquity, which is possibly nothing but the prettiest climax of the Germanic love affair with the South," and whatever belies that ideality, the less glamorous "reality" of antiquity, which Nietzsche crucially fails to elaborate (pp. 251, 253).[120] Expressions of this gap today are, on the one hand, the negative, idol-shattering, and skeptical tendencies of philological method ("reservations and doubts," which give philology, in its "overall character [*Gesammtcharakter*]," itself the look of something "completely dubious," p. 253). On the other are its opposite tendencies toward wholeness and haleness (Goethe's healthy classicism is cited as an exemplary inspiration). How the gap might ever be healed is anything but clear. The naming of antiquity alone—of "the so-called 'classical' antiquity" (p. 249)—betrays its projective character. In what sense is antiquity "one"? The problem haunts the idealist and realist aspirations alike.

If the essay in its first half is troubled with doubts about philology, in the second part about Homer the essay strives for wholeness—strives, but ultimately without attaining its aim. As we have seen, the drift and logic of the essay go another way, effectively eroding any confidence one might have in the coherence of the idea of wholeness itself. Nietzsche is deploying two strategies in his essay, while covering over their traces with a third. Pretending to want to resolve the problems of philology and to restore it to its rightful and "natural" wholeness (p. 253), Nietzsche goes on to make a bizarre and troubling move, one that, as if designed to appease philologists and lay humanists alike but in fact horrifying to both, will take up the remainder of his essay: he runs, so to speak, with Wolfian philology, the bane of classicism, full tilt into the open, waiting arms of Goethe, that movement's greatest exponent. If Nietzsche is attempting to reconcile classicism with historicism, he could not have found a less appropriate way to do so. Wolf and Goethe stand at the opposite ends of the Homeric question. There is simply no harmonizing Wolf's position, which Nietzsche unabashedly names and adopts ("We believe in the one great poet of the *Iliad* and the *Odyssey—just not in*

Homer as this poet"),[121] with Goethe's demands for Homeric wholeness. Early on in the essay, Nietzsche cites Goethe's uncompromising critique of Wolf, from a pungent epigram bearing the title "Homer again Homer."[122] But Nietzsche is not trying to reconcile these opposed tendencies. Quite the contrary, there is a perversity to his position, to his attempt to blow life and unity into the *disiecta membra* of his discipline whose fragmentariness he is the last to deny (centauric, it is in essence, as he says, a "pseudo-monar-chy").[123] Nietzsche's equivocal attitude toward wholeness is evident through-out (the essay is obsessed with totality in its *elusiveness*). His approach to "the so-called Homeric question," which he concedes to be "in fact no longer timely [*zeitgemäss*]," in large part thanks to the achievement of Wolf (p. 254), turns out to be a specific, troubled instance of the same issue, indeed its shimmering reflection: instead of showing the Homeric question to be resolved, Nietzsche seems only to revive it in a magnified form. In pursuing the contradictory positions of classicism and historicism, Nietzsche is, I believe, exploring their internal self-contradictions. What he shows, in effect, is how both tendencies are moving down the same illogical paths toward one and the same goal, and how exposing and living with that goal coincides, or could be made to coincide, with a philology of the future. A brief look at Wolf's Homeric scholarship will help to bring out this larger point and will at the same time illuminate the most puzzling aspects of Nietzsche's essay.

F. A. Wolf and the Hermeneutics of Deception

Wolf's *Prolegomena to Homer*, published in 1795, enjoyed an immediate and lasting *succès de scandale*. In its troubling wake, anyone nourished on the ideals of Winckelmann, Goethe, and Schiller (let alone these last two mon-umental figures themselves) would have to think twice about the historicity of Homer and the unity of his poems. But the real threat posed by Wolf to the ideals of classicism, I suspect, lay not so much in what he had to say about Homer, that prized icon of classical perfection and of natural poetic genius, as in what he revealed about the ways in which classicism went about constructing its ideals. Wolf was neither fabulously original nor was he a confabulist. In "dar[ing] to deprive Homer of some of the renown for that artistic skill which [scholars and layfolk] admire so greatly" (*Prolegomena*, chap. 35, p. 148), he was preceded by a generation or more of academic controversy over Homer. His contentions, moreover, had the backing of ancient sources (Cicero, Plutarch, Aelian, Josephus, and others), which showed that the Homeric poems, even in antiquity, were conceded to be mere compilations in several hands. On both fronts, ancient and modern, Wolf was easily anticipated, nor did he do anything to conceal the fact.[124] Given this background of extensive debate alone, the ideals of classicism do seem more than a little suspect. Mired in disavowal, classicism must ignore the obvious contestability of its own perspectives, while its holism is strictly speaking synecdochal. Much of the evidence of the past (or all of it, Wolf would argue, summoning up "the voice of all antiquity" [chap. 33, p. 137]) had to be overlooked in order to construct that past as a self-contained and harmonious (and directly accessible) whole. The idealized image of "so-called classical antiquity" is self-contradictory and blindly so, Wolf seems to be saying, implicating "the Klopstocks, the Wielands, the Vosses," and other belletrists of the mid-eighteenth century who, bent as they were on viewing the classical world through the mists of poetic reverie, helped swell the classicist revival that not even Wolf's iconoclasm could dampen. Their vision of antiquity, his analysis of Homer could show, is the product of a classicizing aesthetic.[125] Nietzsche would eventually seize upon this last point and make it valid against Wolf himself, who was after all the inventor of *Altertumswissenschaft*, or the study of "all antiquity."

Wolf, for his part, was by no means immune to the lures of the classical ideal, nor was he entirely free of doubts of his own. In fact, his treatise often reads like the product of a scholarly mind plagued with uncertainties and doubts as it watches its own logic unfold, bemusedly and at times with blank fascination.[126] Words like "doubt" and "suspicion," occasionally applied to each other (friends of his "distrusted [his] suspicions"), are in fact leitmotifs of Wolf's narrative of discovery, which bears not a few resemblances to Nietzsche's own wrestling with doubt in his *Democritea*.[127] The demolition of the myth of "Homer" is no easy thing, and Wolf often seems to vacillate as he presses the logic of his position to its last consequences. Clearly, some of this is staged, some of it is genuine (or at least a lingering memory of a once more genuinely felt wonderment and self-doubting), and some of it is a cautious pose that allows Wolf to hedge where he has no definitive answers.[128]

But no such answers were to be forthcoming. Symptomatically, the *Prolegomena* would (like so much of Nietzsche's own philology) remain a fragment, its second part never published, its project never fully realized even in the first installment—assuming the project was even capable of being realized at all.

The *Prolegomena* was conceived as an introduction to a new critical edition of Homer, based on the latest manuscript evidence, but above all on the recently discovered Venice scholia published by the French classicist Villoison in 1788. Derived from Alexandrian commentaries, the scholia shed new light on the transmission of Homer in antiquity, and Wolf was ideally positioned to benefit from them. His *Prolegomena* is in ways more and less than a methodological preamble to the edition. Its primary goal is to attempt a reconstruction of the earliest history of the Homeric texts in antiquity and so to assess the foundations of the texts in their vulgate form. Wolf's edition appeared in the same year as his *Prolegomena*, but the achievements of the edition could only be—and would in fact be—overshadowed by the theoretical justifications made for it in the *Prolegomena*. For in promising to reach back to the most reliable sources for any text of Homer by way of the earliest preserved critical traditions in antiquity, the *Prolegomena* had effectively led to an aporetic result; the tradition was hopelessly incomplete, and to an extent that could never be fully determined. To quote a recent diagnosis of the problem faced by Wolf, "close study of the evidence showed that the work of the ancient scholars could not be reconstructed fully—and thus that a really critical text could not be produced."[129] All that any edition might do is circumscribe a series of losses that could no longer even be imagined—or else could only be imagined. Accordingly, the *Prolegomena* warns us away from any greater expectation; it qualifies, in advance, the pretensions of the edition it introduces.[130]

That, however, is not all there is to the *Prolegomena*, because Wolf does in fact try to imagine what has been lost, as he only can if he is to reconstruct the history and locate the evidence of this loss, in accordance with the program of his subtitle: "Concerning the Original and Genuine Form of the Homeric Works and Their Various Alterations and the Proper Method of Emendation." This is after all one of Wolf's recognized achievements. His reconstruction of the history of the Homeric text in antiquity was the first of its kind; indeed, a vivid grasp of antiquity—its *Vergegenwärtigung*—lies at the very heart of his concept of *Altertumswissenschaft*.[131] And so, even on Wolf's rigorous conception of philology the ideals of classicism are not quite dislodged; instead, they are displaced onto the image of an invaluable and now vanished world whose outlines, at least, are solid.[132] In a moment we shall see just how tenuous that image is. At any rate, in Wolf's philology, negation and reconstruction are intertwined but also at odds. So perhaps his *Prolegomena* does not consist in a single, realizable project after all. What is certain, however, is that the Homeric question encapsulated the question of philology like none other could, for the history of the Homeric text just is the history of philology.[133] And in pressing philological problems to the limit of what could be known, Wolf was pressing the problem of philology itself to new and unknown limits. It was the extremity of this kind of philology, with its exuberant skepticism and high-stakes gamble, that would appeal to Nietzsche, who doubtless had a clearer sense of where the dangers lay than Wolf could afford to admit.

That Wolf sensed the dangers is certain. His voice and his logic are hard to read, but it is possible to pin down a little more closely the source of his vacillations. His real dilemma is not simply that philological skepticism, given free rein, tends to shatter habitual and customary beliefs (such as those surrounding the integrity of the Homeric poems). It is that the ultimate touchstone for the knowing skeptic and the would-be believer in Wolf is one and the same faculty—namely, his aesthetic sensibility as a reader; and it is this selfsame sensibility that leads him down conflicting paths of logic. Thus, it is his readerly (literally, philological) "sense [*sensus*]" that tells him that the *Iliad* is not a seamless whole (specifically, that the last six books are not by Homer).[134] And it is the same sense that persuades him—literally deceives him—that it is.[135] Knowing this, he also knows (or ought to know) that he cannot trust his readerly sense: it might be deceiving him at this very moment, and it may be inherently deceptive as well. These possibilities, but especially the last, infinitely complicate Wolf's task as a philologist, and they will eventually disable his thesis about Homer. It seems likely that Nietzsche, who knew Wolf's treatise well, also knew its stumbling blocks, and that he consequently put these at the center of his own essay on Homer and classical philology. But in order to see why this is so, we will first need to explore Wolf's thesis about what a reader can and cannot know.

Wolf is a shrewd observer of the psychology of reading. He understands something about the capacity of readers to overlook what they know, and in a sense to blind themselves or to be rendered blind by the experience of reading itself. How is it that the different compositional layers in Homer, visibly joined together (as he was able to determine "in the course of very frequent readings"), could have gone undetected for so many millennia? They haven't, Wolf answers, or rather they have and have not:

> True, not even the most erudite readers have felt difficulties of this sort for many centuries, though I would think that no one of even average intelligence could avoid encountering them. Perhaps one reason for this was that the poems' continuous sequence deceived their readers, thanks in part to their high reputation and in part to their own beauty [or: "appearance"] (*sua specie fallens*), and thus banished any meditation on this matter; and that we are almost all naturally more eager to join together things which are disconnected than to disconnect things which are joined together. (*Prolegomena*, chap. 30, pp. 127–28)

In effect, we naturally and unwittingly construct aesthetic wholes thanks to natural and unconscious habits of reading, codified over centuries-long practices.[136] That we do presents a problem for Wolf's reconstruction of Homer. For if his observation about the habits of reading proves true, not even his own judgment about Homer will be reliable, resting as it does on an aesthetic perception, nor will anyone else's. And that is his dilemma.

Some of Wolf's reasoning will be familiar from Nietzsche's essay. The *Iliad* and the *Odyssey* each display what Wolf calls "artistic structure [*artem et structuram*]," a unitary cohesiveness and intentional design (in Nietzsche's phrase, which is inherited—this is their *Plan*).[137] The problem is determining the original seat of this unity, but also its reach. Either the artistic structure subsists in the original form of the poems or it "was derived from the genius of others, who were inspired by the theme of the poems and the ordering of the plot" (chap. 30, p. 127; and chap. 31, p. 131). To propose that the "artistic structure" of Homer's poems "was introduced by later ages" is, as Wolf senses, to move beyond the relatively sure ground of philological skepticism into the deeper waters of hopeful reconstruction. "Even if all the rest were explained away, this would raise a doubt about the entire form of these poems, one which could not be answered [*inexplicabilis dubitatio nasceretur de universa forma*]" (chap. 31, p. 131).[138] Wisely, Wolf retreats ("But we must move on to another kind of argument"). Unwisely, he continues to maintain that Homer, the original epic bard, "was responsible for the larger part and the order of the earlier books" (*Iliad*, 1–18), which display an artistic structure and unity of their own (ibid., p. 132, and passim).[139] After Homer, rhapsodes, revisers, or critics (functionally, these are hard to distinguish for Wolf) "forced" the original episodic remains of Homer, his original centos, "into a single great continuous body" so as to create "a new and more perfect and splendid monument" (chap. 28, p. 122). Later, the Alexandrian grammarians, principally Aristarchus, brilliantly managed to "restore" Homer's corrupted and interpolated text to its "original form" and "miraculous harmony" (chap. 50, p. 210; cf. chap. 35, p. 148). But *which* original form and harmony?

Holding all of this, Wolf has effectively constructed a logical conundrum, one that entails the very "doubt about the entire form of these poems" that, as he feared, "could not be answered." Wolf's recuperative desire is at odds with his philological skepticism, and both seem baffled in each other's presence. He seems, moreover, to be caught in a temporal paradox, as if tripped up by the retroactive effects of his own experience of the poems. The poems are and are not "whole." They seem to be artistically unified, but in what sense are they? Worse, they seem to contain different possible wholes in their variegated stratigraphy.[140] Our sense of the whole(s) may be owing to Homer, or to later rhapsodes, or to grammarian critics, or simply to our self-confirming sense and experience of the poems (as well as our resolute indifference to the poems' palpable blemishes). However we decide the issue, the coherence of the Homeric poems is what it can only be, a shadow and a deception, a mere appearance, for the poems "deceive us by their appearance [*facie fallunt*]" (chap. 31, p. 134). Their formal design is indeed a "phantom," as Nietzsche would say: it is merely the appearance of itself, the illusion that "the whole hovered before [the artist responsible for this illusion, and consequently ourselves] in a powerful instantaneity, as a vivid whole." Indeed, for Nietzsche, and to a lesser extent for Wolf, the sensation of the whole is not something we can even directly experience: it comes mediated by an illusion that somebody else has already had—or rather seems to have had (whether this be an Alexandrian textual critic or the speculated artist-compositor of the Homeric poems). So, for example, the last hands to put Homer's poems into their final form, Wolf concedes, "sought the genuine form of the text." But he crucially adds that "for them the genuine form was that which seemed most to suit the poet": "They sought only what would be in harmony with the continuous movement and art of epic poetry" (chap. 47, pp. 193–94; chap. 30, p. 130). Our illusion is courtesy of theirs. The whole one senses is thus a conjectural form extrapolated from some original set of traces that in turn have only a conjectural existence. Such is the circularity of aesthetic logic, the consequences of which can be paralyzing.

In one sense, this standoff is precisely the desired effect. Wolf is defying his readers to pin down with any certainty the stages in the transformation of Homer's poems, with a kind of skeptical overkill. If he can establish the futility of the attempt, while reinforcing the requirement to do so, he can establish all the more evidently the futility of trying to recover the original design of Homer's poems.[141] That original design, he can confidently show, is as illusory an image as the impression that the poems are seamlessly unified products of art. And so any inquiry guided by "poetic laws" rather than by that which "appears to be probable on historical and critical grounds" (Wolf's programmatic criteria) must concede inadequacy (chap. 30, p. 127). Wolf is partly attacking the anachronistic Aristotelian canon of beginnings, middles, and ends that was pursued with such sterile rigor and "chill erudition" by the Alexandrians, and which he believed had come to dominate the perception of Homer's poems into his own day.[142] But he is also making a stronger argument about the general fallibility of aesthetic perception, its extraordinary tolerance for self-delusion, in favor of the sounder judgment of philology. Hence the assertion that marks the climax of his discussion is disingenuous: "Nor indeed are the poems so deformed and reshaped that they seem excessively unlike their own original form in individual details" (chap. 50, p. 210). The claim conceals a tautology: the notion of an "original form" is precisely what a critical Homeric philology must dispute.[143] Wolf's ironies plainly can be arch, on this, the most generous reading of his writerly strategies. The question is whether he can come away from his puzzle scot-free. It is doubtful that he can.

The problem is that Wolf cannot rid himself of the ghost of the poems' original form. Paradoxically, what keeps the idea of an original form afloat is the very evidence that we no longer have it: the blemishes, the bad joins, the "traces of another poet's imitation" that "lurk in the things derived from Homer," and whatever else betrays "the sinews and the Homeric spirit" of the poems, which is to say of "the original work[s]" (chap. 30, p. 127; chap. 31, p.131). Wolf crucially requires the traces of a lost original in order to be able to eliminate them again convincingly. But the only hard evidence he can bring to his most central claims about the Homeric question is, ironically, the evidence of his own senses.[144] The poems give the deceptive appearance of being all one (*sensus* tells us so); but *sensus* tells us that only "the greater part" is by Homer and that the "remainder" was interpolated by a later tradition.[145] The question, in the final analysis, boils down to a literary one, rather than being a matter of "historical and critical grounds" for judgment. How could it be anything else? Wolf and the received view of Wolf notwithstanding, historicism is not vindicated over aesthetics in the last analysis. On the contrary, history for Wolf is as conjectural as art and is apparently less certain than his own literary (readerly, or philological) *sensus*.[146]

Nor is this all. In pursuing his logic, Wolf has in effect constructed an impossible philological object, one that goes out of focus whenever we try to examine it. Not even literary *sensus*, though indubitable, is finally decisive. It soon loses the trail, or in Wolf's favorite metaphor (which is self-consciously contrived to quicken one of the ancient etymologies of "rhapsode"), the "thread."[147] All that is left is a crumbling text on the one hand and a series of "faint and blurred [historical] impression[s]" on the other (cf. chap. 41, p. 168). At no point does clarity supervene—except in those blinding moments of delusion, when the mists gather and then vanish, leaving us with the most vivid and empty impression of all, the marvel of Homer's poems.[148] No wonder that Wolf was never able to clarify the exact nature of his contribution to Homeric scholarship to his peers (or vice versa): it lay in pressing the problems inherent in the materials and methods of philology to an aporetic extreme. But this was nothing that could be truly assessed by Wolf or by his fellow philologists, because it described a kind of blind spot in their visual field.[149] Plainly, for Wolf and the tradition he embodies, Homer and his texts are not merely an imperfect collection of textual fragments. They are a paradoxical kind of monument, a sublime object, about which it can be said that "*even the ruins have perished*" (chap. 49, p. 209): they exist only in the imagination.[150]

Nietzsche's essay on Homer is evidently playing with the dilemmas of Wolf's philology, but with a vengeance, and with a love of insoluble ambiguity as well. Affecting to take a Wolfian stance, he carries Wolf's logic to an intolerable limit, staging its inner contortions in a numbing blur of (non)distinctions that rival Wolf's own. A good example of this blurring effect is the following proposition (which may well be derived from Wolf's language): "The *Iliad* is not a garland [or "wreath": *Kranz*], but a wreath [or "garland"] of flowers [*Blumengewinde*]" (p. 265).[151] Even the Wolfian-sounding claim that stands at the center of Nietzsche's essay is devious, because it actually reverses Wolf's position while retaining the structure of his argument: "We believe in the one great poet of the *Iliad* and the *Odyssey—just not in Homer as this poet.*" Clinging to a prehistorical shadow, Wolf is vulnerable to Nietzsche's dispute with the entire philological establishment, for Wolf "accepted as secure tradition what antiquity itself set up only as a hypothesis," that is to say, the hypothesis of Homer's identity, which Nietzsche more freely rejects (p. 256). Wolf did in fact hypothesize an original bard "Homer," nor did he ever relinquish this part of his equivocal argument, as the title to his text edition confirms (*Homeri et Homeridarum opera et reliquiae*).

Half of Nietzsche's reproach, then, is spot on. In Wolf, Homer is indeed "a person who has been made out of a concept" (p. 257). This follows from Wolf's own hermeneutical principles, which are author- and intention-oriented, and which clash with his historical principles, which are object-oriented.[152] The other half of Nietzsche's reproach, concerning the ancient "hypothesis," is a provocative piece of distortion, which awards to antiquity a delight in fiction that is, strictly speaking, *Nietzschean*. And yet the source of this conceit derives ultimately from Wolf himself. For, as I hope is growing clear by now, it was Wolf's dilemma regarding his readerly sense, far more than his decision about the poems' authorship, that suggested to Nietzsche a solution to the Homeric question, though it is not one that Wolf elected to adopt. Nietzsche in turn could imply, not without reason, that Wolf *had* adopted this solution, unbeknownst to himself. This other solution, declined by Wolf, spells out the conditions of reading under deception; and it suggests to Nietzsche a rapprochement of historicism with classicism, albeit in a deviant way. All of this needs to be unpacked briefly.

Nietzsche's solution, we may recall, is that "Homer" is a "phantom," the product of an "aesthetic judgment." Wolf would agree, up to a point. But Nietzsche goes on to radicalize Wolf's findings beyond recognition. Against Wolf, he eliminates the historical value of Homer altogether, ironizing it out of existence and replacing it with the singular instance of a deception, namely the very source of deception so perceptively located by Wolf: the natural and conventional habits of reading.[153] It follows that Wolf's Homer must be conceded to be what it always only was in antiquity, either a legend or an illusion. Here, Nietzsche is making a telling point. Wolf *has*, in effect, been deceived by antiquity. As if to literalize the point, Nietzsche credits antiquity with a conscious knack for aestheticization and for deception, while discrediting modern scholars with not being sufficiently ancient-minded, that is, with not being sufficiently accepting of the aesthetics of deception.[154] The famous quip by the fifth-century sophist Gorgias of Leontini would pass perfectly into Nietzsche's model: "The deceiver is more just than the one who fails to deceive, and the one who is deceived is wiser than one who fails to be deceived" (fr. 23 DK). This remark would appear to back up Nietzsche's later claim from "Homer's Contest" (1872): "I fear that we don't understand these [Greeks] in a sufficiently 'Greek' way; indeed, that we would shudder once we understood them in a Greek way."[155] But Gorgias' conceit also contains a paradox, for how does a subject rationally will itself into deception? Nietzsche's reply is that subjects do not: they irrationally will themselves into deception. "Classical antiquity" is one such deception, Homer is another. His essay exists to justify the validity of this logic.

Divesting Homer of all personality, for that is nothing but an aesthetic illusion, Nietzsche renders Homer into a concept that has been made out of a person—the concept he had always been from time out of mind. Nietzsche then reinvests the traits of a reader's deception in the figure of the anonymous final arranger of Homer's lays. But the latter is no more than a conceptual figure; he is a person who has been made out of a concept, a personification, in fact, of aesthetic deception. Thanks to the conscious deceptions of Nietzsche's "one great poet" who is not Homer, readers of "Homer" are unwittingly or semiconsciously deceived into imagining the epics and their author. In point of fact, Wolf can only have arrived at the conclusions he does and with the degree of certainty he has under the influence of such a deception. For on his own admission, "no human wisdom could discern the difference between [Homer] and a first-class rhapsode"—not Aristarchus, and not even Wolf himself (chap. 49, p. 205).[156] And if belief in the historicity of Homer is what ultimately belays Wolf's philological sense of the poems, then he is merely confirming one presupposition with another. Wolf's "Homer" does indeed stand for an "aesthetic judgment," however much he would try to resist this conclusion, whether on historicist or on more narrowly philological grounds.[157] Either way, Wolf is in the end what he was from the beginning: an intuitionist. "For in these matters one needs a certain sensibility [*sensu quodam*] which arguments do not provide" (chap. 35, p. 148).[158]

Wolf's dilemmas bring out the dissonances of an untimely discipline. In revenge, Nietzsche makes these dissonances explicit, and then embraces them in his own essay. Part art, part science, philology consorts closely with "poets, thinkers, and artists" (p. 267). (We may overhear in this triad Nietzsche's earlier approximation of *Denken* and *Dichten*.) Philology must come to terms with its necessarily split nature, on pain of incoherence; yet the only escape from incoherence, Nietzsche is suggesting, is not for philology to evade its nature but to plunge, wholeheartedly, back into its nature. His recommendation does not reconcile historicism with classicism; it *historicizes classicism*, and shows how indispensable to philology the elements of aesthetic deception and self-willed delusion actually are. "Humanism" is not thereby dissolved; it is recalibrated. Wolf's definition of *Altertumswissenschaft*, which he shared with Humboldt and thus made valid for a half-century to come, is "knowledge of human nature in antiquity."[159] At the center of Nietzsche's analysis, by contrast, stands the all-too-human subject of philology, the beholder of antiquity today. Nietzsche thus sketches out a hermeneutics of human deception as an alternative to the humanist hermeneutics of classicism.

If Nietzsche's essay is manifestly paradoxical, it is also chastening. We should be clear about what he is *not* saying. He is not going so far as to credit philology, or classicism for that matter, with a capacity for free invention. He denies to philology the capacity to "invent" antiquity: "Philology is to be sure not the creator of that world" (p. 268). Philology inherits antiquity and its inventions, and only then do the problems begin—anew.[160] Indeed, it would seem that the very idealizing traits of philology are inherited, which renders them all the more inevitable. Thus, on Nietzsche's view historicism and classicism are inescapably conjoined. And he accordingly appears to opt for a third strategy, one that (he would argue) is unconsciously or half-consciously practiced in any case. Classicism, the doctrine of "the untold simplicity and noble dignity of the Hellenic," is an "ideal" that is consciously embraced, while its falsehood, the "reality" behind it, is disavowed (p. 251).

Upholders of the classical ideal would acknowledge their idealism up to a point. Nietzsche asks of them that they also acknowledge the illusoriness of their ideal, its purely aesthetic justification, and its high degree of overdetermination (its historicity, its contingency, and the intricate psychological mechanisms that sustain it). Classicism, in other words, requires a good deal of self-deception. The question is whether it can withstand the shock of the various further requirements that Nietzsche puts upon it. The image of "the fearful-beautiful Gorgon-head of the classical" that he conjures up in the very same passage suggests some of the hidden risks and dangers of classicism. What is unclear is whether the threatening image points to anything but classicism's internal, constitutive contradictions. I doubt that it does.

A truly skeptical philology, such as Nietzsche practices, will never be deluded by the belief that what it knows is to be regarded as safe and sound historical fact. It will always be aware of the fallibility of aesthetic perception, and it will also concede the irresistibility of such a perception. One alternative left to a classicist is to empty out his beliefs of historical foundation and then to believe in them again, skeptically. Another, which is the route that Nietzsche chooses, is to suspend judgment altogether, ephectically. Practicing such "ephexis in interpretation" is the paradigmatic gesture of Nietzsche's philology of the future. It is a philology that forever lies in wait, suspended in time.

In mimicking Wolfian philology, but also in making it conscious of itself and of its own desperate act of bestowing belief upon a philological fiction, Nietzsche is in a sense completing Wolf's project for him. Wolf's great emancipatory "act was not fully understood," Nietzsche writes in "We Philologists" six years later, "because an aggressive, active element, such as attached to the poet-philologists of the Renaissance, remained undeveloped [in Wolf's philology]" ("WPh," 5[107]). Nietzsche, in contrast, is prepared to carry Wolf's revolution one step further, into its "aggressive, active element"—namely, toward a conscious poeticization of the doubtful past. The contrast couldn't be clearer. For Wolf and his successors, "intuition" is a passive faculty subordinate to the claims of reason and knowledge. Its job is to recognize the given, or in August Boeckh's words, to "reproduce the already known."[161] Not for nothing does Nietzsche's talk of "emancipation" recall Democritus' freeing of knowledge from religious superstition.[162] Wolf's Homer, we shall see in the next chapter, has its exact equivalent in Nietzsche's Democritus. Only, Nietzsche's Democritus is a conscious poetic object whose historical validity is inseparable from his reception, first by Plato, then by Epicurus, and finally by the Church itself. Recovering Democritus from the debris of this tradition is conceived by Nietzsche as a critical act of aggression against the tradition, not as a positive act of recovery.

Nietzsche's solution to the Homeric question thus returns us to his philological practices in the *Democritea* and to his reading of Lange. Skepticism and affirmation, or just knowledge and need, go hand in hand: "One may talk about the unreachability of the goal, and even label the goal itself as an illogical demand," but the goal exists in the form of its being striven toward all the same (pp. 253–54). And yet the goal is itself never one, never unitary, and never independent of its postulation as such. It is constantly being remodeled. For "where one abusively speaks about the overthrow of the holies, in fact merely newer and more venerable altars have been built" (p. 254). One of those altars is later said to have been "Homer," on which the unknown poet of the Homeric epics that we have today "sacrificed his name" (p. 266).[163]

Nietzsche's essay closes, as mentioned above, on a confessional note and with a specious appeal to unitary wholeness. The "confession of faith [*Glaubensbekenntnis*]" that Nietzsche makes in the end is all the more doubtful given the context out of which it can now be seen to have arisen. The confession (or profession) is to a faith renewed upon the ashes of philological certainty. It is a faith in skeptical possibilities, a renunciation of the whole in favor of a newly embraced "whole" (always in inverted commas). It speaks "professionally" but only on condition of doing so with a voice that is "of the most personal sort." And, finally, it is in the name of a philology that has been converted over to philosophy, as the inversion of Seneca makes plain. Needless to say, the speaker of these last, intensely personal lines is himself nameless, like the poet of "Homer's" epics, and speciously "whole" besides: "We demand *gratitude*, certainly not in our name . . . , but in the name of philology itself." The reason for this namelessness is given in the space of the ellipsis that I have not introduced into the text but have merely reproduced in a graphic form. The contents of that hiatus are themselves an appeal to an empty void: "*for we are atoms.*"[164]

Wir Philologen (p. 251).

CHAPTER 2

The Poetry of Atomism and the Fictions of Philology

Nietzsche's rediscovery of Greek atomism is of the greatest moment. His completion of Democritus' project, which involved rounding out the missing contours of that philosophy and absorbing atomistic thinking into his own evolving perspectives, would affect all his future undertakings, be these his reflections on ethical or aesthetic problems or his speculations on the will to power. Nietzsche could, and did, easily find precedents in Democritus in each of these areas, though perhaps the most obvious parallels to atomism are to be found in the "physics" of power that Nietzsche elaborated in the last half-decade of his career. In what follows, we will have a chance to trace some of the incipient connections between the *Democritea* project of the late 1860s and the horizons that would eventually encompass them, both within that project and well beyond it. A fuller study will have to wait for another occasion. For now, I would like to focus briefly on what, in Nietzsche's mind, binds the first two realms mentioned above (ethics and aesthetics) and justifies their having fallen within the legitimate reach of atomistic inquiry.

Here, the interest is not in the first instance what could be inferred about the conceptual model of a probable Democritean aesthetics, which I believe Nietzsche found difficult to separate from his understanding of music and rhythm. Nor is it Democritus' ethical theory proper, which Nietzsche significantly regards as the "core" of the atomist's philosophy (3:350). Rather, it is the ways in which the ethical and the aesthetic dimensions are for Nietzsche the "color" of atomism, a part of its texture and tonality (as opposed to its dogmatic substance), and the source of its overwhelming capacity and power. For what Nietzsche admires above all is, in his own words, the poetry that he feels to be constitutive of atomism (a telegraphic entry reads: "Poetry in atomism," 3:346), in addition to the "ethical value" that he finds (possibly again in Lange's wake) to lie precisely in the modalities, not the objects, of Democritus' vision: his *Betrachtungsweise* (3:349).

The connections between these two kinds of value are anything but obvious, let alone simple. The ethical thrust that Nietzsche sees in Democritus' system is literally a matter of perspective. Just to see the world from the perspective of atomism is to bring about a change in oneself and to discover, through science, philosophical happiness in one's life—freedom from disturbance (3:348–50). It is in this sense that Nietzsche would later qualify the Presocratics, Democritus among them, "as individuals who were innocent of the contradiction between being and thought and who clearly demonstrated their theories *praxi*," whether "by their actions" or performatively, in the very articulation of their theories ("ECP," 407). Science here is not empirical investigation, but philosophical reflection. But neither is freedom from disturbance to be understood in any straightforward way. Democritus' philosophy is one of "redemption"; only, it is a redemption without solace that atomism promises. And how can that fail to be fundamentally disturbing? Atomism, to be sure, offers none of the consolations of religion or mythology, not even those of prior philosophy (3:348–50), but only a minimalist picture of reality, one drawn in the starkest possible lines and from which every familiar trace of the world of appearances has been subtracted. Redemption without solace, on Nietzsche's account of Democritus, can only mean that what atomism aims to bring about in the first and last instance is a redemption *from* solace. And that, for Nietzsche, is the source of its attraction.[1]

What Nietzsche admires most of all in the Democritean system is the space it affords to collision and opposition, its flouting of commonplace intuitions and of popular and philosophical beliefs, and its assault on the very structures of representation. In all of this Nietzsche detects what he calls the *dichterischer Schwung*, or poetic abandon, with which Democritus retails the story of mankind's irretrievable fragility: its iffy and chancy constitution (death is the straying apart of atoms, no more), and its susceptibility to beliefs, intuitions, and conceptions, the bulk of which exist to conceal human vulnerability but which atomism lays painfully bare again.

Hence Nietzsche can repeatedly write, with an awe that is genuine,

> In and of itself, there is a magnificent poetry to the atomistic conception, a perpetual raining of diverse, minute bodies, which fall in manifold ways and in falling interlock, so that a cosmic whirl [or "vortex"] comes into being.[2]

Obviously, one of the allures of atomism is the dazzling picture it presents of a world broken down into brilliant motions. But this image, by turns awe-inspiring and painful, is not all there is to the poetic beauty of atoms, for

> the poetry lies not in his system, but rather in the belief that he attached to his system. (3:349)

It is this contrast between poetic beauty and empty horror which in Nietzsche's eyes constituted the animus, not just of his own project to reclaim Democritus from his fragmentary remains (itself motivated by a poetic grasp of the atomist's system) but of the very vision that Democritus' worldview embodies for Nietzsche. This vision or stance, which is the very fiber of atomism, might be seen as a matter of calculated abandon, or of investment in detachment, or else as a redemption of negation through negation (which is difficult to tell apart from affirmation). It is this same contrast that will become the motivation behind Nietzsche's own later ideas (partially elaborated, but more often than not simply enacted) pertaining to "the physiology of aesthetics" and everything that such an aesthetics entails (or destroys).[3] Here, too, he could emulate the paradoxes of the Democritean perspective. Casting a calm, scientific glance on the world, Democritus "contemplates the various aspects [of things] on the basis of which mankind is thrown into disturbance" (3:350).[4] Hence the ease with which

Nietzsche was increasingly able to move between the unsettling spectacle of atoms and void on the one hand, and on the other the richness of *another* perception, glimpsed, as it were, in the interstices of the atomistic system, amid the detritus of basic intuitions that such a vision leaves in its wake.[5]

Nietzsche was not just fantasizing when he wrote about atoms and void in this way. The atomists' conception is defiantly mind-boggling; try as you might to give it a straightforward, dry as dust description, the conception will betray you. And while Nietzsche here is for the most part dealing with problems of attribution and busy organizing the surface lineaments of the Democritean corpus, his notes presuppose a thorough familiarity with the physical theory of Democritus. The same is true of his lecture notes on the Presocratic philosophers, designed for a first run in 1869 and taught again in three subsequent semesters, the last in the summer term of 1876. The lectures in particular are comprehensive, and chronologically arranged. The fifteenth of these is devoted to the physical assumptions of Leucippus and Democritus, but it merely formalizes what was already assumed in the abortive *Democritea* project ("PP," 328–40). Accordingly, a cursory sketch of the Democritean physical system, as Nietzsche could appreciate it, will be useful. Without this background, his glimpse into the "poetry in atomism" would be unintelligible.

Atoms and Void: The Atomistic Conception

In the wake of Parmenides of Elea (fl. early to mid-fifth century), the Greek pluralist successors, starting with Anaxagoras and (a half-generation later) Empedocles, began searching for a viable alternative to the iron-clad logic of Eleatic monism. Parmenides' One Being had the attributes of a Platonic form (being, impassibility, eternality, immobility, unity, homogeneity, continuity, etc.); and his monism rested on the denial of the existence of opposites, under the rubric of nonbeing, and thus of all the attributes that are "not." The atomists in particular found an elegant trump card: they inserted nonbeing into being, and out of the contradiction that resulted within being they generated a pluralistic universe based on a mere two principles. Henceforth there would be void (not-being) and being (atoms, or material particles intrinsically endowed with all the attributes of Parmenidean being), and nothing else beyond these. Atoms, on this hyphothesis, are solid (being "full" and literally "indivisible"), infinite in number and shape, and they lie below the threshold of perception. Their role seems relatively straightforward: they are the building-blocks of the universe, the micro-components of the larger structures that, in the form of compounds and aggregates, constitute all physical things and their appearances (all sensations, perceptions, and conceptions). While the nature of atoms (their sum of characteristics) is by and large uncontroversial, the exact character of void, or vacuum (the "empty"), is a matter of some dispute, and this is perhaps as it should be.

The atomists did not invent the concept of void, but they were the first to grant it, at least at first blush, a non-self-refuting existence and a primary place in cosmology. The atomists' void has been variously understood: as an element on a par with body; as a negative substance; as (empty) place; as an occupant of place; and as a place holder for difference.[6] Void is essential on the atomistic scheme. It provides gaps in an otherwise homogeneous universe, and thus makes for the possibility of motion. With void, atoms can come into contact, and they can stray apart again. Clearly it is the tension between void and atoms that keeps the material world in constant flux. Void is itself an "element," and whatever else might be said about it, the presence of void as a primary constituent in the universe guarantees that a kind of negation will always be immanent to the atomistic physical system. By virtue of its "entirely negative character,"[7] void marks the negation of being and substance, or rather, it creates a paradox within being and for substance. Void is not something, but there is void. Moreover, its location is not just between things that are but also within bodies and shapes that "are" in some secondary sense: void is lodged in the interstices of matter.

As a result, on the atomistic view, things in the world are and they are not. They are not what they appear to be, and they crucially contain what is not. In the simplest of terms, the construction of the world is its destruction or voiding. All unities are precariously pitched on the brink of dissolution. Beheld from up close, the world passes into the dysphoria of sheer pointillism. Much effort has gone into trying to rescue the logical coherence of void, but the best understandings of it have conceded to void its full complement of paradox, and especially a strategic and polemical (and even rhetorical) force. Void, we might say, opens a crisis in the representation of materiality. It pushes to the absolute limit the capacity to conceive the world, which the atomists present in an alienating and inverted form.

This is not to imply that atoms are paradox-free. All of one nature, like bits of gold, atoms (*sōmata*, or particle-bodies) are homogeneously yet discontinuously constituted matter, differentiated in the first instance by positional and relational attributes alone. Apart from contingently possessing some size, shape, and weight, their properties are strictly relational, and it is by virtue of these relations ("position," "arrangement," and "shape" or "trajectory") that everything else is. Things, properties, sensations that we know—hardness, color, taste, time, bodies—are just atoms configured into patterns (through *symplokē*, or *synthesis*). This patterning occurs through the triple agency of (i) vortex motions, (ii) the resulting (and purely mechanical) actions and repulsions of bodies, and (iii) the interlocking of atoms into combinatorial kinds. All this obtains at a primordial, nonphenomenal level, constituting a rigid necessity of sorts, but one that knows no purpose, no rational reasons, and consequently (Democritus could add, with perfect if— to us—estranging consistency) one that approaches the haphazardness of chance (*tychē*)—at least so far as the human mind can determine.[8] There is no reason that might explain why things are the way they are, because they just are what they are; this is the world's objective, unaccountable, and infinitely chancy necessity. Phenomena—whatever appears to us—are nothing more or less than the epiphenomenal effect of the distribution of atoms in eternally substitutive and seemingly random motion within a cosmic whirl.[9]

Matter, on this scheme, is so to speak reinvented. Perforated by void and pieced together again by aggregation, matter and materiality take on new and strange meaning. Paradoxes ensue. By far the most difficult of these is the question whether matter is or is not something familiar from the sense of touch. Matter is not something you can feel, but it has some of the essential traits of tangibility. Atoms are variously "angular, hooked, convex, concave," and so on. Through the rotations of the vortex, they collide, suffer "blows," and tend to be sorted into similar kinds, like pebbles tossed forth "by the movement of waves" onto a beach, "long ones pushed to one place, round ones to another." At a closer remove, bitter tastes are due to a preponderance of large, rough, angular atoms in a compound; sweet tastes are due to large, round, smooth atoms. Pungency comes from atoms that are "round, small, with angles and bends," etc. The sounds you hear are "streams of atoms," that is, of atomic film-images, variously called *aporrhoiai* and *eidōla* in Greek (better known as *simulacra* from Lucretius' Latin translation). These are produced when the voice, cast into the wind in "fragments," beats the air into like-shaped bodies (viz., films), which then "tumble along" together with the air and finally "penetrate into the whole of the auditor's body, but principally into the organ of hearing," which is most receptive because it is most "empty."[10]

Not even the apparent world can free itself of the specter of atoms jostling one another in the void. Air, crevices in the body, and the spaces in which the restless motions of visible matter obtain all assume, on the macroscopic level of sensation, the place of void on the microscopic level. Motes dancing in a sunbeam, waves beating on the shore, and sound echoing through an amphitheater reenact for our senses the cosmic spectacle of atomism and are for that reason recurrent elements in the philosophy's repertoire of images.[11] Nietzsche stands in awe of the "sensuous clarity and comprehensibility" of the accounts that Democritus could give to natural events (4:82),[12] and that is the source of his gushing, and no doubt calculatedly shocking, commentary on the "poetic" quality of the Democritean physical landscape. Nietzsche captures this quality in a graphic image of his own. Always in a state of contradiction, Democritus resembles a Greek statue, "to all appearances cold, yet full of concealed warmth" (3:349). But the image is itself a paradox, because it turns on its head the Democritean inversion of appearances: it ought to be the hidden world of atomic figures that is cold, in stark contrast to the warmer, more familiar touches of the phenomenal world. But the livelier image by far is the cold interior of atomism.

This presents a problem, one that Nietzsche is quick to point out. The qualities of atoms are in fact primary quantitative features ("all qualities may be traced back to quantitative differences");[13] they mark a formal difference within materiality. Thus, atoms, being mere quantities and of one nature, "differ only according to *rhysmos* [*schēma*], *diathigē* [*taxis*], and *tropē* [*thesis*]," which is to say, according to their relative disposition. Aristotle reports as examples the differences between the letters "A and N," "A N and N A," and "Z and N."[14] But as the analogy to letters by itself shows, these differences already suggest a minimum quantum of sensibility, as if in anticipation of a future impingement on our sensation of the more familiar "secondary" qualities: the features of atoms represent a minimum of projected sensation onto the assumedly nonphenomenal conditions of sensing. Nietzsche will label the source of this paradox central to atomism a *prōton pseudos*, or false premise, thereby indicating how the theory rests on a fictional foundation that in principle must be effaced for the system to get on with its own business.[15] The very conceivability of atomism is problematical. But instead of effacing this liability, atomism brings it right into the foreground. The differences that structure our perception of the world and the terminology used to describe them are richly evocative, and they blatantly phenomenalize nonphenomenal properties. Atoms not only assume shapes in their arrangement; they "quiver," are "squeezed out," and so on.[16] This suggests a high degree of self-consciousness on the part of atomism's founders, and especially Democritus, whose vivid coinages were admired in antiquity. Even so, the poignancy of the atomistic worldview, which Nietzsche will never cease to exploit, is due more to a series of contrasts than to any mere heaping of graphic details: the small scale of the elements well below the threshold of the visible and the large canvas of theoretical speculation in which they become visible again; the restricted economy of the minima and the general profusion of their effects; the positing of quanta and their endless qualification; the uncanny resemblances that obtain between sensible and atomic reality on the one hand, and the vast discontinuities that run through both on the other.

Atomism is more than an account of nature. It gives an account of ourselves. The contrasts just described bring home this relevance in a few different ways. Most immediately, atomism points to discontinuities between ourselves and what we experience; and it installs discontinuities in our own bodies. Consequently, not only is the stability of the world, on this philosophical view of it, forsworn; our contact with the world and with ourselves (who are no more than a gathering of atoms) is constitutively disrupted. "Touch," the primary condition underlying all sensation and all sensibles as well, "is not direct; rather, it is mediated by *aporrhoiai* [the streaming of atoms]. These latter penetrate the body, via the senses, and are spread out among all its parts: whence arises the representation of things" ("PP," 338). It is a representation that, we can be sure, is commensurate with reality just by being, so to speak, out of touch with it. Void ensures that atoms are forever literally contingent things: fleetingly tangent with one another, they are never blended into organic wholes. Nor, ultimately, are we.

This last point deserves to be emphasized, because it points the way to the ultimate value of atomism in Nietzsche's thinking, both at the time and later on. There is a remarkable coherence but also a dissonance between the form of the atomistic hypothesis and its philosophical aims. The starkly reductive materialism of atomism breaks the world apart and leaves in its wake a welter of atoms streaming aimlessly in the void. In the same breath, atomism lays bare the conventions of meaning and representation, which are shown to lack any intrinsic or natural justification and, consequently, to have the status of mere myths. Atomism is a potent dissolvent of all naturalized illusions.[17] Simply to think about the way the world appears to us in its *phantasmata* (the simulacral impressions caused by atoms) is to think about the way meaning is made; and it is to unmake meaning, to grasp it as a phantasm. On the atomistic hypothesis, meaning and representation, like sensation itself, are artifacts not just of our physiological nature, which is one more fragment of a now precarious and alienating world (Democritus speaks of the "movements" that can sweep through the "great intervals" of the soul, itself a mere collection of atoms.)[18] They are also artifacts of our culture, which has no more stable a foundation than unfounded nature. Sensations exist *nomōi*, by convention and opinion (fr. 9 DK). Worse still, "in reality we grasp nothing precisely, but as it shifts according to the disposition of our body and of the things that enter into it and press upon it" (ibid.).[19] Thinking is nothing besides this rhythmic process of shifting and shaping: it is an *epirhysmiē*, an "epirhythm," or influx and reshaping of atoms.[20] Atomism, plainly, is not a doctrine for the faint of heart.

The view that meaning is a fragile thing, a myth of the mind, isn't merely one of the doctrines of atomism; it is built right into the very conception of Democritus' philosophy. Just to imagine the atomistic hypothesis is to face a threat to one's own sense of intactness, to one's ideas about self and world as coherent and coherently distinct entities. An affront to human intuitions and beliefs of all kinds, atomism leaves no assumptions protected by the look of self-evidence untouched: it denatures them all. For Nietzsche, atomism offers more than a genealogy of the apparent world. It offers a corrosive glimpse into our construction of that world. Atomism thus makes for a stark contrast with later philosophies, such as anodyne Socratism or Platonism, because it ultimately exposes the "unreason" of human existence, which is the condition of all human suffering and of the universe as a whole: in Democritus, that unreason is projected onto the cosmos.[21] "The [Democritean] world is unreasonable, also not measured and beautiful, but merely necessary. Unconditional rejection of all myths. The world can be grasped. He embraces the *polis* (instead of the Epicurean garden); that was a possibility of Greek life."[22] Physical speculation thus slides effortlessly into cultural reflection, and from there into a certain cultural skepticism, for these amount to the same thing. Atomism thus has a revolutionary potential that takes it well beyond its appearance of being a scientific hypothesis, at least in Nietzsche's eyes: "Democritus [is] in a battle with his times"; he is one of the "*forerunners of a reformation of the Greeks.*"[23]

To read Democritus in this way (as Nietzsche is wont to do) is in part to round out his image, not illegitimately, with some of the better attested evidence of Lucretius. Lucretius accorded an ethical function to the mere contemplation of the hard physical qualities of life: simply to look upon the spectacle of atoms, the emblem of life's reducibility, provides inter alia a moral test of one's character and of one's commitment to the ideal of tranquility.[24] Nietzsche's reading of the "poetic" Democritus who "contemplates the various aspects [of things] on the basis of which mankind is thrown into disturbance" is in this sense Lucretian.[25] But it is also a good guess as to Democritus' ethical posture, which, as we saw, Nietzsche considers to be the "core" of the atomist's philosophy. Atomism is ethical in the sense that it braves the illusions of culture; and for Nietzsche that critique is transmitted through every form of the atomistic hypothesis and not just in the cultural histories and moral genealogies that the atomists are thought to have produced and later to have inspired.[26] No doubt for these reasons, Nietzsche found the atomistic model of intellectual subversion both congenial and, within the limits that the term always implies for Nietzsche, emancipating. Finally, with a consequentiality that is rare, the destructive character of atomism can be turned against itself, in the exposure of its own fictional and uncertain foundation (its *prōton pseudos*); it is (true to its own principles) nothing more than a string of phantasms. Consequently, one believes in atomism at one's peril. There is something exhilarating and tragic about this Presocratic insight, at least for Nietzsche.[27]

Democritus the physical scientist (the *physiologos*), could be taken for a forerunner of Comte and other scientific positivists bent on discovering a causal explanation of nature. But Democritus the metaphysician and conceptual artist—arguably his primary distinction—gives an entirely different appearance: that of a wry, daring thinker, whose every thought is a paradox to common sense and whose science is framed by methodological doubts that betray, in every sense of the word, a bottomless appetite for an ever-receding knowledge: "In reality we know nothing. Truth is in the depths" (fr. 117 DK). As Diogenes Laertius reports, at the head of his list of Democritean doctrines, apart from atoms and void, "everything else is merely an object of belief" (or else "a matter of convention" [DL, 9.44]). It is no accident that a disciple of Democritus, Metrodorus of Chios, used atomism to expound skeptical doubt, and from Democritus' already deep ambivalence to a more thoroughgoing skepticism—that is, to "la méthode de redoublement du doute sur le doute"—is just a short remove.[28] The true nature of the Democritean physical universe is, in the words of one recent scholar, "structurally unknowable" and "a permanent aporia of reason."[29] Perhaps not everyone today would agree, but the ancients could see things differently. The conceptual challenge of atomism leads to the consequence, apparently drawn by Pyrrhonians around the time of Epicurus, that atoms have a notional existence: they are themselves a "myth."[30] Whether it is a consequence that Democritus would have drawn himself is entirely open to question.[31] The affinities between Pyrrho and Democritus are stated by Nietzsche in his final notebooks: "Pyrrho goes back, through Protagoras, to Democritus" (*WP*, 437 [1888]). The same tendency to correlate the two thinkers is present in the earlier, philological notebooks and in his published writings as well.[32]

A contrast with Epicurus suggests itself, and Nietzsche does not hesitate to draw it. Compare the following entry:

> The deliverances of the senses, according to Epicurus, give us the truth itself. Cf., e.g., [Cicero] *De finibus* 1.63. *This wasn't the view of Democritus.* Epicurus passed *from atomism to realism*. According to Democritus we have absolutely no knowledge of truth. Sext. Emp. *Adv. math.* 7.135: "Democritus demolishes what appears to the senses and says that of these [appearances] nothing appears as it truly is, but only as it is opined to be. The truth concerning what exists is that there are atoms

and void—'for we do not know how each thing is or isn't in reality.'"
(3:328; emphases added)[33]

Nietzsche prepares the contrast with Epicurus by way of the following:
"[Democritus'] motto remains, 'The thing in itself is unknowable,' and *that
separates him from all realists forever*" (3:327; emphasis added). This is why
"one must not overlook the idealist in Democritus." The qualification of
"idealism," transparently clothed in a Kantian idiom, and to which Nietzsche directly adds, "but he believed in its [the thing in itself's] existence,"
points up a genuine tension in Nietzsche's own thought. It is one that he
inherited directly from Lange:[34] Democritus is "the first rationalist," who
sought to liberate thought from the shackles of mythology (4:63); yet the
lever by which he moved the Greek mind was itself conditioned by a certain
idealism, one that constituted a philosophical mythology in its own right.

Nietzsche is far from depreciating idealism, under a certain description of
it. What he in fact finds so attractive about Democritus' peculiar brand of
idealism—his critical idealism, if you like—is the way it "bites into its very
own children." Nor does Nietzsche need to be claiming to have got a purchase on atomism that atomism in its earliest form did not get on itself:
there are plenty of signs that Democritus' atomism was meant to be illustra-
tive of the predicament that, for Nietzsche, it inescapably embodies. Compare the following fragment: "Democritus had the senses say to the mind:
'Wretched mind, taking your proofs from us, do you wish to overthrow us?
Our downfall will be your overthrow.'"[35] Of course, the reverse of this statement holds too. Atomism crucially depends upon the senses, but it depends
no less upon their impeachment: sensuous knowledge delivers only simulacra of reality. The atomist who attempts to account for his own theory in
terms of the theory itself thus arrives at an uncomfortable impasse. To quote
another fragment from Democritus, perhaps his most broodingly skeptical:
"Yet it will be clear that to know in reality what sort each thing is, is baffling," an "aporia" (fr. 8 DK). Reality does look to be "structurally unknowable" and a permanent aporia after all. What value, then, does Nietzsche discover in Democritus' troubled idealism?

First of all, it is an idealism waged, paradoxically, in the name of materialism. Requiring a minimum of commitments, truth is not transcendentally

located but immanent in the world, much like void among atoms, or as Democritus prefers to put it, "in the depths." Atomism thus has an ideological component that Nietzsche can admire: irrespective of its ultimate cogency as an account of reality, materialism is a potent weapon, one that can be effectively wielded against the most pervasive and popular myths (even when these reassert themselves in philosophical contexts). Secondly, philosophical commitments in atomism are based on methodological necessity, not on secure knowledge. Endlessly revisable, like the mobile contents of reality itself, reflection never attains a stable endpoint, nor does it approximate to one. This constitutes a major, and troubling, revision in the notion of what counts as "true." Idealism, in fact, can only exist as a discourse that disrupts itself; and Democritean idealism embodies this dilemma in a concentrated form. Finally, demolishing the conditions of all mythological credence through philosophical reason, Democritus, we might say, believes in a myth but not in belief itself. His belief is an impossible one, at most (Nietzsche will argue) the expression of a fallible "human need," of a predicament that not even the Greek atomist could avoid. Such a belief, when it is expressed with the greatest possible rigor, is forever submitted to its own contingency.[36]

It is, at any rate, this that for Nietzsche contributes to the "poetry" of the Democritean system: the belief that reattaches, provisionally and unstably, to what has been voided of meaning—most prominently, the phenomenal world as it once appeared to the senses and that subsequently reappears in the world below the threshold of sensation, but more devastatingly, the very sense-bearing structures of language and thought. Viewed from one perspective, the cosmic whirl and its jumble of contents—this *tourbillon de signes*, as Saussure would say (recalling the Lucretian *turba*)—describes a semiotic vortex of sorts, the generative source of signs and sense.[37] From another, it describes the constitutive undoing of all sense and sensation, for the world in its primary character is both restlessly chaotic and inconceivably featureless. In this way, the primary constituents of the atomistic system put into drastic relief the apparitional, which is to say perceptual and representational, structures that are imposed on them but that they in no way ground.

Hence the corrosive effect of Democritean physics, which cuts to the quick any epistemology, all intuitions, and all stable certainties—including, it stands to reason, the verisimilitude of the atomistic hypothesis itself. To anticipate a theme that will haunt Nietzsche's reflections on the will to power in his last productive decade, chaos and even inconceivability seem all too conceivable; the void of atomism is not the void it depicts but only its self-voiding. Nietzsche expresses much the same view in *Human, All Too Human*, when he looks upon void as the semantic negation of all ontological assumptions: "Perhaps we shall then recognize that the thing in itself is worthy of Homeric laughter: that it appeared to be so much, indeed to be everything, and is actually empty—namely, empty of meaning" (*HA*, I:16; trans. mod.). That "Homeric" laughter, like its object, semantic void, is at least in part informed by the hilarity of a *Democritus ridens* (3:333; 4:59), just as Homer and Democritus can never be entirely extricated from one another or from the philology that holds them in a common embrace, endowing them with a life they otherwise never would have. "For we are atoms."

Atoms of Language

Democritus is increasingly recognized by Nietzsche to be not an innovator but a systematizer, and not only of the doctrines of atomism's founder Leucippus—for "the disciples are the systematic ones"[38]—but of whatever his mind encountered. From Aristotle to timeless popular wisdom (attested in a comic fragment of Damoxenus) to latter-day Epicureans like Philodemus in the last century B.C.E. (4:102), the evidence is unanimous: Democritus is recognized to have been a voracious intellect, and his intelligence restlessly— and systematically—"took in the whole world" (4:76; 4:91). The preexistence of any given sphere of inquiry with plausible ties to physical speculation now can be taken as prima facie evidence that, if a subject is represented on the list of titles or among the fragments and bears any of the "primary traits of atomism" (4:49), Democritus, the "universal mind" (4:59), will have genuinely explored it. It is this reasonable assumption about Democritean methodology (its "multifacetedness," underpinned by a deeper coherence) that converts the scattered items of Democritus' attested interests into logically and methodologically necessary correlates. The edifice of evidence, once crumbling and labile, is now fortified to a degree of strength previously unseen.

Thus, the ethical theory can be viewed as a direct and even "necessary consequence" of his physics (4:42; 4:64). Elsewhere, the point is put more strongly still: "The key to Democritean physics lies in his ethics" (3:364). This daring hypothesis about the coherence of ethics and physics in Democritus would have to wait until the following century for systematic exposition.[39] A similar fate befalls the grammatical (philological) and musical writings, as well as those on the visual arts, all of which are viewed by Nietzsche as forming the actual pinnacle of Democritus' philosophy and as closely linked to the ethical ideal of *ataraxia*, or freedom from disturbance ("The *telos* is *otium litteratum*" [3:364]).[40] This is a remarkable assessment. These last areas represented perhaps the furthest extreme of what could plausibly fit into the atomistic frame of reference. (Handbooks such as Zeller's *Die Philosophie der Griechen in ihrer geschichtlichen Entwicklung* (1856–68) had next to nothing to say about them, although Lange lists "music" as one of the attested interests of Democritus, after natural inquiry and mathematics.)[41] Why, after all, should a physicist be at pains to comprehend art? Epicurus famously took up a hostile stance toward the theory and practice of the arts. But viewed against a better informed historical picture and in the light of a revised picture of Democritus, these titles are eventually granted full and unqualified "restitution."[42] Even as unlikely an interest as rhythm and harmony, attested in the Thrasyllan catalogue of titles (DL, 9.48), can be imagined as integrally available to physical speculation, which is now the only criterion that matters.[43] The list of concessions could be extended, but the point is sufficiently clear. Nietzsche's volte-face is complete, and his sympathies overrun the limits of the fragmentary evidence—and the then *communis opinio*—to achieve a new, deeply coherent view of Democritus' philosophical position.[44]

It is a fair question whether Nietzsche could have achieved the coherent picture of Democritus that he does without the confirming echo of poetry within the Democritean system that could return to Nietzsche his own speculations. An admittedly aesthetic whole, Nietzsche's Democritus is poetic to the core. And so it happens that the very tenor of Democritus' writings, their "poetic style" and "poetic abandon"—comparable only to the qualities shown by Lucretius and emphatically in contrast to Epicurus ("His is a poetic mind, like Lucretius'" [4:78])—in addition to the "sensuous clarity and comprehensibility" of his language, indeed his entire vision of the world, conspire to authenticate the titles that pointed to Democritus' interest in these same subjects. Taken together, all this makes Democritus into *"the only philosopher who is still alive today"* (4:84). Nietzsche, more than any other of his contemporaries, felt the truth of this proposition.

Nietzsche's interests plainly follow Democritus' own (at least as Nietzsche chooses to understand them). What is striking, from this point on, is the degree to which the reference to Democritean atomism becomes a part of Nietzsche's own thinking, at times explicitly so, but more often than not implicitly. "Atoms" and "void" become conceptual signs for Nietzsche. They come to designate not so much the system of Democritus as his centrifugal force and dispersal, whether in the subsequent history of philosophy or (more often) in the form of his ramified, nameless presence, wherever the questions of matter and sensation arise. In a word, Nietzsche is learning to *deploy* the reference to atomism in the course of his own engagement with the problems of materialism and idealism, appearance and reality, plurality and identity, or (more abstractly) quantity and quality, once the counter-philological project of restoring Democritus to his rightful and doubtful place has been achieved. Tracing these connections in Nietzsche's subsequent writings would require a separate study. Here, however, it is Nietzsche's immediate uses of atomism that will be of interest, particularly in the realm of language, sound, music, and rhythm. Other, more indirect elaborations of Democritus will be discussed in the chapters that follow.

One of the insights gained from Nietzsche's early study of Democritus is into the intimate link between the analysis of language and conceptuality and their critique. Just to submit language and thought to analysis of the atomistic kind is to critique them. Viewed atomistically, language and thought suddenly take on a simulacral, vertiginously contingent and uncertain appearance: they dissolve into a welter of meaningless elements.[45] Although the evidence for Democritus' views on language, its workings, and its aesthetic properties is hardly conclusive, a number of suggestive clues have survived.[46] Nietzsche knows (or intuits) enough about the atomist to be able to say, "Democritus likewise knows how to explain 'speech' [*Sprechen*] atomistically" (3:333), and even to challenge Cicero's debunking critique of the analogy between the letters of the alphabet and atoms. The analogy appears to stem from the first-generation atomists: "A tragedy can be thrown together [as one would cast dice] from the chance combination of letters [pace Cicero]" (3:385).[47] Nietzsche here defends the conceit, in the course of his fascinating but rambling discussion of teleology since Kant, in which he comes down decidedly in favor of a theory of nature as ruled by chance: "The storm that drives things around is chance" (3:386; cf. "PP," 337). Clearly, this storm is a latter-day atomistic *dinē*, or cosmic "vortex," although Nietzsche's allegiances are anything but straightforwardly in favor of a theory of mechanism. Rather, he is weighing the metaphysical implications of natural worldviews and rejecting as inadequate both the Kantian and the Democritean explanations of the problem from which both start out, namely the question, How can we account for life in nature? (3:385–89). The crossover of ideas from his *Democritea* is startling but understandable. Significantly, Nietzsche's thought now takes on a freer, more independently associative turn. With the lessons of atomism assimilated, his attentions are focused on subjects and in ways that go beyond the explicit doxography on Democritus: he is beginning to "speak atomistically." Nietzsche's mind is cautiously toying at the limits of the ancient testimony, and experimenting in the light of its obliquest illumination.

What is most striking in the notebooks from this period is the insistent juxtaposition of Democritean atomism with the many desultory sequences of notes on rhythm, music, the origins of language, rhetoric, and so on—topics that would preoccupy Nietzsche in so many of his future writings, always with an eye to the corrosive effects of their literal analysis into unfamiliar elements. I take it to be no accident that Nietzsche pursued his *Democritea* concurrently with his speculations on the nature of language (in particular, its empirical attributes), all of which sowed the seeds of his future studies in poetic and rhetorical language. The two pursuits, atomism and language, are linked by an invisible thread of implication; indeed, the two interests could exist side by side, and occasionally their borders could be explicitly overrun and their contents could spill to either side. It is important to note a few examples of this development, in part because this story has never been told, and in part because Nietzsche himself is for the most part too quietly engaged in his ideas to be explicit about the connections he is learning to draw (or else redraw, in the course of a "successful" reconstruction of a probable Democritean aesthetics). A handful of examples will suffice to make the point that needs making.

A typical juxtaposition is found in a notebook from 1868/69 that contains a page devoted to "Aesthetic Principles" (5:206). Here, Nietzsche experimentally worries about the mainsprings of art and aesthetic pleasure. Let us begin with this one page, where it is deliberated from (presumably) two points of view whether art is a function of semiconscious deception ("The experience of art is a matter of being deceived and of *consciously* letting oneself be deceived") or of wholly unconscious affection. If the former experience is on the first view wholly psychological, the latter experience is on the second view the product of the musical elements of art, whose basis is physiological: the unconscious experience of art ultimately resides in rhythm, which is the "common denominator" of all the art forms (5:206).[48] Nietzsche's own solution to the problem is indeterminate. Not clearly identifying himself with either viewpoint (which are not necessarily at odds), he seems to agree that "the essence of art lies in the unconscious": "Poetic art is only art insofar as it contains musical elements." "*Melos* [song]," he continues,

is the enhanced and enchanted sensation in which everything appears to be new and beautiful. Far more powerful than the word—that impoverished sign—is the beat [*Schlag*] of the rhythmical pulse.

Art is the reflection of another world lying hidden beneath things in a heightened dream-experience [*Empfindungstraume*].

In the world of the unconscious there is no intentionality: artistic production is the activity of the instinct.

Color line arrangement—harmony melody rhythm.

These last comments bring us back to the question of deception again, which was central to Nietzsche's reading of Homer. Art is the experience of a dreamy sensation, but possibly it is the experience of sensation itself, only in the form of a pleasant dream. What is it that is ultimately revealed in art? The note resumes: "Painting and plastic art ask that we believe in an enchanted world, that stones should come to life for us and that life should approach us from the canvas: all this takes place through the power of melody and of rhythm." Art, or Nietzsche's view of it, seems to vacillate between illusionism and the blurry communication of instinctual reality. Perhaps all that art reveals is the instinctual impulse to illusion that we have, our desire to be deceived into enchantment, the wish to sublimate, as it were, our own pulse rate. Whatever the case may be, the terms of this discussion strike a familiar chord, in the light of *The Birth of Tragedy* and beyond. Greek musical and aesthetic theory are what inform Nietzsche's language here (as they do in the late writings, which retrace the radical meaning of classical "aesthetics" as physical sensation, combined with illusion). What is particularly striking, beyond this consistent set of interests, is the co-occurrence in the sequel of another, and on the surface remoter, set of issues, which in fact offer a kind of gloss on the passage above. Some forty pages down in the same notebook (which otherwise is devoted exclusively to philological questions) there appears a newly titled section, "Problems and Work to Be Done." This segment begins with a consideration of issues diversely related to the *Democritea* project and then slowly modulates in the direction of Aristotle, by way of a telegraphic jotting: "Influence of Democritean ethics on Aristotle," on the heels of which comes the following:

> The issue of *effect* is taken up in the Aristotelian definition of tragedy: but the problem is to indicate just what this *katharsis* gives rise to:
> Aristotle: actions *eliciting* fear and pity are actions that have the former or latter effect.

Then apparently without batting an eyelash, Nietzsche comes full circle back to atomism:

> The sources of Epicurean doctrine:
> Sources of the canonic [a branch of Epicurean inquiry into the criteria of truth and logic]: only psychical images are true.
> Whence does the epistemology of Zeno and Epicurus derive?
> (5:207–8)

This confluence of ideas is striking. Atomism, its ethics, Aristotelian ethics and poetics, the doctrines of simulacra and *phantasiai* (mental images), truth and falsity, and the question, left dangling and wide open, as to the sources of these things, all point nonetheless to a common root—in Democritus. Another note from the previous year follows an identical trajectory, this time in numbered outline form, which suggests that we have here the projected lines of Nietzsche's never-completed argumentation: "Influence of Democritus on the ethical views of Aristotle. . . . The priorities of functions [are] reoriented from the necessary and the useful to the beautiful; cf. *Politics* 7.14, 1333a30. Compare what Democritus has to say about music."[49] If Nietzsche leaves the positive link between Democritus and Aristotle unexamined, one needn't be dismayed. The topic remains vastly unexplored to this day.

The vagaries of Nietzsche's thoughts in the first sequence examined above suggest that an intimate link exists in Nietzsche's mind between the rhythmical pulsation of atoms and that of the human physiology stimulated by (or to) music. Do atomic effects constitute a physiological equivalent of unconscious melodic patternings ("the beat of the rhythmical pulse"), as the source of instinctual behavior and the buried cause of outward effects? What causal connections are there to be drawn between instinctual, pulsional acts (*Instinkthandlung*) and tragic action (*Handlungen*)? The notes trail off just where one might hope to find an answer. Be that as it may, aesthetics and atomistic physiology are in these pages colluding in tentative, loosely worked out ways. Their imbrication, however implicit, is unmistakable. Here it is no longer a question of "reconstructing" a Democritean physiological aesthetics. Rather than merely producing arguments for atomistic aesthetics (or if you like, aesthetic atomism), Nietzsche is reproducing, behind these startling juxtapositions, the probable contents of such an aesthetics without making any arguments as to their historicity.

At one extreme, Democritean ideas shade off into Nietzsche's own. Take his lectures on "The Greek Lyric Poets," delivered in the winter semester of 1878/79. The manuscript resumes, partly verbatim, notes first set down in 1869, and at one point reads:

Lyric is the oldest form of poetry. Epic develops out of a certain kind of song, that of hymns to gods and heroes. Lyric [is] everywhere bound up with religious cults[;] where music and dance are conjoined with lyric, rhythm invades words. Rhythm colors thoughts, permits a certain selection of words, *groups together the atoms of the sentence* [or "clause," *Satz*]; rhythm in conn[ection] with *logos* is called *metron*. (*KGW*, 2.2:379; emphasis added)

This thought may not be quite matched in any other of Nietzsche's writings during his student or teaching days (though it clearly owes much to his ideas on Greek rhythm, and to fifth- and fourth-century ideas about this topic, as will become apparent in the next chapter).[50] But the thought sticks, and it reappears in the later writings, almost verbatim, in a passage from *The Gay Science* in which "The Origin of Poetry" (which is to say, rhythm) comes under discussion: rhythm, Nietzsche writes, is "that force which *reorders all the atoms of the sentence*, bids one choose one's words with care, and gives one's thoughts a new color, making them darker, stranger, and more remote" (*GS* 84; emphasis added).

The phrasing is elusive. What constitutes an atom here? On one view, the analogy will be between sounds and letters, a comparison that won't be of Nietzsche's making, as the Greek analytical lexicon from the late fifth century onward suggests: there, *stoicheion* is synonymously "letter" and "physical (or componential) element," while for the atomists "letters" are analogous to "atoms" (both of which get combined into higher-order compounds). The musical and rhythmical theories put forward by Aristoxenus in the fourth century B.C.E. make this connection explicitly, as Nietzsche well knows.[51] In their wake, sensualism as well as a kind of physical reductivism color the literary theories of some strains of Hellenistic literary criticism down to Dionysius of Halicarnassus in the last century B.C.E. Although nothing survives that might confirm beyond the shadow of a doubt Democritus' role in these developments, the catalogue of his titles and other connections of the sort drawn by Nietzsche point favorably in this direction. At the very least they suggest that in antiquity the inference to some kind of conjunction between atomism and aesthetic speculation, or physiology and art, was not felt to be impossible. Nietzsche's later projected "physiology of aesthetics" is conceived in the same spirit as the ancient theories of aesthetics in their most critical moods. It is fleetingly announced in *On the Genealogy of Morals* (III:8) and then again in *The Case of Wagner*, in a more binding—more complete—promise of a forthcoming work ("in a chapter of my main work," *CW*, 7; presumably, *The Will to Power* is meant). The aim in each case is to unsettle contemporary idealizations and ideologies of art through a disturbingly frank, though not quite "honest," naturalism, by appealing to reductivist foundations (say, to the physics of sound). Those foundations, however, turn out to be riddled with hidden complications: at bottom, naturalism for both Nietzsche and the ancient critics is a guise masking a deeper, thorough-going conventionalism (one attuned to the conventions of nature), which in turn is scarcely immune to critique. Naturalism is thus a stance, one that is useful for loosening the deeply seated conventions and habits of aesthetic, and ultimately cultural, perception.[52] Democritus in his own way appears to have made similar moves.

As we shall see, while Nietzsche's phrase, "the atoms of the sentence," suggests the analogy between letters and sounds, there is good reason to suppose that the reference is not to quantities of sound but to quantities of *time*. A Democritean influence is to be suspected even here, but it cannot be proved. Of related concern is the "analogy" that Nietzsche is keen to draw at this time between the qualitative representational structures by which "matter" is either taken in by the senses or "produced" by a subject (depending on one's philosophical preferences) and those pertaining to "music" (*KSA*, 14, 114 = *KGW*, 3.5.1:907): in each case, relations between quanta (whether quantities of sensation or of sensible matter) yield a registry of qualitative differences, for instance distinctive qualities of sound or tempo. Nietzsche is plainly exploring (and exposing) the root meaning of *aesthēsis* (sensation and perception). And in general, the primordial structures of perception are frequently compared in Nietzsche's corpus, both early and late, to those of music, rhythm, and tone, as in one notebook entry in which a dichotomy between "number" (quantity) and "will" (qualitative force) is posed in relation to similar polarities in music (*KSA*, 7, 3[23]; 1869/70). The Pythagorean section of the lectures on Presocratic philosophy makes the same point:

> Music as such exists only in our acoustic nerves and in our brain: outside of these or *in itself* (in Locke's sense) it consists of sheer numerical relations: namely, in the first place, according to its quantity, with respect to rhythmical measure [*Takt*], then according to its quality, with respect to the levels of the musical scale, viz., both in its rhythmical and in its harmonic element. ("PP," 343)

Merging together Pythagorean and Democritean ideas, Nietzsche decides that the world's essence, of which music is a "copy," is expressible in numbers, inquiry into which today is "strictly speaking the purview of chemistry and of the natural sciences. . . . In this sense, our science is Pythagorean." More precisely, in chemistry "atomism and Pythagoreanism" are "conjoined" (ibid., 343–44). The underlying theme here, as in the studies on atomism, is not just a physiologically based theory of aesthetic experience (as one might expect to find in any blending together of atomism and art). It is the principle that all quality is reducible to relations and proportions of quantity (ibid.; cf. ibid., 333–34, on Democritus), which are in turn volitilized by some dynamic factor (be it motion, force, or will).

The same thought runs through Nietzsche's contemporary lectures on Greek and Roman rhythm, in which beat (*Takt*) and rhythm represent for Nietzsche "the simplest forms" of the pulsional "drives" (*KSA*, 7, 1[49]; 1869). In the lectures on the Presocratics (1869–76), these drives are conceived as "forces [*Kräfte*]," but Democritus is explicitly said to have denied the identity of atoms with teleological factors such as "intelligence" and "force" [*Nous und Atomkräfte*]: "he recognizes only a mechanistic causality" (4:83)—although Nietzsche can vacillate on the question whether atoms constitute a kind of force or not, that is, whether mechanism can be reduced to its purest conceivable form and drained of all interior animation.[53] The ever unstable relation between matter and force is the paradox driving Nietzsche's speculations in "Teleology since Kant," just as it was a central preoccupation for Lange. Ultimately, Nietzsche will never entirely resolve the issue: it becomes a standing aporia in his later writings, more of a device for generating critical speculation than a question capable of natural solution or explanation. For the ultimate source of motion in any hypothesis about the world, Nietzsche concludes, lies in the mind of the subject that beholds and thereby animates it. This problem properly belongs in the ambit of Nietzsche's later concept of genealogy, which is designed to elicit (rather than solve) questions about rational explanations of the world and their intelligibility. Atoms invite such speculation. Indeed, they seduce us into making it, with their deceptively sensuous palpability, even as they void all final answers of meaning, first by reason of their intrinsic lack of meaning and then by reason of the fallacy of their construction as such—as, precisely, endowed with sensuous traits they strictly cannot have. Atoms are, in other words, a genealogical trap and a prototype of Nietzsche's later method of genealogical hypothesizing and its constitutive snares. But this is not the place to make the case for this interpretation of "genealogy."

At any rate, it is undoubtedly Nietzsche's wayward insight into the truly "lost" Democritus, the philosopher of language and of aesthetics, indeed "the Humboldt of the ancient world" (3:364),[54] that finally justifies his observations about the poetic élan that pervades Democritus' physical system and that, as it were, gives atoms their force. It is certainly this faintest of preserved connections that Nietzsche revives in his ongoing speculations on the affective sources of music, as in the following, a mere page of notes that is somewhat mysteriously, but not inexplicably, lodged in the notebooks dedicated to the *Democritea*:

An aesthetics of music has to take as its departure-point the effects

A (1) of a note [qua tone]

(2) of a sequence of notes

(3) of an interval

B (4) of rhythm

C (5) of the consonance of notes

A. Cause of the note. A language of affect. Cf. the singing of animals.

Source, therefore, in passions, in the will.

Parallels between language and music. Language consists of sounds, like music.

The interjection and the word.

The former is already musical. In the word, musicality (sonority [*das Klangliche*]) is impoverished, but as soon as affect appears [musicality, sonority] comes to the fore. Original root of music and poetry. (3:351)

Here as before, Nietzsche is tentatively exploring the physiological sources of language, and these turn out to be irreducibly tied to the problematics of sound viewed as pure sonority, musicality, tonality, and rhythm—and to their purely simulacral status (as appearances). But Nietzsche does not let the problem rest here. The dynamics of the "atoms of the sentence" (or "bodies of sound [*Lautkörper*]") have to be viewed as animated by instinctual, unconscious forces that have their own physiology, a parallel dynamics, but also, qua animus and stimulus, properties of their own. In this version of the theory at least, the properties of atoms are not quite reducible to mechanistic causes (for instance, to the arrangement of phonic materials by sequence, modulation, combination, etc.)[55]—let alone to the sense-bearing structures of language.[56] Democritean physiology can thus be implicitly blended together with a Schopenhauerian reflection on will (as here), at a primary level that exposes the will's complicity with a materialist hypothesis. Note how the interjection of the will brings us back to the materiality of linguistic sound in its purely sensuous dimension (*das Klangliche*), which lies at the heart of music—a far cry, incidentally, from Schopenhauerian linguistic expressivism.[57] What we find here, in other words, and possibly for the first time, is no simple speculation about the sources of language, but a curious mélange of models that are mutually interrogating. From a Schopenhauerian point of view, atoms do not so much exist as they are the imaginary products of the will, or else an attempt to account for this will in mechanistic terms.[58] In revenge, Nietzsche seems to say, the Democritean hypothesis is not so much wrong as it simply reflects the punctual essence of the will, whose rhythmical pulsation (the will's self-negating *rhythmos*) in itself resembles a kind of atomism. This particular conflation of models—of atomism and Schopenhauer, to the critical disadvantage of both—is characteristic of Nietzsche's most speculative thinking at all points in his career.[59] Indeed, the punctual, atomistic essence of the will, which lives on in the later fragments on the will to power, seems to be no more than a cipher for the will's own questionable and *ex hypothesi* status. In his search for a starting point of language and of sentience, Nietzsche will never look anywhere beyond this insoluble and irreducible contrast between rhythm and rhythm's "force," between physical quantities and their enlivening subjective qualities, between patterns of punctual elements (much like dots of ink on a page) and the will, or whatever it is that comes to animate them. What he finds in each case are primordial patterns of rhythmical modulations, made up of individual elements (*individua*, atoms) riven within by the image of their own wholeness. Needless to say, the ultimate incarnation of these figures is the individual human subject, their actual inventor.

Democritus: "The Freest Man"

It was Nietzsche's abiding interest in the stark physical landscape of atomism, stripped bare of anthropomorphic distractions, that provided the model for these experimental forays into the lowest thresholds, if not quite foundations, of language, thought, and sensation.[60] The minimalistic complexion of atomism, with its enviable simplicity and its economy of assumptions (allowing for a maximum of complexity), holds great attractions for Nietzsche quite apart from the philological puzzles that are involved.[61] Through atomism, the kinds of relations that he was exploring during the late 1860s could find a highly concentrated and almost allegorical expression: not just the oppositions but also the shared intimacies of subject and object, force and matter, passion and indifference, figure and ground, epiphenomena and materiality. The basis of all these terms is anything but scientific. Nietzsche is patently projecting conceptual models onto a limit—the limiting condition of atoms shifting places in a void—that (he knows) is itself the result of a projection.

This emerges most clearly in the essay from 1867/68 on post-Kantian teleology, where Nietzsche's thoughts on atomism are driven to another level of reflection beyond what Democritus may or may not be thought to have held, and where they mingle freely and disturbingly with Kantian motifs, as they would do so again in a sketch on temporal atomism from 1873. In both instances the crossing of perspectives is to the detriment of the two kinds of conception, atoms and things in themselves, which for Nietzsche clearly have no more validity than derives from their being speculative models of the natural world.[62] How certifiable are the properties of atoms? Their "blows" and "weight" are as hypothetical and as unprovable as the existence of the atoms themselves.[63] Yet we cannot even think of atoms in the absence of features borrowed from our experience, including their most basic attributes: "extension, impenetrability, shape, number [viz., numerical identity]" ("PP," 333). Following an insight made by Lange—namely, that "order and disorder are not found in nature" but are merely forms of experience[64]—what Nietzsche comes to see in the natural world is not the sturdy structure of existence but its mere conditions of possibility, made intelligible ex post facto by a projective, or rather retroactive, causal reasoning. This is in ways a Kantian idea (and an old one for Nietzsche),[65] but it also goes against Kant inasmuch as what Nietzsche appears willing to entertain is not a continuum of possibilities but the *interruption* of any such continuum—for instance, "the continual intermission of all rigorous necessitation." Interruption (Nietzsche holds, in reaction to Kant) is the result of the very attempt to "think" causality without agency ("TSK," 375). What conditions Kant's conditions of possibility? Agency (purposiveness) has to be imported into nature, "here and there," as a series of "interpolated motives." Nature cannot be imagined unless the traces of the mind that imagined it are structurally a part of the very picture of nature itself. The picture is thus a self-interrupting one, and it cannot help but lend itself to the most powerful fascinations. In a hauntingly beautiful phrase directed partly against Lange, Nietzsche writes that existence is not filled with wonder, it is "perforated" with wonder.[66] The metaphysical discontinuities presented by void are not far away. Perhaps this is the value that Nietzsche finally sees in atomism: by positing a reality that lies at the limits of what is conceivable, atomism underwrites its own evacuation. So does Kantianism, though in its purest form, in Kant, the immanent impossibilities of the system (its conditions of impossibility, so to speak) are strongly disavowed.

The remainder of the essay ("Teleology Since Kant") is given over to speculations about the stuff of life: chance, variety, mechanism, projected orders of meaning and intelligibility. Democritus is summoned throughout as a witness to the frailties of scientific models, and to the terrifying prospects that are opened up by his own system. Nietzsche hails Democritus as a blatantly antiteleological thinker, though Nietzsche is not himself quite prepared to embrace the consequences of mechanism, which after all is just one more model sprung from the mind: "NB The 'whole' is itself but a representation." The "form" of life, its purposiveness, is contradicted by its endless variation ("eternal becoming is life"), which may still prove to be nothing but the combinatorial characteristics of the play of dice, of letters thrown by chance onto a page, and their resultant synthesis: a tragedy that on any other throw could have been a comedy.[67] If Nietzsche is critical of a purely mechanical view of nature, he never entirely rejects the possibility that organic nature is ruled by principles identical to those that govern inorganic nature. "Life" is in many respects as uncertain as a chance collocation of elementary particles or letters, as evenly composed of successes as it is of failures, of nonteleological factors as of aims. Ultimately without form ("TSK," 387), in another respect life operates not according to chance but by a necessity of sorts, though it is one that Nietzsche claims to be blind: it is a "*purposeless causality*, an *anagkē* [necessity] *without aims*," conformable to the "most rigorous lawlike behavior, *only not according to rational laws*."[68] A later expression of this same idea is found in the fragments on the will to power, as for example: "'Necessity' not in the shape of an overreaching, dominating total force, or that of a prime mover; even less as a necessary condition for something valuable" (*WP*, 708).

In all of this, Nietzsche is allowing Democritean notions to infiltrate and confound a Kantian (and Schopenhauerian) view of the conceivability of teleology. Democritean cosmology yields a purposiveness without any purpose—but it does this with a vengeance. It is undoubtedly this that prompted Nietzsche to endorse Democritus' theory of the origins of the cosmos: the world, endlessly recomposing itself, is the fortuitous result of the sheer logic of its own necessity; it is its own cause, and just is what it is, having *become what it is* (3:334).[69] Democritean atomism is hyperallergic to the idea of natural ends. It thus makes a sharp contrast with the earliest Presocratic forerunner to Aristotelian teleology, Anaxagoras' conception of *Nous* or "Mind," a principle of intelligence in nature that, Nietzsche says, is "far too *full* to explain something as simple as motion." The allusion is again to void (the source of atomic motion), and to Democritus' well-known hostility to the Anaxagorean conception (DL, 9.35). Democritus, in contrast, offers not a method of science but a "method of critique," in the form of a "*renunciation*" (*KSA*, 7, 23[30]; 1872/73; emphasis added). His relative lack of hypotheses, the simple and sparse formalism of his system, can thus be read both as a distillation of scientific discourse and as its repudiation. This radical reduction of truth to its empty "kernel" is incarnated in what Nietzsche will later call "the ascetic ideal" (*GM*, III:27). In Nietzsche's eyes, and not without a reminiscence of Lange, the discourse of science will forever be striving to reattain the rigor, the purity, and the elegance of the Democritean system—that shimmering myth of natural inquiry from antiquity. Nietzsche's deep ambivalence toward and even fascination with the ascetic ideal, the death-drive of human consciousness, is evident at both ends of his career. His thought and writing will thus remain haunted by the empty, senseless specter of Democritean cosmology.

Democritus is the very picture of enlightened, demystified rationality and clear-eyed sobriety (3:364; 4:83). His vision is not just lucid: it is searing. The world he depicts is drained of moral and aesthetic significance, as we saw. Viewed against the featureless background of atoms and void, meanings appear more starkly than ever to have been imposed and invented.[70] Propounding a zero degree of meaning and exposing its empty outlines, Democritus comes to figure these as well: his name gradually disappears in Nietzsche's writings, and the signifying structure that he embodies (as it were, the personality, not the person) comes to be filled with ever new contents. That was the case in the critical encounter with Kant just above, in which Democritus is not named but is everywhere implied. This dispersal of Democritus' substance in Nietzsche's writings mirrors the historical fate of the philosopher, as he passes into the tradition of materialism for the most part namelessly, evoked more often than invoked, as alluring and repulsive as matter itself.

If the atomistic hypothesis continues to fascinate Nietzsche, this is surely because of the paradoxical extremes it embodies, which lend themselves to seemingly endless qualification. Alongside his histories of the Presocratic philosophers ("Philosophy in the Tragic Age of the Greeks" [1873]; the lectures on the Preplatonic Philosophers [1869–76]), Nietzsche finds new ways to insert Democritus—again, the personality, not the person—into his ongoing projects. These include his speculations on rhythm, on time (what Nietzsche terms *Zeitatomistik*, or temporal atomism), on language, or on Schopenhauer's model of the will—not to mention the various forms of materialism that Nietzsche probes throughout the coming years. Democritus literally ghosts Nietzsche's writings. As a consequence, Democritus can appear in places where he is least expected, as in *The Birth of Tragedy* ("It was in dreams, says Lucretius, that the glorious divine figures first appeared to the souls of men" [*BT* §1]) or in chance phrases that recall the specter of atoms and void. Democriteanism will return with a vengeance in the last productive half-decade of Nietzsche's life in his never fully developed "doctrine" of "the physiology of aesthetics," which is a direct carryover from the earlier forays into music and aesthetic perception à la Democritus in the late 1860s, as well as in the fragments on the will to power. There, the physics of atomism once more occupies the center of Nietzsche's thinking, now as the target of adverse criticism. The discussions are enhanced by more recent conceptual developments in atomism (Boscovich and Fechner), but the later theories are always reconsidered from the perspective of their earliest, most economical expression in Democritus' fragments and testimonia. Most striking of all is the quiet incorporation of Democritus into the theory of the will to power itself, which is a literal extrapolation of atomism: the physical trappings are shed and only the conceptual outlines remain (the postulate—and *prōton pseudos*—of punctual atoms of will).[71] Nietzsche never seemed able to finish his *Democritea*.

Democritus has a further value for Nietzsche, one that is nearly as grand and as ambitious as his earliest plans to reconsider the whole of Greek literary history in terms that would themselves be critically literary and historical. What Democritus represents to Nietzsche, throughout his career, is one particular version of that history—and its total transformation. By virtue of being a philosopher whose teaching is embedded in a philological tradition, and in view of the radical nature of his teaching, Democritus plays a singular role in this literary history—which is to say, in the recovery of the ancient past. What is more, given the overwhelming symmetries that obtain at the various levels involved (the principles of atomism, the forms of their transmission, and the philology that must embrace both of these aspects), Democritus is uniquely positioned to represent the dazzling traffic jam of Nietzsche's thought in his early years. And so too, his lifelong appropriation of atomism is perhaps best viewed not as a recuperative history but as a revisioning of the Western philosophical tradition from a historical and philological perspective, one that is not only philosophically informed but also philosophically implicated. Democritean philology, elaborated—circularly—in the course of the recovery of Democritus himself, is a case in point.

This skein is perhaps too tangled to be completely unraveled. It wasn't really meant by Nietzsche ever to be unraveled in its entirety: it contains too many insolubles. But we can at least begin to see how intricate and overdetermined Nietzsche's massive project is if we return to the set of problems from which he began, those concerning the authenticity of the Democritean corpus. For it is here that philosophical and literary-historical perspectives, by all accounts incommensurable, show a tendency to converge on one another again, and in interesting ways. Compare the following observation, from Nietzsche's lectures on the Presocratics, concerning the useful frailties of heuristic ventures, of the value in maintaining, even while exposing, a *prōton pseudos*, or false premise, that acts as one's enabling assumption:

> Materialism is a valuable hypothesis of relative truth, even after the *prōton pseudos* has been exposed: it is an idea that facilitates natural science, all of whose results still contain truth *for us*, albeit no absolute

truth. It is after all *our* world, in the production of which we are always actively involved. ("PP," 339–40)

This conclusion reflects a blend of Lange ("relative truth") and of Schopenhauer (*prōton pseudos*), but it is also distinctively Nietzschean.[72] The position expressed here virtually diagrams the path that Nietzsche took in the late 1860s en route to reaching the conclusions he did about classical philology by way of his inquiry into philosophical materialism. Philology works by negating its own assumptions, which can be shown to be false in a way that its results cannot: whatever is salvaged from the classical ruins "remains the truth *for us*." This salvaging operation is in fact a kind of necessary, healing redemption, not so much of the past as of the present. Delusion, whether conscious or not, inescapably plays a part in this process.

It might be tempting to say that Democritus is himself to be viewed as one such *prōton pseudos*, postulated by Nietzsche only to be withdrawn again, as a heuristic fiction that makes philosophy into a form of literary confabulation. But this approach, all too conveniently susceptible of a certain cynicism (Democritus as *Witz*, as a mere *jeu d'esprit*), is inadequate, and far too easy a way out of a far more troubling circularity.[73] For one thing, the self-skeptical ironies of the heurism in question are on Nietzsche's understanding arguably Democritus' own, and they are expressly said to leave the relative truth and value of materialism confirmed and intact. What is more, Nietzsche foresaw this interpretive move, and it was one to which he was hostile on other grounds. A cynically conceived Democritus lay too close to Nietzsche's initial intention, which was to expose the "pseudo-Democritus" upon which ancient traditions and modern philologists had heaped nonexistent attributes, thereby feeding a self-perpetuating philological hoax.

The picture that Nietzsche draws while musing upon this last idea, which he will reject, is as fantastic as it is diabolical. Alexandrian scholars in Egypt (Thrasyllus, Bolus, and their ilk), given over anyway to exotic possibilities, sought to "place Democritus on a sublime pedestal," perhaps as a way of relativizing Aristotle's own monumental achievements, which would henceforth stand diminished by an even more monumental predecessor. In this way, the "many-sided accomplishments, the worldly exposure [especially in the Orient], and the prolific writings" of this falsified Democritus, Nietzsche reasoned, could be set up as a phantom-other to Aristotle's systematic inquiry into all known subjects. Later Peripatetics would have retaliated in kind, by ascribing phantom-writings to their master's already considerable body of treatises—and thus would a history of philosophy be written out of pure *ressentiment* and into the vacuum of fiction (3:270). At the core of this story is Nietzsche's early hypothesis, here somewhat overblown and no doubt consciously so, but nonetheless accurate in the essentials ("Perhaps there were as many as 200 false titles"). But as we have seen, he soon found that he had to abandon the quest for pseudepigraphy (and with it Valentin Rose, under whose spell he was operating): the phantoms had all too much reality to them; they were too persistent and haunting, while reality, as a representation, carried too many phantoms of its own. The stakes had grown, Nietzsche could now see. It was Democritus' philosophical materialism and its troubling uncertainties that had entered him into world history, pitting him against a spiritualism that, in its most canonical form, was cast as Platonism. And so it was not the number of titles that mattered to Nietzsche in the end, but only the depth of Democritus' achievement and his impact.

Nietzsche nowhere claims to be recovering in a positivistic way the true scope of early atomism once he makes his volte-face, but neither is he freely inventing. Democritus falls within the literary-historical project that guides Nietzsche's philology; and within that project, Nietzsche is at the same time writing a genealogy of the philosophical tradition that sought to erase, from the very start, any traces of its debt to Democritus and his materialism. As we saw, Democritus was no sooner registered by that tradition than he was rendered opaque, a cipher, illegible. Beginning with Plato's first and failed attempt to erase an important part of the atomist's legacy, followed by an entire tradition of obliteration and hostility, whether open or secretive, conscious or not (3:340), and culminating in Kantian idealism, Democritus is the bane and scourge of some of the most successful forms of philosophy in the West. Paying tribute to the much maligned and feared atomist is Nietzsche's way of exposing this history at its origins:

> We owe Democritus many more sacrificial victims yet, in order just to begin to make amends for the injuries visited on him by the past. In fact, seldom has an important author had to suffer so many attacks actuated by so many different motives as Democritus has. Theologians and meta-

physicians have heaped on his name the inveterate grudges they hold against materialism. (3:347; cf. 3:277).

Plato is an exemplary instance. In the immediate sequel, Nietzsche relates once more the apocryphal story of "the divine" Plato's aborted "private auto-da-fé." Driven by his resentment against materialism, and against Democritus in particular as the most spectral embodiment of that philosophical view of reality, Plato "was stopped by the consideration that it was too late: the poison had already spread too far."

Philosophy neither begins nor ends with Democritus. But in an important sense for Nietzsche it revolves continuously around his figure, whose ghostly survival represents not only "the incarnation of pagan antiquity" but the very antithesis of Western idealism (ibid.). Nietzsche's Democritus is accordingly not a "pseudo-Democritus" but a counter-Democritus, a Democritus who is never merely invented as a fiction but a resistant figure who can only be written against, like the postulate of matter that he himself propounded, lacing it ("perforating it") with skeptical doubt and poeticized belief. In Nietzsche's eyes, Democritus' importance does not lie in his being an originary figure, or even an original invention by Nietzsche. Quite the contrary, Democritus represents the falsehood of all such origins. The systematic disciple of Leucippus and not the originator of atomism (not atomism's *prōtos heuretēs*), Democritus stands, we might say, for the impossibility of any absolute philosophical beginning. If anything, he stands for the internal debt-structure of philosophy, its historical conditions, and its innermost rivalries, the way Platonism owes more to Democritus than Plato's jealously ever allows, or the way idealism in general (Christianity included) constructs itself as a negation of the material world, drawing whatever force it has from this denial, lavishly attending to the very world it would deny.[74]

Democritus, so conceived, is not a *chiffre* for materialism, pure and simple, any more than Nietzsche should be considered a materialist, even though Nietzsche's sympathies clearly lie that way, especially whenever dwelling on matter and sensation provides him with a chance to confound Platonism—which is to say, idealism in the broadest sense, whether of the metaphysical variety or in its more immediately cultural and ideological forms. Allergic to reductionisms of all kinds, Nietzsche ensures that the Democritus about whom he writes will be irreducibly complex as well. Part serene and a disparager of mankind, part brooding and self-doubting skeptic, part historical specter, Democritus is for Nietzsche the paradigmatic instance of the *problem* of materialism—the problem that materialism poses within the Western philosophical tradition, and the problem that it poses for itself. This is so even if reductive materialism turns out, as Nietzsche claims it does, to be little more than an inverted Platonism, a form of idealism in its own right. Nietzsche can relish this outcome too, because it marks the ultimate embarrassment to Platonism, its deepest scandal: the contingency of its identity on what it would most deny. Nietzsche thus takes a view of materialism that turns matter into a fatal question mark of meaning. The body, on this polemical view of it, is not an object of knowledge but a threat. It continues to enjoy all the stigmatic features that are heaped upon it in the loftier spiritual traditions, which include Christianity and other "decadent" forms of social activity, while darkening those traditions with its own questionable substance as well. The question that the body on this view of it implicitly raises is "What if Platonism is merely *an inverted materialism* . . . ?" Far from underwriting the origins of philosophy, Democritus—as lost, and as persisting nonetheless like a stain in the philosophical tradition—is rather a figure for the failure of Western philosophy to originate itself, to free itself from its own constraints (history, matter, the derivation of ideas from some prior source), and to attach itself to a purer mission (timeless, disembodied truth). And so it happens that Nietzsche's complex reconstruction of Democritus, Nietzsche's heurism rather than his rediscovery or reinvention, ultimately results in a massive realignment of the whole of the philosophical tradition. His object, in the end, is not so much philosophy as it is philosophy's history, which, in part unwritten and in part unfinished, is no less constitutive of philosophy than are its various recorded teachings. At once heralding and challenging the materialisms of the nineteenth century and thwarting all purer forms of idealism, Democritus is one of the very real phantoms that haunts philosophy today. Such is his "afterlife."

A crowning irony of Nietzsche's philosophical project is that it remains an eminently philological one. For the recovery of Democritus owes as much to a revisioned philology as to anything else. And so too, Nietzsche's pointed reversal of Seneca's Latin aphorism (*philosophia facta est quae philologia fuit*) is only apparent: it is transparently veiled by its own classicism. The ends of philosophical discourse, Nietzsche seems to be saying, can be viewed only by considering the history of its obliterations, and—perhaps nowhere more urgently than in the present case—by confronting philosophy with its own (abnegated) philology, its denied origins.[75] Philology, the origin of philosophy? In an important sense, yes. In another, not exactly, for the very shape of philology is itself philosophically and historically conditioned. And here we enter into a circle that one might wish to call vicious. Nietzsche would simply call it inescapable. If Nietzsche will never have done with Democritus, perhaps now we can see why. The project of reclaiming Democritus—"*the freest man*"[76]—is precisely endless, because being without origin, it had no sure place to begin.

'Habent Sua Fata Libelli': Diocles of Magnesia, Nietzsche's 'Laertiana,' and Democritus' Nachleben

The foregoing account of Nietzsche's philology has focused primarily on his notebooks, which were never finished and never intended for publication. Hence, one might wish to object, the impression that Nietzsche's philology oversteps the bounds of scholarly convention and decorum has to be misleading: surely not all of his projects were as wayward as these make him appear to be. The question can be briefly addressed, but to do so it will be necessary to turn to those writings by which he made his mark as a scholar at a still tender age (he was not yet twenty-six years old when the last of these articles saw the light of day) and for which he was chiefly remembered in philological circles at one time—until, that is, scholarly opinion finally cast Nietzsche into outer darkness.[77] These are his three published studies on the philosophical sourcebook from the late third century C.E., Diogenes Laertius' *Lives of the Philosophers*.[78] Sharing affinities both of subject matter and of a deeper kind with the philosophical philology of Nietzsche's *Democritea*, the Laertian studies (two of which are in Latin) can be as fantastic in their conception as anything else he wrote at the time. Strangely, for all its prominence, this face of Nietzsche's scholarship, the imaginative framework of the Laertian studies, is passed over in utter silence in the literature. This silence is telling, and needs to be addressed. Accordingly, a quick overview of the Laertian materials is in order. Doing so will enable us to highlight from another perspective the most salient features of Nietzsche's wayward conventional philology, and it will give us a deeper insight into the recuperative project we have been tracing so far.

Nietzsche made his name, though not his debut, as a philologist with his studies on Diogenes Laertius' *Lives* (his first publication, on Theognis, appeared in 1867). If not in his own eyes then at least in those of others, his career as a philologist is to all intents and purposes identical with these studies. The theme of his research while he was at Leipzig in 1866, the *Laertiana* became the occasion for a first collusion between Ritschl and Nietzsche. Ritschl was well aware of Nietzsche's research on Diogenes' sources when, with a wink and a nod, he set a prize-essay theme for the following year on the topic *De fontibus Diogenis Laertii* ("On the Sources of Diogenes Laertius") ("Rückblick," 311). When the essay was finally submitted, it bore as its epigraph a prophetic quotation in Greek from Pindar: "Become what you are."[79] Nietzsche plainly felt that he was following his own destiny. The essay carried off the prize and eventually appeared in two installments in Ritschl's journal, *Rheinisches Museum*, in 1868 and in 1869. (Two more Laertian studies were to follow, both appearing in 1870.) More would hang on these studies than Nietzsche could imagine. It was on the basis of the published *De fontibus* and on his earlier article on Theognis (likewise published in *Rheinisches Museum*) that he was offered an assistant professorship of classical philology at Basel in 1868, again with Ritschl's influential backing. Under the pressure of the offer, Nietzsche was awarded a doctoral degree *honoris causa* from Leipzig, his publications being accepted in lieu of a dissertation. Promotion to full professor came a year later, likewise (in no small part) on the basis of the Laertian studies.[80] Finally, it is on the basis of his *Laertiana* as a whole that, in the words of one classicist, Nietzsche's "standing as a scholar is . . . largely determined."[81]

The studies were innovative indeed and full of novel insights. More vigorously systematic than their predecessors in this area, they contained vital implications for a new understanding of the entirety of Diogenes' *Lives*, a crucial source of information even today for the history of philosophy in antiquity. Clearly, the *Laertiana*, approaching two hundred printed pages and representing half of Nietzsche's total published output, are a work to be reckoned with. What the world saw in them seems fairly evident. What

Nietzsche saw in them is a separate question. As they have been treated only in passing above, a word or two will be needed to address the matter of their relevance to the *Democritea*.

We have already seen how the two projects overlap, and how the note-books can bear witness to either or both simultaneously. In point of fact, the two studies share an astonishing degree of similarity and focus, but one that, given the sprawling contours of both, is all too likely to escape notice. Each by itself justifies Nietzsche's later comment from *Ecce Homo* on the spurious, skeptical narratives of his philological "novellas": "My old teacher Ritschl went so far as to maintain that I conceived even my philological essays like a Parisian *romancier*—absurdly exciting" (*EH*, IV:2). And as a rule, Nietzsche knew full well the hazards of ancient biographies: "In general the tradition about lives and circumstances of poets in antiquity is very uncertain and sparse." As he also was aware, Theodor Bergk had rejected an earlier schol-ar's reconstruction of Theognis' personality and circumstances for being the "novella" that it was.[82] The philosophical tradition was no more secure. Nietzsche's response was to supplement both traditions again (his noveliza-tion of Theognis, ever full of complication, will be discussed in chapter 5). As we shall see, Nietzsche's *Laertiana*, in their conceptual framework, reen-act the drama of his *Democritea* and in fact are inconceivable apart from these latter studies.

Nietzsche's *Democritea* are written in the context and spirit of irretrievable loss. The effect is enhanced by the wide historical and philosophical dimen-sions spanning past and present that Nietzsche builds into his perspectives, within which philology, materialism, and Platonism converge in a coherent if troubled whole, while Democritus steadily recedes from the picture as its central vanishing point. In adopting this view, Nietzsche appears in fact to be aligning himself with a surprising figure: Diocles of Magnesia, a doxog-rapher whose *Summary of the Philosophers* (dated by Nietzsche to the first century C.E.) he postulated as the principle source for Diogenes' *Lives*. Nietzsche's reconstruction of Diocles as a source is highly speculative,[83] but no less telling for that. Nietzsche takes Diocles to have been, if not an Epi-curean, then at least a sympathizer (pp. 87–90),[84] based on only the slightest of indications. This judgment is clearly willful and tendentious, but it is essential to the story he tells. He reasons that Diocles composed, inter alia, the life of Democritus, whom Diocles admired as "the greatest of the pre-

Platonic philosophers" (p. 221, cf. p. 223); that Diocles in places consciously arranged his materials so as to counteract Plato's antipathy toward Democritus (cf. p. 223); and, ironically, that it was the epitomizing handiwork of Diogenes (a mindless copyist and a poet) that produced an abbreviated exposition of Democritus' teaching (p. 221). On this telling, a longer exposition in Diocles was fatefully tossed aside by Diogenes (p. 219), while a similar fate befell the list of Democritus' titles. At one time more elaborate in Diocles, the signs of this portion of the catalogue, especially the physical writings, are now reduced to a faint trace in Diogenes (p. 231). The loss of all this material is incalculable.

Here, Nietzsche is plying a philology based in part on personalities, as in his reconstructions of Democritus and Homer, and in part on his by now familiar skepticism, which deprives Diogenes of the authorship not only of much of his work but even of passages written in the first person. Nietzsche's "central hypothesis" about the singular source of Diogenes' *Lives* (p. 203), which he sometimes calls his "Dioclesian hypothesis" (p. 221), is buttressed by wild speculations about the singular personalities involved and their motives. Classical scholars naturally seize upon Nietzsche's elegant, if reductive, philological hypothesis, ignoring the scenery and stage effects. But this is to miss his point, which lies, precisely, in the theatrical conditions in which his argument plays itself out and in the hunches about the dramatis personae of his narrative. For although it is not pronounced, the Laertian source studies give the appearance of being a reconstruction, by way of a late ally of the atomists, of the historical antagonism between Plato (or Platonism) and Democritus (and, to a certain extent, his succession, including Cynics, Pyrrhonists, and satirical writers in the so-called Menippean genre). These are the topics that frame the last of Nietzsche's three published articles on Diogenes Laertius, and together they represent the conception and the form by which the studies, taken as a whole, are underlain.

Nietzsche's *Laertiana* thus do have a coherent shape, although it is one that is partly hidden from view. This is unsurprising in itself: concealment is a characteristic of all of Nietzsche's writings. But one should also compare his letter to Deussen of 4 April 1867, where this very feature of the *Laertiana* is already envisaged: "My whole endeavor is, this time round, not to let the logical skeleton [of the essay] to be as readily transparent as it is in my study on Theognis, which is enclosed. [85] [To do] this is, let me assure you, quite difficult. At least for me. I want to give things of this kind a somewhat artistic garb." Nietzsche's choice of Diocles and the decisive role that he allots to him is a powerful piece of creative philology, or else a violent and gratuitous hypothesis, depending on whether you share Nietzsche's point of view. It also inverts the accepted historical relationship between Diocles (first century B.C.E.) and Thrasyllus (early first century C.E.): Nietzsche establishes Diocles as Thrasyllus' younger contemporary,[86] but his argument makes the most of a marginal uncertainty, and it is at worst circular. Wilamowitz's pupil Ernst Maas would later savage Nietzsche's chronology as a "pipe dream."[87] Nietzsche clearly went out of his way to cast the *Lives* in a particular light, and it was a light that he for the most part was happy to share. But this is not the end of the story. For it is ironic that on this imaginative but unprovable hypothesis, Democritus' ultimate nemesis, doxographically speaking, should turn out not to be Plato's jealousy (at one point, Diocles is briefly made into the inventor of the anecdote about Plato's auto-da-fé [4:98]). Nor is it the misguided ambitions of the neo-Pythagorean and failed philologist Thrasyllus, who rearranged Democritus' titles in the form in which they have come down to us. It is rather something far less exalted, and closer to the workings of dumb chance—namely, the negligence of a mediocre poet who moreover made his mark by writing imaginary epitaphs, in epigrammatic form, on dead philosophers (Nietzsche calls them "burial inscriptions [*Sepulcralinschriften*]," p. 193).[88] Diogenes' *Lives*, preserving at least his own epigrams intact, turns out to be a haphazard graveyard for philosophers.[89]

Even so, one of the morals of Nietzsche's *Laertiana* is that histories, however hazardous, are never indifferent or disinterested, and they never cease to be free of little ironies. If it was the scholarly consensus at the time that Diogenes was an Epicurean ("even" the otherwise "skeptical" Rose rides this bandwagon [p. 199]), it was Nietzsche's aim to demolish this view by unmasking the true nature of Diogenes' ghost-writings. If anything, Diogenes reveres Plato—even if he never read a word of him—as a "doctor of the soul," while his "epitaph" on Epicurus is derisive and malicious (pp. 198–99). Curiously, the tables at this point turn on Diogenes, in Diocles' (and so too, Democritus') favor. For Diogenes could produce no more than what he found in his source. And here Nietzsche claims to be able to establish that the doxographical account of Plato was actually reduced from the start. On Nietzsche's argument, the very inclusion of the Platonic account in Diocles' work is presented by Diocles—not Diogenes, for the first person has been mindlessly transcribed by him—as a favor to his addressee, a learned female "philo-Platonist" whose importunate whims he indulges only begrudgingly (her desire more than anything else is to hear about Plato's teachings "'over all the others'"). And so, contrary to his custom, which is to supply both summary and detailed accounts, Diocles offers a summary of Plato's views in "elementary outline" only, "lest" the biographical portion should appear naked without it. A fuller account, he says with utmost tact, would under the circumstances be "taking owls to Athens" (DL, 3.47; pp. 193–201).[90]

A Final 'Witz'? Thrasyllus

It has been proposed by one of the very few scholars to pay the *Democritea* any attention that in Nietzsche's imagination Thrasyllus stands emblematically as an alter ego from antiquity.[91] In the light of the foregoing, I think we can safely say that this thesis is not so much wrong as it is incomplete. True, resemblances of a kind can be said to obtain between Nietzsche's "philological *Witz*"—his inspiration, mental agility, and above all his knack (as he himself describes it) for "comparison, by leaps and bounds, of hidden analogies, and the capacity to pose paradoxical questions"[92]—and Thrasyllus' own *Witz*—namely, his attempt to view Democritus as a continuator of Pythagoreanism, if not Pythagoras' direct disciple.[93] But Nietzsche makes it plain that despite his apparent interest in Pythagoras, Democritus was his own thinker, committed by virtue of his atomism to a line of inquiry that ran counter to Pythagorean metaphysics ("the differences are enormous").[94] Thrasyllus' ambitions led him to try to comprehend Democritus' output within the "straitjacket" of Pythagorean categories, along the lines of his index to Plato's titles (likewise arranged in tetralogies).[95] In both cases, the procedure yields a total of fifty-six titles, an all-too-convenient and patently mystical figure (the halo is assured in any case by the ever "holy" tetralogy-concept), stretched somewhat desperately from fifty-two by an act of double counting (counting both titles and book-numbers within titles [*KGW*, 2.1, 229]). But the method suffers from an added constraint. In a moment of blazing insight, Thrasyllus compared the versatile Democritus to a "pentathlete,"[96] and so, Nietzsche hypothesizes, he embarked on a painful but consequential process, further grouping the thirteen tetralogies into five divisions conceived according to content. The last of these (*ta technika*, the so-called technical treatises) was a catch-all and thus even more patently a pure contrivance, thanks to which the formal integrity of his scheme, and thus his initial inspiration (his *Witz*), could be "saved" (4:99).

How close, in fact, are Nietzsche and Thrasyllus? Their resemblances are, like those between Thrasyllus and Democritus, superficial at best, and they are crucially overshadowed by huge differences in Nietzsche's mind.[97] Thrasyllus' genial but "unphilological" idea "lays the foundation for a bad building" (4:99); *Witz*, as Nietzsche conceives it, lays the foundation for "methodological rigor," which always has connotations of a skeptical withholding of belief and a complex inquiry into the conditions of possibility of philology itself.[98] Thrasyllus, by contrast, is gripped by a "belief higher than any reason" (4:96). So far is Thrasyllus from being possessed of any such rigor, he is responsible for having definitively hobbled the transmission of Democritus' catalogue of titles, either reducing the number of titles from three hundred (on Ritschl's speculation) to fifty-six, or contaminating it with who knows how many spurious works, but in any case disfiguring it with an arbitrary schematism. Such were the catastrophic effects of Thrasyllus' "incomprehensible" *Witz*, which Nietzsche sets out to expose.[99]

Thus, any hint of sympathy with Thrasyllus gives over in the end to a philological "correction": Nietzsche's stated aim is to restore Thrasyllus' misguided catalogue "according to its [original] form and intention," on the way to replacing Mullach's edition of the fragments, which means correcting Thrasyllus' Pythagoreanizing tendencies and going behind him so as to arrive at "older pinakographic [viz., Alexandrian] arrangements."[100] But Nietzsche will ultimately realize his correction of Thrasyllus when, paradoxically, he decides to forgo the ambition to do so. For he can safely call Thrasyllus' intention to restore the Democritean catalogue to its original arrangement "delusional" only when he recognizes the futility of the attempt: there is simply no way to determine with any degree of precision, let alone recover, what has been irreparably lost. In many ways closer to Nietzsche's self-image as a philologist striving to preserve the memory of Democritus, likewise in accordance with "the latest philological methods for ascertaining authenticity and inauthenticity" (4:97), is the shadowy figure of Diocles of Magnesia, whom Nietzsche presumes to have been an Epicurean, not a Platonist, and certainly not a Pythagorean. Ironically, it was Thrasyllus who (on Nietzsche's inverted chronology and on his fantastic imagining) represented to Diocles the cutting edge of philology (ibid.). This did not, however, prevent Diocles from retrieving further titles over and above the Thrasyllan catalogues, which he sought out in the lists compiled by earlier scholars.[101] But, as we noted earlier, Nietzsche's philology is itself modeled after Democritus' methodological rigor (his "rigorous standard of scientific method" [4:44; "SWB," 101]); and that encompasses bracing skeptical tendencies and a suspicion of all dogmatic truth, which in turn causes the very effort to reclaim the historical Democritus to spin off into vertiginous self-reflection. The only check on this endless regression is the fact that for Nietzsche self-reflexivity has no value as an end in itself. Its primary purpose in the present case lies in its capacity to trouble an otherwise quiescent history of philosophy, and the philology that underwrites it.

So, rather than forcing Nietzsche into the straitjacket of one kind of commitment or another, we should recognize that his many identifications are never wholly guided by sympathy. They tend, on the contrary, to be partial and contradictory, and to be guided, rather, by theatrical purposes, for his writings put on display the complex investments (epistemic, cultural, and ideological) that are always at stake in philology. Nietzsche is, if you like, at once Thrasyllus, Democritus, Diocles, and even, at another level (as we saw), Plato. This insight prompts the following general observation about Nietzsche's philological method. All philology for Nietzsche mirrors its subject, which is to say, the philologist. ("A fact without subjectivity is nothing," he once wrote to his friend Gersdorff, 20 February 1867.)[102] But not every object caught in that reflection is an image, pure and simple, of the subject. There are a number of reasons why this is so, but two immediately stand out. First, the asymmetry of self-reflection for Nietzsche lies in the very nature of subjectivity, which is constantly at war with itself and pulled in antagonistic directions (for example, in the directions of *Denken* and *Dichten*, or rigor and invention). The subject, itself no simple entity, is at best a contradictory ensemble of impulses that never achieve anything more than a partial unity: it is riddled with dark spots eluding self-reflection. This is not to say that these opacities are not mirrored somewhere in the domain of self-reflection. They are. Only, they make themselves apparent in the noncoincidence of the self with its various reflections, and in the multiplicity of contradictory identifications through which subjects are formed. This is perhaps the most fundamental and unchanging fact about Nietzsche's sense of the self. In ways, the development of his writings over the course of his career is just the gradual unfolding of this fact.[103]

Second, historical fissures and overlays always have to be taken into account, and these serve to interrupt the process of self-reflection (as its obstacles) and actually condition the process as well (by belonging to its prehistory). Nietzsche never forgets, and in fact he always foregrounds, the uneven differences that are constituted by historical distances. This is evident throughout the whole of his *Democritea* and the philology associated with it, but we might compare the avowed asymmetry and incommensurability between Thrasyllus and Nietzsche,[104] or consider how Nietzsche's entire project of "reclamation" is suffused with the sense of loss and unreachable impossibility—a sense that he embraces, intensifies, and lays into the very foundations of his philology. The subject is victim to both kinds of influence outside of its control, to historical conditions and losses that turn out to be constitutive of the subject and its undertakings. Philology is only one of the more prominent instances of this unwitting influence.

Thus, subjectivity for Nietzsche is never the starting point of analysis, except in the sense that it is the most immediate "given" for a philologist, and often the most undetectable factor as well (often taking the form of unreflective bias). "Subjectivity prevails," but not without a long prehistory of struggle and contest, of which the philologist as subject is only the most recent symptom (this was one lesson of the essay on Homer). Torn, willy-nilly, between "rigor" and "invention," the philologist ultimately must come to grips with the harsh reality that neither factor is spontaneously given in the world or ever found in some pure form. Rigor and imagination enjoy only the most tenuous and contingent of identities, because of their inevitable contamination with historical predecessors (there being no such thing as pure invention) and their contamination with each other (rigor is always something of an accepted and conventionalized fiction). This realization only compounds the sense of dislocation that pervades Nietzsche's philology, the upshot of which for us is that simple reductions in Nietzsche or about Nietzsche, even at this early stage, are hazardous indeed.

As a result, the possibility that Nietzsche is practicing a purely "fantastic" and "romantic" brand of philology is out of the question.[105] At the other extreme, arguments against any notion of Nietzsche's "unscholarly levity" miss the mark as well.[106] Nietzsche's critical philology is neither irreducibly "fantastic" nor is it irreducibly "scholarly"—even if one of its guiding aims is to reflect, through a kind of exaggerated and negative distortion, the unpalatable truth that conventional philology is forever driven by the fiction of its own rigor. This is what, in the tradition, is known (and partially obscured) as "intuitionism." Nor were philologists ever completely unaware of this fact about their work, given their frequent admissions about the crucial necessity of intuitive leaps (as in the case of Wolf). Nietzsche simply does not hesitate to bring this truth about philology disturbingly into the foreground again.

One final comment deserves to be made about the irresolvability of the question that drives so much of the *Democritea* and that cries out for attention: just how many works can Democritus be said to have written? If Nietzsche never resolves the issue, this is perhaps due to his shift of attention to what the works themselves contained. But in point of fact the question is not so much dropped as it is blurred. The notes leave the issue unresolved, and in the one place that it is addressed in print by Nietzsche (the *Analecta Laertiana* of 1870) the problem is conspicuously, and, we might now add, symbolically elided. Tottering on the brink between two hypotheses, those of Rose and Ritschl, Nietzsche's argument in the end clinches nothing. Ritschl's conclusion, pegging the number at around three hundred titles, is demolished, thanks to a forceful counterconjecture by Nietzsche that succeeds in erasing—yet again—Democritus' name from the historical record (from a passage in Diogenes on ancient polygraphic writers, DL, 1.16). The implications of this move for Rose's pseudepigraphical thesis, which Nietzsche mentions and which is itself vague, are nowhere drawn, whether here or anywhere else in Nietzsche's writings. (Democritus, Rose says, published "only a few" books—Nietzsche takes this to mean fewer than twenty titles.)[107] In his lectures on the Presocratics, given variously over the years from 1869/70 to 1876, Nietzsche likewise leaves open the question of the exact number of titles in Democritus' corpus. In fact, he leaves the question pretty much as it was before he began his inquiries: "Very encouraging grounds for undertaking a fresh collection of the fragments. The problem of the falsified tradition ["pseudepigraphy"] likewise remains unsolved: Rose, for example, takes all the ethical fragments to be spurious."[108] And similar signs of openness may be found elsewhere in other contexts in the philological writings after 1870.[109] Nietzsche never touched the question again. But then, he never really needed to do so either.

With the depth of Democritus' achievement assured, or at least gauged, the exact number of his works and their range remains forever hazy, contestable, and troubling. And here, Nietzsche might be seen as deliberately leaving in place the stain of Democritus within the tradition that variously embraced him. Such is Democritus' afterlife. Overcoming that kind of stain, whether positivistically or idealistically, but without ever looking it directly in the face, is what for Nietzsche most characterizes the motivating impulse of traditional philology. Coming face to face again with what philology most wants to avoid is what characterizes Nietzsche's counterphilology, which in its own way, and in its own afterlife, has created a stain for all subsequent philological undertakings.

CHAPTER 3

Being on Time:
The Studies in Ancient Rhythm and Meter (1870–72)

Es ist Zeit, daß es Zeit wird.

— CELAN

The concept and phenomenon of rhythm are a constant motif in Nietzsche's writing throughout his career. Their significance to his later thinking, though not well recognized, is indisputable. One need only recall the prominence given to the "wave beat of [musical] rhythm" and its "formative power" in the early and closing sections of *The Birth of Tragedy* (1872), or the identification of this same plastic power, "that continual urge and surge of a creative, form-giving, changeable force," with the species activity of mankind in the later writings ("Man is a creature that fashions form and rhythm"), let alone the finely described dynamics of the will to power—its pulsations, its inner metabolism, its "forms of intermittence," and its varying tempos and rhythms (1885–87).[1] At one point, in a synthetic gesture, Nietzsche will even go so far as to characterize the Apollinian and Dionysian states in terms of "a difference in tempo," that is, as an alteration in the ordinary perception of "time and space," which is itself already in some rhythmic shape (1888).[2]

Nietzsche's later thinking on the topic is in turn indebted to his first encounter with rhythm as a philological problem during his studies at Bonn and Leipzig and then as a professor at Basel. The concepts and even the terms of the later reflections are all derived from this early phase, as is the tendency to surround the question of rhythm with philosophical perspectives, whereby rhythm tends to be viewed as a "symbolics of the drives"—so, already, a notebook entry from the fall of 1869, vaguely influenced by Schopenhauer.[3] But then so, too, is the further tendency to put these perspectives in the service of a wider-ranging critique of cultural perception, for rhythm is nothing if not a perceptual phenomenon, a "symbolics," if you will, that is variously shaped by history and culture. That, at least, was the lesson of Nietzsche's first philological reflections on the subject. As with his other investigations at the time, philology could give even the most abstruse of philosophical issues a historical dimension, a sense of their being time-bound rather than timeless. And rhythm, even more so than meter (for reasons that will emerge below), proved to be an object-lesson in this regard. It was a study in the dimension of time itself.

Alongside his interest in rhythm more abstractly conceived, Nietzsche dwelt at surprising length on the particulars of rhythm in the Greek and Roman world. The second of his publications was an article on the Danae fragment by Simonides and the problem of its rhythmical form (1868).[4] Although the study was conceived in 1866, his interest in the problem dates back to 1864 while he was at Bonn.[5] Not long afterward, Nietzsche showed signs of a budding interest in the more general question of classical rhythm and meter (a review from 1869 of an edition of a Greek text on rhythm; scattered but persistent notebook entries, which already regard "the beat of the rhythmical pulse" as a foundation of aesthetic phenomena in general; a plan from 1868 contemplating future lecture courses, one of which is to be on "rhythm and meter").[6] An intense burst of activity while at Basel followed. There, Nietzsche treated the topic of rhythm in lectures between 1869 and 1874, twice devoting a whole course to it (1869 and 1870/71). And having made a series of unconventional and innovative insights into Greek and Roman rhythm and meter, he filled four notebooks on the subject between 1870 and roughly 1872, with an eye to future publication—a plan that, like so many others, never materialized.

Even so, rhythm and meter in antiquity never ceased to be a concern to

Nietzsche. The *Nachlass* of the next decade occasionally points to a revival of the notebook projects from the early 1870s, and there are quiet allusions to the early insights in most of his subsequent discussions of rhythm, both in the notebooks and in the published works. Invariably, "rhythm" continues to be used either in the strict sense of music, dance, and language, or in the extended philosophical sense of the sort described above (although as we shall see, this distinction was never a hard and fast one for Nietzsche). Most remarkably of all, however, he continued to defend his earliest, unorthodox views about the subject down to the very end of his career, mainly in correspondence with his long-standing friend and confidant *in rebus musicis*, the musician and musicologist and former member of the charmed Wagner circle, Carl Fuchs. At these moments, Nietzsche would relive his own arguments as vividly as when he had first discovered them. Compare the following letter from mid-April 1886:

> Finally a word about a quite large theoretical difference between us,
> namely with regard to classical metrics. Admittedly, I am hardly entitled
> to talk about these matters anymore—but I would have been entitled to
> do so back in 1871, a dreadful year that I spent reading the Greek and
> Latin metricians, but with a most peculiar result. At that time, I felt
> myself to be the most marginally placed metrician among all classical
> philologists: for I demonstrated to my students how the whole develop-
> ment of metrical theory from Bentley to Westphal was the history of a
> fundamental error [*Grundirrthum*].

The letters to Fuchs (two more follow, in late 1888, all three quite detailed) show Nietzsche to have considered his reflections on rhythm to be worthy contributions to classical philology. But he also considered them to be a critique of modern philology and the culture of which it was a part—and every bit as valid in 1888 as they had been in that "dreadful" period from 1871. It is these early views of Nietzsche's, his ambitious theory of rhythmical perception in the ancient world and its consequences for the modern world, that will be the subject of the present chapter. Although his findings were absorbed quietly into the mainstream of classical philology, they have nonetheless suffered near total neglect. There are good reasons to rescue them from this state.

The bulk of the notebooks from the time of his lectures, some two hundred and thirty printed pages, were published posthumously, and they make for a fascinating if at times bewildering set of documents.[7] Ferociously erudite and in places chaotic, the notes can rival the ancient materials that they cover, both in fragmentariness and in exhibiting divergent threads of thought. If Nietzsche's notes have received scant attention in the past, this is in no small part due to their formidable appearance. Appearances aside, the notes are uniquely situated to throw a revealing light on Nietzsche at a critical phase of his career. An obvious source of their attraction is the glimpse they offer into the musical imagination of Nietzsche at the very moment he is formulating his ideas for *The Birth of Tragedy*, which originally was to have included a section on Greek metrics.[8] But of equal importance is the place they occupy in Nietzsche's developing thought as he continued to articulate for himself some of his deepest lifelong concerns, usually in the form of paradoxes: not only the thematics of musical and linguistic rhythm (the early notebooks being his most sustained reflection on this subject) but also those having to do with time, physiology, the analysis of quantitative and qualitative differences, agonal struggles with form, ancients and moderns, cultural history, and the history and criticism of the present—the very sorts of issues, in other words, that had preoccupied him in his dealings with Democritus, just as they would two decades later in his more polished writings, and not only in his notes on the will to power. The notebooks on rhythm point to the inseparable nexus of these two kinds of concern for Nietzsche: to speculate about Greek culture just is to speculate about philosophy, about classical philology, and about modern culture; more pointedly, to speculate about any one of these areas is to speculate about them all. And this is equally true of Nietzsche's later writings. Thus, even when it is not immediately apparent, Nietzsche's references to rhythm in the later writings conjure up the world of Greece and its rhythms; and they look back to and frequently echo his earlier analyses. His corpus is forever revisiting itself: it is itself in a kind of rhythmic motion.

For all of these reasons, a sketch of this aspect of Nietzsche's philology is worth attempting. At the same time, an important caveat is needed. The subject of ancient rhythm is technical in the extreme, recondite even for classicists, and clouded to an unknown degree by what little survives of the ancient theories (whose descriptions of various rhythms give us our main

entry to the ancient phenomenon of rhythm itself). All in all, it is a treach-
erous and uncertain business that remains controversial even to this day. I
have absolutely no intention of assessing the validity of Nietzsche's reconstruction, even assuming that I could. But neither can his notes, which are
complex as well as tentative, be arraigned before any one tribunal. They pass
back and forth freely between two kinds of historical reconstruction, the one
tracing developments of rhythmic theory in antiquity, the other tracing the
evolution of rhythmic practices. And they can slide into speculative scenarios that, themselves as much an element of his polemics with modern German culture as anything else, color his reconstructions as well. That said, the
main lines of Nietzsche's argument are salient enough, and it is to these and
their polemical thrust, and not to every technical detail, that we will be
attending in what follows.

'Atoms of Time'

Nietzsche's studies in classical Greek and Roman theories of rhythm coincide
closely with his interests in Democritus. We have already seen how Nietzsche could trace the dynamics of rhythm in the trajectory of lifeless atoms
streaming through empty space, in their *rhysmos* (their trajectory) and *epirhysmiē* (their flowing in and out of our sensorium), and more generally in the
"poetry" of atomism that enlivens but also falsifies Democritus' account of
the world. We have also seen how Nietzsche could make suggestive connections between the first known abstract theories of aesthetics in the Sophistic
period and the physical theory of the early atomists. Obviously, the two kinds
of historical study could overlap and intersect in Nietzsche's mind. And
although it would be misleading to state that he ever sought to discover historical traces of atomism in the ancient theories of rhythm (and he nowhere
claims to have done so), it is not far wrong to say that he overheard echoes of
atomism in those sources, as is perhaps only natural. The affinities between
the two forms of inquiry, with their common roots in the Greek Enlightenment, can be striking.[9] If atomism presents an abstract and rational model of
the natural world, rhythm as grasped by the rhythmicists (*rhythmikoi*) is one
such model incarnated in sensation itself—only here, the relation is a frankly
aesthetic one. But there are more tangible connections as well.

Democritus is known to have written not only on acoustics (as several fragments attest) but also on rhythm and harmony, alongside euphony and poetry (bare titles, or just topics, survive).[10] These connections were thoroughly explored by Nietzsche (as we saw in the previous chapter).[11] To these, we may now add the consideration, which surely would have played a part in an atomistic conception of rhythm, that Democritus conceived of time itself in purely phenomenal terms. "Time is an appearance [*phantasma*]," a mere simulacrum, "*resembling* day and night," hence unreal:[12] it is a sensation generated epiphenomenally from configured bits of material reality, a *synthesis* with only a psychological reality. The thought would have been congenial to proponents of one of the earliest theories of rhythmic sensation, especially as Nietzsche reads them. These rhythmicists stood in a tradition of musical theory that, in the words of one recent scholar, sought to explain its objects "not in terms of the physics of sound production or by abstract mathematical considerations [as in the Pythagorean school] but through principles inherent in our experience of sound as musical, and depending ultimately on *aisthēsis*, on what we perceive as melodious, concordant, and the like."[13]

Following phenomenalist principles in their own way, the rhythmicists, for their part, could conceive the units of rhythm as minimal "atoms" consisting of indivisible *chronoi*, or time-lengths (quantitative durations of time). "The first duration[s] that can be grasped by perception," *chronoi* are the minima of rhythmical *synthesis*, or composition, that get thrown into complex interrelations, the perceptual effect of which is rhythm. They are, in effect, *atoms of rhythm*.[14] The connection to atomism here is loose and conceptual, to be sure. Atoms of matter are the smallest imperceptible constituents of the world; atoms of rhythm are the smallest perceptible elements of perceived musical time (although as we shall see, "durations" are not directly perceived—they are perceptually inferred). At most, a common model about the construction and articulation of perception is perhaps all that is shared. Nor is the connection ever anything more than implicit in Nietzsche's view. We might recall his comment from a lecture about Greek lyric and music on the way in which rhythm "colors thoughts, permits a certain selection of words, *groups together the atoms of the sentence*," and then compare how in his notes on rhythm he can claim that for the Greek ear rhythm is an "undular beat: every word is perceived in an aesthetic way, at the very moment it is spoken and heard, as *a group of times*" (p. 338). The meaning of the first phrase emerges only in the light of the latter set of notes: the atoms in question are of *time*.[15] And although the rhythmicists would not have considered themselves to be atomists of any kind, and would have taken no position on the metaphysical nature of time, they did hold that rhythm is the sensuous division of time, the means by which time is divided into recognizable parts (*chronoi*) and so becomes aesthetically palpable, as an appearance and a perception (*aisthēsis*).[16] Rhythm here seems to occupy the elusive place of time on the atomistic theory, that of a mere relative duration, while the nature of abstract time, time uninflected by rhythm or rhythmic perception, is left invitingly open. As one of the ancient musical theoreticians says, and as Nietzsche underscores in the first pages of his notes, "Time does not divide [lit., "cut"] itself"; it must itself be divided, into parts and through the agency of a material body (p. 104).[17] Similarly the atomists: "Since [time] *depends for its existence on the bodies whose motion etc. it measures*, it certainly cannot exist per se."[18] But beyond these glancing comparisons there is the shimmering prospect, for the modern mind at least, of recovering in Democritus and in the rhythmicists the principles of an archaic sentience, "the Greek *aisthēsis*," which is not ours (p. 109). And that is what motivates Nietzsche's studies on rhythm.

Nietzsche's Innovation

Nietzsche excitedly announces his "discovery" of "a new metrics" in a letter to Rohde from 23 November 1870. His finding, he feels, proves the modern theory developed by scholars from Hermann to Westphal to be a magisterial "error": "Laugh or sneer as you wish—for myself, this whole matter is quite astonishing. There is a lot of work to do, but I will gulp down [book] dust with pleasure, because this time I have absolute confidence and find I can impart an ever greater depth to my underlying idea." As we shall see, Nietzsche's theory, far from inhibiting scientific and other speculation, installs within the "ground" of his inquiry ever greater and receding "depths."

Like so many of his other philological undertakings at the time, Nietzsche's study of rhythm is ambitiously conceived. What he was seeking to establish, beyond the narrowest confines of classical philology, were the rules implicit and felt in the practice of spoken and written (chiefly, poetic) language, as these evolved over the millennia. The aim, in a word, was to determine the changing sensibilities of the Greeks, and then of the moderns, with respect to the sound qualities of language, its "music," and to the movements of language and sound through time.[19] Not only did he intend his study to be radically revisionist, which it was. He also conceived it as one more object lesson in the pressing need of his discipline to reevaluate its own methods and goals, as the title to one of the several prefaces he contemplated attests: "Introduction: The Philologist of the Future" (p. 331). Here, in the field of rhythm, Nietzsche felt he could actually demonstrate how hopelessly out of touch with the past classical scholarship actually was. Faced with mute texts, texts that can no longer be sung or even read aloud, scholarship is at an utter loss. It cannot reproduce, let alone comprehend, the classical realities of poetry and music, so alien is the ancient phenomenon of rhythm to the modern sensibility—or rather insensibility—to time: "Now, suddenly, a complete radicalism is necessary, a genuine return to classical antiquity—even at the risk that in some key areas we might no longer be able to enjoy an empathetic connection [*nachfühlen*] with the ancients; and that this would have to be confessed."[20] An "abyss" (not to speak of a degeneracy) separates the two cultural realities. Nietzsche believes he has discovered, if not the sounds then at least the principles of ancient Greek rhythm, in the light of which the more recent scholarly tradition can be discredited on the grounds of anachronism: this latter is classicizing, Kantian, and above all *German*. Much like the scandalous truth-seeker of "On Truth and Lying," who "hides an object behind a bush and then seeks and finds it there," classicists have compensated for their inability to conceive rhythm in a Greek way by "first *projecting*" onto the past "what we later admire"—in other words, by imposing in a Kantian fashion ("our modern habit") a quasi-transcendental "schematism" upon the ancient phenomenon, that of "rhythm *an sich*."[21] The entire development of the modern view, from Bentley to Westphal, is accordingly "the history of an error."[22]

Nietzsche's argument is principally against the existence of a dynamic "stress-accent" (the so-called ictus) in the ancient theory and practice of spoken and written Greek. Quite simply, "the ictus is nowhere attested by the ancients" (p. 274; cf. p. 135). That, he claims, is a projection of modern rhythmical sensibilities. It is false to attribute to the classical languages the more recently evolved feature of dynamic accentuation, whereby measures are marked by "prominence" or volume of sound and frequently correlated with stress or emphasis in meaning (in English and German the ictus tends to fall on syllabic word-roots). In contrast with this later development, which is at first gradual (beginning with the "decline into Latin vocalism") and then accelerates, the specifically Greek sense of linguistic time, Nietzsche argues, was quantitative and purely temporal. It was organized around a system of temporal durations (*Takte*), arranged in potentially complex ratios of arsis (upbeat) to thesis (downbeat)—for instance, of 1:2 or 2:3 (these contrasts supply the rhythmical "pulse") and coupled somehow with a register of tonalities (melodic "pitch" accents). All of this occurs independently of metrical considerations, which are based on the syllable and its absolute equality of measures (*Taktgleicheit*).[23] *Takt*, which covers "time," "measure," or "beat," but also "tact" and feeling, derives from the Latin *tangere*, "to touch," and Nietzsche never loses sight of this sensuous connotation either. Nor did the ancient musicologists. Aristides Quintilianus, for instance, writes that "rhythm in general is perceived by . . . sight, . . . hearing, . . . and touch, by which we perceive the pulsations of the arteries."[24] "Pulse" or "impulse" might therefore serve the purpose just as well; on occasion Nietzsche will speak of the *Pulsschlag*. Word-accent is a completely unrelated phenomenon; it is at most a "difference in the modulation of the voice," possibly endowed with qualities of pitch, but not with rhythmical stress (pp. 273–74, 303).

In the quantitative picture, rhythm is disengaged from the customary semantic material of language, such as syllables or phrases, to which rhythm is in fact heterogeneous. These same factors are standardly associated, in English and German, with *word*-stress (the ictus). Indeed, the lack of correspondence between language (as a conveyor of meaning) and rhythmic measure was one of the characteristic sources of Greek rhythm's beauty—so much so, Nietzsche writes, that the coincidence of sense and sound defeated aesthetic pleasure and was felt as "unrhythmic" (p. 209).[25] By contrast, the modern-day contamination of rhythm with meaning (stress, emphasis, *the phrase*, and generally, *expressivism*), Nietzsche insists, only hinders our comprehension of the ancient practice. In attributing a functional role to the ictus, philologists, Nietzsche could complain with reason, take a metrical view of rhythm.[26] Similarly, on Nietzsche's view Greek music, closely associated with rhythm, is banished from any proximity to modern music, which for the same reasons is a hindrance to comprehending the ancient sensibilities.[27] Counterpoint and harmonic dissonance, not to mention the consonance of chords and all melodic conventions, have to be forgotten if a clear view of the Greek practice is to be attained: "The nature of classical music must be reconstructed. . . . Originally (in citharodic music), *the note functions as a measure of time*" (p. 322; emphasis added).[28] Again, it is the introduction of the ictus (Nietzsche claims) that erases the quantitative characteristics of the Greek sensibility: "The soul of our *melody and harmony* is expressed in the *ictus* of our compositions" (p. 137), or rather in their *Hopsasa* and "frightful tick-tock [*Tiktak*]."[29] For Nietzsche, music and rhythm lie at the root of all cultural perception, being as it were its simplest and most fully symptomatic form. Consequently, "the more we draw on modern music for understanding [classical] metrics [viz., time's measures], the farther we estrange ourselves from the reality of metrics in antiquity"—and indeed from the reality of classical antiquity *simpliciter*.[30] This insight will have a bearing on any reading of *The Birth of Tragedy*, and we will want to take it up again toward the end of this chapter.

Nietzsche's argument turned out to be one of his most lasting contributions to classics. It did indeed entail a drastic revision of existing scholarly theories about the Greek language and Greek rhythm and meter, namely, the treatments by Boeckh (1809 [1814]; following Bentley's lead), Apel (1806, 1807, 1814), Hermann (1816), Geppert (1835 [1848]), Lehrs (1848), Rossbach and Westphal (1854–68), Westphal (1861, 1865), Schmidt (1868), and others. This, in essence, was the cream of nineteenth-century German scholarship, which Nietzsche could criticize, not without justification, for being too "Kantian" in their attempt to uncover the pure and so to speak intemporal "form" or "law" of rhythm in the ancient Greek theory and practice of music and poetry (pp. 126, 268).[31] His theory was later taken over wholesale by Paul Maas, Wilamowitz's pupil and the author of an influential study on Greek meter from the early part of this century. Even so, Maas' study buries Nietzsche's contribution in three brief mentions and in a series of unacknowledged, often nearly verbatim, borrowings.[32] And despite challenges from various quarters, the theory of quantitative rhythm has largely stood up.[33] Be that as it may, Nietzsche's own aim is to lay bare the false premise, the *prōton pseudos*, of contemporary scholarship (p. 267). His goal is manifestly destructive. The aim is to restore some of the original strangeness of the classical past, but without providing in turn any affective relation to the past that a classical scholar might be able to enjoy: any such connection is proscribed, as it were, a priori by Nietzsche's alternative theory of rhythm. At the very most, one might hope to take "enjoyment," if that is any longer the right word, in the bare "schema" of time's measures. And that is "a tall order," Nietzsche concedes. "In our modern education there is nothing comparable; all one needs to learn is to beat a drum" (p. 134).

Nietzsche's project is as arch as it is novel. The idea of deliberately embracing the object of philology not only as a lifeless thing but as utterly inaccessible—as an entity, and an aesthetic entity at that, which can be abstractly known but never again felt, heard, or even truly understood—is extraordinary indeed. Rather than putting one more lost relic from antiquity high up on a pedestal for veneration, his project is designed to frustrate. Nietzsche bristles with disdain at the classicizing romanticism of his profession: "Individual strophes have been compared to the finest works of Phidias, strophes by Aeschylus have been called hoary ruins of a Doric temple in the early morning sunlight," etc. (p. 267). The source of this attitudinizing is the classicism of the previous century. Even Humboldt could hold that "the most primitive and the oldest verse-form of the Greeks, the hexameter, is the essence and the keynote of all the harmonies of mankind and of the whole of creation; . . . [it is] the basis of all the other poetic rhythms."[34] And so too, the project on rhythm, based as it is on Nietzsche's "skeptical views about meter" ("my *skepticism*" [p. 134]), is of a piece with the skeptical challenge to philological positivism that typifies his early philology.[35] Nietzsche's "Pyrrhonism" is partly directed against the posture of the infallible philologist. It is one thing to accuse your predecessors of a magisterial error (Westphal called Hermann's theory a "fantasy";[36] Hermann in turn had called Apel's "an ephemeral *phantasma*";[37] while Boeck had attacked both predecessors for committing errors of anachronism[38]), and quite another to debar the contemporary present from a vivid and sure grasp of the past. "In what way does the *aisthēsis* grasp the *chronos prōtos*?" Nietzsche asks, by which he means the constituent parts of ancient rhythm and thus the whole phenomenon of rhythm (p. 136).[39] That is the guiding question of Nietzsche's inquiry, as it was for the ancient rhythmicians. Only, Nietzsche's postulation of the question has an urgency to it that theirs does not. It is tinged with aporia.

Henceforth, the alienating uncertainties of ancient measure (*Takt*), conceived as rigorously temporal and proportional, and devoid of the warmer spectrum of chromatic possibilities known to us today, must replace the "dithyrambic tones" of the modern, gushing scholars who pour out their all-too-German souls into the empty, soundless vessels of Greek verse.[40] An "*abyss*" dividing the present from the "Hellenic" must be acknowledged, at whatever cost to ourselves it may entail: "That is my task" (p. 268). As with his *Democritea*, Nietzsche has only bitter truths to offer philologists, who must now be faced with phenomena they no longer can make sense of. "So, less enjoyment and apparently less understanding of the individual cases—these are, to be sure, hardly enticing prospects!" But prospects they are, and in the sequel Nietzsche proceeds to demolish the errors and mystifications of modern thinking—offering, in exchange, the "undying attraction of an unassuming *truth*" (ibid.). But this hardly captures Nietzsche's overarching purpose, or its wayward perversity.

Aristoxenus and the Ancient Theory

At the center of Nietzsche's studies is an insight he takes over from Aristoxenus of Tarentum, the preeminent theorist and historian of music in antiquity from the second half of the fourth century B.C.E., known later simply as "the musician."[41] (We have already encountered Aristoxenus in a somewhat different guise above, namely as the devoted Peripatetic credited by later tradition with passing down the story about Plato's failed attempt to destroy the writings of Democritus by fire.) The Aristoxenian theory represented a synthesis of earlier generations of musical thinkers (excluding the Pythagoreans) and a highly original contribution to musical theory as well. As Aristoxenus' works are only imperfectly preserved and his influence was vast, Nietzsche's studies are often an attempt to sift through the later traditions for evidence of Aristoxenian theory (an approach paved by Westphal less than a decade before).[42]

Aristoxenus' insight, disarmingly simple in appearance but which Nietzsche views as philosophically significant, is that "rhythm is not identical with any of the objects made rhythmic."[43] Aristoxenus "speaks in a *philosophical sense* about rhythm" (p. 103). One of the variants of this doctrine, which Aristoxenus admits may be harder to grasp, is the idea that "rhythmic composition [*rhythmopoiia*]," which is to say the making rhythmic of an object, "and rhythm are not the same."[44] The distinction we are being prepared for is between the shape of a rhythmic composition and the shape of a given rhythm, and, more generally, between rhythm and its objects.

Some of the grounds for this distinction are given earlier in the second book of Aristoxenus' treatise, the *Elements of Rhythm*, which is all that remains of that work:

Of the bodies whose nature it is to be shaped, none is identical with any of the shapes; the shape is rather a disposition of the parts of the body, arising from the fact that each of them is placed in a particular way, which is why it is called "shape." Similarly, rhythm is not identical with any of the objects made rhythmic: it is rather one of the things that dispose these objects in a particular way, and make it like this or like that in respect of durations [*chronoi*]. (*Rhyth.* 2.5; trans. Barker; modified)

So stated, the point that rhythm is not identifiable with the materials it shapes or forms, or rather on which its characteristics supervene, puts us in mind of the Aristotelian notion of form and potential: different objects are naturally capable of assuming different shapes. "Shape" is, after all, the original graphic sense of *ryhthmos*; Democritus used the term to name the paths described by atoms in their free fall. But this cannot be the whole thrust of Aristoxenus' distinction. For the relation of a composition to its shape is complicated by a further ingredient. In language and music, rhythm has two objects upon which it acts: a bodily medium and the element of time. And Aristoxenus' conception is designed to capture the distinctness of rhythm from both of these things. It is this aspect of Aristoxenus' theory that Nietzsche seizes upon, the duality of objects that is implied but not entirely clarified in the analogy of shape as applied to time and language or sound (the double articulation of rhythm). It is the fact that rhythm supervenes not only on material bodies but on time itself.

No wonder that rhythmical and metrical analysis are in ways incommensurable (a point that is basic to Nietzsche's quarrel with modern scholarship): they describe different shapes, and in some cases different bodies or objects. This has to do with the peculiar nature of rhythm, the identity of which is bound up with time, while time is of an essentially different order from, say, words. Words divide up into bits of words, but how do words divide up into time-lengths? Strictly speaking, they don't: it is words and their parts (e.g., syllables) that *divide up time*. But words do not thereby constitute the measure of rhythm, "because the syllable does not always have the same duration" in rhythmic composition.[45] On the Aristoxenian view, patterns of rhythm are divided up not by syllables but by lengths of time ("durations").[46] On the other hand, *"time does not divide* [literally, *"cut"*] *itself."* It must itself be divided, into parts and through the agency of a material body, or rather through a rhythmed body: "The object made rhythmic [*rhythmizomenon*] must be capable of being divided into recognizable parts, by which it will divide time" (*Rhyth.*, 2.6; cf. 2.9). But this still leaves us with the problem of the relation between time, time's parts, rhythm, and the medium in which time and its parts are to be rhythmically articulated and actuated. Rhythmic objects ("objects made rhythmic") and time's divisions come into view simultaneously; but they are as distinct, Aristoxenus insists, as rhythm and its objects.

The identity of rhythm seems precarious. Rhythm is inconceivable apart from its objects, from "the matter that is to be shaped, e.g., sound, language, marble" (p. 103), in the absence of which rhythm cannot even be perceived; but it remains elusive in its relation to them nonetheless. If rhythm isn't identical with its objects or with their articulation (through movements of the hands, feet, or voice, thanks to which time is divided and rhythm is actuated), let alone with rhythmic composition, where does rhythm lie? Supervening on its objects as a division of time, rhythm is at once sensuous and abstract; it is "made perceptible to the senses," but it is less a sensation than the shape of one. What supervenes on objects made rhythmic is in fact a system of relations (ratios of time-lengths, or durations [*chronoi*]), literally a structure of signs.[47] Nietzsche's reformulation of Aristoxenus brings out this perceptual tension that is basic to the phenomenon of rhythm: "*Chronoi* are the cuts of *abstract* time" (p. 104; emphasis added). Rhythm, incising itself into time, carves out *chronoi* (durations) and *Takttheile*, the parts of measure (the formal divisions into thesis and arsis and their accompanying subdivisions) that can be recognized by the ear or eye only in their juxtaposition and in their proportional differences, but not heard or seen as such, while rhythm itself is the structural identity of this perception. What is perceived is not rhythm per se but bodies made rhythmic. Aristoxenus speaks about the perception of durations (*Rhyth.* 2.2), but what he clearly means is the perception of their "combination and arrangement" and the recognizability of the parts of rhythm. All of this takes place at the limit of the "movements" to which the durations correspond (whether these are movements of the voice, the hand, the foot, etc.; ibid., 2.6–8, 11). Thus, what the ear hears is not the absolute sound of letters or notes but rather proportions of time marked by the rhythmic pulses of arsis and thesis (roughly: upbeat and downbeat). Strange as it may seem to us, what is perceived, in fact, are structures of *relations*—of time.[48] Thus, rhythm is not "in" the visible or audible metronome of the foot or the hand, for instance the rise and fall of the foot in dance, corresponding to gestures up and down of the hand or finger of a choral or orchestral leader. Arsis and thesis, whatever else they are (and they remain mysteriously elusive today), must be divorced from the locus of their sensation. They have nothing to do with ictus but are instead correlative to whatever it is that the rise and fall of feet (or the hand or voice) are correlated to—namely, to the boundaries of time that mark rhythm. Rhythm is this boundary effect.[49]

Sensuous in its own right, indeed mere "sensuous matter capable of movement [*sinnlicher Bewegungstoff*]," an object made rhythmic is a potential "carrier" of rhythm (p. 104). But with the advent of rhythm, an object comes to be inhabited at once by sensuous and nonsensuous elements (durations and relations): it is inhabited, in other words, by a system. This abstract relation of rhythm to its objects is reflected in rhythmic theory, which in its most rigorous form abstains from treating the intricacies of rhythmic composition that obtain in sequences of rhythmic "feet" (the structural units of rhythm). That is why, Nietzsche infers, larger rhythmical structures are absent from Aristoxenus' account, and why it is a fallacy for contemporary scholars to go searching for the laws governing larger "periods."[50] Inhabited by rhythmical relations but lacking rhythmical form, sequences of rhythm are "no longer made perceptible to the senses through the keeping of time per se, but only through melody or phrasing or both," while "only that which can be *meas-*

ured in time [*taktirt*] falls within the realm of rhythm" (pp. 165, 164).[51] As if to illustrate the point, Nietzsche speculates a historical development in the evolution of rhythmic measure. According to this picture, rhythm was gradually emancipated from its bodily origins in dance; timekeeping ceased to be regulated by sound sometime during the archaic period; and Aristoxenus' theory, occurring at the end of this evolution, captures the final abstraction and autonomy of rhythm: "Dance movement emancipates itself naturally from the movement associated with keeping time [*Taktbewegung*]. More accurately, arsis and thesis are no longer meaningful to the art of dancing [viz., as a lifting and lowering of the foot]; from now on they are only a measure of time [*Zeitmesser*]" (p. 320).[52] No longer parts of the body of the rhythmed, nor even strictly speaking "audible," arsis and thesis become instead parts of the body of structure.[53] Supervening on its objects, rhythm as it were vanishes sensuously into them, all the while remaining rigorously "external" to them.[54] That is the consequence of Aristoxenus' insight into the sheer difference of rhythm to its objects, its virtual noncoincidence with them.

Questions immediately arise. Are durations, which divide time, parts of time or partitions within a material medium that generate time, or rather *a sense of time*? Is rhythm nothing more than this generation of a sensation? And is it time that is abstract (colorless, unmarked, uninflected) or is it rhythm, that "higher unity," which is an abstraction, the mere presence of a system of relations within a sensuous body?[55] The tendency toward quasi-metaphysical speculation, illustrated by questions like these, ripens over the course of several notebooks. But the starting point is clearly indicated in the ancient sources, especially in the Aristoxenian tradition to which Nietzsche feels himself drawn almost as a partisan in the war on modern, degenerate sensibilities. If rhythmic composition installs rhythm in an object (whether in melody, language, or a body), what is made sensible through rhythm is *nothing other than time itself as a formal structure*. Here we have the first hint of the wider significance of rhythm, the implication of which is spelled out in another, roughly contemporaneous notebook: "*Rhythm* [*Takt*] is to be understood as something utterly fundamental, i.e., as the most primary sensation of time, as the very *form of time*."[56]

Recognizing that time is differently perceived at different cultural moments, Nietzsche sets himself the task of mapping out the cultural evolution of rhythm, a "history of rhythmic sensations," as he grandly rephrases his project at one point (p. 309). The ambition widens. The aim henceforth is to take up the larger philosophical problem of time and its measures, "the entire metrical problem of time," as the fourth and final notebook announces to the world (p. 308). The study will constitute a "philosophy of rhythm" (p. 309), even if the starting point was always in its own way "philosophical."[57] Labeling itself "*Inquiries into Rhythm, by Friedrich Nietzsche*," the later and final study is clearly imagined for eventual publication. Nietzsche's ideas here begin to look forward to his later speculations on the more familiar themes of being, becoming, and appearance, not to mention the will to power, its relational quantitative measures (*Maß*) and "rhythms."[58] Indeed, the last page of the philological notebooks on rhythm provides the following glimpse into what is yet to come, although perhaps it is more correct to say that the later speculations look back to the earlier ones:

Rhythm is an *attempt at individuation*. For rhythm to exist, there must be multiplicity and becoming. Here, the rage for beauty shows itself to be a motive for individuation. Rhythm is the form of becoming, [and] generally the *form of the world of appearances*. (p. 338)[59]

One of the stranger and more rarefied offshoots of this line of speculation is the handful of notes on temporal atomism from 1873, which in more ways than one are a startling precursor to the theory of the will to power (*KSA*, 7, 26[11–12]). But we need to go back now to Nietzsche's philological argument and its gradual perversion.

Quantitative Rhythm

As we saw, Nietzsche's point of departure and his innovation is his insight into quantitative rhythm and its sheer incommensurability with modern dynamic rhythm.[60] The specifically Greek sense of linguistic time, he maintains, was quantitative and purely temporal, and not based on the criteria of sound (for instance, volume [*intensio vocis*], of which ictus is a species). That sensibility suffered an immense erosion, which Nietzsche is all too keen to characterize as a degradation of a faculty that was on its way to becoming anemically modern: "Gradually, the robust feeling for time disintegrates [*zerfällt*] in [every-day] speech" (p. 307). Some change did occur within the Greek-speaking world of later antiquity, involving the gradual preeminence of the stress accent over the earlier tonal (pitch) accent and, evidently, a corresponding loss in the quantitative system of rhythm.[61] But the seeds of this change were planted earlier. And so, although the decline was "into Latin vocalism," the change can be traced back to the end of the classical period in Greece.

As the last witness to rhythm in its pure form for Nietzsche, Aristoxenus is thus located on the cusp of the transition between two otherwise incommensurable worlds, classical antiquity and postclassical modernity. After him, and when the decline sets in, theory is corrupted by altered sensibilities and by the effects of a language evolving away from the purities of the classical period: Aristoxenus' epigones produce competing and eclectic models of the same classical Greek base, in the deceptive, because timeless, idiom of methodological truth, often reversing distinctions they no longer even understand (much like today's moderns). Tracing lines of descent in these later sources, distinguishing false tracks from genuine leads, is crucial to Nietzsche's undertaking and essential to any reconstruction of Aristoxenus' system, but also beyond the scope of this sketch.[62] What matters here is the fact that Nietzsche charts the decline of the classical sensibility, in theory and in practice, into what he calls "Latin vocalism" (p. 307), which is to say, the fall *into* vocalism generally, into an accentual system of rhythmical notation (according to "stress"), in a direction away from the temporal quantities of earlier speech.[63] Of course, there is something awry in the tracking of a sensibility's decline, as if such a pattern could be tracked across time and languages in a quasi-organic, linear fashion.[64] That this is indeed the premise of Nietzsche's argument suggests that we are in the midst of what later will be called a "genealogy" (here, a genealogy of rhythmic sensibility). But if so, then we must attend closely to the complications that ripple through this narrative of decline, because Nietzsche's genealogies are never innocent, and never straightforwardly historical. His studies on rhythm testify to this fact to an exasperating degree. As his notebooks evolve, complications that were latent in the earlier pages begin to surface. More strikingly, the history he relates grows increasingly bizarre.

According to the scenario proposed by Nietzsche, which starts to become strangely personified in the last of the notebooks, the syllable takes on an unprecedented prominence, slowly effacing temporal duration. "Gradually, the robust feeling for time disintegrates in [everyday] speech," while the melodic pitch accent and syllabic stress (ictus) come into functional prominence and eventually into collusion, "representing, as it were, a violent survival of the word": the word henceforth becomes a literal battleground of opposing forces (p. 307–8). The picture Nietzsche paints gets grimmer and increasingly melodramatic, not to say more physical, with each new detail. "From this point on, the spiritual life of the word concentrates itself in the accented syllable." As the ictus and the accent overpower, by "breaking through" their "quantitative barriers," the low-pitched syllables die off, functionless, with nothing to do (higher pitches being associated with the stress accent). Temporal proportions come abruptly to an end. And "the new accentuated syllable sucks up every trace of life," while everything around it withers away.[65] Language is now uttered through "explosions," and the earlier negotiation of times (the "rhythmic alternation of times") gives way to a negotiation of forces (the "rhythmic alternation of *strengths*" [p. 308]).[66] Intensities of voice gain the upper hand, "fatally" undermining the nonaccentual rhythms of classical Greek; henceforth, the accent is placed on force (pp. 269, 302). The theme of force might appear an unexpected turn in the theory of rhythm, more characteristic (say) of the later philosopher than the early classicist. Nietzsche will soon be discussing what he calls the "physiological foundation and explanation of rhythm (and its *Macht*)" (p. 322), which he locates in the rhythms that obtain within the body: "The entire body contains a countless number of rhythms" (ibid.), and "physiologically, life is . . . a continuous rhythmical movement of cells. The influence of rhythm seems to me to be an endlessly small modification of this rhythmical movement" (p. 325). In the bare outline-sketch of a future table of contents, which he probes for its possibilities and tests with the title *Prolegomena to a Theory of Rhythmics in Antiquity*, "Physiology of Rhythm" follows upon "Philosophy of Rhythm" directly (p. 323), before the assault on modern theory held by scholars from Bentley to Westphal and Schmidt officially begins. And in later pages, the metaphors of physiology and technical rhythmics blend together unnoticeably, as if they always had. But the change in emphasis is deceptive: the force of physiology was implied from the beginning. The term *Pulsschlag*, wherever it appears in the notebooks, is regularly employed in both a literal and a derived sense to signify the beat of the pulse or the pulsating beat.[67] This is a superficial reminder of the physiological basis of rhythm and its "sensuous" power, a concept that Nietzsche had earlier explored in connection with his study of Democritean physiology.[68] What is more, the picture that Nietzsche gives of the gradual erosion of a sensibility is complicated by another perspective that is developed alongside the first. And here physiology, indeed a kind of vitalism, plays a more prominent role from the start. Only, the more that physiology comes into prominence, the more *symbolic* does it become. It is this latter development, which is even more characteristic of Nietzsche's later thinking, to which we must now turn.

'Zeitleben' and 'Tonleben'

In the same passages on the ictus and the accent that we have just been examining, Nietzsche's reflections take a different turn, inspired by the simple question, "Is *Zeitleben* ["the life of time," viz., the regime of cadences established by temporal differences] really prior?"[69] that is, prior to its modern counterpart, *Tonleben* (the life of the accent, of vocality, stress, and so on) (p. 308). The question casts a pall of doubt on the entirety of the plot line that has been developing until now, which in the next breath is unexpectedly reversed: "*Once, Tonleben was freer*; then it was hemmed in and almost overwhelmed by *Zeitleben*; and finally it emerges victorious again" (ibid.; emphasis added). It might appear as if Nietzsche is affirming, against his own express purpose, the antecedence of the modern sensibility (the dynamic accent) to the ancient (quantitative) one. But the sequel makes it impossible to characterize this new move as a simple reversal of a linear scheme:

> At the very earliest stage, struggle [*Kampf*] between *Zeit*- and *Tonleben* (side by side)[70]
>
> Victory of *Zeitleben* over *Tonleben*
>
> Decline of *Zeitleben* and victory of *Tonleben*.

The previous narrative of decline, until now the governing paradigm in Nietzsche's study, here stands in a puzzling light. In fact, it no longer applies at all, because the opposition on which it rests, between time-quantities and stress, is no longer a simple and exclusive one: their difference is primordial; it lies at the origin of linguistic rhythm, as a basic antagonism, and is no longer figured as a contrast in historical extremes. "Vocality" turns out to have been "freer," not because it was antecedent to the "classical" sensibility to time but because of the relative freedom it enjoyed, or rather wrested for itself in a kind of standoff vis-à-vis that sensibility. Nietzsche's revised historical scheme does not replace the earlier one. Instead, it frustrates both the likelihood of a straightforward, linear progression, in virtue of that history's split origins, and the prospect of a resolution, for the very same reason: a resolution, insofar as it is imaginable at all, could only mean a return to conflictual, irresolute origins. But then to what degree, one might well ask, is the scheme any longer even historical? Nietzsche's revised history of sensation not only puts the perspective of decline that he has been reconstructing all along into a radically altered light. It causes the whole of his recuperative effort to vacillate indeterminately. Which account is right? This irresolvable doubt is played out in the sequel in interesting ways.

When Nietzsche next turns away from his "History of Rhythmic Sensations" to contemplate the "Philosophy of Rhythm" (p. 309), his reflections bring out what was already latent in the whole of his discussion of Greek rhythm: namely, the fundamental insolubility of ancient rhythmical patterns. That is the warning issued in one of his many experimental prefaces: "In contrast with individual rhythmical schemata, *on my theory there are no sure decisions, but many possibilities*" (p. 268; emphasis added).[71] Taken by itself, the point might be no more profound than the realization that Greek rhythm wasn't dictated by language or melody (that is, by syllabification, which is linguistically fixed, or by scalar notes) and so can't be read off the surface of surviving texts. (Indeed, in practice it was rhythm that clarified the character of melody and meter, and not the other way around.)[72] Tempo is another factor that renders rhythm hard to read: the length of rhythmic durations is given by the tempo, and tempi are not recorded in the ancient scores we have. As Maas would say in Nietzsche's wake, "the problem of rhythmic values in the ancient notation is still wholly unresolved."[73] But the surrounding arguments suggest that there is more to Nietzsche's point than that. At issue is the very indeterminacy intrinsic to rhythm itself. "We have absolutely no laws for [rhythmic] sequences, and everything that Westphal and Schmidt infer about them is pure invention" (p. 199).[74] Aristoxenus invites such a conclusion: "The interlacing of measures and their analysis into divisions is not part of the abstract theory of rhythm" (p. 144).[75] But the fact that larger scale rhythmical patterns have no place in the theory of rhythm abstractly conceived does not have anything near the poignancy for him that it has for Nietzsche. At issue is the recovery of the principles of an archaic sentience. "In what way does the *aisthēsis* grasp the *chronos prōtos* [the primary duration]?" (p. 136).[76]

This uncertainty was behind Nietzsche's publication on the Simonides fragment preserved by Dionysius of Halicarnassus in chapter 26 of *On the Composition of Words*, where Dionysius endeavors to show how "melodious metrical composition . . . bears a close similarity to prose." At one extreme, then, verse makes contact with speech. At the other extreme, Greek lyric, through the sheer profusion of its polyrhythms, was felt to approach the fluid rhythms of prose again, in what could be described as a "wandering" of rhythm and meter (*to peplanēmenon*) in which the precision of measure effaces itself to the point of unrecognizability. For Nietzsche, these two facets are intertwined: the basic indeterminacy of Greek temporal quantities was the source of their great "pliancy" and of their rich potential for interpretation and performance, as well as their unrivaled aesthetic value.[77] If a series of strophes from Simonides could be made to look like a period of prose, even if by the mere suggestion of the fact, then fundamental questions concerning the objectivity of rhythm, as opposed to its supervenient or else simply interpretive nature, could be raised. (To prove his point, Dionysius "reads" a fragment from the great lyric poet according to its "divisions" of sense, thus obscuring the original rhythms and meters.)[78] It is worth noting that Dionysius' Simonides fragment (fr. 37 Bergk, the famous Danae fragment) was worked over by generations of scholars (including Nietzsche in 1868 and later Wilamowitz) seeking to restore its original strophic form;[79] and even today it has left the philological establishment all but completely baffled as to the solution of the mystery. It is generally conceded that Dionysius cannot have deliberately misquoted a poem that was in popular circulation. But then, he would not have needed to either. Whether Dionysius has deliberately tripped up his readers or not (by shearing off parts of the poem and camouflaging the results), his point and its power are not refuted. Nor is it contradicted by Nietzsche's later statement that, however "incomprehensible" the fact may seem to us, "in the judgment of the ancients, it was ordinary everyday speech itself that could very easily contain perfect verses" (letter to Fuchs, end of August 1888). Canons of aesthetic judgment are the function of culturally ingrained, or manipulated, perception—as our "incomprehension" in the face of Greek rhythmical patterns verifies, as it were *ex contrario*.

Similarly, Aristoxenus' descriptions fall short of clarifying the exact nature of rhythm at every stage. Does the problem lie in the attempt to capture rhythm through the abstract conventions of science after all? Did he even grasp the phenomena he sought to describe?[80] Whatever the answer may be, Nietzsche will not hesitate to draw some of these consequences for Aristoxenus, thus realizing the radical potential of the rift between rhythm and the rhythmed in a way that Aristoxenus could not. For Nietzsche, the distinctness of rhythm and its objects becomes symbolic of a historical divide—or more accurately, symbolic of time as this divide itself—that is absolutely unbridgeable. What is more, this same divide was implicitly written into the perception of rhythm which was held, or rather felt but not quite understood, by the Greeks themselves. At stake is nothing less than the objectivity of rhythm, which Nietzsche proceeds to put into doubt from both the modern and ancient perspectives. Explaining all of this will take a little unpacking.

Contemplating the two contrastive orders of rhythm, temporal (ancient) and forceful (modern), Nietzsche turns, in a more philosophical mood, to the similarities they now can be said to share. Both orders of rhythm are "symbolic" expressions of the will and of differences in culture.[81] Additionally, each seems to exist only in the mind that beholds them, as a feeling. Thus, speaking about the quantitative sensibility, Nietzsche writes, "The strict, basic proportions are *only ideally present*; it is by these that we measure, in our perception [or "sensation," *Empfindung*], the profusion of the actual times" (p. 309; emphasis added). The same applies to the way in which actual "degrees of strength" are measured. The point is not that ideal standards strive but fail to measure up to rhythmical realities, but rather the reverse, namely that ideal standards give us the only criterion we have of what ought to count as an actual rhythm: "'The mathematical structure of proportions in terms of time or strength is *ideally* present as a regulator or measure of the actual degrees of time and strength.' What does this mean physiologically?"[82] (ibid.). Nietzsche's overarching historical contrast, we can now see, thus turns on the difference between two types of idealism: "the idealism of tonality and feeling [that is, of the moderns], as against the idealism of space and light (appearance) of the Greeks" (ibid.). Sensation is in both cases already in the realm of the symbolic. There is no way of evading ideality: no matter how far down the scale we go, from the ideal to the actual, everywhere we look we will find that "representation [*Vorstellung*]"— which is to say, symbolization and idealization—"is already underway and at work" (ibid.). Thus, rhythm, taken as a perceptual phenomenon (a "sensation"), is first and foremost a representational structure, and the latter is so thoroughly superimposed upon the experience of rhythm as to be constitutive of that experience. Nietzsche is here taking to an extreme Aristoxenus' perception-based theory.[83] But even for Aristoxenus, rhythms are conventional patterns, acquired through culture, reinforced by habit, and limited only by our physiology.

Nietzsche then fleshes this idea out in a tantalizing if obscure way. Evidently, temporal proportions are given in the very appearance of the Greek language, which is an aesthetic phenomenon through and through and primordially shaped by rhythmical feeling, just as dynamic differences appear to us in our own. This constitutes a primary level of idealization, or, if you like, of simplification. While "rhythmical feeling" is the principle accomplice in the formation of language, poetry first makes evident and then "solidifies" this feeling for rhythm, by enforcing a regard for language in its palpable substance, which is to say, in the rhythmical proportions of time that the Greek language assumes (ibid.).[84] We might think of language as a vast manifold of differences of sound, the very specification of which already bespeaks a symbolization (the way, for example, phonemes—the smallest bits of meaningful sound—are conventionally delimited). Sounds are at least to a minimal degree temporally distinguished (in the Greek language, evidently to a large degree). "Temporal differences do indeed exist," Nietzsche writes—as "an endlessly fine symbolic" (ibid.). But the simplifying process hardly ends here, which is to say at the first level of specification in terms of time or force. Differences of time (to stay with the Greek system) are next brought under increasingly "large rubrics" (up a ladder that runs from temporal quantities to ratios of quantities, and then on to cola and periods). A "new symbolic" is now possible, that of the whole sentence or clause (*Satz*). This still leaves the finer temporal differences intact as a "manifold" rippling beneath the larger rhythmical patterns, one that presumably is too subtle to be consciously organized but that can be felt nonetheless to resonate through the large-scale effects of rhythm, both disruptively and aesthetically.[85] It is these fine differences that constitute "the actual times," whose "profusion" (if not precision) is measured by the senses and their sense of rhythm, attuned as they are to the ideal proportions of time. Actual times, then, are not so much excluded from sensation by a given idealization as they are "tolerated" (or "permitted" [*erlaubt*]) by it; and they are themselves already conditioned, possibly just subliminally, by rhythmic sensibility. In the Greek context, actual times are the dissonances that run through the rhythmic ideals, the "light dissonances" and irrationalities that underlie the ideal patterns of so-called rational rhythms. To these can be attributed, Nietzsche believes, an aesthetically functional role (they are a source of variety), as well as a dark and unwitting attraction. Dissonance, however, is less actual than it is ideal: it represents an ideal point of failure in the constitution of rhythm and is legible only against a rhythmic background.[86] We will come back to this point below.

Of course, Nietzsche's account is in its own way an idealization and a simplification, a fact that subtly calls attention to its contrived nature despite its initial plausibility. Rhythm is an idealization of time, and what is equally important—and endlessly fascinating to contemplate—the perception of rhythm is itself an idealization of what is perceived: rhythms never obtain except ideally, because "two beats are never equivalent in a mathematically exact way" (p. 205). Be that as it may, in Nietzsche's current scenario time and force are, one has to assume, always present and the very ingredients of consciousness. Accordingly, to speak of "time" and "strength" is misleadingly reductive. What is required, but difficult if not impossible to conceive given the habits of rhythmic conventions, is rather something like a concept of "time-strength."

The components of "time-strength" can (let us speculate) be isolated, proportioned, ratioed, or quantified, but always only through some kind of idealization and simplification. On the other hand, simply to conceive "time-strength" is to return it to some conventional setting, as the very terms that make it up suggest by themselves; it is, after all, only our way of designating "the problem of time" in the traditions familiar to us. Conditioned in determinate ways, rhythmic sensibilities follow a cultural dominant, shaped, as it happens, either quantitatively (in terms of time) or qualitatively (in terms of force), at least in the two cultures that stand in Nietzsche's limelight. The point would seem to be that the division of time into quantities is itself an instance of force (what Nietzsche in one place calls "the shaping force of temporal proportions" [p. 330]), while force, Nietzsche recognizes on occasion, is at least minimally quantitative. After all, dynamic accentuation is itself durational.[87] In short, time-strength displays itself in two ways and with reciprocal dissonances: in the division of time into (ever slightly antagonistic) times or into (ever durational) quantities of force. Idealism, then, would consist in the determined pursuit of one factor in the absence (viz., to the suppression) of the other, in the attempted evasion of their necessary co-presence and mutual dependency. And dissonances within a given cultural dominant forecast the dissonances between cultures, their mutual opacities and incommensurabilities.

'Alogia'

The theory just sketched out is consistent with the stymied genealogy of rhythm witnessed above, which showed temporal and forceful factors to be antagonistically co-present ("side by side") from the very beginning of things. It is also consistent with Nietzsche's general account of Greek rhythm and its fundamental "irrationality," which is to say, its nonobedience to an exact equivalence of measures (*Taktgleichheit*). The irrationality of Greek rhythm can be perceived—or felt—in the "light dissonances" it continuously displays, its ever-varying and modulating character—in a word, in its precarious and elusive relation to its objects, not to mention to its capture by theory.[88] Irrational rhythms could be felt as well as analyzed (up to a point), and they did present themselves in practice. It is to the credit of Aristoxenus that he could accommodate them in some form in his theory.[89] The ancient musicologists reserved the dissonances of so-called "irrational" rhythms to an area that Aristoxenus calls "intermediate between two ratios that the senses can recognize."[90] By definition, such rhythms are at the limit of sensation: to experience them is to experience sensation's boundaries as well, and it is this that contributes to their effect (which is often described as "ecstatic"). Going well beyond the conclusions of the ancient theorists,

Nietzsche holds that language and music just are discrepant mediums, wherever they represent the intersection of time and a body. (Here, the insight into the noncoincidence of rhythm and its objects receives a radical twist.) No measure will be precisely rational unless rhythm and especially sensation make it appear so. Consequently, irrationality is a central feature of all Greek rhythm: quite simply, it obtains all the time.[91] Nietzsche's starting point is the perceptual basis of rhythm, its status as an appearance. Presumably, the Greek ear was accustomed to detect and to accept as rhythmic irrational deviations from regular rhythmic norms. On the other hand, a strict equivalence of measure is psychologically painful, Nietzsche claims, and so it is a constant of human nature to vary rhythms and to yearn for the dissonances that will, in any case, inevitably occur in them—within the limits of the expressive means of a given culture (p. 205). Perhaps the ultimate dissonance lies within us (be we Greeks or moderns), in our conflicting desires for an ideal conformity of measure and its opposite.[92]

Rhythm here takes on the remarkable role of a dissimulator: "The facts of feeling, which grasp a dactyl (- ˅ ˅) as a *logos isos* [as "rational"], have nothing to do with the mathematical description of the way the dactyl comes out when spoken" (pp. 278–79), even if the one kind of measure is no less ideal than the other. The only equivalence that can exist between a long syllable and two short syllables is accordingly rhythmic—which is to say, thanks to a rhythmic convention.[93] Nietzsche accordingly declares the dactyl to be *alogos*, an irrational rhythm (p. 298), on the assumption that "alogia is a light dissonance in a beat that in other respects is regular" (p. 327). In the dactyl, the first long and the two shorts that follow are strictly speaking in an irrational ratio; but the dactyl is not an officially recognized irrational rhythm. (It generally signifies the eminently rational ratio of 1:2.) Acknowledging this, but stressing the fact that the dactyl has, as it were, been rationalized, Nietzsche reaches conclusions not drawn by the ancient musicologists. This is not to deny the existence of the irrational rhythms officially recognized by Aristoxenus and others. It is to distinguish the irrationalities codified by feeling and sensation from those that eluded the sense of rhythm, only to return in a "subtactile" effect.[94] In fact, Nietzsche speculates, in certain cases deviations might be taken for instances of rhythmic modulation (*metabolē*), or changes from one genus of rhythm to another—an assumption, he quickly adds, that was easier for the ancients to make than it is for us, given their finer sense of time (p. 260). But deviations were marked and were in ways less subtle than those that the ear overlooked when it interpreted as rational the ever so slight irrationalities of workaday rhythms like the dactyl and the iamb. The inequalities are not thereby effaced;[95] they simply go underground, only to reemerge elsewhere, for instance in the dappled effects of rhythmic composition. (These could be distinguished, up to a point, from those arising out of the canonical irrational rhythms.) Nietzsche seems to believe that the fundamental dissonances (the irrationality) of all Greek rhythm are submerged at the level of the individual foot, but that they surface strongly and almost irrepressibly as feet accumulate in larger rhythmic patterns.[96] Rhythm is thus strangely indeterminate, for all its specifiability.[97] The contrast is with our modern sensibilities, which are infinitely "naive" as compared with those of the Greeks (p. 260). Delicately balanced on an abyss, Greek rhythm in Nietzsche's eyes displays a clear antagonism of measure— a precarious equilibrium of time and force—in the suppleness of its rhythms and in its proportioned quantities of sensation. By contrast, modern rhythm brutally overpowers this balance and obscures its tensions, tipping the scales in favor of force and losing out in sensuousness in the bargain. Force under modern conditions is reduced to the monotony of a metronome.

Aristoxenus is responsive to the precariousness of rhythm, and Nietzsche draws attention to this fact already in the very first pages of his notebooks: "Aristoxenus maintains that irrational rhythm occurs *when one part of the measure oversteps its legitimate limit by a tiny fraction of time*" (p. 105; emphasis added). Nietzsche's description is telling, because the production of irrationality in rhythm is treated here as a virtual encroachment of and within quantitative forces. At this point, an intriguing possibility suggests itself. Was the "irrationality" recognized on the theory of Aristoxenus the first intimation of that theory's ultimate demise, of a future breakdown of temporal barriers that would render the temporal system otiose? If so, then we have a further confirmation of the narrative scenario sketched out above (pp. 144–47), whereby the modern accent made its first appearance when the accent "broke through" its "quantitative barriers." Prior to that, vocality had been "almost overwhelmed" by the temporal-based system, which would suggest that the accentual property was a latent feature of the quantitative system and was tamed and "confined" by the limits imposed by that system. Irrationality, on this reading, would represent the ideal point of failure in the constitution of quantitative rhythm, the precarious stability of the classical system. By what force did the constraints of time manage to hold back the breakthrough of "accentual" life? One answer lies in "the physiological foundation and explanation of rhythm (and its *Macht*)," although Nietzsche never develops this possibility beyond a few hints. But if physiology is to count for anything, then the quantitative system, which is in its own right an expression of biological power, can no longer be neatly opposed to force. Once again, Nietzsche's categories seem to frustrate easy encapsulation.[98] Another answer is a version of the first. It has to do with the paradox of a philology that is able to grasp only what lies within its reach—a form of philology irretrievably infected with modernism, in other words, of which Aristoxenus has to be reckoned the precursor.[99]

The elusiveness of rhythm in relation to its objects, it follows, should be seen as a reflex of the theory that sought to capture rhythm theoretically and even to contain it by way of the exclusive and rigorous considerations of time and its quantitative barriers.[100] Aristoxenus, in that case, would have to be numbered among the first of the moderns, as somebody already caught in the toils of decline and prophetically forecasting the eventual conquest of temporal quantities by vocality. He would, in other words, be a threshold figure of the kind that appears so frequently in Nietzsche's writings on antiquity, such as the early Greek tragedians, or else the archaic moralist Theognis of Megara, another remnant of an earlier glory likewise caught in the toils of decline.[101] A rare biographical comment by Nietzsche on the personality of Aristoxenus, from the earliest of the notebooks on rhythm, lends some support to the hypothesis of Aristoxenus' postclassical modernity: "Importance of Aristoxenus, his oppositional stance toward the more recent art. Reminiscence of the old art of music [or "culture" (*mousikē*)]. Degeneracy already with Sophocles" (p. 126).[102] Reverence for the past is a sure sign of modernist decline: German classicism is a good case in point, and Aristoxenus' resistance to recent change and his enshrinement of what he took to be classical rhythm in his own theory—in his, as it were, museum of a faded sensibility—is surely another. Not by chance do these two potentials flow together in Rudolf Westphal's 1861 study of Aristoxenus, which may be Nietzsche's immediate source for this portrait of Aristoxenus.[103] Nietzsche will himself later adopt Aristoxenus' view of Sophocles in his writings around *The Birth of Tragedy*.[104]

The question that this line of interpretation leaves open is whether Aristoxenus had the wherewithal to reach back past a century of decline to capture or even appreciate rhythm in its purer form, prior to Sophocles. That he did not was a thesis that had been put forward by the German musicologist Carl Fortlage in 1847, albeit with a set of assumptions different from Nietzsche's. Nietzsche, who was familiar with Fortlage, could air suspicions against Aristoxenus, mainly by way of implication, but he stops short of undermining the authority of his key witness to the classical sense of time. Instead, he is content to lodge his doubts about the reliability of Aristoxenus, which only adds to the uncertainties of Greek rhythm, and then to make refinements of his own, using Aristoxenus as a deficient but necessary baseline.[105] Could Aristoxenus' theory of quantitative rhythm be a misreading of the classical practices, and even an attempt to "classicize" them, by endowing them with stately proportionalities and abstract (and soundless) beauties? Either way, that is whether Aristoxenus did grasp the realities of classical rhythm or merely sought to re-create them in his mind, Aristoxenus is a witness to a decline, and that is all the evidence that Nietzsche needs or wants.

Whether a degeneracy is to be found in Sophocles or in Aristoxenus, on Nietzsche's account Greek rhythm would have to be seen as suffering not from external encroachments but only from dissonances that are internal to itself, in relation to which it could establish itself only as an aesthetic ideal. Pursuing one set of aesthetic criteria (those of time) to the detriment of others (those of force) is therefore in some sense an exercise in illusion, even if it is only an aesthetic one. Such a pursuit generates *a* sense of rhythm and *a* sense of time, and consequently, a "history." Thus, the history of rhythmic sensation—as Nietzsche posits it and conducts it—is a philosophical one before it is a historical one. It pits two "idealisms" against one another (p. 309). And it is as convoluted as it is only because, as is so often the case in Nietzsche, he has to invent his history in order to dismantle it. What remains unclear to the end—and it is a question that nags all of Nietzsche's writings—is whether the history he describes has any validity apart from the perspective of his contemporary modernity; that is, whether to detect in antiquity, say, an element of force, of *Tonstärke* and *Tonleben*, is anything other than a telltale projection from the present. It is doubtful that anyone could ever resolve such a question, which probably explains why Nietzsche can give his various scenarios no more than an apparent validity.

Ancients and Moderns

Nietzsche's notebooks on rhythm reveal two forms of idealism, one modern, one ancient. Their relationship is put in an interesting light. The idealism of the Greeks has a decided advantage over that of the moderns. The moderns fail, paradoxically, because they are possessed of an all-too-successful, too robust (and simplifying) sense of aesthetics, one that as it were underwrites its own success. The advantages of the Greeks lay in the rich rhythms of their language, which their theories sought but failed to capture.[106] Discussing modern composers, Nietzsche would later write,

> The premise on which they build—*that* there is a correct, i.e., *one* correct interpretation—seems to me to be psychologically and experientially *false*. The composer, whether at the moment of creation or of reproduction, sees these *subtle shadows* only in a most precarious equilibrium: every fortuitous event, every heightening or weakening of the subjective feeling of power, forges unities out of fields that are larger one moment and necessarily more *contracted* the next. In short, says the *old classical philologist* drawing on the whole of his philological experience, *there is no unique, saving interpretation* for poets or for musicians (a poet is absolutely *no* authority for the meaning of his verses: the most peculiar proofs exist to show how fluid and vague their "meaning" is—). (Letter to Fuchs, 26 August 1888)

In place of "meaning," Nietzsche might as well have said form or structure, for it is this he declares himself willing to renounce in favor of a much richer declension of "possibilities," in lieu of any "sure decisions." It was this inherent fluidity of rhythm, its manifold and minute articulations of the whole ("little hesitations and abbreviations," p. 338), or rather its alertness to these possibilities, its general openness and vulnerability to contrary constructions, that for Nietzsche characterizes Greek rhythm and distinguishes it from its modern descendants. This, more than anything else, seems best to characterize the near-indeterminacy of Greek rhythm—in short, its vacillation of *signs*. But this is also what narrows the gap between modern and ancient rhythms to a paradoxical vanishing point, for the very same features that distinguish the infinitely fragile ancient practice already forecast the dissolution of Greek rhythm and the advent of its modern counterpart.

The passions of language were for the Greeks expressed in its "positional laws" and formal properties that were buried deep within it (*in der Sprache verborgen*, p. 331).[107] These properties of the Greek language held at bay, by their temporal distribution, forces that would otherwise overcome them (the force, for instance, of another reading that remains insensible to the pathologies of time, such as modern classicists would eventually offer, following the canons of German taste and habit). Such was the fate that the Greek language bore within itself: namely, to be overpowered by another rhythm, out of an incommensurability to its own. Thus, the possibilities of Greek rhythm, which were a part of its cultural unconscious, were incomparably fragile, to the point of undermining their own chances. "The language felt the longs and shorts even more finely than the poets could make use of them," Nietzsche writes, with more than a trace of wistfulness (p. 331).[108] Turning its back on the past, modern rhythm masks its own incommensurabilities with that past by means of the one art that might be thought capable of nearing it again: imitation of ancient ways (cf. p. 309); only, it is the poets, not the language, that the classicizing moderns know (and only know— abstractly, or else deludedly) how to imitate. "But an inhabitant of the ancient world would have heard none of *these* charms, still less would he have thought that he was hearing *his* meters" (letter to Fuchs, mid-April 1886).[109]

Despair with regard to the moderns, resigned agnosticism with regard to the ancients. It is the Germans, more than any other nation, who come in for stinging criticism and, characteristically, it is the French who provide the chastening counterexample. Only the French, Nietzsche declares, have any feeling for the syllable as an element of time (ibid.), which proves that a purely time-quantifying metrics is conceivable in principle; Maas makes the identical concession in a fleeting afterthought.[110] The general insensibility to time in nineteenth-century conceptions of rhythm, in Nietzsche's eyes, gives them their irrational character and their inner fatality: it is what marks contemporary rhythm's peculiar modernity.

Nietzsche is plainly using his history of rhythm to paint a critical picture of his contemporary modernity, and not just of philology. But the force of that critique lies for the most part in its implications. Perhaps the most intriguing fact about Nietzsche's reproach has to do with the peculiar blindness to history that the question of rhythm brings to the fore in the modern, ahistorical present. Isn't this the substance of the reproach he levels at philologists who project contemporary assumptions anachronistically onto the past? The history of rhythmic sensation traces a fateful downward arc in the thesis of culture, falling now—more recently—in the resounding ictus of stultifying repetition, ironically through a fateful insensibility to the very condition of this lapse: time itself. But this criticism is itself in ways pure irony. For what is the history that Nietzsche purports to tell? As we have seen, he is not content merely to offer a substitute for the going accounts of Greek rhythm, and certainly not in the timeless idiom of methodological truth. Indeed, it isn't clear that he offers any single account. We could write this off to the provisional quality of the notebook form, but that hardly accounts for the underlying, seemingly *systematic* vacillations in Nietzsche's thinking. Not only are his formulations to a certain degree self-effacing; the purity, not to say clarity, of the concept of Greek rhythm is left endangered by this very uncertainty.

A case in point are his views on the ictus. We find a remarkable, indeed a troubling, emphasis on the presence of ictus, not just prior to the advent of the Greek ideal as captured by Aristoxenus (as one of Nietzsche's competing historical frames would have it) but also within the phenomenon of Greek rhythm itself. Thus, at times it would seem that Nietzsche is still leaning on a version of the ictus-theory, as when he tries to account for irrational or compensatory lengthenings and retardations or changes in tempo through the concept of "secondary ictus and accent [*Nebenictus* or *Nebenton*]."[111] Yet this is the very feature he would deny elsewhere in the notes, and again in his letter to Fuchs from the end of August 1888.[112] Either Nietzsche vacillates or he has two competing models going. How could he hold both theories with any consistency? And yet, for all his opposition to the modern anachronistic readings of Greek rhythm, the latency of the ictus is never relinquished.[113]

As tempting as it might be to connect up this flaw in the conceptual purity of Greek quantitative rhythm with *alogia*, or the irrationality of rhythm, and from there with Nietzsche's contemporary interest in the physiological and metaphysical abysses of Dionysianism, this hardly points a way out of the problem of rhythm. For the resort to Dionysianism in the context of rhythm only raises further questions about its pertinence to and its role in Nietzsche's largest schemes, conceptual and historical. Let us consider just a few of these issues.

Dionysian Music: A Modern Phenomenon?

The association between Dionysus and the irrational (*alogia*), force, and dissonance is attested by a handful of passing allusions in the notebooks on rhythm. How decisive is this link? It is unclear how decisive any such link could in principal be. A number of purely theoretical considerations, already discussed above, tell against the easy reduction of the uncertainties of Greek rhythm to a Dionysian disruption. Suffice it to say that in Nietzsche's view, dissonance and irrationality are not identical terms, because dissonance just is the intrinsic feature of *all* measure: no two times can be strictly equivalent. And it is this "fine dissonance," which suffuses and disrupts Greek rhythm from within, that Nietzsche takes to be the most compelling feature of the rhythms of Greek music and verses; it is the source of their great "pliancy [*Gefügigkeit*]" and of their rich potential for interpretation and performance. Dissonance for Nietzsche is not only a commonplace feature of even so-called rational measures (which have nothing to do with Dionysus). Their dissonance, he goes so far as to venture, is "stronger," more effective aesthetically, than that of genuinely irrational and "ecstatic" measures, because the disruptions are quieter, subtler, and more pleasurably irritating. And the same applies to changes of rhythm and of tempo: Greek quantitative rhythm works its greatest effects—which is to say, is most psychologically compelling—through its finely modulated character, in contrast to the "tick-tock" of modern rhythm, which mechanically follows a strict equality of times (*Taktgleichheit*) (p. 260).[114]

A second consideration: Nietzsche has already shown how "force" is itself an ideal quality, made possible only through a symbolic representational framework. This strikes two blows against construing the Dionysian as a primordial and preclassical force of the irrational. Given Nietzsche's general alertness to the pitfalls of idealism, could his account of Dionysianism in rhythm, such as it is, be critical of the phenomenon it undertakes to describe? At the very least, recognizing the idealizing streak within Dionysianism would require a revision in our understanding of this all-too-easily clichéd phenomenon, which would in any case have to be aligned somehow with "the idealism of tonality and feeling [that is, of the *moderns*], as against the idealism of space and light (appearance) of the Greeks." To be sure, such a tack runs us into problems of periodization and of historical characterization. As it happens, these problems are reflected in Nietzsche's dating of the Greek Dionysian rhythms in the notebooks. Let us look at the evidence.

Although Nietzsche gives no absolute dates for the incipit of the Dionysian rhythms, he does date them in a relative way, and this is revealing. In the first notebook, he associates them with early cultic practices ("earlier, [choreic rhythms were called] *'baccheioi'* in the cult songs of Dionysus and Demeter").[115] In the final notebook, the same rhythms, notable for their exploitation of rhythmic changes and "dissonances in time-measures" (p. 329), are more closely dated. They appear to be a later, and in any case postquantitative, development in musical sensibility:

> The nature of ancient music must be reconstructed: the mimetic dance, *harmonia* [viz., musical scales], *rhythmos*. Essential differences in so-called melody, in rhythm, and also in dancing, among the moderns [*bei den Neueren*]. *Originally* (in citharodic music), *the note functions as a measure of time.* The nature of the *scales* needs to be discovered (acutest feeling for proportions of height [viz., intervals]). What allowed the Greeks to deploy quarter-tones? Harmony was not drawn into the realm of the symbolic for them. Establishment of the ancient [viz., classical (*antiken*)] symbolic. *The Dionysian innovations in tonality* [or "key" (*Tonart*)], *in rhythm* (*alogia*?). (p. 322; emphases added)

Dionysianism, an "innovation [*Neuerung*]"? The chronology here, as elsewhere in the notes, is elusive, or better yet, symbolic. Presumably, the earlier-mentioned cults are archaic and post-Homeric, and yet the aesthetic system that the Dionysian "innovations" act against is patently quantitative and classical. For this same reason, the Dionysian innovations, said to be "in tonality," are likely to be just *of* tonality, as contrasted with the essentially temporal character of the classical note and its corresponding scales (*Tonleitern*). These last, thanks to their peculiar restrictions, are not "tonal" in the modern—or relatively modern and Dionysian—sense of the word. We may further recall how in Nietzsche's historical picture it is tonality (*Tonleben*) that threatens to undo the proportional symmetries of time (*Zeitleben*), which is to say the classical symbolics of rhythm. Irrationality is an encroachment upon temporal barriers that naturally, or at least historically, give way to changes in vocality and tone, to the rise of the accentuated pause, and finally to the functional ictus ("the upbeat has sense only for the ictus" [p. 338]). And even if the two principals (tonality and time) are locked in a primordial antagonism, this does not alter the evolutionary picture. The Dionysian irrationalities of measure seem to play a specific part in this evolution (if they do not represent this evolution altogether). The Dionysian phenomenon emerges against the backdrop of the classical order of things.

That it does represent this very change, or its incipient moment, is corroborated by a passage from *The Birth of Tragedy* in which Nietzsche comes at the problem once again. There, Nietzsche is concerned to underscore the specifically innovative character of the Dionysian reveries, wherein one is reminded that "pain begets joy, that ecstasy may wring sounds of agony from us." The passage needs to be quoted in full:

> The song and pantomime of such dually minded revelers was something *new and unheard-of* in the Homeric-Greek world; and the Dionysian music in particular excited awe and terror. If music, as it would seem, had been known previously as an Apollinian art, it was so, strictly speaking, *only as the wave beat of rhythm*, whose formative power was developed for the representation of Apollinian states. The music of Apollo was Doric *architectonics in tones, but in tones that were merely suggestive*, such as those of the cithara. The very element which forms the essence of Dionysian music (and hence of music in general) is carefully excluded as un-Apollinian—*namely, the emotional power of the tone, the uniform flow of the melody, and the utterly incomparable world of harmony.* (*BT* §2; emphases added)

The parallels between the two accounts of change are remarkably close. Again, the innovations appear to take place in a post-Homeric but still archaic Greek world; yet the aesthetic regime that is overturned is the Apollinian, classical, and (quite plainly) quantitative system of rhythmic proportions. And again, it is tonality, or vocality, that paves the way to change. The note, originally "architectonic" and "merely suggestive," and functional only as a "measure of time," steps boldly into the foreground, as an emotional, forceful, even "pathological" tone, connected now with melodic and harmonic structures.[116] Stately proportions yield to dynamic movements. Temporally defined rhythm yields to "music" in a new and unheard-of sense of the word. That sense, it remains to be shown, is a thoroughly familiar one, at least to Nietzsche's contemporary world.[117]

Dionysianism plainly appears to be a postclassical phenomenon, if not in historical time then surely in tendency. This relatively late invention of the Dionysian puts Dionysian symbolics in a disturbing light. Can Dionysianism possibly be associated with the *decline* of classical sensibilities—that is to say, with the advent of the modern sensibility, whether as its harbinger, prelude, or first instantiation? The notebooks on rhythm and *The Birth of Tragedy* suggest that it can. The progression described in both is toward music in a thoroughly and unmistakably modern sense. Dionysianism captures the moment when "the other symbolic powers suddenly press forward, particularly those of music, *in rhythm, dynamics, and harmony*" (*BT* §2; emphasis added; trans. mod.). And these last, as we have seen, being the principal ingredients of the modern sensibility to time, are for Nietzsche thoroughly out of place in any account of Greek quantitative rhythmics, which represents the classical sense of time. Nietzsche knows very well the difference between "Greek music as compared with the infinitely richer music known and familiar to us" (*BT* §17), which is to say, "the utterly incomparable world of harmony" (*BT* §2). Hence, to quote again from his letter to Ritschl which was cited earlier, "The more we draw on modern music for understanding [Greek] metrics, the farther we estrange ourselves from the reality of metrics in antiquity" (30 December 1870).[118]

Nietzsche is crystal clear on this point, and unfailingly consistent. Melody was not felt by the Greeks as a harmonic power; what they could feel, he asserts, were the architectonic *Raumdifferenzen*, or spatial differences (intervals), in the passage from note to note (elsewhere he calls these *Zeiträume*), which were also deemed somehow "mimetic" (an idea that receives only a mention here [p. 321]).[119] Pitch was measured by "relations of height, and thus, ultimately, by numerical differences."[120] Melody as such did not exist. Rhythm, the actual "creative" element, dominated, at the expense of melody, whereas today the situation is the reverse: melody compensates for an "incapacity to span *large-scale* relations rhythmically—[it reflects] a degenerative form *of rhythm*," which now is valid only as "*a means of expressing affect*" (letters to Fuchs, end of August 1888). "The feeling [of the Greeks] was *depotentialized* [i.e., desensitized, or else simply insensible] with respect to harmonic conditions (which are the creative agent in the German folksong)" (p.

322). Rather, melodic relations, such as they existed, filled out the verticalities of linguistic experience and provided a sense of scalar space ("harmony" in Greek musical theory simply means "attunement" of a musical scale within an octave, and it has nothing to do with accords[121]). Temporal relations, stretching across the horizontal expanses of space, boldly charted out new territories for aesthetic acquisition, and so on. Then comes the contrast we set out from: "The Dionysian innovations in tone, in rhythm (*alogia*?)" (ibid.).

Again, in the passages from *The Birth of Tragedy* just cited and in the corresponding notebook entries on Dionysian rhythms, it is the quantifying characteristics of the Greek sensibility that are erased (Nietzsche claims) by the introduction of the criteria of the ictus, counterpoint, and harmonic consistencies (crucial to the modern idea of dissonance), all of which run through the emotional intonings of the modern scholarly establishment: "The soul of our *melody and harmony* is expressed in the ictus of our compositions"; and so, where harmony and melody are lacking, as in Greek quantitative rhythm, the ictus is too (p. 137). This thought is available to Nietzsche at least as early as the fall of 1869, and it is a constant in his notebooks down to 1872.[122] Due to its association with force and the encroachment on the barriers of time, irrationality in rhythm of the Dionysian kind is suspiciously familiar. We have seen how irrationality is to be conceived as the forerunner of the modern stress accent, which in turn, being tied to sense, is a "*logical accent*": stress and meaning go hand in hand (p. 172).[123] Is the Dionysian urge, then, at bottom a *logical* phenomenon? Or worse, a sign of the irrationality of modern rationality and modern idealism? Elsewhere, Nietzsche is keen to make this very association, as for instance when he lampoons contemporary philology and its cult of (Apollinian) beauty for its pathetic, excessive, and impassioned enthusiasms. There, philology is shown to rest on an unconscious, or else willfully ignored, anachronism. Nietzsche makes all due apologies to the reader for having swept away so much "*pleasure*" and "*enjoyment*" with a single stroke of his theory; quantitative measure, alienating and uncertain, is hard to square with the "dithyrambic tones" of the modern critics:

Individual strophes have been compared to the finest works of Phidias [etc.]. The latest, H[einrich] Schmidt, is completely filled with enthusiasm for the beauties of eurythmia—his own.[124] Even if you deduct the sense of triumph one feels with one's own discoveries, which now and then seduce a person into dithyrambic tones, there is an enjoyment left over that I must compare with the enjoyment one takes in the beating of a drum [i.e., the ictus]: as far as my feeling goes, a pathetic glorification of the drummer's enjoyments has something comic and cheerful [*Heiteres*] about it. (pp. 267–68)

In point of fact, this Dionysian ecstasy, sublimated in a comic serenity, amounts to no more than a "frightful tick-tock" and a mechanical "drumbeat." This is the source of the "equivalence of measures [*Taktgleichheit*]" that Nietzsche so fiercely opposes throughout his notes. Making for a caricature of the ancient meters and rhythms, the accentual, ictus-based rhythms are in reality a self-caricature: they derive from nowhere else than the *Hopsasa* of the German language and the corresponding forms of modern feeling.[125] Meanwhile, let there be no mistake about it: "the ictus is *not* to be used to explain irrationality" (p. 159). In a word, what Nietzsche's emphasis (the little there is) on Dionysian rhythm reveals in his notebooks is a correspondence between philology and the "invention" of the Dionysian as a recognizable category of Greek mythology, or rather of our mythology about the Greeks. *The Birth of Tragedy out of the Spirit of Music*, as the title of Nietzsche's work in its first edition (1872) read, appears to do nothing so much as to fulfill the very program announced (and partly disguised) in its title. Surely the hope expressed in that work for a return *ad fontes* and to a musical spirit that could be reclaimed today as "our own" is overshadowed by the very sorts of impossibility that Nietzsche is demonstrating in his lectures on rhythm at the very moment he was composing his first book.[126] For the most that book can hope to offer is a sublime misprision, best encapsulated in the trio of names Nietzsche gives to the "mothers of being" who act as the titular guiding spirits (and virtual epigraph) of this other project: *Wahn, Wille, Wehe* ("Delusion, Will, Woe") (*BT* §20). But neither are Nietzsche's writings on rhythm innocent of this mythologizing and invention of antiquity, as we saw.[127]

The seemingly ineradicable presence of the ictus in Nietzsche's theory of quantitative rhythm, which the ictus in fact disturbs, is exemplary in this respect. It is a sign that Greek rhythm can never be comprehended independently of the framework that tries to grasp it. Nor is it the only example we have seen of Nietzsche's self-disrupting frameworks. Indeed, self-disruption is the trademark of his early philology. As we saw, Nietzsche's own historical scheme injects, almost willfully, the notion of the vitality of the accent and of force into an account of temporal and quantitative barriers that strictly doesn't call for it. Is that scheme itself infected with modernism, much like the conscious anachronism of Dionysian music in *The Birth of Tragedy*? Everything would suggest that it indeed is. Nietzsche's construction of Greek rhythm is to this extent a reflex of the modern philology it simultaneously critiques.[128] But to the extent that it asks to be read in this way, it is not.

Here we see again what was shown above and will be repeated below. Nietzsche's vision of history might be thought to be continuist, when it is in fact neither continuous nor disjunctive, but only a commentary on the specular and asymmetrical processes of representation that have fashioned historical consciousness to date. Rhythm is an appropriate vehicle for making this comment, because the conditions of rhythm are the conditions of historical consciousness itself. Rhythm, after all, is "the most primary sensation of time, the very *form of time*." And what Nietzsche demonstrates in his writings is the immense variety of forms that time can assume even from within the single vantage point of a given cultural perspective—most impressively, the modern and quintessentially German perspective.[129] Outwardly inconsistent, his writing displays the dissonances of contemporary ideals. The moderns have always reinvented the Greeks in their own image. Nietzsche plays with that image in order to portray what is so problematic about a specular consciousness that not even he can elude.

CHAPTER 4

Inversions of the Classical Ideal:
The "Encyclopedia of Classical Philology" (1871)

I want to sit in the theater not as an ancient but as a modern: my observations may well be pedantic; but at first I must wonder at everything so
as to comprehend it all afterward.

— "PROLEGOMENA TO THE 'CHOEPHORI' OF AESCHYLUS"[1]

During the summer semester of 1871, two years into his professorship at
Basel and a little over half a year before the publication of *The Birth of
Tragedy*, Nietzsche delivered a lecture course on the methods of classical
philology. Laboriously entitled "Encyclopedia of Classical Philology and
Introduction to the Study of the Same," the lectures, preserved in note form,
are intended as a general guide to the study of philology.[2] But they are in fact
much more than this. In the guise of a professional primer for aspiring classicists, the lectures explore the relation of the classical discipline to the contemporary situation of classicism in German letters and philosophy at large.
More pointedly, they expose the uneasy relation of classical studies to their
own inevitable classicism. The "Encyclopedia" course is at least in this sense
a continuation of Nietzsche's critique of contemporary culture in his lectures
and notes on Greek rhythm, begun the previous semester. Only, now the
focus is inverted and the strategies are reversed. Whereas in the earlier writings Nietzsche is happy to foreground the elusiveness of the Greek world of

sensation and to indict modern scholars for trying to capture that world with their own misplaced feeling, in the "Encyclopedia" the focus is on the feeling for antiquity that a classicist must cultivate just to approach this lost world in any of its manifestations. In the later lecture Nietzsche strangely seems to encourage an untimeliness toward the past. And yet, as in the studies on rhythm, the net effect here, too, is to bring out all the more visibly the essential anachronism of classical scholarship in the modern world on the one side, and the definitive loss of antiquity on the other. The two studies are thus complementary faces of a single, if still puzzling, critique. In order to unravel this puzzle further we must turn now to this later phase of Nietzsche's philology.

Philological Encyclopedism

In their form and scope, Nietzsche's "Encyclopedia" lectures fall squarely within the genre that became *de rigueur* among professing classicists ever since the formation of the discipline at the end of the eighteenth century, in the wake of F. A. Wolf's landmark formulation of *Altertumswissenschaft*. Wolf himself had lectured on the "Encyclopedia of Philology" from 1785 onward at Halle and then later at Berlin (the lectures were published in 1831), whether inspired by Johann Matthias Gesner (1691–1761) or by Christian Gottlob Heyne (1729–1812).[3] Some eighty years later Nietzsche had followed lectures by Ritschl on the same subject at Bonn or Leipzig.[4] The philological encyclopedia was evanescent but by no means dead in 1871 (August Boeckh's *Encyklopädie und Methodologie der philologischen Wissenschaften* would appear posthumously in 1877 and be reissued in 1886). Yet the encylopedic genre did not so much disappear as it ceded its function, which was governed by an ideal of disciplinary rigor, to the seminar and the curriculum of modern philological programs. These continued to embody, at an institutional level, the original Wolfian aspiration, which was to comprehend what was thought to be the whole of classical antiquity in the totality of its aspects. The force of this ideal is still to be felt today.[5]

A great weight of tradition hung heavily upon this kind of teaching, every aspect of which reeked of disciplinary formation.[6] The conventional encyclopedias, whose outlines Nietzsche's lectures mimic, sought to offer and by their very existence to defend an all-encompassing definition of the field in its systematic coherence, against the background of the long march of philology from Alexandria in the age of the Museum (third to first centuries B.C.E.) to the modern present. Imposing in their breadth, selectively detailed, and representing an impersonal knowledge, the encyclopedias wore all the signs of unassailable mastery. This is not to say that classicists strove through their teaching to dissolve facelessly into the tradition the way Nietzsche urges them to do in his essay on "Homer and Classical Philology" (1869). On the contrary, the philological encyclopedias, which were generally destined for publication (even if only posthumously), stood out as signature works written not merely with the aim of transmitting the tradition, but with the hope of shaping it definitively.

The format of these encyclopedic works and lectures was more or less fixed: a cascade of sweeping and programmatic segments, organized under broad rubrics, which could be arranged, divided, and subdivided or regrouped at will. Divisions typically included the history and methodology of philology, hermeneutics (the science of interpretation), textual, literary, and source criticism, grammar and language, and thumbnail portraits and histories of the different subdisciplines (religion, fine arts, philosophy, science, and so on). Philology, so viewed, took in everything with any conceivable historical connection to antiquity, including—admirably—itself. Yet what is truly remarkable about this hallowed tradition, less than a century old in 1871, is how unlike itself it can actually be.

No two encyclopedias are identical, whether in their formal organization or in their contents: disputing either aspect was half the raison d'être of an encyclopedic work. To take a prominent example, Wolf in his encyclopedia had placed numismatics in its own category, alongside architecture and epigraphy and within the general ambit of art, archaeology, monuments, and other material remains. But that is absurd, August Boeckh complains a generation later in his own encyclopedia, and about his own teacher no less: "In evidence here is a total inability to form concepts—par for the course, among philologists."[7] The inscriptions of numismatics, Boeckh reasons, are literary, while the coins themselves have to be treated partly as manufacture, partly as money, and partly as plastic art. Thus, numismatics has no place in the history of the fine arts, while epigraphy has its proper place in the history of literature.[8] Boeckh's logic against Wolf might appear overfine (you might think it to be a reductio ad absurdum of encyclopedic divisions), but it also concedes more than any sane philologist bent on systematicity ought perhaps to do. For what is to prevent its reapplication to any of the categories left undivided, and therefore laterally unconnected, by Boeckh himself (for example, literature, religion, mathematics, or economics)?[9] At any rate, where one drew a line around a field or subfield all depended on how one viewed the general contours of the discipline. Finding holes and filling them was another way of nudging tradition aside.[10] And as the nineteenth century wore on, encyclopedias could offer a further line of defense against, or else a justification of, the disciplinary fractioning that came with increased specialization (a trend that Nietzsche knew about and resented, as his frequent notebook references to philologists as "factory workers" show).[11]

Clearly, each new encyclopedia not only redistributed and rearticulated the material of the ancient world; it altered the image of that world. And yet given these individual disparities, which could be considerable, one is entitled to ask just what is being transmitted in the philological encyclopedic genre: is it a body of knowledge or a way of organizing or conceiving this knowledge? Barometric in the extreme, encyclopedias at least provide the comforting illusion that even if times change, antiquity no longer does. Problems of frameworks aside (for instance, the problem of theory-dependence, which was usually named and disowned as "subjectivism"), what passes in the nineteenth century for a stable (if approximate) object of knowledge, encompassed by successive concentric rings of encyclopedic effort, may turn out to be no more than a commitment to the mere belief in the ultimate existence and organizability (and distant objectivity) of such an object. (Boeckh's famous and resounding definition of philology as "knowledge of the known," *Erkenntniss des Erkannten*, is one way of securing this distanced objectivity.)[12] The philological encyclopedia, whether in the lecture hall or as a published manual, is above all the sign and the embodiment of this belief, made possible by another, which is in fact its founding presupposition: the belief in the integrity of classical antiquity itself. Viewed in this light, the project of the encyclopedia seems at once wishful and self-fulfilling. Nietzsche recognized this to be the case, but then so did the classicists who wrote and professed the nineteenth-century encyclopedias of philology.

A concrete instance will help make the point. Gottfried Bernhardy (1800–1875), a disciple of Wolf and a pupil of Boeckh's, had published his

Grundlinien zur Encyklopädie der Philologie in 1832 in the hope of consolidating Wolf's gains in the unified study of antiquity, in the face of new obstacles and challenges. To be combated were the centrifugal forces of classical studies on the one hand ("a tendency toward *realia*, historical polymathism, [and] the splitting up of classical antiquity into classical antiquities") and a symptomatically modern indulgence in "subjectivity" on the other.[13] Like Nietzsche in his inaugural lecture, Bernhardy, too, is anxious about how—and indeed whether—antiquity, in the "totality of its effects," can be aptly "named."[14] Much hangs on the question, starting with the idea of wholeness itself. Is the very desire for totality itself a symptom of a dividedness within?

Bernhardy's anxieties are again telling. He freely admits that "the existence [*Dasein*] of the modern world," in contrast to its antique counterpart, "is immortal"—it has a timeless universality to it—"as is its goal, the ideal."[15] Just how this claim about idealism is supposed to be cashed out, rhetorically or methodologically, is not entirely clear. Idealism for Bernhardy is, as we shall see, a liability that also has its advantages. Is he lamenting or celebrating this feature of the modern mind? One thing is certain, however. Bernhardy's forthright admission that idealism is peculiarly modern is itself a performance of what it states, for in it antiquity and modernity are conceived as two discontinuous, incommensurable, and ideal totalities—a picture that is borne out elsewhere in his encyclopedia, for instance just a few pages earlier: "The antiquity of the Greeks and the Romans, those genuine *veteres*, appears in its innermost essence to be a self-enclosed structure, which is accessible to the moderns only to a minimal degree" (p. 36). A little later on we read: "The ancients completely exhausted their being [*Dasein*] and brought it to perfection without any posthumous echo; and a standard of measure that would apply to both [ancients and moderns] is out of the question," literally "impossible" (p. 39). How trustworthy is such a picture, given that it is itself an expression of idealism? The problem pales beside the question of how such a view can be consistently maintained, which it is not in Bernhardy's case. His position is in fact self-refuting, for *he knows too much* about the antiquity he is describing, far more than his own strictures ought to allow. Compare the sequel to the statement above: "The antiquity of the Greeks and the Romans, those genuine *veteres*, . . . is accessible to the moderns only to a minimal degree, because the symmetry [of antiquity], that most delicate tissue of life's fullness, is supported by *mysteriously hidden* threads" (p. 36;

emphasis added). This looks like forbidden knowledge, but no matter. Purported incommensurability and mutual incommunicability are belied elsewhere in the same work by influences and communications of all kinds that are said to exist between the two "worlds," ancient and modern; indeed, the very characterization of antiquity as a "world" is itself the product of one such communication. Qualifications are quickly needed, in fact in the next breath: "But neither people developed and preserved, for itself or in common, one and the same nature; although we are in the habit of embracing the totality of [the admittedly diverse life of ancient Greece and Rome] under the same name." The addendum shows Bernhardy, the circumspect scholar, to be critical of the reduction of classical antiquity to a singular phenomenon. But his admission only underscores his dilemma. Bernhardy simply fails to confront the contradictions of his encyclopedia. Or rather, he confronts them and then shrinks back again from them.

These problems are built deeply into Wolfian philology, which underwrites totalizing encyclopedic constructs like "classical antiquity" but views with suspicion and as characteristically modern the conscious production of aesthetic wholes. The ancient world surely cannot be allowed to be the idealized construct of modernity.[16] And yet that is exactly the consequence classical philology is compelled to draw if it wishes to elude the circularity of its own premises. For how can the "all-encompassing reflection" that characterizes the "modern whole," the speculative totality that is modernity, hope to take in the "firmly rooted particularity and multiformity" of the ancients—without obliterating antiquity altogether, through its *Aufhebung*? That is Bernhardy's problem:

> The concepts of universality in culture and history were connected [in the modern world] with [an] unfettered striving for the very first time; the essence of the modern world is as immortal as its goal, the ideal. Thus, the tendency of the moderns is no longer a plastic one, that is, an expression of sensuous beauty; rather, it is a rational one, whose horizon is universal and is at home in both the past and the present. . . . Insofar as the modern totality extends its perimeters by canceling out [*durch Aufheben*] the particular and through all-encompassing reflection, the power of individuality fades away, which was the source of the firmly rooted particularity and multiformity of the ancients. (pp. 41–42)

Under these conditions, how indeed can modern philology avoid canceling out its cherished object of study? And yet how else can it proceed? Nietzsche, in his own "Encyclopedia," will mimic this dilemma of the modern classicist and its repressed incoherence, its attitude of compromise that runs, "I know very well that the very idea of classical antiquity is a gross oversimplification (there was too much disparity and even strife among its constituents for that, and anyway scholarship is too fragmentary to comprehend antiquity as such), but (*for these very reasons*) I will treat the ancient phenomena as though they belong 'under the same name' ('classical antiquity') just the same."[17] Bernhardy is perhaps unusual in bringing the dilemma so close to the surface with his admissions. But his plight, and his ultimate disavowal of the problems, are by no means exceptional.

Nietzsche's lectures outwardly resemble the conventional philological encyclopedias. His subject divisions, twenty-one in number, are similar to those used by Bernhardy and Boeckh, though his are loosely concatenated, not rigorously hierarchical. In places, the contents showcase Nietzsche's own actual or hoped-for contributions to the field, but they can also be unenergetic and dutiful, or else—being, after all, notes to lecture by—merely telegraphic. They also contain a few surprises. So, for example, the sixteenth lecture on "rhythm and meter" resumes several of the high points from the notebooks devoted to this subject and proudly blazons forth Nietzsche's discovery ("We must give up the rhythmical ictus and follow Aristoxenus, who knows only *temporal rhythm*. . . . The error lay in taking our music to be identical with the ancient system" [p. 399]). This is an admission that, as we shall see in a moment, sits awkwardly next to his general position in the lectures. The eighteenth lecture on philosophy oddly reads as though Nietzsche had never even started a notebook on Democritus or published a word on Diogenes Laertius.[18] Similarly, the quotation from Seneca, so spectacularly inverted at the end of Nietzsche's inaugural lecture, is here simply cited, without inversion, as one piece of the puzzle of ancient testimony about the original meanings of "philology" (*quae philosophia fuit, facta philologia est*) (p. 343).[19] There is a glancing reference to Apollo and Dionysus as a pair, a rare discussion of statuary (Nietzsche was never much given to archaeology), and a fascinating excursion on ancient religion (to be discussed below) which throws a troubling sidelight on *The Birth of Tragedy*.

The sole formal departure from the inherited scheme of the encyclopedias comes in the opening, methodological sections, in a lecture on the
"Genesis and Preparation of the Classical Philologist" (§6), which com-
mences with the problem "How does one *become* a philologist? [*Wie* wird *der*
Philolog?]." The question is one that simply wasn't asked in the encyclopedic
tradition, most likely because the answer was thought (or was wished) to be
self-evident, as the following remark by August Boeckh suggests: "What
Ruhnken says about criticism, *Criticus non fit, sed nascitur*, also applies to
interpretation: *Interpres non fit, sed nascitur*" ("An interpreter doesn't become
what he is, but is born").[20] Nietzsche's partial answer to his own question
only begins to point to his divergence from the tradition: "Every profession
must correspond to a *need*, every need to a *drive*" (p. 366; emphases added).[21]
Underlying this analysis is the worry, or at least the spectral possibility, that
will be expressed in the notes to the never completed essay "We Philologists" four years hence (1875): "The philologists of the future—will there be
any then?" ("WPh," 7[3]). Small wonder that the later essay, originally projected as a fifth *Untimely Mediation*, was according to one of Nietzsche's
plans to have opened with the very same problem as the sixth lecture of the
"Encyclopedia": "Genesis of the present-day philologist" ("WPh," 2[3]).
The two questions are clearly linked. To understand how one becomes a
philologist today is to be armed with a knowledge of how to produce philologists of the future. Even contemporary philology, if pressed, would admit
that this was one of its principal concerns. Philological encyclopedias are a
case in point: they are designed to extend the tradition of disciplinary formation, and so too the discipline itself, from one generation to the next.
Nietzsche's "Encyclopedia" is in this respect no different from its conventional predecessors.

Superficial resemblances notwithstanding, Nietzsche's lectures are a most
curious example of the encyclopedic genre in at least three respects, all of
which are related to the question of philology's future: in their vigorous protreptic (exhortative) function; in their explicit focus on the formation of the
subject of philology (the philologist); and in their obsessive foregrounding of
the historical contingency of philology. The dissonances between content
and form that result are immense. Not only are the lectures opposed to the
mission of the philological encyclopedia conventionally defined. They also
seem at times to work against their own ostensible purpose, or rather pur-

poses. And so, Nietzsche's lectures constitute a kind of anti-encyclopedia within the encyclopedic genre—assuming we can even tell these apart, so fundamentally confused are the signs of either label in Nietzsche, and so greatly at odds with itself is the genre of the encyclopedia already, as we glimpsed above in the cases of Bernhardy and Boeckh. Nietzsche exacerbates the inherited tensions in the philological encyclopedia to the point of its perversion.

So, for instance, despite the overtly protreptic character of his lectures (the attempt to recruit and enlist philologists of the future), the student envisaged by them is not exactly turned toward classics, at least not in any straightforward way, but is rather turned *away* from antiquity and from its present form of study. And far from underscoring the coherent development of philology and its mastery of its subject matter, what the lectures demonstrate through their performance, and at times what they argue, is that philology cannot escape the paradoxes of its own temporality—its peculiar "untimeliness" and frequent incoherence. Correspondingly, the notion of mastery becomes increasingly elusive, as indeed it is everywhere else in Nietzsche's philology. One can only imagine the effect the lectures must have had on their audience. Nietzsche was evidently banking on scandalizing his pupils, although this hardly exhausts his aim. Indeed, as I hope to show, Nietzsche's "Encyclopedia" is a ranging reflection on temporal paradoxes and historical contradictions. It is also—or rather, for these very reasons—a perfectly consistent example of his earliest philological thinking, which taken as a whole is a general reflection on modern culture and its historical contradictions.[22] But let us turn to the lectures.

Nietzsche's "Encyclopedia"

The opening thesis is astounding. The study of the classics, Nietzsche claims, is literally the study of modernity. Ostensibly, the aim of philology is immersion in the past. "We want to grasp the [classical] phenomenon at its highest level and to grow with it," he writes, characterizing the process in the optimistic language of eighteenth- and nineteenth-century hermeneutics, of which Wolf's intuitionism, discussed earlier, is merely one instance. *Hineinleben* may be "the goal" (p. 345), but such immersion, whatever else it entails, is for Nietzsche in the final analysis a form of aesthetic intuition: its "precondition" is "a highly active aesthetic impulse [*Schönheitstrieb*]." By this is meant a faculty for imaginative projection, which is the opposite of deep familiarity with antiquity. Required, instead, is that the philological subject step back from the past as from an impressionist painting, that he close his eyes to the blur of historical detail. Only so can the past come into view, in the present case as "that most beautiful *idyll*" that we call "classical antiquity."[23] Perception of the past necessarily involves a kind of perspectival illusion, and it is conditioned by our position in the present. This being the case, Nietzsche reasons, the single most important means of making oneself "receptive" to antiquity, and the final criterion of a philologist, is "*to be modern*," to steep oneself thoroughly in the best of modern thinking, especially poetry and philosophy. Heavy doses of Winckelmann, Lessing, Schiller, Goethe, and Kant are commended to the aspiring classicist, who must first become a "*moderner Mensch*" in order to become a philologist (pp. 345, 368). "What a difficult job it is to prepare somebody for the enjoyments of antiquity!" he exclaims, reiterating a central imperative of the classical tradition (p. 345). Needless to say, bad philology—micro-erudition of the institutional kind—is carried out by scholars whom Nietzsche despises for being of a grossly "unaesthetic" cast of mind (p. 367). They have no modern culture, and hence no talent for idealizing. Or so it would seem.[24]

Were this all there is to Nietzsche's critique of philology, the "Encyclopedia" would be at most a remarkably unsparing document, at worst an uncompelling argument, and in any case strangely inconsistent with his other critiques of the discipline from around the same time.[25] Wasn't the point of the lectures on rhythm, from a few short months ago (and vividly recalled in the lectures here), to *deprive* contemporary classicists of their projective enjoyment of the ancient rhythms and meters, which (his argument went) are so constructed as to baffle modern ears with their absolute inaccessibility? And are not classicists everywhere else in Nietzsche's early notes under attack for being *too modern*, and not sufficiently in touch with ancient realities? But we have hardly begun to appreciate the intricacies of the "Encyclopedia."

Hints that something is awry are available on the first few pages, which literally dissect in a philological fashion the conventional title of the lectures they introduce, and that seem to take delight in lingering over a series of disconcerting facts. Fussing over its own nomenclature is a standard element in the repertoire of the encyclopedic genre, a pastime that could be indulged in with ease only once the term "philology" had gained ascendancy. Not so in the earlier stages of the discipline, however, when Wolf could go on for pages weighing the various inherited options ("philology," "classical learning," "ancient literature," "humanities studies," "fine sciences," etc.) before finally grounding his own coinage (which survived as an ideal but soon gave way to "philology"), in part by way of a dubious appeal to cultural elitism and a disdain for non-European values: *Alterthums-Wissenschaft*.[26] Hard as it may be for us, one has to imagine what it must have been like to study in a field that as yet had no clear perimeters and not even an agreed-upon name.[27]

In his apparent return to the earlier humanism, Nietzsche doesn't quite plunge his audience into Wolf's foundational doubts, but his preface goes well beyond the usual line of duty in disciplinary self-scrutiny. He does not hesitate to point out, for instance, how the very term for the genre in common use at the time ("encyclopedia") is itself the result of a philological mistake: it stems from a manuscript error in Quintilian, transmitted unsuspectingly by a major sixteenth-century French classical scholar (Henricus Stephanus [Henri Étienne]) and later translated into the modern vernacular, which gives us our word and its meaning today (p. 342).[28] Nor does Nietzsche leave undiscussed the debated origins and meaning of "philology," a term he accepts but not without misgivings. Sifting through a handful of testimonia, he briefly airs the ancient disagreements (which seem to have reached no clear consensus) and then decides on what he takes to be the original meaning of "philology." His solution, which is clearly willful, reduces the ancient practice to an ethical quality: "In antiquity, *philologia* is by no stretch of the imagination a science, but only a general pleasure in knowledge of all sorts, a quality." But then he points the problem back at the present: "Now what in antiquity corresponds to what we understand by 'philology'?" (p. 343).

Where the successors to Wolf would prefer to see stable continuity and evolution in the philological tradition from antiquity to the present (hence Rudolf Pfeiffer's exponency, in this century, of *philologia perennis*),[29] in Nietzsche's overview of the discipline the modernity of philology and its uncertain or at the very least self-made origins are put troublingly on show. He will eventually call for a return to something like an ethical as opposed to a scientific view of philology, evidently aligning himself with Seneca, this time extracting the original thrust of Seneca's saying: "'Love of knowledge has become a mere study of words,' mere knowledge with no impact on one's ethical behavior" (p. 343). As for the term "classical," Nietzsche raises the problem of its meaning in a gloss on the title of his lectures, in which the political echoes latent in the Latin etymology of the word are explored.[30] "Classical" in a sense that begins to approach our own is a relatively belated usage even by ancient standards. As the antiquarian from the second century C.E. Aulus Gellius famously remarks, *classicus* originally designates the propertied tax-paying classes, in contrast to the lowest proletarian classes (*proletarius*), before being transferred to contexts of literary value (p. 341 n. 1). In the same note Nietzsche observes that the application of the term to the whole of Greek and Roman antiquity was a practice that began only in the Renaissance. Then comes a brief verdict, principally addressed to the notion of "classical antiquity" itself: "An aesthetic judgment lies therein." The shift in focus is significant. One might expect Nietzsche, the presumed aristocratic elitist, to thrill to the original sense of the term "classical." Instead, he embraces its aesthetic implications, and these, as we shall see, are highly equivocal.[31]

Consider his claim that classical scholars are of an "unaesthetic" cast of mind. It is not, in point of fact, because classicists have no talent for idealizing or for being modern that Nietzsche despises them. It is because they disavow the presence and influence of contemporary culture in their philology, and not least of all their own idealism. And so when he asserts that the study of the classics comprises nothing but "aesthetic judgments," he is not suggesting that philology take up the practice of aesthetics for the very first time. He is describing its unstated and ongoing practice. If antiquity appears to us today as a "phenomenon [*Erscheinung*]" that must be "judged from a standpoint that is both transhistorical and spatially removed" (p. 374), the logical consequence is plain to see. Receptivity to the past requires immersion in the only mode of apprehension available to us moderns, disavow this as we may: that of the aesthetic ideal. Judgment of the appearances of antiquity can only ever be "aesthetic," and the classical ideal (to be discussed below) is but one more expression of this fact.[32] The appeal to the modernist foundations of classical philology is therefore an ironical one, like the label "unaesthetic" itself: Nietzsche's position is as critical of the hidden (because unconscious or simply disavowed) but in any case modern *préjugés* of classical studies as it is of those studies themselves. And although Nietzsche is himself not concerned to use the term here, we will not go far wrong to see in his exposure of the aesthetic biases of philology a critique of modern "ideology"—that is, of the ideology of modernity in German culture since the Enlightenment, as this is expressed in classical philology.

Nor is the connection all that hard to make, and in other nearby contexts Nietzsche is keener to make it himself. The discipline of classics was after all the cornerstone of the entire educational system in Germany during Nietzsche's century (what he elsewhere ridicules as "the euphemism of '*klassische Bildung*'").[33] In the words of one scholar, "As a common treasury of ideas and experiences, [classical philology] linked almost all educated Germans, shaping into common forms the thought and language of men who in other respects agreed on nothing."[34] What is striking and original in Nietzsche's case is the way he succeeds in fusing the critique of modern ideology with a critique of classical philology, as if the one phenomenon were immediately reflected in the other. The study of the classics, he seems to be saying in all of his philology (with varying degrees of explicitness), gives a unique purchase on modernity—its imagined identity and its aesthetically fashioned self-image. It does so, however, in an inverted and alienated form, for "antiquity has in fact always been understood only *from the perspective of the present*" ("WPh," 3[62]). The myth of the classical world *is* the ideology of modernity in the German nineteenth century; and so too philology, in its untimeliness, expresses the inverted reality of modernity.

Viewed in this light, Nietzsche's paradoxical program for the aspiring classicist makes perfect sense: "Let him learn to speak and write Greek and Latin, [but] keep him completely away from the higher literary forms and from *realia*. Instead, bring him closer to the modern poets, make him wholly modern, put the present vividly before his eyes"—all in the name of "lovingly immersing oneself in antiquity" (pp. 344–45, 368, 390). To study the classics is inevitably to study them in a modern way; that is "the antinomy of philology" and the condition of its peculiar untimeliness ("WPh," 3[62]).[35] Hence, there is no contradiction in Nietzsche's mixed advice that cannot already be found in his discipline. After all, the very attempt to approach antiquity hermeneutically, through empathetic immersion and intuitive understanding, is an invention of the recent tradition of classical studies in Germany. And here the tradition is unanimous: "*Hineinleben* is the goal," indeed. As Goethe had declared to Herder in July of 1772, "Pindar is where I live these days."[36] Wolf, in his *Encyclopedia*, postulates for classicists a natural ability and "a certain fluency" and "facility of the soul" that allow the soul to "immerse itself empathetically [*hineinzustimmen*] in alien ideas" and thereby "imaginatively make present [to itself] a remote past."[37] Bernhardy, following suit, remarks (as we saw) on the "universality" of the modern spirit, which allows it to make itself at home (*einheimisch*) wherever it casts its gaze, whether in the past or in the present: its "horizon" is seemingly boundless. Boeckh, for his part, talks about "feeling" one's way through the barricades of the hermeneutical circle (which were erected in part by no less an authority than the skeptically minded sophist Gorgias of Leontini in the fifth century B.C.E.): "In certain cases, a complete understanding is achieved for the faculty of *feeling*." Here, "congeniality is a requirement" for "hermeneutical artists," who know how to draw on their native productive faculty, to wit "fantasy" (which is why for Boeckh philologists cannot be made but must be "born"). Apparently not even Gorgias can obstruct our view of the past: Boeckh has his number too, or so he thinks.[38] Hermann arrives at a similar view, though without the pretense of hermeneutical sophistication: one must be so intimately versed in ancient letters as to become practically an ancient oneself (*quasi ipse factus sit antiquus*), if one wishes to be able to retrieve the original sense and to inspire others with the same.[39] In urging classicists to aspire to immersion in the past, Nietzsche is plainly repeating the conventional gestures of classical philology—and then drawing the moral that others could not even afford to see, namely, that proximity to the past so conceived is by necessity aesthetically achieved, a matter of pure projection: it is a transferential effect.[40]

The implications of this insight, once they are brought to the fore, can be disorienting (not to say alienating). Nietzsche seems to delight in the havoc you could say he is sowing, although he is really only laying it bare. A letter to Rohde from 7 June 1871 confirms this impression: "I am now giving my lecture, 'Introduction and Encyclopedia,' to the amazement of my audience, who can scarcely recognize themselves in the picture of the ideal philologist that I am sketching." How Nietzsche's students actually received the lectures we can only guess. But another set of lecture notes, this time on Aeschylus'

Choephori, allows us to extrapolate some of what Nietzsche's procedure in the "Encyclopedia" course must have been like. In these other notes, Nietzsche actually scripts in his theatrical cues, in what appears to be an introductory segment to a lecture. The passage is worth citing in toto, so rare and informative a glimpse into Nietzsche's teaching style in the classroom does it provide:

> No one among us has seen the *Oresteia*; no one has heard it: an elaborate and backbreaking *guesswork* is required to understand things that would have been simple and easy [to follow] at the performance. Here goes one attempt to view things as real: I will tell you what I saw there. Naturally, much of this will be sheer fantasy. But we need to experience an *effect*; once we have that we can form an opinion about the artist. I want to sit in the theater not as an ancient but as a modern: my observations may well be pedantic; but at first I have to wonder at everything so as to comprehend it all afterward.
>
> I have a certain impression of the *Choephori* and I want to describe it. But what does it matter to us, you will say, what my impression is? Why don't I appeal to yours? Or to the work?—An impression is something rare. To attain it one has to add so much—which not everyone is able and willing to do.
>
> One shouldn't talk about poems, as Socrates says in the *Protagoras*. But I want to investigate for once what this *impulse* [*Trieb*; viz., to discuss poetry, especially Greek poetry] *is really worth*. Through one example [namely, the *Choephori*].
>
> Result: you students will be proved right in the particulars [if you don't follow my approach]: but on the whole, it [namely, the standard approach] is an act of insolence. How little there is to know at that point where knowledge first starts to be of value! That cannot possibly be the goal of a science! Critique of conjectural criticism.[41] (*KGW*, 2.2:34–35)

Nietzsche's parting shot nicely brings home one of the points of this exercise in paradox. If the posture of deliberate anachronism he is commending seems far-fetched, how can conjectural criticism—the art and science of restoring classical texts through supplements, deletions, and corrections— possibly seem justified in turn? Isn't the textual editing of (say) a play by Aeschylus ultimately like taking a front seat at a Greek theater and imagining oneself as present—as an "ancient"? Isn't this the peculiar presumptuousness, the "insolence," of scholarship itself? But how, on the other hand, is one to proceed otherwise, in the absence of the posture of knowing intimately, like an eyewitness, what was or wasn't the case? Isn't the appeal to presentism the only honest response one can give to the problems of historicity? Something like this—this puzzling lesson, and no doubt this exemplary method, which consists in playing havoc with the assumptions and expectations of his students—is the upshot of the "Encyclopedia" lectures as well, to which we may now return.[42]

Now, if the ultimate aim of the course of study Nietzsche recommends in the "Encyclopedia" is not greater proximity, whether to the past or the present, but greater alienation ("so as to feel the distance" and "the difference"),[43] the distances one learns to feel are not exactly the historical differences between modernity and antiquity. Rather, he is suggesting that a greater distance be put between classical antiquity, whatever it "really" may have been, and our conception of it. As elsewhere in Nietzsche, the "reality" of classical antiquity designates less what is true about the past, which is never really known as such, than what is false about its current idealization. That idealization is the product of the "classicizing" (typically, Hellenocentric) tendency whose "aim," detectable even in its most sober positivistic strains, "is to uncover a buried ideal world and to hold it up before the present day as a mirror of what is eternally valid," as Nietzsche puts it in his controversial inaugural lecture on Homer from 1869.[44] It is this tendency that produces the so-called classicalness of antiquity, its *Klassicität*, which can be known and exposed as false for the same reasons that the reality of antiquity cannot be known: classicalness exists alone for a modern subject. It is, after all, "*for ourselves* that we talk about classicalness, for our modern world" (pp. 345, 390).[45]

The classicalness of antiquity is not some intrinsic characteristic of the past but is rather *produced* by "understanding what is *classical* [*das Klassische*]" about the past. That, Nietzsche writes, "is the philosophical precondition of classical philology," as well as its "goal" (pp. 345, 368; cf. pp. 370, 390). Here he is repeating, in effect, the motto to his earlier inaugural lecture, with its transformation of philology into philosophy. His recommendation of Kant has its place here too, though not without a certain irony: philosophical idealism is useful above all for its ability to "correct" [!] naive conceptions of reality (p. 372). (In this respect, and to this end, Kant compares favorably to

Plato: their "union" is something the would-be philologist should strive to bring about [ibid.].) A vigorous aesthetic evaluation of the phenomena of antiquity is the prerequisite to their apprehension. The past has to be—and perhaps can only be—idealized; the capacity to produce this idealization has to be "instinctive" to the philologist, and so on. All this goes to show why "intimate familiarity" with the great neoclassicists and philhellenists of the preceding century is indispensable: only so can "we learn to feel, as it were with them and through them, *what classical antiquity means for the modern person*. We must awaken the impulse, the longing desire [*Sehnsucht*] [for the past] . . . *in order to feel the distances*" (p. 368; emphases added).

Nietzsche encourages his audience not to "shrink back in fear" before the "apparent paradoxes" that philology, by its very nature, must entail (p. 372). But it is far from clear just what a lucid and fearless stance toward the problem might add up to. Nietzsche's own position is archly perverse. At the very least, the shock of alienation urged upon the listener stands in a troubling tension with the imperative to familiarity. At the worst, Nietzsche is demonstrating how alien, not to say unreliable, the very concept of the familiar can in fact be.[46] Recommending in effect that the philologist *become what he already is*, he is critiquing the status quo in the form of its affirmation. The risks of such a strategy are evident. Nietzsche's engaging in a two-handed rhetorical practice could easily be mistaken for a desire to set classics on a humanistic footing again, in the wake of its contemporary drifting into austere positivism and historicism.[47] But to read him in this way would be to erase the alienating thrust of Nietzsche's critique, the aim of which is precisely to confront philology with its least wanted self-image, to make it uncomfortably conscious of what it least consciously is and does—which is, to produce an "idyll" of antiquity. Nietzsche's rhetoric is *deceptively* two-handed, or rather double-edged.

In the course of confronting classical studies with its repressed classicism, he is also out to revise the conceptions of "humanity" that underlay the classical humanism of the eighteenth and nineteenth centuries. With their assumptions about "'Greek cheerfulness'" and their prettification of the past (the view that everything classically antique must be "*as beautiful as possible*"), the humanism of classicism is plainly "false" and "naive"; hence, "beware of the expression 'Greek cheerfulness'" (pp. 370, 371).[48] But this rare moment of explicit critique directed at classicism, though it points ahead to Nietzsche's revaluation of cruelty, passion, and turbulence in the classical world and to his general (or rather quietly pervasive) critique of classicism within the lectures themselves,[49] has a more immediate purpose: it points back to the contradictions in Nietzsche's own apparent position. For how does one aestheticize the past—without aestheticizing and idealizing it? Is not his own "idyll" of antiquity meant to be of a "most beautiful" sort and the source of unrivaled pleasure? Nietzsche certainly cannot himself avoid this paradox. Oblivious to his own advice, he goes on to admire the "ideal" traits of Greek humanity: its profundity, mildness, artistic nature, and political sense . . . all "beautiful, noble forms" (p. 371). Nietzsche's Greeks, those splendid "works of art," in the final analysis are decidedly (and classically) "naive" (p. 437). Marked by "the stamp of simplicity," they represent a "transfiguration" of history and a retreat from it as well: Greece, he declares on the last page of the lecture notes, is a "place of refuge for every seriously minded person" (ibid.). Perhaps the greatest risk the lectures run in the end is incurring the charge not of idealism, but of self-contradiction.[50]

A notebook entry from the time, outlining the contents of the lectures, leaves little doubt as to where Nietzsche's true sympathies lie: "Weeks 7 and 8. *Classical* antiquity (against Wolf, Winckelmann, Goethe)."[51] Other notes show that this attitude was already formed in 1869/70: "against the new Hellenism [*Neu-Griechenthum*] (the Renaissance, Goethe, Hegel, etc.)"; "the 'Hellenic' since Winckelmann: an intense superficialization."[52] Nietzsche's position toward classicism in its canonical form is undeniably critical, and it runs beyond his desire to indict the classical profession for its disguised or failed classicism. To be indicted, in his view, is the very substance of classicism. By itself, this does not yet account for the style of his critique, but it does suggest that there is more to the apparent classicism of the "Encyclopedia" than meets the eye. The perverseness of Nietzsche's stance in the lectures, I want to suggest, lies not so much in his apparent identification with the biases of Winckelmann, Humboldt, and the philologists in their wake, as in his *overidentification* with their idealism—his excessive commitment to the classical ideal, the relentlessness with which he draws out its consequences, and the utter candor with which he inscribes into his program the tensions already present in classicizing discourse. Nietzsche here is something like a fanatic who, in his very fanaticism, in the sheer overproximity to the truth of the belief he embodies, repels even the most entrenched of his fellow believers at the mere sight of himself. In this way, Nietzsche manages to expose something of the inner, repressed perversity of classicism—including the repressed classicism of even the driest forms of historicist philology that were taking hold as the nineteenth century wore on, at the cost of the earlier humanism that had been the chief inspiration in the philological tradition until then.[53] Stating the obvious (so to speak), he shows what classicism already knows—namely, that its idealism is a product of modern German idealism and its yearnings. This was the admission that is all but fully explicit in Bernhardy, as we saw above. And it is on the verge of conscious awareness in all forms of classicism from the eighteenth century onward, whenever an honest glance is thrown at the abyss that separates glittering idealities from historical realities and the contingencies of the ideal, or whenever the hidden inner contradictions of idealism bubble up to the surface.

A brief look at the discourse of the classical ideal is needed at this point if we are to appreciate Nietzsche's running dialogue with this all-important tradition, but also if we are to grasp why classicism is not an option that Nietzsche can lightly recommend. The classical ideal and its various features in Nietzsche's lectures—its aesthetic form, its Platonism, its striving for totality, its separation from reality by a yawning "abyss [*Kluft*]"—are all derived from this tradition, as are the ensuing aporias, which Nietzsche merely puts on stage. Undoubtedly the most alluring of these is the aesthetic consistency of the classical ideal, its anchoring in a fantasy of beauty that is presumed not to be our own and yet incites us to identify with it—indeed, to make it our own.[54] This fantasy, which is the aesthetic illusion of classical antiquity itself, is a site of deepest incoherence and disavowal, and at times openly so. As will become evident in a moment, classicism can provide Nietzsche with no alternative to the disavowals of classical philology for the simple reason that *classicism constructs itself as a form of disavowal*, and is precisely the very element that philology most disavows about itself. Nor is Nietzsche any more aware of this fact than were his classicizing predecessors, who could close their eyes to their own practices at will so as to be able to perpetuate their undertakings, adopting the by now familiar gesture: "I know very well . . . , but just the same." In advocating a return to classicism as a program and a stance that has to be consciously assumed, Nietzsche retraces not so much classicism's fantasy of antiquity as the mere form of this fantasy, by restating its bare formal requirements—for instance, the unconscious imperative that one should aestheticize antiquity. Retraced in this way, and in Nietzsche's hands, the incoherencies of the doctrine are not only reproduced but embarrassingly magnified. A brief glance at a canonical vision of the classical ideal will help to illustrate how classicism could construct itself around a disavowal of its own aestheticizing program; and how this disavowal names the very logic of classicism that Nietzsche's lectures, through their performative contradictions, lay bare.

Wilhelm von Humboldt and the Classical Ideal

If Johann Joachim Winckelmann (1717–1768) was the chief inspiration behind the classical ideal in Germany, the chief architect of this same ideal was without a doubt the classical humanist and educator Wilhelm von Humboldt (1767–1835). A brilliant synthesizer and visionary, Humboldt exercised a powerful influence on his immediate contemporaries in the Weimar-Jena circle (most intimately, Goethe, Schiller, and the classical scholar and Homerist F. A. Wolf). He also had a lasting influence upon German culture, not least of all thanks to the central role he played both in the founding of the University of Berlin in 1809–10 and in the gymnasial curricular reforms of the Prussian state during the same period, which were eventually extended to the rest of Germany. The diffusion of his ideas was great, even if in the main indirect.[55] This explains why on at least one occasion Nietzsche (like countless other nineteenth-century philologists) seems to know enough to be able to reproduce an almost verbatim echo of Humboldt's views; whether this comes through an intermediary or through sheer intuition is unclear and for present purposes irrelevant.[56] Of interest to us here will not, in the first instance, be the specifics of Humboldt's writings, but the logic of his position, which is characteristic of German classicism and which was perfectly available to Nietzsche.

Humboldt's view of classical antiquity is complex, but it is consistent with the classicism of his contemporaries and that of later generations. The complexity of his view betrays the difficulties of its conception, but that, too, is typical. Ancient Greece, the *locus classicus* of all classicism, is for Humboldt a sunlit world unsullied by the divisions that run through modernity. Painfully remote from modernity, but also painfully close, it is a reminder of lost and seemingly unattainable possibilities. Winckelmann appeals to the ideal of classical perfection by way of its images in art, sensuously apprehended and quickened by the imagination. Humboldt, by contrast, appeals directly to the fantasy of that ideal, whether in its abstract formulation or as embodied in the imaginary objects of this fantasy, the ancient Greeks themselves, before whom one must kneel "as before images of gods."[57] These gods made flesh—who for Humboldt are a vanished "humanity," and more precisely the Greek Spirit incarnate—are extraordinary creatures who conveniently avoid the banes of a debasing "materiality" (which only "dulls one's strength") and who live, much like Nietzsche's later "free spirits," a winged existence "so as not to be impeded in the strivings of their power." Following the dictates of their nature, they "prefer to dwell in the more easily joined [parts of the] sensuous world . . . , now chimerical and boastful, now eager for fame and heroic, now sublime and idealistic [*idealisch*] in . . . their thought, poetry, and creativity," their lives completely bathed in "the intensity of a powerful mobility, . . . a naturally correct and uniform composure, . . . clarity, correctness . . . , [and] consequentiality"—all of which conspires to make them "capable of ideality."[58] Humboldt's Greeks are spontaneous idealists. So, too, are Nietzsche's own noble inventions (the archaic Greeks of the earlier writings and their avatars in the later writings), but that is another story.[59]

Humboldt is quick to concede the idealism of his own project, which has reality only in one sense—namely, as an incentive to moral self-improvement through emulation. That is the thrust of his much-cited imperative that one acquire a "knowledge of humanity in antiquity."[60] But he is equally quick to concede the quandaries that flow from his project—or rather, we ought to say, that are constitutive of it. For on closer examination, idealism isn't merely the postulation of an ideal; it is the construction of a conscience-racking dilemma, usually sanctioned by a moral imperative, and always designed to be irresolvable, as the following excerpt from one of Humboldt's seminal sketches on classical antiquity shows:

> Since every creature can be something only insofar as it is not something else, a genuine, ineliminable [*nicht aufzuhebender*] conflict comes about, an unbridgeable gulf [*Kluft*] between any two of even the most similar individuals and between all individuals and the ideal; [consequently,] the imperative to attain the ideal on the level of individuality is

impossible to execute.

Nevertheless, this imperative cannot be eliminated [*aufgehoben*].[61]

Is the self-inflicted painfulness and virtual masochism (in Nietzsche's later vocabulary, "asceticism") of the idealist program part of its attractiveness? Whatever the case may be, the point is simply that idealism constructs itself as an (ideal) contradiction. Translated into history and into classical studies, this means that the idealism of the Greeks is not merely found, as an ideal to emulate; it is invented, as ideally unreachable (for the road from any finite entity to the infinity of the ideal is itself "always only idealistic").[62] We have already seen some of the effects of this irresolvable dilemma in Bernhardy. The unbridgeable gap (*Kluft*) that exists between individuals and the ideal, or more generally between life and the ideal, also exists between antiquity and modernity, as it only can. For Humboldt and others, this historical and ideological gap is felt as a painful "contradiction" and dilemma (for how can the two worlds ever be joined?);[63] it exists to be felt, in order to reveal the deficiencies of modernity. Indeed, interest in the ideal past springs from dissatisfaction with the contemporary world, and so classical idealism is inevitably conceived as a form of cultural critique (as Nietzsche also recognizes):[64] the image of antiquity constitutes a standard by which modern culture can only fall miserably short, unless it promises to reform itself along the lines that classicism proposes. Salvation ("healing") is to come only through the study of antiquity and the cultivation of the humane self.[65] But how does this resolve the "contradiction" mentioned above, the precipitous abyss that exists "between all individuals and the ideal"? And what can the status of "knowledge of humanity in antiquity," so conceived, actually be?

Classicism plainly requires a kind of leap of faith. And with an enviable economy, the same leap leads both into and out of its dilemmas. Humboldt's solution to the contradiction just named, which is the contradiction of idealism itself (this "incessant schism"[66]), is imaginary and idealistic at once: it is a mental and spiritual glimpse of the impossible. The solution to idealism is, in other words, idealism all over again:

> An actual resolution of this contradiction, a true and genuine union of the ancient and modern species [*Geschlechts*] in a new, third species, is *inconceivable*, even on the most generous premising of infinite

perfectibility.

The only compensation is the fact that the truly highest (and not, as with the Greeks, symbolically highest) [ideal] by virtue of its nature cannot be represented in all of its totality in the being of an individual or nation. In reality, it can manifest itself only partially: it can be viewed and intimated as a whole—but only by the mind's thoughts, only in the depths of the breast, and *only in isolated, fortunate moments*.[67]

Clearly, classical idealism is by definition an aporetic doctrine that solves itself by its own means—idealistically. Idealism amounts to a willful blindness, for only so can the glaring inconsistencies in the image of the Greeks and in the very act of imagining them be overlooked, or rather, disavowed—whether this be by the classical idealists themselves or by their later interpreters. The tendency, especially in the latter case, is to skirt the tensions in the classical ideal and to view them as complementary and resolved in a "hard-won" higher unity rather than as strained and insolubly so.[68]

So much for the classical ideal. When we turn back to its representatives, the ancient Greeks, we find that Humboldt's image of them is far from being contradiction-free. This ought to come as no surprise, given what we have just seen of the classical ideal: how could Humboldt's Greeks fail to embody its contradictions? They are literally contradictory types, and he occasionally acknowledges as much himself, as if bemused by "the otherwise incomprehensible [!] contradictions" in their character, which he nonetheless views as ultimately "unified."[69] At one point, he proceeds to enumerate some of these: extremest sociability and an impulse to communication as opposed to a pathological need (*Sucht*) for withdrawal and loneliness; dwelling in light sensuality and art versus plunging into deepest speculation, not to say morose and metaphysical melancholia; "the most despicable stupidity and immense inconsistency, the most incredible fickleness, wherever agility and susceptibility to external stimuli [or "irritability," *Reizbarkeit*] gained the upper hand," versus "paradigmatic steadfastness and severest virtue, wherever their fire gathered itself together as a serious force in the depths of their spirit."[70] On a more general level, and pervading all of Humboldt's writings, is the contradictory claim that the Greeks are the essence of humanity and yet removed from humanity in its modern form by an unbridgeable gap.[71] Further, they "did not exactly shine in the perfection of moral education," living as they do (to coin a phrase) beyond good and evil, even if they are at the same time the moral exemplars for all civilization.[72] They "are chimerical"; and they are not—not "chimerical and fantastical," or rather "never" this; and so on.[73] The similarities with Nietzsche's Greeks are often overwhelming, as is the shared desperateness of the attempt to unify these contradictions in a single image.[74] Humboldt's characterizations and their irreconcilabilities would play themselves out for over a century to come (witness Bernhardy, above).[75] A result of this rapprochement between Nietzsche and the tradition, which ought to be disconcerting, is that to the extent that one buys into Nietzsche's image of the Greeks, whether taken by themselves or as prototypes of the *Übermensch* of the future, one has to take on board the classical ideal and its inconsistencies as well. But let us continue with Humboldt's dilemmas.

As one might expect, it is the Greeks' capacity for idealism that allowed them to unify—or efface—"the otherwise incomprehensible contradictions" in their character.[76] Humboldt's Greeks, we might say, are only ideally harmonious. In reality, they are riven by dilemmas that betray a desired ideality—that which they would exemplify. Nor is it the case that they achieve a higher spiritual synthesis by sublimating the antitheses in their character, as Humboldt and others would have us believe.[77] On the contrary, Humboldt's picture of the Greeks, and possibly their own self-portrait, vacillates, as if unable to decide whether to focus on a given trait or its opposite.[78] All the features of the Greeks are preciously theirs, but which are definitive? In the end, the only trait that matters is their ideality, which draws us to them. But that touches all their features—and, no doubt, their attractive irreconcilability. Inconsistencies such as these are but the extremest symptom of a project that superimposes its ideals, but also, inevitably, its modernity, upon the ever supple and forgiving mythology that is classical antiquity.

A curiously self-confirming circularity ensues. Spontaneous idealists, Humboldt's Greeks are "always *in search of* the necessary and the idea."[79] It is not enough that they should embody "the highest form of life, i.e., . . . the most human existence imaginable": they must "yearn" to represent such an existence, which can come about only in the wake of this desire, and, so too, in the form of an ideal.[80] In fact, a case could be made that for Humboldt it is the Greeks' yearning and their sense of self-deficiency, more than any triumph of perfection wrested from the hindrances of their own nature, which is the real source of their admirable "depth": "The ideality of a character depends on nothing so much as on the depth and the kind of desire [or "yearning" (*Sehnsucht*)] that inspire it."[81] One way of describing this restless striving is to say that *Humboldt's Greeks desire nothing so much as to become what they already are*, "pure and complete beings."[82] But the very superfluousness of this desire (why should the Greeks want to be what they already are?)[83] gives away its true source: such is the remarkable *compliance* of Greek antiquity in the face of a projective modern desire. This pattern will become patented, and it will affect anyone working in the shadow of the classical ideal. An example is the classical scholar K. O. Müller, whose portrait of the Dorians (1824) follows Humboldt's suit: the defining and unifying trait of these imagined *Ur*-Greeks is likewise "*a striving for unity in the whole.*"[84] They, too, desire nothing so much as to become what they already are: racially pure Dorians, which is to say, ideal Greeks. We will want to come back to Müller's troubled classicism below.

The compliance of the Greeks is worth pondering for a moment. What is astonishing about Humboldt's Greeks is how they can at times seem unexpectedly *modern*, and never more so than in their desire to be ideal Greeks. "Striving for ideality," after all, is a quintessentially modern desire, as Humboldt is the first to concede and as Bernhardy later confirms (as we have seen). Strictly (or ideally), Humboldt would have striving after the ideal be a universally human essence.[85] Thus, the German nation surpass the French, and "possibly even" the Greeks, Humboldt muses, insofar as the Germans strive after ideal, unattainable objects, while the French are content to find what they seek at the level of reality (in a "real object of striving"[!]).[86] But there is no point in belaboring the issue, which is obvious and clouded only by Humboldt's waverings: if the Greeks are sometimes said not to strive after what they naturally exemplify,[87] the moderns eternally—and embarrassingly—strive to become *what they are not.*[88] In any event, Humboldt's attempts to hold apart such poles as "classical" and "romantic" or "modern" and "Greek" all stumble over the antinomies of the ideal noted earlier.[89] He is at least occasionally frank about the anachronism of his conception: it is contrived so as to be intelligible, and seductive, to contemporary *Germans*.[90] The Greeks are a modern ideal, not a historical reality.

This point about the ahistoricity of the ideal Greeks cannot be emphasized enough (and, needless to say, it will be an important factor in Nietzsche's critical staging of classicism). Humboldt's Greeks are not merely a symbol and a norm for humanity in its most perfect form, as he says and as commentators reiterate for him.[91] They are, quite simply, a symbol of their own classicizing mandate, which they fulfill through their own most active faculty, the imagination, and through their desire for ideality. They *fantasize* their own ideality. That is also what makes them so appealing to the modern imagination, if not altogether modern: they do the work of the imaginary for us and, as it were, in our absence, and therefore in a purer form.[92] In this way, they do more than fulfill the classical ideal. In their disguise of antiquity, they reenact the very disavowal that is constitutive of the classical ideal. Desire and imagination, after all, are the instruments not only of idealization but of disavowal. The mirroring of Greeks and Germans, down to this last detail, is perfect.

Humboldt had set up the Greeks as a frankly ahistorical ideal that exists solely for the self-advancement of modernity: "For us, the Greeks are not only a people that is useful to know historically, but an ideal." And more radically still: "For us, . . . the Greeks step completely out of the circle of [history]. . . . Knowledge of them is not simply pleasant, useful, and necessary for us; in them alone do we find the ideal of what we ourselves should like to be and to produce. . . . They move us, *not by compelling us in their way but by inspiring us in our own way*" to strive after the idea (and ideal) of complete perfection. In other words, the Greeks, thus modeled and in their ahistoricity, inspire us not to be more like them but to be *more ourselves*.[93] Humboldt's educational ideal was destined to become the official model for the German gymnasial and university systems for the century to come. It must have succeeded in attracting as many generations as it did, not in spite of but precisely on account of the open duplicity of its pragmatic and, as it were, realistic idealism. Here, disavowal is made into an art form: belief in the classical ideal can be self-willed, and it can even be denied (say, as a "fantasy") in the way that it commonly is denied in classicizing discourse, so long as the ideal, vaunted for its "usefulness," does not threaten us (its exponents) with a refutation of our "real" existence; and so long as we continue to *act* as if we believe in the ideal, despite its sheer impossibility.[94] Winckelmann had left the door similarly open with his wry paradox that "the only way for us to become great, and indeed—if this is possible—inimitable, is by imitating the ancients," who are themselves inimitable.[95] There was a certain attractiveness to this position, which played into the hands of the cultural projects of the nineteenth century: the self-fashioning of German identity, its fantasy of Germanness, which could be built on top of the fantasy of Greekness. Nietzsche is keenly aware of this larger dimension of classicism, and his exposure of its mechanisms are for this very reason tied directly to his critique of contemporary culture. Let us briefly consider some of the ways in which Nietzsche's critique treats classicism as a producer and consumer of cultural illusions.

The Logic of Disavowal

Plainly, classicism is staked on a disavowal of its own premises and of its own impossibility. The classical ideal could come about in no other way. Classicism could only succeed—not as a belief but as a persuasion—if it disavowed itself, in effect by disavowing its own disavowals. It offered a high tolerance of self-awareness in return for a high quotient of illusion. We have already seen how open Humboldt can be about the unattainability of the classical ideal, about its "idealism" in this precise sense. He does not commit his metaphysical sins unawares, nor is he under any illusions. And in this respect, too, he is entirely typical. Classicism is not a blind delusion, despite its frequent caricature as such. It is a *clear-eyed* delusion, a delicate form of disavowed consciousness. Advocates of the classical ideal knew full well that they were misreading antiquity. They could occasionally chide each other for overidealizing the past, the way Friedrich Schlegel could repeat, rather than divulge, the open secret that "everyone has found in the ancients what he needed or wished to find: *chiefly, himself.*" Goethe had like things to say about Winckelmann in the course of promoting him as a cultural icon, in the same way that Schiller could accuse his contemporaries of "Graecomania" while blithely persevering in his own mania for the Greeks.[96] And so on. They knew exactly what was at stake, and they wrote this knowledge into their projects—in the form of its disavowal. Classical antiquity may be a "deception," but it is at least a "necessary deception" (so Humboldt in a letter to Goethe, defending their common stance, not apologizing for it).[97] Hence the contradictory gestures of the classicizers, the many confessions and denials, all attesting to the sheer impossibility at the heart of the classicist undertaking. "We imitate their models with an awareness of their unattainability," Humboldt would write, and that is the source of their greatness and their ideality.[98]

What could not be acknowledged and probably not even perceived by the exponents of classicism was that the "necessary deception" of the classical ideal had no necessity to it at all: its fundamental contingency was the one major blind spot in the classical ideal. Thus, the actual deception lay not in the fantastic, projective illusion of Greece (which was plain for all to see), *but in the very illusion of its necessity*.[99] An all too frank recognition of the stakes of this delicate game would taint it irreparably, ruining the lure of the ideal by dragging it down to the level of a crude utilitarianism, precisely by exposing the emptiness of the classical ideal, its absence of any foundation, its utter lack of intrinsic necessity, and hence vitiating its justification as a source of potential truth and value. To adopt a Nietzschean idiom, the classical ideal was driven not by a necessity but by a *need*, and not least of all by the need that the ideal should at all costs appear to be compellingly necessary. This need was what had to remain opaque to the agents of classical self-deception.[100] Nietzsche's inquiries into the irrationality of necessity, into the existence of a "necessity without aim," in his overlapping studies of Democritus and Kant (discussed earlier), would have warned him away from any overvaluation and idealization of the concept of necessity and of the belief, as it were, in the necessity of necessity: like "the concept of a whole" or "totality," the idea of necessity "resides not in things, but in us"; it is "our work," and a mere "representation."[101] Nietzsche's thoroughgoing skepticism sets him definitively apart from Humboldt's shrewd but ultimately naiver posture.

It is not by chance that classicism resembles the phenomenon that Nietzsche would later call by the name of Christian belief, but which in fact stands for the whole realm of cultural persuasions by which contemporary subjects live: "Above all, [Christianity] knows that it is in itself a matter of absolute indifference whether a thing be true, but a matter of the highest importance *to what extent* it is believed to be true" (*A*, 23). To appreciate the irony of this remark, one has to realize that by "Christianity" Nietzsche means to designate the Christianity of practicing Christians themselves, who know but deny the true nature of their convictions. Only so can he account for the irreducible fascination exerted by a believer's highest hopes and ideals: for these "cannot be refuted by any actuality"—or be "*done away with* by any ful-filment."[102] This, incidentally, throws an interesting light on Nietzsche's later concept of *ressentiment*, which designates not so much the emotion of resentment as the calculated play of affect within a subject, along the lines just described (and following the literal sense of the word): it is a form of self-manipulation. The impossibility of the classical ideal is one instance of this play of affect and its fascination. The absolute elusiveness of what classicism holds out in the form of a promise (sublime elevation, immersion in an alien, vanished world, imitation of the inimitable) is the source and not the refutation of its never-ending attractions. But Nietzsche's exposure of the mechanisms by which classicism establishes itself has a further implication that needs to be mentioned before we turn back to the "Encyclopedia."

Perhaps the most fundamental deception of classicism is the assumption that its illusions are self-willed, as it were consciously adopted and then just as consciously forgotten; and what is more, that its illusions are restricted to the realm of classical antiquity and are not symptomatic of modernity at large. Classicism thus makes itself plausible as an illusion that one can choose to have, and on rational grounds (the classical ideal is "necessary" to human enlightenment, growth, perfectibility, and so on). What classicism thereby represses (disavows) is the fact that illusion is itself a basic con-stituent of human action in the world today. Avowing the necessity of a lim-ited deception, as classicizers pretend to do, is a way of disavowing the actual necessity of deception, its utter pervasiveness in contemporary human life, its "timeliness," and its ineliminability as such. This, then, is the ultimate object of Nietzsche's critique, which is culturally critical in the broadest sense: it takes in the illusions that are constitutive of culture. In the nine-teenth century, classical antiquity is one of the constitutive illusions of mod-ern culture. Classicism is, in other words, an accomplice of modernity.

If this is the farthest-reaching object of Nietzsche's critique, there is a correspondingly far-reaching consequence to it as well. In miming the ges-tures of classicism and, at least in his "Encyclopedia," in setting forth a pro-gram for its cultivation, Nietzsche is asking classical idealists not only to avow their disavowal (to accept the fact that antiquity is an aesthetic illusion) but to ponder the limits of their capacity to do so. Ultimately, Nietzsche's critique has a deeply disturbing moral: it points to the fact that idealism is not some privileged category that can be elected at will but is rather an ineradicable fact of our culture and of our subjectivity. Disavowal may be avowed, *but it cannot be eliminated*, while idealism is the presumption that it can. Even when it is avowed in classicism, idealism always reappears, as a form of disavowal, in some other sector of contemporary life where it is least expected. One instance of this is to be found in the phenomena that Nietzsche will later collect under the heading of the "ascetic ideal" (atheism, science, and historical consciousness are three of its products).[103] Disavowal and self-deception are thus by no means limited to the safer and controlled realm of classicism, while classicism is beginning to look like a desperate defense against this very uncontrollability. A profound blindness lies at the root of disavowing mechanisms, and it is these, finally, that Nietzsche's exposure of classicism brings painfully to light. Thus, Nietzsche's critique takes in its sights a fundamental feature of modern subjectivity of which classicism is but a special, albeit a significant and instrumental, instance. As a result, the mechanisms of classicism can be seen to enjoy an unexpected pervasiveness and even banality in contemporary culture, while the historical contingency of classicism reveals something essential about the organization of modern desires. Here, Nietzsche would heartily agree with Humboldt's brilliant insight that one's character is defined by the style and shape of one's desires.[104] Nietzsche's "Encyclopedia" is ultimately a study in the modern shapes of desire. It is a study in the modern imaginary and its fascinations.

Philology as Philosophical Prejudice

Given the psychological irrefutability of the classical ideal, Nietzsche can at best hope to mine it from within, by exposing its various, competing logics. He is not, in any case, interested in ruining the lure of the ideal, for that is what furnishes the lure of his own critique. He is interested, rather, in exploiting this fascination and all the paradoxes of classicism. In restating the ideal in a literal way and by urging that philologists become what they already are, Nietzsche in his "Encyclopedia" is doing more than merely retracing the logic of classicism: he is mimicking its perversity.

If Humboldt's scholars become classicists in order to become fully modern, Nietzsche's become modern in order to become complete classicists. The circle is the same; Nietzsche simply steps into it from the opposite end, with disorienting results. Plainly, the imperative "Become what you are!" is no less a leitmotif for the earlier Nietzsche than it is for him later on (*GS*, 270; *Z*, IV:1). (The Greek original, taken from Pindar, supplies the epigraph to his 1867 prize-essay *De fontibus Diogenis Laertii*.) The imperative is a nonsensical one, adding nothing to what a subject is or does, because what it enjoins is what a subject most naturally and spontaneously (and unconsciously) does anyway. It has no literal meaning, but only a strategic one. In the case of the "Encyclopedia," the imperative is at once the implied moral of the lectures and part of their alienating thrust. In this way philology can be made, for once, into the problem that it is: "*Philologists* who speak about their science never get to the *root* of things, never represent philology as a problem. Bad conscience? Or absent-mindedness?" ("WPh," 5[135]). On the other hand, "critical" philologists are not being asked to practice a fundamentally novel kind of philology. Quite the contrary, they are being encouraged to be more like the philologists they already are—to become what they are and to assume to an even greater degree the antinomies that their position vis-à-vis the past and the present already entails, to the extent they can at all. Small wonder that Nietzsche's ideally envisaged pupil should resemble the contemporary classicist in more ways than one. In his unconscious activity ("He should learn nothing besides immediate action"); in his presentism ("Keep him completely away from the high [Greek and Latin] literary forms and from *realia*"); and in his "sentimental enjoyment" of the past (à la Schiller, but also Humboldt),[105] the pupil is a modern *tabula rasa*: "He understands absolutely nothing about antiquity. Nor anything about philosophy." All that he knows is how to "speak and write Greek and Latin" (p. 345)! Nietzsche's shrewd (if baffling) critique lies in his stating what is the case in the form of an earnest imperative.

Nietzsche's exposure of classicism as a form of aestheticism runs parallel to his critique of teleology in philosophy as a disguised form of aesthetic intuition.[106] His conscious adoption of aestheticism in the form of anachronism plays into his inversion of classicism. Humboldt explicitly warns against overvaluing an aesthetic appreciation of antiquity, to which he opposes a deeper, historical knowledge (much like his contemporary and close friend, F. A. Wolf). He would never concede that classicism is itself an aestheticizing view of the past, for obvious reasons. But then he seems never to have clearly thought through the puzzles of his position either, for as we saw he also abandons historicity in favor of a transhistorical (or ahistorical) ideal that centrally involves, once again, an aesthetic dimension that is irresistible in its attractions.[107] In contrast, Nietzsche resists these circumlocutions and makes the aesthetic criterion itself, as an experience one has, directly into the ideal: "The *aesthetic* . . . is a matter of ascending to the highest heights of the ideal" (p. 374). Ironically, if you want to find out what this means, Nietzsche's best counsel is that you read the likes of Humboldt: read the idealists, cultivate their peculiar form of modernism, follow their program, accommodate yourself to their dilemmas—and then you will discover how classical idealism is in fact *produced*, as an aesthetic illusion. Although superficially out of tune with his own ostensible program, his passing critique of classicizing meters à la Goethe has its place here, too. "Our imitation in ancient meters is an illusion: our hexameters and that of the Greeks have nothing in common" (p. 399). The Greek rhythms, the soul of their poetry ("the principle element that created the perfect form" in Greek culture [p. 397]), have a consistency we cannot even imagine—or else can *only* imagine. "It is hardly possible for us to have any feeling at all for a purely quantitative rhythmics" such as the Greeks enjoyed, Nietzsche would maintain throughout his life.[108] This dissonance is only one of the many indices that there is trouble afoot with the classicism of Nietzsche's lectures—and yet how else can one approach the ancients today except by "reading with Germanic accents" (p. 398)? In a word, Nietzsche's most powerful instrument for exposing the contingency of the classical ideal is simply naming its modern sources—so that we may "feel the distances." His reduction of Homer to the product of an "aesthetic deception" (as we saw in the context of Wolf's *Prolegomena*) is part and parcel of this critical alienation of the present.[109]

As the duplicities of Nietzsche's project heap up, they continuously curve back upon themselves. Nietzsche in effect shows aspiring classicists (which all classicists by definition are) how one can become the idealist one already is. Eschewing the delicacies of his predecessors in classics, for whom idealism stands for the mere desirability of a desideratum (as opposed to its attainability), Nietzsche locates idealism immediately in the structure of (modern) subjective identity itself. Idealism is, quite simply, desire *tout court*, the unhinderable desire for ideal and imaginary solutions, identifications, and disavowals—quintessentially, the desire to disavow one's modernity and the actual *banality* of idealism. Idealism is pervasive. Is classicism an attempt to dignify desire? Philologists of a more positivistic mindset would object, but for Nietzsche they are scarcely an exception. Nietzsche knows very well that classical philologists who may appear to have "skeptically abandon[ed] the Hellenic ideal and completely pervert[ed] the true purpose of antiquarian studies [*Alterthumswissenschaften*]"[110] in the name of a desiccated historicism and once classicism had begun to fall out of fashion in Germany earlier in the century, are in fact the true contemporary adherents of classical idealism. That is implied in the very idea of a unified (and venerable) object of study, the charms of which never fail to attract no matter how severely the discipline is conceived. Nor does the commitment to an edifying ideal ever fade.[111] The value of their antiquity is an aesthetic and (so too) a philosophical one, a point that was likewise made in the inaugural lecture on Homer: "I would like to try to make clear through a single example how the most significant steps of classical philology never lead away from the ideal antiquity but rather *to* it, and how it is exactly in those places where one abusively speaks about the overthrow of the holies, that *in fact merely newer and more venerable altars have been built*." The latest and most venerable of these is not the personality of Homer, for research since F. A. Wolf's historicizing labors had rendered that issue "no longer timely [*zeitgemäß*]" and had shown Homer to be "not an historical tradition but an aesthetic judgment," and thus something far more pervasive and therefore less salient as an altar of worship: it is the "whole magical world" of classical antiquity itself, the object of an undimmed "reverence." Hence, today's scholarship continues to "take comfort" in telling tales "about the divine figures of a distant, blue, and fortunate magic land"—and in not doing so as well (at least by assuring itself that this is not the case).[112] To help bring classicists more readily to this admission, Nietzsche encourages them to take up Plato, the Greek idealist, and his modern counterpart, Kant, so as to come all the more directly into contact with the "philosophical precondition" of the study of antiquity, the classical ideal (p. 345).

Nietzsche's effective inversion of Seneca ("What was once philology has now been made into philosophy") made sense against the background of his *Democritea*, but that move seems oddly out of place here in the "Encyclopedia." The concept of classical antiquity may well be an "aesthetic judgment," but in what way is it "philosophical"? In the same way that it is an aesthetic judgment, Nietzsche will reply, for by "philosophy" he means to designate no more than what falls within the realm of prejudice, ideology, or the hidden mainsprings (and aesthetic criteria) of belief and action—including, if need be, the very denial of philosophical prejudice itself: philosophy is all of these things, and it is never anything but them. Nietzsche's later comment from *Beyond Good and Evil* is entirely apt in the context of his "Encyclopedia," and it also helps bring out a further dimension to the original meaning of the earlier motto: what philosophers vaunt as their "truth" is "at bottom . . . an assumption, a hunch, indeed a kind of 'inspiration'—most often a desire of the heart that has been filtered and made abstract—that they defend with reasons they have sought after the fact" (*BGE*, 5, "On the Prejudices of Philosophers"). This reasoning *post festum* may be dignified with the term "philosophy," but that merely disguises as a prejudice what is cultural in the broadest sense. *For culture*, in Nietzsche's eyes, *is nothing but the sum of illusions and denials by which we live*, as well as the "philosophical" justification of their rightness. This is a point that will be deepened in the *Birth of Tragedy*, and not only under the more pronounced influence of Schopenhauerian existentialism. Another name for this kind of justification is "aesthetic" (a point that will be notoriously central to this same work).[113] Nor is philology immune to either tendency. Compare the following from "We Philologists" (1875), a passage that looks back to earlier notes and incidentally paves the way for Nietzsche's "doctrine" of the will to power:

> It is the job of all education to reeducate conscious activities into more or less unconscious ones: and the history of mankind is in this sense its education. The classical philologist now exercises a vast number of activities unconsciously in this same way: that is what I want to investigate one day, how his power [*Kraft*], i.e., his instinctive doings, are the result of formerly conscious activities that gradually he hardly any longer feels as such: but *that [former] consciousness consisted in prejudices. His present* power rests *on those prejudices*. . . . Prejudices are, as Lichtenberg says, the *artistic drives of mankind*. ("WPh," 5[87]; Nietzsche's emphasis)[114]

The example of prejudice given here is the privileging of *ratio* (reason) by Bentley and Hermann (presumably, the "Kantian" assumptions in their theories of metrics and time discussed earlier), but other examples are easily imaginable.[115] The "philosophical preconditions" of philology go right to the heart of the ideology that rules classical studies, and nowhere more so than when these assumptions are concealed or denied.[116] Such "preconditions" are centrally involved in what Nietzsche in his "Encyclopedia" calls the "unconscious construction of parallels" between past and present in the hermeneutic effort to approach antiquity today (p. 373).[117]

As it happens, and as we have occasionally witnessed above, classical philologists of the nineteenth century do in fact bring philosophical presuppositions in the narrower sense to their philology. Sometimes they do so blithely, sometimes disguisedly or unawares (as in the appeal to self-evidence), sometimes reluctantly, but in any case always by way of a justification of their enterprise.[118] August Boeckh's uneasy regard for philosophy is well known.[119] Yet his uncertain designation, in his own *Encyclopedia*, of the essence of the philological object as "that which the philosophers call the *principle* of a people or an age, the innermost kernel of its total being," and his identification of that object with "antiquity *an sich*," or rather its "idea," is just one example of this kind of justification, done in bad faith.[120] The view that antiquity is a totality that scholarship must laboriously approximate, however imperfectly, had been the foundational premise of classical studies ever since Wolf. Not unjustifiably, then, could Nietzsche say of Boeckh that he had "perfected the concept of *Altherthumsstudien*."[121] What Boeckh understood by this concept emerges from his definition of one of philology's main tasks: "removing the falsification of the ages and prior misunderstanding, [thereby] unifying into a whole what does not appear as whole."[122] Significantly, Boeckh will call the approximative striving of philology "ideal" ("The task . . . is admittedly only an ideal, never to be fully attained," etc.), but not the target of the approximation.[123] The justification he gives, which was cited earlier, shows how irretrievably bound up with contemporary conceptual grids philology at its purest can be. Let us look at the fuller context:

> A commonality [*ein Gemeinsames*] has to be found in which every particular is contained. This is what the philosophers call the *principle* of a people or an age, the innermost kernel of its total being [*Gesammtwesens*]; something else it cannot be, for anything else would be strange, brought in from without. The particulars should not be *deduced* from this principle, which is impossible in things historical, but rather they

should arise out of a general intuition [*Anschauung*], and this must in turn prove true of each of the individual parts; this [intuition] is the soul of the body . . . [and] its organizing causal principle . . . : thanks to this animation, science becomes, precisely, *organic*.[124]

To whom, precisely, does this intuition belong? Seeing how Boeckh goes on to identify the intuition with "the idea of antiquity *an sich*," it is safe to say that this idea is itself an ideal, one that is circuitously written into the philologist's object.[125] Nietzsche's real target is thus a whole series of legitimizing assumptions that are betokened by these philosophical borrowings and their multiple anachronism. Like Humboldt, Boeckh's greatest failing is his unwillingness to accept what Nietzsche takes for a fact: philology's inescapable presentism.[126] Meanwhile, positivism, which Boeckh partially fostered, suffers from the same delusions, in the guise of a demystified glimpse into "timeless" and "eternal" scientific reality: the belief that knowledge can be demythologized is itself mythological.[127] The hidden classicizing biases of philological positivism, which could also take the form of "historicism," will be discussed in more detail in the next chapter, as will the underlying cultural frameworks that made these intellectual moves possible.

"Nobody enters into antiquity with a leap out of the blue," Nietzsche writes in the contemporary lectures "On the Future of Our Educational Institutions."[128] One must first awaken "the feeling for the classical and the Hellenic" through the example of "the leaders and mystagogues of classical education," Winckelmann, Lessing, Schiller, Goethe, and Wolf, "under whose guidance alone can be found the correct way that leads to antiquity, . . . the land of desire, . . . Greece."[129] The attempt to go unaccompanied to the source, to leap into antiquity from nowhere, gives rise to the prevailing "deceptions" and "misunderstandings" in today's pedagogy: it is the "delusion that one can disavow the German national spirit and leap, as it were, directly and in the absence of any bridges, into the alienated [*verfremdete*] Hellenic world"—alienated, that is, by classical humanistic education. Only by cultivating "the feeling" for the classical (*das Klassische*) can one enter into communion with the past and learn to appreciate "the Greeks as Greeks," a capacity that has evidently withered away. Humboldt would only have agreed.[130] But when was this capacity ever fully possessed? As we saw, Humboldt's very own Greeks are in search of this same desire. Nietzsche qualifies the delusional wish to project oneself into the past as "un-German, practically foreign or cosmopolitan." But of course nothing is more characteristically German than this kind of leap out of the blue into antiquity: it describes the very leap of faith that is the daily routine of classicism itself, which on the contrary projects itself *as* "un-German, practically foreign or cosmopolitan"—ideally, as Greek.[131] This is surely the final unstated irony of Nietzsche's commentary, put in the mouth of a fictional "philosopher," in praise of the German ideal of classical education. Hence the imperative, uttered near the close of the same passage, to seek out the German spirit wherever it may be in hiding, in any of its guises, whatever its "fashionable trappings" may conceal it to be: "One has to love [the German spirit] and not be ashamed of it even in its shriveled form" today.[132]

Classicism, Nietzsche seems to be saying (while appearing to deny it), is a typically modern, and especially modern German, "delusion."[133] His critique could easily apply to Bernhardy's overconfidence in the universality of the modern spirit that "feels comfortably at home [*einheimisch*]" wherever it casts its gaze, whether in the past or in the present, its universal "horizon" seemingly boundless. That is a claim that, as we saw, sits awkwardly next to its corollary about the absolute incommensurability of antiquity and modernity. In attempting to hold these irreconcilable ideas together, Bernhardy is merely exemplary. Humboldt, for his part, could hold that "nothing modern is comparable to anything from antiquity"—and yet the Greeks are "flesh of our flesh, bone of our bone."[134] In reproducing these irreconcilabilities in another form, and in reminding classicism of its sheer distance from antiquity, Nietzsche is mimicking, rather than endorsing, the German, un-German condition of the classical world "today."

Classical 'Bildung'

In their pedagogical implications, Nietzsche's "Encyclopedia" lectures have a more pragmatic reference in the modern world: the educational institutions by which culture is shaped and passed on. This was also the lesson of his inaugural lecture on Homer, which opens with the thesis "that philology, in its origins and at all times has simultaneously been the science of pedagogy"—indeed, the central core of pedagogy ("ECP," 250). Historically, this is a valid observation, and it continued to be valid thanks to the educational reforms instituted by Humboldt at the turn of Nietzsche's century and until their drastic modification at the end of the century.[135] Nietzsche's appreciation of the nexus formed by classicism, classical study, and the educational mandates of society is deep, and it speaks directly to the material production of knowledge and of cultural subjects. It is also of a piece with his earliest philological thinking, which displays a strong interest in "the social position" and educational formation of philosophers and of philologists in antiquity and the present. It is partly out of this perspective that his "history of literary studies in antiquity and modernity" was to have been written.[136] And although he does not use the term himself, these institutions are best described as the manufacturers of modern ideology. We might compare the following note from Nietzsche's unfinished essay "We Philologists," his most extended tirade against the discipline, although identical sentiments are expressed much earlier:

> Classical philology is the seat of the shallowest possible form of enlightenment: always dishonestly used, [it has] gradually become utterly ineffectual. Its net effect is one more illusion for modern man. Actually, what is involved here is just a professional class of educators, not priests: the state has a vested interest in this. ("WPh," 5[124]).

The modern state has a vested interest in the formation of classicists and in their role, which is to be otiose, precisely because it is their function to be completely absorbed in the maintenance of modern ideological illusion. Their status as agents of mystification (*Zauberei*) must be invisible, not only to society at large but also to themselves (this is what in *The Birth of Tragedy* is called "the powerful mythical foundation" of the modern state and its "unwritten laws").[137] Nietzsche's analysis is penetrating, and it is prompted by actual developments.[138]

In his public lecture series from the early months of 1872, "On the Future of Our Educational Institutions," Nietzsche speaks prophetically of an extension to all parts of Germany of the Prussian state educational reforms enacted in the earlier part of the century. That trend would lead only to an acceleration of education's effects ("pseudo-education"), "the hasty and fruitless production" of scholarship (the "disgraceful production of books" for its own sake, or more crudely, for income), and a kind of Taylorism of intellectual labor, through specialization, that turns academic researchers into "factory workers" and "drones."[139] This was the beginning of a debate that would become known as the *Kulturkampf*, through the activity of Rudolph Virchow in 1873 (Virchow was among other things a promoter of the Prussian state reforms against the hegemony of the Roman Catholic church). Nietzsche, ever resistant to the militant connotations of *Kultur* and favoring the old-fashioned idiom, would designate the stakes of the battle with the word *Bildungskampf*.[140] At the center of this turmoil stood classical studies, which happened to be closely allied in name and mission with the study of German classical writers: together these constituents of the "so-called *klassische Bildung*" formed the privileged foundation of the educational system in Nietzsche's century, especially at the gymnasium (secondary) level. Classicists did indeed seem to participate in the general, "national" economy of state-sponsored culture (the term cited by Nietzsche and in circulation at the time was *Kulturstaat*). On his analysis, culture at the level of the state was governed by an economy of overproduction, and its aims were exhausted in the production of production, in the creation of empty needs and their illusory fulfillment (self-contentment and happiness, in both a material and a psychological sense).[141]

Nietzsche's worries are not limited to the institutional forms that impinge on classical study. Of equal concern to him are the peculiar ways in which those constraints have been internalized and legitimized, and the implications of these processes for cultural formations at large. Not the least of his concerns has to do with the way in which these constraints become internalized in the form (and the formation) of the modern category of the subject. Hence the distinguishing marks of the classicist, which are also those of the modern cultural subject: "flight from reality" and "from the self," cleverness in disguise and mendacity, the unwitting "antinomies" of historical self-definition.[142] In each case, classical antiquity furnishes what looks like a compensatory instance: the flight into an imaginary past provides a flight from reality; the Greeks' naive simplicity and lack of disguise may be vicariously savored, and so on. Yet paradoxically these compensations are a lure, for in each case imaginary displacement, which for Nietzsche is an essential trait of modernity, is in fact the reality that is being fled. As a result, the act of fleeing is itself imaginary, a mere dreamt-of flight. To delight in simplicity in its

Greek form is the height of (disavowed) cleverness, just as the presumed linear progression of history, with its neat division into past and present, is the reassuring product of a circular and reflexive definition of history: it is the product of a certain ahistorical thinking, in the eyes of which, by contrast, the humanism of classicism (the appeal to the classical ideal of Winckelmann and others) could likewise appear to be a flight from historical reality. Meanwhile, the opposite impulse to historicism (the new and opposed tendency of the nineteenth century) could pretend to escape this charge.[143] Nietzsche is critical of both perspectives, as will be shown in the final chapter. The "Encyclopedia" brings these same antinomies to light and to a head in another form, following yet another strategy, to which we may now turn.

The Logic of Classical Time

Philological inquiry into antiquity is plainly an exercise in contradiction ("untimeliness"). Only, the aestheticization of the past is what *produces*, not what heals over, this contradiction. To train oneself in the ways of modernity as any classicist must do (and in this respect Nietzsche's "Encyclopedia" offers a completely characteristic apprenticeship) is to reproduce what is modern about antiquity today; it is to reproduce the *symptoms* of a classicized antiquity, while antiquity itself is but a symptom of the present. Classical studies, Nietzsche seems to be saying, have both invented and alienated their object, in unwitting concert with the dominant cultural ideologies of the modern age, especially over the recent century. What those studies take as their object is an ideal antiquity, which is an aestheticized image projected from the present. A paradox of Nietzsche's critique is that it attempts to alienate alienation, as it were, by reproducing (and thus rendering visible) the very symptom it seeks to dislodge. We might think of this in Brechtian terms: everyday, transparent alienation is here subjected to a further critical distancing, not from some outer Archimedian point (for that would simply be to reproduce the initial alienation, on the pretense that a "safe" distance can be assumed), but from within (reproducing the very symptom of alienation, in all its incomprehensibility). Nietzsche accomplishes this effect by exposing and identifying with the symptom of classicism—a deeply alienating set of moves, because it estranges the projected image of the classical past and returns it to the present, in a disturbing proximity. Hence, all talk of immersion and empathy notwithstanding, alienation is the ultimate object of Nietzsche's lectures. To put this in the language of the lectures, it is only by aestheticizing antiquity in a conscious way that one can come to sense the fundamental "distance" that irreparably divides the "alienated" past from modernity.

Needless to say, this distance is an ideological and not a historical one: it is the distance that contemporary thought produces between itself and the past. The distance can be collapsed by drawing it closer to its source. Thus, instead of critiquing the classicizing premises of philology, Nietzsche ironizes them. In this way, the tension between philology and its objects is heightened; the very viability of philological practice is put into question; and the way is paved for a more sweeping critique of the larger cultural issues that are at stake in the conduct of classical studies. Philology must proceed by foregrounding its own conditions of possibility and laying them radically bare. It must avow disavowal. But it can never do this with complete consistency, any more than Nietzsche can, for "we philologists" are irretrievably modern. As always, Nietzsche is his own object-lesson, an accomplice of the prejudices he would dispel.

As we have seen, sometimes Nietzsche's critique is outspoken, but more often and most intriguingly it is implicit, whether this be in his own practice of philology or in the temporal logic of his writings on antiquity. It is this last feature that I want to dwell on for a moment, not least because it is so intriguingly on display in the lectures of the "Encyclopedia." As a rule, Nietzsche's writings on antiquity exhibit a curious structure that is generally tautological: the more layers of the past one strips away in order to reach back to the pristine past, the more of the modern subject, the modern philologist, stands revealed. Features of the past presented as antique begin to accumulate, repeat, and uncannily look ahead to and resemble the philological prejudices that were used to unveil them. The linearity of history thus curves back on itself, in the form of a tautology. And philology is shown to be trapped within this circle.

Philology can never step outside the shadow of its own history. And so (Nietzsche's argument goes), modern philology has to be seen as continuous with its forebear, Alexandrian philology: both are driven by the impulse to recover the simultaneous object and cause of a common desire, an antiquity that is identified only when it has been lost. Here, however, Nietzsche gives this commonplace an unexpected twist and veers provocatively away from what professing classicists of any age might be willing to accept: *for it is the supposed loss of classical antiquity that gives rise to the belief in its initial existence.*[144] Ironically, the closest that the modern classical tradition comes to confessing this fact about itself is at the historical moment of its reinvention of classical antiquity, at the point when it discovers that classical antiquity represents a loss that is irreparable. Humboldt can again be our witness:

> [The Greeks] return us in every respect to our very own lost freedom again (*assuming one can lose what one never had but to which one was entitled by nature*), inasmuch as they cancel out [*aufheben*] the burden of time for an instant, and through their inspiration strengthen that force in us which is designed to overcome this burden automatically, all by itself.[145]

"The burden of time" is what prevents us from leaping "out of the blue" into a world we can only imagine as real. And yet, to entertain this imagining is itself to leap into classical antiquity, to act as if an immediate contact with the alien past were possible, despite the knowledge that it is not. German Hellenism, with its simulated belief in the classical ideal, was plainly capable of Nietzschean insights, but it would never draw the drastic conclusions that Nietzsche would. It kept up the pretenses of belief that Nietzsche will expose for being what they were, merest pretenses that are necessary to the cultural identity of modernity in its current form. Classicism is a symptom of the modern world, not its corrective. Belief in the classical ideal, even if it is only simulated, reinforces rather than corrects the imbalances of modernity, its divisions, its failed humanism, its false historical consciousness, and so on. And philology's disavowed classicism is entirely in keeping with the classicizing program, indeed a part of the latter's repertoire of evasions.

For Nietzsche, then, philology is a sign not of a falling away from the golden classical era but of that era's mythical status. This last point is crucial, and I state it fully aware that it goes against one of the most widely assumed features of Nietzsche's narrative of the classical past, namely the slow decline in culture from antiquity to the present, starting with fifth-century Greece (especially Euripides and Socrates). I want to suggest that this picture of decline, like that of an unrivaled classical (or rather preclassical) grandeur, is itself a myth for Nietzsche, and consequently that both of these pictures need to be reevaluated.

Nietzsche's stance is complex, and it is affected by a number of considerations. To begin with, the narrative of decline is one of the standard features of classicism: it is built into the very idea of the "classical," which designates, in a confused way, the notion of pristine cultural origins, variously divided into elements and phases but essentially one, followed (with greater apparent precision) by a steep falling off at the end of the fifth century B.C.E.[146] To rehearse a well-known plot line, decline leads to a phase of Greek culture that is no longer productive but merely reproductive, during the no longer properly "Hellenic" but instead only "Hellenistic" age of the Museum (the library of Alexandria) from the third to the last centuries B.C.E.; an all but extinguished memory of that memory survives in the centuries following, which are no longer even productively reproductive. It is during the age of the Museum and in the wake of its cataloguing activities (of which the Callimachean *Pinakes*, preserving the titles of Democritus and other Greek authors, are the most brilliant example) that the venerable, frozen classical past becomes canonical in a definitive way. And indeed most classical scholars from Wolf on would concede that they stand closer to their eponymous ancestors, the Alexandrian philologists, than to earlier Greeks, and that they are trying just as desperately as their learned predecessors to shore up the fragments of a lost and irretrievable splendor.[147] This fragile if equivocal connection to antiquity is affirmed in the opening pages of the philological encyclopedias, which by an unstated convention trace the genealogy of their discipline back to this earlier secondary age and to the first scholars to call themselves "critics" and "philologists."

Nietzsche's critical maneuver against this ingrained historical perception of a past in irretrievable decline is, first, to reinforce the familiar and then to estrange it again. Turning the concept of decline into a nonfunctional puzzle and a narrative stumbling block is a consistent strategy of Nietzsche's throughout much of his philology, though it also persists into the later "genealogical" writings. A typical argument is found in the notes from 1875, to which we may briefly turn.

The attitude of veneration, which has only grown over the centuries, ought by itself to be a sign of the continued decline of culture in the West. Yet Nietzsche takes veneration as a symptom not of objective decay but of cultural pessimism, and ultimately as a puzzle for the historical imagination. Conceived as a "classical collection of exemplars" worthy of imitation, Greek antiquity is "the pessimistic foundation of our culture," Nietzsche claims, because this view of the past diminishes the present. The classical past is culture's way of "understanding" itself and its times, of "passing sentence" on those times, and finally of "overcoming" them ("WSB," 6[2]). But isn't such a critique, leading to an overcoming of the present, Nietzsche's goal? Evidently, self-understanding and self-overcoming cut two ways, and they may turn out in the end to lie beyond our reach.[148] Nietzsche's position, consequently, is either itself pessimistic or else it is just remorselessly caustic. Whatever the case may be, reverence for the past, like the desire to overcome the present, not only obliterates the value of the present; it also points to the objective lack of value in the present, its fundamental weakness of will, and its utter submission to the pulls of the reproductive imagination: "One cannot understand our modern world unless one recognizes the immense influence that the purely fantastic has had on it" ("WPh," 7[1]). Accordingly,

> reverence for classical antiquity . . . , which is the only serious, unself-serving, self-sacrificing reverence that antiquity has received to date, is *a monumental example of quixoticism*: and that is what philology is at its best. . . . *One imitates something that is purely chimerical, and chases after a wonderland that never existed.* (ibid.; emphases added)

By the very same token, however, neither does the decline of antiquity itself have any real existence, except in the form of yet one more imaginary projection. And while it may be that to behold the past with the regard of a classicist is to look upon the world with "a retrospective weariness" (to feel that the future is a thing of the past and to believe "that one is a latecomer and epigone"),[149] the alternative is anything but clear. The narrative of decline begs the very question that Nietzsche wants to put before us: What is classical antiquity viewed apart from its imaginary wholeness or its equally imagined decline? No good answer is forthcoming.

The problem, on Nietzsche's construction of it, is to find an instance of antiquity that doesn't exhibit the same structure, if not the same sense, of transferential loss. Not only is the chimerical appearance of antiquity a myth inherited from the Alexandrians and then from the next surge of Greek cultural belatedness, the classicizing Atticists of the so-called Second Sophistic in the Roman imperial period (ibid.); looking backward seems to be a constitutive element of Greek culture from Homer on:

> The same impulse [to veneration] runs through classical antiquity: the way in which the Homeric heroes were copied, the entire traffic with myth has something of this [impulse]. *Gradually, the whole of ancient Greece was made into an object worthy of Don Quixote.* (ibid.; emphasis added)

As a result, the slow decadence of antiquity is not only much harder to date than on its customary understanding, but also harder to characterize. For what has to be reckoned with is not only a steady linear progression of fallings off from an ever more distant height but a retroactive process whereby the past rewrites itself at every step along the way. Prior losses are reinscribed in imaginary recuperations that bury the past in ever more inaccessible layers of construction, each supposed loss giving rise to an even greater desire for an ever greater impossible recovery.

Nietzsche's reading of time here might be said to be symptomatic as opposed to chronological. It is not far different from what we encountered in his lectures on rhythm and meter, in which the very form of time is put into question, or in his lecture on Homer and classical philology, in which Homer and his Alexandrian recuperation describe two interconnected vanishing points of time (with "Homer" disappearing into an imaginary blur at both ends). As with the phenomena of rhythm or the Homeric poems, so too with the image of antiquity itself: the more intensely antiquity is sought out, the more it fades off into the imaginary. And as a rule, in every aspect of Nietzsche's writings down to and including *The Birth of Tragedy* and beyond, his image of antiquity mimics but also embarrasses the narrative of decline that is central to the mythologies of the modern present. At one level he is describing an antiquity that exhibits aestheticizing and idealizing tendencies of its own. But insofar as these are to be traced back to the agency of a protective "envelope of the unhistorical," a willful and necessary blindness that is the premise and condition of all historical perception (*UM*, II:1), Nietzsche's image of the classical past as declining from a lost height into the present is less an objective description of the past than an ambivalent and critical repetition of a mode of historical thinking. What is disturbing to the modern gaze is not the appearance of a lost historical past but the appearance in that past of the very loss, the blind spot, around which the modern historical project constructs itself. The very identity of modernity is here put at risk. If modernity can no longer invent antiquity for the simple reason that antiquity has already invented itself, how can modernity *invent itself* (and thus be constitutively modern)? In a word, in his several accounts of the past Nietzsche is not only describing the myths of antiquity; he is also, and primarily, describing those of modernity. I want to substantiate these claims in what follows through a reading of the nineteenth section of the "Encyclopedia" and an examination of its larger implications. At the very least, the lecture gives a fascinating glimpse into Nietzsche's mythological imagination at the moment he is about to put *The Birth of Tragedy* into final form. A revised and more ranging picture of Nietzsche's conception of antiquity will be offered in the concluding chapter below.

The Birth of Greek Mythology

The nineteenth lecture of the "Encyclopedia," entitled "On the Religion and Mythology of the Ancients," confronts the problem of mythological reconstruction directly, and it consciously plays havoc with various strands of modern (mainly German) scholarship in this field (from Heyne and Voss in the previous century to Creuzer, K. O. Müller, Ludwig Preller, Friedrich Gottlieb Welcker, and others in the nineteenth century). Nietzsche's starting point is a rejection of the "tedious" search for origins (whether euhemerist, symbolic, or comparative), but especially "the current favorite" approach, which is to trace the meanings of gods back to corresponding natural functions (whereby Apollo's "atmospheric" associations can variously explain why he is a god of light, of herds, of music, of healing, and so forth). All this searching, Nietzsche argues, is a pointless exercise, for what is of value in religious thought comes to light only once "this coarse subsoil [of primitive perceptions] has been overcome and spiritualized" (p. 412). And so, rather than "trace ethical ideas back to sensuous perceptions" that are universally shared among primitive peoples anyway, and rather than peer endlessly into "a wholly unknown prehistory [*Urzeit*]," the more pertinent project is to investigate how the Greek gods gradually evolve into entities charged with ethical meaning and how this evolution specifically reflects the changing ethical attitudes of the Greeks themselves: that is, "once again," the true "task of the classical philologist" (ibid.).[150] This move away from the material origins of culture, which are all too frequently confused with Nietzsche's later concept of "genealogy," might seem uncharacteristic of him even in these early years. But it is in fact entirely in keeping with an even more significant tendency of Nietzsche's thought throughout his career, which is to disparage the fact of origins ("The more insight we possess into an origin the less significant does the origin appear") and to focus instead on their *invention*.[151] A question that the lectures implicitly go on to pose is whether the invention of Greek religion is a historical phenomenon or whether it is not rather the product of a certain historicizing tendency, namely that of the philologists of the recent nineteenth century who strove to understand the creation of Greek religion *aus sich selbst*, as a self-creation (p. 410).[152]

Such, at any rate, are the questions that guide Nietzsche's own approach, and what he finds is a mixed lot. Greek gods seem on his analysis to evolve in two directions at once, from shared identity to difference and from difference to shared identity, which raises the problem of how they really can be said to evolve at all. On the one hand, he describes a process that illustrates the progressive specification or particularization of "the selfsame divinity"—that is, of a single *concept* of the divine (as it were, a Platonic Form of the divine), whereby "all individual gods were so many passing revelations of the One, of the divine power that permeates Nature."[153] Formally different, the gods are substantially the same; they share an essential identity at every point in their evolution: "the selfsame divinity is established at different levels of formation, and so there are several manifestations, one after another, of a *single* essential Idea [*Grundidee*]" (p. 414 n. 37).[154] On the other hand, there is the "boundless syncretism" of Greek religion, its essential "leveling and blending together of cults," coupled with a "theocrasic" tendency whereby plural gods are conflated into a single identity. And both of these processes, the differentiation of gods by "metamorphosis" and their indifferentiation through syncretism and theocrasy, go on simultaneously.[155] The picture is of a great melting pot of myth and religion, into and out of which the gods are poured and repoured. Identities are continually conflated, but then they were never essentially distinct to begin with. With this hypothesis Nietzsche has neatly evaded the problems of origins and thereby significantly complicated the narrative of decline to come. For "theocrasy is not at first a symptom of decline," he writes ominously (p. 414). On the other hand, syncretism, which is "as old as history," ultimately renders the effects of "metamorphosis" syncretistic again, and so later changes make no difference to the evolutionary process. Only the look of the gods changes: all that evolves is the process of evolution itself. Behind everything is the question that is nowhere stated but everywhere implied in Nietzsche's lecture: does Greek religion objectively decline or is it degenerative *in its very essence*?

Given the tendencies just described, the fact that gods were distinguished at all cries out for an explanation, and Nietzsche's answer, partly spelled out in a lengthy addendum to his text, is shocking: their distinction is the result, on the one hand, of a "process of beautification [*Verschönerung*], through poetry and especially through figurative art," and on the other, of a greater rationalization that is palpable partly in poetry and art and partly in the work of the early prose-writers and the learned mythographers who attempted to produce order in a disorderly body of cultural materials, even if this effort was merely productive of further "conflations" (p. 415 and n. 37).[156] Ultimately, however, these two processes are indistinguishable, for rational thought just is a form of aestheticization, as the sequel shows.[157]

In the same addendum and in the rest of his text Nietzsche traces "the gods' ethical evolution" in Pindar, then in tragedy, and finally in the later pagan period.[158] The plot is a familiar one, and it is largely (and surprisingly) Hegelian. Myths pass through three stages of ideation: "It is the way from the sublime to the beautiful and then to the symbolic," which is to say, to allegory. The picture, so viewed, is one of decline. At the same time, the process brings with it, in the age of Greek tragedy, the evolution of justice into an abstract ethical ideal, as well as a waning belief in myth and a rehabilitation of previous, darker superstitions ("the blinding daimonic force of ruin, a residue of the belief in Titanic divinity," p. 415 n. 37).

Meanwhile, an opposite tendency becomes pronounced, though it leads to identical results. Starting with Sophocles, there is a marked turn inward: there is a search for a "metaphysical solution" to the mysteries of life (or what amounts to the same thing, to the baffling nature of the divine); a Beyond (*Jenseits*) looms into view for the first time; philosophical speculation surpasses religion—it is deeper; the divinities suffer "an ethical degeneracy";

"the whole of mythology becomes a phantasm and a farce, because all deeper natures satisfy their metaphysical need in the mysteries [viz., mystery cults]. The only rehabilitation available to the gods is through a general symbolization and allegorization," and so on (p. 416 n. 37). The passage warrants fuller quotation:

> In the midst of this religious development stand Aeschylus and Sophocles, the one looking back, the other turned toward the end to come. It is the way from the sublime to the beautiful and, finally, to the symbolic. A strong yearning for justice is in evidence in Aeschylus. God and man [stand] in close association. The div[ine], justice, morality and *happiness* are all connected. [God][159] Titan and man are measured according to this standard. The gods are reconstrued accordingly. The popular belief in the blinding daimonic force of ruin, a residue of the belief in Titantic divinity, is corrected; the daimonic force is made into an instrument of a righteous Zeus. . . .
>
> Aeschylus discovers sublimity in the severity of the Olympian administration of justice. Sophocles, in its *inscrutability*. He restores the popular perspective. The enigmatic [and] apparent unreason of fate is his tragic premise. Suffering is understood here as something that sanctifies. The gap between the divine and the human is immeasurable: pious resignation is the most appropriate response. . . . Aeschylus continuously struggles to discover justice in every appearance: Sophocles considers this region [viz., appearances] unilluminable. *Life* does not solve the riddle; he presupposes a metaphysical solution; and Oedipus, shrouded in mystery at the moment of his vanishing, gives us a hint of the only place where the solution lies. Already here we see for the first time the looming into view of a Beyond [*Jenseits*], of which the older periods down to Aeschylus knew nothing. We see how the gods of beauty and justice cannot withstand the philosophical spirit as it gains ground. The deeper conceptions go over their heads; an ethical degeneration of the divinities sets in, the whole of mythology becomes a phantasm and a pose, because all deeper natures satisfy their metaphys[ical] need in the mysteries. The only rehabilitation available to the gods is through a general symbolization and allegorization. (pp. 415–16 n. 37)

These two accounts, the one rational and Aeschylean, the other irrational and Sophoclean, are nonetheless two faces of the same coin, two kinds of "reconstruction" internal to Greek mythology, about which Nietzsche can claim, in a revealing aside that is set off by a dash: "The divine world of beauty *produces* [*erzeugt*] the chthonic divinities [viz., the "horrible" world of "Hades, Persephone, Demeter, Hermes, Hecate, and the Erinyes" and "then Dionysus"[160]] *as its own supplement* [*Ergänzung*]. These latter, more formless in themselves [*an sich*] and closer to the Concept, increasingly gain the upper hand and [then] cause the whole Olympian world to vanish together with the heroes, as symbols of *their* [that is, the chthonic gods' own] secrets" (p. 415 n. 37; first two emphases added).

What is fascinating about this last aside is the reversed genealogy it introduces into Nietzsche's proposed evolutionary scheme, rupturing it from within: the striking claim about the invention—the aesthetic creation—of the dark chthonic divinities (among whom the younger god Dionysus figures with increasing prominence) out of the brighter Olympian world, the origination of the mysteries and of a realm beyond (*Jenseits*), not to mention ecstatic orgies, initially absent from the scene (p. 413)[161]—in short, the invention of the Dionysian godhead out of an Apollinian framework. As I wish to show, this reversed genealogy is in fact not a challenge to Nietzsche's evolutionary scheme but is rather a specification of its inner logic.

The idea of the relative lateness of the Olympians is a commonplace in nineteenth-century scholarship, but confusions reigned about the chronology and nature of earlier divinities.[162] Here, Nietzsche is following K. O. Müller, who in his *Prolegomena to a Scientific Mythology* (1825) had boldly speculated that the Titan divinities, in the form in which they are known to us, are younger than the Olympians (thus reversing Hesiod's genealogies, according to which Zeus and the bright Olympians emerge "out of darkness"): "One can say that here, in point of fact, the children produced [*erzeugten*] their parents."[163] While Müller is likewise explaining a general feature of mythological constructions (cults "historically portray," which is to say invent, their own origins), Nietzsche's formulation is more radical, more visionary, and more holistic than Müller's. The aesthetic supplement of the pre-Olympians, Nietzsche maintains, is at bottom philosophically motivated: it constitutes a response to a deep "metaphysical need." Perhaps this explains why the chthonic divinities can be both "more formless in themselves [*an sich*]" and "closer to the Concept"; for the Concept in question is none other than the concept *of* the In-itself, which is the condition of any metaphysical Beyond, at least in the German speculative tradition that affects everyone from Creuzer on.[164] The irrational is thus clearly marked as a rational construct, one that is given aesthetic form in the mythology of the Greeks. The decline mapped out by Nietzsche is, in other words, *into* the abyss of the irrational, into philosophical speculation about metaphysics, and eventually into a (presumed) condition of mythlessness: "The individual details of mythology were given up long ago, long before Lucian [in the second century C.E.]. Only in art did mythology stay alive, but more as a burden than as a support: it was deemed boring" (p. 417). It is in this context that the mysteries of Dionysus, the yearnings for a hereafter and the like, would flourish—as a practice unsupported by the illusions of classical mythology.

So viewed, the "Encyclopedia" throws a shadow on the work that is exactly contemporary with it, *The Birth of Tragedy*. Quite simply, the inversion described here—the invention of the Dionysian out of the Apollinian—stands the surface narrative of *The Birth of Tragedy* on its head.[165] There, we should recall, the world of the Titans and of Dionysus, embodying an "abysmal and terrifying view of the world" and associated by Nietzsche with the pre-Homeric "folk wisdom" of the Silenus (*BT* §§3, 4), is said to be antecedent to that of Olympian Apollo,[166] who does indeed give birth, but merely, so to speak, to himself, as the "father" of the Olympian world: "For the same impulse that embodied itself in Apollo gave birth to this entire Olympian world, and in this sense Apollo is its father" (ibid.). And although Nietzsche does not avail himself of the terms "Apollinian" and "Dionysian" in this section of the "Encyclopedia," these are plainly on his mind, a fact that emerges two lectures earlier, where a synopsis of the "riddle" at the core of *The Birth of Tragedy* is given (without, however, any hint as to the existence of this work in the making). The "riddle," Nietzsche says, lies somewhere in the relation between "the chorus, the ideal actor, . . . the opposition between the musical Dionysus [or "Dionysianism"] and the Apollinian, . . . etc." (p. 403).[167]

How do we explain the dissonance between the two writings? We could say that Nietzsche vacillates. He clearly can tell the difference between the two views when he wants to; he knows that the question of the priority of the Olympians to the Chthonians is controversial and open to opposed constructions, as his correspondence shows,[168] but also as the present text shows by itself. For the "Encyclopedia" in fact presupposes a multiple reading of divinity, allowing for its successive "manifestations," while preserving their underlying identity. So, for instance, Nietzsche can make "the age of the Titans and of Cronos and of the Olympians with Zeus . . . fundamentally identical" (p. 414 n. 37), which is to say, manifestations of a single *Grundidee*: "The selfsame divinity is established at different levels of formation, and so there are several manifestations, one after another, of a *single* essential Idea" (ibid.). So on this (for want of a better word) hendiadic reading, Olympians and Chthonians, or Apollo and Dionysus, are merely two faces of one and the same divine conception, differentiated aesthetically but at bottom not essentially distinct. On this view, art is indeed an aesthetic supplement that answers to a metaphysical need. It is, in this sense, a *Verschönerung*, even if the exact nature of that need has yet to be determined. But clearly it is not hard to perceive how the aesthetic invention of darker (chthonic) forces might satisfy some kind of metaphysical need; and how the assumed, or just fictional, priority of the chthonic gods might fit into this larger design—for instance, how their eventual repression and the triumph of Olympian beauty might provide a relatively safe dose of "metaphysical comfort." Another possibility, a more troubling one, is that *The Birth of Tragedy* can and perhaps should be read in the light of the kind of multiple reading that is found in the "Encyclopedia," which in that case can be seen as supplying a shrewd commentary on the published work, while the latter might be seen as commenting, obliquely, upon itself.

There are, after all, traces of the nineteenth lecture to be found in *The Birth of Tragedy*—for example, the claim in *The Birth of Tragedy* that the appearances of art are "not merely imitation of the reality of nature but rather a metaphysical supplement [*Supplement*] of the reality of nature, placed beside it for its overcoming" (§24), while tragedy is fundamentally a purveyor of "metaphysical comfort" (§§7, 8, etc.); or Nietzsche's location, at the height of the archaic period and in Aeschylus, of "an immovably firm foundation for metaphysical thought in [the] mysteries" and a corresponding "skepticism" toward divinity, especially one that is "vented against the Olympians" (*BT* §9). The reference here is to the Prometheus trilogy, and specifically to Prometheus' threatened vengeance against Zeus' Olympian regime. Evidently, Nietzsche is backdating the Sophoclean phenomenon witnessed above ("[Sophocles] presupposes a metaphysical solution"). Or else he is bringing out a feature of Aeschylean tragedy that was simply understated in the "Encyclopedia" lecture (justice is, after all, a metaphysical "concept" even for Aeschylus, while already for him, too, "the belief in myth wanes").[169] At any rate, if Aeschylus, in *The Birth of Tragedy*, takes over Sophocles' role and announces the decline of Olympus in the face of deepening metaphysical speculation, the end result is the same: the "twilight of the gods" intimated by Aeschylus (*BT* §9) will eventually "cause the whole Olympian world to vanish together with the heroes, as symbols of [the chthonic gods' own] secrets." This is an obscure phrase from the "Encyclopedia." But I believe that here, too, *The Birth of Tragedy* can help us out. Prometheus, the Titan who forecasts the "twilight of the gods," contains some of these secrets within himself, just as the "Dionysian truth" that he represents "takes over the entire domain of myth as the symbolism of *its* knowledge" now in the form of tragedy and "dramatic mysteries" (*BT* §10).[170] As in the "Encyclopedia," the passage in *The Birth of Tragedy* is likewise from myth to mystery, only the implication there, if one reads that work closely, is that the passage is less a sequence than it is an identity, one that is masked as a succession. Compare, for instance, the end of the first section of *The Birth of Tragedy*, where "the mysterious primordial unity" (to which tragedy gives access and against which it protects the Greek spectator), Dionysian metaphysics ("the Dionysian world-artist"), and the Eleusinian mysteries are all viewed as part of the selfsame phenomenon. Dionysianism does not merely "live on" in the mysteries; it is one itself. Is it also "degenerate" then? In the balance in both of Nietzsche's accounts is not simply the resolution of a trilogy but the very health of tragedy. On both accounts tragedy literally dies by "suicide."[171] What other correlations are there? What other secrets? The logic of the "Encyclopedia" lecture will lead the way.

By itself, Nietzsche's speculation about the aesthetic invention of the darker mysteries and of the Dionysian realm greatly complicates the meaning of the historical evolution of Greek mythology, for that evolution is shown to be an evolving retroactive construct by the Greeks themselves. "Thus did the Delphic God *interpret* the Greek past," Nietzsche would put it in *The Birth of Tragedy*. Similarly, "overweening pride and excess are regarded as the truly hostile demons of the non-Apollinian sphere, *hence* as characteristic as of the pre-Apollinian age—that of the Titans; and of the extra-Apollinian world—that of the barbarians" (§4; emphases added). Here we have the retroactive creation, by interpretation, of the Titans after all: "the divine world of beauty" does indeed "produce the chthonic divinities as its own supplement."[172] But Nietzsche's speculation in the "Encyclopedia" also throws a curious light on the Dionysian element in Greek culture, which at least on this narrative version of it appears as a belated, *postclassical* (at least in tendency), and increasingly significant phenomenon, a possibility that again reverses the surface narrative of *The Birth of Tragedy*. The possibility does, however, chime with the inner logic of that work,[173] and with the parallel perspectives from Nietzsche's contemporary notes on rhythm and meter, as was seen above. "With Alexander, this impulse [to the Beyond] sets in once again: it is characterized by the expansion of Dionysus-worship" (pp. 416–17). As the ages go by, down to late antiquity, the tendency ripens, only to blossom in the late antique "mysteries of Dionysus, Hecate, Venus, Sabazius, Isis, Mithras—everyone [living at the time] is unanimous about that. As a result, the character of the here and now [*Diesseits*] changes" (p. 417). It does indeed, for Christianity is but a short step away. In fact, these Greek worshipers are essentially Christians, and Dionysus has metamorphosed into Christ, "for the goal of existence is [now] referred to a Beyond" (p. 418). But no matter, for Nietzsche has already disputed the relevance of the distinction between Greek and Christian religion: the real issue, he writes earlier in the "Encyclopedia," is not what decides between paganism and Christianity, but between pessimism and optimism. And on that score, the antique past and the more recent Christian present share too many features to allow for a clear decision: "Both in Christianity and in paganism there are quite serious [viz., deeper and darker] attitudes, e.g., the mysteries, the underground of tragedy, Empedocles, the whole sixth century, while in the secularization of the Church and its political pretensions there lies a pagan, i.e., optimistic element" (p. 370).

Questions about Dionysus abound. One suspects that it is only in hindsight that his "emergent" traces can be detected in earlier Greek myths, by way of a back-projection. If so, then we have in Dionysus a characteristically *Alexandrian* phenomenon (but one that is perhaps only legible today from within a Christianized tradition). Still, in case the analogy between Christians and Dionysiac cultists should seem far-fetched, especially to readers of

Nietzsche habituated in the opposite expectation (which is fostered, in part, by the later writings),[174] one should compare a note from "We Philologists":

> A critique of the Greeks is simultaneously a critique of Christianity, since the foundation of the belief in spirits, of religious cult, [and] of the enchantment of nature, is the same.
> *This would be a task: to characterize Greek culture as irretrievable* [viz., *"unrepeatable," unwiederbringlich*], and *with it Christianity too, and the foundations on which our society and political life have been built until now.*"[175] ("WPh," 5[156]; Nietzsche's emphasis)

The continuities between Christianity and Dionysian antiquity are remarkable, and overwhelming. As Nietzsche could hold in 1870/71, "The Hellenic world of Apollo is gradually overcome *within* by the Dionysian powers. Christianity was already *in place*."[176] And in fact, reversals of the expected scheme, of the sort we have been witnessing all along, are already sketched out in 1870: Dionysianism is consistently reckoned to be an accomplice of the degeneration of ancient Greece; classical mythology etiolates; mysteries gain ground; and Christianity, joining forces with Dionysianism, takes over.[177] Perhaps more surprising than these earlier "critiques" of Dionysianism, which trouble the apparent drift of *The Birth of Tragedy* but which are detectable even within that work, is the persistence of this same pattern into the later writings, as for example in a note from 1887/88: Christianity's onslaught against "the *classical* ideal" is in fact a "translation into the needs and level of understanding of the *religious masses* of the time: of those masses who believed in Isis, Mithras, Dionysus, the 'great Mother,' and who sought in a religion: (1) a *Jenseits-Hoffnung*; (2) the bloody phantasmagoria of the sacrificial animal, 'the *mysterium*,'" and so on.[178] The conclusion to which all of Nietzsche's thoughts are leading in the "Encyclopedia" seems to be the same. At the very least, the evolving conceptions of divinity traced by Nietzsche are a train of *idealizations*. And the Dionysian element of Greek culture, the much prized feature of Nietzsche's critique of modernity (as this is usually read, starting belatedly with *The Birth of Tragedy*), turns out to be *one of these idealizations*: "Strange idealism of the Greeks in their worship of narcotism" and *"wine"* (*KSA*, 7:3[43], 1869/70).[179]

But what of modern philology? It stands directly in the line of succession, and emblematically so, for "our whole modern world is entangled in the net of Alexandrian culture" (*BT* §1). Its forebear, Alexandrian philology, is contemporaneous with the resurgence of Dionysus-worship and of the orientalizing tendencies of Greek cults, transplanted now to Egypt (Alexandria), where the new "unification of Greeks and Egyptians" is consecrated through further religious syncretism (p. 417). Indeed, philology must reckon among its ancestors the likes of a Thrasyllus, Tiberius' court astrologer and the late editor of the Democritean corpus, for he fits right into the picture: "The influence of astrologists was immense" (ibid.). Philology, with its bowed, reverential posture toward the past, may even be the latest manifestation of the earlier described theocrasic tendencies. Theocrasy eventually is transformed into a political instrument and a means of cultural adaptation: it occurs wherever "gods lose their national character" and a general "*identification with Greekness*" rules (pp. 417–19). As before, the process of identification and differentiation rolls on, as gods die and are reborn in new guises, only now they take on the disguise of not having one at all. The Romantic slogan "We are all Greeks" is here given an unexpected twist of meaning.[180]

If any of this is at all plausible, then far from revealing the dark truth of antiquity, as readers of *The Birth of Tragedy* still imagine, the Dionysian bespeaks a less welcome truth. The Dionysian state of mind is one of "selfforgetting" and "narcosis" (*BT* §1). I want to suggest that the Dionysian condition is a figure for *historical self-forgetting*. The tendency is, in fact, said to be one of the defining characteristics of the Greeks in one of the later notes: "Given to lies. Unhistorical" ("WPh," 5[70]). But the attribution is tricky. Appearing to concede to the Greeks a trait of their own, Nietzsche has also discovered in the Greeks something that Humboldt and others would find "useful" as a way of approaching them: "For us, the Greeks are not only a people that is useful to know historically but an ideal," Humboldt had confessed. The ahistorical talents of the Greeks in Nietzsche prefigure, in fact, the projection of more recent, decidedly ahistorical readings of the classical past—a contemporary form of theocrasy, as it were: "The Greeks are for us what their gods were for them; flesh of our flesh and bone of our bone," in Humboldt's own words. Dionysianism, after all, represents for Nietzsche "a return *to itself* of the German spirit" (*BT* §19; emphasis added). And if in his "Attempt at a Self-Criticism" (1886) Nietzsche can describe *The Birth of Tragedy* as "a piece of anti-Hellenism," the work is by the same token a piece of "romanticism": "Is it not itself something 'equally intoxicating and befogging,' in any case a narcotic, even a piece of music, *German music?*" ("Attempt," 7). Classical antiquity is *our mysterium* today.[181]

On one level, the Dionysian is a thoroughly *modern* myth, myth, as it were, *Wagnerisé*.[182] That it would become this in Nietzsche's wake is incontestable. In 1881, Karl Blind, for example, would write to his friend Heinrich Schliemann, "Those Thrakians—blue-eyed, red-haired, according to an indication by Xenophanes, 500 years before our era—were a most martial and a highly musical people, much given to Bacchic habits, but also to philosophical speculation. . . . Do not these martial, musical, Bacchic, and philosophical traits point strongly to the Teutonic stock?"[183] Nietzsche is merely preying upon this fantasy of identification, which, as will be seen in the next chapter, is deeply rooted in the German classical tradition. The general thought concerning the modern provenance of Greek myth is in any case consistent with the leading insight of the nineteenth lecture of the "Encyclopedia," which is established from the start: Greek mythology as we know it is a reconstruction. The very idea of "understanding" Greek mythology, whether through comparative analysis or "on its own terms" and "out of itself [*aus sich selbst*]," which is to say, "as a product of the Greeks," must in any case be historicized for being what it is: a most recent scholarly project (p. 410). And so, even if Nietzsche appears to be following some of this thinking in some of its strands (the principles of religious syncretism, historical evolution, acculturation, the relatively late date of Dionysus-worship, the tendencies to "spritualization" and to an eventual rapprochement with Christianity, not to say to decline), he is not following them innocently.[184] In a sense, by welcoming them all he is confounding them in their own mutual self-contradiction. For the logic that Nietzsche traces is ultimately one not of historical evolution but of retroactive attribution: the aesthetic production of antiquity is here palpable in the form of its scholarly mythology. As he had said earlier about the very idea of the classical world, "An aesthetic judgment lies therein." The extreme aestheticism of the view of a classical, Olympian antiquity—which is to say, of a mythology that invents itself in the name of some aesthetic value (whether this be coherence, truth, or beauty)—is perfectly in keeping with this same verdict. The question posed here in the lectures and again in *The Birth of Tragedy*—"What terrific need was it that could produce such an illustrious company of Olympian beings?" (*BT* §3)—has its ultimate reference in contemporary views about the classical past, whether these are outwardly classicizing or even (as in Nietzsche's case) apparently anticlassicizing. This is a point that will be brought home in the concluding chapter of this study.[185]

If on one level, then, the Dionysian is a thoroughly modern myth, on another level the Dionysian is a symbol for the ineradicable *need* for myths in modernity. Nietzsche thus uses the Dionysian to expose, in a rhetorical rather than declarative way, the most transparent and therefore most invisible myth of all: *the myth of mythlessness* that prevails in the modern world, its presumed "timeliness." Philology as a discipline is what helps to sustain this myth and the modern needs for myth in the contemporary present. That those needs are said by Nietzsche to be consistent with religious needs that develop in antiquity is only a sign of the deeply rooted nature of the phenomenon described and of its seeming ineradicability.[186]

Traditional philology is the agency that helps to sustain the mythical shape of the present, in part by alienating myth as an object of dispassionate study. It is one of the forms that forgetfulness assumes. Exposing this condition is the work of a critical philology. And because there is no philology that does not stand in the shadow of its own history, philology for Nietzsche must become a self-reflexive, self-critical, and often paradoxical undertaking. Nietzsche's "Encyclopedia of Philology" is but a case in point.

CHAPTER 5

After Philology: The Reinvention of Antiquity

Given the complexity of Nietzsche's early projects in philology between 1867 and 1871, his view of the classical past cannot be reduced to a single formula. Nevertheless, his readers tend to assume that he does have a consistent conception of antiquity, at least starting with *The Birth of Tragedy* (1872), if not earlier. I want to challenge this assumption in the present chapter. Nietzsche has no single view of antiquity, and certainly no consistent view of it, at any point in his career. Disparities, whether in the form of internal tensions or of outright contradictions, can occur not only from essay to essay or from note to note but within any view of antiquity that he may choose to adopt at a given moment. As a result of these imbalances and of the corresponding effort on the part of interpreters to cast his thinking in a more manageable form, Nietzsche has come to be surrounded by a number of myths, many of them incompatible: myths about his commitments to classicism or romanticism, about his place within the nineteenth-century struggles between historicism and humanism, or about his alleged view or views on religion, philosophy, art, and the irrational in classical antiquity.

It is not my intention to settle these disputes here. What I do hope to show is why Nietzsche has occupied so sensitive a place in the framework according to which we understand our relation to Greek and Roman antiquity today, and why it is that to disturb Nietzsche's place in that framework is to risk disturbing the framework itself. In order to demonstrate all of this, it will be necessary to look beyond the materials covered thus far in this study and to turn to *The Birth of Tragedy*, to some of the philological writings that postdate that work, and to references to antiquity in Nietzsche's later published and unpublished writings. We shall see, once more, why Nietzsche's philology is irreducible to philology as we commonly know it (it is indeed a kind of *Afterphilologie*). We shall also see how the philological references in the nonphilological writings extend rather than repudiate his earlier approaches to antiquity. We may begin by turning to one of the most significant and widespread set of myths about Nietzsche, namely those that surround his invention of a counterclassical antiquity.

Nietzsche's Archaism

The usual way of making sense of Nietzsche's conception of antiquity is to take *The Birth of Tragedy* as a point of reference and to see him as offering, more or less from this point on, a *Schreckbild*, or frightening counterimage, of antiquity, one that threatens the complacency of the idyllic perfections of Greek culture familiar in Germany from the time of J. J. Winckelmann (1717–68). Winckelmann embodies what Nietzsche takes to be the most prevalent, if often denied and suppressed, attitude to classical antiquity in his contemporary world, the reverential idealism of German classicism ("Greek 'cheerfulness'").[1] Thus, at a stroke, popular conceptions of antiquity, classical scholarship and classical education, and hallowed traditions all can be seen to come under attack. Nietzsche's conception of antiquity is on this view decisively anticlassicist and unpalatably so.

A good index of the shock waves that Nietzsche's *Birth of Tragedy* could send through the contemporary establishment is given by Wilamowitz's counterattack in his pamphlet *Zukunftsphilologie!* (1872). Their clash is often taken as an example of the historical rifts within the discipline of classics. Above all it is taken to be emblematic of the clash between a now faded humanism, whether that of traditional classicism or of a romanticism that may have exhausted itself before it could ever fully establish itself within the discipline of classics, and the new positivist historicism that had gained ascendancy in the nineteenth century. Yet Wilamowitz's reactions tell a slightly different story: they are more finely tuned than some of the later reductions of his impassioned polemic or of this particular crisis in the discipline let on. Wilamowitz does indeed rally to the defense of his field, piqued by Nietzsche's rebuff of the cherished "historical-critical method" and by his accusation that (in Wilamowitz's misquotation) contemporary Germany had "'completely misrecognized the study of antiquity.'" All this, Wilamowitz adds, "at a time when philology in Germany had been lifted to a height never before imagined, thanks above all to the services of Gottfried Hermann and Karl Lachmann," the two leading lights in the science of textual criticism from earlier in the century. In contrast to the likes of these, Nietzsche offers as exemplary counterexamples, "apart from Schiller and Goethe, only Winckelmann."[2] Wilamowitz continues:

> To be sure, he is writing only for those who, like himself, have never read Winckelmann. Whoever has learned from Winckelmann to see the essence of Hellenic art in beauty alone will shrink back with horror from the "world-symbolics of the primordial pain of the primordial unity," from the "joy taken in the destruction of the individual," the "joy taken in dissonance." Whoever has learned from Winckelmann to grasp the essence of beauty historically, [i.e.,] the way it manifests itself differently at different times . . . , will never talk about a "marked degeneration of the Hellenic spirit" or about an inartistic spirit in the age when Zeuxis and Apelles, Praxiteles and Lysippus . . . created a beauty . . . [that is] admired and worth admiring in perpetuity. . . . Does Mr. Nietzsche dare to maintain that he knows Winckelmann?[3]

Correct in his assessment of the reader's anticipated reactions to the work, which are also his own (shock and horror), Wilamowitz is obviously confused about Nietzsche's intentions, and rightly so. Nietzsche does invoke the authority of German classicism, even if he acknowledges that "heroes like Goethe and Schiller could not succeed in breaking open the enchanted gate which leads into the Hellenic magic mountain" (*BT* §20). Why, then, does Nietzsche construct an antiquity that is so patently unclassical?[4]

The standard way of proceeding here is to ignore the contradictions in Nietzsche's own exposition and to fasten onto the anticlassical features of his picture of the ancient Greek world—for example, the "inhuman" traits of his ideal Greeks, or the "terrible and wicked background" ("depth") that puts their deeds in an eerie and alienating light.[5] In terms that are all too familiar from *The Birth of Tragedy*, this is the "Dionysian" face of Greek culture, which is then generalized to account for the majority of Nietzsche's subsequent views about antiquity. Sometimes a resort to a periodizing shift on Nietzsche's part is taken, usually by classicists seeking to render the strangeness of Nietzsche's thinking familiar again, or at least intelligible. His favorite Greeks are said to live in the rough and tumble world of archaic Greece, the post-Homeric world of Archilochus, the Presocratics, Theognis, Pindar, and Aeschylus, prior and in contrast to the conventional zenith of Greek culture, the Athenian fifth century, the brighter world of Pericles, Sophocles, and Phidias that was so much admired by Winckelmann and his succession.[6] In this way, Nietzsche can be credited with having anticipated and even inaugurated a new vision of antiquity, not to mention a new vogue and a research focus within classical studies that would culminate in the next century.

A string of discoveries (or rediscoveries) is conventionally linked together on this logic: his discovery of the archaic age as a self-standing period of Greek culture, his discovery (or "invention") of the Presocratics, his "unprecedented insights" into Greek religion or into the true darkness and irrationality of the Greek mind.[7] Such generalities as these are not easily maintained, whether in the face of the evidence of Nietzsche's own texts or as arguments in their own right.[8] And they risk substituting one idealized conception of Greece for another. The shimmering mirage of an earlier, healthier condition such as the Greeks enjoyed has skewed many an analysis of Nietzsche.[9] And besides, isn't that the premise of classicism all over again?[10] A further, hidden cost of this now orthodox view of Nietzsche is that while his conception of archaic Greece becomes retrospectively plausible, in the wake of the twentieth-century revaluation of archaic literature and religion, his view of subsequent developments in Greek culture, starting with Socrates, becomes highly implausible.[11] How many views does Nietzsche have of classical antiquity, and how many views must we, accordingly, have about them? Whether Nietzsche can be credited with so much originality is another question altogether.

Did Nietzsche discover archaic Greece? The temptations and the difficulties of such a view aside, to accept Nietzsche's shift in historical focus at face value is a move of desperation. Is he to be vindicated on historicist grounds after all? Doubtfully. Nietzsche's vision of antiquity obeys no ordinary chronologies. The world he professes to admire in, say, "Homer's Contest" (1872) is labeled "pre-Homeric," and it designates a state of mind and of character that can reoccur in any age, rather than being bound to a fixed timeline. That is also the basic premise of Dionysian metaphysics and of the hoped-for "rebirth" of Greek tragedy: Dionysianism is presented by Nietzsche as an insight into a transhistorical truth that in fact underlies all reality, but which may prove to be no more than an idealization of reality itself and, what may amount to the same thing, a German myth (*"the rebirth of German myth"* [*BT* §23]). Then there are the palpable infractions of his own chronologies: Homer is and is not an instance of Dionysian insight,[12] is and is not "pre-Homeric," is (in the more usual sense of the term) a shadowy pre-Homeric poet and a later poetic illusion of the same, which is to say, a post-Homeric "myth."[13] Heraclitus, Pindar, and Aeschylus come too late in the time scheme to allow for a neat cut-off point in the late sixth century: they straddle the fifth century, and their poetry reflects this. Sophocles flourishes at the height of the classical period and nonetheless is claimed as an instance of archaic (Dionysian) insight. Democritus is a contemporary of Socrates and outlives him. But then, "Socratism is older than Socrates,"—it exists as a kind of pre-Socratic Socratism.[14] And so on. And in general, wherever one looks in Nietzsche's historical pageants, those Greeks who are supposed to be most representative of privileged moments turn out to be not teeming with historical possibilities but ambivalent, Janus-faced, and transitional figures, filled, whether they recognize it or not, with a foreboding of their own imminent or actual decline. Here, time starts to flow in reverse: decline seeps into even archaic Greece from the decadent Alexandrian period, which is inaugurated—so Nietzsche's master narrative from 1870 on would have us believe—by Euripides and Socrates. It is enough to read just

The Birth of Tragedy closely to find that the signs of decline are detectable in Sophocles, then in Aeschylus, and finally in the very first glimmerings of Greek cultural life.[15]

Nietzsche can tell no one story about antiquity because he has no one story to tell, and he cannot even tell the stories he does have to tell in a straightforward, easily traceable way. But this only gets at the surface of the problem, for Nietzsche's views about antiquity, I want to suggest, are not easily reducible or even easily deducible as such, *because he in fact has no views about antiquity.* What his writings offer us instead is a series of often competing accounts of antiquity, which in turn are best read as a series of exploratory postures and attitudes toward antiquity understood as a problem. Instead of views, Nietzsche gives us poses, mere possible positions, which are reflexive and self-interrogating rather than positive and fixed. What is more, they tend to be derived from contemporary attitudes to antiquity and then are reflected back, provocatively, upon these sources in a distortive mirroring. Such is, I believe, the provisional nature of the stances that Nietzsche adopts in his war on received assumptions. Nietzsche *uses* antiquity as a strategic element of his critique of the present. And while his stances, when they are not merely opportunistic, are often marked by contradictions and paradoxes, they are not reducible to these things. For in general, just as contradictions in Nietzsche are never innocent but are always telling, so too are his historical perspectives (which all of his writings about antiquity necessarily are). Like his frequent inversions of time and of historical processes of the sort discussed earlier in this study, his contradictions signify in an elusively allegorical way. Meaningful in their own right, the contradictions that in point of fact constitute Nietzsche's conceptions of the ancient past bear, by virtue of their bald inconsistency, directly on the projective capabilities of moderns in relation to antiquity and *their* inconsistencies. The question they pose is whether we, as moderns, can coherently construe antiquity. Through their irreconcilabilities, Nietzsche's various sketches of the past point to what is problematical about the attempt to make straight sense of antiquity. At issue in them all is "the problem of time" itself, as he puts it in his lectures on Greek rhythm and meter—not time in some inert sense but taken as a perceptual problem. At stake, in other words, is the very concept and meaning of history, viewed as a determinant of cultural perspectives, and above all the problem of the contemporary construction of its own historical past. These are, I believe, the reasons why Nietzsche disappoints the customary clichés that surround him, and even the redeeming judgments that would certify his most lasting contributions to the field of classical studies. Nietzsche is not interested in discovering new research foci. He is drawn to whatever is problematical about the identification of the past as a safely secure and stable moment. In their inconsistency and often in their sheer incoherence, his accounts of the past stage the insoluble antagonisms that definitions of the past, which are invariably acts of self-definition, exist to cover over.

In order to justify this account of Nietzsche's provocative chronologies, let us consider a few instances of the individual moments that make them up. Only so will we be able to appreciate how hazardous any characterizations of historical time can be in Nietzsche's images of antiquity. The examples of the fifth and fourth centuries are a good place to start. Restlessly in transition and in fact filtered, for Nietzsche, through a complex overlay of historical perceptions (and thus never isolable in their own right), they are perfectly consistent with his characterizations of the archaic period as described above. Consider the following statement, from the lecture notes on Greek rhythm (1870/71): "Importance of Aristoxenus [of Tarentum], his oppositional stance toward the more recent art. Reminiscence of the old art of music. Degeneracy already with Sophocles."[16] Is Sophocles' degeneracy a fact or a perception—and if the latter, whose?[17] The problem of verification is in fact built directly, and insolubly, into Nietzsche's portrait of the fourth-century musicologist Aristoxenus, a highly problematic figure for Nietzsche for any number of reasons. A precarious witness to a sensibility that, as we saw, also happens to be equivalent to the sense of time itself, Aristoxenus crystallizes in his person, or rather in his emblematic position as a theorist of an artform he may no longer even be able to grasp, the sheer difficulties of historical reconstruction.[18] He is, in other words, a threshold figure, or *Grenzfigur*, of the kind to which Nietzsche endlessly found himself drawn, such as the sixth-century moralist and elegiac poet Theognis of Megara, the subject of Nietzsche's valedictory thesis while at Schulpforte in 1864 and of his first publication in 1867.[19] Given the centrality of Theognis to Nietzsche's writings early and late, we should turn briefly to Nietzsche's portraits of this figure, which are riddled with questions of historicity.

Although frequently pictured as an analogue to Nietzsche's alleged aristocratism, especially in the light of *On the Genealogy of Morals* (1887) where he appears as the "mouthpiece" of a powerful Greek nobility, Theognis is for Nietzsche on the contrary a deeply compromised figure who has to be situated in the context of the "breakdown of the old aristocracy." Himself a "Junker" in decline, "deteriorated," "down at the heels," the bearer of a "somewhat corrupted and no longer securely noble bloodline," "filled with deadly hatred for the rising mob" and "feelings of vengeance," "despair," and "resignation," Theognis is, in short, "a twisted Janus-face, since to him the past appears so beautiful and enviable, while what lies ahead, [although] of equal merit in and of itself, appears repellent and repulsive."[20] His poem records, moreover, one of the versions of the pessimistic "wisdom of Silenus" (the claim that it is "better not to have been born"), which will become a leitmotif of *The Birth of Tragedy*. Not only is Theognis himself not clearly a noble; he risks being an instance (in Nietzsche's later vocabulary) of *ressentiment*, which typically projects wished-for values where these are most conspicuously lacking. Nobles, in a mind like that of Theognis, are a fantasy—that of a resentful, clouded spirit.[21] Worse, they may prove to be a fantasy of later ascetic culture itself. For at the end of these notes from 1864, the logic of Theognis' resentment is complicated by a devastating speculation, this time about the provenance of the Theognidean corpus itself: "Was the author [of the most questionable—or most objectionable—portions of the poem] a simulated, fictive ancient [*ein fingierter Alter*], a monk?"[22]

This last suspicion, a consequence of Nietzsche's "skeptical" philology, gives the substance and originality of his first publication, "On the History of the Theognidean Collection of Maxims" (1867).[23] There, Theognis is viewed as a literal philological construct, a composite (literally, "aggregate") of voices from antiquity, including his own (*aus den disiectis membris poetae*). His final unity, such as it is, is superimposed (or rather, further ruined) by a later falsifier of the transmitted Theognidean corpus, a "parodist" who sought to discredit the pagan aristocrat from a moralizing and presumably Christian perspective at some point in later antiquity. "[The redactor] sought out weapons to damage [Theognis]: he deliberately introduced shadows here and there into the pure image of Theognis' character. To this end, he assembled parodies of Theognis and *threw in verses of Mimnermus*," a sensuously minded predecessor, "which, soft in tone, made for a strange contrast with the hard, energetically robust, often gloomy and grim thoughts of

Theognis."[24] These two portraits of Theognis and the redactor may be somewhat fantastic, but Nietzsche is not inventing at random: he is exploiting contemporary perceptions. One point of reference, apart from the textual critical tradition represented by Friedrich Gottlieb Welcker (1826) and Theodor Bergk (1845), is K. O. Müller's widely influential history of the Dorians (*Die Dorier* [1824]), or rather, we should say, the aristocratic, Prussian, and *Blut und Boden* ideology that is reflected in that history (as Momigliano and others have noted).[25] Müller turns out to be a crucial touchstone in Nietzsche's thinking about antiquity generally, and he provides an essential context to Nietzsche's understanding of Theognis in particular. A few comments about Müller are in order. He will be indispensable to us again below.

August Boeckh's most brilliant pupil, K. O. Müller (1797–1840) sought to locate the essence of Greekness in a desperate way. His study opens with a highly speculative reconstruction of *Völkerwanderungen*, set in the recesses of prehistorical time, and then traces the subsequent vicissitudes of the Dorian race on mainland Greece.[26] For Müller, Greekness in its pure form is located not in democratic Athens but in the archaic and aristocratic culture of Sparta, Athens' greatest Greek rival. At first sight this looks like a powerful move against the classical ideal, and it holds obvious attractions for Nietzsche, both early and late. In Müller's imagination, "*martial valour* was deeply implanted in the Dorian nature"; the Dorian people are measured and harmonious; "the general accent of their language carried the impress of a command or apothegm, not that of a question or request"; they display "a sound disposition that is aware of its own principles, and this not through studied reflection but through sudden illumination"; "their gaze is directed not at *becoming* but at *being*"; "the terms 'good' and 'bad'" signify political rank and lineage, not moral attitudes; and so on.[27] The parallels with the Greek nobles for whom Theognis acts as a spokesman in *Genealogy*, I:5, are remarkably close: "*esthlos* signifies one who *is*, who possesses reality, who is actual, who is true." But how does Theognis fit in?

Theognis, with his complaints about decline, is a troubling figure for Müller, but then so is every instance of pure Dorianism after its initial prehistorical appearance. Its only pure moment lies in the mists of prehistory, which is to say in the mere postulation of Dorianism: the rest is gradual but inexorable decline.[28] Dorianism in its historical appearance is thus a kind of living monument, or else, in Müller's own words, a monumental "ruin" standing in "foreign surroundings," by which he means, strikingly enough, the surrounding Greek tribes.[29] If Müller has little to say about Theognis in his *Dorier*, in his *Geschichte der griechischen Literatur* (1841) he tries to rescue the poet as an instance of "older and noble Doric customs."[30] Theognis plainly encapsulates in his person the dilemmas of Müller's reconstructed *Doriertum*, which is among other things an ambivalent instance of classicism: it is inflected with both the bright, clear, and measured Apollinian impulses of classicism and the darker, more brooding, and degenerative traits of classicism's counterpart, or rather its underside. These latter include passionate outbursts from the depths of the soul; gazing proudly and conservatively— or is it longingly?—back onto the past; a steep "dualism" and conflicted darkness within Apollo's realm itself; not to mention furtive *Knabenliebe*. Nor did Müller sense any contradiction here.[31]

Müller may not have, but Nietzsche certainly did. In his earlier set of notes, Nietzsche paraphrases Müller's classicism, especially the latter's depiction of the Dorian religious mentality, which provides a crucial background to Theognis' society: "It shows itself to be a thoroughly *idealistic* tendency of mind, and it conceives divinity less in connection with natural life than with the free activity of men"; hence it is "clear, . . . light, cheerful, and free-spirited." But then Nietzsche goes on to subvert this picture by featuring Theognis as its internal contradiction.[32] The move is not entirely original. Wilhelm S. Teuffel had already in 1852 painted Theognis as a depressive aristocrat, whose "dark subjectivity" and whose "pride of consciousness against the humiliations of life" betray his aristocratic pretensions.[33] Nietzsche heightens the tensions in his notes by juxtaposing Müller's views, which seem to be on a par with Theognis' own disavowing instincts, with Theognis' darker shades. (Dorians can appear as free-spirited as they do "because," Müller writes, "depressiveness and gloom were *kept at a fair remove* from exuberant and brightening feelings.")[34] In Nietzsche's publication, the same effect is achieved by filling out the "pure," which is to say original and uncontaminated image of Theognis, with a less than pure set of features: "the hard, energetically robust, *often gloomy and grim thoughts of Theognis*." How secure are any of these images of Theognis?[35] These uncertainties have an immediate bearing on *The Birth of Tragedy*, where Müller's influence on the pictures of Dorianism and Apollinianism drawn there has been well established. Looking farther ahead, Nietzsche's portraits confirm at a distance the unwanted implications of his own divided picture of nobility in *On the Genealogy of Morals*, and more generally of the kindred spirit they are supposed to exemplify, the controversial "blond beast" of this work and the later writings. These figures, too, are contaminated by the very resentful traits that their definition is supposed to exclude.[36]

In Nietzsche's philological portrait of Theognis as the "mouthpiece" of a bygone nobility, each new detail added to the whole renders Theognis—and the idea of nobility itself—less accessible and more complex, a riddle of overdeterminations and imaginary accretions. Bergk had already rejected Müller's account of Theognis as an unfounded romance; Nietzsche would displace Müller's philological fiction by means of another, the freely invented figure of Theognis' redactor, "hostilely inclined towards Theognis."[37] But a more general lesson can be read out of Nietzsche's moves. The thesis about Theognis' compilation, accepted by Bergk and others, had two flaws to it: it treated Theognis' case as exceptional; and it failed to account for the projective mechanisms of the history of literature, mechanisms that Nietzsche is not only uncovering but also exemplifying in his fanciful historical reconstruction. Nietzsche's practice here anticipates his thesis about Homer in "Homer and Classical Philology" (1869), where the focus is likewise on the text's transmission—figured by an imagined and deceptive redactor—and not on the transmitted text.[38] As with Theognis, Homer's identity is not isolable as such. On the contrary, it is wrapped up in a chain of overdeterminations, rewritings, and idealizations: it is a product of the natural and unconscious habits of reading and of perceptions (and misperceptions) that have been codified by centuries-long practices and institutions, and to which we owe the images of antiquity that are in circulation in the contemporary cultural present. "A mythical monster that has gone through the strangest [historical] transformations," Homer is a "ghost,"[39] but then so is Democritus, as we saw. All of the "personalities" reconstructed by Nietzsche from the past have this complex indexical and even ghostly quality to them, which makes them difficult to read, but in the absence of which they would be unreadable by us. Nietzsche's lesson is plain, and it should be familiar by now. Antiquity can be read only through the traces of its transmission. We can have no unmediated access to it.[40]

Pindar and Aeschylus fare no differently from Theognis or Homer: in

Nietzsche's hands, they are equally complex and symptom-ridden. Pindar, who marks the closing parenthesis of the lyric age and possibly of the archaic age as a whole (*BT* §6), can be a hopeless melancholic (a trait elsewhere reserved for Euripides),[41] while Aeschylus, inaugurating the tragic age (in the narrowest sense), represents a brooding mysticism and a deeper underlying "skepticism" toward divinity, a kind of nihilism vengefully enacted against Olympus: his *Prometheus* projects nothing less than the "intimation of a twilight of the gods" (*BT* §9).[42] But what is finally tragic about Aeschylus is that he "came too late": he appears at the beginning of the end of Greek culture (whence, no doubt, his "skeptical moods").[43] And yet, too late for what? To prevent the decay of Greek culture, or to be untouched by it? "Aeschylus vouches for a height of the Greek spirit that dies out with him"—hardly an unequivocal guarantee.[44] A study preparatory to *The Birth of Tragedy* and dating from 1870 gives a more precise reflection of this equivocalness. There, Aeschylus is periodized into two phases according to a corrupting taint that seeps in from Sophocles ("the quite gradual decline begins with Sophocles"), and that works a reverse influence upon the elder playwright: Aeschylus literally straddles the apogee and the demise of Greek culture.[45] Elsewhere, Sophocles, who "alone" has a truly "tragic *Weltanschauung*" (Aeschylus' here is "still that of epic"), is said to be carrying out a tendency found in Aeschylus, in leading tragedy to its dissolution.[46] Caught in these conflicting and conflicted patterns, Aeschylus is neither unique nor is he a reliably periodizing figure. On the contrary, his dilemmas are typical of Nietzsche's narratives about the Greek past, all of which reflect a crisis of historical characterization.

If the traits of Aeschylus are expectedly close to those of his earlier archaic contemporaries, the Presocratic philosophers (they tend to be treated together by Nietzsche), so, too, is the predicament they share. Yet the look these latter figures wear is considerably different from what one might expect of Nietzsche's proud invention of an archaic, preclassical and anticlassical period. Far from typifying an exalted "tyranny of the spirit," teeming with cruelty, arrogance, and vitality and heralding a new style of human being that presages the *Übermensch* of the later writings, and despite his claims that they constituted the "zenith" of Greek culture (*HA*, I:261), Nietzsche's Presocratics are, strangely, a *failed* type, "*forerunners of a reformation*" that never took place. With the Presocratics, "the Greeks were *about to discover a still higher type* of man than existed previously." Nothing came of their efforts.[47] Even at their acme in the sixth century, "the Greeks never achieved their best."[48] All that was achieved was "a *tragic age* of the Greeks," no more than an empty "promise." And yet what is tragic about these thinkers resides not in the enormity of their failures but in the modality of their achievements. Proudly tyrannical, presumptuous, ascetically hardened, joyfully in possession of truth ("never" was such joy greater), the Presocratics have a knowledge that ultimately rests on mere "belief." Their boastful individuality is illusory, a mere phantasm: "Even their independence [from one another] is only apparent. In the final analysis, each philosopher is chained to his predecessors. *Phantasm to phantasm.*"[49] On another reading of this remark, each of these figures is *himself* a phantasm. This would conform to Nietzsche's general assessment of individuals from antiquity as "mythical" abstractions, and indeed as mere "ideas" and "idealizations," whether of their own making, of their society's, or of a more recent vintage.[50] Nietzsche's stance in these same notes is correspondingly detached, "mournful," even "ironic": "It is odd [or "comical," *komisch*] to take everything so seriously."[51] In his final judgment, "the whole older philosophy [has to be viewed] as a curious labyrinth [literally, a "maze of missteps and wanderings": *Irrgarten-Gang*] of reason. *It has to be sung in the key of dreams and fairytales.*"[52] Hence, an adjacent note could apply equally well to Nietzsche's story about the Presocratics or to their own philosophy: "Ironic novellas: Everything is false."[53]

The Presocratics taken as a whole are an empty illusion, destined to nonexistence. When Nietzsche goes on to ask, *"How does this age die off? . . . Where lie the first germs of the corruption?"* the question contains its own answer. The corruption is within: "They have a hole [or "deficiency," *Lücke*] in their nature."[54] Inner contradiction ("here everything is so inventive, sensible, audacious, despairing, and full of hope"[55]) and pathetic failure (constituted by imaginary success), more than anything else, mark Nietzsche's archaic age, which as we are beginning to see cannot even be consistently drawn. Similarly, Aeschylus' "skeptical moods" stand in contrast to his own "immovably firm foundation for metaphysical thought in [the] mysteries" (*BT* §9), while the latter tendency is in contrast to the Presocratic "ascetic" will to truth and belief. How can all of this be reconciled? Worse still, on Nietzsche's own criteria, Plato has to be reckoned a notional Presocratic, as does Socrates ("Every Greek was a tyrant in his secret desires").[56] But then so do we, for as Nietzsche writes in notes to "On Truth and Lying in an Extra-Moral Sense," "all occurrences of having truth are at bottom only a belief that one has the truth," and thus "no one can firmly believe himself to be in possession of the truth without some *delusion*."[57] Perhaps the Presocratics exist simply to point away from themselves: "There are still very many possibilities that have not even been discovered yet: *because the Greeks did not discover them*."[58] Only, the Greeks now seem to point toward ourselves. Whether Nietzsche's tragic age philosophers are any less "classical" for all that remains to be seen.

Nietzsche's "invention" of the archaic period and the significance it is supposed to have risk proving to be an invention of his interpreters, starting perhaps with Richard Oehler, a coeditor of some of the later popular editions of Nietzsche's works (the revised, complete edition appeared in 1901–13) and the author of *Friedrich Nietzsche und die Vorsokratiker* (1904), the first study of its kind. Appearing a year after Hermann Diels' landmark edition of the fragments of the Presocratics and Karl Joël's *Der Ursprung der Naturphilosophie aus dem Geiste der Mystik* of the same year, Oehler's study bears all the marks of a myth in the making: it is plainly an attempt to turn Nietzsche into a prophet of a new and (Oehler hoped) newly emerging vision of the Greeks.[59] To do so meant, however, establishing a coherence in Nietzsche where there is either none or not the kind that Oehler wished for. The aim of Oehler's study is to unify Nietzsche's image of antiquity and to harmonize this image with Nietzsche's philosophy of Dionysian, life-affirming power. Yet the fact that there is something flawed in Nietzsche's picture of the Presocratic age is obvious even to Oehler: "True, the way for the decline and fall was paved already in their time, and it had also already partially commenced." But no sooner is this partial concession made than it is just as quickly erased: "That is why Nietzsche also depicts [the Presocratics] as reformers, as combatants pitched against the dangers and corruptions of the Greeks."[60] In the end, Oehler would succeed. "Scarcely had Diels's edition appeared when Nietzsche immediately displaced it and all others."[61] Thus was born a myth about the philosophical movement that Nietzsche did not invent but only problematized. His preclassical Greece is not archaic. It is at best an affected archaism.[62]

If, on the other hand, we look away from the controlling images of *The*

Birth of Tragedy, which govern every reading of Nietzsche's archaism, and consider his philological publications by themselves, we find a quite different story. Apart from Theognis, who as we saw may not even count, Nietzsche never published his discovery of archaic Greece in a learned form, and even his only essay on the "Preplatonics," "Philosophy in the Tragic Age of the Greeks" (1873), remained a posthumous fragment.[63] What he did publish in scholarly journals (between 1867 and 1873) shows an extraordinary historical range, with a predilection for the *post*classical period, which is marked by its problematical transmission of the prior Greek canon: an early article on the lyric poet Simonides, which is less about Simonides and his Danae poem than it is about the first century B.C.E. Roman critic Dionysius of Halicarnassus who preserves the poem (and conceals, Nietzsche argues, its true strophic form); three studies on the third-century C.E. epitomizer of Greek philosophers and their lives, Diogenes Laertius; and apart from those reviews treating Hesiod, Theognis, and the Anacreonta, reviews on Eudocia (a Byzantine compiler of earlier Greek authors [the work is heavily interpolated]), the falsified epistles of Heraclitus, Aristoxenus, Platonism, and Lucian. All this is in line with his earliest ambition to write "a history of literary studies in antiquity and modernity" as well as a history of philosophy through its transmission ("Diogenes Laertius, Stobaeus, ps.-Plutarch, etc."), of which his studies on the authenticity of Democritus would have formed a part.[64] In addition there are his projects on Aristoxenus and later rhythmical theorists, on Greek and Roman rhetorical theory, and on sundry other subjects that spilled over into his teaching as well. Summing up, we can say that Nietzsche's research interests are not defined by one period or another. They are defined by the transmission of classical antiquity itself.

One of his more lasting contributions is his article on the *Certamen Homeri et Hesiodi*, published in two parts, in 1870 and 1873. While its thesis has been revindicated, often with a vengeance,[65] we should be careful about reclaiming the argument itself for an all-too-orthodox philology. The article makes a critical point by virtue of its selection of materials alone: it traces a then neglected and maligned Florentine manuscript (a treatise on an imaginary contest between Homer and Hesiod) back to its sophistic origins at the turn of the fourth century. Ascribing the work to Alcidamas of Elaea, a pupil of Gorgias', Nietzsche proudly declares it to be "a product of the classical period," thus throwing a shadow on this periodizing concept.[66] He then claims that his finding opens a window onto the "whole history of the concept of the contest."[67] The never-published essay, "Homer's Contest" (1872), gives a fuller and at times dizzying glimpse into that same history, and we will want to come back to it below. The point is that to focus on Nietzsche and his archaic period is to get the accent all wrong. His abiding interest is not in ancient authors for their own sake but in their exemplary status (they are generally "types," not individuals), and above all in their reception and construction by a tradition that stretches into the contemporary world. Even his sketches of the archaic age are drawn in this trembling light. The studies on Theognis, witnessed above, are a case in point. The same applies to his studies on Democritus, which for all their desire to recover this exemplary Presocratic are deeply invested in a larger historical and self-reflexive project, namely, the inquiry into what it is that governs the needs and limits the efforts to reclaim antiquity for the present.[68] I believe that all of Nietzsche's philological activity is conditioned by this question. To try to get hold of the archaic period in a direct and unmediated way is to take precisely the opposite course.

Looking back, we can see that all of Nietzsche's representative Greeks are shot through with ambiguity, as if to reflect their incapacity to signify so much past and present meaning. They are suffused with a sense of their overwhelming historicity, by which should be understood not their recoverable positive historical identity but exactly the opposite: their irrecoverability, which is what provokes the question about their identity and the search for their historicity. Without exception, Nietzsche's representative "personalities" from antiquity are all slightly out of focus and troublingly so. "What attracted me," he writes about his interest in Theognis, "was the confusion of the fragments. Not the ethical dimension. But rather what was problematical about the fragments."[69] In his essay on Homer, published in a vanity edition in 1869, Nietzsche describes more precisely the source of his interest. It is what he calls the "original kernel" of Homer's identity, which is, significantly, as "empty" as Homer's name: an insoluble void that gains in potency and fascination as time wears on, this "kernel" has a markedly *retroactive* character as well. Homer's identity, or rather the question of his identity, *die Persönlichkeitsfrage*, is "the fruitful kernel of an entire cycle of questions."[70]

Nietzsche's perspective is, characteristically, retrospective and modern. If the typical representatives of Nietzsche's literary and cultural histories bear the marks of their patent construction, that is a result of his philology by *Persönlichkeit*, which allows him to indulge and retreat from the fiction of a person at will. "The contest! And this denial of the individual! These aren't historical but only mythical people. Even the personality [*das Persönliche*] enjoys glory only (as in Pindar) if it is wrapped in distant myths" (1871/72).[71] By virtue of its literary-historical succession, philology is a successor to the ancient mythologies of the "person." And so too, if in the representatives of his freshly discovered archaic period Nietzsche evokes the figure of the *Spätling*, or the one who arrives "too late," he is evoking a figure of time's passing itself: they embody their own elusive historicity.[72] Indeed, the problem with Nietzsche's preclassical Greeks is that they resemble, if anything, *the postclassical moderns*, written over as they are from the longing perspectives of their later audience. The notion of the epigonal *Spätling*, or latecomer, is, after all, a commonplace of nineteenth-century mythology about *itself*.[73] And it is this contamination of ancient and modern traits that finally renders the precise location of Nietzsche's figures problematic. They all have something phantomlike about them; they are all, like Homer, products of a later "deception." It is not only that isolating discrete historical periods, tagged by personalities, is a problematical approach for Nietzsche. He is drawn to moments that put into doubt their own historical characterization. And all the moments that comprise his version, or rather versions, of antiquity do just this.

The most dramatic case is also the most touted. The Dionysian satyr choruses of *The Birth of Tragedy* are as purely archaic as anyone could hope to find in Nietzsche. And yet on closer inspection they turn out to be infected with Socratism,[74] and what is worse, with Platonism. But then so is the whole of Greek culture: "The Platonic distinction and evaluation of the 'Idea' [that is, Form] in contrast to the 'idol,' the mere copy, *is very deeply grounded in the Hellenic character.* . . . Using Plato's terminology we should have to speak of the tragic figures of the Hellenic stage somewhat as follows: The one truly real Dionysus appears in a variety of forms" (*BT* §10; emphasis added). As Nietzsche's language leaves no doubt, *Dionysus is in fact a Platonic Idea*, as are all Greek appearances, all the phenomena of Greek culture.[75] Is this what Nietzsche's famous "inversion of Platonism" amounts to? Or should we say that the modern view of antiquity is necessarily—*Pla-*

tonic?[76] Needless to say, circularities of this magnitude confound the logic of Nietzsche's surface narratives, to the point where moments of "evolution" prove impossible to distinguish from moments of "decline" or "corruption." Even the Homeric Achilles is pictured as already "mourning . . . the decline of the heroic age" (*BT* §3). The question that needs to be asked about Nietzsche's vision of antiquity is not when did decline set in, but *when was there ever no declining?*[77] That is the difficulty that besets all of Nietzsche's largest cultural histories, and not only in the inverted history of Dionysus given by his "Encyclopedia of Classical Philology," in which Dionysus and the pre-Olympian gods are said to be an aesthetic invention, after the fact, by Apollo (as we saw in chap. 4), or in the competing and unresolved histories of rhythmical sensations that are sketched out in the notebooks on rhythm, whose very indecision enacts the agony of describing, in a neutral way, a historical progression (as we saw in chap. 3).

Narrative problems like these present supreme obstacles to any reductive reading of Nietzsche's views of antiquity. The challenge they raise is not to the going paradigms of historical perception alone but to the very *coherence* of historical perception. The self-consuming dimension of Nietzsche's narratives of the antique past is in fact their most characteristic feature. What is more, I believe, they contain within themselves a warning about how we read the past through its mythological construction. Nor is this warning concealed: they wear it on their sleeves and in their very *form*. For this reason alone, Nietzsche's models of antiquity cannot be simply reduced to pro- or anticlassical models. Their very complexity and their multiply allusive texture prohibit any such easy reduction. To view them in any other way is to substitute one myth for another. Nietzsche, in effect, dares us to try not to do just that.

His retelling of Hesiod's myth of the ages offers a good illustration of the point. Nietzsche knows Hesiod in different forms, but the most striking of these is surely the account in the First Essay of *On the Genealogy of Morals*:

> I once drew attention to the dilemma in which Hesiod found himself when he concocted[78] his succession of cultural epochs and sought to express them in terms of gold, silver, and bronze: he knew no way of handling the contradiction presented by the glorious but at the same time terrible and violent world of Homer except by dividing one epoch

into two epochs, *which he then placed one behind the other*—first the epoch of the heroes and demigods of Troy and Thebes, the form in which that world had survived in the memory of the noble races who were those heroes' true descendants; then the bronze epoch, the form in which that same world appeared to the descendants of the downtrodden, pillaged, mistreated, abducted, enslaved: an epoch of bronze, as aforesaid, hard, cold, cruel, devoid of feeling or conscience, destructive and bloody. (*GM*, I:11; emphasis added)

On the surface, the Hesiodic myth of the five ages or races of man appears to chart the inexorable decline of mortal existence, from a once golden era, when men consorted with gods, through a succession of deteriorations (silver, bronze), to a puzzling interlude (the heroic age), which seems to stall the downward trajectory momentarily (heroes being perhaps better and more just than brazen bronze men [Hesiod, *Works and Days*, v. 158]). Then comes a final decline (the iron age of the present). Nietzsche's reading of Hesiod marvelously exploits the logical and structural ambivalences of the myth. Are the heroes better men than their predecessors proved to be? Nietzsche seems undecided and will have it both ways. In this passage he places them first, ahead of the bronze age of man, possibly in line with Hesiod's tacit meaning, but against his express sequence. In the earlier version from *Daybreak* (189 [1881]), alluded to in the *Genealogy* passage above, Nietzsche seems to do it the other way around.

Either of these approaches to the archaic poet is meaningful only if Nietzsche took the sequence to be linear, but there are plenty of signs that he wished us to take it as nonlinear. Indeed, there is evidence to suggest that Hesiod himself took the sequence to be cyclical, for instance in his exclamation, wrung from the depths of pessimism: "Would that I were not among the fifth race of men, / but had either died earlier or been born later!" (*Works and Days*, vv. 174–75). But in both of Nietzsche's versions, time in fact appears to follow a logic that is neither linear nor cyclical, nor even geometrical in any clear fashion, but simply puzzling, projective, and critical. If Hesiod's bipartite audience are truly descendants of the heroic/bronze age (as in the *Genealogy*), let alone their contemporaries (as *Daybreak* might appear to suggest),[79] then the current age is no different from its predecessor, and the whole notion of progression or degeneracy is suspect: history merely repeats itself in differently imagined colors, but with a wearying sameness. If, on the other hand, the descendants know of the past only through its memory, then there is only the present and no past but merely the projection of one—the making of "*two* [strictly, it is three] *ages out of one*" (*Daybreak*, 189).[80] Nietzsche's Hesiodic genealogy is a commentary on the mechanisms of this retrojection. It is a study in the devices of memory. And it brings mythical ideality, whether painted in dark or bright colors, back to the level of its all-too-human and all-too-"grey" foundations of the present, whether this be Hesiod's or, by analogy (which is, after all, the point of the exemplication in both passages), our own.[81] Let us consider this last point briefly.

Embedded within Hesiod's "concocted" succession of cultural epochs is a literary memory, the memory of another contrivance, namely Homer's epics and their ambivalent world of glory and violence. An original contradiction—glory rests on violence—is resolved into its elements and then projected onto a new chronology: in essence, two incompatible perspectives (heroic glory eclipses violence; bronze and brazen violence is without glory), each of which throws its partial light on a contradiction whose meaning escapes both views. Those perspectives originate in the present, in the divisions between two classes of subjects who gaze resentfully or fondly on the past, as the case may be: the downtrodden (or their descendants) can make past pain and suffering meaningful, while the "nobles" can see in their own somewhat shabbier image the justification for their savage practices, if not the nostalgic hope for a renewal and reascendancy to absolute, "blissful," or just blissfully violent, power. Contradictions from the present are thus projected onto the screen of the past, where they can be resolved and even explained, through a spatializing distance in time, a kind of monumentalization perhaps, but one that monumentally confuses history and myth, and worse, one that conceals and confuses the contradictions of their actual source in the present. History is the contradictory expression of the present and its confused memory—the invention of a sequence that clarifies nothing but merely records and obscures a "dilemma" in the present. Nietzsche's retelling of the fable warns us against a naive reading of genealogy and about the risks of confusing history and mythology. Greece is one such mythology, and Nietzsche's inventive "Hesiod" is one of the myths of that mythology.[82] In both its form and its content, Hesiod's fable represents the mythological projection of history, a fact to which Nietzsche's reading of the myth draws attention in a pointed and hermeneutically violent way. Once again, the modern subject finds itself in the archaic past—projecting the myth of an archaic past.[83]

Even though these retellings of Hesiod are late, they are well in line with Nietzsche's earlier ways of reconceptualizing and problematizing antiquity. As with Theognis just a few sections earlier in the same work, in the present case, too, Nietzsche has actually gone back to his own philological notebooks for inspiration. Compare, for instance, the following from the lecture notes to the "Encyclopedia of Classical Philology": "The age of the Titans and Cronos and the Olympians with Zeus are *fundamentally identical*: in the same way, the myths of heroes and the original sagas about the gods are fundamentally identical. *So, too, the iron age and the age of the heroes.*" What is the reason for their eventual distinction? The answer, as we have seen, is astonishing: "A process of beautification," whereby "the divine world of beauty produces the chthonic divinities [viz., its chronological predecessors] as its own supplement."[84] Idealization, in other words, produces distinctions *where there were none before*, a glorified world of violence and its paler reflex in the present. Does the contrast possibly mask a grayer, more banal reality that corresponds to neither of these "beautifications"—one that is closer to the condition of the iron present?

Other notes from the time (1871/72) preserve similar traces of a rewriting of Hesiod's myth of the ages,[85] which as it happens are closely linked to Nietzsche's early conception of "pre-Homeric violence." And as we saw, there is even a telltale clue to this reversed and retrojective chronology in *The Birth of Tragedy*, which in turn would need to be reapplied to the whole of that work ("Thus did the Delphic god interpret the Greek past" [*BT* §4]). The parallels all converge in a simple pattern, which is one of disguised projection and distortion: the earliest, pre-Homeric phase of violence thus seems to be a later invention, much like Nietzsche's archaic period itself. And the disguises are at best half-hidden, and thus half-known: "The effects wrought by the *Dionysian* also *seemed* 'titanic' and 'barbaric' to the Apollinian Greek; while at the same time *he could not conceal from himself* that he, too, was inwardly related to these overthrown Titans and heroes" (ibid.; last two emphases added). Nietzsche's reading ranks with any of the attempts by classical scholars to solve the apparent contradiction in Hesiod's myth, namely, the curious place of the heroic age in the sequence of the five ages.[86] It would be wrong to state that Nietzsche's reading qualitatively differs from the philology he ordinarily critiques. His predecessors could in their own ways be as wild and eccentric as Nietzsche often is. He simply excels at these traits.[87]

A final, baffling example of "anti"-classicism gone awry is Nietzsche's invocation, in his posthumously published essay "Homer's Contest" (1872), of "the pre-Homeric abyss of horrible savagery, hatred, and pleasure in destruction."[88] This is another Hesiodic—which is to say, projective and critical—conceit, and quite literally so, since Nietzsche affects to derive the principle from Hesiod's account of the pre-Olympian divinities, the Titans and the daughters of Night: Strife, Death, and Old Age, but also Desire and Deception (p. 785). The anticlassicist implications are plain to see, and Nietzsche is quick to draw them: Homer can no longer be imagined to reflect "the springtime of the people, etc.," without a background ("winter") of horror and cruelty.[89] The view that these "frightful" and "irrational" creatures are pre-Homeric was the received wisdom even among adherents of classicism (here, Welcker and Müller).[90] Classicism *consisted in the very story that Nietzsche is telling*: the idealization of horror—of this "violent" and irrational "chaos" with its "dark, unfathomable *Urgrund*" and "terrors"—is what classicism is all about. Violence is foundational to classicism in this precise sense.[91] What mileage can Nietzsche hope to gain from retelling it again? And what, we might well ask, has happened to the notion that it was Apollo who invented the world of the Titans and projected it back in time as pre-Homeric? At the very least, Nietzsche owes us an answer, in the first case as proof of his anticlassicist credentials, and in the second for the sake of consistency. The answer, I want to suggest, lies in the concept of the pre-Homeric itself.

Judging by its name, the "pre-Homeric" condition described ought to be a temporal condition of Greek civilization. It is in fact recurrent, as it can only be if the threat of its anticlassicist implications is to be made to stick.[92] That is Nietzsche's innovation vis-à-vis the going views of antiquity in nineteenth-century histories of Greek religion, mythology, and culture: not the rediscovery of the pre-Homeric world (for that was already a given) but its unmooring from history and the insight into its potential for universality. The problem, however, is that the pre-Homeric world recurs in the wrong ways. A brilliant example of the condition is the early fifth century Athenian general Miltiades when he suddenly loses the protection, or cover, of socially sanctioned contest and commits hubristic outrages. At this moment we steal a glimpse into the "pre-Homeric" abyss (and by extension into Dionysian horror): Miltiades falls into vengefulness; "he becomes wicked and cruel"; he "*degenerates*"; "*in a word, he becomes 'pre-Homeric'*" (p. 792; emphases added). The figure of Miltiades, freely embroidered upon in Nietzsche's account, is an example of the self-betrayal of the Hellenic spirit in Athens and Sparta; he points the way, not to the valuable return of the repressed in Greek culture, but to the definitive demise of that culture and to the coming age of Alexander. That is how Nietzsche chooses to close his essay, in a *panic* of logic. The naming of this final disaster, for all the bafflement it occasions, is perfectly consistent with the logic of the conceit, or rather paradox, around which the essay is formed: joyful, violent combat (the contest) is what protects Greek culture from its own (pre-Homeric) horrors; horror ("horrible savagery, hatred, and pleasure in destruction") is a defense against horror, which is to say, *against itself.*[93] Nothing self-consistent could possibly follow from such a premise, and nothing does. And generally speaking, the sheer contradictions in Nietzsche's image, or images, of antiquity, which can be extreme but which have yet to be appreciated, fall into this same pattern.[94]

Consider how the Greeks can be held up as paragons of supreme moderation ("The *moderation* of the Greeks in their sensuous expenditures, eating, drinking, and the pleasure they took in these . . . —that shows what they were") or as the victims of an uncontrollable sensuousness ("The Greeks lack sobriety. Excessive sensitivity, abnormally heightened activity of the nerves and brain, vehemence and passionateness of desire"). They can be naive and credulous (evincing a "child's nature") or treacherously false and deceptive (*lügnerisch*). They can display extremest "cruelty in battle and dispute" or else "pliancy" and "exaggerated sociability." They can be endowed with the capacity to transfigure the present moment into a state of utter sublimity ("*into the immense and eternal*") or be given to "myth, the lazy bed of thought," depending upon Nietzsche's mood. Such irreconcilabilities, which can appear in the space of a page or even within a paragraph, are one of the least noticed features of Nietzsche's narratives of classical antiquity,[95] as is their ultimate source, which lies not in antiquity but in the modern conceits about antiquity, which Nietzsche is merely reflecting in all their disparity and more than occasional incoherence. In the present case, Nietzsche's Greeks are virtually indistinguishable from Humboldt's, who could display all these traits at once, or from those of the classicist Christian Lobeck, Gottfried Hermann's pupil and the author of a study of religion ridiculed by Nietzsche in *Twilight of the Idols*: "'When the Greeks had nothing else to do,' [Lobeck] says (*Aglaophamus*, I:672), 'they used to laugh, jump, race about, or since man sometimes feels a desire for this, they used to sit down and weep and wail. *Others* later came along and sought some reason for this striking behavior; and thus those countless myths and legends arose to explain these practices.'"[96]

To be sure, in cases the Greeks are capable of displaying contradictions that might in principle be their own (their penchants for mythological belief or for cold abstraction and rigorous scientific knowledge, etc.).[97] Yet these eventually, and suspiciously, become intertwined with traits that are all too familiarly modern: scholarly cold abstraction and rigor, leitmotifs of Nietzsche's meta-reflections on philological method, can produce mythical beliefs about the Greeks, his commonest complaint. Not for nothing are the Greeks an essentially ahistorical race ("Given to lies. Unhistorical").[98] Like their later extrapolation, the nobles of *On the Genealogy of Morals* who are models of "forgetfulness," Nietzsche's Greeks reflect back, in their ahistoricity, the ahistorical projections of the more recent present, which Nietzsche discovers even in the so-called historicist tendencies of classical scholarship, what Odo Marquard has called, in a Nietzschean vein, "the latent ahistoricity of the historical sense."[99] Similarly, the deceptive naïveté of Nietzsche's Greeks, which reflects back the self-deceptions of the naive classical ideal today.[100] Models of historical projection, Nietzsche's Greeks betray the blemishes of their own construction, but in an inverted and therefore misrecognizable form. They are models of historical misrecognition in Nietzsche's contemporary present. And, to the extent that Nietzsche's images of antiquity continue to fascinate us today, we are part of that present.

The Myth of "Classicism"

At the end of his career, Nietzsche makes the following remarkable statement: "I owe absolutely no such strong impressions to the Greeks; and, not to mince words, they *cannot* be to us what the Romans are. One does not *learn* from the Greeks—their manner is too strange, it is also too fluid to produce an imperative, a 'classical' effect. Who would ever have learned to write from a Greek!" (*Twilight of the Idols*, "What I Owe to the Ancients," 2; trans. mod.). Could his arguments have only an occasional validity? I believe this is so. In all of them, he is merely trying on a pose. Thus, when it suits Nietzsche to do so, he can treat Homer as an "individual being," as an emblem of the naive artist, as a fantasy of the Greek mind, or as the effective cause of Greece's decline, "the actual *fatality* of Greek culture," its panhellenically available (hence leveling, and in any case tyrannically oppressive because seemingly unsurpassable) myth.[101] In this last case, Nietzsche postulates that the centralization and the effects of dissolution occur "early on," prior even to the more recognizable archaic age—as he only can given his understanding about the history of the Homeric epics.[102] Elsewhere we see the sequelae of this process in the archaic age. The "pre-Homeric" mentality compels Greeks to violence not so much against others as against themselves and in the realm of the "imaginary": asceticism, feelings of guilt, and ritual purification ("Orpheus, Pythagoras") are its symptoms.[103] Is the decline—the decadence—of Greece possibly to be pegged as *pre-Homeric*?

It would doubtless be more convenient if Nietzsche's ancient perspectives were consistently anticlassical. The fact is that his subversiveness is harder to pin down (his inconsistencies can appear like slips of the pen) and ultimately less acceptable than one might wish to suppose. True, he often appears to propose an alternative picture of antiquity that flatly goes against the humanistic ideal consecrated by Winckelmann and his successors. And yet Nietzsche's own pictures of the past, even of his archaic period, are at the same time filled with those very idealizing features he claims to reject: naïveté, geniality, originality, spontaneous creativity, instincts to art, worship of beauty, illusion, simplicity, unity, healthy body-consciousness, elitism, self-cultivation and self-fashioning (whether individual, ethical, or political), and so on, not to mention his overarching biases, philhellenism and Hellenocentrism, which are likewise inherited and confirmed rather than overthrown ("*beauty* seems to be uniquely Greek"; Romans are "shallow" by comparison).[104] Which is more horrible, one might well wonder: Nietzsche's alternative "horrifying" antiquity or his self-inconsistency?

A striking instance, which takes us back to the heart of the archaic period, is to be found in the picture of Heraclitus that emerges from the never-finished essay "Philosophy in the Tragic Age of the Greeks" (1873). In apparent contrast to the "deep mystical night" that dwells in Anaximander's principle of becoming, Heraclitus' philosophy represents an Apollinian dream world, one that is all light and harmony, cheerful in tenor (in express contrast to Schopenhauerian pessimism), untroubled by contradiction, and founded on a purely "aesthetic" perception of reality.[105] He thereby also stands worlds apart from the anemic abstraction of his great successor Parmenides, whom Nietzsche goes on to disparage as "un-Greek."[106] These two sets of contrasts are all the more remarkable, seeing how a few pages earlier the argument was that the Presocratics were all "carved from one stone."[107] The metaphor is doubly significant. It alludes to the principal belief (it is in fact a "metaphysical article of faith") that in Nietzsche's eyes unites all the Presocratics, or rather their desperate life-affirming urge to unify reality into a harmonious, ideal picture (hence their virtual motto, "Everything is all One"); and it is a reflection of Nietzsche's very own idealization of the Presocratics, of that "marvelously idealized philosophers' society" (they are all one).[108]

Nietzsche had good precedents. Jacob Bernays, the Jewish philologist from Bonn and Nietzsche's early model for a "philology of the future," had made similar moves in his foundational studies on Heraclitus (1850 and 1854);[109] and Heraclitus had already been claimed by the classicizing tradition—by Goethe, Schleiermacher, Hölderlin, Hegel, and others. What attracted them all to Heraclitus' system was its reconciliation of opposites (of the sensuous and the ideal, of strife and justice, etc.).[110] In German eyes, and certainly in Nietzsche's (at least, here), Heraclitus seems to stand in a special symbolic relation to his Presocratic philosophical peers (it was Schleiermacher who famously organized them into a whole):[111] Heraclitus' indifference to contradiction allows him to unify their contrasts and to lend them the light of his harmony. Supreme aestheticians, mythologists, mystical intuitionists, and metaphysical idealists, all driven by an "ideal need for life," the Presocratics are for Nietzsche (and for his predecessors too) classical objects par excellence.[112] This is still more emphatically the case in the lecture notes on "The Preplatonic Philosophers" from a year later. Drawing on his earlier fragment, Nietzsche renders Heraclitus into a Presocratic Schiller, an exponent of the aesthetics of *Spieltrieb*, or the instinctual urge to play,[113] while the

Presocratics generally are said to be "after all, *contemporaries of the classical period of classical Greece*, principally of the sixth and fifth centuries, contemporaries of tragedy [and] the Persian wars."[114] Finally, Heraclitus, ever the Apollinian philosopher, viewed the recent upsurge of the Dionysian cult "with complete hostility" and with no trace of sympathy.[115] Has Nietzsche displaced classicism, or has he simply backdated it?

Nietzsche, I want to suggest, has done neither of these things. He has merely *diagnosed* classicism. He knows very well that classicism is an idealization and a simplification of antiquity. Compare a note from 1869/70:

> The "Hellenic" since Winckelmann: an intense superficialization [*Verflachung*]. Then the Christian-Germanic conceit that one was completely beyond it [viz., beyond antiquity in its classical form]. The age of Heraclitus, Empedocles, etc. was unknown. One had the image of a Roman, universal Hellenism, of Alexandrianism. Beauty and superficiality in league, indeed necessary! Scandalous theory![116]

The lesson in plain: classicism is a postclassical phenomenon, the "image of a Roman, universal Hellenism." It is the projection of a desire, and it is simultaneously the disavowal, in bad faith, of this very projection, in a curious ruse of logic that runs "Let the Greeks disavow their heaviness, their materiality, and their darker traits so that they may assume the attitude of cheerful lightness and ideality—that way, we don't have to be troubled by *our* disavowal." At times (as here), Nietzsche waves the Presocratic Greeks like a banner of anticlassicism. But not so whenever he begins to scrutinize them in any detail. Then they reveal themselves, in their aesthetic rage for purity, ideality, and unity, to be as indebted to disavowal as are the exponents of German classicism: they "close their eyes" to reality, to their own self-contradictions, and to what they are.[117] Later on Nietzsche would call this suppression of differences "the lie of unity," and he would do so in a criticism of Heraclitus.[118] But in 1873 he is already aware that Heraclitean harmonies are a "lie." That is what gives them their *beauty*.

Nietzsche does not fall into the error that he critiques in the notebook entry quoted just above: he does not move "beyond" classicism. On the contrary, he repeats its inability to move beyond itself. But then, his myth about archaic Greece has only a strategic, "polemical" value anyway: "Polemical side: against the new [image of] Greece (the Renaissance, Goethe, Hegel, etc.)."[119] He is combating one myth with a countermyth; his archaic Greece brings out the antinomies in the classical model, but it also reflects these, inevitably, in itself.[120] It would be wrong, in any case, to say that Nietzsche's counterantiquity is a rejection of classicism. Instead, it reflects, much like K. O. Müller's parallel project before him, the attempt to construct a *purer* form of classicism: it is the myth of the archaic essence of Greece itself. That myth was available even to Humboldt and his successors, who viewed Greek culture in its earliest manifestations to be at its most natural, "unmixed," and most racially pure.[121] Classical antiquity is merely this myth of archaism in a classical form. It is the myth of the pristine quality of the past itself.

There are two further factors that make resorting to an easily legible anti-classical Greece in Nietzsche problematic, and both are related to this last point. First, while it is true that Nietzsche displaces the long-standing canonical emphasis on fifth-century Athenian culture (an emphasis that stems at least from the Alexandrian period, if not from the end of the Periclean fifth century itself), it is not true that the emphasis of classicism was always and only laid there, as we just saw. Classicism in the form that Winckelmann and Humboldt gave it was of several minds: it had a number of competing views about antiquity going at the same time, and for the most part it drew whatever coherence it had from a general lack of precision in its ideals, which benefited in part just from being vague and untraceable to concrete historical instances. If you have any doubts about this, just try locating, say, a concrete instance of a genuinely classical body. Winckelmann admits to having troubles in this regard. In his *History of Art* he confesses that "not all statues of Apollo have the high degree of beauty" of the Apollo Belvedere.[122] And in his successive draft descriptions he must literally talk himself into an unqualified approval of even this statue, whose blemishes he initially concedes ("the mouth is drawn downward at both ends, . . . the cheeks are flat, the ears a little deep, but larger than the practice of the ancients generally allows for. . . . The ringlets of the hair . . . are not done up with all that much attention," although "the muscles and the whole skin are done fairly sublimely," etc.).[123] His drafts thus retrace the founding disavowal of classicism, as they progress from a hesitant skepticism to blind faith (or its posture). If the genuinely classical is hard to locate, this in no way diminishes its appeal. Ideals have a way of seducing us with their very nonlocatability.[124] That is their chief source of power, which is purely ideological: they present the requirement, and the illusion, of consensus, which in turn masks over a good deal of uncertainty, contestation, and difference. Classicism's construction of the classical ideal is shaped in response to the very impossibility of discovering it in the works that are beheld. Indeed, the very concept of what is "classical" is divided within, appealing as it does to "competing awarenesses of *different* classical esthetics."[125] The problem is one of surfeit: there are too many "antiquities" vying for the title. Is classical antiquity Greek or Roman? Is antiquity in all of its manifestations (times, peoples, places, objects) classical? And if it is not always this, then in what sense is it ever "one" and "whole"? This basic incoherence was one of the greatest problems bequeathed by modern German classicism to the study of classical antiquity. In the application, so to speak, of the classical ideal to classical studies, the greatest achievement of German philological classicism (*Altertumswissenschaft*) proved to be its greatest stumbling block—namely, the very idea of "classical antiquity" itself. The aim, nobly enough, may have been to grasp the phenomena of antiquity in their totality and as a totality. But just what does that mean? The history of philology in Germany into the twentieth century is a record of a series of attempts to wrestle with this insoluble difficulty. Bernhardy's dilemmas, discussed earlier, are merely symptomatic, as were Wolf's before him.

The pronounced (if wavering) Hellenocentrism that marks the whole of German classicism in the face of these questions, starting with Winckelmann and from then on to Humboldt, Schiller, Goethe, and beyond, was one way of minimizing this particular dissonance within the ideal. It is a prejudice that lives on today.[126] Yet not even Hellenocentrism could defend itself against the unsustainable logic of the classical ideal. On this score, Humboldt fares no better than Winckelmann. His answer to the question "What is classical?" is characteristically roving and selective, not to say idiosyncratic (his personal canon of classical authors consists of Homer, Pindar, Sophocles, and Aristophanes; he later adds Aeschylus);[127] but Humboldt's preference, for the most part, is to retreat into a more general Hellenocentric vagueness. Although his classical ideal may be vaguely antique, it is nonetheless the opposite of a timeless world. Pindar, who was neither Athenian nor part of its fifth-century canon, is claimed by Humboldt as an instance of Greek "tranquility" and "cheerfulness." Humboldt is concerned to locate Pindar "historically" (as allegedly here) before he does so "critically" and "purely philosophically." Telling these characterizations apart is another question.[128] Homer is an uncontested instance of classicity, yet how does he fall into an Athenocentric paradigm? One justification for the adoration of Homer by classicists, at any rate, was the claim that "one shouldn't dwell at length on only those periods in which the Greeks were at their finest and most cultivated; on the contrary, one should also single out the first and earliest periods. For it is in these that the kernel of the true Greek character actually lies; and it is easier and more interesting to observe in the sequel how that character gradually changes and *finally degenerates*." So Humboldt, conspicuously failing to specify which early periods he has in mind.[129] Evidently, the problem is not locating classical antiquity but locating *just one instance of it*. There is an elusiveness, indeed a fleetingness, to the classical ideal that is part of its very nature and its allure, and that surrounds it with the penumbra of sadness, melancholy, loss, and desirability, but also with ambivalence and inconsistency.[130] Classicist idealism in its traditional form is not all light and airy "Greek cheerfulness," as Nietzsche knew and as we tend to forget today. The idealism of the Greeks is the surest sign of their fascinating and enigmatic "depth."[131] This last point is Humboldt's, but Nietzsche would only nod in approval.[132] In his consistent idealization of antiquity, Nietzsche is indistinguishable from his classicizing predecessors.[133]

The inheritance of the classical ideal was double: it consisted in a rich imaginary vision and a wealth of contradictions. This is no doubt part of the reason why the classical ideal proved so powerfully attractive and influential, not only among belletrists but also in the field of classical philology as well. Nietzsche will be keen to draw attention to all these factors—the richness, the imaginariness, and the contradictoriness of the classical vision. But there are other, related reasons for this broad historical fascination with the classical ideal. In its structural antinomies, the classical ideal seems to provide a precise reflection of German society, in addition to being a contributing factor in that society's formation. A sociological explanation suggests itself. The turbulences of the eighteenth century, as Germany lurched into modernity, involved massive social and political shifts that entailed new enfranchisements and corresponding disenfranchisements. There was a polarization of society, brought about on the one hand by the rise of *Beamtertum*, the caste of civil servants, to which the noble and elite classes attached themselves, and by the rise of a bourgeois cultural elite (*Bildungsbürgertum*) on the other, largely in reaction. This polarization was reflected in the new social *habitus* of the latter classes. Flight from society into the worlds of books, intellectual productivity, or nature; the concept of the ideal made absolute; and sundry forms of sentimentality (melancholy, resignation, and introversion) have all been named as typifying this reaction of the middle and professional classes to their exclusion from political power and activity. This exclusion may not, however, have been as rigid as it is often made out to be, and it may have been more of an ideological perception or even posture than a reality, especially toward the end of the century.[134] Philologists, historians, philosophers, and literary writers were at the forefront, but the collective effects of these new modes of thinking and feeling eventually flooded the whole of society, coloring it indelibly. By the end of the nineteenth century, these tendencies and pressures would take on a new scale, but they remained fundamentally unchanged. Nietzsche is himself a witness.[135] A question that will preoccupy us below is to what extent classicism vanishes from the study of antiquity in the nineteenth century. Professions of classicism may fall out of fashion, but—to put the question in a more salient form—to what extent does the *habitus* of classicism vanish or persist? Does the *fascination* with Greece in any way diminish as the century wears on?

These questions can be refocused in the following way. The prestige of classicism owed much to the ideological role that attitudes toward antiquity enjoyed in the formation of modern German identity. At the core of the problem of classicism, seen as a reflection of social divisions, are questions of identity, and these are bound up with uncertainties about class-belonging, cultural aspirations, and (as we shall see) national identity. But what is of equal significance, questions of *identity* express themselves in dilemmas of *identification*. And the inhabitants of the ancient world provided a perfect screen on which to project these dilemmas. In an essay from 1796/97 on the eighteenth century, Humboldt writes, "One can never sufficiently call the external activity of mankind back to the constraints of necessity, and never sufficiently invite its mind into the region of infinity."[136] It is not by accident that the impossible splitting of the subject's mandates expressed here is exactly mirrored by Humboldt's classical Greeks, who represent and perform both imperatives, and thus embody the dilemma at the heart of Humboldt's program for the modern subject. Questions of identity are everywhere apparent in classicism. In the German cultural imaginary that forms the background to the present study, the seemingly innocent question "What is Greek?" is intimately bound up with the anxiety "What is German?" These questions do not disappear but only intensify over the century to come. And so, correspondingly, do the dilemmas of the classical ideal. Evasion and disavowals are the least visible hallmarks of this process: they are hidden in the very form that the classical ideal assumes, in its sheer apparent otherness. The very obsession with "noble simplicity and tranquil grandeur" alone betrays a consciousness that is less than completely comfortable with its sequestered middle-class location. Nietzsche's pretensions to elitism and aristocratism fail to mark him off as in any way different from his predecessors: classicism is inherently elitist, however much it may broadcast humanist values. Nietzsche was quite capable of seeing through the inconsistencies of German classicism and its ruses. And it was dilemmas of identity like these, and not just the positive classicizing values, that shaped his attitude toward Winckelmann and company and that give the ultimate thrust of his critiques. Nietzsche was, in this sense, no more at odds with classicism than classicism was at odds with itself.

This brings us to the second objection against Nietzsche's alleged anticlassicism, which is the one from which this chapter started out. To adduce Nietzsche's counterclassicism is to ignore the very justification that he often gives for it—namely, classicism itself. Nietzsche can be wildly self-inconsistent, and one might wish to view his occasional classicism as a sign of this very inconsistency. But it would be as wrong to arraign him for inconsistency as it would be to smooth over the discrepancies by way of a reductive reading in favor of either his classicism or his anticlassicism. The classical ideal, as we saw, is notable for its waverings, and Nietzsche's articulation of his own "counter"-classical ideal matches in its waverings those of its counterpart exactly. The incoherence of classicism was not something Nietzsche felt he needed to refute. Instead, he chose to embody it by assuming the inconsistencies of classicism and exaggerating (or simply exposing) them. Brought to light in his various accounts of antiquity is not an alternative antiquity of his own making but rather the complex strategies of identification that were mounted by his predecessors. Nietzsche's writings thus spell out the consequences of classicism that those strategies were designed to evade. As in his "Encyclopedia," with its exaggerated and embarrassing classicism, this kind of mimetic criticism takes the form of an identification in an exponential form: that of *over*identification.

A better way to view Nietzsche's approach to the ancient world of Greece and Rome, in other words, is not as a spectral *Schreckbild* of classical antiquity but as a *Zerrbild*, or caricature and distortion, of German classicism. Thus, whenever Nietzsche is describing the classical past, we have to bear in mind the polemical intent of the images he puts on offer. And while it is true that his images of antiquity have no value in themselves but are meaningful only against the backdrop of a tamer, idealized, and classicized antiquity that he took to be the pervasive model for interpreting the past deep into the nineteenth century, this still fails to get at the ultimate thrust of Nietzsche's critique and its implications. He does not replace the classicizing model from without so much as he scandalizes it from within, by drawing out the internal incoherencies of classicism itself—as if to reproach classicism for having been *inconsistently classicizing* and not sufficiently true to itself. A glance at a few further examples from the classicist tradition will show why Nietzsche could feel justified in embarking on this strategy of exposure and will help make more plausible the claim that Nietzsche's writings in fact embody, rather than displace, the gestures of classicism. At the very least I hope to show how his views of antiquity are far more entrenched in classicism than his apparent anticlassicism, or rather the reductive views of his anticlassicism (and of the phenomenon of classicism itself), let on. But first we need to turn one last time to the classical ideal in the canonical and classical form that it had in Nietzsche's day.

Classicism conjures up images of "a world of serene, whole, and happy individuals, living in the eternal springtime of mankind; it is a world of beauty, lightness, form, and order, which reflects the brightest aspects of the Olympian pantheon. The irrational side of Greek religion and culture is ignored or suppressed."[137] Such an account goes only so far, however, and it tends to be written from the perspective of the conventional teleology: classicism—Nietzschean revolt. It is true that classicism often lays stress on the condition of perfection and harmony, on visual beauty, and on the childlike naïveté of early Greece. That is its most desired *myth*, the story it would most like to tell about itself. But qualifications are immediately called for. Irrationality is not ignored or suppressed in classicism even on this picture; it is openly acknowledged and then sublimated, but in such a way as to be written into the substance of classicism. On an alternative view, the irrational and the passional can be seen to be in fact part of classicism's constitutive features: they are built directly into the classical ideal, which requires a kind of homeostatic balance between rational and irrational forces, whether these are said to exist within the Greek psyche or in Greek culture as a whole. One of the most famous passages in Winckelmann, announcing his innovative aesthetic criterion of classical perfection, contains both elements prominently:

> The universal and predominant characteristic of the Greek masterpieces is a noble simplicity and tranquil grandeur [*edle Einfalt und stille Grösse*], both in posture and expression. Just as the depths of the sea remain forever calm, however much the surface may rage, so does the expression of the Greek figures, in the throes of their strongest passions [*bei allen Leidenschaften*], reveal a great and dignified soul. Such a soul is depicted in the face of Laocoön, and not only in his face but also in the throes of his most violent torments [*bei dem heftigsten Leiden*]. The pain which is evident in his every muscle and sinew, and which, disregarding his face and other parts of his body, we can almost feel ourselves simply by looking at his painfully contracted abdomen—this pain, I maintain, nevertheless causes no violent distortion either to his face or to his general posture. [*Thoughts on the Imitation of the Painting and Sculpture of the Greeks* [1755])[138]

The strictly pastoral vision of "serene, whole, and happy individuals," what Schiller would later call "naive," is in Winckelmann flagrantly contradicted by the image of heroic grandeur and a body pitched on the brink of extinction, writhing in mortal agony. This is literally the case in the example just given; it is more pronounced in his later and final description of the statue in his foundational *History of Art* (1764);[139] and it is more subtly evident in the thematics of other works described (or interpretively supplied) by Winckelmann, for instance the Apollo Belvedere, in Winckelmann's eyes the most canonical embodiment of the classical idea: "Disdain sits on his lips, and the anger he is containing within flares the nostrils of his nose and runs right up to his haughty brow." So reads Winckelmann's final description of Apollo, fresh from the slaughter of the Python and precariously pitched, like Laocoön, in classical repose.[140] The same attention to violent passion is derivatively true of countless other instances of the ideal adduced by Winckelmann, whether in the (inevitable) form of mutilated fragments, such as the Belvedere Torso, or in the dismembering attention paid to the details of individual sculptural remains.[141] Passion, for Winckelmann, is not merely a necessary element of classical art. It is the contrast with passion that allows the ideal to appear at all: like any devotional ideal, the classical ideal is literally constructed out of pathos.[142] Gloominess and melancholy play their part here too.[143] Humboldt is keenly aware of this fact as well: "No people has known how to intensify the feeling of melancholy as did the Greeks, because in the most vivid depiction of pain they did not deny the most luxurious kind of pleasure its rightful due, and because they even knew how to obtain serenity [*Heiterkeit*] and grandeur [*Grösse*] *from pain*"—not from its suppression.[144] As in Humboldt later, there is a kind of redemptive vision operating in Winckelmann: classical beauty has transfigurative powers. And in the example of Laocoön, we find out just what it is that beauty exists to transfigure and without which it would be unthinkable. Pain is transfigured into beauty, while beauty is transfigured into itself, and thus is rendered a classical ideal. Pain and passion at any rate are in the full view of the classicists' audience.

In this light, Nietzsche's revision of classicism is in some respects less dramatic than it at first appears to be. His account, say, of Raphael's *Transfiguration*, like his account of Greek tragic experience, is remarkably similar to Winckelmann's account of the Laocoön group. Nor should this be all that surprising: Raphael had already been claimed by Winckelmann as an instance of "noble simplicity and tranquil grandeur" in his *Thoughts on Imitation*, in the sequel to his treatment of Laocoön.[145] The *Transfiguration*, as described in *The Birth of Tragedy* §4, in particular makes for an interesting comparison with Winckelmann. Nietzsche divides its canvas into two parts, a "lower half" (like the contracted bowels (*Unter-Leib*] of Laocoön), which "shows us the reflection of suffering, primal and eternal" ("the whole world of suffering"), and an upper half ("a radiant floating in purest bliss, a serene contemplation beaming from radiant eyes"), the two planes corresponding to the two new aesthetic principles, "that Apollinian world of beauty and its substratum, the terrible wisdom of Silenus."[146] Of central importance is "their necessary interdependence," according to which Apollo "shows us how necessary is the entire world of suffering, that by means of it the individual may be impelled to realize the redeeming vision, and then, sunk in contemplation of it, sit quietly in his tossing bark amid the waves" (*BT* §4). This is what defines Nietzsche's view of the birth of tragedy—not raving Maenads and Bacchic orgies, but their mere *spectacle*, recollected in aesthetic tranquility. Similarly, Winckelmann in the same work: "The soul becomes more expressive and recognisable in powerful passions: but it is great and noble only in the state of unity, the state of rest." Hence, bodies depicted in art must be "at rest yet at the same time active."[147] They must rest quietly, "like the eye of the god who causes Olympus to shake and who is in eternal rest, as on the surface of a still sea, bobbing." The form of a classical body, Winckelmann says elsewhere, must be "a unity like the sea's surface, which for a stretch appears to be as even and still as a mirror, even if the sea is in motion all the time and tossing in billowing waves."[148] The illusionism of the calm is striking.

Nietzsche's halcyon image, conjuring up a sensation that is part rapture, part serenity, is a direct inheritance from German Hellenism, and it remains a leitmotif of Nietzsche's even after *The Birth of Tragedy*.[149] Epicurus, for example, can exhibit a tranquility born of suffering that is not all that far removed from Winckelmann's Laocoön: "Such happiness [as Epicurus possessed] could be invented only by a man who was suffering continually" (*GS*, 45 [1882]). Epicurus here is emblematically Greek: "The Greeks directed their idealistic tendency precisely toward the passions and loved, elevated, gilded, and deified them" (ibid., 139). He is also emblematically classical: "[His] is the happiness of eyes that have seen the sea of existence become calm, and now they can never weary of the surface and of the many hues of this tender, shuddering skin of the sea. Never before has voluptuousness been so modest" (ibid., 45). Is Nietzsche describing the Greeks—or is he describing the Germans who invented them? Nietzsche claims to identify with the happiness of Epicurus ("Whenever I hear or read of him, I experience the happiness of the afternoon of antiquity") and to be alone in this experience (ibid.). But the very language used, which is inherited and by now conventional, gives the lie to the claim. Perhaps Nietzsche is basking in the joys of a *Spätling*-culture—his own—and *its* afternoon of antiquity? Nor was he exactly alone in seeing in Epicurus a consummating instance of classicism. Winckelmann's ideal of flesh rendered transparent and finally unseen (a prerequisite of idealization) is explicitly supported by a reference to Epicurus' account of the form in which the gods appear to mankind; and his classical ideal in general is suffused with features that have been argued to be drawn directly from the same Epicurean ideal: the gods of Epicurus preeminently display grandeur in tranquility (*ataraxia*) and are ideals of human happiness—despite, or perhaps because of, their essential inhumanity.[150]

One should be on one's guard in any case. Nietzsche's attitude to Epicurus is hardly uniform and it is often equivocal: at times pagan and anti-Christian *avant la lettre* (*A*, 58), Epicurus is frequently the equivalent of a Christian and a romantic, and is for that reason "undionysian."[151] Yet even this last tag is misleading, for just as often as not Epicurus can be associated with "Dionysian" traits.[152] The complications in Nietzsche's image of the Greeks, early and late, are no less formidable. Whatever the complications, Nietzsche's postures are consistent, and so are, we ought to say, his self-contradictions. He is in point of fact consistently classicizing, for classicizing traits—sunlit clarity, but also its precarious instability—run through all his writings about ancient Greeks. Six years after the publication of *The Gay Science*, in 1888, he would write in a letter to his musical confidant Carl Fuchs, "The delivery of the classical rhapsode was extremely passionate (—in Plato's *Ion* there is a vivid description of gestures, tears, etc.): symmetries of time were felt to be a kind of oil upon the waves."[153] And nearly identical statements are found in the earlier published works too.[154] Clearly, if we focus on this strand of Nietzsche's thinking, and even if we include the apparently anticlassical rhetoric of Dionysian ecstasy (which is arguably more of an appeal to Germanness than to Greekness),[155] not to mention the "Apollinian" form of ecstasy (which he dubs "the classical style"), Nietzsche's Greeks come out in no way different from Winckelmann's; both can speak of "ecstasy," but that is the ecstasy of classicism itself.[156] Compare a later note, from 1888, in which "Apollinian intoxication" is described: "The classical style essentially represents . . . tranquility, simplification, abbreviation, concentration—the *highest feeling of power* is concentrated in the classical type."[157] Is Nietzsche's theory of the will to power possibly an instance of classicism too?

In the light of this discussion, we should acknowledge that *The Birth of Tragedy* shows a deep familiarity with the tensions within the classical ideal and is in crucial ways in conformity with Winckelmann's classicizing aesthetic and not its antithesis. Wilamowitz, it seems, was dead wrong. But then so are the conventional histories of literature and ideas that assign to Winckelmann and Nietzsche the roles of polar opposites. There are complications on both sides, and there are interesting and largely unexplored lines of communication running between them. The ever so faintly implied connection between pain and the Dionysian in the account of Laocoön might suggest a contrast between Apollo and Bacchus.[158] But elsewhere in Winckelmann, these are two nearly equivalent ideals of beauty, and Bacchus has no obvious connection with pain or passion (and certainly holds no more erotic fascination for Winckelmann than does Apollo).[159] Is Nietzsche, in his *Birth of Tragedy*, reacting to this soft-lensed idealization of the Dionysian, as though classicism had disavowed its primary impulses? On the surface, he undoubtedly is. And one might adduce the criticism of Winckelmann by August Feuerbach (*Der vaticanische Apollo*, 1833) as a corroborating, intermediary link, or Schelling's laying bare of the "pain" hidden in the classicist transfigurations of beauty. This is what Schelling in his *Philosophy of Revelation*, developing his "Dionysiology," calls the "*secret* pain (that] transfigures, ennobles, and as it were sanctifies the beauty of Greek images," that "whole beautiful world of appearance."[160] But to accept these nineteenth-century arguments at face value is to accept their overstatements as fact. Feuerbach is actually defending Winckelmann against himself, salvaging classicism along with the evident place of pathos in it,[161] while Schelling's words read more like a polemical unmasking of the open secret of classicism than a revelation of a deeper truth. The stances of both are, in any case, part of the discursive wars in fashion at the time. And as a rule, histories of classicism can be as reductive as they are simply by ignoring such discursive constraints and by repeating, in effect, the tendentious misreadings of classicism by the Romantic generation. Classicism seems, in effect, to have been canonized in a classical form, which is to say simplified and flattened, in the generation after Humboldt. In the process, what gets obscured is the presence of "non"-classical values in classicism and the persistence of classical values in the later, allegedly nonclassicist movements.[162] The battle lines are not so easily drawn as one might like to think.

Nietzsche's own uses of Dionysus are highly stylized and idealized. They are, to be sure, a product of the Dionysian tradition that runs from Herder to Friedrich Schlegel, Creuzer, Schelling, Heyne, Bachofen, and beyond, a fact that his contemporaries could see in a way we no longer do.[163] But they are also a polemical commentary on this tradition, which is to say on the

German obsession with Germanic traits, in the guise of Hellenism and Dionysianism. Hence his criticism, in *Human, All Too Human*, of "the modern spirit, with its restlessness, its hatred for bounds and moderation," which brings to mind nothing so much as the Dionysianism of *The Birth of Tragedy*, and to which are now opposed, as representative Greek traits, "artistic conscientiousness," "charm," "simplicity," and self-imposed "constraint."[164] The critique is meant to wound. But it does so by implicating the modern spirit in its own fantasy. Why the persistent and general fascination with Greece? Is there something restless and immoderate about classicism too? The adverse reaction to Winckelmann, once his faddish popularity waned, suggests there was: what was registered now was his overinvestment in the classical ideal ("the very tone of excitement, the language of enthusiasm," and the "ecstatic descriptions . . . were what alienated us" [Anselm Feuerbach, 1833]).[165] The very form that classicism assumed, we might say, belied its principles of "tranquil grandeur." But that is not all. Given the obsessive and repeated conjuring forth of horror as material for idealization in both classicism and its successors, the question we should also ask is, Why is there this general fascination with the *unclassical* (pain, passion, the Titanic, the monstrous, the abyssal, the pre-Homeric)? But ultimately classicism, even the classicism of so-called anticlassicism, has the last word: its images of horror are steeped in ideality; they are ideal counterimages supporting (masking) the myth of a purer ideality. Classicism is more than a self-deception. It is a disavowal of its own premises, and ultimately of its own founding fascination with violence.[166]

Even more striking than Nietzsche's critique of modern Dionysian pathos is the Apollinianism of his Dionysianism. In *The Birth of Tragedy*, Dionysus is, as I have mentioned, an ideal form fashioned in a "Platonic" mold and only illusorily distinct from Apollo: both figures are the result of a classicizing transfiguration (cf. *BT* §10). Although violating the purported metaphysics of that work, this is entirely in keeping with its aesthetics, which exists to show how in art, and above all in tragedy, "Dionysus no longer speaks through forces but as an epic hero, almost in the language of Homer," which is to say, "with Apollinian precision and lucidity" (*BT* §§8–9).[167] "Nature as it appears is not disavowed [by the Greeks]," Nietzsche later writes, as if to defend this seeming retraction of his own Dionysianism; "it is only *arranged*."[168] In question here is the "regulated discharge" of nature, which is to say of passion and irrational violence, on predetermined festival and cultic days (for example, at tragic performances). This statement and its logic, which is the logic of sublimation, reanimates the voice of denial itself. Thus, the Greeks typically, and their poets emblematically, "take pleasure in individual realities of every kind and don't wish to deny them but only to moderate [and "restrict"] them so that these realities won't become all-deadly."[169] What is "human, all too human" about this regulated discharge of nature, as a later reformulation of the earlier note puts it, is not the terrible reality of the Greeks' natures but the inexplicable need for sublimation and the accompanying denials.[170] A later expression of the same insight, and per-fectly consistent with the earlier passages, is to be found in *On the Genealogy of Morals* (1887), in an account of how the "Greeks used their gods precisely so as to ward off the 'bad conscience,' so as to be able to rejoice in their free-dom of soul." An outbreak of violent hubris elicits from the gods the cry, "How *foolish* they are!" "'Foolishness,' 'folly,' a little 'disturbance in the head'"—these are the sorts of labels that get put on such behavior in Greek culture, Nietzsche notes with customary satisfaction: "foolishness, *not* sin!" But then he continues:

> Even this disturbance in the head, however, presented a problem: "How is it possible? how could it actually have happened to heads such as *we* have, we men of aristocratic descent of the best society, happy, well-constituted, noble, and virtuous?"—thus noble Greeks asked themselves for centuries in the face of every incomprehensible atrocity or wanton-ness with which one of their kind had polluted himself. "He must have been deluded by a *god*," they concluded finally, shaking their heads. . . . This expedient is *typical* of the Greeks. (*GM*, II:23)

Nor is it the case that the Greeks ignore the concept of guilt (or pollution); they merely dispatch it: it was the virtue of their gods that "in those days they took upon themselves, not the punishment but, what is *nobler*, the guilt." Quite manifestly, the Greeks here, in this darkly ironic passage, are models of (all-too-human) self-deception. Their very conception, as living out an existence "before morality" (and with a good conscience), is itself an expression of the same impulse today.

Nietzsche's Greeks, plainly, do not live beyond the complacencies of modern disavowal and of self-deception. Mirroring a modern utopic desire, they reflect back its deepest impulses as well. And as with classicism, so with its later counterparts, which attempt to disavow their own hidden classicism: Nietzsche is theatrically rehearsing the inner contradictions of both aesthetics, their mythologies and constitutive incoherencies, without replacing them with a positive vision of his own. Dionysianism is too ridden with symptoms, too compromised, and ultimately too incoherent to serve as a substitute for classicism. It names the disavowal not of the irrational in antiquity but of the modernity of the classical ideal and its own obsessive formation in part around the problem of the irrational (pain and passion), and in part merely as a modern and irrational obsession. If Apollinianism is idealism in its purest imaginable form, then Dionysianism is the irrationality of idealism, idealized again: the problem is telling these apart in Nietzsche, or in classicism for that matter. And so when he writes in the same passage from *The Birth of Tragedy*, quoted earlier in connection with Raphael and Winckelmann, that "the 'appearance' here is the reflection of eternal contradiction, the father of things," he is performing three things at once. He is naming, inter alia, the contradictions of classicism; he is commenting on their sources (in an all-too-human condition that is unhinderable and in that sense "eternal"); and he is performing a contradiction of his own. "The 'appearance'" is vague in itself; presumably it refers to the despairing, lower half of the *Transfiguration*—but is that a Dionysian image or already Apollinian, just by virtue of being an image and aesthetically accessible? "The 'appearance'" gives rise in turn to a "world of mere appearances": "from this appearance arises, like ambrosial vapor, a new visionary world of appearances," namely, the Apollinian world of beauty. Try as we might to sort this out logically, the conceit resists all literal understanding. But then so does that of the classical ideal, whose confusions carried over into philology and would prove to be definitive for over a century and a half to come.

The Hidden Classicism of Historicism (and Vice Versa)

We have seen how Nietzsche, at various moments, alludes to the competing strains within classicist ideology. Indeed, his figurations of the past are in ways a perversion of these various strains, inherited as elements of a discourse of antiquity that was never quite coherent and whose incoherency is taken to new heights in Nietzsche's hands. The unmanageability of these contrasts in Nietzsche's approaches to classical antiquity, I want to suggest, reveals itself in the (often spectacularly) competing views that have surrounded Nietzsche and his place in philology. It is to these debates, usually phrased in a somewhat different vocabulary, that of humanism and historicism, that we should next to turn. The problems here, as we shall see, run a course parallel to the one we have been pursuing up until now within the classicizing tradition and its putative rejection in the nineteenth century.

Within philological circles, it is generally thought that Nietzsche either perpetuates a form of humanistic classicism against the historicist, anticlassicizing tendency of nineteenth-century scholarship or that he displaces humanism with an anticlassicizing vision of antiquity of his own. The first is by far the minority view. There are good reasons to support either view of Nietzsche, and even better reasons to reject them both. It was once part of a fashionable if guarded defense of Nietzsche to claim him for a revived humanism in the wake of the so-called Third Humanism promoted by Wilamowitz's pupil and eventual successor in Berlin, Werner Jaeger, during the latter half of the 1920s. Jaeger's movement came to a head in the famous Naumburg conference of 1930 on the topic of "The Problem of the Classical and Antiquity."[171] Jaeger was operating against the historicist tendency that came to dominate nineteenth-century philology, a tendency that culminated in Theodor Mommsen (1807–1903) and that was smiled upon by Wilamowitz in his anticlassicist moods. To side against Wilamowitz was automatically to side with Nietzsche, who, as we saw, puzzlingly enlisted classicist arguments against historicism, and not only in *The Birth of Tragedy*. These gestures could subsequently be read, or rather claimed, as supporting the humanist cause.[172] Yet the very ambivalence with which Nietzsche could be enlisted as a forerunner of a revived humanism suggests the limits of such a recuperation. Karl Reinhardt, mentioned in the Introduction above, is a good example. His verdict on Nietzsche is troubled to the point of confusion. Excused from the history of philology, Nietzsche "would have coming to him an even higher place in German humanism, were its history ever to be written[!] . . . And yet, a humanistic attitude as deeply probing as this [i.e., as Nietzsche showed] could come only from a philologist who strove, as a philosopher, to tear off the veil from the age in which he lived."[173] Reinhardt's logic is self-evidently strained.[174]

Another problem is the very difficulty of the distinction between historicism and humanism (the latter being effectively inseparable from classicism). The idealism of classicism was in fact born of an insoluble tension between these two duties, and the divided allegiances of classicism to the exemplary functions of humanism and to a historical foundation were never resolved. Humboldt's hypothetical division of his study of Pindar, as mentioned earlier, into three parts, "historical," "critical," and "purely philosophical," is typical of the conflicting impulses of this age. So, too, are his later warnings, issued in the name of "historical rigor and conscientiousness," against trusting in our "so-called aesthetic feeling" in our commerce with Greek poetry or culture if we wish to avoid projecting our whimsy upon the past—"the worst possible thing that can befall anyone working on the ancients."[175] Is Winckelmann's *History of Art* an example of historicism or humanism?[176] What about F. A. Wolf's philology? The question is badly formed. Just as there is often no felt contradiction between these two ways of approaching the classical past in either writer, so too there is ultimately no conceptual distinction to be made between these two approaches: each validates the other, and neither aspect can exist in the other's absence. It is this complicity of factors that provides the ultimate justification of, and that grounds, what might be called "humanistic hermeneutics," the prerequisites of which are the intimate relation between (in the language of this tradition) "feeling" (or "art"), "cultivation," and "understanding." What such a hermeneutics calls for is that both object and interpreter must be of an adequate level of humane cultivation.[177] Indeed, so rigorous is this prerequisite, it is not at all clear that a nonclassical object can be comprehended humanistically and historically—a problem that leads to the "humane" exclusion of non-European cultures from the scope of classical study (see below).

The distinction between humanism and historicism, a cliché of the discipline's self-understanding, ultimately leads astray: far more interesting to observe than the perhaps unexpected historicism of classicism is the quiet classicism of so-called historicist philology. As Nietzsche says in "Homer and Classical Philology," there is "an inner and often so heart-rending . . . contradiction within the *concept*, and the ensuing activity, of classical philology."[178] We might recall how Wilamowitz claims Winckelmann against Nietzsche on both counts, humanist and historicist, as somebody who showed us how to "grasp the essence of beauty *historically*"—an essence that is in itself "eternally" valid and compelling. Classicism and humanism run persistently throughout the changing fortunes of eighteenth- and nineteenth-century literary and historical ideologies. Applied in some pure and opposable form, the generic classifications "humanism" ("classicism") and "historicism" cannot be made to stick.[179]

One reason why they cannot is the uncertain reach of "classicism" itself. The point would seem obvious but it needs to be made, in part because the "anticlassical" reaction to classicism during the nineteenth century is sometimes typified as a Romanticist revolt (Schelling) or, more elaborately, as a romanticizing return to *Sturm und Drang* values. Yet all three movements idealize antiquity, reverence it, and accept fundamental assumptions that derive from the conventional warehouse of classicizing prejudices. What is more, all three literary movements could coexist in a single mind. The young Humboldt, who helped coin classicism, steered a course that intersected with Romanticism (his Greeks, as we saw, could be given to sudden bouts of melancholy, exuberancy, dark religious nihilism, and flights of fancy). Or else he continued to cling, at least in appearance, to so-called *Sturm und Drang* tendencies—to the extent that such categories are useful at all. Classicism is never as pure as it would like itself to be.[180] The incoherencies that result from this mixed stance repeat themselves in the field of philology, where the values of classicism may occasionally be pushed back or forward in time, but they never disappear. K. O. Müller, touched on above, is a textbook illustration, and we will return to him shortly.[181]

Classicism colors all strains of nineteenth-century philology, even the most positivistic and allegedly antihumanistic. As one scholar has recently written, "The greatness of the great classical authors was so to speak taken for granted," even by the most fiercely historicist of scholars.[182] The latter were reacting to the rhetoric of a previous generation but not to the value of the classical past, which was never disputed and was frequently taken to be paradigmatic in the Humboldtian and Goethean sense of *vorbildlich*. Scholars working in the name of dry historicism showed themselves to be true adherents to idealism in their very attachment to the object of their discipline, in the way they integrally conceived it, and in the supreme value they accorded to it—an argument that Nietzsche would make himself.[183] One quarrel within the ranks of the historicists will suffice to illustrate the point. When in 1856 Theodor Mommsen laid claim to imperial Rome and to Caesar as a counterparadigm to J. G. Droysen's (already anticlassicist) Hellenistic Greece and Alexander, he drew up the contrast in the following way: "That the past glory of Hellas and Italy forms a bridge to the prouder structure of modern world history, that Western Europe is Romanic, that Germanic [*germanische*] Europe is *classical*, that the names Themistocles and Scipio have another ring for us than Asoka and Shalmanesar, that Homer and Sophocles do not, like the Vedas and Kalidasa, attract only literary botanists but rather bloom for us in our own garden—all this is Caesar's doing." In a word, Caesar's monumental activity "stands squarely for what we call eternity."[184]

To be sure, political and especially nationalistic motivations (as here) play an increasingly important role in this hijacking of an effaced tradition, philhellenism.[185] But these motivations had always played a role, ever since the generation of Winckelmann and Herder. What stands out in Mommsen's case is the appeal to the legitimacy of that earlier tradition's values and some of its rhetoric, even as that tradition is being shoved aside. Nor is Mommsen averse to affirming the "unity" of his antiquity—another telltale inheritance from classicism.[186] Rudolf Pfeiffer's suggestion that the distinction between humanism and historicism, and its congener *Sach-* and *Sprachphilologie* (text- and object-based philology), are an invention of the latter half of the nineteenth century, indeed a "mirage," is attractive. His adoption, nonetheless, of the same contrast as historically real and definitive, and his final resort to the claim that "the idea of *humanitas*" is in fact traceable to antiquity itself, is symptomatic of the very phenomenon he is critically reacting to.[187] The history of modern classical philology is the history of such inconsistencies and disavowals. The contrast between historicism and humanism was perhaps the invention of the nineteenth century. But if so, it was never more than a polemically aimed ideological distinction, and never clearly (or coherently) articulated at that.

The battle lines drawn up between Wilamowitz and Nietzsche are only one of the most famous cases of this illusory clash. Wilamowitz would go on to be named as a leading exponent of the new historicism, and he was more than happy to take up the banner himself. A much-cited moment is Wilamowitz's proud declaration in 1900 that the ideal of classical antiquity was dead: "Antiquity, as a unity and as an ideal, is gone: scholarship itself is what destroyed this belief."[188] His agitations against the epithet "classical" are both famous and infamous in philological circles. Classicism was a concept that he felt, with justification, to be intrinsically incoherent: "Whenever I read [Jaeger's neohumanist journal] *Die Antike*, a millstone starts turning in my head. But the stone grinds no meal, not for me at least.—I have an idea what classical physics is, and there is classical music. But besides that?"[189] He would drop the epithet from his *History of Philology* (1921), justifying this move through an appeal to the substantive objects of classical philology themselves: it is these, not the adjective "classical," that determines what philology is.[190] The move is deceptive. The ideal unity of antiquity is not jettisoned; it is simply transferred over to the objective historical reality of antiquity: "Graeco-Roman culture in its essence and in all the manifestations of its life . . . is a unity." The move is really just a way of moving in place and ultimately of not moving at all. But this was only one of the tactics available to the displacement of the faded classicism of the past century.

Another was to locate unity no longer in the past but in the activity of the philologist, in what Wilamowitz would call "the common belief in the dignity and unity of philology."[191] Philology can only be as unified as its objects, and the language of unity quickly slides into a recommendation of the old *Totalitätsidee* of the earlier humanism—and its underlying darker shadows, which will be touched on in the final section of this chapter.[192] Is Wilamowitz protesting too much?[193] The tensions and contradictions in Wilamowitz's positions over his career have long been apparent, as have been his underlying sympathies toward some of the very classicizing influences that he would spend his life joining in uneasy battle (Lessing, Humboldt, Goethe, and the philologists Boeckh, K. O. Müller, and Welcker).[194] Strangely, the most striking evidence for Wilamowitz's sympathies is the most easily overlooked. It is the pamphlet *Zukunftsphilologie!* itself, with its passionate defense of Winckelmann and Schiller, the (inherited) value it places on "Aeschylean magnificence," which in its unconscious achievement towers beyond Euripides' rational perplexity with the poetic process,[195] and on "the eternally cheerful amiability of Sophocles, in harmony with himself and the whole world"—not to mention Wilamowitz's solemn vow, in the second installment to his pamphlet, to "seek to draw near the light of eternal beauty which art, and every appearance in its own way, radiates."[196] Needless to say, the same influences that worked upon Wilamowitz worked upon Nietzsche as well, though not unequivocally either.[197] The underlying affinities between Wilamowitz and Nietzsche, which are perhaps only to be expected from near classmates at the same preparatory school, and above all their shared ambivalences, are the unstated irony of their nineteenth-century conflict. The story of the deeper affinities between these two figures has yet to be written.[198]

Wilamowitz in any case was wrong about the death of the ideal of antiquity. The ideal was far too alive to be declared dead, a fact that might be inferred from the very redundancy of his polemical claim to the contrary. Nor was he by any means the first to proclaim its demise. In 1830, Droysen, the historian who helped to legitimate the age of Alexander, felt that with a revaluation of the postclassical world "the privilege of humanistic studies [was] shaken."[199] Ernst Curtius, whose concept of Greek contest culture Nietzsche freely adopted and also turned inside out, would blithely affirm his faith in the classical ideal in 1894, virtually as if nothing had changed over the last century, though perhaps the gesture had a quaint defiancy about it by then.[200] In the next generation, Wilamowitz's students would rebel against him and assert the value of humanism again. And some seventy years later, a British classicist would contradict Wilamowitz (in the belief that he was aligning himself, at least in sympathy, with Nietzsche): "To the classicists, with whom Nietzsche's standpoint has so much in common, the ancients had supplied a pattern, an ideal standard of excellence; for the historicists with their relativistic outlook no such thing could exist. . . . Even in modern conditions, and in our new awareness of the dangers of historicism, we cannot renounce the idea of *Altertumswissenschaft* as a unity; if only as an ideal notion, it must still be kept in mind."[201] But no matter: not even Wilamowitz himself believed that the ideal of antiquity was "gone." Not only did he know better, as he himself acknowledges.[202] His claim is flanked, before and after 1900, with passionate affirmations that Greek and Roman antiquity is an "ideal unity," "whole," "immortal," and "divine."[203] Small wonder that Wilamowitz's opinion would be cited and marveled at, but not believed. And yet at the risk of sounding paradoxical, I want to suggest that no one would believe Wilamowitz, or Droysen for that matter, because no one had ever really believed the fiction of antiquity's wholeness to begin with.

That antiquity is a heuristic fiction was an open secret, the anxiously disavowed premise of philological study and of classicism alike. How could it ever be anything else? At stake in the premise of a coherently conceived antiquity is nothing less than the very coherence and meaning of one's attitude toward the past, whether this is reflected in the (desired) coherence of the discipline of classical studies or that of the less scholarly (humanistic) devotion to the same subject matter. Philologists naturally take it for granted that their discipline has a fundamental meaning and unity; they assume, or wish to believe, that the discipline is as coherent as its objects—even if there is a certain circularity to this premise, since the objects of the classical discipline surely derive some of the coherence they enjoy from their disciplinary definition. Classicism, I want to suggest, provided (and continues to provide) this sense of coherence and legitimacy: it gives meaning to an activity where there may be none at all, often producing in the process a very different kind of meaning from the kind sought after and valued. As the preceding chapters have endeavored to show, Nietzsche was always attentive to these other kinds of meaning.[204]

Something like this was one of the reproaches made against historicism in the name of the new Third Humanism mentioned above. To be sure, what surfaced at the time was not that the idea of antiquity is a heuristic fiction, but rather the observation that classicism had persisted into the present in a disavowed form. The point, pressed home most forcefully by Jaeger's pupil Wolfgang Schadewaldt, touched the difficulty of shaking off a conception that had been so thoroughly drummed into the minds of students of antiquity not only throughout the last century but over the last two millennia.[205] "*Even denial*," Schadewaldt added, in a shrewd turn worthy of Nietzsche (whom he invokes without naming), "*is a concealed acknowledgment*."[206] Putting his finger on the repressed and concealed classicism of classical studies ("whether we affirm it or deny it"), Schadewaldt may have deliberately been stirring up old ashes, for a similar point about disavowal had been made by Ernst Rohde (or was it just Nietzsche, dictating to Rohde?) in the pamphlet *Afterphilologie*: sheer historical objectivity is "illusory," because "we stand facing a ruined and scattered wonderland" of antiquity, a mere heap of fragments, "in search of a unity that we can in turn obtain only by virtue of the unified character of an intuitive knowledge that has its source within ourselves." In Montaigne's "well-aimed" phrase, which Rohde redirects, "*Il est impossible, de ranger les pièces, à qui n'a une forme du total en sa teste*," nor can "anyone deny the innermost nature of his whole way of thinking, which is inborn and developed by reflection."[207] Both arguments by Schadewaldt and Rohde recall Nietzsche in different ways. But they also recall the intuitionism of Wilamowitz, which in turn has a troubled history that runs back to the origins of modern philology in the person of F. A. Wolf, whose quandaries (whether to trust his readerly instincts, and if so, which ones) were discussed above. Wilamowitz must have seen in Nietzsche a grotesque reflection of himself and of the conflict of interests that they had both inherited from the philological tradition.[208]

Both Nietzsche and Wilamowitz acknowledge that the ghosts of the past speak to us only when they are fed with our "blood."[209] Nor is either classicist saying anything new or unknown, but only what tends to remain unsaid, or not said very loudly, about the study of the antique past. As Humboldt had remarked about the Greeks, without giving away his hand entirely, "They are for us what their gods were for them; flesh of our flesh and bone of our bone." Here again, it is Nietzsche's proximity to the tradition, not his distance from it, that is his least well recognized trademark. And it is this proximity that makes Nietzsche's position within classical studies so troubling. An unwanted reminder, his writings represent in a grotesque form the dilemmas that run through the project of reclaiming antiquity for modern life.

The Wild Darkness of Modernity, or, the Tyranny of Germany over Greece

Nietzsche crystallizes the problems of the profession of classical studies—not its momentary crisis during the 1870s, but the intrinsic dilemmas that defined those studies as a discipline and then accompanied them as their ongoing and perpetual crisis. This is their condition of "untimeliness," by which we should understand not the necessary anachronism of the study of antiquity in modernity but the special relation that such study, and indeed the whole attitude of gazing back on a past, has in the formation of the identity of modernity. The various myths about Nietzsche treated so far, his relation to classicism, his invention of a counterclassical archaic period, his discovery of the irrational in Greece, or his place in the humanist-historicist debate, are not so much myths about Nietzsche as they are myths about this untimely relation, which Nietzsche disquietingly brings back into view. They are the stories that modernity tells about itself and that constitute it as such, as the modernity that it is.

We have seen how the premise of classicism, actual or denied, is the myth of a pristine moment as yet untouched by the ills of the present or by its own memory of a past: it is the myth of pure possibility itself. Nietzsche's positing of one such pristine moment in the archaic period is full of internal complications that return, in a kind of grotesquery, the image of the present to itself. His discovery of the irrational in Greece is another such myth, one that is perhaps the harder to come to grips with because it is itself founded upon a kind of irrational wish—the wish to discover the original essence of irrationality. Nothing could be more misleading than to link this discovery of the irrational with the discovery of the archaic period. Irrationality is not the preserve of Nietzsche's preclassical Greeks. Apollinianism, bathed in light (and in the darker language of dreams), is as suspect and as irrational as the image of Dionysian Greeks at one with the natural world. That this last image is a modern "idyll" follows both from the language in which it is couched (which is blatantly Schillerian and romanticising) and from the very desirability of that image today.[210] And so, if Nietzsche "discovers" anything at all, it is the irrationality of the modern mind that he brings to light.[211] A further set of reflections will help to make the point.

It may be that "knowledge of classical antiquity" produces the equivalent of a "Goethean" antiquity, but this is not to say that philology always produces a harmless image of antiquity.[212] Quite the contrary, one of the ways in which Nietzsche effectively "outs" classical studies, especially in their German form, is through the reflection in his writings of the racism and nationalism that run like an unbroken thread through classical philology from its modern inception to well beyond Nietzsche. Racism and nationalism are profoundly irrational components of the classical ideal. This, too, is an aspect of the tyranny of Germany over Greece that Nietzsche is keen to expose and to problematize, and it will furnish a final example of the way in which Nietzsche's uses of antiquity are a cultural mythology of the present.[213] One chain of references will have to suffice not simply to make the point, which has been made before (albeit too rarely and too unconditionally), but also to reveal the anxieties that are constitutive of the logic of "purity" that runs through so much of German culture at the time and through the philology that is one of its expressions. The discussion will return us to texts already cited, but it will oblige us to view them in a somewhat darker light.

Consider, to begin with, the allusions to Aryanism that appear only in section 9 of *The Birth of Tragedy*, but which profoundly color the whole of that work. There, Nietzsche confronts two myths and two races, the story of Prometheus as told by "the Aryan community," and that of the Fall as told by the "Semitic" peoples. "What distinguishes the Aryan notion," Nietzsche writes, "is the sublime view of *active sin* as the characteristically Promethean virtue" (Nietzsche's emphasis); the Semitic counterpart is marked by "curiosity, mendacious deception, susceptibility to seduction, lust." The ethical significance of Prometheus' acts and the question of its legibility from within the Judaeo-Christian framework of sin and atonement had long been debated by nineteenth-century scholars. Welcker, for instance, in the second volume of his *Griechische Götterlehre* from 1860, will have none of this "Christian dogma" that scholars since G. F. Schömann earlier in the century were eager to read into the Greek myths.[214] Is Nietzsche's approach to ancient Greece possibly Christianizing? On the other hand, Nietzsche's remarks are not just made en passant. He expressly links the Aryan mind to Dionysian wisdom, namely, the insight into "the misfortune in the nature of things, which the contemplative Aryan is not inclined to interpret away—the contradiction at the heart of the world reveals itself to him as confusion of different worlds" (*BT* §9). He designates Prometheus as "a Dionysian mask."[215] And the first edition of *The Birth of Tragedy* prominently sports a vignette of Prometheus Unbound as its frontispiece.[216] One consequence of these equations is that whenever we speak about Nietzsche's prelapsarian Greeks in *The Birth of Tragedy*, down to Socrates and Euripides at the end of the fifth century, we are in fact talking, or should be talking, about *Aryans*. A decade and a half later, Nietzsche's Aryan Greek returns, no longer a Dionysian reveler but still very much a model of "sublime" and "active sin": he is the "active" (as opposed to "reactive" and resentful) and "noble" "blond beast of prey," one of whose "mouthpieces" is said to be "the Megarian poet Theognis."[217]

If Nietzsche's later myth of the blond beast would occasion embarrassment and confusion, his earlier myth would not, at least not immediately. There are good reasons for this complacency. The language of racism was surprisingly common in the philological tradition, thanks in part to the impetus, in the fields of ethnology and linguistics, of Herder and then later of the Indo-Germanicists Friedrich Schlegel and Franz Bopp.[218] As the reference to Theognis in the *Genealogy* gives away, one of Nietzsche's sources for his racial characterization of the Greeks in that work is K. O. Müller. Müller's Dorians, representing the racial purity of Greece itself, are a virtual template for the active, impetuous, and incalculable nobles of the *Genealogy*, and indeed for Nietzsche's characterization of the will to power in its "active" form generally. Another equally pertinent source for Nietzsche's vision of the Greeks is Müller's devoted pupil and emulator Ernst Curtius, whose essay "Der Wettkampf" (1856) provided Nietzsche (and Jacob Burckhardt) with one model for interpreting Greek culture, and who offers a further confirmation of the often unconscious or simply accepted racial mythologies of the modern classical tradition in Germany.[219] Like Nietzsche in *The Birth of Tragedy*, Curtius, too, resorts to a contrast between Semitic and Aryan civilizations. Unlike Nietzsche, he tries to ground this racial contrast in a historical division at the origins of culture, in line with contemporary paradigms.[220] The latter (Aryan) tribes "received as their inheritance all the masculine impulse to pleasure in activity [*Thatenlust*]," whence their competitive urge, their restless exploitative "energy," and their terrifying "displays of power." As they spread from the biblical lands, in a movement that one can follow today only "with a rapid act of mind [*ein rascher Gedankenzug*]"(!) they developed—much like the blond beasts in Nietzsche's *On the Genealogy of Morals* (II:17)—into "state-founding peoples." Eventually they were transformed into "that Apollinian people," "the representative[s] of classical antiquity," whose purest exemplars are, needless to say, the Dorians again. Curtius' language in places gives a verbatim echo of K. O. Müller.[221] Preserving only the essentials and universalizing Müller's findings, he has essentially compressed Müller's two-volume treatment into a powerful symbol that runs a mere fifteen pages. The connection with the present is likewise more explicitly brought out by Curtius in his appeals to the nationalistic instincts of his audience. "The Germans have indeed been handed the honor of being confided with a special understanding of the Hellenic nature," and the imaginary identifications made possible by the myth of Dorian Aryanism are living proof of this claim.[222] Leaving nothing to chance, Curtius goes on to make these identifications explicit in a series of "analogies" between Germans and Greeks that reverberate with the nationalist aspirations of modern, pre-Bismarckian Germany.[223]

Nationalism here takes a curious and instructive twist. The German "tribes [*Stämme*]" show their commitment to the nationalist ideal in a way parallel to the Apollinian race of Greece, not by conforming to the nationalist imperative to Prussian centralization and unification but, remarkably, in their very *resistance* to it. Antagonistically struggling against the imposition from without of any state formation that would "level" their particular differences and leave them with only a universal identity, the German peoples produce, from within, an even more impressive form of nationalism, comparable only to that of the dissident Greeks. Here the essence of the analogy finally comes to light: "Here, like there, national unity has remained a spiritual, inner possession, an idea hovering over the individual tribes and states." Curtius is working out the dilemmas of identification that affect classicism generally of the sort witnessed above and in the previous chapter: first, the "naming" of "classical antiquity" as a coherent entity; and then, the identification with its inhabitants by way of an imaginary projection. Thus, for Curtius the ancient Greeks are and are not a unified whole; Dorians represent the essence of this whole that is not one and that is in fact founded upon their exceptional status, in their very negation of the unity they nonetheless are supposed to represent. National consciousness, like this very picture of the Greek heritage, is an expression of an "idea" and an "idealism" (Curtius' terms): it has a purely idealistic content, and it is *for that very reason* all the more compelling and imperative a form of submission.[224] The real force of nationalism can be rendered by the economy of logic that runs, "I know nationalism conflicts with my freedom, but it is just an idea that I can freely choose, and besides we have been chosen to choose it."[225] Curtius has thus put his finger not on the essence of nationalism as this is usually understood (as a form of blind identification with a higher cause) but on its inner *antagonism*, which is what makes nationalism so compelling and so endlessly elusive.[226] Müller's occasional reluctance toward the Prussianization of Germany has to be read in the same light.[227] The concept of conflict (the contest form, or *agon*) is a reflection, in fact, of the deeper antagonisms within the classical ideal, the illogic of its construction, and some of its more troubling implications. And this pattern of aggressive exclusions and underlying anxieties—this panic—around the ideal of the contest and its Doric (Spartan) connotations, is traceable to the first stirrings of modern German classicism and classical philology from the time of Winckelmann; and they are jointly bound up with fantasies of racial purity and with those of nationalism as well.[228]

The absolute propriety of the fantasies of racial purity to modern German philology and to classicism can be established through two quick examples. In his *Darstellung der Alterthumswissenschaft* (1807), F. A. Wolf justifies his conception of classical antiquity and his seminal definition of its discipline as a "self-enclosed" totality by means of a powerful exclusion. Gazing back upon the great *Völkerwanderung* of the distant past, and then fast-forwarding to the emerging cultures of the more recent millennia, Wolf's eye rests on the Mediterranean Near East, which elicits the following comment: "One would very much like to comprehend all such peoples [of this place, which has to be considered "the most beautiful region of the ancient world"] within a single scientific object; yet several reasons make a division necessary and permit us not to put *Aegyptians, Hebrews, Persians*, and other nations of the Orient on a par with *Greeks* and *Romans*. One of the most significant differences between the latter and the former nations is that the former did not at all, or only barely, raised themselves above the level of cultivation that should be called *civil order* or *civilisation*, in contrast to *higher, genuine intellectual culture*," which only the classical world can be said to attain.[229] Classicism constitutes classical antiquity as a "whole" that is "a self-enclosed world" ("ours") in this precise sense.[230] Müller will take the same orientalist principle to another extreme: Ionians make a weak contrast to Dorians because of their "commerce, already in the earliest times, with their Asiatic neighbors": they are now "effeminate and enervated," while Dorians are landbound, ingrown, nonmiscegenating, and so on.[231] As with classicism in general, these gestures literally take the form of the logical evasion "I know very well . . . ," acknowledging the assailability of the constructions being made and yet still making them nonetheless.[232] It would thus be a mistake to consider humanism as innocent of these exclusions and to focus single-mindedly on the following from the pen of Wolf, written in a more Winckelmannian mood: "Through the simplicity and dignity and the great, encompassing sense with which they give expression to what is true and noble and beautiful, do the ancients forever lay a rightful claim to being the teachers and inspiration of all posterity." The very purism of this kind of humanism, pretending to a *certain* universality, is suspect: it is the telltale sign of a purism of another, less palatable kind.[233] Unfortunately, most histories of classicism and of classical philology pass over such moments without murmur or demur.

Now to Humboldt, who in a private letter to Goethe from 1804 begins in an eminently quotable way:

> A verse of Homer, even an insignificant one, is a sound from a land we all recognize as a better one and yet as one not distant from us. There are lots of factors that make this the case. . . . But the actual explanation for me lies in the times of barbarity. Through Christianity and the state of wildness in society (the Greeks knew only the wildness of nature), man became so worn-down that natural tranquility, undisturbed inner peace, were forever lost to him; and both of these things can be wrested back again today only through a hard-won victory. Man's nature was split, pure spirituality was opposed to sensuality, and he was filled with ideas of poverty, humility, and sin that would never more retreat.

Here we need to pause. To "the wildness of nature" known to the Greeks, Humboldt juxtaposes another characteristic and another morality:

> Contrite within, due to a mixture of Gnostic sophistries and fanaticisms and the petty-minded, terrifying concept of Judaism, man was terrified and plagued by arbitrary violence from without, which violence, however, always required submission in the name of law and justice (like no tyranny in antiquity).

In the sequel, we are returned to the cheerier prospect of the antique past, and advised to "fall down prostrate" before the Greeks and their works, "as before images of gods" (and in a most un-Jewish way, one might add).[234] Elsewhere, Humboldt makes a point identical to Wolf's: when we look upon the Greeks we behold "a race of mankind [*Menschenstamm*] formed out of a nobler and purer stuff," incomparable to any other.[235] Nietzsche will make similar exclusions in a matter-of-fact way in his "Encyclopedia of Classical Philology," though with a certain frankness that is not found in the conventional moves. The exclusions are justified, he writes, because classicism has its ultimate point of reference in ourselves: "For we speak about 'the classical' for *us*, for our modern world, not with a view to Indians, Babylonians, and Egyptians."[236] In outlining the actual stakes of classicism, Nietzsche disturbs its paradigm. But as we have already seen, he is equally capable of bringing out the confusions in those stakes (for instance, in the question of

racial purity), and we will have a further opportunity to witness this disturbance of the paradigm in a moment.[237]

While Humboldt was also capable of agitating for Jewish rights,[238] and
while there are notable exceptions to these various modes of misperception
among classicists, the classical ideal and the mythologies of racism and
nationalism were never entirely unlinked in German scholarship during the
eighteenth and nineteenth centuries.[239] Nor do these prejudices simply go
away in the twentieth.[240] My point is not to claim that the Aryan fantasy of
classicism was straightforwardly racist or anti-Semitic. Nor do I wish to
claim that this fantasy was the exclusive property of Germans (as a glance at
Matthew Arnold's *Culture and Anarchy* [1st ed., 1869] will show), or that it
was simply available to appropriation by later Fascists. Meanwhile, those
rare exceptions among scholars who do pay any attention to these tendencies
crucially neglect to observe the tensions within, and not just between, the
Aryan and the alternative models.[241] The Aryan fantasy was nowhere close to
being as pure as it purported to be, or as it is taken to have been. Inevitably,
the Aryan agents betray their non-Greek origins in the projective modern
mind. In a moment, I will want to show how such unwanted convergences of
identity obtain virtually all the time. But the point I wish to underscore now
is that racism, nationalism, and classicism prospered together even when
some of these elements were not explicitly linked up with the others.
Together they formed a complex of factors that puts into question the innocent face of classicism and that connects it more closely to the realities of its
social contexts than its exponents would have liked us to imagine. In the passage above, Humboldt has uncannily anticipated the culture wars between
Greece and Judaea that would become a central motif of Nietzsche's later
writings, as in the First Essay of *On the Genealogy of Morals* with its speculative history of Jewish *ressentiment* and the associated "fanaticisms" and legal-
istic "terrors." *The Birth of Tragedy* marks the first public appearance of this
motif, but the thought is present in Nietzsche's earliest notes (e.g., "destruction of Greek culture by the Jewish world" [1869/70]).[242] In his first book,
Nietzsche is at the very least making reference to this well-established,
indeed hallowed, conceptual paradigm.[243] The question is just what else he
is doing with it.

The reference to Aryanism in *The Birth of Tragedy* is troubling, but it is
also troubled. It has more than an air of paradox about it. There is little

point in belaboring the obvious, for instance that, Nietzsche's protestations notwithstanding, the myth of Prometheus *is* preeminently a myth about "mendacious deception [*dolon*]" and, in its aftermath, about "susceptibility to seduction," "curiosity," and "lust" (Pandora); or that "the whole flood of sufferings and sorrows with which the offended divinities have to afflict the nobly aspiring race of men" pertains every bit as much to the divine wrath of Yahweh as it does to the Olympians. Elsewhere, both in contemporary notes and in later writings, Nietzsche owns up to these mythical facts.[244] Here, he seems to be advertising the very untenability of his racial contrast, which consequently looks to be either self-refuting or cunningly willful. What is more, the "*dignity* [that the Greek myth of Prometheus] confers on sacrilege" would appear to be an effort to dignify a triter state of affairs; it is as if it were *the Greeks themselves* who were seeking refuge in this Aryanization of a Greek tale.[245] This possibility is less far-fetched than it might at first seem. Apollinian culture is, after all, a form of self-glorification ("in order to glorify themselves, its creatures had to feel themselves worthy of glory; they had to behold themselves again in a higher sphere, without this perfect world of contemplation acting as a command or a reproach" [*BT* §3]). And Prometheus is the hero "of every ascending culture" (*BT* §9). Connected with this, Apollinian culture is fundamentally defensive; it is a "bulwark" protecting a certain autochthony against the racial barbarian other (§4). What is more, the Dionysian/Promethean principle of "universalism" is supposed to rise above "all the rigid, hostile barriers that necessity, caprice, or 'impudent convention' have fixed between man and man"; only, that principle squares rather badly with the passage in which it is announced.[246] An accomplice of Apollinian illusion, Dionysianism seems to be *itself* one such illusion—while the cheerful appearances of Apollo are another, a façade of beauty masking "a political structure so cruel and relentless," and not only in Dorian Sparta.[247] As a contemporary notebook reads, "Here we arrive at the *cruel* reality of a *culture*—insofar as it builds its triumphal arches on top of enslavement and annihilation."[248] In a later fragment, dating from 1874, Prometheus produces the illusion of Greek culture itself, which in turn produces him as an empty myth.[249]

Is this illusoriness the "contradiction at the heart of the world" that the "contemplative"—or is it "active"?—"Aryan is not inclined to interpret away?" If so, then Aryanism turns out to be this very inclination, disguised by an attempt at self-glorification ("the glory of activity"). Only, what Aryanism reveals is not "a clash of different worlds," divine and human (Kaufmann's rendering), but something quite different: what is revealed is rather a "confusion" or "muddle" of different worlds ("*ein Durcheinander verschiedener Welten*"). Kaufmann's mistake is to translate *ad sensum*, not *ad verbum*: what the sense requires is a word like "clash" (for instance, "between men and gods"), but Nietzsche cheats us and gives us a "muddle" instead. The contrast between active and passive, or Aryan and Semitic, is another such "muddle." It merely reveals itself, as the myth of Aryanism that it is.[250] The more consoling prospect that Nietzsche is alluding to Goethe's hymn to Prometheus from 1774, which is fostered by a misdirection by Nietzsche himself (*BT* §9), cannot be sustained. The ultimate source for this Aryanized Prometheus is not Goethe, although Nietzsche is happy to implicate Goethean idealism in this inherited racial mythology,[251] let alone Byron and the whole modern idyll of antiquity, which exists to furnish an "optimistic glorification of man as such" (*BT* §19). It is rather the discourse of Aryanism in Germany and elsewhere, which standardly viewed Prometheus, the son of Iapetus, as an heir of the biblical race of Japeth—a glorification of man in a slightly different key.[252]

The source of the muddle, of this identification gone awry, is the irony that the Aryan people *was once itself a Semitic tribe*, a confusion that lies at the heart of nineteenth-century Orientalist fantasies.[253] Welcker, in his *Griechische Götterlehre*, would accept the Aryan myth but resist the Semitic derivation.[254] Nor does this irony escape Nietzsche. "The two myths [Aryan and Semitic]," after all, "are related to each other like brother and sister," which is to say, by blood (*BT* §9). How racially pure, in fact, are the Dorians? In nearly contemporary notes, Nietzsche resoundingly—indeed, almost heretically—opposes the ideal of racial purity as transmitted by Müller. In "We Philologists," Nietzsche will ask, "What are 'Greeks by race' [*Rassengriechen*]?" His reply, confounding the ideal of racial purity, is that the Greeks had absorbed both "Mongolian" and "Semitic" blood into their veins; "the Dorian *Wanderung* is a later impact, once everything had already been gradually inundated."[255] Nietzsche's criticisms of Müller, who is to be understood here, could elsewhere be unqualifiedly damning. "How remote from the Greeks must one be to credit them with so narrow-minded an autochthony as [K.] O. Müller does!" he would write again in 1875, having already ridiculed the idea of "upright Indo-Germans [*biedere Indogermanen*]" three years earlier.[256] Nietzsche's later stance, in the *Genealogy* and the *Antichrist*, is that Germans are not blond except in their fantasies, and that anti-Semites are themselves, horrifyingly, virtual Jews.[257] Curtius' fantasy, which was in Nietzsche's mind in 1871, would have passed easily into the framework of Nietzsche's later critique. Indeed, Nietzsche's later critique is arguably already at work in *The Birth of Tragedy*. The whole project of this work is premised on a German national endeavor, namely, the attempt to discover itself in ancient Greece without the mediation and contamination of alien influences: it is "to establish a permanent alliance between German and Greek culture" without "being attached to the lead strings of a Romanic civilization" (*BT* §20). Nietzsche's well-known distaste for German nationalism aside,[258] the irony, again, is that to produce such an alliance one has to return to the Semitic lands of Babylonia, to the Sacaean festivals, to the "prehistory" of Greece in Asia Minor (§1), and to the Judaeo-Christian feints and deceits that "dignify" sacrilege, sin, and suffering. The hatred of the racial other is not only a fascination with the other but also an identification with the other—and simultaneously a hatred, fear, and negation of oneself.[259]

Here we have a glimpse of what is a general phenomenon in Nietzsche. Nietzsche frequently deploys the discourse of nineteenth-century racism. But instead of merely mouthing that discourse, he preserves its most embarrassing traces. The racial fantasy of Aryanism reveals itself to be *faithfully* represented by Nietzsche, in all its essential *incoherence*. This is one reason why attempts to whitewash Nietzsche's writings, a pastime of Nietzsche scholars since the 1950s, are of no avail. Nietzsche's blond beasts cannot be freed of racial contamination, or rather of the essential impurity of racist fantasies. Even more astonishing than the occasional attempts to confront the problem, especially those that do not convict Nietzsche of downright racism, is the general silence that shrouds it.[260]

We have already seen how Nietzsche manipulates Müller's Dorian fantasy in the person of Theognis, in part merely by bringing out what is already latent in that fantasy. Nietzsche could with good reason understand his portrait of Theognis to be a faithful rendering of the contradictions internal to the images of antiquity propagated by Müller and others. Above, we saw the hints of a similar trajectory in *The Birth of Tragedy*, where Müller's perplexed account of Doric culture (the manifestations of *Doriertum* in aristocracy, lyric poetry, and architecture) is an important source of allusions in *The Birth of Tragedy*. While some of these allusions to Müller have been traced, usually under the label of borrowings or dependencies,[261] what too easily escapes notice is that in this work Nietzsche is alluding not only to the content of Müller's findings *but also to their very perplexity*. And as for Nietzsche's appropriation of the concept of "contest" from Curtius, we have seen how entangled the logic of purity can become, to the point where features of decline and of power are not only indistinguishable but also paralyzing and bewildering (recall Miltiades).[262] In each case, Nietzsche's approach is identical: what appears to be an instance of cultural superiority and purity turns out to be a troubling instance of degeneracy, decline, and impurity.[263] Nietzsche is teasing out a strand of anxiety that runs through all racial discourse and that happens to be strongly pronounced in the philology he inherited. Mirroring contemporary philological discourse, he mirrors its failings as well.

Let us pursue this thread of anxiety, which can be more closely documented. What the various scenarios of the contest-ideal reveal is the hysterical core of racism, which unwittingly produces a fantasy-image of its own hysteria in its ideal types. These latter are depicted, after all, as restlessly roaming and agitated creatures, forever securing their own positions and attesting to their own reality, as if unsure of themselves, doubting themselves, and needing to reassure us and themselves of their superior status. Such is the paradox of purity: the very signs that mark something off as pure attest to an anxiety about purity itself. Isn't this what lies behind Müller's Dorians, who are perpetually in decline and anxiously "gazing upon the past" so as to ward off the future, as though (like Hegel's classical-age Greeks) prescient of their own fate and yet (unlike Hegel's Greeks) closing their eyes to it at the same time? Hence the self-enclosure and conservatism of Dorians, "keeping at a fair remove" their own least wanted features. The same holds for the "dualism" that Müller discovers in the Dorian cult of Apollo, a finding that transparently reproduces the antagonisms of the Dorian ideal and its historical vicissitudes in miniature. For Müller, Apollo is "a *corrupting*, *vengeful* and, simultaneously, a saving, protective nature." As a consequence of this "contradiction"—of these "dark" shades and this "impureness"—within the "purity, brightness, and clarity" of Apollo, of so to speak *ressentiment* within blue-eyed activity, "the deity is not represented [in his cult] as realizing his whole being, but rather as [forever] producing *antag-*

onistic effects," which are the effects of impurity itself.[264] The circularity is apparent. The racial/classical ideal is here reduced to a radical, literally self-threatening, uncertainty.[265]

Curtius confesses to the same worry when he states, midway through his essay, that the very "flourishing" of the Greeks in the sixth century already contained within itself "the seed of degeneration."[266] This is not an empirical observation; nothing compels him to this conclusion, apart from a theory about power that has no basis in anything besides an anxiety about power. Power, as depicted by Curtius, is a fragile thing, its possession most uncertain, almost too precious a gift for human hands. "The more the noblest states of antiquity perceived that their calling lay in the free unfolding of all human talents . . . , the more rapidly did their powers consume themselves and waste away, and the more short-lived were their states."[267] The same worry returns in still more concentrated form in the paradox of Nietzsche's essay on contest: contest (Hesiodic *eris* in its "good" form) is what protects Greek culture from pre-Homeric (Hesiodic) horrors and violence (*eris* in its "bad" form). Combat is "the cure, the salvation," a defense against the brooding darkness of a pre-Homeric existence, but "the cruelty of victory won [in combat] is the culmination of life's jubilation."[268] Violence is double-edged, inflicted on and against itself—and that is its fatality. Significantly, what compels Nietzsche's Greeks to contest-like behavior is not just a glimpse into "a world of battle and cruelty" but a feeling of "nausea toward existence"; what stands revealed is a "view of existence as a penalty that has to be expiated," indeed, a "belief in the identity of existence and a state of guilt." Here, Nietzsche adds, Greece betrays its affinities with the Orient.[269] Evidently, the Greeks are not so much terrible cruel beasts as they are anxious metaphysical subjects, cringing before oppressive superstitions and suffering in a crisis of nerves.[270] At the bottom of all this existential agony, there is something deeply *banal* about the Greek condition, *and that, for Nietzsche, is the source of its actual terror.* Horror in its sublime form (as in the mystery of Dionysian wisdom) is merely a protective screen, an Apollinian illusion, and an instrument of self-glorification: it is a fantasy about power. Thus, if Miltiades can represent both the pinnacle and the nadir of power, that is because power is the fantasy through which such contrasts become legible at all. This insight into the phantasmatic dimension of power, its fragility, and its essential proximity to (and often indistinguishability from) impotence,[271] will be fundamental to Nietzsche's later theory, or rather staging, of the will to power, whose motto might as well have been "phantasm upon phantasm."[272] Nietzsche's Greeks are wrapped in a protective, delusive halo at the very core of their being. So conceived, they are paradigms of modernity and its delusions.

It is tempting to see in the worries that course through the troubled narratives of Müller and Curtius, and which are rendered all but intractable in Nietzsche, a characteristically nineteenth-century concern with dissipating energies, or else a symptom of widespread cultural pessimism. No doubt these historical trends helped to shape the fears that were traced above. But as suggested earlier, the fears and the thematics are in fact rooted in the classical tradition and its eighteenth-century origins. Nor is pessimism universal in the nineteenth century (Nietzsche is a good example, but then so is August Boeckh before him).[273] Wolf's humane Greeks, for instance, are driven by a passionate (and competitive) *need* to cultivate themselves, and they are every bit as restless in this pursuit—they literally "*hurry* from one object to another," to the point of distraction—as are Müller's and Curtius' Dorians and Athenians.[274] Humboldt, for his part, turns out to have an extraordinary obsession with energetics that strikingly anticipates Nietzsche's theory of the will to power.[275] The approximation betrays, once again, the classical impulses behind that theory. And Humboldt's own image of Greece is heavily inflected with Dorian colors, as was Winckelmann's before him.[276] Indeed, the idea of "contest," as a productive and ultimately ruinous cultural form of experience, runs throughout classicism and is part of its very fiber, as are the associated Doric racial connotations.[277] Cutting across all these cultural expressions is a characteristically German worry about identity, as even Goethe would attest.[278] And Nietzsche's writings are nothing if not an inquiry into this troubling question. The filtering of problems of race, class, and identity through classical ideals is merely one of the more startling expressions of such problems. Classicism is plainly a way of "thinking through" these issues in the eighteenth and nineteenth centuries.

Epilogue: Horror Vacui

"Greece, the only form in which life can be lived: the horrible in the mask of beauty." So an early notebook entry from 1869/70, blurring the lines of

Nietzsche's customary analysis in an intriguing anachronism.[279] Here, it is not some dimension of Greece but *Greece itself* that is experienced through "the mask of beauty." Greece is an aesthetic deception. It is necessary in the sense that it fulfills a need. We have seen plenty of evidence that "Greece" does at least that. But wherein lies the horror? Not in the fascinatingly "unclassical" contents of the classical imagination or in the terrifying truths of Dionysus: all these are masked by their own metaphysical ideality, as we have also seen. The horror that Greece shields us from has a more proximate actuality, one that obtains somewhere in "life," not in the dead past. And Nietzsche's writings on antiquity pose a threat precisely because they expose the proximate presence of this horror. On one approach, we might say that their threat resides not in revealing contemporary views about antiquity to be a fantasy, but in *fulfilling* these fantasies. In bringing them too close, Nietzsche's writings make the reigning fantasies about the past too much a part of the present; at the extreme, they eliminate the present altogether by dissolving its own fantastic consistency, a consistency that crucially relies upon the image of an estranged antiquity. Isn't this the real threat of a "rebirth" of antiquity? Yet the fascination that runs through the contemporary world from classicism to the present is not only with a horror held at arm's length but ultimately also with the problematic substance of antiquity itself—with its actual inconsistency, its disobedience of ideal norms, its seeming refusal of classicism, and so on, or else—what can be equally disconcerting—the *excessive* obedience of antiquity to norms imposed from without, its all too easy acceptance of ideals, its infinite malleability, indeed its very *classicism*. Perhaps what is horrible is not something that the mask of beauty hides but the possibility, which no subject can consistently face, that the mask hides nothing—nothing apart from its own self-masking.

Nietzsche's images of antiquity are, I believe, in different ways an expression of this suspicion. Antiquity, touched by art and science, is a seduction to life in the actual present. That is his starting point in his inaugural speech at Basel in 1869, "Homer and Classical Philology." It is not the past that is revived through the apprehension of antiquity. On the contrary, in the bright light of antiquity "the most day-to-day reality appears . . . utterly new and compelling, indeed as a thing just born and experienced now for the first time, as though through the power of an enchantment [*Verzauberung*]."[280] The "magic mountain [*Zauberberg*]" of antiquity promised by *The Birth of*

Tragedy is likewise the result of this spell (*BT* §§3, 20). In its diverting of a modern subject's gaze, this spectacle, too, is but a seduction to life in the present. The ultimate transfiguration wrought by "the mask of beauty" is thus not of the past but of the present, of the everyday, and of the sheer banality of contemporary existence when it is bereft of all such ideality. Could this be the ultimate horror concealed by antiquity? Dionysianism, after all, is a confused avoidance of "the horror" and "absurdity of existence" and of the "everyday" (*BT* §7). The view that the Dionysian is anything else, for instance that it is an exalted metaphysical condition, is the result of a classicizing transfiguration and a mere metaphysical "illusion" (*BT* §18). And what else is Nietzsche's myth of the birth of tragedy if not "a return to itself of the German spirit" and "a blessed self-discovery" (*BT* §19)?[281] The mythical nature of the return ensures the blessedness of this discovery. What it conceals is ultimately the "horror of oneself."[282]

Seen from this perspective, Nietzsche's images of antiquity are not a rich imagining of the past, nor are they a wild fantasy. On the contrary, they are a form of imaginary destitution: they deprive themselves of credibility; and they require this destitution, willy-nilly, on the part of their beholder. That is the source of their violence as well as of their value. They carry out a critique of culture upon the subject of culture itself in its most vulnerable spot, in the very heart of a subject's imaginary. Such are the ways and means of the philology of the future.

"The aim is to characterize Greek culture as a paradigm and to show how all culture rests on conceptions that are invalid" ("We Philologists").[283] The Presocratics, with their desperate metaphysics, give one confirmation of Nietzsche's point. Pericles gives another: "The Funeral Oration of Pericles is a great, optimistic mirage, the sunset glow by which one forgets the bad day—night comes hard on its heels."[284] And modernity, with its illusionary antiquity, gives us a third.

Reference Matter

Notes

1. "Attempt," 3. (See at n. 28 below.) Or compare his critique, from late 1888, of the philologist C. A. Lobeck (*TI*, X, "What I Owe to the Ancients," 4).

2. That Nietzsche annotated his notebooks after the fact seems evident. See n. 52 below and n. 59 in chapter 3. What remains unclear is just how late the annotations in question actually are. The phenomenon has not received sufficient attention.

3. Porter 2000, developing the argument of Porter 1995b.

4. *The Seductions of Metaphysics: Nietzsche's Final Philosophy* (in progress), developing the arguments of (inter alia) Porter 1998 and 1999.

5. Cf. *KGW*, 2.2:29–30.

6. "TL," 252 = *KSA*, 1:883; first emphasis added.

7. Cf. "WPh," 5[87] (1875). For Nietzsche's later views on unconscious forgetting, see Porter 1998.

8. See "WPh," 5[31]: "*It is in the interests of a class [that is, that of the philologists] not to allow purer insights into antiquity to flourish: especially the insight that antiquity makes [one] untimely in the deepest sense*" (Nietzsche's emphasis) ibid., 5[55]: "If the greater public found out how untimely a thing antiquity really is, philologists wouldn't be appointed to the job of educators any longer." Cf. ibid., 5[197].

9. "*Philisterei*" (e.g., "WPh," 3[40]); cf. "*Bildungsphilister*" (e.g., "WPh," 3[65]). Nietzsche is not averse to attaching pejorative labels like *kleinbürgerlich* (petit bourgeois) or *bieder* (bourgeois) to his contemporaries either.

10. See the notes "Toward a History of Literary Studies" from 1867/68 (*BAW*, 3:336–42); "WPh," 3[26]: "*Overstraining of the memory*—quite common amongst philologists, [and accompanied by] a comparatively weaker development of judgment"; and *UM*, I:2; *UM*, II:passim.

11. "WPh," 3[74], ("4").

12. Hermann 1826, 6–7.

13. That Hermann was indeed vulnerable to his own accusations is a point that was made by the French classicist Joseph-Daniel Guigniaut in 1835. See Judet de la Combe 1993, 326–27.

14. Cf. Nietzsche's searing critique of Kant in *Beyond Good and Evil*, 11: "'How are synthetic judgments a priori *possible*?' Kant asked himself—and what really is his answer? *'By virtue of a faculty'* [*Vermöge eines Vermögens*]."

15. "WPh," 5[142].

16. "WPh," 5[53]; 3[68].

17. "HCP," 251.

18. Nietzsche, of course, was acutely aware of the difficulties of being read and understood, and his constant reflection on these problems tends only to compound them. Cf. the following note from 1885 (drafted around the time of *Beyond Good and Evil*): "I would like to know whether this book has been understood by anybody: its backgrounds belong to my most personal possessions. . . . I have absolutely no faith in the possibility that anyone today is in a position to hear the totality of its notes ringing: also, understanding it presupposes the kind of philological (and more than philological) work that nobody today will apply: they don't have the time" (*KSA*, 11:38[15]). The autism gestured at here recalls nobody so closely as one of Nietzsche's philological predecessors and models, Valentin Rose, whose watchword, as Nietzsche observed and admired from a distance, was *sibi quisque scribit*. Cf. also *GS*, 102.

19. *EH*, XV.

20. See Diels to Zeller, letter of 26 July 1897: Nietzsche is "just as attractive psychologically as he is otherwise repulsive" (Ehler 1992, 2:183; in print: Diels 1901, ix); Zeller is equally divided (letter to Diels, 24 July 1897; ibid., 2:184)—the reaction is typical (cf. Porter 1998, 172 n. 36; 179 n. 50). Equally telling, and impressive, is the number of classicists who have pilgrimaged to the Nietzsche archive for one reason or another; see Cancik 1995b. On Nietzsche's often unacknowledged influence, which helped to shape debates in classics both in Germany and beyond, see Howald 1920, 21, 27; Henrichs 1984; Mansfeld 1986; Schlesier 1994; Most 1995. Further instances will be cited below, mainly in the notes, as they relate to the topics under discussion.

21. Pfeiffer 1968, ix. For Pfeiffer's ambivalent devotion to Wilamowitz, in whom he moreover rightly saw great ambivalences of his own, see Pfeiffer 1960, 269–76; id. 1961, 19–20; and Lloyd-Jones 1982, 263–65.

22. *BAW*, 3:319, 323 ("Every identity is imaginary").

23. Pfeiffer 1968, ix; also, id. 1960, 288.

24. Pfeiffer 1961, 18; cf. p. 3; and Pfeiffer 1968, vii: "We do not want to know what is obsolete and past forever, but what is still enduring, . . . the continuity of knowledge, the *philologia perennis*."

25. Not only are Pfeiffer's affirmations self-refuting (viz., consisting themselves in generalizations with a "philosophical" tint); his history, turning as it does on the gradual manifestation (a coming to "self-consciousness") of an idea, that of the clarification of poetic meaning, is fundamentally Hegelian. See Porter 1992b, 71–73.

26. *BAW*, 3:338 (1867/68)

27. "WPh," 3[62]. Nietzsche couldn't set his face against current classical scholarship any more directly if he wanted to. Cf. Boeckh 1877, 15: "It is precisely in infinity that the essence of science lies; it is only where [one's] subject-matter [*Stoff*— Nietzsche's word, too] is completely limited, and scarcely even there, that it is possible for science to be fully attained: where infinity ceases, science comes to an end." If Boeckh's logic is that of a romantic view of knowledge, celebrating the infinity of knowledge, postromantic positivism would carry on the torch by dividing the stuff of knowledge into ever-diminishing, infinitesimal objects, and thus securing the everlasting mission of science.

28. "WPh," 3[70].

29. *KGW*, 2.3:331 (*der zukünflige Philolog*).

30. See Nietzsche's letter to Rohde, November 1872, describing the painful circumstances of the lectures on rhetoric held in the winter semester of 1872/73, which drew no classicists and only two students, a Germanist and a law student. See also his letter to Wagner of 7/8 November 1872: "Up until the last half-year, my enrollments were steadily on the rise—and now suddenly it is as if they have simply evaporated."

31. Wilamowitz 1928, 130; and id., in Gründer 1969, 55.

32. Reinhardt 1966, 345.

33. See Silk and Stern 1981, 90–131 (here, p. 131), for a fair sampling of opinions in this vein, issued mainly by philologists. A number of able defenses of various aspects of Nietzsche's philology have been put forward, and references will be made to these as required below.

34. Rohde's polemic is reprinted in Gründer 1969, as is Wilamowitz's reply to Rohde, a second installment (*Zweites Stück*) of *Zukunftsphilologie!* (1873). Some of Nietzsche's directives appear in two letters to Rohde from 18 June and 16 July 1872. The title *Afterphilologie* was suggested by Franz Overbeck; see Silk and Stern 1981, 98, on some of its connotations. The term *Afterphilosophie* is found in Lange 1866, 14 (and in earlier writers), and later in Nietzsche himself, in *UM*, III:4.

35. Overly historicizing approaches to Nietzsche (one of the surprising lines of defense available to his sympathizers; see chap. 5 below) risk losing sight of his healthy and deliberate anachronism, and his provocative use of antiquity at times as a foil to modernism, at times as the construction of modernity. As will become apparent in chap. 1 below, it was Lange himself who may have encouraged this way of thinking about the present in terms of reflexes and atavisms from the (philosophical) past. Even Karl Joël, writing in 1905, recognized the fallacy of viewing Nietzsche's antiquity as historicizing: "I can scarcely find a place in him that justifies his study of the Greeks on the basis of the particularities of the Greeks" (p. 280). Joël aligns Nietzsche with the "Graecomania" of the Romantics (the "un-Greek enthusiasts of the Greeks"), for example the Schlegels and Hölderlin, but depicts Nietzsche as an unwitting follower (ibid., e.g., 282 and 287). For Wilamowitz's despair at antihistoricism of *BT*, see *Zukunftsphilologie!* in Gründer 1969, 31, 55, and passim.

36. Nancy 1973.

37. See Porter 1998 and 1999.

38. Barthes 1968, 2, 32–33 (emphasis added).

39. Following the text of *GA*, 17:329, which reads: "*Denn eine Thatsache ist etwas Unendliches, nie völlig Reproducirbares*," where the *KGW* editors print: . . . "*ein völlig Reproduzirbares*." Logic favors the *GA* reading. Facts are endless for the same reason that they are never fully reproducible—because of their ongoing constitution in the contemporary present.

40. "PTG," 846 (1874). Cf. *WP*, 565: "Qualities are insurmountable barriers for us; we cannot help feeling" that qualities are irreducible to quantitative differences, because "qualities are an idiosyncrasy particular to man." This is Nietzsche's earlier argument too. Cf. "PP," 333, where the primary (but in point of fact, secondary) qualities of atoms are an aspect of them that cannot be "thought away." The examples of this underlying continuity in Nietzsche could be multiplied.

41. Grafton 1983, 181. One of Nietzsche's nineteenth-century predecessors, Theodor Bergk (1845, 407), calls this operation "cleansing" (*säubern*): the philologist scrapes away encrustations of falsehood until arriving at the purest available (or imaginable) form of the transmitted object, the equivalent of Pfeiffer's "text as such, in its purity, truth, and authenticity." So, too, Ritschl (1866–79, 5:7): the goal of philology is the "purification and cleansing [*Reinigung und Säuberung*] of its sources."

42. *BAW*, 3:341–42; "OF," 745 (cf. *UM*, II:18; and "WPh," 3[60]); *GM*, II:24.

43. *BGE*, 208, 34. Cf. *BGE*, 209; *GM*, III:passim; *A*, 54: "Great minds are skeptics."

44. Compare P. Michaelis's review of *Beyond Good and Evil* from 1886 in the Berlin *National-Zeitung*. Michaelis acutely recognizes, in a way that few readers have since, that Nietzsche is an ultra-skeptic "for whom nothing is holy," and least of all the very gesture of doubting itself: Nietzsche, he observes, is "himself in doubt about doubt" (cited and discussed in Porter 1998, 184 n. 62). The only scholar to connect this feature of Nietzsche's thought with his philological method, to my knowledge, is Andler (1920–31, 2:96), who, as usual, has read every word of Nietzsche, made interesting sense of it, and then put the point well: "One can follow, in the *philologica*, the moves and countermoves of this new method [that is, philological skepticism] that is searching for itself. They symbolize the general movement of Nietzsche's thought. . . . How can we fail to recognize that Nietzsche is thus projecting, in the impersonal history [of ideas], the evolution of his very own thought? Isn't it he himself who will give himself over, fondly, to grand models, and then doubt them, only to reestablish in them all that will have provided the crystal-clear evidence of this doubt?" Michaelis's reading of Nietzschean doubt is, however, the sharper of the two.

45. "WPh," 3[63] (1875). Cf. *BAW*, 3:348 (1867/68), where this spectacle is projected onto the Greek landscape itself: the sight of Democritus and his "restless" philosophical style and life was "offensive" to his classically minded, "harmonious" contem-

poraries. See Wilamowitz 1913b [1892], 2:114: classicists too often act as "if antiquity had had a single spirit that was shared by all writers who were read in the schools (Homer, say, and Ovid, or else Plato and Demosthenes) and even by those who weren't selected for the young lads. But in that case, the materialism of Democritus, the critical skepticism of Carneades, and all the exact sciences must admittedly seem unancient [*unantik*]," if not unclassical. Wilamowitz and Nietzsche are unwittingly on the same side of this issue. See further ch. 3 n. 64, ch. 4 n. 184, ch. 5 nn. 195, 198, 208–9.

46. *BT* §20; cf. "WPh," 3[4], 3[62].

47. "WPh," 5[53] ("overcoming" antiquity). More perversely, the "goal" is to engender "hatred" for classical antiquity (ibid., 3[68]).

48. *Der Florentinische Tractat über Homer und Hesiod, ihr Geschlecht und ihren Wettkampf* (*KGW*, 2.1:273–337). Parts I and II appeared in 1870.

49. See Cancik 1994, 84–86, 92–93, for an overview of Nietzsche's activities during the transitional period 1875–76, and passim for a detailed account of the corresponding archival materials, notably "WPh," "SWB," and the sketch to a book of aphorisms that blends into *HA*, "*Die Pflugschar.*" What might be added here is that surprisingly little emerges from Nietzsche's attitude toward antiquity or philology during this transitional period that wasn't already present in the notebooks and correspondence from the Bonn and Leipzig days.

50. Or perhaps not: judging from the bulk of Nietzsche's output, it is no exaggeration to say that his favorite medium is the fragment—the note, the darting jab of words—and not the finished treatise, and this is as true in 1868 as it is in 1888.

51. I am aware of only Wismann 1973 and Nancy 1973; Ducat 1990 has a brief afterword by Nancy. See also Porter 1992a.

52. While the materials collected in *BAW* are vastly superior in quantity and in accuracy to those in any prior edition, they are not exhaustive either. A fresh look at the manuscripts might throw a new light on details and might add considerably to our fund of knowledge; but it is unlikely that the originals, which I have not been able to consult, would dramatically alter the overall impression given by the printed materials. A forthcoming reedition of the *Democritea* and related materials is promised for the *KGW* series. Ducat 1990, the only translation known to me, is misleadingly selective. On Nietzsche and the Presocratics generally, see the collection of essays edited by Conway and Rehn (1992). But the neglect is also symptomatic of a wider syndrome in Nietzsche studies. With the advent of the new, monumental critical edition of Nietzsche's works initiated in 1967 by Colli and Montinari, increasing attention has been paid to the notebooks from 1869 to 1873, especially as these relate to *The Birth of Tragedy* or to Nietzsche's early theories of language. But these notebooks are in their substance often continuous with or else simply resume the earlier, more "philological" notebooks. The philological *Nachlass* is being slowly edited or reedited, although (so far) minus any critical apparatus, which it is essential to have. It will be years before the early *Nachlass* can be adequately assessed. For most of the material to be used below, one has to rely on the editors' chronologies, which are not

always as clearly arranged or explained as one would like. But then collation of the notes must be a hazardous task in any case, given the general lack of internal dating. See, for example, the editorial note in *BAW*, 3:419, to pp. 246–79, describing the notebook labeled by Mette as "Mp VIII, 6" (cf. *BAW*, 1:lxxx), a notebook filled only on the left-hand column, which allowed Nietzsche to add to this (and no doubt others like it) at will. A new edition of "Wir Philologen" by Hubert and Hildegard Cancik is forthcoming.

53. *WP*, 428.

54. *BAW*, 4:84.

55. Cf. "TL," 247: "For what does man really know about himself! If only he could ever see himself perfectly, as if displayed in an illuminated showcase! Does not nature keep nearly everything secret from him, even about his own body, in order to hold him fast under the spell of a proud, delusionary consciousness, unmindful of the windings of his entrails, the swift flow of his bloodstream, the intricate quiverings of his tissues! She threw away the key; and woe to the fateful curiosity that ever succeeded in peering through a crack out of the room of consciousness and downward. . . . " We should not imagine that the sheer materiality of the body alone is what horrifies the mind. Cf. Lange 1866, 485: "If it was once amazingly hard for people to conceive the solid earth on which we stand, that picture of stillness and steadiness, as a thing in motion, it will be even harder for them to recognize in their own body, which is for them the picture of all reality, a mere schema of representation, a product of our optical apparatus," etc. This is Nietzsche's view as well.

56. *KSA*, 13:14[99], 277 (1888); *BAW*, 4:55 (1867/68).

57. *KSA*, 13:14[87] (1888). The full note reads: "The ancient philosopher from Socrates onward has the *stigmata of decadence*: moralism and happiness. High point in Pyrrho; the level of Buddhism is reached. *Epicureanism* in *Christianity*. *Ways to happiness*: signs that all the major forces of life are exhausted." Cf. *NCW*, "We Antipodes" for similar sentiments.

58. *KSA*, 13:14[100]; 14[99], 227; cf. 13, 312; 14[129], 312. Such remarks are typical (cf. *A*, 30), even if Nietzsche could also appear to vacillate (*A*, 58).

59. "WPh," 5[156].

60. "That we may not despair utterly of the German spirit, must we not conclude that, in some essential matter, even these champions ["heroes like Goethe and Schiller" and "Winckelmann"] did not penetrate into the core of the Hellenic nature, to establish a permanent alliance between German and Greek culture?" (*BT* §20). Ironically, proof for Nietzsche of a successful grasp of the Hellenic essence will be a successful appeal to German thinking. Put differently, the philhellenists failed not because they were insufficiently appreciative of the Greeks but because they were insufficiently modern in their appreciation of them: they did not acknowledge the anachronism of their ideal; and their ideal was not anachronistic enough. By contrast, Nietzsche's ideal will be even more anachronistic (and successful) than theirs; and he will acknowledge this by adopting his ideal skeptically.

61. "HC," 784.

62. The phrase *die Idee des Antiken an sich* is from Boeckh 1877, 57, based on lectures whose contents were familiar to Nietzsche, at least in outline form (*BAW*, 4:6–7). Boeckh's defensive and contradictory stance (ibid., 6) is typical of the age, and summed up in such slogans (which he rightly calls "philosophical principles") as: "*Philosophein* ["the practice of philosophy"] is something even the untutored masses can do, but not *philologein* ["the practice of philology"]," or, "There is more production in the reproduction [of philological facts] than in many a philosophy, even though the latter purport to operate in the realm of pure production" (ibid., 68, 12, 14). For useful discussion, see Rodi 1979; Boeckh's position is discussed in chapter 4. On the need within the classical philological discipline to maintain an institutional autonomy from philosophy, especially as Hegelianism was spreading through the German university systems in the first half of the nineteenth century, see Wolf 1869, 2:893–94 (*Darstellung*); Turner, 1980, 75, 90–92; Nietzsche, "OF," 708. But philology's ostensible distinctness from philosophy is a given from the Alexandrian grammarians to Wolf and to Pfeiffer 1968 (88, 226–27; id. 1961, 3)—as is its quiet grounding in philosophical conceptions of all kinds (see n. 25 above).

63. See further Conway and Rehn 1992; Niehues-Pröbsting 1980 and 1996; and others to be discussed in chapter 5 below.

64. For a discussion of this (largely misunderstood) area in Nietzsche, see Porter 1994.

CHAPTER I

1. Nietzsche of course had thought about Democritus and ancient atomism at least since his studies preparatory to his prize-winning essay on the sources of Diogenes Laertius (awarded in October of 1867). Preparations for that essay began intensively in the latter part of 1866 ("Rückblick," 311; letter to Mushacke, November 1866), but they also were a continuation of earlier studies (e.g., work done on the sources to the *Suda*; *BAW*, 3:137; Janz 1978–79, 1:190; cf. *BAW*, 3:221–22, 3:254–59). See further Janz's comments in Salaquarda 1978, 254, 255. In what follows, references in the text and in the notes by page only will be to *BAW*.

2. For a useful overview of the uneasy relation between philosophy and philology in the nineteenth century, see Selden 1990. In Nietzsche's case, their separation was reinforced thanks in no small part to the pressures exerted by his teacher Friedrich Ritschl; see "Rückblick," 305. Ironically, Ritschl would comment apropos of another of Nietzsche's extracurricular pursuits that his protégé was "also a gifted musician, which is irrelevant here," viz., in an assessment of his philological talents (letter to Kießling, cited in Stroux 1925, 33, without date [December 1868]).

3. *BAW*, 3:74 (1864); letter to Mushacke, 20 September 1865 (where *mein höchst geistloser Theognis* could also signal Nietzsche's momentarily flagging inspiration for his project).

4. See Barnes 1986; and the penultimate section of the next chapter.

5. Nietzsche to Rohde, 25 October 1872; repeated verbatim in a letter to Wagner of 7/8 November 1872.

6. Letter to Rohde, 6 June 1868.

7. The *Democritea* project is intensively underway by 26 September 1867 (letter to Ritschl), although no mention of it is made in his autobiographical essay ("Rückblick"), covering developments down to August. The notebooks appear to give continued attention to the project (or its topic) into late 1868, when it enjoys a sudden spurt of renewed enthusiasm (letter to Rohde, 9 December 1868), and apparently another in 1870 (*GA*, 19, *Verzeichniss*, 422: "Mappe VII, 7: mit Zusätzen aus Basel 1870"). It had never really ceased to be on Nietzsche's mind, and it continually crops up alongside other budding interests (*KSA*, 7:2[7] [winter 1869/70–spring 1870]), where the heading "Democritus" follows "Socrates and Tragedy," and ibid., 2[29] (1870): "Democritea," etc. It is overlapped, moreover, by the notes on the project it parallels and supplements, the study of Diogenes Laertius and his sources. The *Democritea* thus finds expression in notes that can belong to either project, as well as in the Diogenes Laertius publications themselves, which give oblique, capsule formulations of the Democritus project, occasionally lifting materials verbatim from the notes and drafts of a year or two earlier. (In all of this, one must remember that these datings are not exact—Nietzsche does not date his notebooks—and they are often just relative, though correspondence and other external evidence help to confirm the general lines of the chronologies.)

8. See the letter to Deussen of April/May 1868, which mentions all three projects, and more accurately identifies the theme of the post-Kantian project as "the concept of the organic since Kant," viz. "physiological inquiry since Kant."

9. The Senecan original (*Epistle* 108.23) reads: *quae philosophia fuit facta philologia est* ("The pursuit of wisdom has turned into the study of mere words"). Whether wittingly or not, Nietzsche is repeating nearly verbatim the defiant gesture of a Renaissance predecessor, the humanist scholar Justus Lipsius, who wrote in 1581: "I was the first or the only one in my time to make literary scholarship serve true wisdom. I made philology into philosophy [*ego Philologia Philosophiam feci*]" (translation after Grafton 1991, 39). But then, Seneca, too, was concerned about the philologist of the future, the *grammaticus futurus* (*Epistle* 108.24).

10. The language is reiterated almost verbatim in *TI*, IX:49, with the same sense of irony (pace Kaufmann 1974, 281, and others): "Goethe . . . aspired to *totality*; . . . he disciplined himself to a whole, he *created* himself . . . with a joyful and trusting fatalism, in the *faith* that only what is separate and individual may be rejected that in the totality everything is redeemed and affirmed."

11. See also the letter to Rohde of 30 April 1872, where Nietzsche comments that his essay on Homer in its unpublished form already elicited the comment, possibly from Ritschl: "One more step like that and he's ruined!"

12. See Nancy 1973 and below.

13. *KGB*, 2.2:8, 175; see Behler 1989, 150.

14. *BAW*, 3:321 (1867/68).

15. Cf. "The Life of Democritus" (one of several titles in a laundry list of philological projects still to be completed), *KSA*, 8:22[10] (1877).

16. See Janz 1974 for a definitive account of Nietzsche's teaching duties, public and private, in the decade between 1869 and 1879. Of special interest is a seminar taught by Nietzsche in the winter semester of 1875/76, devoted to Diogenes Laertius' chapter on Democritus. (Nothing of this has been published to date, unless his lecture notes were drawn from already existing notes; Nietzsche in any case broke off the seminar at the end of February due to illness.) And there are his lectures on the Presocratic philosophers (taught four times between 1869 and 1876), the fifteenth of which is devoted to Leucippus and Democritus ("PP," 328–40). Democritus figures, moreover, as an important point of reference in the fragment from 1872, "Philosophy in the Tragic Age of the Greeks." This work, a chronologically ordered essay on the Presocratics, breaks off with Anaxagoras and presumably would have resumed with Democritus. He also figures in the never finished "Science and Wisdom in Battle," which is contemporaneous with "We Philologists," as well as in a scattered series of planned but never executed works related to all of these titles (for example, *The Justification of Philosophy by the Greeks: A Festschrift*, by Friedrich Nietzsche; *KSA*, 7:19[316] (1872/73). Remarkably, the name of Democritus drops out of sight in the notebooks until 1884, an entry that states that the Presocratics, including Democritus, "are *fuller*" than "Kant, Hegel, Schopenhauer, Spinoza"; *KSA*, 11:26[3]. By "speculative writings" I have in mind the Schopenhaueresque notes from 1870/71 and the sketch on *Zeitatomistik*, or temporal atomism, from 1873. See Introduction.

17. *BAW*, 3:252–53; 4:99; *KGW*, 2.1:229–31. Nietzsche's figures are based on Ritschl's, who had proposed that the Alexandrian catalogues of Democritean titles numbered anywhere from 215 to 400 (Ritschl 1866–79, 1:185). Democritus' literary output is ranked fourth among the ancient philosophers known to Diogenes Laertius, behind Aristotle, Epicurus, and Chrysippus (DL 1.16)—a passage in which Nietzsche, emulating his teacher's zeal for conjecture in the same passage, later proposed to emend Democritus' name to "Demetrius" (of Phaleron), in his *Analecta Laertiana* (1870), thus demolishing Ritschl's evidence, and strangely some of his own (*KGW*, 2.1:175–76; cf. *BAW*, 5:174, 264). We will come back to this problem below.

18. One abandoned note from 1872/73 reads, "I haven't made it easy for those who will only take a *learned* satisfaction in what they do, because in the end I haven't even given them a thought. The citations are missing." Misleading readers through spurious and missing quotation marks will become a strategic element of Nietzsche's later writerly arsenal; but the impetus is philological. Cf. *BAW*, 3:246: "One only had to remove the quotations from Chrysippus' work, a malicious Epicurean opined, and one would see that empty paper was all that was left."

19. *BAW*, 4:70–72; more bluntly, letter to Rohde, 8 October 1868 (fin.); *KSA*, 10:1[45], 22, on the "gestures" that language possesses in great "wealth": "length and

brevity of phrases, interpunctuation, word-choice, pauses, the sequence of arguments" (1882). This thought, too, goes back to Nietzsche's philology, here his studies on rhythm and meter. See chapter 3 below.

20. Janko 1990, 48.

21. *BAW*, 3:212–26; cf. esp. 215. See n. 67 below.

22. Rose 1854, 6–10; cf. p. 7: "*ut uno certe plures . . . , ita paucos tantum libros ipse Democritus edidit.*" On Nietzsche's later reckoning, this hypothesis would lead to assuming the existence of fewer than twenty authentic titles (*KGW*, 2.1:176).

23. The Byzantine document, Nietzsche speculates, is following an ancient source, possibly the mid-second century B.C.E. Stoic Panaetius, but in any case a grammarian from the first century B.C.E., Demetrius of Magnesia (3:254–59). This number could be (and may well have been) surmised from the corpus of Leucippus' own works, which evidently numbered two, a figure Nietzsche later would reject in the case of Democritus (4:78).

24. Letter of 9 December 1868; *BAW*, 3:254; *KGW*, 2.1:230; cf. "ECP," 407 (see chap. 4, n. 18 below). Similarly, Rose 1854, 9 ("*Mullach multos quidem . . . fontes . . . negligens*" while many of the sources he did collect are "plainly false," viz., spurious). Mullach's edition of the Presocratics of 1860 (*Fragmenta philosophorum graecorum*, vol. 1) set the standard—not a very highly regarded one—until Hermann Diels' edition of the Presocratics appeared in 1903.

25. "Pyrrhonism" was the contentious banner of the moderns in the *Querelle des Anciens et des Modernes*; see Hazard 1968, 1:48–77. Fuhrmann 1959, 207–8 (on the Homerist Abbé François Hédelin d'Aubignac); Wolf 1985, 117 n. 84 (chap. 26) (on Wolf's conflicted stance toward d'Aubignac's "Pyrrhonism"); and Momigliano 1994, 46.

26. Dionysius Thrax, *Ars Grammatica* §6 (Uhlig). Is there any possible connection to be made between the rise of skepticism as a philosophical school after Pyrrho in the third century and the contemporary emergence of philology and its practices?

27. Remarkably, classical philology was not even a clearly recognized discipline when F. A. Wolf, the founder of *Altertumswissenschaft*, petitioned to study classics at Göttingen in 1777 (8 April, a day Nietzsche would later call "the birthday of philology" ["WPh," 3(2)]); on the legends surrounding this event, see Pfeiffer 1976, 173. Cf. Turner 1980, 83, on developments a generation later: "The tradition of research spawned in the *Vormärz* period [1815–1848] by the vigorous philological and historical disciplines stressed specialization, rigor of analysis, and negative criticism." This is generally right, but the tendency is more ingrained than Turner suggests, and more conflicted.

28. Cf. Wolf 1985, 118–19 (chap. 27) ; in chapter 29, p. 126, Wolf scoffs at "the rules which schoolboys now learn from Batteux," viz., neoclassical aesthetics. A parallel development takes place in classical art history. See "ECP," 384, on Anton Raphael Mengs ("the first doubter").

29. See *BAW*, 3:341, extolling "the more recent research, which does not mince

matters, which took the wreath off of Homer's single head and tossed it to the four winds, which invented the bold title, *Aristoteles pseudepigraphus*," etc.

30. On the term "doxography," which was coined either by Hermann Diels in 1879 or by his teacher Hermann Usener, see Pfeiffer 1968, 84 n. 6; and Mejer 1978, 81–89.

31. See generally Grafton 1990. The ancient critical traditions, aware of this, often adopted the attitude of uneasy acceptance of textual evidence and transmitted knowledge (the Homeric scholia being a case in point). See Porter 1992b.

32. *BAW*, 3:270.

33. *BAW*, 4:93, 98–100 (on Thrasyllus' "factory"); ibid., 367 (his "Faustian nature").

34. *BAW*, 3:248–49.

35. *BAW*, 3:341–42.

36. *BAW*, 3:341, 368.

37. See most recently Burkert (forthcoming). I am grateful to Professor Burkert for sharing this article with me in advance of its publication.

38. "[D]*ie schöne Form . . . , nach der ich suche.*"

39. Letter to Rohde, 3 November 1867.

40. A paradigmatic instance coincides, not by accident, with the extreme, skeptical reduction of Democritus' genuine works to a mere two titles in July–September 1867 (3:257–59). This claim, which Nietzsche traces inferentially as far back as he can (to the last century B.C.E.), puts extraordinary pressure on the ancient traditions. Investigating its authority reveals hopeless dissensions and uncertainties within the very tradition that has to be made to vouch for the claim. If the (hypothesized) reductive notice by the grammarian Demetrius of Magnesia is right, then Theophrastus (three centuries earlier) is wrong (Theophrastus took one of the two titles in question to be a work not by Democritus but by Leucippus). But if the latter is wrong, which is to say, "if Theophrastus had no trustworthiness as a witness to the most significant work by Democritus," then "*what authority is left* if we don't respect that of Theophrastus? . . . And doesn't exactly the same hold for Aristotle [a generation earlier]? Suppose he held the *Great Diacosmos* to be genuine and Theophrastus did not?" (3:258; emphasis added). Faced with this quagmire, Nietzsche replies in kind: "These general skeptical remarks will lend some significance" to the notice that reduces Democritus' titles to two; but "*it is asking too much that we believe it*" (ibid.; emphasis added). Whether or not this moment represents a turning point in Nietzsche's thinking, or whether he is already in the midst of a dramatization of doubt (about which more below), the moment and the stakes are surely symptomatic of his venture as a whole. Blind skepticism would demolish the basis of philology, paralyzing it from without. Further, the logic of skepticism requires not belief but the application of skepticism to itself, the consequence of which is another, deeper kind of paralysis, this time from within. A way out of these dilemmas lies in a passage from one extreme to another, in a complete and unexpected reversal of skepticism: the

1

near-total validation of the tradition that favors Democritus as the author of his own works. Nietzsche heads off that way on the next page, but no conclusions are drawn yet, at this still relatively early phase of his research.

41. *BAW*, 3:275, 334, 350; 4:64, etc.

42. A good overview of Democritus' achievement is to be found in Guthrie 1965. Briefer but convenient and pointed are the treatments by Barnes 1982, Farrar 1988, and Furley 1987. A fair sampling of fragments and testimony (with commentary) is to be found in Kirk, Raven, and Schofield 1983, based on the edition by Diels and Kranz. The most complete collection is Luria 1970.

43. Rose 1863, 268–75 (Aristotle); id. 1854, 9 (Democritus).

44. *BAW*, 3:350.

45. *BAW*, 3:335.

46. *BAW*, 3:334; cf. 3:328: "The physics of Democritus has to be fully excavated [*eruiren*] from the remains of Epicurus." Cf. Sedley 1982 and Lange 1866, 245–46, 354–57. Henceforth in this chapter, Lange's work will be cited by page number, after the edition used by Nietzsche (1st ed., 1866).

47. *De fin.* 1.6.20, cit. 3:327. On the so-called "cone fragment," see Furley 1967, 100.

48. *BAW*, 3:278.

49. *BAW*, 3:334.

50. Cf. *BAW*, 3:257; DL 9.40; also 9.37, where Thrasyllus brilliantly makes Democritus into "the one present but unnamed" in a questionable dialogue, *The Rivals*, "if it is indeed a work by Plato." Further, *KGW*, 2.1:223.

51. Aristotle's work is variously attested: Simplicius, *De Caelo* 294.33; DL 5.26 (= 68A34 DK).

52. Cf. *BAW*, 4:98. Nietzsche was conscious of the deepest rivalries between Plato and the atomists, not to speak of Plato's likely indebtedness to him (*KGW*, 2.1:223), on which see further Guthrie 1965, 430, 462, 502.

53. This is in line with the testimony of DL 9.40. Earlier (*BAW*, 3:258 n. 1), Nietzsche calls this idea "nonsensical," pursuing the same logic into nonsense of its own: Plato's hatred must have been directed only at the philosophical writings of Democritus; but all the writings were in question and at risk; therefore there were *only* philosophical writings in Democritus' corpus, which accordingly cannot have been all that large. Book burning was not unknown in antiquity. Protagoras' works were said to have been confiscated and burned in the Athenian agora ca. 415 B.C.E., in retaliation for his alleged impiety, but that was by official decree. See Pfeiffer 1968, 31; and Long 1978, 81, affirming Aristoxenus as the source of this story. And, of course, there is the anecdote relating how Plato destroyed his own verses by fire upon meeting Socrates (DL 3.5; *BT* §14).

54. Rose 1854, 7.

55. For example, *BAW*, 3:279 (emphasis in original).

56. Letter to Rohde, 1–3 February 1868.

57. *BAW*, 4:105 (Nietzsche's emphasis); 4:64 (emphasis added).

58. Another possible instance concerns the grammatical and musical writings, whose "restitution" parallels that of the ethical writings (*BAW*, 4:82). Their coordination is historically verified. They were linked in the thought of Hippias, a fifth-century sophist attacked by Plato, who also, like Democritus, combined interests in astronomy, geometry, and arithmetic. Interestingly, here Nietzsche proceeds from a mention of *orthoepeia* (lexical and grammatical correctness, usually termed *orthotēs logōn* or *onomatōn* ["correctness of words" or "names"]), to a consideration of titles reflecting Democritus' multifaceted interests in grammatical and poetical theory. Nietzsche then turns to *orthotēs grammatōn*, "correctness of letters," which is connected by Hippias (Plato, *Hippias Minor*, 368b) to "correctness of rhythms and harmonies." At first, Nietzsche seems to deny the connection between *orthoepeia* (grammatical knowledge) and letters and sounds (*BAW*, 4:85), but then he joins the notion of "correctness of letters" to rhythmical and harmonic properties (*BAW*, 4:86: "Knowledge of the one goes hand in hand with knowledge of the other"), as if to restore the connection previously denied. (One of the works by Democritus cited in this context is ostensibly concerned with "euphonious and dysphonious letters," which is to say with the aural properties of the alphabet, viewed as phonic material and organized into changeful configurations—of sounds juxtaposed, blended, patterned, rhythmed, etc., presumably by analogy with the commotion and interlacing of atoms. Perhaps that gives all the physical connection that Nietzsche feels he needs.)

59. Letter of 16 February 1868.

60. This emerges clearly from what looks like an outline of the planned work (*BAW*, 4:81–82), which moves dialectically from doubts to "restitution," and then opens onto new "consequences" for understanding Aristotle (seemingly, against Rose's own judgment), although these last are never more than suggested in the notes we have.

61. Letter to Rohde, 9 December 1868.

62. The illegible word in the manuscript (see frontispiece) may just possibly be "*Mannes*" ("the writings *of the man*"), but this is far from certain. Either way, Nietzsche will have unnamed Democritus here. Cf. *BGE*, 7, which describes, as it were, the revenge of Democritus, in the form of Epicurus' prolificness as a writer; and thus echoes (and reverses) the Aristoxenian anecdote about Plato and Democritus' writings: "[Epicurus], that old schoolmaster from Samos, . . . sat, hidden away, in his little garden at Athens and wrote three hundred books—who knows? perhaps from rage and ambition against Plato?"

63. Lange 1866, 269.

64. Letter to Ritschl, 10 May 1869, a remarkable disclosure.

65. See *KSA*, 7:29[8], 624–25: "No one can so firmly believe himself to be in possession of the truth without a certain amount of *delusion*: [otherwise,] skepticism is bound to reassert itself. . . . Delusion after all is merely belief in truth. . . . Even skepticism contains in itself a belief: the belief in logic."

66. The image of a snake that bites into its own tail recurs in *BT* §15 and in *TI*, ix, 24.

67. In a paper read before Nietzsche's fellow students in January of 1867, Rose's

assumptions and conclusions about the transmission of Aristotle's corpus are shown by the young Turk Nietzsche to "stand on feet of clay" (*BAW*, 3:226). The later *aperçu* is more hopefully aimed.

68. See Rose, 1854, 1–2, which provides a general historical justification for suspecting falsifications in the literary tradition, but no systematic criteria of discernment. Rose's final arbiter is self-evidence. Cf. Rose 1863, 26: "*omnino autem de Aristotelis ingenio iudicaturo testis fide dignus extat nullus praeter ipsum Aristotelem*"; and cf. n. 101 below.

69. Lange 1866, 67.

70. Ibid., 261.

71. Lange's importance for Nietzsche's philosophical outlook has long been suspected, at least as early as Vaihinger 1911. See the two relevant articles by Salaquarda 1978 and 1979, the study by Stack 1983, and the discussion in Crawford 1988, with their respective bibliographies. Despite this sizable interest, the more radical spirit of Lange's first edition has not been the object of much attention among scholars.

72. On these historical continuities, see *BAW*, 3:333 (following Lange); 4:82; and Furley 1987, 123. Cautions about overestimating the continuities are voiced by Melsen 1952 and Barnes 1982, 343–45.

73. An heir of Lange on this point is Adorno. Cf. Adorno 1982, 143: "For philosophical thought, dualism is a given [*vorfindlich*], and just as inevitable as it is shown false in the continued course of thinking."

74. Protagoras thus approximates to Kant, as revised by Lange. Cf. Lange 1866, 15, 305. An interesting echo and confirmation is provided by a late note in Nietzsche: "Our contemporary way of thinking [viz., critical skepticism toward morality] is to a great extent Heraclitean, Democritean, and Protagorean: it suffices to say that it is Protagorean, because Protagoras represented a synthesis of Heraclitus and Democritus" (*WP*, 428 [1888]).

75. See Nietzsche to Gersdorff, end of August 1866. The error in question presumably concerns the graphic display of eroticism and intimacy in a devotional painting, a point that was widely debated in Goethe's day (see Hatfield 1964, 204–5). Lange's remark offers a new, philosophical twist on this stale debate.

76. *BAW*, 4:5; cf. "ECP," 374.

77. Lange 1866, 251, 268; Nietzsche to Gersdorff, end of August 1866.

78. "Dominated by the prevailing materialism, scholars had become fatally ambitious to emulate the positive and concrete achievements of natural science" (Lloyd-Jones 1982, 176); cf. Reinhardt 1966, 339.

79. So great was his passion for the subject, Nietzsche was ready at one point to abandon philology and to take up molecular chemistry. This, at least, was the intention that he coolly announced one day to Rohde (letter of 16 January 1869). The interest is an abiding one. In 1873, while at work on "Philosophy in the Tragic Age of the Greeks," Nietzsche discloses that he has immersed himself in "the strangest of studies," which he took to be prerequisites to his ongoing philological project:

"[modern] mechanics, chemical atomic theory, etc.," including even the dreaded study of mathematics, his weakest flank in grade school (letter of 5 April 1873, to Gersdorff). But he was already making similar connections in the late 1860s ("Test for the intuitively talented: physics and chemistry," *BAW*, 3:343; 1867/68); and the attraction to natural science itself came early, at least by the age of eighteen (as instanced by the intriguing essay from 1862, "Fatum und Geschichte"). Cf. *BAW*, 2:255 (from that essay): "History and natural science, the wondrous legacies of our entire past, the harbingers of our future, are the only secure foundations on which we can build the tower of our speculations." After 1866 Lange contributed to his zeal no doubt, but so did Nietzsche's own readings in Presocratic natural philosophy. This point deserves to be underscored. Lange's influence is neither pure nor is it exclusive. Nietzsche's reading of Democritus and his speculations in philosophy prior to and then independently of Lange informs his reading of Lange every bit as much as it is informed by Lange after 1866. They were after all breathing in the same atmosphere of a post-Kantian Germany. Lange, like Schopenhauer and even Democritus, was in ways merely confirming Nietzsche's own native inclinations.

80. Cf. Hayman 1980, 92, who rightly notices this emulation.

81. Lange 1866, 377.

82. Cf. *BAW*, 5:268: the "natural scientific way of viewing antiquity"; *HA*, I:1: "Chemistry of concepts and sensations"; "WPh," 5[88]: "—Thinking and inferential reasoning: but this is something you learn not *from* the ancients, but at most *in the course of dealing* with them, by means of scholarship. In addition, all historical inference-making is highly conditioned and uncertain: that of the natural sciences is to be preferred."

83. *BAW*, 3:336. Cf. also *MusA*, 1:292–93 (spring 1868).

84. See further *BAW*, 5:127–28, for a series of reflections on the limits of "discursive" inquiry, the heuristic play of hypotheses, and the role of intuition, though here the proximity of philology to natural scientific method is not well marked. See discussion of the latter in Figl 1984, 123–24, without reference to Lange or Democritus.

85. Lange 1866, 498.

86. See *BAW*, 3:340–41, on the variability, in meaning and function, of "commonsense reasoning" across time and cultures, and within them as well.

87. See Introduction.

88. *A*, 52. Cf. also *BGE*, 209, a tongue-in-cheek hymn to skepticism, in which "the unconquerably strong and tough virility of the great German philologists and critical historians" is praised: "Viewed properly, all of them were also artists of destruction and dissolution."

89. Letter to Rohde, 9 December 1868. Nietzsche's attitudes toward Jews and Judaism will be treated in the final chapter.

90. On the former, see *BAW*, 4:63: "Epicurus denied the existence of Leucippus. Sign of impudence"; ibid., p. 59: "To deny Leucippus is not possible (Epicurus not

withstanding)." On the latter, see "PP," 336 n. 39, although the ethical implications of the swerve are not discussed here—but see Lange in n. 91 below.

91. This line of reasoning is explicated a few years later: "The Stoics simplified Heraclitus through their rereading and misunderstanding of him. The Epicureans likewise smuggled flaccid ideas into the rigorous principles of Democritus" (*KSA*, 7:19[114] [1872/73]). In the same mood, *KSA*, 12:1[123], a note from 1885/86, railing against the beatitude and bliss of "beautiful souls" and "pietists," in addition to "Spinozan or Epicurean happiness"—in short, "against any form of resting in contemplative states." For Epicurus' antireductionism and his arguments against Democritus, which Nietzsche could have inferred even without piecing together the evidence of the published but still unedited transcriptions of Epicurus' *On Nature*, see Sedley 1983 and 1988. Finally, cf. Lange 1866, 27: "Physics stands in the service of ethics in Epicurus, with the consequence that this subordinate status inevitably works to the detriment of his account of nature."

92. Cf. the preface to "Philosophy in the Tragic Age of the Greeks" ("PTG," 801): "I want to bring out in every system [of the philosophers under discussion] that point which constitutes a bit of *Persönlichkeit*." Barnes 1986, 21, rightly notes that Nietzsche is here following the anecdotal approach to philosophy found in Diogenes' *Lives of the Philosophers*—but then Nietzsche has gone Diogenes one better and applied the approach *to Diogenes himself* (on this, see *BAW*, 4:214–16; 5:129, 172: "The personality of Laertius"; and see pp. 116–21 below on Democritus' *Nachleben*). Diogenes is not the only inspiration: Zeller (1856–68, 1:10–12) and Lange lie close by too, and the two kinds of influence wrought a mutual and lasting confirmation for Nietzsche, whose instincts were in any case already formed before he arrived at Bonn; see *BAW*, 5:254, a retrospective account: "At Schulpforte one usually leaves behind a literary monument . . . : to this end I wrote my essay, which in my hands turned into a character-sketch of the Megarian Theognis." Nietzsche's attempt to capture a *Gesammtbild* ("comprehensive picture") of the personality of Democritus is strikingly similar to Zeller, ibid., 1:11: "Every philosophical view is in the first instance the thought of a certain individual," his "way of thinking"; "our first job is therefore . . . to connect the views of every philosopher into a *Gesammtbild*" by locating the single organizing "principle" of the system of any given thinker. Questions of personality die hard. For a recent application, see Mejer 1978 (approving of Nietzsche's approach on p. 46 n. 96). That such questions and investments have always been inseparable from philological activity is Nietzsche's point in his essay on Homer and elsewhere (see below).

93. The phrase recalls a much earlier entry from 1861, which in turn informs his later critique: "Finally, there is a whole series of poems noteworthy for the way in which [Hölderlin] tells bitter truths to the Germans—truths that, alas, are frequently all too well founded. In his *Hyperion*, too, he hurls slings and arrows against German barbarity [*Barbarenthum*]" (*BAW*, 2:4).

94. Cf. *BAW*, 3:321: "individual personality has only as much [historical] influ-

ence as it works upon the masses"; all "great 'ideas'" are thus always pale shadows of themselves (*BAW*, 3:324). Contrast Lange's more romantic cultivation of genius: "Ideas are the poetic offspring of the individual person, powerful enough perhaps to master entire periods and peoples with their spell, but never universal [*allgemein*] and still less immutable" (1866, 346). Jakob Burckhardt's positive treatment of the person as "typical" may be influential here, that is after 1869 (Niehues-Pröbsting 1983, 281–83), but then Nietzsche will in that case have complicated, darkened, and ironized Burckhardt's model.

95. "It seems natural to me that you would smell in the lines written here the aroma of a Schopenhauerian kitchen" (ibid.). The "strongly pessimistic" flavor of Nietzsche's view is not metaphysical; it stands specifically in relation to philology and to literary history; and his view of historical "needs" is quite alien to Schopenhauer's depreciation of history (*W*, 2.2:§38). Likewise, Nietzsche's claim that a "new cult of genius lies concealed" in his reflections refers to the specific cult that is revealed by them: the historical tendency described and critiqued by Nietzsche. See further, chapter 5, n. 50 below.

96. See *BAW*, 5:251, anticipating the critique of philology on similar grounds from *UM*, II:9: "I don't want exactly to say that I fully belong to these philologists of resignation [*Resignationsphilologen*], but as I look back on the way I traveled from art to philosophy and from philosophy to scholarship, and how here in philology I find myself in an ever narrower field, it nearly looks like a conscious act of renunciation [on my part]"; cf. *BAW*, 3:297, again linking melancholic resignation and scholarly asceticism to the name of Schopenhauer. Cf. further the letter to Deussen of September/October 1868 for similar sentiments.

97. *BAW*, 3:319–26; here, p. 323.

98. Ibid.

99. Ibid.

100. Ibid., 324; cf. Lange 1866, 268 (with Porter 2000, 13–14).

101. Rose is hardly innocent of making decisions based on the presumptive personal profile of an ancient thinker, which only confirms Nietzsche's point. See Rose 1854, 104, for the judgment as to what is or isn't "abhorrent to Aristotle's mind [*mens*]," to his "character" or "genius" (*ingenium*).

102. Letter to Deussen, April/May 1868 (ad fin.).

103. On Wolf's achievement, see Pfeiffer 1976, 173–77; Jebb 1887, 107–10; and the introduction to Wolf 1985, 3–35.

104. The current state of the problem is usefully laid out in a few pages by Janko 1990. For a detailed survey of the Homeric question, see the introduction to Parry 1971.

105. Foucault, "What is an Author?" in Foucault 1977. Foucault, who has both Nietzsche and Homer in mind, gives expression to a by now familiar thought: "Here, as well, it is necessary to distinguish a 'return' from scientific 'rediscoveries' or 'reactivations.' 'Rediscoveries' are the *effects of analogy or isomorphism* with current forms

of knowledge that allow the perception of forgotten or obscured figures" (p. 134; emphasis added), such as Democritus. Analogy as an interpretive trope is of course central to Nietzsche's essay and to his philology as a whole. In what follows, references to "HCP" will be by page only.

106. Cf. also *BAW*, 5:280 ("Where lies individuality?") and esp. p. 281: "Homer is thus the first singer of the heroic song. Concede this, however, and his personality eludes us completely. It flees back into an unfathomable prehistory [*Vorzeit*] and changes into a mythical person. . . . This figure of Homer was reborn in ever new forms: it went through the whole evolution of epic poetry and gradually passed from an ideal, [that of] a marvelous creature [*Wundermann*], into a human transformation." The early idealism of Greek culture (see n. 112 below) is worth noting; it will recur with some frequency below.

107. Cf. "ECP," 373: "How much effort is needed not to regard Homer as a literary product, the way *Wolf* was the first to do!"

108. Summarizing the results of his study in a letter to Rohde, Nietzsche describes Homer as a "ghost," "a mythical monster that has gone through the strangest [historical] transformations" (9 December 1868). Cf. *BAW*, 5:197, 221, on the parallel problems that surround Hesiod's "image." For a historical survey of the problem of Homer's identity as variously fashioned by his readers down to the Renaissance, see Lamberton and Keaney 1992.

109. *"Dies wird um so vollkommener gelingen, je bewusster der anordnende Künstler die aesthetischen Grundgesetze handhabt: ja er wird selbst die Täuschung erregen können als ob das Ganze in einem kräftigen Augenblicke als anschauliches Ganze ihm vorgeschwebt habe."*

110. "HCP," 257. See the notes to lectures on tragedy from a year later, where these ideas are developed further and along slightly different lines: "The unity of tragedy is that of a concept [*Gedankens*], not of a *form*" ("IST," 38). One point made here is that the very idea of dramatic closure springs from a desire that is both "deceived" (falsely gratified and denied) and "rekindled afresh": "At the end of the whole [tragedy] one is allowed to see not the *full* form but only the conceptual *threads* connecting the parts," nor are the connections in any way *"logically necessary"*—it is only the power of illusion that makes them seem so (ibid.). Nietzsche's insights here and elsewhere into such aesthetic expectations as closure and totality—the poetics of sense and meaning—would be well worth studying. Cf. further *KGW*, 2.2:26 on Homer and tragic tetralogies.

111. "If we compare the great so-called cyclical compositions [that is, the materials of the epic cycle], we see that the indisputable merit of the final designer [*Planmacher*] of the *Iliad* and *Odyssey* lies in his having accomplished the relative best that he could with his conscious technique of composition. . . . Are all those weaknesses and flaws, which are taken to be so very valid but which in reality are on the whole depreciated on highly subjective grounds, and which one is in the habit of regarding as the petrified remainders of the period of the tradition [of the text's transmission], possibly nothing more than the almost necessary evils that this [same] genial poet

had to incur in his so magnificently intentioned, almost unexampled, and incalculably difficult composition of the whole?" (pp. 265–66).

112. Cf. *BAW*, 5:223 (a notebook preparatory to the essay): "The fame of *Homer* must be older than the epics," which were later compiled and transcribed under the name of "Homer" at a time when "Homer" designated an *Idealwesen*, an idealized poetic source (ibid., 222), indeed a "mythological figure" (ibid., 225)—although the idealization was plainly inherited from preliterate times and then rationalized: "Ideals that one powerfully tackles with the help of rationalizations—and with ever sharper weapons" (ibid., 223). Similarly, the Hesiodic corpus (ibid., pp. 222, 232).

113. Nietzsche's term, *Plan*, had already been used by him in a similar way in 1863, in a few pages inspired by Kantian aesthetics: "The mind seeks out a unity in the fullness [of sensations] and unifies and organizes [the manifold] in a flash. [There is] pleasure in this *arrangement*, albeit an apparent one, for it lies in the mind. We believe that we can recognize a *design* [*Plan*] in colors, shadings, etc. In art we have imitated nature and [in our perception of nature] we project art into nature. We spiritualize the *particular*," and so perceive synthetic totalities ("wholes") in the place of particulars, etc. (*BAW*, 2:256).

114. *Fragencyklus* of course contains an allusion to the so-called "Homeric cycle" of poems, whose exact relation to the twin epics is still debated.

115. Cf. *BAW*, 5:232, where Nietzsche decides that the redactor of the first-person proem (preamble) to the *Theogony* (and possibly of the entire Hesiodic corpus) had "not correctly understood" the autobiographical portions of the *Works and Days*. The result is an uneven amalgam of verses passed down under the hallowed name of "Hesiod."

116. Pp. 249, 251, 250. The impetus (*Wucht*) of the personalities of educators is discussed in a notebook from 1870/71 in terms of *Wahnvorstellungen*, or "delusions" (or even "hallucinations"; *KSA*, 7:5[106]).

117. August Boeckh's speech to a gathering of fellow philologists in Berlin in 1850 paints a fairly grim picture of a discipline under hostile attack from a wider public representing "the so-called spirit of the times" (Boeckh 1858–72, 2:183–99, esp. 193–94). The situation seems unchanged forty years later; see R. Hirzel, "Über die Stellung der klassischen Philologie in der Gegenwart," in *Jahresbericht über die Fortschritte der classischen Alterthumswissenschaft* 69 (1892): 145, lamenting the "numerous opponents of philology and of classical antiquity."

118. On Hermann and Boeckh, see Bursian 1883, 2:665–705. Bursian's study literally divides itself around the conflict, with volume 2 opening with the dispute and then subdividing into two histories of philology, each one stemming from Hermann and Boeckh, respectively, and reaching into Bursian's present. For a more careful portrayal, see Vogt, in Flashar et al. 1979. On Wolf, see Fuhrmann 1959. In retrospect, the earlier debate between Wolf and Heyne could be read (and simplified) as the ancestor to the debate between Boeckh and Hermann; such, at least, is Hermann's view (1826, 3). See further chap. 5 below, and chap. 5 n. 187.

119. "HCP," 253, 249; cf. *KSA*, 7:23[18] (*"Theorie der Aggregatzustände. Theorie der Materie"*); and "PP," 236: *"Aggregatzustände"* (viz., configurations of quantitative constituents) vs. "qualities." Cf. Lange 1866, 29. The term conventionally had the stigmatic connotation of matter qua heterogeneous, discontinuous, and unsystematic (as in Kant's *CJ*, First Introduction, §2; Kant is mentioned in the passage from "PP" just cited), of which atoms and void provided the essential stereotype. The association with matter is thus never far off wherever the term *Aggregat* appears in philosophical contexts, as it does in Hegel's identical criticism of contemporary classical philology in 1830 (*Enzyklopädie der philosophischen Wissenschaften im Grundrisse*, §16), and in all subsequent allusions to this stinging critique—for example, Bernhardy 1832, 19 (see below); Ritschl 1869–77, 5:8; and Boeckh 1877, 3 (in the second sentence of his *Encyklopädie*); cf. also Boeckh's letter to Schleiermacher (9 February 1808), where he levels Hegel's complaint against F. A. Wolf (cit. in Bravo 1968, 78, 89); again, in the preface to his *Corpus Inscriptionum Graecarum*, 1:vii (*"rudi . . . variarum rerum congeri"*); and then again in Boeckh 1877, 40. Compare Bernhardy's concession (familiar also from A. H. L. Heeren's *Geschichte des Studiums der classischen Litteratur seit dem Wiederaufleben der Wissenschaften* [Göttingen 1797] 1:1) that philology's many disciplines were once, prior to Heyne (Wolf's teacher), like "aggregates and riven masses [*Aggregaten und zerklüfteten Massen*] lacking any [organizing] principles" (Bernhardy 1832, 19). That the classicists are painfully aware of Hegel's critique is clear from Boeckh 1859, 2:192 (and the whole of that speech). Another source of sensitivity may have been the ascendancy of Hegelians in the German university system (see Turner 1980, 75, 91; Nietzsche, "OF," 708). Ironically, Hegel, in turn, may have derived the term from Wolf himself; see Wolf 1831a, 2–3, where earlier encyclopedias in various branches of learning (including philology, in the 1770s and 1780s) are viewed as "aggregates," though not, evidently, in a pejorative sense.

120. Cf. the identical threat in "WPh," 2[3] ("d."): "The relationship [of the ideal, classical, privileged Greeks] to the real Greeks"—a threat that is never made good on in the expected sense, for reasons that the present study aims to clarify.

121. Cf. Wolf 1985, 209 (chap. 49) : "The Homer that we hold in our hands now is not the one who flourished in the mouths of the Greeks of his own day, but one variously altered, interpolated, corrected, and emended," etc.: so "history speaks."

122. "It was Goethe who, himself formerly an adherent of Wolf's views on Homer, announced his 'apostasy' with these verses [Goethe 1948–54, 1:56, *"Homer wieder Homer"*]: 'Discerning as you are, / you freed us from all blind adoration, / and we admitted [or "allowed": *bekannten*] all too readily / that the *Iliad* is a mere patchwork. / Let no one begrudge us our apostasy; / for it is youth with its fire that disposes us / sooner to conceive [Homer] as a whole / and joyfully to experience [*empfinden*; cf. Wolf's *"sensus"*] him as a whole' ['*Scharfsinnig habt Ihr, wie Ihr seid / von aller Verehrung uns befreit, / und wir bekannten überfrei, / dass Ilias nur ein Flickwerk sei. / Mög' unser Abfall niemand kränken; / denn Jugend weiss uns zu entzünden, / dass wir ihn lieber als Ganzes denken, / als Ganzes freudig ihn empfinden'*]" (p. 252). Goethe's rupture

with Wolf is well documented; see Volkmann 1887; Fuhrmann 1959, 224–28. See also Schiller's sarcastic poem, "Ilias" (Schiller 1943–, 1:259), written for Humboldt in 1795.

123. *Scheinmonarchie* (p. 249).

124. On ancient sources, see Wolf 1985 (chs. 32–33); *Praefatio* to Wolf's 1794 edition of the *Iliad*, in Wolf 1869, 1:205 ("*Ita haec . . . dubitatio nequaquam nova est, uti putabant isti nuper, quibus ea absurda et ridicula videbatur*," etc.). On modern sources, see Wolf 1985, 45 (chap. 2): "But in general no one disputes any of these points. [With regard to] Homer, . . . doubts clearly exist. . . . "; chapter 12, p. 71; chapter 26, n. 84, pp. 116–17; and passim. In an essay from 1788 the Danish archaeologist Georg Zoëga (1755–1809), a student of Heyne's at Göttingen, had proposed that "Homer" was a purely symbolic fiction corresponding to no individual, while the poems were merely collections of earlier lays; the essay first appeared in *Georg Zoegas Abhandlungen*, ed. F. G. Welcker (Göttingen, 1817), pp. 306–15; Heyne's response in a letter of 22 September 1790 to a now lost letter by Zoëga on the same question is published in F. G. Welcker, *Zoegas Leben*, 2 vols. (Halle, 1913 [originally published 1819]), 2:33–34. Whether Wolf knew of Zoëga's hypothesis can only be guessed. See also Volkmann 1874, 47.

125. Cf. Wolf 1985, chapter 33, p. 139: "This is what I found in all these [ancient] authors, and what anyone will find if he takes the trouble to read them attentively and does not, blinded by partisanship and rashly accepted opinions, prefer to be deprived of the light of truth"; and cf. chapter 27, pp. 118–19, where Wolf gently mocks "the Klopstocks, the Wielands, the Vosses" and other belletrists, revealing the source of some of this partisanship. The force of Wolf's arguments can be measured by the reaction he provoked among these same literati (see next note). Cf. Wolf 1884, 235: "Various [readers of the *Prolegomena*] discover, as I anticipated, a way round all my entrenchments, through their own *unhistorical hypotheses*, and take the comfortable route back to the standard old belief." Schiller, too, was capable of condemning the "merely aesthetic" basis of the classicized antiquity of his contemporaries (while perpetuating his own); see his critical annotations to Humboldt's essay (Humboldt 1969a [1793]) in Schiller 1943–, vol. 21, pt. 2:63–65; cit. in Rehm 1951, 144 n. 57.

126. The reception of Wolf's ideas is the history of such dual responses, often within a single individual. "*Man muß mit, wohin der Geist führt*," the classicizing writer and translator Johann Heinrich Voss wrote approvingly to Wolf in June of 1795. But by November, Voss had changed his tune: "I believe in *one* Homer! One *Iliad*! One *Odyssey*!" See Volkmann 1887 (cit. in Fuhrmann 1959, 226 n. 160); see Jebb 1887, 117 n. 2: "Schiller called the theory 'barbaric'"; Wieland and Klopstock had equally adverse reactions, as did Goethe.

127. Cf. a letter to his teacher Heyne from 1795: "It was always my wish to be accompanied only by learned, calm researchers, by men . . . who know the attraction of doubts which no *locus probans* resolves" (Wolf 1985, 234 = Wolf 1884, 234–35).

128. See Fuhrmann 1959, 224–25; and the introduction to Wolf 1985, 33–34.

129. Grafton 1981, 124. This statement of Wolf's problem is more acute than Pfeiffer 1976, 174, and more accurate as well. See Wolf 1985, 196, (chap. 47), on Aristarchus' methods and his contribution: "These and other things cannot today be inferred by certain or even probable arguments."

130. Although the *Prolegomena* bears a later publication date than the edition (1795/1794), they were bound and sold together, with the *Prolegomena* preceding Wolf's text of Homer.

131. See introduction to Wolf 1985, 12–15; Grafton 1981, 108–9; and Wolf 1869, 2:953: "For us moderns, the bond joining the erstwhile sibling arts has long been dissolved; everything is parceled out into isolated workshops of learning, wherein even the most fertile genius can find inspiration only by way of the hard-won imagination [lit., "making present" in the mind, *Vergegenwärtigung*] of an alien past."

132. On classical antiquity as a seat of everlasting value, see Wolf 1869, 2:877 (*Darstellung*); as "a self-enclosed world," see ibid., 892. For this reason, Wolf could resist the "Pyrrhonism" of his predecessor in France, d'Aubignac, whose argument Wolf looked upon as a *Schreckbild* of his own—but with which in the end he felt himself "forced" to agree (Wolf 1985, 117 n. 84 (chap. 26) ; see Pattison 1889, 1:380 on Perrault). As for methodological rigor, Wolf's hoped-for ideal, which he concedes to be beyond reach, is based on an idea of "mathematical rigor and evidence" (Wolf 1869, 2:832).

133. Cf. *Prolegomena*, chap. 38 (p. 155): "The monuments of Homer and his contemporaries [. . .] in a sense forced philological criticism into existence, and had done so before the name of critic or grammarian had come into common use."

134. "Certainly, every time I have come down to those [last six books] in continuous reading, I have always sensed [*sensi*] in them certain things" (Wolf 1985, 133 [chap. 31]).

135. The Homeric poems "deceive us by their appearance [*facie fallunt*], which is uniform *in general* and extremely similar to the rest. For in general all the books have the same sound, the same quality of thought, language, and meter" (chap. 31, p. 134); "Indeed, almost everything in [the poems] seems to affirm the same mind, the same customs, the same manner of thinking and speaking. Everyone who reads carefully and sensitively [*cum sensu*] feels this sharply [*intime sensit*]" (chap. 50, p. 210).

136. Cf. chapter 31 on the way the seams between the numerically last (and for Wolf, compositionally last) six books of the *Iliad* "merged so early with the rest" of the poem, making the seams impossible to detect for scholars—until Wolf came along.

137. It is Wolf's German phrase, too (as in Wolf 1884, 236), and Heyne had used it before Wolf (Wolf 1884, 291). See, however, n. 113 above.

138. Hermann struggled to resolve this issue within a Wolfian framework, but only succeeded in clouding matters anew. See Hermann, *Opuscula*, 5:52, 6.1:70, 8:11; and Jebb 1887, 119–20.

139. Cf. Wolf's *Praefatio* to the 1794 edition of the *Iliad*, on the poems of the original bard *"in quibus tanta conspicitur unitas et simplicitas argumenti et dispositionis"* (Wolf 1869, 1:207). Their unity minimally derives from the logic of the proem (*Iliad* 1.1–7), which announces the theme of Achilles' "wrath," but not (Wolf protests) the later, "new" wrath of the last six books (chap. 27, pp. 119–20; cf. Wolf to Heyne in Wolf 1985, 244–45 = Wolf 1884, 290–91). Sometimes the impression Wolf gives is that uniformity, not unity, is the key to detecting the original Homer (cf. chap. 25, p. 111, on the poem's original "simplicity of thought and language"—referring, inter alia, to what is now understood as "formulaic" diction). But we cannot make Wolf any more precise than he is.

140. These wholes correspond to different sets of clues. There is the "original" and "genuine" form, which we admire (Wolf will say) in its traces, for its traces (but not as a whole, for that has vanished) (chap. 31, p. 31). There are the individual lays, which "may seem to have been composed by Homer and sung for a long time in the same way, that is, separately and without regard for the shape of the whole." And there is "the whole which we now all admire," which is but the showy aesthetic supplement to those traces; it is their extrapolated and conjectural form: that "single great continuous body," that "new and more perfect and splendid monument" (chap. 28, p. 122).

141. This is the very strategy used by Wolf in a letter to Heyne, his former teacher and later critic, whom he deprecates for presuming to know more about the poems than he can account for in historical terms. Heyne has plenty to say about the *"great action, great designs, great passions,"* and so on, "concerning the whole of *Homer's epic poems"*; but "we have never read a syllable of yours in writings or heard one in lectures about how the rhapsodies and so-called poems might have looked before *Pisistratus"* had the poems compiled in the sixth century (Wolf 1985, 243 = Wolf 1884, 289–90).

142. Cf. chapter 29, p. 124, with n. 91, urging that one consider *"how late the Greeks learned to construct wholes [totum ponere] in poetry"* (emphasis in original), a predilection taken to extreme lengths by "our philosophers" (viz., aestheticians) today; and cf. chs. 41 and 49, p. 205, on the Alexandrians' Aristotelianism. Cf. *BAW*, 5:275: "In general, one must not overvalue the composition [of Homer's poems]: Aristotelian deception." Further, n. 157, below.

143. Other claims are less equivocal. See p. 74–75 above ("sought the genuine form"). Even the poems' artistic naïveté, lauded in chapter 12, may be a delusive effect, an *effet-image* of natural genius, produced by sophisticated means in a later age and in the pursuit of an imagined original naïveté. Cf. chapter 11 ad fin., which gives the ironic contrast to chapter 12.

144. Pace Jebb 1887, 110, who wrongly distinguishes the role played by "feeling" from philological-historical considerations: "The whole argument for his *theory*, on the other hand, was essentially external." (Similarly, Howald 1920, 2, with n. 1.) Wolf's own testimony after the fact, moreover, flatly contradicts this: "One can get

around the *external grounds* if necessary, should the *internal* ones not stand up to examination," etc. (in Wolf 1985, 234 = Wolf 1884, 236).

145. Cf. the following statement, equally remarkable for both its confidence and its contradictoriness, from the preface to his 1794 edition of the *Iliad* (Wolf 1869, 1:211–12): "Perhaps it will never be possible to show, even with probability, the precise points at which new filaments or dependencies of the texture begin: but this, at least, if I mistake not, will admit of proof—that we must assign to Homer only the greater part of the songs, and the remainder to the Homeridae who were following out the lines traced out by him" (trans. Jebb 1887, 109). Wolf never changed his mind on this point.

146. See n. 144 above. Wolf's official position—his most fondly remembered dictum—is given in the *Praefatio* to the edition of 1794 (Wolf 1869, 1:210–11): "Tota quaestio nostra *historica et critica* est, non de *optabili* re, sed de re *facta*. . . . Amandae sunt artes, at reverenda est historia" (Wolf's emphases). Fuhrmann 1959, 225, captures Wolf's words but not his practice: "*Nicht ohne Überwindung gab Wolf den normativen Ästhetizismus preis und bekannte sich zur historischen Forschung.*" Thanks to these complications, it would also be a simplification to place Wolf in the camp of the so-called analysts.

147. "The last decisive question [raised by Wolf's inquiry] was simply left *undecided*," as he himself puts it (Wolf 1985, 235 = Wolf 1884, 239).

148. See the *Praefatio* to his 1804 *Iliad* edition, p. xxii, beautifully captured in Jebb's paraphrase in the third person (Jebb 1887, 110): "As he steeps himself in that stream of epic story which glides like a clear river, his own arguments vanish from his mind; the pervading harmony and consistency of the poems assert themselves with irresistible power; and he is angry with the scepticism which has robbed him of belief in one Homer," which is to say, belief in the unity of the Homeric poems, since Homer's historical existence is never doubted by Wolf.

149. The irresolvable debates over property rights unleashed by Wolf's publication are symptomatic in this regard. See the correspondence between Wolf and Heyne reproduced in Wolf 1985, 232–47, for example, the following: "By [your] *duplicity* [viz., vacillations] you put your readers and adherents into an extraordinary confusion." The statement, perfectly applicable to Wolf, was in fact made *by* Wolf—to Heyne (ibid., 244 = Wolf 1884, 291; emphasis added). In Wolf, an earlier generation's quandaries are made into a central problem and a modus operandi (hence, too, the dramatic pro and contra form of his argument in the *Prolegomena*). See also Fuhrmann 1959, 224–25.

150. See Wolf 1985, 47 (chap. 3): "Once I gave up hope, then, that the original form of the Homeric poems could ever be laid out *save in our minds, and even there only in rough outlines*, it seemed appropriate to investigate how far the ancient evidence would take us in polishing these eternal and unique remains of the Greek genius" (emphasis added). Exactly how does one polish a rough mental outline? (The term *expolire* ["polish"] is used, not coincidentally, of the practice and results of the

ancient grammarians throughout the *Prolegomena*.) The flip side of Wolf's argument is that the Homer we have is the product of a deficient age governed by a deficient aesthetic (a point Nietzsche will make good in his own way). "How many are the corpses and tombs of books that lie together there, before our eyes!" Wolf wrings his hands at one point (chap. 41, p. 169). The Alexandrian Museum is a mausoleum, and at its center lies a cenotaph: "Homer." Likewise, Nietzsche (pp. 65–66 above).

151. The equivocation about the form of the poem is probably a glancing allusion to Wolf's own terms (*"corollae . . . collectae"* [chap. 41, p. 167], referring to the anthologizing instincts of Alexandrians, at a time when genuine poetic production was long past its prime). But there may also be a dig at Schiller, who complained that philologists—namely, Wolf—"had torn apart Homer's [victory] wreath [*Kranz*]" ("HCP," 252).

152. Contrast Cesarotti, *Prose edite e inedite* (Bologna, 1882), p. 197 (cit. in Wolf 1985, 131 n. a): "[Wolf] admires and exalts the *Iliad*, and sacrifices Homer without remorse"; Jebb 1887, 109, is more accurate: "But Wolf was far from denying a personal Homer. He supposes . . . a poet of commanding genius." Flashar's contrast (1979, 22–23) between Wolfian (author-based) versus Boeckhian and Schleiermachian (text- or object-based) hermeneutics needs fine-tuning on both sides. See chapters 4 and 5, below, for one alternative (what I there call "humanistic hermeneutics").

153. When one subtracted "all those excrescences, everything flat and substanceless that one believed was to be found in the Homeric poems, one was immediately prepared to lay the blame at the doorstep of the tiresome tradition. What of the individual Homeric essence was left over? Nothing but a sequence of especially fine and impressive *loci*, chosen in accordance with a subjective standard of taste. The essence [*Inbegriff*] of aesthetic singularity, that of the individual who is acknowledged for his artistic capability, was now called 'Homer.' That is the basis of all Homeric errors" (p. 263). Nietzsche is plainly referring to readers of Homer; they proceed in the same way as his arch-deceiver, who merely stands in for a reader's own self-deception.

154. Cf. *KSA*, 7:16[6] (in the context of reflections on Homer and Hesiod from 1871/72): "The poet is only possible amongst a public of poets. . . . A richly imaginative public. . . . Making poetry is only a stimulus and a guide for the imagination." Homer and Hesiod are merely idealized names (ibid., 16[5]; cf. [15]) and aesthetic judgments (ibid., 16[21]; "Cap. VII"). These notes are conceptually continuous with the inaugural lecture from some two years earlier. Nietzsche's invention of the post-Homeric composer would have seemed not merely bizarre but perversely so to Wolf; see Wolf 1985, 235 (= Wolf 1884, 238): "Here and there, people have read into the book that I sought to make one man responsible for the composition of the Homeric songs, one who had made the *Iliad* and the *Odyssey* for us *out of scattered fragments*....I do not know how I could ever have given rise to this bizarre [*abentheuerliche*] opinion, which has long been the object of ridicule." Nietzsche's philology is "absurdly exciting" (Ritschl) in just this way. (See next chapter.) K. O. Müller would likewise have found Nietzsche's imputation about antiquity objectionable. Cf. Müller

1825, 110, wondering how myths, which in their essence are a blend of imaginary ideas (*Ideen*) and facts, come to be believed at all:

The imaginary component [*jenes Ideelle*], someone could say, is nothing but poetry and invention dressed up in narrative form; an invention of this kind cannot be made up by several individuals simultaneously short of a miracle: that would require a striking coincidence of intention and of representational abilities and styles. So a single person really did make it up. And how did this one person convince everybody else about the reality, the factual nature, of his invention? Should we assume that this one person is a sly old fox who knows how to persuade others through all manner of deception and illusion, say by plotting together with like-minded swindlers who would then have to testify to the rest of the nation that they themselves had also witnessed the thing he had concocted [*das Ersonnene*]?

Having made this reductio ad absurdum, Müller goes on to reject the imaginary objector's thesis on various historical grounds (his own theory being the sum of these), but also because the thesis "offends the noble simplicity [*edle Einheit*] of those times" (ibid., 111), which is to say, it is offensive to Müller's classicizing sensibility, which here is clearly doing homage to Winckelmann. Myths are not "invented," Müller reasons; they are the "necessary and unconscious" products of a cultural imaginary; and even if a single individual were responsible for a mythical invention, he would merely be an embodiment of this larger process, as it were the "mouth" through which a nation speaks (ibid., 111–12). An example from *Iliad* 1 follows. Nietzsche knew Müller's work. Did Müller suggest to him the figure of the conscious deceiver in "Homer and Classical Philology"? Preller 1837, vi-viii, shows, at least, that the issue raised by Müller was very much in the air. Cf. further the reference to the *splendidum mendacium* by the Alexandrians in *BAW*, 3:230. More important than any precedents that conceits like these might provide, what they reveal is an underlying anxiety among philologists of the time. Worries about falsification, deception, and (at the far limit) conspiracy are but the fantastic extreme of rational philological skepticism. Nietzsche is playing on these fears with his own brand of skeptical philology.

155. "HC," 784. Nietzsche repeats the gist of Gorgias' famous *mot* in a contemporary notebook: "Die Kunstempfindung ist getäuscht werden und *bewußt* sich täuschen lassen. In diesem Schwebezustand liegt die Freude an der Kunst" (*BAW*, 5:206). See chapter 2, n. 48 below.

156. "Why then should we be surprised if from the discordant testimony of the singers and scribes *Aristarchus could not—even if he had wanted to and had devoted himself to that goal alone—have recovered the genuine and, so to speak, primitive singer? . . .* Thus we can see how dubious was the state of affairs at the time when Aristarchus placed the finishing touches on his Homer" (ibid., pp. 204–5; emphasis added).

157. Wolf is in part attacking eighteenth-century rationalist aesthetics, which

colored his contemporaries' readings of Homer. Oddly, the Alexandrian redactors of Homer's text followed an ancient version of these same poetic principles (chap. 38), which Wolf beholds only with contempt: their modern counterpart is "what our fellow countrymen call aesthetic judgment" (ibid., p. 158; cf. chap. 29). In other words, the poems were put together in their current form with the guiding light of aesthetic judgment. And Wolf, as a connoisseur of their harmony and as a philological detective, is implicated *malgré lui* in the same kind of judgment. Moreover, if philology arose at the same time as "the desire to imitate antiquity" in the Hellenistic age (both are symptoms of decline; cf. chap. 41, p. 167), then Wolf is implicitly classicism's critical partner in a postclassical age.

158. As he later betrays in a letter to Heyne, the seeds for the *Prolegomena* were planted before he could even articulate the grounds for an argument: "Furthermore, I noticed that my initial feelings [from before 1788, concerning the last six books of the *Iliad*, etc.] could be put into words and . . . conceptualized" (Wolf 1985, 233; trans. mod. = Wolf 1884, 231–32; see also Volkmann 1874, 36–37). He goes on in the same letter to concede, contrafactually, the possibility that "an attachment to old sentiments . . . was for once playing a trick upon" his scientific judgment. But how could he know even that? Paradoxically, Wolf's intuition is founded on the ability to read a presumed preliterate bard. The classicist David Ruhnken, to whom the *Prolegomena* is dedicated, may be the inspiration here (see chap. 31, p. 133). Intuitionism, however, is doubtless in the air (and continues to be so into the next century, even among classicists), and it plays into Wolf's rejection of rationalist aesthetics. See further Wolf 1869, 2:816, on the "boldest flights of scholarly divination," etc. Intuitionism is also a long-standing feature of philological criticism. Panaetius (second century B.C.E.) is said to have called Aristarchus a *mantis* ("prophet") for his ability to divine Homer's meanings (Athenaeus 634c; cf. Plato, *Ion*, passim, and *Laws* 634e). See further *KSA*, 7:19[74–78] (1872/73), for reflections on the role of intuition in the construction of meaning.

159. "*Die Kenntniss der alterthümlichen Menschheit selbst*" (Wolf 1869 [*Darstellung*], 2: 883). On Humboldt and Wolf, see Stadler 1959, esp. 53–55; Grafton 1981, 108–9.

160. Cf. "WPh," 7[1] (quoted on p. 210 below), on the fantasy-like nature of "classical antiquity," which so greatly influences the modern world, but which originally runs through the ancient world, at least starting with the Alexandrians: we are infected with their fantasies as well.

161. See *BAW*, 5:128, for the same endorsement of "intuition," viz., "poetic, unifying perception." Boeckh 1877, 25, speaks of philology as an art, albeit as an art of knowing and of historical reconstruction.

162. See "WPh," 3[2]. The specific reference is to the circumstances surrounding Wolf's matriculation at Göttingen (his legendary switch from theology to philology) and his conversation with the rector of the university and his future teacher, Heyne; see the note on this passage at *KSA*, 14:556; and n. 27 above.

163. The closer you approach "the one Homer" the further he recedes. One rea-

son, undiscussed until now, lies in the nature of individuality itself, which is essentially "undefinable" and "inaccessible" (pp. 257, 262), but not for organicist or Romantic reasons. Cf. "TSK," 379: "In reality, there are no individuals; rather, individuals and organisms are nothing but abstractions. . . . These unities . . . are in turn multiplicities." Thus, if Nietzsche's essay on Homer appears to explain historical impossibilities through philosophical ones, the reverse also seems true, and ultimately neither kind of reasoning taken by itself is satisfactory or privileged in the essay.

164. This last thought (about atoms, individuals, and the evaporation of the singular element into the greater whole [pp. 268–69]) is scarcely new to Nietzsche. Compare the concluding lines of a talk from July 1867, close to the inception of the *Democritea*, entitled "The Battle of the Singers on Euboea" (*BAW*, 3:230–44), on the fabled contest between Homer and Hesiod in which Homer loses. The "contest" (preserved under the same title) raises questions about the synchronicity of the two poets but also about the authenticity of the report and the date of its origins. As in "HCP," instead of solving his purported academic problem by philological means, Nietzsche leaves every issue uncomfortably open to the very end, including the problem of each poet's *Persönlichkeit*: "Whether the positive claims [made by scholars, beginning with Aristotle and then the Peripatetic Alexandrians; cf. pp. 237–38], for example, that Homer lived during the Ionian migration [i.e., before Hesiod], are positively more factual than the *agōn* [contest] and the *isochronia* [synchronicity of the two poets], is another question. In the same way, my investigation deliberately fights shy of the question whether *the atomistic evaporation of the person* [Persönlichkeit] *of Homer into the aether of Homer* [that is, into the concept "Homer," the canonically enshrined monumental poet], as our age loves to have it, is really a logical conclusion to make or whether it is only a concession to *certain recently and very widely held philosophical or aesthetic views*" (p. 244; emphasis added). "HCP" constitutes a further elaboration of this mysterious closing, and a further mystification (for, we are all "Alexandrians," and so "recent" in Nietzsche stands for everyone after Homer who tries to construe Homer). His letter to Ritschl from 17 February 1868 reveals how deeply congruent the two studies on Homer are; another, to Deussen (April/May 1868), draws attention to Nietzsche's love of "paradox" in this connection (see at n. 102 above). The piece on the "contest" eventually appeared in *Rheinisches Museum* in two parts, in 1870 and in 1873 (*KGW*, 2.1:273–337), as a companion to the edition of the *Certamen* that Nietzsche published in 1871 (*KGW*, 2.1:341–64).

Without going any further into this fascinating conjunction of ideas here, let us simply note how bringing this essay into the picture makes explicit the dimension of Nietzsche's early profile that we have been tracking so far: its decidedly sophistic, self-dissolving element (cf. "HCP," 253, where Nietzsche briefly poses as a sophist). The *Contest* (*Certamen*) that we have is filtered through the sophistry of Gorgias' pupil Alcidamas of Elaea, the "Homerist" and author of a lost work, the *Mouseion*. This work turn conjures up a whole prehistory of "rhapsodic contests, sympotic riddling games, and the earliest Homeric studies" (*KGW*, 2.1:337; cf. *BAW*, 3:234–35); Nietzsche was the first to identify Alcidamas as the source of the preserved *Contest*, and his hypothesis, today widely accepted and acknowledged, was later corroborated by two papyrus finds; see O'Sullivan 1992). The *Contest* ends with a riddle: "Dear sirs, you hunters of the sea's prey," Homer asks, "have we caught anything?" "All that we caught," the fishermen reply, "we left behind, and we are carrying off all that we didn't catch." Nietzsche's lecture, "Homer and Classical Philology," is nothing less than a repetition of this riddle, and its commentary too.

CHAPTER 2

1. Compare the remarks on redemption as a "flight *into* reality" toward the end of *GM*, II:24.

2. *BAW*, 3:332; 4:44; cf. 3:349; 4:63.

3. See *GM*, III:8; *CW* 7; and the fragments of *The Will to Power* collected under the title "The Will to Power as Art" (*WP*, 794–853), although the editors could have as easily adopted the chapter title preferred by Nietzsche in 1888, "Towards A Physiology of Art" (*KSA*, 13:16[71], 18[17]).

4. "Being unbeholden [to anything] is his ideal, a calm, scientific life" (ibid.). See DL 9.45: "The end of action is tranquility [*euthymia*], which is not the same as pleasure [the Epicurean ideal], as some have misunderstood it, but a state in which the soul remains calm and strong, undisturbed by any fear or superstition or any other emotion" (trans. Hicks, mod.). Cf. *BAW*, 3:277, where we find Nietzsche's gloss for the Democritean ideal of "well-being" (*euestō*, of which Democritus was the living embodiment, according to some of his portrayals in antiquity): "He did not let himself be frightened by *eidōla* [that is, atomic films or images]," which is to say, by the reduction of appearances to such films.

5. Not insignificantly, Nietzsche's predilection for Lucretius over Epicurus (to be discussed below) is in line with Lange's similar view. But Lange deprecates slightly Lucretius' poetic talents (his language is "rough and simple," etc.) and the drier, unpoetic didactic portions of the poem, while praising the sublimity of his ideas: he shows "a *Schwung* [élan] of belief and phantasy" that takes him beyond the bland and "harmless serenity [*Heiterkeit*]" of Epicurus (pp. 37–38). Nietzsche, more consequent than even Lange on this point, and transferring, as it were, Lucretian attributes onto Democritus, sees no difference where Lange saw one: the élan of Democritus' thought *is* his poetry. Elsewhere, Lange concedes to others what he denies to Lucretius; cf. Leibniz's "*Poesie der Begriffe*" (p. 214).

6. See generally Sedley 1982.

7. Ibid., 176; cf. "PP," 331–32: "'Not-Being is as real as Being.'"

8. "PP," 335 ("blind chance" is in fact "*die zwecklose Causalität, die anagkē* [necessity] *ohne Zweckabsichten*"). Aristotle, *Physics* 2.4; Barnes 1982, 423–26; Guthrie 1965, 414–19.

9. *Dinē*, Nietzsche's *"Wirbel"*; cf. *BAW*, 3:332; *KSA*, 7:23[32].

10. DK 68A37; fr. 164; A135; A128. Cf. "PP," 333, 338–39.

11. Lucretius, *On the Nature of Things*, books 2, 4 (esp. 2.114–31); for Democritus, see previous note.

12. See Sedley 1982, 181, on the atomists' lexical innovations; von Fritz 1939, on the vivid character of their language, which includes aural as well as visual characteristics (ibid., 29); "PP," 331 ("Dionysius [of Halicarnassus, *On the Composition of Words*, chapter 24] calls [Democritus] a paradigm for writing, next to Plato and Aristotle. On account of his élan [*Schwung*] and his figures of speech, Cicero [*De orator* 1.11.49, *Orator* 67] compares him to Plato . . . ; his clarity was renowned; Plutarch . . . marvels at his élan"). Cf. also *KSA*, 7:1[7], 13: "Even in prose [there is] poetry," where Democritus is named as an instance; and *BAW*, 4:59, on Democritus' distinctive traits: "need for knowledge—clarity—poetic abandon [*dichterischer Schwung*]."

13. "All qualities are *nomōi* [by convention]; *onta* [all things that exist in nature] are only quantitatively different. Thus all qualities may be traced back to quantitative differences" ("PP," 333).

14. Ibid.

15. *Prōton pseudos*: "PP," 339–40; "secondary qualities": ibid., 333, *BAW*, 3:332, and *KSA*, 7:23[39] (1872/73).

16. Galen makes this point in *De medic. empir. fr.* (Democritus, fr. 125 DK). Further, Farrar 1988, 210 with n. 82. See *HA* I:15: "As Democritus transferred the concepts Above and Below to infinite space, where they make no sense, so philosophers in general transfer the concept 'inner and outer' to the essence and phenomena of the world" (resuming a critique from "PP," 335–36).

17. Cf. Lange 1866, 285: "The genuine materialist will always be inclined to direct his gaze at the vast world of external nature and to regard man as a wave in the ocean of the eternal motion of matter. . . . To be sure, in practical philosophy he will likewise have recourse solely to the nature [viz., "physiology"] of man," and will not be inclined to award it "godly attributes." Democritus is literally the starting point for Lange's historical inquiry, but see ibid., 67, on Democritus as the "starting point" for all subsequent scientific method.

18. Fr. 191 DK.

19. Trans. Guthrie, 1965, p. 44.

20. Fr. 7 DK. On this term, see Langerbeck 1935. Cf. *KSA*, 7:23[39] (= "PP," 331, 337): "Thought is a movement" (which echoes verbatim Zeller 1856–68, 1:617); cf. *BAW*, 4:74 ("B7") and 75 ("B7"): "*to phronein* [thought] consists in the mixture of the body" and its particles. Nietzsche could also describe belief as a mere physiological error, which is not far off from the Democritean conception. The idea is widely prevalent in the early notebooks, but cf. "WPh," 3[76], 38; 5[5] (1875), where the context is a discussion of the favorite cultural target of the atomists, religious belief.

21. "SWB," 6[25] (1875). Nietzsche could have speculated that this is what lies

behind the meaning of the Democritean phrase "man, the microcosm" (fr. 34 DK); cf. Porter 2000, 205 n. 16. The *KSA* passage reads: "With Empedocles and Democritus, the Greeks were on the best road to *a correct assessment* of human existence, its unreason, its suffering; *they never arrived, however*, thanks to Socrates. An impartial view of mankind is absent from all the Socratics, whose heads are filled with abominable *abstracta*, [such as] 'the good,' 'the just.'"

22. "SWB," 6[50].

23. *BAW*, 4:86 (1867/68); "SWB," 6[18] (1875). In a similar vein, because it is based on these same notes from 1875, *HA* I:261 ("The Tyrants of the Spirit").

24. See *On the Nature of Things*, esp. bk. 3.

25. See nn. 4, 5 above.

26. See Democritus fr. 5 DK (the texts given in Diels 1951–52, 2:135–38); Vlastos 1945–46, esp. §IV ("Man Makes Himself"); Guthrie 1965, 2:473–83, 489–97; Cole 1990. See *BAW*, 3:275.

27. Hence, his name for this period, "the tragic age of the Greeks." Significantly, the Presocratics are linked to each other by mere "phantasms" ("SWB," 6[7]). More on this in chapter 5 below.

28. Dumont 1990, 32.

29. Caizzi 1984, 17–19.

30. Timon of Phlius, fr. 46 Diels (DL 9.40): "Such is wise Democritus, shepherd of myths [or "words" (*mythoi*)], / ambiguous [lit., "two-minded"] chatterer, among the very best I've read"; see Caizzi (previous note), who incidentally takes "chatterer" to refer to Democritus' productivity as a writer. Timon's praise is complex, in contrast to the unambiguous Peripatetic Strato of Lampsacus, who ridiculed Democritean atoms as a "pipe-dream" (Cicero, *Academica*, 2.37.121 = 68A80 DK). On Timon's literary practice, see generally Long 1978. Nietzsche unsuccessfully sought to emend the verses just cited (*KGW*, 2.1:222–24 [1870]; cf. Gigante 1984a, 352) so as to bring out a different point: Pyrrhonian skepticism and Democritean atomism are a "bane" to "myths" (especially those concerning the gods). For what it is worth, Timon's language is sprinkled with terms familiar from atomism, notably "empty" and "vortex"; and Pyrrho is known to have associated with the atomist Anaxarchus (DL 9.111) and (like Timon) to have admired Democritus (DL 9.67).

31. Arguments for Democritus' "Pyrrhonian skepticism" are given by Barnes 1982, 559–64, and by Kirk, Raven, and Schofield 1983, 411. Contra, Farrar 1988, 204–15, opting for Democritus' "agnosticism" instead, as does Zeller 1856–68, 1:632–34.

32. For example, *BAW*, 4:38: "Later Abderites were Pyrrhonians. . . . Democritus was made into a pupil of Xenophanes because they are both skeptics; v. [DL] 9, Pyrrho 7" (sic); *BAW*, 4:90: "Pyrrho and Epicurus base their ethics on Democritus"; cf. *KGW*, 2.1:222–23; *BAW*, 3:332: Pyrrho derives his epistemology from Democritus. But qualifications are also made: Metrodoran ethics seems to exceed the reach of Democritean ethics, though what this means is left vague (*BAW*, 4:49 ["3"]; 63; 90).

Perhaps Nietzsche felt that Democritean skepticism was limited to scientific methodology (the impossibility of proofs, etc.) and epistemology. At any rate, Nietzsche would have found the uncertain foundation of skepticism in Democritus appealing: Democritus reinvests the objects of doubt with poetic belief, a much more daring and dangerous combination than Pyrrhonian blank doubt (which for Nietzsche is a form of nihilism).

33. Nietzsche has slightly conflated two passages from Sextus Empiricus, and taken small liberties with the second (*Against the Mathematicians*, 7.135, 136). The passages are conveniently presented in Kirk, Raven, and Schofield 1983, 410.

34. It was only in the second edition that Lange made explicit this connection between the atom and Kant's thing in itself (Lange 1974, 2:87), which will become a commonplace for Nietzsche, especially in the last decade of his writings. But in the first edition Protagoras had already fallen just shy of making the "leap" to positing a *Ding an sich* that might have saved him from the pitfalls of subjectivism (Lange 1866, 15), and so the inference to a Kantian thing in itself lay close at hand for Nietzsche. (Cf. ibid., 380, where the thing in itself could be either a thing, a force, or a material.) Schopenhauer had in any case made the same critical inference in his critique of atomism (*W*, 1.1:§24). Kant, the source of all these speculations, denied that matter can qualify as a thing in itself, because matter is just a "representation in us" (*CR*, A359).

35. Democritus, fr. 125 DK. Cf. *A*, 14, a virtual quotation of this fragment: "'Pure spirit [viz., mind]' is pure stupidity: if we deduct the nervous system and the senses, the 'mortal frame,' *we miscalculate*—that's all . . . " (trans. mod.). In both Nietzsche and Democritus, the claims made on behalf of the body and of matter are tempered by unknowability; cf. "TL," 247, and *BGE*, 15.

36. This comes out clearly in the later lectures on the Presocratics, where the premise of atomism, on Nietzsche's view of it at least—namely, that "thought is a movement" of atoms ("PP," 331)—occasions the downfall of the atomistic hypothesis. For at the very point at which materialism touches the nature of thought, demolishing the immateriality of the soul by pulverizing it into mobile, fiery bits of matter, something inexplicable happens. The atomistic hypothesis inverts itself; it becomes a demonstration about thought rather than about matter:

> Here, the dilemmas intrinsic to materialism surface, because here materialism begins to suspect its *prōton pseudos*. Everything that is objective, extended, endowed with causal properties, in other words everything that is material, that counts as materialism's firmest foundation, is nonetheless a "given" only in a highly mediated sense and has an existence that is at most relative: it passes through the machinery of the brain and into the forms of time, space, and causality, by virtue of which it presents itself as spatially extended and causally effective in time. From that which is given in this way, materialism now wants to derive *the only unmediated given there is: representation*. It is a huge *petitio principii*. Suddenly, the last link proves to be the starting point on which the first link in

the chain always depended. . . . The absurdity resides in the way in which materialism starts out from what is objective, when everything objective is in fact conditioned in various ways by a knowing subject and, as a consequence, vanishes entirely from sight as soon as one thinks away that subject. (ibid., 339–40; emphasis added; cf. "PTG," §11, against Parmenides).

The atomistic hypothesis inverts itself, but strangely confirms itself in the process: thought is a movement, a *perpetuum mobile*, an inconstant and restless thing.

37. See Porter 1986 for traces of this analogy in Saussure.

38. *BAW*, 4:49, 76, 78.

39. Nietzsche apparently kindled the interest in this project in a colleague who stood utterly in awe of him, Heinrich Romundt (see Romundt's letter to Nietzsche of 30 September 1868), though neither one ever carried out the demonstration. Romundt's letter is a virtual but unwitting parody of Nietzsche (see Nietzsche's letter to Rohde of 6 August 1868). The attempt by Natorp (1898) was superseded by a groundbreaking article by Vlastos, 1945–46. See further Farrar 1988. And see n. 44 below.

40. Democritus' title *On Painting*, known from Vitruvius, is to be linked to his study of perspectival painting (4:59; 4:99). The theory of sound and the mapping of astral bodies are "sibling arts," attested together for Hippias, with similar implications for Democritus (4:93).

41. Lange 1866, 9; cf. ibid., 67.

42. *BAW*, 4:64; 4:82; 4:86. Nietzsche fought long and hard to come to grips with their inclusion in the Thrasyllan lists. Prima facie arguments against the attribution of these and like titles to Democritus included the existence of six homonymous or near-homonymous Democrituses, not to mention the raft of ethical fragments of doubtful authenticity handed down under the spurious attribution to "Damocritus" (cf. 3:271, "*Der Historiker und der Musiker Democrit*"; and DL 9.49). The known forgeries of a later impostor, one Bolus from the Hellenistic period, with attested medical and magical interests of a weird Pythagorean bent, helped muddy the waters further ("*Bolus und seine Fabrik*," 3:259).

In the end, these objections are overcome. The musical writings named by Glaucus already attest to their early date, Nietzsche reasons (*BAW*, 4:47); just as musical studies are attested "before Glaucus," so is "philosophy of language" attested "before Plato" (ibid., 55). The intrinsic connection between music and mathematics (especially number theory) begins to look increasingly plausible, because it now appears "very fitting" to an atomist's program of study (*BAW*, 4:92). Indeed, mathematical interests could already be conceded even when the authenticity of the alleged linguistic, technical, and ethical pursuits could still be denied (*BAW*, 4:47). Equally illuminating is the insight into the close imbrication of musical and philological (viz., linguistic) questions: competence in one field implies competence in both. The connection, already implied by the width of the meaning of *mousikē* (the cultivation of arts and letters), is historically motivated even in the narrower sense of "music."

("The teachers of music and letters were formerly the same people," *BAW*, 4:74, citing an ancient source.) But Nietzsche is making a more fundamental assumption about this mutual entailment: the grounds are purely methodological; physical speculation is justifiable in all of these various domains. With poetics secured, the musical writings in the narrower sense can be rehabilitated: "The musical writings of Democritus are genuine" (*BAW*, 4:86), and so too, the cloud of uncertainty surrounding the homonymity of the two Democrituses is decisively dispelled: "Confusion with Democritus the musician [a contemporary of Democritus of Abdera] is impossible" (*BAW*, 4:64).

43. Hence the confidence with which Nietzsche decides on the issue of the two Democrituses (see previous note). Philodemus knows about both Democrituses in his *De musica* but credits the philosopher with musical and historical interests nonetheless. This Epicurean watchdog is unlikely to have been fooled by a falsified tradition, and Nietzsche may well have taken this factor into account. On Nietzsche's knowledge of the Herculaneum papyri and of Philodemus' writings, see *BAW*, 4:260, 330, 441, 492, etc.; and Gigante 1984b and 1986.

44. Zeller's handbook flatly denies the possibility of a link between ethics and physics in Democritus (1856, 1:653; contrast *BAW*, 4:63: "It would be astonishing if Democritus had overlooked the ethical implications of his system") and has next to nothing to say about the (well-attested) place of aesthetic inquiry in Democritean atomism, although the subject has since become a regular feature of surveys of Democritus. Nietzsche was dependent on Zeller, but not uncritically so. See his letter to Rohde of 11 June 1872; and *UM*, III:8: "I for one prefer reading Laertius Diogenes to Zeller, because the former at least breathes the spirit of the philosophers of antiquity, while the latter breathes neither that spirit nor any other."

45. On the simulacral sources of concept-formation, see (e.g.) *BAW*, 3:327.

46. A list of titles preserved in Diogenes, making up two tetralogies under the general heading of *Ta Mousika*, suggests that Democritus showed a remarkable interest in poetry and its study: *On Rhythms and Harmony, On Poetry, On the Beauty of Verses, On Euphonious and Dysphonious Letters, On Homer or On Orthoepeia and Glosses, On Song [or "On the Art of Song"], On Words, Onomastics* (DL 9.48). How and whether Democritus would have translated the properties of language, atomistically conceived, into his view of poetry is a matter of speculation (one that Nietzsche seems prepared, in principle, to undertake). For one possible sketch, see next note.

47. Cic. *De natura deorum* 2.93. Cf. *KSA*, 7:23[35] (1872/73): Democritus would have viewed a tragedy "as the result of machines." The analogy is common in the atomist tradition. See Ferrari 1981; Wismann 1979; Porter 1989 (with further references), and id. 1995a; and cf. Diderot's similar argument, drawn no doubt from the same sources (and cited in Lange 1974, 2:752), about the composition of the *Iliad*.

48. The first viewpoint looks like an allusion to the fifth-century sophist Gorgias (Plutarch, *De Glor. Ath.* 348C = fr. 23 DK). The second viewpoint is compatible with Gorgias' theory of aesthetic ecstasy, but also with much else in early Greek musical

theory. On the other hand, Gorgias' aesthetics, being sophistic, constitute a paradox (Porter 1993), and so may Nietzsche's position here. Another instance was hinted at above (p. 78). If Gorgias creates the puzzle about how a subject can rationally will itself into deception, Nietzsche's answer, I suggested, is that subjects *irrationally* will themselves into deception. This seems like a further paradox, or else not much of an improvement. But if I am right in my speculation about Nietzsche's "response" to Gorgias, we can see how Nietzsche can ultimately blend the two viewpoints presented in *BAW*, 5:206 into mutual compatibility. The view that "art is conscious self-deception" belongs, Nietzsche writes, to the "rationalist"; the claim that "art is an unconscious effect" belongs to the "philosopher." Both are right: art is the irrational (because) conscious production of unconscious effects in a subject. It is a form of self-deception. Dotting the i's, Nietzsche adds that the "artist" in the face of his own future work of art is equivalent to the spectator in the face of the finished work of art (ibid.): both of these will themselves, consciously and irrationally, into self-deception and unconscious states. In other words, the deceiver and the deceived are one. (Identically, *KSA*, 7:5[90] [1870/71], on the "pathological interest" that is the "prerequisite" of all art: "The ideal is that [the poet] knows how to deceive himself," in addition to deceiving his audience.) See Porter 1993, 296 for an argument that this is in fact the meaning behind Gorgias' original dictum. Finally, for an argument that art for Nietzsche—at least in *The Birth of Tragedy*—is in some sense the experience of sensation itself, that is, a consciousness of what is unconscious in sensation, see Porter 2000.

49. *BAW*, 4:81 ("C.5."); 1867/68.

50. The underscored portion alludes again to a proposition by Gorgias, this time from his *Encomium of Helen* ("poetry is *logos* plus *metron*"; fr. 11 DK). In this famous speech, Gorgias expounds a corpuscular account of language that is reminiscent of atomism (he talks about the tiny *sōmata* [bodies] of *logos*, as well as a general view of aesthetic responses as a form of ecstasy that might or might not follow from atomism. The repeated allusions to Gorgias in Nietzsche would be worth a study in itself, the more so given the misleading impression his early *philologica* too often leave scholars with that Nietzsche was relatively indifferent to the fifth-century sophists. His notes on Alcidamas (a pupil of Gorgias'; see chapter 1, n. 164, and chapter 5, p. 239 below), and various other clues from his thinking at the time, tell a different story.

51. See Aristoxenus, *Elements of Harmony* 1.27; *Elements of Rhythm* 2.8 (to be discussed in chapter 3 below).

52. See Porter 1989, 1995a, and forthcoming, on this ancient critical tendency and its strategic use of naturalism.

53. See "PP," 334; and *KSA*, 7:23[30], where Democritean atoms are recognized as "forces" or as instances of a kind of force.

54. The allusion is ambiguous. It is preceded by: "The *telos* is *otium litteratum* [learned leisure], to be unhassled." This points to the classical humanist, linguist, and

aesthetician Wilhelm von Humboldt enjoying the simple pleasures of his villa in Tegel, and whose classicism pervades all of German Hellenism (see chap. 4). The sequel, with its reference to Democritus' impoverishing travels (see Lange 1866, 7), points to Wilhelm's brother, the scientist and explorer Alexander von Humboldt, but also away from the *telos* just described. (A famous portrait of Alexander late in life shows him surrounded by his towering library—which he had had to sell to his butler, who stands off to the side.) In any case, if the *telos* here seems discrepant with the ways and means that lead up to it, it is no more this than the shocking spectacle of atomistic nature which sits uncomfortably next to the goal it is supposed to produce: *ataraxia*, or freedom from disturbance.

55. Cf. "PP," 338–39, which resumes Democritus' theory of acoustics (sound as a streamings of atoms, of acoustic simulacra); cf. DK 68A135 and fr. 164 DK). The titles of Democritus' writings on poetry listed above (n. 46) suggest that acoustics and aesthetics must have intersected in his thinking. Moreover, atoms are literally rhythmical in their motions for Democritus; one of their differentiating attributes is *rhysmos* (their "trajectory" or "shape"). Hence the proximity of the analogy to letters of the alphabet discussed earlier (see von Fritz 1938, 26, and Allen 1973, 96).

56. Elsewhere, Nietzsche discusses the interjection as the origin of language, only to replace this with a more intriguing concept: "The interjection [as] the mother of language: whereas it is actually the negation." This statement arguably could be taken in two ways: negation (not interjection) is the mother of language; or (more probably) interjection (qua pure sonority, *das Klangliche*, and pure affectivity) is actually the negation of language. "*Vom Ursprung der Sprache*" (1869/70), *MusA* 2:467–70; here, 470.

57. Cf. *W*, 1.1:§51: "Rhythm and rhyme are a very special auxiliary resource [*Hülfsmittel*] for poetry," and thus subordinate to its main purpose, which is to "communicate ideas."

58. Cf. "dreamt up atoms," "a mere phantom," etc. (*W*, 1.1:§24).

59. See, most immediately, "The Dionysian Worldview" (1870), *KSA*, 1:574: in various painful agitations of the body, "there seem to be expressed certain 'forms of intermittence' of the will, in short (in the symbolics of the language of musical sound), *rhythm*. The fullness of the will's intensification, the alternating quantity of pleasure and displeasure, is recognizable again in the *dynamics* of musical sound." See chapter 3 below on the quantitative analysis of rhythm undertaken by Nietzsche during these same years. The conflation of atomism and Schopenhaueresque reflections binds together Nietzsche's speculative musings, in their style and their content, from the late 1860s to the notes on the will to power.

60. Cf. "PP," 334: "Now, for the first time [that is, with Democritus], the entire anthropomorphic, mythic view of the world is overcome."

61. Cf. *KSA*, 7:23 [30], [39]: "Democritus: greatest possible simplification of hypotheses," etc.

62. The mingling is invited by Kant himself in an early cosmological essay cited

in "PP," 334–35: "I do not deny that the theory of Lucretius or of his predecessors Epicurus, Leucippus, and Democritus, has a great many similarities to my own. . . . Give me matter, and I will make you a world."

63. Cf. *KSA*, 7:7[147]; 19[159]; 19[121].

64. Lange 1866, 197 (where he adds, "We find order in everything that conforms to our nature, disorder in everything that is alien to it"); *BAW*, 3:375.

65. "We have no acquaintance with things in and of themselves, but only with their images in the mirror of our souls. . . . All *abstracta*, properties, that we ascribe to things are composed in our mind," etc. (*BAW*, 2:255 [1863]), a remark from a few pages inspired by Kant and Schiller.

66. *BAW*, 3:375 ("*mit Wundern durchlöchert*"). Contrast Lange's way of phrasing the problem. Reasoning that order and disorder are not intrinsic to nature but only forms of experience, Lange concludes: "It follows directly from this view that there can be absolutely no wonder in nature" (Lange 1866, 197). For a later variant of this motif, see *WP*, 620–22, where the wondrous lies not in nature (e.g., in "force"), but in our capacity to imagine that it does—and to forget that it is we who posit the miraculous (e.g., force) in nature.

67. "TSK," 381, 385; cf. ibid., 374: "Chance can discover the finest melody." Cf. *KSA*, 7:23[35] (1872/73).

68. "PP," 335; emphases added.

69. "Also on the question of the formation of the universe Democritus is right. An unending series of years, all the millennia [being but] a little stone upon a little stone, and the earth finally becomes the way it is [*wird endlich so wie sie ist*]"—an echo of the Pindaric slogan borrowed already at this time by Nietzsche: "Become what you are!" See n. 79 and chapter 5, n. 112, below.

70. *KSA*, 7:23[35].

71. See Porter 1992a; 1998, 187–88. The later atomism of the will to power arises out of the conflations and deformations of Democritus, Leibniz, and Schopenhauer that Nietzsche experiments with in 1869/70. This is developed in a book in progress.

72. Lange 1866, 277 ("relative truth"); Schopenhauer, *W*, 1.2, "*Kritik der Kantischen Philosophie*," p. 538 (*prōton pseudos*). Schopenhauer accuses Kant of subjectifying the object of sensation, of making it (always) "already" into a cognized representation, which thus lays the ground for Kant's "fatal [elsewhere: "hybridistic"] commingling [*Vermischung*] of intuitive and abstract cognition." For Lange, as for Nietzsche, such a "fusing together [*Verschmelzung*]" is an inevitable, unstable, and provocative starting point for any theory of experience (Lange 1866, 304–5, 483, 493, 543 ["a contribution by the mind finds its way (*mischt sich*) into even the most rudimentary form of sensory activity"], etc.). Here, in "PP," 339–40, Nietzsche is actually deforming Schopenhauer's use of *prōton pseudos* by making it equivalent to the *hypothesis*, cherished also by Schopenhauer, of an objectively constituted matter. In his contemporary essay "On Schopenhauer," Nietzsche had described Schopenhauer's own flawed premise—that of the "will"—as itself a *prōton pseudos*, and the source of an

"obscurity" equal to any that Schopenhauer finds in Kant ("OS," 356). I discuss this critique of Schopenhauer in Porter 2000.

73. Pace Nancy 1973, whose thesis stands in need of modification.

74. Cf. on Parmenides, a forerunner of Plato, in "PTG" §§10–11; and cf. *GM*, III:11.

75. See also Niehues-Pröbsting 1983, 277–79. In his lecture "On the Future of Our Educational Institutions" (1872), Nietzsche regrets the current reduction of philosophy to a tamed historical ("philological") study at the university—that is, to an academicist philosophy. But these remarks are directed against other targets, and they occur in another context ("OF," 742–43).

76. *KSA*, 7:23[17] (1872); Nietzsche's emphasis.

77. See Barnes 1986, 36–38, for a thorough review of this change in Nietzsche's scholarly fortune, and the apparently decisive role played—again—by the hostility of a single scholar, Ulrich von Wilamowitz-Moellendorff.

78. *KGW*, 2.1:75–245. References below by page only will be to the *Laertiana* published in this same volume. Preliminary notes and sketches take up the bulk of *BAW*, vols. 4 and 5.

79. *Pythian Ode* 2.72. Cf. the letters to Gersdorff of 24 November/1 December 1867, and to Rohde of 3 November 1867 and 1–3 February 1868. Nietzsche's quotation is selective, as is well known: he leaves off a final word (*mathōn*, "learning" or "discovering"), thereby altering the meaning of a phrase that is puzzling in the original as well. But Nietzsche nowhere discusses the reasons for this truncation, and we can only speculate as to its significance, apart from its intensifying the paradox in Pindar's language.

80. Promotion was awarded in April of 1870. See Stroux 1925, 66–67, for the documentary record ("In recognition of his performance to date"); further Janz 1978/79, 1:350. Nietzsche was plainly a rising star.

81. Barnes 1986, 17; cf. 39–40. This is the standard view that even Wilamowitz seconds, in the wake of Usener's judgment in the latter 1870s (Wilamowitz 1928, 129). More critically, Gigante 1994. Naturally, opinions vary. For Pöschl 1979, 154, "the greatest philological discovery by Nietzsche" was his insight into the nonexistence of verse-ictus in antiquity (see chap. 3).

82. *KGW*, 2.1:55; Bergk 1845, 227, repeating K. O. Müller's own term: "*Und so lässt sich . . . ein kleiner Liebes-Roman zusammensetzen*" (Müller 1875–76, 1:203). Bergk's critique is aimed generally, and not just at Müller's reconstruction (ibid., 226–29).

83. See Barnes 1986, passim.

84. In his contemporary lecture-course, "Introduction to the Study of the Platonic Dialogues," Nietzsche states flat out that "Diocles was an Epicurean" (*KGW*, 2.4:30).

85. Or possibly: "which is in progress [*mitfolgenden*]."

86. *BAW*, 4:230–33; *KGW*, 2.1:85–88, 204–5. This is also the picture given in the brief résumé of the same argument in Nietzsche's lectures on the Platonic dialogues

from the winter semester of 1871/72, where Diocles' *floruit* is dated to shortly after Nero's reign (*KGW*, 2.4:30).

87. Maas 1880, 15. The study, which appeared in the new series coedited by Adolf Kiessling and Wilamowitz, *Philologische Untersuchungen*, has a handsome dedication to Wilamowitz, Maas' dissertation director at Greifswald (ibid., 7), and a correspondingly handsome (and floridly Ciceronian) twenty-two-page validation of its theses by Wilamowitz himself. The occasion was clearly designed to demolish the credibility of Nietzsche's one major, and professionally decisive, philological achievement, while Wilamowitz managed to accuse Nietzsche of ignorance of Greek in the bargain (ibid., 145–46). See further Barnes 1986, 37, with nn. 73, 74 (citing Wilamowitz 1929, 129).

88. DL 1.63. The title of this work was *Pammetros* ("Epigrams in Various Meters").

89. Compare a note from "Laertius Diogenes and His Sources" (*BAW*, 5:126, 1868/69): "What is Diogenes Laertius to us? Nobody would waste a word on the philistine character of this writer were he not by chance the clumsy night-watchman guarding treasures whose value he hasn't a clue about. He is the night-watchman of the history of Greek philosophy; no one can enter it without getting the key from him."

90. Cf. *BAW*, 5:146–47 (1868/69). The natural way to read this passage in DL is to view the dedication as issuing from Diogenes in the first person, not from Diocles or from any other source. Nietzsche inverts all this with his "central hypothesis." To pull off this stunt, he must make Diogenes into a mindless copyist indeed. For a more recent defense of this solution, crediting as a predecessor not Nietzsche but Usener (*Epicurea*, 1887, xxxiii with n. 1, crediting no one but himself), see Mansfeld 1994, 106, with the following additional observation: "Diogenes needed a sentence describing the contents of the account that was meant to follow. . . . He transcribed it . . . lock, stock and barrel, no doubt intending to rephrase it when completing the final version of his work." If Nietzsche thought of this last possibility, he suppressed it. Similarly, cf. DL 10.28, in the life of Epicurus. There, Diogenes, whose *Lives* "are almost wholly impersonal works" (Barnes 1986, 27), does indeed appear to be quoting a first person Epicurean source verbatim; to suspect, with Nietzsche, that "Diogenes may have thoughtlessly copied someone else . . . is not wholly wild," although the attribution here to Diocles by Nietzsche (*KGW*, 2.1:89–90, 199) is unfounded, as is Nietzsche's allegation that Diocles was an Epicurean (so Barnes, ibid.). And if that piece of the puzzle falls, so does the logic of Nietzsche's narrative framework—one further indication of how fragile Nietzsche's reconstruction is, as Nietzsche was the first to admit (letter to Rohde, 8 October 1868). See Gigante 1997, 320, who gets right to the point, calling Nietzsche's study "fundamentally contradictory": claiming to rescue the historiographical value of Diogenes' work, Nietzsche in fact shows Diogenes to be a blundering copyist.

91. Nancy 1973, 63.

92. Letter to Rohde, 9 December 1868.

93. Thrasyllus "would have made Democritus into a disciple of Pythagoras had not the tiresome fact of chronology entered a veto against this" (*BAW*, 4:96). Nietzsche is paraphrasing Thrasyllus' words as quoted in DL 9.38.

94. *BAW*, 4:62. Hence, on the question of the origins (and so too, the essence) of language, Democritus comes down firmly on the side of the conventionalists, "turning against Pythagoras" (*BAW*, 4:86; cf. 4:62): language is not something *physei* (a natural occurrence) but *thesei* (a human product). Pythagorean number theory would have been useful insofar as it could be adapted to the framework of atomism; for in principle it accords well with some of atomism's purposes ("*die Zahlenlehre ist ja sehr passend für Atomistik*" [*BAW*, 4:92], an opaque remark that probably represents Thrasyllus' purported reasoning). And so, "to be sure, it is easy to give Pythagorean number theory a twist when it steers [as it did under Thrasyllus' tutelage], with sails fully hoisted, into the harbor of atomism" (*BAW*, 4:100; *KGW*, 2.1:227–28). But the foundational concepts of atomism owe nothing to the concept of number (ibid.); indeed, the two philosophies are separated by "mental gulfs" (*BAW*, 4:102), a point that is reaffirmed elsewhere: "There is nothing in [Democritus] . . . that recalls Pythagorean *philosophy*. The concept of number does not have the meaning for him that it has for his contemporary Philolaus, who appears to have founded Pythagorean *philosophy*" ("PP," 330–31; Nietzsche's emphasis; cf. *KGW*, 2.1:227–29).

95. *BAW*, 4:99. Cf. DL 3.57 (on Plato). Nietzsche's discovery of this possibility, which would be remembered in the scholarly literature, is doubtless one of the products of his own "philological *Witz*" (letter to Rohde, 9 December 1868).

96. DL 9.37. The epithet was earlier given to the Alexandrian polymath Eratosthenes of Cyrene, who was also called *Beta* for having finished second in all undertakings but, like a successful pentathlete, first overall. Undoubtedly for Thrasyllus, Democritus is second only to Pythagoras. Thrasyllus seems to have been inspired by a dubious work of Plato's, *Rivals*.

97. The resemblances reside "only" in the universal tendencies in learning that each figure shows, the one in an atomistic, the other in a Pythagoreanizing way (*BAW*, 4:99); the resemblances are projected rather than real (cf. 4:44: "similarity to [his] image of Democritus, namely 'the Pythagorean Democritus'"). The same thought is repeated in print (*KGW*, 2.1:226–27), where, however, the "delusion" and "violent schematism" of Thrasyllus' philology are underscored.

98. Letter to Rohde of 9 December 1868. The compatible pairing of "methodological rigor [*strenge Methodik*]" and *Witz* (the felicitous "combination" of moves and materials) seems to stem from Ritschl; see Nietzsche's "Rückblick" (p. 300).

99. See *BAW*, 4:99–100; *KGW*, 2.1:229–31.

100. Nietzsche to Rohde, 9 December 1868.

101. Nietzsche showed, against Mullach, why the *asyntakta* or "unarranged works" (consisting in explanations of natural phenomena) could not have figured in Thrasyllus' original scheme (they are not, inter alia, tetralogized). They must there-

fore be a later interpolation, and possibly spurious (*BAW*, 4:555, an earlier notice), but possibly not (*KGW*, 2.1:231, Nietzsche's later, considered opinion). Nietzsche's view was adopted by the German editors of the Presocratic philosophers, Diels and Kranz (2:91, n. ad l. 12), who however decided in favor of the inauthenticity of the titles in question (pace Diels 1905, 316). How scholarship could accept as plausible Nietzsche's finding without taking on board the rest of his fanciful conceit is baffling in itself. One alternative is to assume that Thrasyllus' catalogue included a set of titles not arranged in tetralogy form (so Mansfeld 1994, 104), but Nietzsche won't hear of that.

102. "In and of themselves, events are empty husks. What counts is the way we are disposed toward them: the value that we give to an event, the value it has for us." See pp. 55–57 above.

103. See Porter 1998 and 1999 on the later expressions of this insight in Nietzsche.

104. *BAW*, 4:99–100.

105. Nancy 1973, 63–64, 71–73. However contradictory it may seem, "rigor [*strenge Methodik*]" is as much a delusory and a separate requirement as is imagination (another convention of scholarship), and they are at least as irreducible to each other as are Nietzsche's method and the philology that he critiques with it. Thus, Democritus, unlike Thrasyllus, is a model of rigor (*strenge Methodik*) and of poeticism, and so he is worthy of admiration and of emulation (cf. *KGW*, 2.1:175: "*Thrasyllos, criticus modicae tantum severitas*"). But both Thrasyllus and Democritus are the product of Nietzsche's philological rigor and his philological invention (within the limits just given).

106. Barnes 1986, 39 n. 86.

107. *KGW*, 2.1:175–76; Rose 1854, 7; cf. above, on the Thrasyllan catalogue, where Nietzsche abstains from making any inferences about authenticity; and *KGW*, 2.1:229–31, on the "unassigned works," which leaves the door open again to speculations about further lost works.

108. "PP," 331.

109. For example, "ECP," 344 n. 5, on the preserved titles concerning poetry, rhythm, and music ("Whether the books are genuine?") and p. 407 ("countless historical writings have disappeared" of the sort that would throw light on the remains and teachings of Democritus and other Presocratics).

CHAPTER 3

1. *BT* §2: ([*der*] *Wellenschlag des Rhythmus, dessen bildnerische Kraft*, etc.; cf. ibid., §25, and ibid., §22 ["as if he saw before him, with the help of music, the waves of the will"]); *KSA*, 11:38[10], 608 = 11:42[3], 692 (1885): "*Der Mensch ist ein Formen- und Rhythmenbildendes Geschöpf*" (cf. *BT* §1: Mankind is "the great shaper [*der grosser Bildner*]"). On the will's "rhythmical" dynamics, see, for example, *KSA*, 12:7[18], and 13,

11[76] (on pleasure as a "sequence of small, painful stimuli"); ibid., 12:291; 7[8], p. 291 (on the rhythm of contemporary nihilism: "Its tempo is slower, but the quality of its measure [*Takt*; viz., "rhythm"], by contrast, is much richer"); and more grandly *KSA*, 12:9[62], on the "difference[s] in the *tempo* of becoming." The term "the forms of intermittence [*Intermittenzformen*] of the will," glossed by "rhythm," is from *KSA*, 7:3[19] (1869/70) and from "DW," 574, likewise in connection with pain and pleasure (see Porter 1992a); the term may derive from Dühring 1865, whose critique of Schopenhauer's view of music may have had an impact on Nietzsche. The connections between the motions of becoming and rhythm are traditional and nearly automatic; see Lange 1866, 285 (quoted in n. 17 of chapter 2 above); and cf. Heraclitus' vision of becoming, "ebbing and flowing in the brazen beat of rhythm," which leads to an insight into the abstract form of time itself ("PTG," 823); Democritus availed himself of similar imagery (used of the sorting actions of the cosmic vortex); cf. DK 68A135, cited on page 87 above.

2. *KSA*, 13:14[46]: "There must be a difference in tempo in [and between] both conditions." He goes on to describe the Apollinian condition in terms of a "slowing down of the sensation of time and space," but never finishes the contrast; presumably the Dionysian is an acceleration of these sensations. If the thought recalls a *Gedankenexperiment* from the lecture on Heraclitus in "The Pre-Platonic Philosophers," that is no accident. There (pp. 267–69), Nietzsche is working with the hypotheses of Karl Ernst von Baer (1860), who was concerned to locate the subjective basis of perception in physiology by isolating the minima of temporal sensation ("the time it takes to register in our consciousness an impression on our sense organ"), but also the proportional relation of the pulse rate to the rate of conscious sensations. These are precisely Nietzsche's concerns in his lectures on rhythm, in the notes on temporal atomism, and, evidently, in the later notebooks as well. On Nietzsche and Baer (but with no reference to the lectures on rhythm or to the continuity of these interests in Nietzsche), see Schlechta and Anders 1962, 64–66, 152.

3. *KSA*, 7:1[49].

4. *Beiträge zur Kritik der griechischen Lyriker I: Der Danae Klage* (*KGW*, 2.1:59–74). No further installments were made.

5. See Nietzsche's letters in draft to Georg Curtius from November/December 1866 and to Deussen from 2 June 1868; and Howald 1920, 5.

6. On the aesthetic speculations, see *BAW*, 5:206 (1868/69, a notebook from Leipzig). See previous chapter for discussion of this and related passages. The lectures are listed in *BAW*, 4:123.

7. The notebooks are printed in *KGW*, 2.3:99–338. Below, references by page only will be to this volume. The dates just given are necessarily conjectural. All four notebooks are dated by the editors to 1870–71, "and (at the latest) the beginning of 1872" (ibid., v). The first notebook (101–201) bears the title of his lecture course ("Greek Rhythmics"). The others are not lecture notes per se but are evidently based on these and clearly envisaged as leading up to a major publication (as their various

title pages and tables of contents show). According to Nietzsche's own official and unofficial reports (see Gutzwiller 1951 and Janz 1974), he offered two courses on classical metrics and rhythm, first in the summer semester of 1869 (a *Paedagogium*, taught at the gymnasial level but not at the university, which explains its absence from Stroux's catalogue [Stroux 1925, 95]), and then again at the university in the winter semester of 1870/71. The only treatment of Nietzsche's study known to me (Bornmann 1989) makes no mention of the earlier course, and conjecturally dates some of the notebooks to 1872/73 and one of them to a later date still. In the definitive edition by Bornmann and Carpitella the dates for all the notebooks are revised down to 1870/71, without arguments for any of the datings. Nietzsche's insights are at any rate firmly in place early on. His "discovery" of the modern philological "mistake" (*Verirrung*) about ancient rhythm is announced in a letter to Rohde from 27 November 1870, and then reiterated in a letter to Ritschl from 30 December of that same year. One needn't wait for the third notebook ("On the Theory of Quantitative Rhythmics") to find Nietzsche's revolutionary insight into ancient rhythm expressed (pace Bornmann, ibid., 477); it is found in the earliest pages of the preserved notebooks: "only time" (p. 104), viz., "only temporal differences" (p. 135; cf. "ECP," 399: "only *temporal rhythm*"), constructed by variously grouping "units of time" (p. 104), give the proper criteria of rhythm. See the discussion of "abstract time" (ibid.) below. The lectures entitled "Encyclopedia of Classical Philology" contains a segment on rhythm and meter (§16) that resumes the findings of his earlier studies. Nietzsche taught this course in the summer semester of 1871 and again in the winter of 1873/74. The idea of completing the project on rhythm persists in the notebooks through mid-1877.

Nietzsche's interest in rhythm develops slowly, and its progress is hard to document. In January of 1869, prior to his appointment at Basel, he published a review of Paul Marquard's 1868 edition of the fragments of Aristoxenus' *Harmonic Elements*, with its appendix containing a critical edition of the fragments of Aristoxenus' *Elements of Rhythm* (rpt. in *KGW* 2.1: 374–76; cf. *BAW*, 5:247–48); residues of this contact are found in the notebooks from 1869 (see below). But this was hardly his first encounter with the subject. See his letter to Mushacke of 27 April 1866, where a casual reference is made to his bedtime reading at the time: "Schopenhauer or Westphal's *Metrik*."

Nietzsche never lost interest in his earliest studies in rhythm and meter. He briefly revisited them in the summer of 1877 in a letter to Carl Fuchs (29 July) and in his notebooks (cf. also *KSA*, 8:22[10]: "Skeptical Views about Metrics," imagined as a chapter-title in a collection of philological essays; it is preceded by "The Life of Democritus"), and then extensively again in three more letters to Fuchs, assigned by editors to mid-April of 1886 and the end of August 1888. In addition to possibly annotating his earlier notebooks on occasion (as may well be the case on p. 338, a passage to be discussed below), he also actively kept up with literature in the field of Greek and Latin rhythmics. Edmond Bouvy's *Poètes et Mélodes. Étude sur les origines du rhythm tonique dans l'hymnographie de l'église grecque* (1886) and W. Meyer's *Anfang und Ursprung der lateinischen und griechischen rhythmischen Dichtung* (1884) are two examples cited in the notebooks from 1886/87 (*KSA*, 12:6[5]).

8. Traces of this intention can be detected in the notebooks on rhythm, not least in the passing allusions to Dionysian cult (for example, pp. 322, 329, 331 ["Dionysus and Apollo"]), but also to "Socrates and Greek Tragedy" (p. 145). Cf. further *KSA*, 7:3[37] ("XIV"), 7[178] (1870/71); "DW," pp. 572–77; *KSA*, 7:16[1], [2] (summer 1871–spring 1872), where "Greek rhythm" is integral to a list of current cultural-critical projects (but where the separation of rhythm from *BT* seems already to have been effected). Further references in Silk and Stern 1981, 389 n. 81 and 393 n. 127. The earliest documented connection is from the fall of 1869 (*KSA*, 7:1[46], [49]). And the first of these two notes strikingly anticipates Nietzsche's "discovery" from the end of the following year. The question as to the relative priority of the two projects (rhythm, *The Birth of Tragedy*) is overshadowed by Nietzsche's largest views on the relationship of Greek culture to modernity (see below).

9. See Burkert 1959. See n. 14 below, on "conceptual" or "theoretical atomism," a model that arises during this period, is later found in Plato and Aristotle, and finally becomes commonplace in postclassical treatises.

10. Acoustics: cf. "PP," 338–39 (discussing DK 68A135 and fr. 164). Music: see esp. fr. 15c, 16, 25a DK. See West 1992, 243.

11. These titles are reeled off again in "ECP," 344 n. 5, where Nietzsche reaffirms Democritus' authorship of these works, and then parenthetically wonders whether he is right to do so (probably just giving voice to a position he no longer holds, or reenacting his dialectic of doubt).

12. Sextus, *Against the Mathematicians* 10.81 (DK 68A72). See Guthrie 1962, 429–30.

13. Barker 1978a, 16. See further id. 1978b; 1984; 1989, 123–25.

14. Aristoxenus, *Elements of Rhythm* 2.11 (henceforth, "*Rhyth.*"): *chronos prōtos* ("primary time-length" or "duration"); Aristides Quintilianus, *De musica* 1.14: *prōtos . . . chronos atomos kai elachistos* ("the primary duration is indivisible and smallest," etc.). If durations are, as it were, the "atoms" of time, what might their corresponding "void" be? The answer is an "empty duration," of course, which is to say, a "rest" or "pause": "An empty duration is one without sound, adopted to fill out the rhythm. A 'pause,' in the context of rhythm, is the smallest empty duration [*chronos kenos elachistos*]" (Aristides, *De musica*, 1.18; trans. Barker). Yet as we shall soon see, all durations are "empty" from a certain perspective: they mark mere formal and abstract divisions in a system of relations. The formula "first and smallest element" is used in a variety of analytical approaches in antiquity (in the areas of medicine, physics, astronomy, grammar, etc.). These approaches exhibit what might be called "conceptual" or "theoretical atomism" (the analysis of systems of relations—whether these are made up of sound, of bodies, or of times—into constituent, irreducible ["indivisible"] elements). Translations of Aristoxenus below will be from Barker 1989 and

Pearson 1990, with occasional modifications; those of Aristides are from Barker 1989.

15. *BAW*, 5:372 = *KGW*, 2.2:379 (a transcript of a lecture on Greek lyric poets from 1878/79, but very likely resuming notes from a decade earlier; emphasis added); *KGW*, 2.3:338 (emphases added). The second statement is reproduced almost verbatim in "ECP," 401, where the emphasis this time is given by Nietzsche (unless the statement was appended to the notes on rhythm at the time of "ECP."). See above, pp. 101–102.

16. See Aristoxenus, *Rhyth.*, 2.2: "We have already pointed out that rhythm is concerned with time-lengths [*chronoi*] and the perception [*aisthēsis*] of them, and we must say it again now, because this is in a way the starting point for the study of rhythm" (trans. Pearson).

17. Aristoxenus, *Rhyth.*, 2.6.

18. Long and Sedley 1987, 1:37. The statement just quoted occurs in a summary of Epicurus' view, which is better attested than Democritus' and doubtless derivative of it. Cf. Asmis 1984, 33: "Time [for Epicurus] is nothing but the relative duration of properties," viz., perceptual properties.

19. Cf. *KSA*, 7:1[7], 13 (1869): "Earlier, [there was] poetry even in prose," where the examples cited are "Heraclitus, the Pythian priestesses, Democritus, Empedocles"; cf. "*Verses* in speech" (p. 275) and the discussion on pp. 276–77; and the letter to Fuchs, end of August 1888: "In the judgment of the ancients, it was ordinary everyday speech itself that could very easily contain perfect verses."

20. Letter to Ritschl of 30 December 1870. Cf. the letter to Fuchs of mid-April 1886: "It is hardly possible for us to have any feeling at all for a purely quantitative rhythmics." In both places, the operative term is *nachfühlen*. Compare Maas 1962, 3–4, who is explicitly in Nietzsche's debt (but lacking the complexities of his predecessor): "Scarcely any facet of the culture of the ancient world is so alien to us as its quantitative metric. We lack here the most important prerequisite of all historical study; for we can never attain that kind of 'empathy' [*Einfühlung*] by which all other manifestations of the art, literature, science, philosophy, religion, and social life of the ancients are brought so near to us that they become an essential part of our own culture. . . . Our feeling for rhythm is altogether dominated by the dynamic rhythm of our own language and metric. . . . We have no means of reading, reciting, or hearing Greek poetry as it actually sounded. It may be possible for us *to form a mental notion of it*; but such a notion is too shadowy to serve as a basis for the scientific investigation of the subject" (emphasis added). Maas credits Nietzsche with the discovery of this insight (ibid.).

21. Pp. 268, 126, 260; "TL," 251 (= *KSA*, 1:883); letter to Fuchs of mid-April 1886: "Our rhythmic sense is taken as the *only* and 'eternal' [*ewige*] kind, as rhythm *an sich.*"

22. *Grundirrthum*: letter to Fuchs, mid-April 1886; and *KGW*, 2.3:267; *Verirrung*: letter to Rohde of 23 November 1870; *Grundfehler*: "ECP," 400.

23. Primary durations are "not absolute magnitudes of time" but are determined in their length "only" relative to the tempo (p. 107).

24. Aristides, *De musica* 1.13; cf. 2.15 with Barker 1989, 485 n. 162.

25. A not dissimilar point is made by Dionysius of Halicarnassus, *On the Composition of Words*, chapter 26, who notes how poets diversify their language by forcing a noncoincidence of semantic clauses with metrical limits (e.g., via enjambment): clauses of sense are thus made "unequal in length and sound." The effect is to efface the meter and to diversify the rhythm. See nn. 78, 91, 123 below.

26. "The *development* of the *equation* of *Takt* ["rhythmical beat"] and [metrical] 'foot,' above all the theory of ictus, is the *history of modern rhythmics*" (p. 269; emphasis in original). Cf. further p. 128, where philologists are attacked for their rigorous enforcement of "absolute" *Taktgleichheit* (equality of measures), thereby rendering "ancient and modern rhythm identical." Cf. Westphal 1861, 5: "The [ancient] rhythmicians, to be sure, chiefly have the rhythm of song in view, but this rhythm is identical with that of the meter, as this latter rhythm is palpable in the words."

27. Cf. "ECP," 399: "The error [of modern philology] lies in having taken our music to be identical to ancient music."

28. See n. 122 below; and cf. pp. 161–64.

29. Letter to Fuchs, [mid-April] 1886. Nietzsche's arguments are unwittingly restated and confirmed by Zuckerman 1974, 20–21, 25. Briefly, but correctly, Bornmann 1989, 486. A variation (independently made) on Nietzsche's insight is found, strikingly enough, in John Cage: "Schools teach the making of structures by means of classical harmony. Outside school, however (e.g., Satie and Webern), a different and correct* structural means reappears: one based on lengths of time. . . . Harmonic structure is a recent Occidental phenomenon, for the past century in a process of disintegration. [*"Sound has four characteristics: pitch, timbre, loudness, and duration. The opposite and necessary coexistent of sound is silence. Of the four characteristics of sound, only duration involves both sound and silence. Therefore, a structure based on durations (rhythmic: phrase, time lengths) is correct (corresponds with the nature of the material), whereas harmonic structure is incorrect (derived from pitch, which has no being in silence)." (Cage 1961, 63; cf. 20).] See further n. 53, below.

30. Letter to Ritschl, 30 December 1870.

31. The dates given here are those cited by Nietzsche in his notebooks and in "ECP." (Bracketed dates represent those given by Nietzsche that fail to match actual publication dates.) Nietzsche is in part rehearsing familiar arguments, but with his own spin. Boeckh had already criticized Hermann's metrics for being an application of Kantian categories (see Boeckh 1877, 775), and Nietzsche's mentor Ritschl had repeated the charge in his own lectures on the subject (Otto Ribbeck, *Friedrich Wilhelm Ritschl: Ein Beitrag zur geschichte der Philosophie*, vol. 1, p. 67); see Pfeiffer 1976, 178; Lloyd-Jones 1982, 169; and esp. Bravo 1968, 70). Humboldt can use similar language, at times reminiscent not only of Kant but also of Herder: "Everything that the Greek spirit brought forth" draws upon "the eternal and constant laws of space and

rhythm" (Humboldt 1969b, 31). Humboldt's isolation of rhythm as a realm of "pure form, unencumbered by matter" and by "meanings" points in the direction of Nietzsche's own formulations. Cf. further Humboldt 1903–36, 1:429, on Pindar's rhythms [1795]: "Every rhythmical period spans a very large reach that our ear can barely grasp. Never (with only one exception) do two odes have the same syllabic measure." His applauding of German as the most suitable medium for rendering the rhythms of Greek verse points away from Nietzsche again (Humboldt 1903–36, 8:135–36; Humboldt's introduction to his translation of the *Agamemnon* [1816]).

32. Cf. Maas 1962, 5: "The modern scientific treatment of Greek metric began with Bentley, was substantially advanced by Porson, Elmsley, Hermann, Boeckh, Nietzsche, Wilhelm Meyer, and O. Schroeder, and reached its peak in Wilamowitz's book *Griechische Verskunst* (Berlin 1921)." Entombed in this mausoleum of Greek scholars, Nietzsche here finds himself arrayed uncomfortably in a genealogy that culminates in his nemesis. Maas 1962 [1923] is heavily dependent on Nietzsche—much more so than his handful of references to Nietzsche let on. An analysis of Maas' reading, and at times spectacular misreading, of Nietzsche's rhythmical theory would require more space than can be allotted to it here.

33. General skepticism about the quantitative theory is voiced by Chatman 1965 (cit. in Allen 1987, 132 n. 47) and by Allen 1987, 104–39; id. 1973, 275–96. Many of Nietzsche's basic contentions about Greek rhythm do not appear to be undermined by the recent linguistic analysis of Devine and Stephens 1994, although claims as to the irreproducibility of Greek rhythm are contested by these authors; similarly, Stanford 1967, who follows Nietzsche and Maas in their rejection of stress accents (40–42), but rejects their skepticism (cf. p. 48 n. 76, p. 132 n. 31). Greek rhythms, he claims, can be recovered along with the authentic "sound" of Greek. (By the way Greek "sounded" Stanford has in mind mainly pitch-accents, but his discussions of rhythm are as thin as the version of the view he opposes would lead one to expect.) Pearson 1990, xxxiii, likewise rejects the line taken by Maas (and Nietzsche), but his objection that "they identify only *rhythmizomena* ["objects made rhythmic"], not the rhythms" misses the point of their argument. West 1992 accepts the quantitative view but not the argument about the irreproducibility of Greek rhythm.

34. Humboldt 1969b, 37–38.

35. *KSA*, 8:22[10] (1877). See n. 7 above.

36. Westphal 1865, xv.

37. *KGW*, 2.3:127 n. 11.

38. See n. 128 below.

39. This resuming a thread from pp. 103 and 109, one that is central to the whole investigation.

40. Pp. 267–68; cf. pp. 321–22; and see pp. 241, 269, criticizing the equation of rhythmic and metrical feet by modern scholars; and Nietzsche's letter to Fuchs of mid-April 1886.

41. For texts and discussion of this tradition, see generally Barker 1989.

42. Esp. Westphal 1861 and 1865. See *KGW*, 2.2:173, duly crediting Westphal with this discovery.

43. Aristoxenus, *Rhyth.*, 2.5; trans. Barker.

44. Ibid. 2.13; cf. *KGW*, 2.3:137: the feet of rhythmical and metrical patterns are "entirely different" (where Nietzsche is leaning on a valuable, late source for Aristoxenus, Michael Psellus' *Introduction to the Study of Rhythm*, 8; text and translation in Pearson 1990, 21–27).

45. So Aristoxenus, arguing against "the older rhythmicians" (Psellus, ibid., 1 = Pearson 1990, 21; cf. *KGW*, 2.3:121).

46. The kinds of features that an object made rhythmic shows are conditioned not by the nature of the object but only by "the nature of the rhythm [the object] adopts"; nor does there seem to be a theoretical limit on how many different rhythms an object, such as a phrase, can assume (*Rhyth.*, 2.4). Accordingly, rhythmic theory and practice maintain a rigorous distinction between syllabic and rhythmic length: in some combinations, a "light" syllable (viz., a syllable ending with a short vowel) can contain a half-measure more than a "heavy" syllable (viz., one containing a long vowel or ending with a consonant); and depending upon its metrical position, a "light" syllable can assume five different rhythmical values. See Allen 1987, 111; Maas 1962, 38.

47. Cf. *Rhyth.* 2.16; and 2.18: "One *chronos* [duration] cannot make a foot . . . because a single signal [*sēmeion*] does not create time division" (trans. Pearson). Aristoxenus' conception is reminiscent of Saussure. Signs owe their existence to the system of relations that constitute and make recognizable individual signs as such; but neither sign nor system is strictly prior to the other. Both come into view simultaneously, or rather, *retroactively*. How much does Nietzsche's conception of semiotics, at this point or later on, owe to his contact with Aristoxenian rhythm?

48. Cf. ibid., 2.16: "The means by which we mark rhythm and make it perceptible to the senses is a [rhythmic] foot." By themselves, individual durations have no rhythmic significance ("one duration cannot make a foot," ibid., 2.18). Nietzsche grasped this point firmly. See pp. 102, 136–37, 164, 165. Yet, what ear could be so finely attuned as to detect abstract quantities of time? W. Sidney Allen, a linguist who is critical of the theory espoused by Nietzsche and Maas, raises this very question, and cites a modern authority on the theory of meter, who writes, "I do not deny that time is the medium through which meter flows, or even that length itself is a component of 'stress'; what I do deny is that the mind has some elaborate faculty of measuring and identifying time spans and that this is what it does in meter" (Chatman 1965, quoted in Allen 1987, 132 n. 47). Aristoxenus, Nietzsche, and Cage (n. 29 above) all resist this objection. Cf. "ECP," 400 n. 33: "How fine is the ear that recognizes [temporal] length of position!"; *KGW* 2.3:338 (quoted p. 132 above); and "*ECP*," p. 401 (n. 119 below).

49. See Nietzsche's paraphrase (p. 104) of Aristoxenus' theory as found in Michael Psellus, *Introduction*, 6 (see n. 44 above).

In every object which is made rhythmic [*rhythmizomenon*] there is an exchange between moments of stasis and moments of movement. The static pause [*ēremia*, "rest"] finds its expression in the syllable, in the note, in the orchestral dance figure [*schēma*]; movement [*kinēsis*] consists in the transition from note to note, from syllable to syllable, from orchestral *schēma* to orchestral *schēma*. The time of the pause [rest] is knowable by sensation; the time of movement, of the transition, is unknowable by sensation.

Aristoxenus' premise elsewhere, too, is that the time of movement is indeterminate for the senses (cf. Aristoxenus, *Elements of Harmony*, 8.14–10.10 da Rios = Barker 1989, 132–33). But the picture complicates itself with the introduction of the notion of "system":

> The perceptible durations are the parts of the rhythmical structure [*systēma*, viz., series or system of temporal ratios]; the imperceptible durations are but the *limits* of these parts (p. 104).

Within an utterance, the articulations of the singing voice and those of its rhythm do not coincide, except at the limit of an irrational (unrecognizable) quantity. Transitions "from note to note, syllable to syllable," while constitutive of rhythmic patterns, cannot in fact be registered by the ear. It is the stable "pauses," the platforms of voice, which are the sensible durations, and which delineate the places where "the singer will locate each of the notes" (*Rhyth.*, 2.11; trans. Barker); "for the voice [when it sings] moves while it makes an interval, and stands still on a note" (Aristox., *Harm.*, 12.20 = Barker 1989, 134; cf. 12.9).

50. See Rossbach 1854, 68. Westphal (e.g., 1865, 15–16) is an exception in this respect; he knows enough to "reject periodology" (*KGW*, 2.3:130).

51. Cf. 135: "The measure of the longest [rhythmical] foot is the capacity to be 'measured' [*die Taktirbarkeit*]. Does rhythmic structure thereby cease to matter? If rhythm is only signified by the *beat* that is given [or rather, "the time that is kept," *durch den taktirten Takt*], it becomes apparent that larger rhythmic structures do not obtain. . . . Therefore, Aristoxenus cannot have assumed the existence of larger rhythmical structures." This idea had already been grasped by Nietzsche in 1869, and it is central to his thinking about the elusive distance to the criteria of sound and visibility shown by Greek rhythm. See *KSA*, 7:1[46] (fall, 1869): "Through what does the rhythm of motion distinguish itself from the rhythm of stillness (i.e., perception)? Large rhythmical relations can be taken in only through visual perception," whereas the rhythm of motion is the province of "more exact and more mathematical" rhythmic measure (*Takt*). "According to explicit testimonies, it wasn't possible to hear the rhythm of spoken lyric verses unless the feeling was made conscious of the *larger*

units of time through the beat. So long as dance accompanied [verse] (—and ancient rhythmics did *not* develop out of music, but rather out of dance), one could see the rhythmical units with one's own *eyes*" (letter to Fuchs, end of August 1888). This same idea is elaborated, somewhat tentatively, in the notebooks on rhythm (pp. 225, 270–71, 319–20; cf. *KSA*, 1:530), and is bound up with speculations elsewhere about the pause, the rest, the sound or silence of the lowered foot and its motion upward, and the association and dissociation of arsis and thesis from the criteria of sound. Nietzsche has fascinating ideas about whether arsis and thesis, and indeed the criteria of measure generally, are visible or audible, and whether they coincide with a silent pause or the noise of an up- or downbeat. But there is no space to treat these problems here.

52. Cf. *TI*, IX:11 (1889): "The actor, the mime, the dancer, the musician, the lyric poet are fundamentally related in their instincts and essentially one, only gradually specialized and separated from one another—even to the point of opposition." As a consequence of this emancipation from the constraints of bodily motion and especially from sound (viz., the stamping of the foot, and even from instrumental music [p. 270]), arsis and thesis, Nietzsche reasons, can be freely and indifferently correlated with different quantities ("heavy" and "light") and positions (within a sequence). Cf. n. 46 above. Arsis and thesis are thus, in one respect, otiose distinctions ("nothing but completely superficial down- and upbeats," like the metronomic rise and fall of a finger, baton, or foot [p. 229]; cf. pp. 102, 271; "mere signs for keeping time," letter to Fuchs, mid-April 1886). That is so even if in another respect they are essential to providing perceptible rhythmic "pulsations"—though how they do so is never very clearly defined (see, e.g., pp. 268–73, 312–19). Maas 1962, 7, closely (and quietly) echoes Nietzsche here, too.

53. See Cage 1961, 18–21, for (once again) a striking modern parallel:

> Composition, then, I viewed, ten years ago, as an activity integrating the opposites, the rational and the irrational, bringing about, ideally, a freely moving continuity within a strict division of parts, the sounds, their combination and succession being either logically related or arbitrarily chosen. The strict division of parts, the structure, was a function of the duration aspect of sound, since . . . duration alone was a characteristic of silence. . . . The structure, then, was a division of actual time by conventional metrical means, meter taken as simply the measurement of quantity. . . . For nothing about the structure [that is, "this rhythmic structure"] was determined by the materials which were to occur in it. . . . Chance operations determined stability or change of tempo. Thus, by introducing the action of method into the body of the structure, and these two opposed in terms of order and freedom, that structure became indeterminate: it was not possible to know the total time-length of the piece until the final chance operation, the last toss of coins affecting the rate of tempo, had been made. Being indeterminate, though still present, it became apparent that structure was not necessary, even though it had certain uses.

54. *"Äußerlich,"* said of *Takt* (p. 135) and of arsis and thesis (p. 229).

55. P. 104; cf. pp. 103, 110, 144, 235 (all concerning "abstract rhythm").

56. *KSA*, 7:9[116] (1871). The formulation is Kantian, and it is natural that Schopenhauer should have something to say about the form of time himself. See his *Parerga und Paralipomena* II, §147a, against which we may measure Nietzsche's distance from Schopenhauer: "The *form of time* is the very means—and this as if by design—by which we are taught the *nugatoriness* [*die Nichtigkeit*] of all earthly enjoyments" (Schopenhauer's emphases).

57. Aristoxenus' theory was *"philosophical"* in its foundations (p. 103; Nietzsche's emphasis).

58. To name just a few instances of these later echoes, cf. "PTG," 822–23, on the Heraclitean glimpse into the rhythm of becoming (1872); *KSA*, 12:9[62] ("a difference in the *tempo* of becoming"; 1887); *WP*, 568, on the "tempo" of appearances and the relational and quantitative "measure of power" (1888); *WP*, 641: "(1) a resistance to all other forces; (2) an adjustment of the same according to form and rhythm; (3) an estimate in regard to assimilation or excretion" (1883–84); *KSA*, 12:7[18] (on this same resistance, here described as a "rhythmical dance"; 1886/87); *KSA*, 13:14[79]: 259, on the "dynamic quanta" of the will to power (1888).

59. Unless, that is, this is an annotation appended at a later date, or is even appended contemporaneously but out of a different context (for instance, in the course of Nietzsche's experimental reflections in a Schopenhauerian vein from the same period, *KSA*, 7[144–72], [200–204]; 1870/71; see Porter 2000). The content and placement of this fragment suggest as much (a line in pencil divides it from the preceding text), although all this is most uncertain. Cf. the editorial note to *BAW*, 3:246–79 at *BAW*, 3:419, describing one ms. (Mp VIII, 6), "a quarto-notebook lacking a cover . . . , 58 pages almost completely written in the left-hand columns [possibly, this means "sides" of the notebook, as in the ms. to "ECP"] (the right-hand columns contain occasional supplements, which in good part originate from a later time)." At the very least, we know that Nietzsche annotated his own notebooks. But at how much later a date? On the other hand, the two kinds of speculation, philosophical and more narrowly rhythmical, could sit side by side, as in *KSA*, 1:1 [46–47].

60. The title of the third notebook on rhythm reads "On the Theory of Quantitative Rhythmics."

61. See Allen 1987, 94; and West 1982, 162: "This period [that is, the Imperial period] is marked by a fundamental change in the Greek language which spelt the eventual ruin of the traditional metrical system. . . . This was the change in the nature of the accent from being a tonal (pitch) accent to being a dynamic (stress) accent, as it is in modern Greek." West dates the "breakdown of quantitative distinctions" to around 200 C.E. (ibid., 163). The dire language here (cf. ibid., 189–90) echoes the nearly identical account of Maas 1962, 13–15 (e.g., "the only instrument through which a quantitative metric could be effective disintegrated [*zerfiel*]"), which

in turn echoes that of Nietzsche. It is not uncommon to refer to the two metrics that bound either side of the great gap in time as the "Greek" and the "Byzantine" or modern systems (Allen 1987, 150). There is more than a certain (classicizing) wistfulness in all of this.

62. Nietzsche's approach is at the very least ingenious. He detects signs of the pattern of decline in the post-Aristoxenian theorists as they struggle to make sense of Aristoxenus' account, and thus embody the decline without recognizing it as such. By contrast, Westphal (who likewise values the later traditions for what they can reveal about Aristoxenus' system) takes the later metricians to have translated Aristoxenus' terminology into a nonrhythmical context, which allows, harmlessly, for a reverse translation again into Aristoxenus' original intentions (Westphal 1865, 25–32). Nietzsche regards Westphal's procedure as dangerously misguided (p. 241).

63. See West 1982, 187: "Native Latin verse was primarily accentual, with quantity playing a subordinate role"; nonetheless, it too went the way of the Greek language: "in Latin as in Greek, quantity eventually yielded to accent" (ibid., 189).

64. Compare Wilamowitz's closely parallel language, describing a "change that, despite the stubbornly arrested state of writing, fundamentally reshaped language, the carrier of all culture. The nature of emphasis shifts, whereby volume of sound [*Tonstärke*] takes the place of pitch [*Tonhöhe*], and in this way the old difference between longs and shorts vanishes. With this, the old artforms in poetry and prose finally give way, and even music has to seek out a new basis for itself." "Accentuation" is eventually passed on to the West via "church song" (another Nietzschean motif). The decline, which sets in after 300 C.E., is definitive: "When the old gods were dead, the verses of Homer and the songs of Anacreon and the rhythms of Demosthenes no longer sounded, then the old culture was finished" (Wilamowitz 1925–26, 2:7, in a public address from 1897). Similarly, Maas 1962, 19–20. This is Nietzsche's theory *in nucleo*, if by "longs and shorts" Wilamowitz means quantitative durations. The coincidence is as puzzling as it is astonishing: this part of Nietzsche's philological *Nachlass*, on which Maas' 1923 study is based, was not published until 1912. Perhaps by 1897 the tide was beginning to turn anyway. See Bornmann 1989, 487–88. But if Wilamowitz was not entirely consistent about the ictus (see Timpanaro 1981, 19, 29; and Bornmann, ibid., crediting Wilamowitz with having inspired a brief revival of the verse-ictus theory), neither was Nietzsche for that matter (see below). Other noteworthy coincidences of opinion between Wilamowitz and Nietzsche are named and briefly discussed in chapter 5 below.

65. The passage, full of high drama, deserves to be quoted more fully: "Gradually, the robust feeling for time disintegrates in [everyday] speech. Now the accent *and the ictus* appear, representing, as it were, a violent afterlife of the word. From this point on, the spiritual life of the word concentrates itself in the accented syllable. Simultaneously, the old barriers of the accent break down; it wanders backwards or forwards, and to maintain the consistency of the word, it now needs a new pillar, the *ictus*. What are the causes of the word's fatal demise, in its outward aspect? In folk

songs everything is driven forward by trochaic sequences of words; more precisely, an exchange of *stressed* and *unstressed* syllables occupies the place of high- and low-pitched syllables. The temporal relations are displaced because the syllable now lacks tonality [viz., pitch]—or is it the other way around?" (pp. 307–8).

66. Nietzsche's original coinages are hard to render in translation: *Zeitwechselwelle* and *Stärkewechselwelle*. The notion of "alternation" or "exchange" recalls the Aristoxenian description of rhythmic pulses cited in n. 49 above: "the exchange [*Wechsel*] between moments of stasis and moments of movement." The wave imagery refers to what in *The Birth of Tragedy* is called the "wave beat [*Wellenschlag*] of rhythm."

67. Pp. 298, 322 (citing the famous medical tradition that goes back to Herophilus in the third century B.C.E.); cf. pp. 195, 196, 197, 337 for more formal uses of *Pulsschlag* or "to pulse" in the sense of rhythmical pulsation, but where the connotation of the physical pulse is inevitable (as on p. 258).

68. See p. 99 above.

69. "*Ist nun das Zeitleben das ursprüngliche?*"

70. "*Nebeneinander.*" A crucial term in Nietzsche's self-subverting genealogical accounts; see Porter 1992, 76.

71. Cf. "ECP," 400: "It is time for a fresh reconstruction [of Greek rhythmics], one in which we frankly have to give up the desire to know everything."

72. See Aristides, *De musica*, 1.13, 1.23; with Barker 1989, 434 n. 156, 450, nn. 237, 238; and Aristoxenus, *Rhyth.*, 2.4: "The same spoken phrase or sentence, with different arrangements of its parts, each arrangement different from the other, takes on as many differences as there are differences in the nature of rhythm. The same argument applies to melody . . . " (trans. Pearson)

73. Maas 1962, 38; cf. 36 ("We know next to nothing about it"), 4.

74. See Rossbach 1854, 68 (n. 99 below), where rhythmical sequence is described as an "organic whole."

75. See above at n. 50, and further pp. 135, 136–37, 139 ("2"), 144, 164–66 ("rhythm has no caesurae; only objects [that is, words] made rhythmic do"), 209, 229, 234–35, 241.

76. "The primary durations of each rhythm will be infinite," Aristoxenus writes in a fragment from a now lost treatise, *On the Primary Duration* (Pearson 1990, 33; trans. mod.). By this he means that the durations receive their temporal value or magnitude from the tempo (they are not fixed or "absolute" quantities of time but are only defined as the minimal elements of the ratios of time patterned in a rhythmic tempo [p. 107]), while the number of durations required to fill out a rhythmic foot (the basic proportional relation of arsis and thesis) will vary in composition. Both of these factors put time as it were into motion and bring the experience of rhythm and its theoretical capture to the limits of rationality. There are plenty of indications that Aristoxenus sensed how startling and difficult some of the implications of his system could be. In the sequel to the same treatise, for instance, he defends his use of "infinite" as not being inimical to science. It is indeterminacy, not infinity, which is inim-

ical to science (cf. the contrast in the same context, "determinate and limited" versus "unlimited"). Hence, no doubt, his open admission, part way through book 2 of the *Elements of Rhythm*, that "the fact that rhythmic composition and rhythm are not the same is not easy to make clear at this stage" (*Rhyth.*, 2.13). See further Barker 1989, 436 n. 165.

77. Cf. pp. 258–59; "ECP," 399 ("on account of the diverse temporal rhythms").

78. "We may take these lines of Simonides. They are written not according to those divisions which Aristophanes or some other metrician devised, but according to those demanded by prose. Now look at the ode and read it according to divisions: you can be sure that its rhythmical arrangement [literally, "its rhythm"] will escape you, and you will be unable to guess at any strope, antistrophe or epode, but it will seem to you clearly to be a continuous piece of prose" (*On the Composition of Words*, chap. 26; trans. Usher). Dionysius couches his point provocatively: by claiming that poetry thereby approaches prose he means to say that prose often contains (hidden) poetry within itself. See *KGW*, 2.3:275–76 ("verses in speech"), reciting Cicero's argument (*Orator*, 183) that lyric, despoiled of song, is naked speech (*nuda oratio*), speech naked of rhythm. Cicero's point is likewise made to buttress the claim that "there is a certain rhythm in [well-wrought] prose." A parallel suspicion as to the objectivity of euphony is raised in the same chapter of Dionysius' work; see Porter forthcoming. Not by chance is Cicero reckoned by Nietzsche to be "one of the greatest rhythmists that ever lived" (*KGW*, 2.4:403).

79. *KGW*, 2.1:59–74 (Nietzsche's second publication, from 1868); Wilamowitz 1886, 144; id. 1913a. See Smyth 1900, 321, for a survey of the early debate. Smyth adopts Nietzsche's solution, with some misgivings, as the most satisfactory of those proposed to date, and variants of it have been tried out since (see Denys Page, "Simonidea," *Journal of Hellenic Studies* 71 (1951): 133–42; here, pp. 133–40.). Nietzsche cleverly deduced that Dionysius has presented not strophic wholes but the end of a strophe and the whole of its antistrophe, plus an epode. Even so, the more recent scholarship has done nothing to invalidate Dionysius' point; he was "no more honest than he had to be" (Campbell 1967, 389). See now also Rosenmeyer 1991 for an appreciation of Dionysius' strategies of presentation, which are read as offering "proof of the fragility of literary conventions" (p. 11).

80. Cicero testifies to the difficulties of rhythm as a science (as does Aristoxenus, despite his brash confidence): "Feeling (*sensus*) is the judge, in which case it is wrong not to acknowledge what occurs [that is, the presence of a rhythmical pattern], even if we are unable to discover its cause" (*Orator*, 183).

81. P. 309. Cf. "reconstruction of the ancient symbolics [*der antiken Symbolik*]" (p. 322).

82. The internal quotation may be taken from some unspecified source, but it may simply focalize the position about which Nietzsche is speculating.

83. Nietzsche's position is similar to that of Lange, who observes (1866, 482) that

"experience and habit have an impact not only on the interpretation of sense impressions but also on the immediate appearance" given by sense impressions (namely, on the way in which sense impressions appear to us, as in the case of music). On Aristoxenus, see Barker 1978a. It is worth noting that the idealized nature of rhythmic conventions is an insight made by recent linguistic studies; see Essens and Poval (cited in Devine and Stephens 1995). This is so, despite what a superficial reading of Nietzsche's language along Dionysian/Apollinian lines might suggest (one that follows, say, *KSA*, 7:3[27–37], or *The Birth of Tragedy*). The assumption here would be that idealizing belongs to the side of the Apollinian sphere alone; Dionysianism, in contrast, points to the dissonant realities of the actual rhythms. That this apportionment is wrong is hinted at in *KSA*, 7:3[43]: "Strange idealism of the Greeks in their worship of narcotism," viz., the Dionysian "worship of *wine*." See below and the last sections of the next chapter.

84. Rhythmic feeling and linguistic form are thus mutually conditioning and mutually enforcing: "Until now, every *Ur*-phenomenon remains unexplained: the very same rhythmical feeling that invented rhythmical schemata is already active in the genesis of language, governing the succession of long and short syllables—this standpoint is an *important* one to take" ("ECP," 400).

85. This is possibly akin to what in music theory is sometimes called a "subtactile pulse": "a strongly articulated, rock-steady rhythmic unit that lies beneath the level of the 'felt beat,' or tactus, the beat that conductors show. . . . Most 'Western' music of the Germanic 'common practice' period is strongly tactile, with at best a weakly articulated subtactile component. But much music of the rest of the world—Asian or African music; earlier, later or more easterly European music—is intricately coordinated at the subtactile level, allowing overwhelming cumulative processes, or fascinating asymmetrical patterning, or viscerally compelling lurches to take place at the tactile surface" (Richard Taruskin, "A Sturdy Musical Bridge to the 21st Century," *New York Times*, August 20, 1997). With the exception of "rock-steady rhythmic unit," this account matches Nietzsche's (as I understand it) quite closely.

86. See a roughly contemporary note: "One might think of the reality of dissonance, as opposed to the ideality of consonance" (*KSA*, 7:7[116]). But "reality" is another kind of ideality, as we shall see.

87. The ictus in Greek rhythm (which Nietzsche never fully eliminates; see below) has for Nietzsche a temporal function, and emphasis for him may have been underscored by duration as well; cf., for example, p. 136: "What we make manifest through the ictus was expressed by retardations and accelerations." Cf. pp. 337–38, where temporal rhythm is admitted to be a factor in modern music, "though it is now secondary and no longer telling."

88. Pp. 159, 252, 327.

89. Thus, there existed a class of rhythms whose antagonistic distributions of arsis and thesis in ratio worked psychologically upon the mind of the hearer. Take,

for example, the *epibatos*, a potent variant of the *paion* (with a ratio of 3:2). Aristides classes this kind as the "more ecstatic" among rhythms: "It disturbs the soul with its double thesis, and lifts the mind upwards [*es hypsos*] with its long arsis" (*De musica*, 2.15). Nietzsche's translation brings out the intensity of the effects: "The soul of the hearer is both shaken [*erschüttert*] and lifted up to sublimity [*zur Erhabenheit*]" (p. 111). And his commentary brings out well the coordinated tension of a rhythm at formal cross-purposes with itself: "The first [effect occurs] through the inequality of the two heavy parts of the measure, the second through the lack of resolutions [viz., through protraction]." Not all irrational rhythms met with equal recognition, however. Aristoxenus held that some were too complex to be effective, like the epitritic ratio (4:3); but contrary opinions existed too (Aristides, *De musica*, 1.18; cf. *KGW*, 2.3:305).

90. *Rhyth.*, 2.20. Bacchius, for instance, describes "a syllable longer than a short but shorter than a long" as "irrational" (*Isagoge*, 95; see Barker, 1989, 440 n. 190); it is dissonant because the two resulting parts (here conceived as arsis and thesis) fall in the "intermediate" area described by Aristoxenus.

91. A similar thesis could be derived, mutatis mutandis, from Dionysius of Halicarnassus. See Porter, forthcoming. On the discrepancy of time and bodies, see p. 209 (p. 35 above) on the inevitable *décalage* of rhythm from the semantic materials of language (a point frequently made in the notes); and p. 210, where in yet another historical "genealogy" of rhythm Nietzsche imagines the genesis of the quantitative method: at first, there is an original syllabic method of metrical counting, which seeks out uniformities of measure in the refractory medium of language; as nonequivalences emerge, "a nonuniform movement comes about that provides the basis for a varied arrangement and a new foundation—based on temporal measures [*nach Tacten*]." Further, n. 123 below.

92. Nietzsche's taste for dissonance is attested early. See his letter of October 1861 to an anonymous friend (*BAW*, 2:2–3; not in KSB), extolling the virtues of Hölderlin's poetic achievements. Far beyond achieving the "success" of classicizing meters ("In successful Greek meters? My God! Is that what your praise amounts to?"), Hölderlin's poetry attains an unmatched degree of sublimity and beauty, especially in the prose-poem *Hyperion*: "In point of fact, this prose is music: weak, melting sounds, interrupted by painful dissonances, finally whispering in gloomy, uncanny funereal hymns."

93. Nietzsche recognized that the durational units of Greek verse are not strictly equivalent: "In itself, language can develop only the felt contrast of syllables that are long and short, not that of 1 long = 2 shorts. A foot with three syllables will always be slightly different from one with two. -- and -˘˘ will have been approximately equivalent in time, but their division was slightly different" (p. 278). A footnote here reads: "Contrast between mathematical facts and those of feeling"; cf. p. 205: "Two beats [or "times"; *Takten*] are never equivalent in a mathematically exact way." Modern theory confirms this insight into the subtle nonequivalence of quantities in "resolu-

tion," with a precision that is almost too good to believe: "A long syllable in ancient Greek had a duration which was nearer to that of two short syllables than to that of one. The actual ratio may be estimated as approximately 5:3. This means that in the metrical sequence - ⌣⌣, recited in ordinary speech rhythm, the princeps occupied a slightly shorter time than the biceps (5:6), and if a long syllable was used to fill the biceps it had to be dragged a little," etc. (West 1987, 6–7; cf. West 1982, 20). Cf. Nietzsche's similar analysis of the dactyl (pp. 251, 328).

94. See n. 85 above. "[It is] important [to note] that in the major meters in hexameters and iambics," which in principle are rational, "*alogia* occupied an important place" (p. 337), a fact that Nietzsche is quick to infer ("Plainly, [the dactyl] . . . is an *alogos* ["irrational," that is, rhythm]," p. 298). Dactylic rhythm was commonly treated as distinct from the dactylic foot, with which it also could coincide, the way Quintilian (*Institutio Oratoria*, 9.4.48) could say of "the dactyl" (meaning the metrical foot) that rhythmically speaking it is an indifferent matter whether it should have shorts preceding or following the long: "for only time is measured, so that the interval from arsis to thesis remains constant" in a ratio of 2:1 or 1:2. But if that is the case, and if a dactylic rhythm could be recognized to "resemble in rhythm" an irrational *choreios* (Aristides, *De musica*, 1.17), how can we tell them apart? (cf. pp. 240, 254). A similar question could be asked of the dactylic anapaest (-[a.]⌣⌣[th.]) and the dactyl (-[th.] ⌣⌣[a.]) (p. 301). In fact, Nietzsche will say, one can. Only, to do so is to view the fundamental irrationalities of the dactylic foot as rational.

95. Compare Nietzsche's remark that irrationality in the long "is thus for the dactyl *regular*" (p. 278; emphasis added). Nietzsche insists upon the irrational relation between the arsis and thesis of the dactyl, and even claims Aristoxenian authority for it (pp. 328, 329)

96. Cf. p. 205: "In series and periods the individuality [of rhythms] increases; architectonic rigidity is the death of a declamatory speech."

97. Is rhythm that to which we respond or is it what we hear—say, the simplified resonance of a more deeply buried, inaudible rhythmic pattern? This is part of its indeterminacy too. Unlike meter, rhythm has no definite structure, no "members [*cola*]," no caesurae, no periods, and no figures (*schēmata*): it is, as Quintilian says (9.4.48–51), "indifferent" with respect to these kinds of division (which pertain to rhythmic composition alone). Cf. pp. 105–20; and, as Nietzsche says, paraphrasing Quintilian and Aristoxenus both, rhythm is "endless" (p. 214; Aristoxenus ap. Porphyry, *Harm.*, 4 [Pearson 1990, 33; n. 76 above]). This is why rhythmic theory has no "periodology"; the subject falls to metrics (p. 116). Not even the basic units of time (*chronoi*) are identical in rhythm and in their rhythmic composition: rhythmic units are empty, waiting to be inflected compositionally and by their assignment of a tempo (which fixes their magnitude). The magnitude of primary durations is not determined outside of their structural relation, but instead is derived from a consideration of the overall tempo: they are not fixed or "absolute" quantities of time, but

only defined as the minimal elements of the ratios of time patterned in a rhythmic tempo (p. 107). Hence, "[there are] entirely different *chronoi* in *rhythmopoiia* [that is, from those of the rhythmic foot]" (p. 137), by which Nietzsche means "differently conceived." Psellus talks confusingly about "a particular *chronos* of the *rhythmopoiia*" as being "either longer or shorter" than a "podic *chronos*" (*Introduction*, 8; Pearson 1990, 23). Intersecting abstractly with its own construction, rhythm thus supervenes on its materials in the sense that it is the emergent effect of their articulation in relation to time. To put this in a different way, the system of durations does not preexist the individual durations, or vice versa: both are wholly systematic in nature, and the one cannot come into view unless the other has. This apparent paradox of perception is in fact less difficult than it seems. For if rhythm is what supervenes on temporal durations, it does so after the fact, retroactively—in other words, only once the rhythmical foot has been established as a whole. The quantities in (say) an arsis must wait for a thesis for the ratios, and for the rhythmic value of all the quantities, to obtain: what is to "count" as a minimum duration that cannot be further divided won't emerge until the larger pattern emerges. (In *De musica*, 1.14, Aristides mentions how mistaken identifications can come about and be corrected in just this way.) A complex rhythmic pattern, allowing for a great number of substitutions, might take several bars before its rhythm becomes plain, which is to say before the question of which durations are primary and indivisible (and thus how they stand in relation to one another) can be answered.

98. Cf. p. 322: "I suspect that the sensuous power of rhythm resides in the fact that two rhythms acting reciprocally upon one another determine themselves in such a way that the encompassing rhythm divides up [and so articulates] the smaller one. The rhythmical movements of the pulse, etc. (of the gait) are rearticulated through *marching* music, the way the beat of the pulse accommodates itself to the step. . . . Everything suddenly is astir according to a new law: namely, not in such a way that the old rhythms no longer predominate, but rather such that they are subjected to a [new] determination." In the same passage, Nietzsche states that "all rhythms" carry out "a direct assault on the body," along the lines described.

99. The violence of Nietzsche's language is reminiscent of Rossbach 1854, 68, who uses personifications and a subdued violence of his own in a discussion of the build-up of larger rhythmical patterns, while pressing an analogy with word-accents in individual words and phrases: "The accent joins together the various syllables into a unity. And similarly, the arsis in individual feet. In a whole clause the accent of a single word takes preeminence [*tritt . . . hervor*] over the accents of the individual words. In this way, the entire clause becomes an organic whole, inasmuch as everything strains toward a single point and emanates from it in turn: the accent of the individual word does not vanish; it retreats into the shadows and is governed by the main accent of the clause. . . . In the same way, an arsis in a rhythmical sequence becomes preeminent over the others, which as a consequence, although they do not

perish [*untergehen*], are nonetheless subordinated." Cf. also Wilamowitz's account (n. 64 above).

100. "Only time" (p. 104)—that is, "only temporal differences" (p. 135; cf. "ECP," 399: "only temporal rhythm")—gives the proper criterion of Aristoxenian rhythm.

101. *BAW*, 3:74. See chapter 5, below, for discussion of this threshold typecasting and its more general significance for Nietzsche's philology.

102. Cf. the notes to the lectures on "The Greek Lyric Poets," a section the editors describe as "addenda" and date to anywhere from 1869 to 1878/79: "Especially important, Aristoxenus the theoretician of music. . . . Opposition of the old classical art in contrast to the modern: like Aristophanes, he is an opponent of modern taste. . . . Aristoxenus names Phrynicus [the early fifth-century tragedian] and Aeschylus as his masters. Sophocles is also faulted. . . . The time of the Persian wars is the classical period" (*KGW*, 2.2:173).

103. Cf. Westphal 1861, 22–23; for an excerpt, see chapter 5, n. 17 below, and cf. n. 18 there as well.

104. Cf. "Introduction to Sophoclean Tragedy " (1870) §§9–10 ("IST," 37–45). For discussion, see Porter 1995b, 483–84; and Porter 2000.

105. There are no reliable checks on Aristoxenus, yet his empirical observations can in principle be rejected as "superficial" and his theory "opposed" (p. 135). Nietzsche does neither of these things, although at one point he derides Aristoxenus' expectations concerning the relative speeds of certain perceptions as a "naive illusion conditioned by the habits of his own perception" (p. 167).

106. A favorite contrast of Nietzsche's runs according to the very same logic: the rich polytheism of the Greeks versus the deadening monotheism of the Judaeo-Christian tradition. Cf. *GS*, 143, 149.

107. The thought is echoed in the lectures on rhetoric from 1870/71: "It is not hard to show," Nietzsche writes there, "that those instruments of conscious art which we refer to as 'rhetorical' were always at work as the instruments of unconscious art within language and its evolution [*Werden*], indeed that *rhetoric is an extension of the instruments of art that are buried in language* [*in der Sprache gelegenen Kunstmittel*], viewed in the bright light of understanding," etc. ("R," 20–21; trans. mod. = *KGW*, 2.4:425; Nietzsche's emphasis). See Porter 1994. See also "ECP," 344, on the proximity of language and rhythm (its "music"), the feeling for which even in antiquity had to be learned and cultivated. At stake, clearly, are culturally embedded sensibilities: and in general for Nietzsche, even at this point in his career, culture is the realm of the unconscious (see Porter 1998 and 2000).

108. Cf. pp. 210 (where language seems to have a will of its own), 278 (on the simplifications—read: idealizations—wrought by linguistic feeling and *habitus*). Cf. *BT* §17: "The Greeks are eternal children . . . who do not know what a sublime plaything originated in their hands and—was quickly demolished."

109. Cf. "ECP," 399: "For that reason our imitation in ancient meters is an illu-

sion: our hexameters and those of the Greeks have absolutely nothing in common." Like Nietzsche, and indeed because of him, Maas was critical of classicizing meters of the sort that could be found in Goethe or Platen. If Maas can write that such imitations, which are in fact "misread[ings]," "scarcely ever recapture the impression of the original," it is emphatically not because we have access to the original and thus a positive means of disconfirming the purported resemblance; any such resemblance is ruled out as a priori impossible (Maas 1962, 20–21).

110. Ibid., 4.

111. As on pp. 119, 171, 172, 196, 237–238, 249–50, 252.

112. Cf. p. 136, where changes in tempo are said to be expressed by the length of notes, the Greek equivalent of our ictus, while evidence for the latter Nietzsche finds utterly wanting ("Important: the absence of a true *ictus*"). Cf. "ECP," 398: "I found that the rhythmical ictus is entirely unattested, that no force is to be ascribed to it." Maas 1962, §127, rejects the ictus on these grounds too.

113. Pace Bornmann 1989, esp. pp. 482–83, who gives no indication of this troubling persistence. The ictus-theory is reinstated even after it has been rejected—for example, on p. 252 ("*Nebenictus*"), on the heels of p. 221 (rejecting the ictus as "unattested"). Here, where Nietzsche's inconsistency is, so to speak, absolutely consistent, there can be no question of a dialectical procedure (a "negation of negation") of the sort found in the *Democritea*. See below for reasons why.

114. See p. 337: "-‿‿ and ‿‿- [are] *real alogiai* (irrational rhythms); -- [is a] *rational* measure. Thus the dissonance in -- was *stronger* than in -‿‿ and ‿‿-." Identically, p. 329. The "rational" spondee (--) is more strongly dissonant presumably because the expectation of an exact equivalence between two longs is stronger than in a dactyl (-‿‿), and the disappointment of this expectation, accordingly, is all the greater, given that "two beats are never equivalent in a mathematically exact way" (p. 205); and presumably because its irrationality is more variable and less certain than in a dactyl: either long can be longer than a long (see: "*a-* or *-a*," where "*a*" stands for "irrational length" (*alogia*) [p. 337]).

On *Taktgleichheit*, see p. 255: "Aristoxenus denies to all livelier compositions any strict equality of times. Modulation (*metabolē*) is the prime instrument for achieving an effect." Now, modulation can occur in a number of ways: most obviously, through changes in the tempo or in the movement from one rhythm to another (and rhythmic composition is nothing if not the art of varying tempo and rhythm through intricate combinations of both). But less obviously, modulation occurs, or rather simply transpires, in the mere performance of any single rhythm. That, at least, is the core of Nietzsche's claim (which again takes an Aristoxenian insight beyond its native bounds). "Every irrational length is evidence of a modulation in rhythm," principally because "irrationality belongs to the realm of tempo, just as in general tempo is the decisive factor [in rhythm]" (pp. 252, 159). (The grounds for this connection are easy to see on the quantitative theory of rhythm: rhythmic tempo is determined strictly by the "size of the interval between one thesis, or arsis, and the next" [Aristides, *De musica*, 1.19].) For Nietzsche, then, the only constant in Greek rhythm appears to be its modulating character, which is its "irrationality," whence rhythm derives its most distinctive character and its greatest effect.

115. Pp. 112–13; cf. pp. 327–29.

116. "IST," 11, for the contrast between the "lawful architectonic character of music" ("Apollonian") versus "the pure musicality, indeed pathologicalness, of the tone" or "note" ("Dionysian").

117. We might compare his public lecture from January 1870, "*Das griechische Musikdrama*," where the proximity between the rhythms of modern German folk songs and of Greek music is asserted (*KSA*, 1:529). But in this case, Nietzsche has an excuse he won't have at the time of *The Birth of Tragedy*: he hadn't yet made his discovery about Greek rhythm (or perhaps, rather, hadn't organized into a "discovery" what he was beginning to intuit since the fall of 1869). On the next page, however, Nietzsche already intimates his future discovery: Greek rhythm stands out for its "simplicity, indeed its poverty in harmony, [and] its wealth in rhythmical expressive means." He goes on to talk about the way in which music is "made visible" to the eye in choric dance and movement, etc. But on the question of Dionysian music, there can be no doubts about its counting as an innovation.

A further confirmation emerges from the sketch "The Dionysian Worldview" (1870). There, Nietzsche depicts the entry of Dionysus ("the new god" with "his new cult") into the Greek world. "Originally, Apollo was the sole Hellenic god of art, and it was his power that restrained [*mäßigte*] Dionysus as the latter came storming out of Asia and into Greece. . . . If one wants to see really clearly how powerfully the Apollinian element suppressed the irrational supernatural quality of Dionysus, one need only consider how in the older musical periods the genos *dithyrambikon* [the dithyrambic class of music] was simultaneously the *hēsychastikon* [the most peaceful class]. The more powerfully the Apollinian artistic spirit evolved [in the direction of classical sculpture "at the time of Phidias"], the more freely did the brother-god Dionysus develop [in creating tragic glimpses into the abyss of being]" ("DW," 556). Probably, "the older musical periods" refers to the "pre-Dionysian age of Apollo" (ibid., 569–70): "The music of Apollo is architecture in tones," etc. (ibid., 557). As the sequel shows, the idea of "music generally" is conceived from a modern vantage point ("even though the need for a *realized*, truly resounding harmony was much smaller among the Greeks than it is in the modern world").

Finally, see *KGW*, 2.2:158–59, from the lecture notes to "The Greek Lyric Poets," a course Nietzsche offered six times between 1869 and 1879, here from a section on the dithyrambists:

> *The dithyrambists.* To be distinguished [are] the archaic, the classical, and the degenerate. The first to develop the dithyramb is Arion. . . . He is supposed to be the inventor of the *tragical* mode (*tragikos tropos*). [Presumably,] these old

dithyrambs of Arion were in the "diastaltic" character [viz., the (pretragic) mode, representing "the deeds of heroes and their corresponding sufferings and emotions (*pathē*)," in contrast to the "systaltic (restlessly moving)" and the "hesychastic" (tranquil and stately)"]. . . . [By the time of Lasus of Hermione, Pindar's teacher and a dithyrambic innovator,] tragedy had evolved. Now the dithyramb takes on another coloring. . . . The classical [viz., early] dithyramb has nothing excessive, immoderate, or unruly about it, its rhythm is mainly calm (datctylic-epitritic), to be sure livelier than the paeon of the hymns, but together these form a common *genos* [class], viz., the "hesychastic" [peaceful, calm class of music] (and the Pindaric epinicians belong to the hesychastic [class]), in contrast both to the *tropos nomikos* (excited erotica, *thrēnoi* [dirges]) and, on the other hand, to the *tragikos*, i.e., the tragic choruses. That is consistent with the fact that the [classical dithyrambic] melodies occupied a middle ground. With this change in *ēthos* [character], there must have been an associated change in key. When it is said of the dithyramb that it was in the Phrygian and Hypophrygian key, this cannot refer to the classical [that is, older] dithyramb; for the former have an exciting and enthusiastic character, and the Hypophrygian spurs a person on to powerful deeds, it is *praktikon*. In all likelihood these accounts refer to the *newer* [that is, degenerate] dithyramb.

An appended outline (p. 159, n. 16) reads:

> *Archaic* dithyramb, diastaltic mixolydian key (explicitly [attested])
>
> *Classical* dithyramb, hesyhastic, modified scale, probably *Doric* (Pratinas) and Aeolic (Pindar, Simonides)
>
> *Newer* dithyramb, Phrygian or Hypophrygian, and otherwise all the keys in alternation

And on the next page, Aristophanes' praise of the earlier dithyrambs is mentioned (he admired them for their "archaic simplicity"); and a resemblance is drawn between Goethe's *Wanderers Sturmlied* and the newer, no longer classical dithyramb. By this final innovation, Nietzsche is plainly referring to the changes wrought most famously by Philoxenus of Cythera and Timotheus of Miletus toward the end of the fifth century, whose "new music" was felt by Aristophanes and other conservatives to be a turn for the worse; Nietzsche calls this "new Attic dithyramb" an "imitation by means of concepts" (the dithyramb henceforth became a virtuoso expressivist medium) and "intrinsically degenerate" (*BT* §17). What this historical account establishes is that any innovations that bring the dithyramb to the realm of *alogia* in the ecstatic sense can only refer to the *degenerate* phase of the dithyramb. And it is only in this phase that Dionysianism becomes recognizably palpable.

118. Cf. "ECP," 399 (n. 27 above). By "metrics" Nietzsche obviously means rhythmics and the measurement of time generally: "I've got myself good and stuck in

the toils of rhythmics and metrics" (same letter to Ritschl); and see his letter to Rohde of 23 November 1870, announcing his "discovery" of "a new metrics."

119. See Nietzsche's later assertion of the numerical "architectonics" of rhythmical times, which is to say, the complex relations between quantity and quality in Greek rhythm ("ECP," 401): "Clauses [measured] against each other were felt architectonically," etc. Cf. further *DW*, discussed briefly in Porter 1994, 239–40.

120. P. 321. With "ultimately" Nietzsche is consciously overstating the submerged Pythagoreanism of Aristoxenus. For a similar criticism that Aristoxenus' phenomenalism partially founders on its structuralist (and number-driven) desiderata, see Barker 1978a, esp. 15–16.

121. Cf. *KGW*, 2.2:376: "*Harmonia* designates the correct relationship of the notes in their sequence, not in their combination."

122. Cf. *KSA*, 7:1[54] (1869): "Harmony is characteristic of the Hellenic; for the moderns, it is melody (as absolute character)." See further *KSA*, 1:530 ("Greek Musical Drama," spring 1870). But that essay already shows signs of self-contradiction; on the previous page, as we saw, the characteristic differences between ancient and modern sensibilities are virtually nonexistent (n. 117 above).

123. Emphasis in original. Cf. Nietzsche to Fuchs, end of August 1888, on the correlation of meaning and stress in German, in contrast to classical Greek. Cf. p. 209: "In Pindar, logical conclusions and rhythmic-melodic closures are divergent"; that is, sound and sense take separate lines.

124. Schmidt 1868, whose study of eurhythmic form is briefly discussed by Nietzsche on pp. 130–31 and again in "ECP," 400. Its premise was that the Greeks "did no violence to their language" through protractions of quantity or pauses. Nietzsche would have found more to agree with in Anselm Feuerbach's book on the Vatican Apollo (Belvedere), which he was reading at the time, though it is not cited in the notebooks on rhythm. Apparently critical of Winckelmannian classicism, or rather its caricature in the likes of a Schmidt, Feuerbach is keen to reintroduce an element of pathos (*Affekt*) into the classical aesthetic of Greek tragic lyrics: "The actual soul of the emotional scene [in tragedy] consists in a certain vacillation between a strict imitation of nature and its pure and ideal transfiguration in art. Affect wrestles with the rigor of the art form; *it struggles to break through the barriers of art*, in order to validate its own force in all of its natural potency. In defense, art puts up a redoubled effort to assert its own power, . . . touching pain with its magical wand; and what in reality obeys itself with the irregularity of a convulsive pulse becomes the measure of rhythmic movement: a symmetrical strophic structure forces apart the individual way-stations of feeling; and out of the laconic brevity of those sounds of pain which break through the surface only here and then again there, there arises the beautiful fullness of a periodic language artfully arranged in chiastic patterns" (Feuerbach 1855, 287; emphasis added). But neither is Feuerbach a straightforward ally for Nietzsche. See chapter 5 below on this intriguing continuator of classicism.

125. In point of fact, this Dionysian ecstasy amounts to no more than a "frightful *Tiktak*" and a mechanical "drumbeat" (pp. 267–68; cf. pp. 321–22). "Drum beat": pp. 134, 268; cf. pp. 128, 260 (*Taktgleichheit*). See pp. 241, 269, criticizing modern scholars' equation of rhythmic and metrical feet; and Nietzsche's letter to Fuchs of mid-April 1886 on the "*Hopsasa*" of the German language.

126. In this, Nietzsche's arguments rival those of earlier musicologists, such as N. Forkel (1788), who tended to be despairing of ever bridging the gap, in sharp contrast with the philologists, who could not afford, professionally, to acknowledge such a defeat. See in general Fortlage 1847, which formed a part of Nietzsche's reading starting in 1865 (*BAW*, 3:99). Evidently, Nietzsche is rehearsing some of this debate, which sets him at odds with Fortlage too. Fortlage's study is premised on a hoped-for return to ancient Greek music (buttressed by its theoretical possibility). Nietzsche knows better. And he could have counted on Wagner to know this too. See Wagner's essay "*Zukunftsmusik*" from 1860, which celebrates modern (viz., his own) music in much the same terms as Nietzsche does in *The Birth of Tragedy*: "entirely unheard of in antiquity, harmony, with its inconceivably rich expansion and its application through polyphony, is the discovery and the single most defining achievement of the last few centuries" (Wagner 1871–83, 7:144). By contrast, Italian opera from the early modern period represents "a relapse into paganism," melodically speaking: its rhythms are regulated by dance (ibid., 145). *BT* §19 elaborates on Wagner's biases. But the whole of that work serves to defeat them. See Porter 2000, 153.

127. Above (including n. 117) we retraced Nietzsche's historical accounts of the dithyramb. His musical accounts of the dithyramb link its innovations with a lapse from classical virtues into recognizably modern ones (tonality, melody, harmony), as we've also seen. The two accounts are slightly dissonant. In effect, degeneracy begins to seep into the earlier dithyrambic forms from the retrospective viewpoint that attempts to coordinate historical and musical factors within a coherent picture. The circularity from without is paralleled by a circularity within: the degeneration of the dithyramb marks in fact a *return* to an earlier, "nomic" (ecstatic) mode of musical composition (p. 157), now under the banner of a degenerate Dionysianism (cf. *BT* §17). Another way of putting the problem is to say that dithyrambic compositions are in the process of ripening and degenerating (becoming classical and then postclassical) even as the tragic form is developing alongside of them (out of a blend of diastaltic and hesychastic features in music); and that tragedy contains the seeds of this degeneration just by carrying within itself the influence of the dithyramb. But even this is a simplification. There is no straightforward way to describe the developments, which are organized in Nietzsche from several directions and points of view at once. The problems are condensed in the idea of a "dramatic dithyramb" (*BT* §§4–5).

A final word on Aristoxenus. It is sometimes thought that Aristoxenus' theory reflects the new sensibilities brought about by this musical revolution from the end of the previous century; and that his dissociation of rhythm from meter, instead of capturing the classical essence of rhythm, is conditioned by these very same changes: his "discussion . . . focuses . . . on the rhythmic configuration . . . at the moment of musical performance, which from the time of Timotheus was no longer linked to the temporal values of the verbal text" (Comotti 1989, 45). But Nietzsche does not see it this way. For him, Aristoxenus' theory can reflect, unwittingly, features of a declining rhythmic sensibility. But Nietzsche squarely locates the dissociation of rhythm and meter within the high classical aesthetic (see, e.g., n. 123 above). Nor is he easily disproved, given the state of our evidence for music in antiquity generally. None of this, however, has any bearing on the complications that Nietzsche successfully (and I believe fatally) introduces into his conception of the Dionysian innovations in music, both here and in *The Birth of Tragedy*, the fundamental traits of which are anachronism and modernism. He can be wrong about Aristoxenus and even about early Greek music; but he leaves us with a massive set of difficulties when it comes to taking a consistent view of Dionysian (tragic) music. And these have not been sufficiently appreciated. See further Porter 2000.

128. This allows for uncanny resemblances such as the following, which is said of Westphal's system: "It attempts to show that the postulates of Aristoxenus are not at all an abstract system, but rather that they contain the living facts of classical art. In this he turns against those who quarrel over the basics and appeal to their *sense* of rhythm [lit., "their rhythmical *feeling*"]" (p. 129, Nietzsche's emphasis; cf. p. 131). The allusion is to Westphal 1861, 6–7; and (e.g.) to id. 1865, 432. Westphal's efforts, however, are directed both at recovering an archaic sentience and at getting Aristoxenus' theoretical principles to correspond to their empirical objects (as in Westphal 1861, 20, resisting the "philosophical abstractness" of the earlier quoted thesis of Aristoxenus that rhythm and its objects are distinct; cf. ibid., 24). See further Boeckh 1877, 776–77, charging certain predecessors (Voss, Apel) with anachronism: they apply modern views of music to the ancient material and ignore the ancient theory and practice of metra, a sin his own earlier work on Pindar he can proudly claim does not commit. Boeckh uses the same negative language as Nietzsche, but different positive arguments: "Hermann's *Grundirrthum* lies in the way he construes the quantitative relationship of arsis and thesis as a causal one. Thanks to his self-invented categories he was likewise misled in his analysis of metra. . . . On Apel's theory, which I once found seductive, . . . only the metra possible from the standpoint of modern music are explained, not those realized by the ancients. The rhythm of modern music agrees in principle with ancient music. But it is more limited in the forms it realizes; and it is freer, due to the arbitrary values assigned to syllables." Significantly, Boeckh recommends combining historical research with an understanding of "ancient philosophy," but no details are on offer here. Wilamowitz's complaints from 1895, again superficially resembling Nietzsche's, are to be explained by the same tradition as Boeckh stands in: "A new metrics, or what has a nobler ring to it, rhythmics, has been conceived, built on allegedly eternal, i.e., modern musical

principles," etc. (Wilamowitz 1895, 1:249). For a still more striking parallel with Nietzsche, see n. 64 above.

129. Is the theory of quantitative rhythm, so understood, itself in ways Kantian too? Cf. "PTG," 857 (reproducing an argument by Parmenides against the reality of time, but in a Kantian idiom): "I can say that my intuitions are sequential; but that only means that we are conscious of them in a temporal sequence, which is to say according to the form of the inner sense. Time is for that reason nothing that exists in and of itself [*an sich*], nor is it a determination that is objectively dependent upon external things." If so, then we also have to say that Nietzsche is deploying Kant against the Kantianism of his contemporaries, who have eyes only for the "eternal" form of "rhythm *an sich*." But in fact only the language of Parmenides' argument is modern; its upshot would have been perfectly acceptable to Democritus, who held time to be a "phantasm."

CHAPTER 4

1. *KGW*, 2.2:34.
2. "Encyclopädie der klassischen Philologie und Einleitung in das Studium derselben," in *KGW*, 2.3:341–437 ("ECP"). Henceforth in this chapter, references by page only will be to this edition, except where otherwise noted. Although announced for the winter semester of 1873/74, official records confirming that the second lecture actually took place are lacking. What we have is a letter from 7 November 1873 to Gersdorff in which Nietzsche somewhat mysteriously writes, "I'm reading my lectures on Plato and unloading the other one [*wälze das andere ab*], which likewise has found takers [a sensitive point, as Nietzsche's enrollments had plummeted after the debacle of *The Birth of Tragedy*], in favor of my eyes," which were already starting to fail him. *Abwälzen* implies that Nietzsche was passing (or intending to pass) the responsibility for the course on to somebody else; but Nietzsche gives no further indications. See Janz 1974, whose results are, however, equivocal and inconsistent. In one summary table (p. 199), he concludes on the basis of Nietzsche's testimony, and in the confirming light of a letter from Gersdorff from 29 May 1874, that the second lecture never took place: "*nicht abgehalten (trotz Teilnehmern)*." In another (p. 203), he writes, "SS 1871; possibly WS 73/74." The editors of *KGW*, 2.3, follow the latter formulation, without comment (p. 339). It is doubtful, in view of the letter to Gersdorff alone, that Nietzsche would have revised the lectures in 1873/74 even if he repeated them. I take it that the notebook we have represents the original (and only) lecture course, with annotations dating from the same semester. See n. 30 below.
3. Wolf 1831a, 1831b; and Wolf 1869, 808–95 (*Darstellung der Alterthums-Wissenschaft nach Begriff, Umfang, Zweck und Werth*, 1807). Wolf's lectures, entitled *Encyclopaedia philologica*, were first given in 1785 (Pfeiffer 1976, 175), and from 1792 on were published from his students' lecture notes (see Paulsen 1919–21, 2:211 n. 2).

See Furhmann 1959, 201, on Gesner; and Bernhardy 1832, 19, crediting Heyne, not Wolf, with originating the idea of *Alterthumslehre*, as it were a unified field theory for classics, viewed for the first time as a comprehensive "totality"; Wolf is the executor of this inheritance. With their bold new encyclopedic perspectives, the classicists seem to have been catching up with the common practice of other disciplines at the time; see Fuhrman, ibid.

4. See the two encyclopedic lectures and notes as well as two further lectures, "Ueber die neueste Entwickelung der Philologie" (1833), "Zur Method des philologischen Studiums (Bruchstücke und Aphorismen)" (late 1850s), "Gutachten über philologische Seminarien" (1863), and "Zur Geschichte der classischen Philologie," in Ritschl 1866–79, 5:1–98. An earlier encyclopedic sketch by Nietzsche, dated by editors to 1867/68, is printed in *BAW*, 4:3–8, but this may represent, in its content, notes taken during Ritschl's lectures on the topic a few years earlier (but not before 1864) and copied afresh (see *Nachbericht*, ibid., 616). In that case, in the later course Nietzsche remakes Ritschl's lectures entirely in his own image (which he undoubtedly does, as the writings by Ritschl just noted suggest). That Nietzsche had by 1868 already envisaged incorporating the encyclopedia as an element of his teaching and research is evident from a notebook from that year, where it is listed among other leading topics (*BAW*, 4:120).

5. Not least of all in the most recent incarnation of the philological encyclopedia, *Der neue Pauly* (1996–), which is consciously modeled after the tradition of Wolf and Boeckh, despite the formal resemblances to the first *Real-Encyklopädie der classischen Altertumswissenschaft* (1839–52), founded by August Friedrich von Pauly, which was alphabetical, lemmatic, and multiply authored. See Hubert Cancik, *Der neue Pauly: Reallexikon der Antike, im Anschluß an Pauly's Realencyclopädie der classischen Altertumswissenschaft: Encheiridion mit Vorstellung des Unternehmens und Hinweisen für Autoren* (Stuttgart 1993), 19–21 (now reprinted as "Altertum und Antikerezeption im Spiegel der Realencyklopädie [1839–1993]" in Cancik 1998). See also Cancik and Schneider 1996, "Vorwort," 1:v–vi.

6. See Boeckh 1877, 37–45, for a critical account of the modern genre down to the 1860s; and 45–49 on the relationship between the encyclopedia (as it were, the high theory and rationale) and *Methodik* (the practice, training, and detailed substance of philology). Boeckh delivered his own "Encyclopedia" lectures between 1809 and 1865 over the course of twenty-six semesters to an audience of pupils reckoned by his editor to be 1,696 strong (ibid., iii). Boeckh's lectures were posthumously published by a pupil, as were Wolf's. See also Hübner 1889. For an overview of this tradition, see Landfester 1979.

7. Boeckh 1877, 41. The resentment runs deep. Between 1803 and 1806 (which is to say, prior to the publication of Wolf's *Darstellung*) Boeckh had "drafted an outline of philology based on Schelling and directed against Wolf" (Gossman 1983, 68 n. 108, citing correspondence from 1824).

8. Boeckh 1877, 43.

9. Boeckh eventually relegates numismatics to a perfunctory "appendix" under "metrology," the arts of measurement, with the warning label that the study of coins constitutes no unified discipline in itself: rather, it is "an aggregate or collection of materials for different disciplines" (ibid., 376). Numismatics is thus much like antiquity itself, awaiting its true systematization, or like bad philology, which either mistakes its materials for its methods (ibid., 43, 719) or else threatens to dwindle into the "small coins" of an overly detailed microphilology (cf. ibid., 14). Boeckh's arguments against the disciplinary autonomy of epigraphy (ibid., 719–20) are equally revelatory, pace Boeckh, of the arbitrariness and fluidity of disciplinary boundaries within classical studies at the time. See chapter 1, n. 119 above on the resonance of the term "aggregate" in classical circles, all of whose registers of meaning are active here.

10. Boeckh asks, for instance, on what grounds Bernhardy, a fellow Wolfian, excludes the history of philosophy but not geography from the category of ancient knowledge positivistically conceived (*reale Wissenschaften*): "You won't find any solid system or any clear conceptual separation here!" that is, in Bernhardy's encyclopedic work from 1832 (ibid., 44–45). No matter that Boeckh had earlier praised Bernhardy's encyclopedia as the best of its kind (ibid., 38). To be fair, Bernhardy (ibid., 52) expressly makes place for research in ancient "philosophy and religion"; his encyclopedia, which is architectonic and rudimentary (and which incidentally notes but does not attack Boeckh's departure from Wolf [ibid., 53]), implies but does not etch in a category for these higher studies of ancient knowledge. But omissions of all kinds occur in the classical encyclopedias. Leaving out the medical writers, for example, seems not to have disturbed any of the encyclopediasts.

11. Cf. "ECP," 369–70: "someone trained as a specialist is like a factory worker who makes his screw year-in, year-out"; similarly, "OF," 670; letter to Deussen, September 1868; *BAW*, 3:329, 338. This is an old reproach (as is the banausic imagery); see Wolf 1835, 297, 289, 291 (cit. in Schelsky 1963, 54); or Ritschl 1866–79, 5:29; it can also be found earlier, for example in Humboldt.

12. Boeckh 1877, 10–12.

13. Bernhardy 1832, 21; cf. ibid., iv–v, vii. Compare Nietzsche's notes, possibly reflecting a more tolerant view of the problem by way of his teacher Ritschl, but possibly not: "There are as many philologists as there are antiquities" (*BAW*, 4:7); cf. "WPh," 5[39] (cf. 5[31]): "It would be most important to know what these philologists [today] *understand* by 'ancient culture.' . . . [There is a] lack of clarity on the question of *which* ancient culture they mean." Bernhardy's encyclopedia is mentioned on the same page in *BAW*, 4, and then again in *KSA*, 7:8[39] (in the latter case, as one of three modern sources to be discussed under the heading projected for the first two weeks of the "Encyclopedia" lectures, "Origins and History of Philology"; 1870/71–72). In the encyclopedic tradition and in philology generally, subjectivity was officially abhorred, not desired (see Diels 1902, 33); it had to be transcended in

the perfect ("impartial") philologist; but how to do this in the modern, "subjectively" constituted world? Hence Bernhardy's dilemmas (pace Whitman 1986, 458–59). Cf. *BAW* 5: 268: "Given the feeling that an all too powerful subjectivity is afoot, an epidemic is breaking out here and there: firm supports are sought for obsessively [*krankhaft*], e.g., for architectonic sequences of numbers, etc., in the overvaluing of ancient manuscripts as an absolute norm, and so forth."

14. Bernhardy 1832, 36–37. See p. 68 above.

15. Ibid., 41; cf. ibid., 38–42.

16. For a parallel case of deep ambivalence, compare Humboldt's warnings from 1816 against trusting too lightly in "the so-called aesthetic feeling," in one's commerce with Greek poetry (Humboldt 1903–36, 8:135), a position that is radically at odds with his earlier classicism (see below) and with his contemporary theory of translation and of linguistic understanding (ibid., 129–30). On the latter theory, fantasy (the source of "ideal forms") is privileged over reality and awarded a foundational, or rather abyssal, place in linguistic expression and communication: language originates in force and feeling, and literally "out of Nothingness." Further, id., 1969d, 95, 96 (III:191, 192), opposing both art and reality to the realm of the Idea.

17. So Bernhardy, paraphrased fairly closely, who is repeating an inherited disavowing gesture. See Bernhardy 1832, 36 (quoted earlier, but out of context): "The antiquity of the Greeks and Romans, those genuine *veteres*, appears in its innermost essence as a self-enclosed structure. . . . But both peoples developed and preserved neither for themselves nor in common one and the same nature; although one is in the habit of embracing the totality of [the diversified life of ancient Greece and Rome] under the same name." Similar reservations touch even the label "classical" itself, because plainly not all products of antiquity live up to this moniker, not even within the Greek-speaking world itself: "The disparity of the Greeks over time was neither negligible nor temporary, as one might only expect, given the variety of its ethnic kinds [*Stämme*], the lively diversity [literally, "fragmentation"] in the life of the cities, the contrasts in politics and culture." "Nevertheless" (Bernhardy continues), for all their dissimilarities, "down to the ascendancy of Philip of Macedon, [the Greeks] converge at a significant height, one that, readily apparent in the art they share in common, duly receives the distinctive label of the *classical-* and antique-minded Greeks [*der* klassischen *und* antik-gesinnten *Griechen*]—however few of them were in fact classical and consummate exemplars of their kind, or however few instances we have of Greeks that transcended the limitations of the ancient regimes of thought and life[!]" (Bernhardy 1832, 37). With his desperate reference to art history (as a privileged metonym for culture) and his narrow Hellenocentric bias, Bernhardy is clearly operating within the Winckelmannian and Humboldtian tradition (cf. ibid., 17–18). With his reference to ethnic diversity and division ("*Stämme*"), Bernhardy is alluding to the problem addressed in K. O. Müller's study of the Dorians (1824), to be discussed in the next chapter. Similar troubles afflict

Humboldt's Greeks; see Humboldt 1969a, 18–19 (I:274–75). And finally, cf. Wolf 1869, 2:820: "*Zwar* . . . ; *demungeachtet* . . . " The formula, "I know very well, but just the same . . . ," is the subject of a seminal essay by Octave Mannoni, "Je sais bien, mais quand même . . ." (in Mannoni 1969, 9–33), where the formula is put to both psychoanalytic and anthropological work. The same formula has more recently been developed into a powerful tool of ideological critique by Slavoj Žižek; see Žižek 1989.

18. See "ECP," 407: "The fragments need to be studied again afresh: Mullach's *Fragm*[*enta*] *philos*[*ophorum Graecorum*] (bad, esp. Democritus), the personal notices in Diog. Laert. Countless historical writings have disappeared"; and ibid., 344 n. 5: "Also Democritus" has to be considered in connection with the rise of philology, to which Nietzsche adds a parenthesis: "(Are the books are genuine?)," and then a list of the books in question, all of which were allowed to stand as authentic in his earlier studies on Democritus: "On Rhythms and Harmony, On Poetry, On Song." That these comments are rhetorical only and have to be taken with a grain of salt is clear from the glancing allusion to another ongoing project in a later lecture (§17): "Then the transition [from lyric] to tragedy: very hard to understand!" a coy remark that is followed by a list of items that unmistakably marks this page as a reference to *The Birth of Tragedy*—about which Nietzsche pretends to know next to nothing, for the problems surrounding the genesis of tragedy (he claims) are all one "big riddle" (p. 403).

19. See pp. 14, 35 above.

20. Boeckh 1877, 87. Another way of affirming the tradition was bewilderment at a different question, which was raised with increasing urgency throughout the nineteenth century from outside the field of classics: "'Why does the study of antiquity make up a major part, indeed the privileged part, of the school curriculum?'" (ibid., 30). Boeckh's effort to stem the tide against pedagogical reform would prove to be in vain.

21. "Drive" or "impulse" (*Trieb*) is, to be sure, acknowledged in the tradition, which wanted to root itself in the nature of humanity. Thus, Boeckh can speak of the "philological impulse" as something fundamental to "civilized peoples"; but this *Trieb* arises from the need to communicate and understand, which is not to be confused with philosophy, which "even the uncivilized" can practice (Boeckh 1877, 11–12). Nietzsche's idea of *Trieb* is as different from this as his idea of humanity differs from the classical ideal of humanity; see below (also p. 14 above).

22. Many of the ideas in these lectures are forecast in notebooks from around 1868/69. See, for example, *BAW*, 5:268–74, pages on *Bildung* and classical philology which are preparatory to the inaugural Homer essay.

23. "One must not want to view a painting from up too close"; that way, one can arrive at "that most beautiful idyll," which can be enjoyed in its illusory status, for instance (to cite Nietzsche's own example), the illusion of Homer's aesthetic integrity (*BAW*, 5:270; 1868/69). See further his letter to Gersdorff from 6 April 1867: "For

we do not wish to deny that what the majority of philologists lack is an elevating, comprehensive view of antiquity [*Gesammtanschauung*] because they stand too close to the image and investigate a single fleck of paint instead of marveling at the broad, sweeping brushstrokes of the whole canvas and—what is more—instead of enjoying it." Nietzsche's Democritus, it will be remembered, is recovered in one such "comprehensive image [*Gesammtbild*]."

24. Similarly, "WPh," 3[62]: "Only through knowledge of the present can one receive *the impulse* [*Trieb*] *to classical* antiquity. In the absence of this knowledge, where is the impulse supposed to come from? When one observes how few philologists there are who live off of this [impulse], apart from those exceptions who do, one can infer that this impulse to antiquity . . . is *practically nonexistent*." Nietzsche's earlier stance, while at Schulpforte, is equally catholic, but also free of the later complications: "One must guard against one-sidedness in one's studies. . . . Indeed, one should study Greek and Roman authors alongside German classics and compare their perspectives with one another" (*BAW*, 1:127, a journal entry from August 1859).

25. And, one might wish to suggest, a throwback to his earlier views; see *BAW*, 5:270 (1868/69): "The enjoyment, the aesthetic exploitation of antiquity, is not enhanced by an extremely thorough knowledge of antiquity, but is on the contrary diminished by such knowledge," a view that is itself manifestly contradicted by his contemporary studies on Democritus.

26. Wolf 1869 (*Darstellung*), 2:814–19; 819: "Indeed, it will be permitted, in the spirit of the ancients, who proudly despised the *barbarians* as inferior human kinds, to restrict the name *Altherthum* [antiquity] in an exceptional sense to both peoples [that is, Greeks and Romans], who were refined through intellectual culture, learning, and art." More on these prejudices in chapter 5 below.

27. Not that there are no vacillations today. In the Anglo-Saxon tradition there seems to be no agreement as to whether to call college and university units departments of "classics" or "classical studies," but little disagreement as to whether antiquity and its study are "classical." The term is burdensome, and it offends with its false precision. Instructively aware of this fact is the *Vorwort* to the most recent encyclopedic venture, *Der neue Pauly* (Cancik and Schneider, 1996–, 1:vi), where the concept of *Antike an sich* is roundly rejected as totalizing and proprietary, and the terms "classical" and "antiquity" appear in scare quotes, in parentheses, or not at all.

28. Boeckh 1877, 34, mentions the manuscript error, but not the philological error. See William Nathaniel West, "Spaces for Experiment: Theaters and Encyclopedias in Early Modern England" (diss., University of Michigan, 1996) on the changing self-definition of encyclopedias from Pliny to the early modern period.

29. See Introduction.

30. The text is printed as a numbered footnote in *KGW*, 2.3:341, but this represents a grossly misleading editorial decision. The ms. of the lectures in fact contains no numbered notes and no footnotes. In question are rather annotations written onto the blank sides of a notebook. Just what the status of these annotations is meant to be

and when they were added is unclear: they may be afterthoughts, clarifications in glosslike form, cues for oral delivery, or genuine intercalations written after the fact and intended as preliminary to a future publication. In the minority of cases they have a kind of footnoting function—namely, that of providing bibliographical references, but such references can appear in the body of the text as well. To judge from the handwriting and from the ink, it appears that the annotations are probably contemporary with the lecture notes, but a more experienced eye than mine would be needed to confirm this. The editorial apparatus of *KGW*, thin as it is, gives no indication that any of this is a problem. It obviously is. But the problem will not make much of a difference in what follows, in which I will treat the annotations as integral elements of Nietzsche's lecture text and as supplementing or spelling out rather than modifying its internal logic—for reasons that I hope will become apparent. To avoid confusions, however, my textual references will follow the conventions of *KGW*, 2.3.

31. Here we can gain a brief glimpse into Nietzsche's "workshop." In the notes that probably stem from Ritschl's lectures on the *Encyclopaedia philologica*, Nietzsche records, without critical comment, the conventional wisdom: "Orig[inally,] connection between Greeks and Romans, later communication, common sources. 'Classical' (*classicus* as opposed to *proletarius* [etc.]), because this was the most richly and freely developed of ancient cultures" (*BAW*, 4:8). Not so the later reworking.

32. "Aesthetische Beurtheilung": p. 374. Similarly, the classicist's claims to classicalness (*Klassicität*) express a "judgment" (*Urtheil*) (p. 370) that rests on an "*aesthet[isches] Beschauen*" (p. 345), etc.

33. See "OF," 686–692, passim, likewise ironically pleading for the "real, solid, and nevertheless ideal goal" in which "culture," "education," and German classicism would be seamlessly coordinated.

34. Grafton 1983, 159. To give an idea of what this meant, in the German gymnasium with a "humanistic" (liberal arts) curriculum in the latter half of the nineteenth century, "instruction in Greek . . . entailed at least six hours of instruction every week for seven years," totaling 240 hours a year, while instruction in Greek and Latin accounted for about half of the entire curriculum (Latacz 1996/97, 13, citing Landfester 1988, 45). Fundamental to any study of German education (including these two studies) is Paulsen's exhaustive history (Paulsen 1919–21; here, 2:292; cf. also Paulsen 1906).

35. See Introduction.

36. "*Ich wohne jetzt im Pindar*" (letter to Herder, beginning of July 1772; cit. by Regenbogen, 1961, 533).

37. Wolf 1831a, 164; 1831b, 273; 1869, 2:953; see Fuhrmann 1959, 219. See "WPh," 3[59], quoting from Wolf 1869, 1:836, on how philology involves translating oneself, via *Versetzung*, into the "mentality [*Geist*] of the ancients." See chapter 5 (esp. at n. 177) on this practice, which might be termed "humanistic hermeneutics."

38. Boeckh 1877, 86–87. Boeckh cites the Empedoclean-sounding phrase, *homoios homoion gignōskei*, "like recognizes like," in support (and against Gorgias).

Gorgias provocatively argued that speakers have different understandings in their heads from hearers. But is that what Gorgias really meant? See Porter 1993. Cf. Boeckh 1877, 114, on "familiarizing oneself [*sich einleben*]" with the peculiarities of ancient genres or authors (such as Pindar) and thus attaining a feel for their historicity and, consequently, for their aesthetic properties: so read (and only so), a poem "comes together in a perfect unity and gains in color and force." In his notes on the need for literary history, Nietzsche turns Boeckh's dictum to critical advantage (see *BAW*, 3:330–31): "Like recognizes like"; but are philologists today, nourished on a "hypertrophy" of scholarship (and "ditto for hermeneutics"), sufficiently "like" the ancients even to understand them?

39. Hermann 1827–77, 7:104 (*De officio interpretis* [1834]).

40. Boeckh (1877, 14) comes close to acknowledging this: "There is more production in the reproduction [of philological facts] than in many a philosophy, even though the latter purport to operate in the realm of pure production." But it will take Nietzsche to finish his thought for him: "Reproduction, however, presupposes creative inspiration" (*BAW*, 5:270 [1868/69]), while his philology will bring this principle to a different extreme. Cf. *KSA*, 7:5[106] (1870/71): "What is *education* [*Erziehung*]? Its aim is that one should immediately subsume all that is experienced under certain delusions [*Wahnvorstellungen*]. The *value* of these representations determines the value of cultural formation [*Bildung*] and education. . . . This influence takes the form of *a transference of delusions*" (Nietzsche's emphases).

41. The brackets represent my best guess as to Nietzsche's meaning in what are, after all, mere notes. The alternatives ("[if you do follow my approach] . . . [my approach]") seem less likely given the sequel ("How little there is to know . . . !" etc.), but are equally plausible when taken independently of the sequel.

42. The remainder of the notes (over one hundred pages' worth) are highly detailed and technical, albeit lively and energetic, half of them consisting in a line-by-line commentary on the play, and full of "conjectural criticism." Again, Nietzsche's critique of this kind of philological criticism (on which, see further Gigante 1997, 316; and *BAW*, 5:127–28), we can only say, is also directed back at himself—and that is part of the demonstrandum. Another insightful glimpse into Nietzsche's teaching preferences is afforded by "Rückblick," 296 (n. 121 below).

43. "ECP," 368; cf. ibid., 389: confronted with antiquity, one has to "immerse oneself" in that which is not shared by modernity (*das Nichtgemeinsame*); ibid., 399: "our hexameter and the Greek hexameter have absolutely nothing in common" (*haben gar nichts gemein*); similarly, "OF," 690 ("to retrace this contrast in one's feelings" (*um diesen Gegensatz nachzuempfinden*), said of French and German culture; and p. 704 ("*das Nichtgemeinsame*"), said again of classical antiquity.

44. "HCP,"249–50.

45. For ourselves, and "not with regard to Indians, Babylonians, and Egyptians" (p. 390): the (conventional) peremptoriness of the label "classical" is plain to see; nor does Nietzsche consistently take this line (cf. "WPh," 3[4] ["2"]: "Indians and Chi-

nese are in any case more humane" than the falsely humanized Greeks of the classicists). More on this exclusion in the next chapter.

46. "If we take a *historical* stance towards antiquity we degrade it in a certain
sense: we lose its cultural-pedagogical value [*das Bildende*]. In general, we philologists
stand *too close* to classical antiquity, are *too familiar* with its details, to feel a deep desire
for it and to take in the whole aroma of it" (*BAW*, 5:269; last emphases added). Thus
a precocious entry from 1868/69 (and a prelude to "HCP," 252, of which this is a
draft). See n. 23 above.

47. Nietzsche's philology is frequently so read. See generally Howald 1920, 9,
and passim; Reinhardt 1966, 345; Pöschl 1979; Cancik 1995a, 83 (with some qualifications). Nietzsche of course encourages this misreading, as in *BAW*, 5:269, cited in
the previous note. But the sequel to this quotation and its congeners (n. 23 above)
betray the extremity of Nietzsche's alternative.

48. Similarly, "We Philologists" from 1875. The "privileging" of antiquity is
based on unreflective "prejudices," which include "a false idealization of [the Greeks]
into paradigms of humanity and of mankind" ("WPh," 3[4]); further, ibid., 3[12] on
the Greeks' essential "inhumanity."

49. See chapter 5; and for later developments, see *D*, 190; and *TI*, X, 3 (attacking
the classicizing aesthetic of Schiller, Humboldt, and others, what Nietzsche calls "the
niaiserie allemande").

50. Nor is classical idealism all light and beauty, or free of contradiction. Nietzsche's mention, in this context, of slavery and of the suppression of women as necessary to the political life of the free-spirited Greek is not just an element of his alternative to humanism, nor does it add anything that neoclassicist humanism did not
already know. Compare Humboldt 1969a, 15 (I:271), a passage that Nietzsche's paragraph seems nearly to replicate, if only fortuitously and intuitively (or else via Wolf;
see *KSA*, 7:7[79]). More on this in the next chapter. A further irony of classical
humanism is that its paradigm is not ordinary Greeks but divinized Greek subjects,
if not Greek gods themselves (like the indifferent Olympians of Epicureanism), who
approach a certain inhumanity by virtue of their very austerity. See "DW," 560 (with
Porter 2000); next chapter with n. 150; and Potts 1994, 164.

51. *KSA*, 7:8[39].

52. *KSA*, 7:3[74]; ibid., 3[76].

53. See *BAW*, 5: 268: "Illusion that philology is over or on the wane because the
aesthetic enthusiasm for antiquity [viz., the "classicism" of the previous century] has
given way to an historical view." The illusion is twofold: philology is not on the wane
any more than "the aesthetic enthusiasm for antiquity" ("classicism") is. Hence the
comment in the sequel on the pathological fears, among classicists, about creeping
subjectivism (see n. 13 above). In this light, we can better appreciate how Nietzsche's
motto "Subjectivity Prevails" (chap. 2) does not signal a resumption of classicism;
rather, it constitutes a laying bare of the everyday pragmatics of classical philology
itself, in which subjectivism and a projective reverence for the past go hand in hand.

Examples of lingering classicism will be given below and then discussed in more detail in the next chapter. It was doubtless this repressed classicism that contributed to making outward shows of classicism so horrifyingly repulsive to those who felt they were beyond it, as Anselm Feuerbach attests (p. 262 below), and as Nietzsche could confidently bank on.

54. See, for example, Humboldt 1969a, 18–19 (I:274–76). The essay closes by pronouncing the knowledge of classical Greek and Roman culture "the property of everyone."

55. Some of Humboldt's writings on antiquity were published in his lifetime—for example, his introduction to his translation of the Agamemnon (1816) and his review (from 1830) of Goethe's *Italienische Reise: Zweiter Römischer Aufenthalt*. His essay-sketches on antiquity in particular (Humboldt 1969a–d), dating from around the turn of the century but published only a century later, circulated first by way of correspondence and from there found their way into print through quotation, paraphrase, and summary, and ultimately in less visible and traceable ways. Wolf, for instance, borrows freely and in all of these ways from Humboldt in his published lectures on antiquity (see Wolf, *Darstellung der Alterthums-Wissenschaft* [1807], in Wolf, 1869, vol. 2). The first of Humboldt's sketches (1969a [1793]) was expressly written for Wolf and commented upon by Schiller (Schiller 1943–, vol. 21, pt. 2: 63–65); the others were probably written in 1806/7. For discussion, see Humboldt 1960–81, 5:368–98 (the commentary and notes by the editors of the Cotta edition); Stadler 1959, 54–56; Fuhrmann 1959; Grafton 1981. Nietzsche knew Wolf's publications well, and he was undoubtedly familiar with other similar inheritances from Humboldt in German letters. Humboldt's correspondence with Wolf was partially published in the first edition of Humboldt's collected writings in 1841. His correspondence with the classicist F. G. Welcker was published in 1859 by Rudolf Haym, the author of the first biography and philosophical study of Humboldt (1856), in addition to an influential study on Schopenhauer (1864). Humboldt's letter to Goethe of 1804 was put into print by Goethe himself in his essay on Winckelmann (1805). In a notebook entry from 1880/81, Nietzsche mentions the correspondence with Schiller (*KSA*, 9:9[7]), and then again in print the following year (*D*, 190), in both places with a view to a critique of classicism's idealism.

56. See n. 50 above for just one example; and n. 72 below for (possibly) another.

57. Letter to Goethe of 23 August 1804 (Humboldt 1960–81, 5:215).

58. Humboldt 1969b, 53–54 (III:161–62)

59. See Porter 1998.

60. Humboldt 1969a, 1 (I:256). This formulation was coined and made famous by Wolf, incorporated by Humboldt (see letter of Humboldt to Wolf, 23 January 1793; Humboldt 1841, 18) and much quoted thereafter, once Wolf appropriated Humboldt's views (and words) into his conception of philology (see n. 55 above).

61. Humboldt 1969b, 27 (III:138).

62. Ibid., 29 (III:140): *"Zu dem Uebergange vom Endlichen zum Unendlichen, der immer nur idealisch ist. . . ."*

63. See the letter to Goethe cited in n. 57 above: "No one has ever actually deduced the modern world from the ancient world, and no one can. There is a gulf [*Kluft*] there" (pp. 215–16). And cf. Humboldt 1969c, 71 (VII:615): "Diese[r] an sich geradezu nicht zu lösende Widerstreit des Antiken und Modernen."

64. Cf. *BT* §19, where Renaissance humanists, forerunners of the German classicist humanists, "combated the old ecclesiastical conception of man as inherently corrupt and lost, with this newly created picture of the paradisiacal artist." Schiller's naive artist is adduced in the immediate sequel as a successor to this idyllic view of antiquity.

65. Humboldt 1969a, 19 (I:275).

66. Humboldt 1969c, 71 (VII:614).

67. Humboldt 1969c, 72 (VII:616); emphasis added.

68. So, for example, Stadler 1959; Hatfield 1964; Menze 1965 (e.g., p. 164 [n. 77 below], though cf. pp. 155, 168–69), and others. Hatfield's comment, ibid., p. 195, that Humboldt "was basically a true if rather sophisticated believer in a Hellenic ideal" points in the right direction.

69. Humboldt 1969b, 54 (III:162).

70. Ibid. On melancholy, see ibid., 44 (III:153): "No race has known how to intensify the feeling of melancholy as did the Greeks."

71. Cf. Humboldt 1969a, 19 (I:275): the Greeks embody "for the most part [!] the original character of humanity in general"; id. 1969c, 69 (VII:613 ["IX"]): "the ideal of all human existence . . . , the pure form of the human condition"; and passim. On the "gap," see id. 1969c, 65 (VII:610): "This [that is, the Greek] spirit differs from the modern one in the same way *that reality differs* from an idealistic image of any kind"; id. 1969d, 100 (III:196): "Nothing modern can ever be compared with anything ancient"; and passim.

72. Humboldt 1960–81, 1:565 (VII:659); see id. 1969c, 68 (VII:612), on the "moral energy" that the Greeks exemplify; and cf. id. 1969a 3 (I:257–58). Yet, too proud for fetters of any kind, Humboldt's Greeks are capable (a page later) of immorality on occasion: "Religion exercised absolutely no power over beliefs and attitudes, but instead was confined to ceremonies . . . ; and similarly, ideas of morality clapped no fetters on their spirit" (id., 1969a, 18 [I:274]). It is not virtues and responsibilities, nor considerations of utility and harm, but only "ideas of beauty and liberality" that guide these Greeks, and that is their virtue. Cf. *BT* §15 on the "dubious excellence" shown by the Greeks "in their mores" and their "ugly vices" (where Nietzsche is voicing some unidentified segment of the modern recipients of Hellenism). Humboldt's Nietzschean concessions and self-contradictions come out rather flatly as a classic instance of disavowal in Wolf 1831b, 33: "Morally speaking, there were a number of deficiencies. . . . But we can't pay any heed to that when we

are talking about intellectual cultivation." Such questions took on a different cast in England; see Arnold 1996, e.g., 148–49.

73. "Now chimerical and boastful": Humboldt 1969b, 54 (III:162); "never chimerical": id. 1969c, 69 (VII:612).

74. Cf. Humboldt, 1969a, 8 (I:264): the aim is to identify the ways in which "*the character of a nation possesses multiplicity and unity*—which are in principle one" (Humboldt's emphasis). The parallels with Nietzsche's Greeks will be drawn in the next chapter.

75. For a quick sampling, see the quotations collected in Billeter 1911, 125–33. It is perhaps natural that characterizations in terms of "sensuousness" and "receptiveness" should slide into "passion" and "overflow/excess," whether in Goethe or in the classicist Theodor Bergk (ibid., 131), though not so for the more prudish Schopenhauer (see Rawson 1969, 325 n. 1). As convenient as it is, Billeter's survey is radically incomplete (and inevitably stops short of the early twentieth century). The Greeks' "melancholia" in fact runs from before Humboldt through K. O. Müller to beyond Nietzsche, but not in Billeter (see Rehm 1951 for the literary tradition and the next chapter for a few hints about the philological tradition); and Billeter acknowledges opposing currents in the mainstream and on the margins, but has no eye for the self-opposing currents that are everywhere to be seen.

76. Humboldt 1969b, 54 (III:162).

77. For example, Menze 1965, 164: "Humboldt in no way overlooks or denies tensions and oppositions in the character of the Greeks. Their harmony is rather the result of tensions that are overcome." Sometimes this sublimation is described as an "Apollinian" achievement (ibid.). See Stadler (1959, 156) on the "Nietzschean" resolution of the dilemma between Greek "cheerfulness" and "melancholy," which "astonishingly" is already to be found in Humboldt's *Goethezeit* belief that "Greek cheerfulness is not a lightly won gift of the gods, but rather a gift wrested in a bitter battle with the dark depths of existence." Two passages on the deep religious sentiments of the Greeks are often cited in support, Humboldt 1969b, 43–45 (III:153–54), and 1969d, 93–94 (III:189–90), but these do not quite bear out either description ("overcoming" or "wresting"); Humboldt's language is couched, rather, in terms of an eclipsing, etiolating, and rejection (read: denial) of unwanted features. Elsewhere, "cheerfulness" obtains without any apparent struggle; it is a natural feature, and simply given as such. See further the Pindar essay (1795): "One who possesses ["the greatness of existence, of being, of life"] enjoys untroubled tranquility, . . . and is at one with the gods and with fate. That is the source of the tranquility, cheerfulness, and radiating sublimity that distinguishes Pindar [viz., his portraits of Greek excellence] so preeminently" (Humboldt 1903–36, 1:422). Readers of the early classicist tradition look ahead to Nietzsche more often than Nietzsche scholars look back to Humboldt. But there are hidden complications at both ends, and it is these, not the apparent coincidences, that make for a genuine continuity of sorts. See chapter 5 below.

78. This is true not only from essay to essay, whereby vacillations are more easily accounted for, but often within a given essay, as witnessed above.

79. Humboldt 1969c, 68 (VII:612): "*Er* suchte *immer das Nothwendige und die Idee, mit Hinwegwerfung der zahllosen Zufälligkeiten des Wirklichen*" (emphasis added).

80. Humboldt 1969c, 68 (VII:612): "*Von solcher Sehnsucht beseelt, konnte das Streben der Griechen nur auf Darstellung des höchsten Lebens, d.i. des menschlichsten Daseyns, gehen.*" The previous sentence reads, "And instead of continuously pining away for these things without any satisfaction, the Greeks produced themselves again and again, ever new and ever more beautifully: hence, the fullness, purity, and strength of their spiritual life."

81. Humboldt 1969d, 110 (III:205). Constantly in search of themselves, Humboldt's Greeks must reinvent themselves at every moment; they are in this sense their own "work of art" (Humboldt 1969c, 66 [VII:610]); cf. "ECP," 437: "They have something of a work of art about themselves." Indeed, for Humboldt "character" is actually defined by the style and shape of one's desire (1969c, 67–68 [VII:611–12]; 1969d, 110 [III:205]). On the gloomier and deeper regions of the Greek spirit, which are explicitly coordinated with its capacities for idealization (and with religious feeling), see further 1969b, 43–45 (III:152–54), and, for example, ibid., 45: "Man's truer instinct is his deep, inner passion [*Leidenschaft*]"—that is his real "condition."

82. Humboldt 1969d, 117–18 (III:211–12). Not that the Greeks always were what they are. In a letter to Welcker (Humboldt 1859, 79), Humboldt expresses his interest in explaining "how the Greeks became Greeks" in a historical sense, as they assimilated foreign influences and achieved their own identity. But history inevitably shades off into circular ideality again, for what is it to become a Greek? For Humboldt, it is to be striving to be what a Greek is. The classical ideal is not the resolution, but merely the expression, of this striving.

83. Cf. Hatfield's puzzlement (1964, 207): "It is a little difficult to see why one should yearn, and for what, if one is already total."

84. "Das Streben nach der Einheit im Ganzen" (Müller 1844, 3:394).

85. Humboldt 1969a, 3 (I:257), and passim.

86. Cf. Humboldt 1969b, 55 (III:163); cf. 1969a, 21 (I:278); 1969b, 33 (III:144), where, however, the Greek predecessors do not search for but merely find the ideal; 1969c, 70, 71 (VII:614, 615); 1969d, 110–11 (II:205–6), and passim.

87. Humboldt 1969b, 32–33 (III:143–44).

88. Humboldt 1969c, 70 (VII:614), and passim.

89. As in Humboldt 1969c, 71–72 (VII: 615–16).

90. "Therefore, let their [that is, the Greeks'] impulse [*Trieb*] be named with a word that is intelligible only to the Germans: *Sehnsucht* ["yearning"]," and more specifically, "the striving for ideality" (id. 1969c, 68 [VII: 611]). The standard literature on Humboldt greets such passages without a murmur—for example, Menze 1965, 163, who stands out for at least allowing that Humboldt's treatment of the ideal can be both "fairly arbitrary" and bleakly impossible (ibid., 155, 168–69). Rehm

1951 gets at only one face of the problem (melancholy) and leaps to the Romantics' *interpretatio christiana*, without accounting for this constitutive feature of classicism. See also Lloyd-Jones 1982, 66, who takes a lexical approach to the problem (*Sehnsucht* renders the Greek word *pothos*), without any sense of circularity or anachronism.

91. Humboldt 1969d, 123 (III:217).

92. They represent, at least in the intention, fantasy in an exponential form, the fantasy of a fantasy: their fantasy ought to achieve in "reality" what the modern imagination apparently cannot, except through the fantasy of its possibility. The Greek achievement is not real but only ideal, and it is for this very reason a repetition of a modern wish. Similarly, see nn. 70 and 77 above, on the Greeks' melancholy. That the Greeks operated this play of affect upon themselves suggests a self-manipulation that again points back to the construction of the ideal in the modern present, the modern self-manipulation that aims to produce and operate upon itself the effect of an idealization.

93. Humboldt 1969c, 65 (VII:609); id., 1969d, 92, 94 (III:188, 190; emphasis added). Cf. id. 1969a, 18 (I:274): "*The fantasy* (or "imagination" [*Phantasie*]) *of the Greek* was so *sensitive to the external world* and *he was himself so lively and responsive within* that he not only was highly receptive to every impression but he also allowed these impressions to exert a great influence upon his formation, by means of which his own proper character could at least assume another, different one" (Humboldt's emphasis). The fantasy of the Greeks is a transparent image for German identification with Greek culture, projected onto Greek culture itself. As already noted, the essay closes, true to form, by pronouncing the knowledge of classical Greek and Roman culture "the property of everyone."

94. See, for example, Humboldt 1969d, 93 (III:189): "Precisely the deep awareness of the gap [*Kluft*] that fate placed eternally between them and us incites us to lift ourselves . . . to the heights opened up to our view. . . . We imitate their models with an awareness of their unattainability; we fulfill our imagination [*Phantasie*] with the images of their free, richly endowed life with the feeling that this is just as much denied to us as the light existence of the inhabitants of their Olympus was denied to them." Nietzsche's insight from another context is particularly relevant here: "Men flee not so much being deceived as being harmed by deceit" ("TL," 248; *KSA*, 1:878), where in question is in the first instance *self*-deceit, the "tendency to let oneself be deceived . . . without *harm*" ("TL," 255; *KSA*, 1:888; and passim).

95. In Nisbet, 1985, 33.

96. Athenaeum fr. 151 [1798] (emphasis added); Goethe, "Winckelmann und sein Jahrhundert," in Goethe 1948–, 13:419; Schiller, "Griechheit" (1796) in Schiller 1943–, 1:348 (= *Xenien* §§320–22); cf. Rehm 1951, 138–39, 144, on Schiller's critique of Humboldt's aestheticism. On the contemporary critique of Schiller's own Graecomania, see Rawson 1969, 316. For these reasons, criticizing "the self-evidence with which classicism believed it had correctly understood the message of antiquity" (Himmelmann 1985, 23) doesn't come anywhere near the reality.

97. 23 August 1804 in Humboldt 1960–81, 5:216. See Humboldt, 1969–81, 2:414–15 (VI:547–48), a review (1830) of Goethe's *Zweiter Römischer Aufenhalt*: "No age known to us has experienced the formative contrast of an earlier age the way ours has done—an age [viz., classical antiquity] that is completely historical, but which, in part because there are so many holes in what we know about its reality and *in part because we overlook [that reality] of set purpose*, stands there before us rather as a creature of the imaginative powers. *For we plainly view antiquity more ideally than it really was, and rightly so*, for through its form and its position relative to ourselves we are truly driven to go searching in the past for ideas and for an effect that reaches beyond life, including the life around us" (emphases added). Humboldt goes on to defend the reality of this effect, which he denies "rests on any deception."

98. Humboldt 1969d, 93 (III:189); cf. id. 1969c, 65 (VII:609), 70 (VII:614).

99. Cf. Humboldt 1969c, 65 (VII:609): "This is no accidental viewpoint, but rather a necessary one." The same requirement is reflected (and thereby affirmed) in the ideal of the Greeks themselves, in their striving after "the necessary and the idea," to the detriment of "the contingent." The contingency of the relation between ancients and moderns, whether historical or other, is rarely confronted and then only glancingly by Humboldt—for example, id. 1969a, 21 (I:277).

100. Cf. Humboldt in the letter to Goethe cited in n. 97, defending the necessity of the deception as a "sublime" force (*Gewalt*) that is "irresistible" for anyone who encounters it, and therefore not merely "subjective"—all this despite the acknowledged "gulf" yawning between antiquity and modernity. Humboldt's "Über das Studium des Alterthums" (1969a) is an essay, in fact, on the utility (*Nutzen*) of the classical ideal. Nietzsche's later essay, "Vom Nutzen und Nachteilen der Geschichte" (1874), has to be read in part against the background of the Humboldtian project, whereby history is treated as a useful self-deception. For Nietzsche, however, the deception consists in the presumed usefulness of the deception, while its harmfulness is too easily overlooked.

101. "TSK," 375, 379, 381; and cf. "WPh," 5[58], comparing historical and natural science: "There is this divinization of *necessity* in natural science too." The idea of a sublime necessity coursing through literary and vernacular history fares little better: "that is a deception," while natural necessity, the only kind there is, is in itself "nothing sublime, beautiful, or reasonable" (*BAW*, 3:322–23 [1867/68]); it approximates, instead, to chance and unreason.

102. A thought perfectly available to Nietzsche at this time. See *KSA*, 7:5[25], cited in chap. 5, n. 283 below.

103. See *GM*, III:19, on the paradoxes of modern idealism, which "likes to call itself 'idealism' and at any rate believes it is idealism," but only by dint of a "dishonest mendaciousness—a mendaciousness that is abysmal but innocent, true-hearted, blue-eyed, and virtuous," etc. The whole of the Third Essay of that same work exists to show how successive attempts to rid the world of idealism, by stripping its illusions away (for example, through science), merely conceal the ideal's further entrench-

ment. Humboldt confronts the problem a bit differently. For him, moderns can be idealist but only Greeks can be ideal: "[The ancient Greek] spirit [*Geist*] differs from that of the modern spirit the way reality differs from an ideal image of any sort" (Humboldt 1969c, 65 [VII:610]), a view that interestingly puts the activity of idealizing on the side of reality and thus complicates the account of Humboldt's position given above.

104. See n. 81 above.

105. Humboldt 1969b, 25 (III:136): "There is a fourfold enjoyment to be taken in classical antiquity: in reading ancient authors; in beholding ancient art; in studying ancient history; in living on classical soil."

106. "TSK," 375 ("Teleology is, like optimism, an aesthetic product").

107. Cf. Humboldt 1969a, 1 (I:256); Humboldt to Wolf, letter from 1794, in Humboldt 1841, 5:82 (cit. by Horstmann 1978, 65 n. 49); and n. 16 above. On Wolf, see chapter 1 above.

108. Letter to Fuchs, mid-April of 1886; cf. the letter to Ritschl of 30 December 1870 cited in chapter 3, n. 20.

109. Compare the ironies of the following from "On the Future of Our Educational Institutions" (1872), especially against the background of the "Encyclopedia" lectures: "Who amongst you will arrive at a true *feeling* for the sacred seriousness of art if you are spoilt by methods that teach you how to *stammer* independently, where one should teach you how to speak; to *aestheticize* independently, where one should guide you in how to be pious in the face of works of art; to *philosophize* independently, where one should force you to *listen* to great thinkers—the upshot being that you remain eternally distant from antiquity and become slaves to the fashion of the day" ("OF," 687–88; last emphasis is Nietzsche's).

110. *BT* §20.

111. Discussing nineteenth-century developments in philology, Mansfeld (1986, 45) writes, "Curiously enough, esthetic values still played a part, although they had considerably faded. The greatness of the great classical authors was so to speak taken for granted." Ritschl's conflicted position (and contradictions) are as good an example as any. Trying to patch up the differences rent open in the field between Hermann and Boeckh a few decades earlier, he wants to make textual philology more historically rooted and responsive, not simply a matter of ("subjective") "ideal reproduction," but of ("objective") "real reproduction" (Ritschl 1866–77, 5:13, 17, 25). Instead of discovering a golden mean, Ritschl alternates between excoriating the term "classical" (preempting Wilamowitz and others later in the century, and no doubt inciting Nietzsche to reexamine the term) and embracing it wholeheartedly (ibid., 15, 25), professing in the process an utter commitment to idealism: "*Classische Alterthumsstudien* give ideal nourishment and resuscitation, in the absence of which all higher culture of the modern world grows narrow, effete, and impoverished" (ibid., 25); cf. ibid., 30: "NB: It is not a question of moral idealism [alone] (that is something the pure pedagogue can also have); rather, [classical studies] also provide

an intellectual idealism." Cf. his unblinking *Totalitätsideal*, ibid., 3 and 7: classical antiquity is "a self-enclosed whole," expressive of a single "Idea"—a formula that rolls off the pen of German philologists from Wolf to Bernhardy and beyond. Confirming examples will be given below.

112. "HCP," 253–54, 263, 268 (emphasis added). Cf. Boeckh 1877, 31, on the necessary centrality of classics to the contemporary curriculum; Bernhardy 1832, 19 and 40, praising the Greeks as a "source of the beautiful" and for their "rhythmical confidence and strength of character, their pagan self-trust that draws its resources from nature alone, their plastic talent that unfolds itself tranquilly across polished surfaces according to the law of the beautiful," etc. And Hermann 1827–77, 8:463–70 ("Andeutungen über das Antike und moderne" [1847]), who, while warning against "illuminating antiquity with the faltering light of an aesthetic torch" and other sources of anachronism (p. 466), nonetheless succumbs to the aesthetic charms of the ancient world, conceding it to be in "many" areas the indisputable essence and legislator of "the natural" and "the truth," for example, in the area of plastic art, which was "spontaneously bound up with nature," etc. (p. 465), or in religious feeling, where "the greatness and sublimity of antiquity" finally shines through (p. 470). All three scholars and countless others after them bear out Nietzsche's later remark that "even the historical knowledge of classical antiquity is mediated by reproduction [and] imitation," and thus produces, willy-nilly, the equivalent of "a Goethean antiquity" ("SWB", 6[1]).

113. "For it is only as an *aesthetic phenomenon* that existence and the world are eternally *justified*" (*BT* §5)—a pronouncement that arguably is not metaphysical but is in fact critical of an "eternal" predicament of culture, with special bearing on the present day. See Porter 2000.

114. Cf. "TL," 252 = *KSA*, 1:883, on the "creative art" of forgetting oneself. And cf. *KSA*, 7:19[75] (1872/73) on the unconscious character of thought-processes, which Nietzsche synonymously terms "aesthetic" and "philosophical." This last idea, which is Langean, has its first philological application in Nietzsche's *Democritea* (see chaps. 1 and 2 above) and is later developed in the essay "On Truth and Lying."

115. For a predecessor to these ideas, see *BAW*, 3:319–25, notes entitled by the editors, "Toward a History of Literary Studies in Antiquity and in Modernity," which were discussed in chapter 1; and possibly Democritus' view of education as a "reshaping" of the soul, which parallels Nietzsche's idea here of "reeducation [*Umbilden*]": "Nature and teaching are similar. For teaching reshapes [*metarhysmoi*] a person, and in doing so constitutes a person's nature," which is to say, naturalizes itself (fr. 33 DK).

116. Otto Jahn, whom Nietzsche knew from Bonn and detested, seems to have boasted—famously—that he had never read a philosophical book (so E. Rothacker, *Einleitung in die Geisteswissenschaften* [Tübingen, 1920], 134; cit. by Landfester 1979, 157).

117. " . . . our understanding of antiquity is a continuous, per[haps] unconscious *construction of parallels* [*unbewußtes Parallelisieren*]." Cf. Behler 1997, 524, citing Nietz-

sche on the characteristic trait of the moderns, which lies in "transposing their dispositions involuntarily into the past." Behler rightly calls this (central) aspect of Nietzsche's philology "provocative."

118. Welcker's *Götterlehre der Griechen* is conceived as a "philosophical-historical" study; so self-evident is this designation, no methodological justification for it is needed (Welcker 1857–63, 1:x) or forthcoming. His conception of Greek divinities and of their emergence as ethical beings out of a natural state is indebted, he says, to the anthropological insights of Kant and Schiller; see, for example, ibid., 233.

119. See Introduction above, n. 62, and Bravo 1968, 90–91. Boeckh's reliance on philosophical concepts and his appreciation of philosophy are frequently confused in the secondary literature, with the latter too often overstated; qualifications are everywhere to be found in Boeckh.

120. Boeckh 1877, 56, 57.

121. "ECP," 365. Nietzsche will have formed this opinion based either on Ritschl's discussion in his own encyclopedia lectures (see *BAW*, 4:6–7) or on reports from friends like Mushacke, whom Nietzsche begs for details "again" about Boeckh's lectures, which presumably would have included his famous and still unpublished encyclopedia course (see letter to Mushacke of 11 July 1866). If we take Nietzsche at his word, he would have been interested in Boeckh's lectures on formal and methodological grounds only: "Basically, what drew my attention in most of the lectures [I attended] was not at all the subject-matter [*Stoff*], but only the form in which the academic teacher distilled his wisdom to his pupils. It was the method that I was most excited about; and yet I saw how little was learned in the way of subject-matter at university, and how the value of those studies was nonetheless pegged at the highest conceivable rank. Then it dawned on me that the exemplarity of method, of the way one went about negotiating with a text, etc., was the source of the truest and most lasting impact." This, Nietzsche claims, is also why he rarely attended lectures in their entirety, but only picked up "a few sad bits and pieces" from them ("Rückblick," 296).

122. Boeckh 1877, 15; cf. p. 308; and see Introduction on Pfeiffer's more recent version of this concept, *philologia perennis*.

123. Boeckh, 1877, 15.

124. Ibid., 56 (emphases in original).

125. Cf. a variant of this: "The whole is attained in every single idea; but nobody can grasp all the ideas" (ibid., 15). For more recent statements of this position, guaranteed by but also guaranteeing an "organic" self-enclosure (now in self-conscious, slightly anxious scare quotes), see Pfeiffer 1960, 173; and earlier, Wilamowitz 1880, "Vorwort" (with an explicit appeal to Boeckh and probably a direct allusion to the passage quoted earlier): "We want to go about our job, each working on his own part [of the whole that philology is], but everyone starting from a view [*Anschauung*] of the whole and striving towards the illumination [*Veranschaulichung*] of the whole." Cf. Ritschl 1866–79, 5:29.

126. Nietzsche takes this to be a general (inescapable) as well as a particular (descriptive) truth. Even Pfeiffer could concede the validity of this description for scholarship at least "since the middle of the nineteenth century" (no final terminus is given; presumably he means until early in the next century)—namely, that "it had brought antiquity into an all too familiar proximity with the present" (Pfeiffer 1960, 172). But neither does Pfeiffer allow that these influences might bear on his own conception of philology.

127. Cf. *BAW*, 3:340: "Methodologically healthy research does not leap like Athena ready-made from the head of Zeus, "whereby Nietzsche means to take on Auguste Comte and his "erroneous" belief that "scientific thought instantly becomes visible the moment metaphysical and mythical conceptions are swept aside." The sequel attacks the view that there is a "common root" in the mind by virtue of which common sense and reason can put "the ages of Pericles and Bismarck" in touch with one another and attain "something that lasts for all time." Cf. ibid., 365.

128. "OF," 686.

129. Ibid., 685–87. Cf. Humboldt 1969b, 25 (III:136): "Antiquity seems like a better home, to which one gladly returns every time." Cf. *WP*, 419 (1885), on "the Greek world" where one finally "can be at home": "To be sure, one must be very subtle, very light, very thin to step across these bridges!" which is to say across "the rainbow bridges of concepts" that lead back to Greek antiquity. "But what happiness there is already in this will to spirituality, to ghostliness almost!" The double-edged ironies are the same, early and late.

130. "OF," 689. Cf. Humboldt 1969c, 66 (VII:610) on the need to cultivate "the feeling for antiquity," which is to say, for classical Greece.

131. "Let everyone be a Greek after his own fashion, but that's what he should be!" (Goethe 1948–54, 13:846).

132. "OF," 689–90.

133. The second lecture closes with the stunning and depressing revelation that classical education is an airy and absolutely unreachable "ideal," a mere "phantom"; see "OF," 691–92, and the beginning of the next lecture, where the philosopher and his two interlocutors are depicted as utterly shattered and speechless. Nietzsche's critique is of course a leitmotif of the later writings, long before *Ecce Homo*, III.1, which repeats the argument from the last quoted passage of "OF" in a less shielded way: "This 'education' which from the first teaches one to lose sight of *realities* so as to hunt after altogether problematic, so-called 'ideal' objectives, 'classical education' for example—as if it were not from the first an utterly fruitless undertaking to try to unite 'classical' and 'German' in *one* concept!"

134. Bernhardy 1832, 41, and passim. Humboldt 1969d, 100 (III:196); 1969c, 65 (VII:609).

135. See Paulsen 1919–21, vol. 2; Schelsky 1963; Landfester 1988.

136. *BAW*, 3:370 (1868): "One should observe what kinds of scientific types emerged at the time. E.g., how the concept of 'philosopher' or 'philologist' takes

form. What role the 'mathematician' played. The social position of the philosophers"; *BAW*, 4:128; and *BAW*, 5:268–272 (1868/69), the latter being notes that
again spill over into the drafts of the inaugural lecture and its critique of contemporary philology.

137. "WPh," 7[6] (here, p. 124); *BT* §23. Some of these unwritten laws and the
state's normative role ("*der Staat . . . normiert*") in the regulated economy of philological education are detailed and reaffirmed in Wilamowitz 1913b, 104–5, and passim ("Philologie und Schulreform," 1892).

138. Nietzsche's term *Erzieher-Stand* ("class of educators") designates the historical succession to the *Gelehrtenstand* of the previous century, which evolved into the
professional class of educators in the nineteenth. Humanist classicists were the core
of both; see Turner 1983.

139. Cf. "*Ameisenarbeit*," "WPh," 3[63]; "OF," 667–71; and see n. 11 above.

140. "OF," 687; and *BT* §20.

141. "OF," 667.

142. "WPh," 3[16], [13], [62]. See the third lecture of "On the Future of Our
Educational Institutions" for an analysis of this classical state formation, esp. pp. 667,
706–9; and see the fifth lecture for the "ascetic" consequences of contemporary education, including a "flight from the self" (p. 747). For historical overviews of the concept of the *Kulturstaat*, see Schelsky 1963, 134–73; Cancik 1995a, 46–48.

143. So Howald 1920, 9, calling classicism a "refuge" for nineteenth-century
minds put off by the reigning "historical spirit" of the day, and identifying Nietzsche
as one of these refugees. More will be said about this trait of classicism and its persistence throughout the nineteenth century in the next chapter.

144. This is as it were a crueler form of the parable from "On Truth and Lying in
an Extra-Moral Sense" (1873), about the rationalist who hides an object behind a
bush only to "discover" it thereafter as if for the first time ("TL," 251–52/883).

145. Humboldt 1969d, 65 (VII:609); emphasis added; cf. id. 1969d, 93 (III:189):
"translating ourselves" into the Greek world we are translated into "our original, not
so much lost as never possessed, human freedom."

146. See, for instance, Humboldt 1969d, entitled "History of the Fall and
Demise of the Greek Free States"; and the excerpts from Bernhardy in n. 17 above;
or compare Winckelmann 1972 [1764], who operates with his own four-part scheme,
inherited from Scaliger (see Most 1989, 3), but which nonetheless follows the general parabola of summit and decline retraced by later classicism.

147. See Pfeiffer 1961, 1968.

148. This ambivalence toward self-overcoming will become the dominant feature
of Nietzsche's writing in the last decade of his career; see Porter 1998, 1999.

149. *GM*, Pref., 5; III:25; *UM*, II:5; cf. ibid., 1. See Chapter 5 n. 73 below.

150. Similarly, Nietzsche abandons the linguistic and grammatical approaches of
comparative mythology, which are in any case self-eliminating (p. 410), in favor of
developing an account of the (competing) historical perspectives that surround an

indifferent origin. The emphasis on the ethical dimension of later, Olympian divinity is Welckerian (see Welcker 1857–63, 1:233–35, and passim), with roots in the classicizing tradition (see Schlegel 1958– , 6:47 ["Geschichte der alten und neuen Literatur" (1814)]; Moritz 1981, 2:613 ["These higher powers are nothing less than moral beings"], 639).

151. The quotation is from *Daybreak* 44. Cf. "PTG," 806: "Questions as to the beginnings of philosophy are completely irrelevant, because everywhere at the beginning of things it is the same story: the uncooked, the unformed, emptiness, and ugliness; and because in all things only the higher levels matter." For a first attempt at a revised view of Nietzsche's concept of genealogy, see Porter 1992a; 1998; also p. 104 above (a more elaborate treatment is forthcoming).

152. For example, Welcker 1857–63, 1:iv: "*Griechische Mythologie ist als Griechische . . . aus sich selbst erwachsen*," a thought that entails the "concept of an ["organic" and self-enclosed] totality" (ibid., cf. ibid., vii n. 5).

153. This, at least, is how the metamorphoses of the gods look "in the Dionysian myths" (p. 414). Similarly, "PP," 222 (a lecture course on the Presocratic philosophers), in a section on "the preliminary, mythical stages of philosophy" in which Orphic, Platonic, and Neoplatonic cosmogonic materials sit awkwardly side by side: "Zeus [is] like the breath that permeates the universe" and "the essence [*Inbegriff*] of all things." On the parallel anachronism of the *Grundidee*, see below.

154. The reference to n. 37 here and below is to the text (an addendum) as presented in *KGW*. See n. 30 above; and my review of *KGW* 2.1–5 (*IJCT* 6.3 [2000], 409–43).

155. The entirety of the addendum is devoted to explicating the idea of metamorphosis, which "is not to be confused with theocrasy"; it covers the entire historical "process," from the ethical evolution of the gods to their final and fatal reduction to allegorical "husks" (p. 416 n. 37). Despite Nietzsche's own attempt at distinctions, questions remain. Is the Dionysian version of mythology (with its "revelations of the One") theocrasic or self-specifying? Is the "specification" of the one Idea of the divine itself just another form of theocrasy, appearances notwithstanding? Whatever the case, these uncertainties (which may just be symptomatic of the phenomena being described) are overshadowed by a further question: in exactly what does the decline of Greek religion consist?

156. Similarly, "PP," 219: "To the continuous *theōn krasis* [*theocrasy*] is opposed a *theōn krisis* [a "distinguishing of the gods"]. It was especially hard to bring the age-old order of the Titans into relation with the Olympians." In "ECP" we find out to what lengths the Greeks went so as to put order into their gods (see below).

157. This is evident in one predecessor, Schlegel, for whom the ennobling and beautifying activities of the poets served to "veil and mitigate" what in the earlier divine sagas "offended moral feeling" (Schlegel 1958– , 6:47). The logic of beauty is thus already fundamentally allegorical, conceptual, and morally rationalizing. Nietzsche will only agree.

158. This addendum is remarkable in another respect. By far the longest and most complex addition to the lectures (it is a tightly structured lecture in miniature), it miraculously takes up the two interleaved sides that were left free as Nietzsche entered his running text into the notebook. And unlike all the other addenda to the text, which as I stated earlier (n. 30 above) probably stem from the time of the lecture's delivery, this addendum is in an untidy hand, as if written in haste or excitement. Whatever the explanation, it is one of the more fascinating bits of ratiocination and narrative in Nietzsche's philological notebooks.

159. "Titan" is a correction for "God," which is crossed out in the ms; hence the brackets.

160. Cf. "ECP," 413: "Extremely important are the chthonic Gods, with which secret worship is connected. One supposes that the creation of the secret cults is connected with the suppression of the old, indigenous populations." Nietzsche continues: "To the group of chthonic gods belong Hades, Persephone, Demeter, Hermes, Hecate, and the Erinyes. Then [that is, still later] Dionysus (but not his surroundings). All are gods of *fertility*: horrible, because they live in the darkness and they inflict infertility as a punishment. Because the underworld is where the dead end up, the destiny of whom was deemed to be a function of their ethical behavior, they [that is, the chthonic divinities] are also ethical powers," and also, therefore, late, on Nietzsche's adapted, Welckerian scheme. Nietzsche dates the emergence of these cults to roughly 900–700 B.C.E. (ibid.). Finally, "all the gods group themselves around Demeter or Dionysus," a standard identification (see Müller 1847–48, 2:291).

161. "Orgia (originally not the ecstatic [kind])." These are evidently repressed into existence. Waves of immigrating "knightly" tribes suppressed the indigenous populations, presumably along with their older indigenous cults; these latter went underground and became "mysteries" (p. 413). This speculation (*man vermuthet*) brings to mind K. O. Müller's theory of *Völkerwanderungen*. This is not how Müller represents things in his *Prolegomena* (but see Müller 1847–48, 2:292; and Preller 1837, 276), although he does argue for the relative lateness of the Orphic mysteries and the Bacchic cults (esp. that of Dionysus Zagreus), which he views as linked (see Müller 1825, 71, 382–96); cf. further "PP," 265, dating the Dionysian cult to before the time of Heraclitus in the late sixth century (when the cult was "still fairly new," but also "extremely potent"); and finally, *BT* itself: "The song and pantomime of [the Dionysian] revelers was something new and unheard-of in the world of Homeric Greece; . . . With what astonishment must the Apollonian [viz., classical] Greek have beheld him!" (§2); and ibid., §11: "the sixth century with its birth of tragedy, its mysteries, its Pythagoras and Heraclitus." But Nietzsche doesn't let things stand here: "But that would only be a first beginning, which leaves the magnificence of their [that is, the chthonic mystery cults'] subsequent development completely unexplored" (p. 413), for what is the "need" that these practices fulfill? This pattern of a practice's being repressed into existence, whereby the original value of an entity (be it a chthonic cult or the modern sense of freedom or any ideal) is recognized only

retroactively as having existed at all and as having any value, is standard in Nietzsche (see, e.g., *GM*, II:17–18; and see n. 170 below, for a parallel but different account of the rise of the mysteries). A similar pattern is applied by Nietzsche to the modern notion, or mysterium, of classical antiquity itself.

162. Cf. Müller, ibid., 241: "It is clear . . . that the Homeric Olympus and the artistic world of divinities, in which every direction of the human mind, every activity and every talent, finds its ideal representation, was not the original form of divine worship in Greece, but rather was formed by [a process of] gradual unification"; and Welcker, 1857–63, 1:243: "these new, ideal gods, reposing on themselves." See further Wilamowitz in Gründer 1969, 133 (cited in chap. 5, n. 261 below), where the earlier gods are likewise said to be "formless." Lange 1866, 4, follows this line too: "The masses believed far less in the whole realm of Olympus, which was populated by the poets, than in the popular local divinities of the towns and countrysides, whose images in the temples were revered as especially holy," etc. When he alludes to a Greek priestly order (ibid.), Lange is diverging from Müller and Welcker. See further n. 177 below.

163. Müller 1825, 372; cf. 373–75. The immediate sequel to the sentence just quoted confirms the link between Nietzsche's version of this reversal and Apollo: "Old singers and prophets, filled with the idea of a bright and pure god, Phoebus Apollo, who was born to the world and who came to light out of darkness, called the greatest god 'the' god preeminently, and they called his parent "hiddenness," *Leto* [playing on *lēthē*, "forgetfulness," "hiddenness"], and gave to this goddess in turn a mother, the Bright One, Phoebe," viz., a Titan ancestor.

164. Müller also has the view that the Titans are more generic: "They nearly all stand closer to allegory," which is a later phenomenon influenced by poetic activity (ibid., 373; 219–20; cf. p. 71); but this was more of a commonplace in the nineteenth-century histories of religion (cf. Welcker 1857–63, 1:265: "idea[s] clothed in a mythical riddle"; "empty forms") than Müller's reversed sequence, which Welcker goes out of his way to deny (Welcker, ibid., 789; cf. ibid., 152, 261). For Müller, the emptiness of the Titans is simply evidence of their being as it were unmarked by historical differentiation (Müller, ibid., 120–21); for Nietzsche, their generality seems to fulfill a generic need, one that answers to a philosophical drive.

165. "Contemporary," because the narrative shape of *The Birth of Tragedy* is already well in place at the time of the "Encyclopedia" lectures; see *KSA*, 14:41–43, and *KSA*, 1:533–640. I say "surface narrative," but perhaps one should say "surface narratives," because Nietzsche in fact has no single, coherent story to tell about Apollo and Dionysus, either here or in *The Birth of Tragedy*. For an exposition of these (meaningful) contradictions in the latter work, see Porter 1995b, 2000.

166. "Out of the original Titanic divine order of terror the Olympian divine order of joy gradually evolved through the Apollinian impulse toward beauty" (*BT* §3). Indeed in 1872, Wilamowitz (in Gründer 1969, 36–37; cf. ibid., 119–21), citing Aristarchus and Lachmann but not the latest fashion, Müller, would fault Nietzsche's

divine chronology in *The Birth of Tragedy* for failing to represent the Titans and their associated realm as post-Homeric and post-Olympian. There is an irony to this, in the light of the "Encyclopedia" lecture, which preempts the criticism, as Nietzsche so often does.

167. " . . . *der Gegensatz des Musikal. Dionys. zum Apollin.*"

168. In his counterpolemic against Wilamowitz, Rohde, following Nietzsche's explicit coachings (letter of 16 July 1872), would reject Wilamowitz's objections as unfounded, and would reassert the historical priority of a "pre-Homeric" world of the kind represented by the Titans, marshaling the arguments of "Schöman, Preller, and Welcker" (in Gründer 1969, 80–81).

169. After Pindar, who was "already under the influence of the visual [viz., aesthetically formed and perceived] images of the gods," "the belief in myth slackens," even as "the firmly established ideal figures [of the gods] guarantee religion a still long-lasting duration" (p. 415 n. 37). The foundation of belief is disguisedly transferred from myth to mystery, not eliminated. And Aeschylus, coming after Pindar, is clearly part of this development.

170. In *The Birth of Tragedy*, the sequence runs as follows: "the feeling for myth perishes" and only then is myth "seized by the new-born genius of Dionysian music" under tragedy, which "awaken[s] a longing anticipation of a metaphysical world" (§10); the anticipation intensifies, only to be subsumed by the "mysteries." Cf. *BT* §17: "The Dionysian world view born of this striving lives on in the mysteries"; "it had to flee from art into the underworld as it were, in the degenerate form of a secret cult." This tendency, which is an inherited view (cf. Creuzer 1836–43, 4:185, citing Preller on the lateness of the orgy and its typifying a "degeneracy of the religious feeling"), seems programmed from the start of Nietzsche's conception of the birth of tragedy.

171. *BT* §11.

172. In this light, the claim from *BT* §3, that the Olympian divine order "gradually evolved . . . out of the original Titanic divine order" appears as a story that the retroactive creation would like to hear about itself—a Whig interpretation of history.

173. See n. 165 above.

174. For example, *Twilight of the Idols* X ("What I Owe to the Ancients"), 4: "All this is contained in the word Dionysus: I know of no more exalted symbolism than this *Greek* symbolism, the symbolism of the Dionysian. The profoundest instinct of life, the instinct for the future of life, for the eternity of life, is in this word experienced religiously—the actual road to life, procreation, as the *sacred road.* . . . It was only Christianity, with *ressentiment against* life in its foundations, which made of sexuality something impure: it threw *filth* on the beginning, on the prerequisite of our life. . . ."

175. Cf. ibid., 3[13]: "Christianity overcame antiquity—sure, that is easily said. First, it is itself a part of antiquity; second, it conserved antiquity; third, it was not at all at war with the pure times of antiquity. On the contrary, in order to survive intact, Christianity had to let itself be overcome by the spirit of antiquity."

176. *KSA*, 7:7[3]; first emphasis added (*"Das Christenthum fand* sich *bereits* vor".); cf. ibid., 9[31], "on the spread of the Dionysiac spirit" in the modern world, "which [spirit] is in search of a revelation"; this is what—remarkably—qualifies as a "return of the German spirit to itself" (ibid.), a phrase that will reappear in *BT* §19; see further, *TI*, X:2 (n. 179 below).

177. Cf. *KSA*, 7:5[110] (1870/71): "The development of logic dissipated ["the impulse to truth and wisdom," which had been "reconciled" and thus quenched in the tragic worldview] and forced the creation of the *mystical* worldview. The great institutions decline, the states and religions, etc. . . . Absolute music and absolute mysticism develop in tandem. With the spread of Greek enlightenment the old gods take on a *ghostly* character," etc. Two entries later we read: "*Continuation* of the *Birth*." Cf. ibid., 5[94]: "With the [rise of the] oriental-Christian movement, *the old Dionysianism* inundated the world, and all the work of Hellenism seemed in vain. A *deeper* worldview, an inartistic one, established itself" (emphases added). These are conventionally patterned insights, available in Creuzer and Müller, and digested in the secondary literature by Nietzsche's time. Cf. Creuzer 1836–43, 4:664, 669. And cf. Lange 1866, 20: "So far as religious belief is concerned, it is worth observing that contemporaneously with the loosening of belief, which radiated out from the theater under the influence of Euripides, numberless new *mysteries* came into existence." As the enlightened elites began to stand aloof of religious custom, the "half-educated masses grew uncertain and restless" and started to grasp after "every conceivable bit of foolishness, in order to exalt these to the level of religion. Asiatic cults, with fantastical and in part unseemly practices, had the greatest resonance. Cybele and Cotys, Adonis-cults, and Orphic prophecies based on impudently falsified books, spread in Athens as in the rest of Greece. Thus was the way paved for the great religious syncretisms that united East and West starting with the campaigns of Alexander, and that so significantly laid the groundwork for the later propagation of Christianity." Lange does not mention Dionysian cults in this context, but he does so toward the end of his study (ibid., 544); no historical dating is given for the cults there, but presumably the dates, too, would have followed the by then conventional accounts that Nietzsche follows in turn. See also *BAW*, 2, 432–33, a notebook from 1862 that contains excerpts from Mundt 1856. According to Mundt, the undermining of the Greek state "by mysteries and philosophy" led to an approximation with Christianity, and in fact these were its "anticipation" ("*Vorahnung des Christenthums in der Antike*").

178. *KSA*, 13:11[295]. Part of this is repeated verbatim in *A*, 58, which adds that the subterranean cults are a "latent Christianity." Cf. further *D*, 72 (1881), of which these later passages are the continuation and development. As Silk and Stern (1981, 121) observe about *BT* (pointing to passages in §§12, 17, and 23), "Christianity . . . is not even opposed to Dionysus. Christianity itself is taken to be an expression of the Dionysiac impulse." But they draw a conclusion opposite to the one drawn here: "Nietzsche does not say so overtly, because the admission would give Christianity a

dignity he is reluctant to allow it," and that he later on will be keen to repudiate (ibid., 287); similarly, Joël 1905, 309. The later evidence alone contradicts this reasoning.

179. That was the lesson of the transformations of the gods "in the Dionysian myths." "So many revelations of the One," they resemble phenomenal exemplars of a Platonic Form (here with pronounced Hegelian overtones), a notion that is possibly inherited from Creuzer (1836–43, 4:21, 116, 168, 408), though see also Moritz [1791] 1981, 2:639: "Because the imagination is predicated on no particular sequence of its appearances, often one and the same divinity will manifest itself in different guises." The same language of Platonism and of "revelations of the One" appears in *The Birth of Tragedy* as applied to both Apollo and Dionysus (where Creuzer is clearly an inspiration); see Porter 1995b, 481 and passim; id. 2000. Cf. "ECP," 369 (without the Dionysian connection): "The Greeks have a much higher idealism [than the Romans], to which especially Plato contributes." But the tendency to idealism and idealist conflations is already attested in the note from 1869/70 just cited: "Worship of *wine*, that is, worship of narcotism. This is an idealistic principle, a way to the annihilation of the individual. Strange idealism of the Greeks in their worship of narcotism" (*KSA*, 7:3[43], 1869/70; emphasis in original). In his own way, Humboldt would only concur with Nietzsche's verdict. Idealism is what gives the Greeks and their religiosity (which approaches "mysticism") a fascinating "depth"—and vice versa: the one is a reflex of the other. See Humboldt 1969b, 43–45 (III:152–54), on "their brooding speculation" and "allegorizing mysticism" that led them "deeper and deeper" into the "secrets" hidden beneath the apparent physical and historical world; and id. 1969d, 94 (III:190). For Nietzsche's later attitude, which is his earlier one too, see *TI*, X:2, indicting Plato as "an antecedent Christian"; he "went to school with the Egyptians" and conceived a "fascination" for the "'ideal.'" Similarly, *A*, 58. Is Dionysus a (dissimulated) projection from the culture of *ressentiment*—that is, a symptom of modernity? Undoubtedly. See Porter 1999, 171–72, and 2000.

180. Shelley, Pref. to *Hellas* (1822). See Gourgouris 1996, chapter 4, a fine discussion of the fantasy of modern philhellenism. The fantasy and the phrase are found from the very beginnings of this movement, as we have seen. But then, fantasy projection could coexist alongside its avowal, the way Goethe could notice about Winckelmann that the latter sought and then found in classical Greece whatever it was that corresponded to an internal need of his own (Goethe 1948–54, 13:416–20). The very identification of Greek antiquity as a "totality" that is intelligible only *aus sich selbst* (cf. n. 152 above) is a principle of Alexandrian philology (cf. the famous maxim of Aristarchus, aimed at Homer) that has enjoyed a long afterlife from Casaubon in the Renaissance to Pfeiffer in this century; see Porter 1992b.

181. Cf. *BT* §24: "From this abyss the Dionysian song rises to our ears to let us know that this German knight is still dreaming his primordial Dionysian myth in blissfully serious visions. Let no one believe that the German spirit has forever lost its mythical home. . . . "

182. See Silk and Stern 1981, 214, for a discussion of Wagner's known interest in Dionysus; and ibid., 215, where more could be made of the significance of "syncretism" for Nietzsche.

183. In Schliemann 1884, 359. Blind continues, "Arēs had his home in Thrakē. So had Orpheus. Pittakos, the son of the Thrakian Hyrrhadios, was the teacher of Pythagoras. Hermippos avers that Pythagoras had adopted the Thrakian philosophy," etc. The desperate etymologies that are deployed to buttress the identification, for example, that "'Thrax' (*Thrakk-s*), or Threïx (*Threïk-s*), as a Thrakian was called by the Greeks, may be connected with Frakk, Frank, Phryg, or Fryg, and "free," or *frei*," these umlaut-changes "being easily proveable [*sic*] in other cases, both in the Greek tongue and in Germanic idioms" (ibid., 358), are mocked in the opening sections of *On the Genealogy of Morals*, First Essay. I owe my knowledge of this letter to Mihalis Fotiadis.

184. His sources are for the most part those he names on p. 410, without identifying the works he drew upon: Creuzer 1836–43 (1st ed., 1810–12; 3rd ed., 1842–43); K. O. Müller, 1825; id., *Eleusinien* (1840; rpt. in id., 1847–48, 2:242–311); id., *Handbuch der Archäologie der Kunst* (1830); L. Preller 1837, and other writings; and Welcker 1857–63. These writings variously appraise the Dionysian cults. See Rehm 1951, 161, 353 n. 97, on Creuzer. On Creuzer, Müller, Preller, and Welcker, see Baeumer 1976, 179–84 (duplicating the findings of Andler 1920–31, 2:219–74); and Schlesier 1994. I am grateful to Sally Humphreys and to Albert Henrichs for helpful discussion on the question of Nietzsche's sources in the scholarly tradition. One document that might in places read like a verbatim source (were it not too late to be one) is, surprisingly, Wilamowitz's lectures on the history of Greek religion, delivered and published in Frankfurt in 1904 ("Geschichte der griechischen Religion: Eine Skizze," Wilamowitz 1913a, 169–98). To list only some of the more striking correspondences in Wilamowitz, there is the devaluation of origins ("which everywhere admittedly look pretty much the same") and the focus, instead, on processes of historical evolution (p. 170) in terms of universalizing syncretism and theocrasy (pp. 173–74, 175); the role of poets in this process (p. 176); the moralization of the gods, starting with Hesiod (p. 178); the dimly understood but powerfully felt religiosity, increasingly expressed (from the sixth century on) in the search for "another, purer" existence and eventually in the concept of a *Jenseits* (pp. 181–82)—the onset of this tendency coincides with, and is "abetted by," the "irruption" of the Dionysiac cult from the Thrace to the north and Phrygia to the east (p. 177); the feeling (which is ambiguously felt by both the Presocratic-age Greeks and by Wilamowitz himself) that "*a single, wondrous order penetrated everything*, that all becoming was only a transformation of *the eternal One*, which was the beginning of everything" (p. 183; emphasis added), possibly another inheritance from Boeckh (cf. Boeckh 1877, 60: "On both science and religious doctrine or inner religion as knowledge," with the note about Plato on the same page); Platonism (p. 185) as the culmination of Greek religiosity (where Nietzsche would speak of a Platonism that predates Plato); the ebbing of Greek vitality

"towards the end of the 3rd century" (p. 189)—here Wilamowitz, often celebrated as a great champion of the Hellenistic era, severely disappoints: "And the world is so cold, the poetry is only mere formal art, philosophy is mainly dialectical verbal and conceptual duelling," and (unlike Nietzsche) he skates over this period as being dry, religiously speaking; a period of *Götterdämmerung*, or a "twilight of the gods," which follows, namely, the Roman imperial period (p. 190; cf. *BT* §9, for the same phrase, applied—characteristically for Nietzsche—to the time of *Aeschylus* [!]), leading to a definitive "decline" in the second century C.E. (p. 195); and a final, lurching, and troubling approximation of Greek religion and Christianity (p. 197). There are differences to be sure. But the overlaps are astonishing, given the hostilities between these two great scholars, but not given their shared intellectual backgrounds (see next chapter). For a general discussion of these lectures in the context of Wilamowitz's views about Greek religious feeling, see Henrichs 1984, 226–27 and 1985, esp. 277–78, who in correspondence suggests that "the successive historical stages which Wilamowitz reconstructs here [in the 1904 lectures] owe more to the second part of [Erwin] Rohde's *Psyche* [1894; 2d ed., 1898] than to any other scholar." If Rohde is indeed behind Wilamowitz, one wonders how much of Nietzsche is in Rohde. See Silk and Stern 1981, 126–28, for a preliminary discussion of this question. The ironies of this possible hidden influence are formidable.

185. Creuzer (see previous note) is frequently read as devaluing a classical conception of Greece and as a Romantic working against the classicist grain (J. H. Voss took him that way, as do Andler 1920–31, 242–44, and Baeumer 1976, 180–81). If so, then why does Creuzer (1836–43, 4:38) say about "the Greek character" that it typically reconciled differences, and that it was "granted a happy life and serenity [*Heiterkeit*], features that remained the hallmark of the Greek religions"? The point actually touches the core of Creuzer's project. Herodotus' cheerful acceptance of the mutual agreement and in cases identity of Aegyptian, Orphic, Bacchic, and Pythagorean religious covenants—"this connecting up together of such disparate elements"—not only "accords with the Greek character"; it also provides a much-needed confirmation of Creuzer's syncretistic thesis and, what is more, it mirrors Creuzer's own practice (ibid.). The validity of the distinction between classicism and anticlassicism will be queried in the next chapter.

186. Cf. *KSA*, 13:11[282] (1887/88), a preliminary note to *The Antichrist*: Paul "understood *the great need of the pagan world*" and developed his interpretation of Christianity accordingly. Of course, the notion of pagan need is itself another interpretative device in Nietzsche's hands.

CHAPTER 5

1. Cf. *BT* §9: "The misunderstanding of this concept as cheerfulness in a state of unendangered comfort is, of course, encountered everywhere today." Cf. further "WPh," 3[4], on the "false idealization" and privileging of antiquity in the name of

contemporary humanism and classicism. And see *TI*, VIII:3, where German universities are critiqued for producing "cheerfulness."

2. Wilamowitz in Gründer 1969, 31–32. Wilamowitz's quotations from *BT* are frequently inexact, possibly deliberately, otherwise embarrassingly so. (For Nietzsche's puzzlement about this, see his letter to Rohde of 16 July 1872; *KSB*, 4:24.) Here, Wilamowitz's quotation corresponds to *BT* §20, where Nietzsche actually says that philologists and pedagogues have brought about the "complete perversion of the aim of all studies of antiquity." The substitution of "misrecognition" for "perversion" is telling but not worth pursuing here.

3. Ibid., 32–33. The "quotations" are again inexact, but they correspond roughly to *BT* §§6, 24, 25, 19.

4. "Who would want to confound the essence of naive art as Schiller expounds it with this Nietzschean reverie and *Schönheitsspiegelei*?" (Wilamowitz, ibid., 37). The term *Schönheitsspiegelei* indicates Nietzsche's perversion, through his faulty "mirroring," of classical aesthetics.

5. "HC," 783; "WPh," 3[12]; "WPh," 3 [12], 3[17]; cf. *KSA*, 7:11[1]; p. 352 (draft of the foreword to Richard Wagner of *BT*; 1871; identically *KSA* 7, 7[91]). "There is no truly beautiful surface that has no terrible depth" (these last two words reappear in the German, not the English, of *BT* §3: "an abysmal and terrifying view of the world").

6. *BT* §6: "The period between Homer and Pindar"; ibid., §11: "as if there had never been a sixth century with its birth of tragedy, its mysteries, its Pythagoras and Heraclitus."

7. See Oehler 1904; Joël 1905; Lloyd-Jones 1976, 1982; Borsche 1985; Mansfeld 1986, 55–56; Most 1989, 1995; Cancik 1995a, 35–49. The last of these views (concerning Greek irrationality) first gained credibility in the English-speaking world in the early decades of this century through the work of the Cambridge ritualists, especially F. M. Cornford and Jane Harrison, and culminated in E. R. Dodds' *Greeks and the Irrational* (1951); see Lloyd-Jones 1982, 174–75; and Henrichs 1984, 227–32.

8. See Most 1989 for sensible cautions about the periodicity of the "archaic" age. Histories of mentality are elusive (see Lloyd 1990 for a critique; further, Christopher Rowe, *Journal of Hellenic Studies*, 1983) and overdetermined (see n. 135 below).

9. "The Greeks, ... the truly healthy ones ... " ("PTG," 805). Cf. Rawson 1969, 330: "The Greece [Nietzsche] loves is the Greece of the sixth and early fifth centuries, naive and spontaneous, productive of great aristocratic individuals—the lyric poets, the early philosophers."

10. See Mansfeld 1986, 56.

11. The "two great *innovations* [of *The Birth of Tragedy*] are, firstly the understanding of the *Dionysian* phenomenon in the case of the Greeks—it offers the first psychology of this phenomenon, it sees in it the sole root of the whole of Hellenic art—. The other innovation is the understanding of Socratism: Socrates for the first time recognized as an agent of Hellenic disintegration, as a typical *décadent*" (*EH*,

"The Birth of Tragedy," 1; trans. mod.). This story is accepted in some quarters, for example by Silk and Stern 1981, 154, 156, who would deny the "historicism" of Nietzsche's "insight" but, strangely, not its validity. Contrast Behler 1997, 519, who ends up with problems of a different kind: Nietzsche's "discovery" of the Presocratics is ("perhaps") his "most important contribution to our knowledge of the ancient world," while his treatments of Plato, Socrates, and Euripides "smack too much of myth-making and personal projection into history to be taken as scholarly work."

12. This is too little noticed. If in *BT* §6, Homeric naïveté is opposed to "sentimental" Dionysian art (e.g., music), in *BT* §3, Homer in his naïveté represents "the complete victory of Apollonian illusion" over "the terror and horror of existence" and a "reversal" of the Dionysian insight—which is precisely the effect of Dionysian tragedy. Hence, Homer's heroes suffer pain, and (arguably) no differently from tragic heroes (*BT* §3).

13. See chap. 1 above.

14. *KSA*, 1:545 ("Socrates und die Tragödie"). See Romundt to Nietzsche, letter of 25 March 1870, in which the "Socratism" of Nietzsche's lecture is correctly called "an eternal disease," "pre- and post-Socratic." This paradox was deeply rooted in Nietzsche's mind, and indeed foundational to this conception of Greek tragedy and culture. Cf. *KSA*, 7:1[15], an entry from 1869: "Socrates was the element in tragedy, and of musical drama generally, that dissolved tragedy—*before Socrates was alive*" (emphasis added).

15. See Porter 1995b, 2000.

16. *KGW*, 2.3:126.

17. Aristoxenus, ancient sources like Theophrastus, and modern scholars like Rudolf Westphal (1861), are all candidates. Cf. Westphal 1861, 22–23: "Aristoxenus stands already on the limit of the classical age. . . . This is indeed no longer the vital age of the classical period; it is the period when the creative spirit in rhythm had long been dead. . . . In the midst of the old art's depravity, Aristoxenus occupies a very peculiar position," etc.

18. Westphal (1861, 24) does not doubt for a moment Aristoxenus' ability to capture the classical aesthetic in all its (Winckelmannian) "noble simplicity" (ibid., 4).

19. The term *Grenzfigur* appears in Nietzsche's account of another threshold figure, the Presocratic philosopher Empedocles, in "PP," 328, because "with him, the age of myth, tragedy, and orgiastic worship leaves off [*scheidet*], but by the same token in him appears the newer Greek, as democratic statesman, rhetor, enlightener, allegorist, scientist," etc. As I hope to show, Nietzsche's various "personalities" from antiquity are all vexed by similar threshold complications.

20. *BAW*, 3:11, 18, 20, 74 (1864). The initial impression (see Lloyd-Jones, 1982, 171: "[Nietzsche's] early work on Theognis (1864) is interesting chiefly on account of the resemblance of this poet's uncompromisingly aristocratic outlook with Nietzsche's own") is refuted by these notes, as Blunck already pointed out (Janz 1978–79, 1:123–24). Negri, 1985, 3–102, likewise tries to explain the early notes in the light of

the later "doctrines." Cf. Cancik 1995a, 11: "With Theognis, Nietzsche discovers the sixth century B.C.E.; this is where he will anchor his archaicizing construction of Greek culture." Similarly, Joël 1905, 298, though Joël's insight is tempered by a sense of Romantic (or just brutally frank?) irony: "Nietzsche wants to give us a tyrant and instead he gives us a lyric poet" (ibid., 297; cf. p. 302).

21. Theognis (vv. 425–28); cf. *BT* §3; and Schopenhauer, *W*, 2.2: §46. For the general argument concerning *ressentiment*, see Porter 1998. Further, *GM*, II:23: nobility is always *descended*, hence vulnerable to Theognis' worries about declining purity; and "in the end the ancestor must necessarily be transfigured into a *god*" (ibid., II:19). Theognis' fantasy is the very idea of nobility itself; its contents are specified in *GM*, I:5 (see below). Nietzsche's view seems, moreover, to be reflecting a historical reality. For an indirect confirmation, see Stewart 1997, 68: "The notion of a securely entrenched, hereditary aristocracy in sixth-century Attica is a fantasy. The situation was volatile in the extreme," etc. And as the *Theognidea* show, the situation in Theognis' Megara was equally uncertain.

22. *BAW*, 3:75.

23. *KGW*, 2.1:3–58; cf. *BAW*, 3:151–206 (1866); and ibid., 21–64, for the draft of its predecessor, the valedictory essay from 1864. Nietzsche's treatment is chiefly remembered for its view that the Theognidean corpus is arranged by "catchwords." But not only was Welcker the first to propose this idea, albeit not systematically enough for Nietzsche's tastes (see *KGW*, 2.1:17); the catchword thesis is tied directly to Nietzsche's reconstruction of the redactor's aims and, indeed, of his edition of Theognis itself (labeled "*die Stichwortredaction*" at *KGW*, 2.1:25). Cf. his letter to Carl Dilthey of 2 April 1866: "[I have proved] that a certain intention of the redactor is hidden in [the last, reconstructed redaction of the corpus] and I believe I have finally found the principle of this redaction, which also explains the repetitions, which is to say, the catchword (*Stichwort*) principle"; cf. *KGW*, 2.1:17, 18, 28, 35, where the catchword principle is shown to give the redactor a convenient license for falsification.

24. *KGW*, 2.1:29, 37–38. Nietzsche proposes a date of the fifth century C.E. for the redaction by catchwords and of the fourteenth or fifteenth century for further interpolations (*KGW*, 2.1:35–36; ibid., 17; *BAW*, 5:318 [1869]).

25. Momigliano 1984, 272; 1994, 307; Will 1956.

26. Müller's thesis had to wait for over a century to be demolished by Edouard Will (1956); the consensus till then was that Müller's picture was basically unchallengeable (so Wilamowitz 1921, 57–58), even though dissenting voices were audible (for references, see Pflug 1979, 123; Rawson 1969, 328 n. 1; Reibnitz 1992, 150; and Christ 1996, 20, with n. 45). On Wilamowitz's lifelong sympathies for the Dorian paradigm, see Momigliano 1994, 274. For a British representative of the same set of assumptions, see Bury 1900, 62.

27. Müller 1844 [1st ed., 1824], 3:394–96, 382; id. 1875–76, 1:202.

28. Müller 1844, 2:viii, ix, 3:9; see Janni 1968, 31–33 (reading this as a sign of romanticism).

29. Müller 1844, 3:3.

30. Müller 1875–76 [1st ed., 1841], 1:205; see id., 1844, 3:6.

31. Both sets of traits, classical and "romantic," appear on a single page (Müller 1844, 3:395). See below.

32. *BAW*, 3:14; emphasis added.

33. "Theognis," in the *Real-Encyclopädie der classischen Alterthumswissenschaft*, ed. August Friedrich Pauly (Stuttgart, 1839–52), 6.2:1848–50 (see *BAW*, 3:14–15).

34. Cited in *BAW*, 3:14 as "I, 409" (emphasis added). Nietzsche is citing the 1824 edition. The same thought is similarly expressed in Müller 1844, 3:395 (*"entfernen"*).

35. *KGW*, 2.1:37 (emphasis added). In his earlier notes, the image of Theognis that we have is said to be "fairly secure, [even if] perhaps a little too darkly colored" (*BAW*, 3:74). Colored, exactly, by whom? The later treatment leaves it open whether the redactor has darkened Theognis' portrait with similar "shadows," or whether Nietzsche's own reconstruction of Theognis' personality remains colored by the contaminated tradition.

36. See Porter 1998, 162–72.

37. Bergk 1845, 225–29, and passim; *KGW*, 2.1:37. See chapter 2 at n. 82. Nietzsche evidently had the opportunity to follow some lectures by Bergk on Theognis; see his letter to Rohde of 6 August 1868, where Nietzsche revels in his dissemblance at the time: "I sat there as quiet as a corpse, though with enchanted ears: I must have quite resembled your cherished *onos* [ass]"—the allusion being to Rohde's study in progress on Lucian's *Ass*, which Nietzsche later reviewed (rpt. in *KGW*, 2.1: 376–78). Following Bergk 1845, 396–97, Teuffel had suspected that the repetitions, contradictions, and looseness of the Theognidean corpus are due to the "clumsy and mindless" interferences of a later epitimator before Stobaeus' time (viz., at the end of the fourth century C.E.). Nietzsche invests this interpolator with a moral purpose and a personality to match. (Cf. also chap. 1 at n. 3 above.)

38. At the extreme, these two poles of analysis become indistinguishable, and the question of the text merges into that of its transmission. That, at least, is the upshot of the Homer essay.

39. Letter to Rohde of 9 December 1868.

40. It is worth noting in passing that the pattern of projection and falsification from the side of a "monk" to a lost and fantastically ennobled past is a strangely recurrent fantasy in Nietzsche. Thrasyllus, the late redactor of Democritus' corpus discussed in chapters 1 and 2 above, is one such instance. Speculating about his character, Nietzsche says that Thrasyllus "probably shared the monastic [*mönchische*] rigor and gloomy seriousness of his people" (the Egyptians), and that in his emulation of Pythagoras he will have evinced an *"ascetic* lifestyle," to wit, "embarrassing *self-observation*, dismissive, asocial silence, abstinence from meat dishes" (*BAW*, 3:366–67 [1867/68]; Nietzsche's emphases). A later version of this figure is the "ascetic priest" (as in *On the Genealogy of Morals*). Nietzsche's fantasy of asceticism is intriguing, and it permeates his thought (significantly, it is what binds Zarathustra to his opposites;

see Porter 1998). Whatever else we make of it, one of its earliest expressions is in these two philological studies.

41. "Deep melancholy in Pindar" ("SWB," 6[20]). Euripides: *KSA*, 7:8[13] ("1"). Cf. Cancik 1995a, 41, for the intriguing comment that for Nietzsche "Pindar is not naively archaic, he archaizes sentimentally and in a mannered way; he already affects his archaism." This insight can be deepened and generalized.

42. This last theme was the source of Nietzsche's abiding attraction to Prometheus. See the second of two letters to Wilhelm Pinder from the end of April / beginning of May 1859. Similarly, the later notebooks, for example, *KSA*, 8:8[6] (Aeschylus is "irreligious") and ibid., 11[18], 204 (the Greeks in Aeschylus' day disbelieved in their gods), both dating from 1875.

43. "SWB," 6[42].

44. Ibid.

45. "Socrates and Tragedy" (1870), *KSA*, 1:549. Nietzsche's choice of *Prometheus* as the pinnacle of Aeschylus' achievement exacerbates this division within the playwright. The latest of Aeschylus' preserved plays, it is problematical in other respects, most famously around the question of its authenticity (which Westphal was the first to doubt, in 1869). See Reibnitz 1992, 238–39, for references to the literature on the subject.

46. Cf. "IST" (1870) §§9–10; esp. pp. 39–40. Cf. *KSA*, 7, 1:1[6] (1869): "The time of Sophocles is that of the dissolution." "The death of tragedy [comes] with *Oedipus at Colonus*, in the grove of the Furies."

47. "SWB," 6[7], 6[12], 6[13], 6[18]; cf. 6[27]; and 6[25] (chap. 2, n. 21 above).

48. *KSA*, 7:5[123] (1871); "SWB," 6[34].

49. "SWB," 6[18]; and 6[7], radicalizing Zeller 1856–68, 1:11: "The individual [philosopher] does not stand alone in his way of seeing things [*Vorstellungsweise*]; others attach themselves to him, and he attaches himself to others," etc.

50. See *KSA*, 7:16[9]: "This denial of the individual! They [that is, the Greeks] are not historical but only mythical people . . . , not individuals, but rather ideas." Cf. ibid., 16[6]: "The decision in a contest [*agon*] is only the admission that runs, 'So and so makes us more of a poet; we will follow him, because that way we can create images more quickly.' In other words, an artistic judgment, won through an exciting of the artistic capacity. Not through *concepts*" (1871/72). Cf. ibid., 16[15]. The language and the subject matter here resume Nietzsche's inquiry into the Homeric question, namely, the question whether in Homer "a concept has been made out of a person" or vice versa (see chap. 1). Similarly, *HA*, I:221 (ad fin.).

51. "SWB," 6[7]

52. Ibid.

53. Ibid., 6[6].

54. Ibid., 6 [14], 6[18].

55. Ibid., 6[48], 115.

56. Ibid., 6[7]. Cf. *HA*, I:261: "Plato was the incarnate desire to become the

supreme philosophical lawgiver [viz., tyrant] and founder of states; he appears to have
suffered terribly from the non-fulfillment of his nature [like the Presocratics], and
towards the end of his life his soul became full of the blackest gall. The more the
power of the Greek philosophers declined, the more they inwardly suffered from this
bitterness and vituperativeness."

57. *KSA*, 7:29[8], 624 (1873).

58. "SWB," 6[11]; emphasis added.

59. No doubt in concert with the Nietzsche-Archiv in Weimar. See the biography of Nietzsche by Nietzsche's sister and literary executor, Elisabeth Förster-Nietzsche 1896–1904, 2.1:124 (1897): "Of all the unfinished works of my brother, this is
the work ["Philosophy in the Tragic Age of the Greeks"] he valued the most
throughout his life." It would be an interesting project to trace the way in which this
redemptive myth about Nietzsche, the philologist turned philosopher of the future,
was manufactured and orchestrated by his first editors in Weimar. The success of this
venture may be measured in part from articles like Julius Stern's "Ein Nietzsche des
Altertums" (*Preussische Jahrbücher* 117 [1904]: 515–23), an impressionistic attempt to
establish a deep spiritual link and analogy between Nietzsche and Heraclitus ("Heraclitus, the 'dark,' the aristocrat, the loner, the despiser of mankind and the masses,
the oracular riddler, teeming with contradictions," etc. [p. 515]).

60. Oehler 1904, 49. Cf. ibid., 51 n. 1, the only explicit reference to Diels: "Diels,
too, speaks [in his preface] about a 'blossoming and over-blossoming of the Greek
mind's springtime.'" In contrast to Karl Joël 1903, who evokes Nietzsche, albeit
superficially and inexplicitly, Diels (1848–1922), who the year before had publicly
denounced Nietzsche as an intellectual degenerate in a blistering *Festrede* in honor of
the Kaiser (Diels 1902), was hardly a threat. The source of Diels's own interest is in
"the unbelievably rapid development of philosophy in the sixth and above all in the
fifth centuries," and certainly not "that endless jumble of the Orphics and Pythagoreans" (Diels 1903, v = Diels 1954, vii). Nietzsche would have strenuously objected; see
BT §11 (n. 6 above); *KSA*, 7:16[24] (on Orpheus and Pythagoras) and 16[28]; "PP,"
220, with n. 9 (on Orpheus); and "OF," 701–2. Closer to Nietzsche in this respect is
Joël (1903 and 1906); see further the chapter on "Nietzsche und die Antike" in Joël
1905.

Does Diels' landmark edition of the Presocratics owe a debt to Nietzsche?
Doubtfully, any more than do Bywater's Oxford edition of Heraclitus (1877); G. T. W.
Patrick's *The Fragments of the Work of Heraclitus of Ephesus on Nature* (1889); John Bur-
net's *Early Greek Philosophy* (1892); or Paul Natorp's *Die Ethika des Demokritos* (1898);
let alone the first volume of Zeller's *Geschichte der griechischen Philosophie* (1856), with
its some eight hundred pages devoted to "Presocratic Philosophy" (cf. Zeller
1856–65, 1: 117, stressing the difference between pre- and post-Socratic philosophy:
"through Socrates a vitally new principle and procedure is introduced into philosophy"); Eduard Meyer's *Geschichte des Altertums* (1901/1902; see Schlesier 1994, 79);
or Wilamowitz's Frankfurt lectures on Greek religion (1904), with their pages on the

Presocratics that resemble Nietzsche's own in so many ways. (See further Wilamowitz 1913b, 183, 197). These studies are all part of the main stream that began flowing at the beginning of the nineteenth century, indeed out of the series edited by F. A. Wolf, the *Museum der Alterthumswissenschaften* (Schleiermacher's edition of Heraclitus was published in the first volume of this series in 1807; his chapters on the Presocratics in his *Geschichte der Philosophie* [delivered in lecture form in Berlin in 1812, and later published by Heinrich Ritter in 1839] were a natural sequel). This field received a further boost from nineteenth-century literary critics like Schlegel and philosophers like Hegel. Cf. Schlegel 1958– , 6:23–24 ("Geschichte der alten und neuen Literatur," lectures from 1812, rev. 1820/21): "With Solon a whole new epoch begins. . . . Not only does the very artistic development of lyric poetry and of the first beginnings of drama fall in this age. A slew of brand new didactic poems attest to an awakening reflection [Solon and Theognis are named as examples]. At the same moment Greek philosophy began with Thales, and prose . . . came into existence." A short eulogy of Ionian philosophy follows, while Socrates is later said to give rise to a "rebirth [*Wiedergeburt*] of philosophy" (ibid., 43). See further ibid., 49–51.

The Presocratics were extensively covered and even moderately fashionable well before Nietzsche's time (Bernays 1885, 1:37–39; Ritter 1829–34, 1[1829]:187–614: *Die Geschichte der vorsokratische Philosophie*, Pt. 1 [*Die ionische Philosophie*], Pt. 2 [*Die Pythagorische Philosophie*], Pt. 3 [*Die eleatische Philosophie*], Pt. 4 [*Die Sophisten*, viz., the atomists, Protagoras, Gorgias]; Mullach 1843, 1860; cf. Creuzer's [1836–43, 4:565] offhand remark: "The great significance of the idea of the world soul penetrating and binding the universe in the system of the Ionian philosophers *is well known*" [emphasis added]); Zeller 1856–68, 1:113: if Thales is the first of the Presocratic philosophers, "Socrates is usually regarded as the next major turning point, for which reason one is accustomed to open the second period [of Greek philosophy] with him." So far has the field developed by Zeller's day that he is concerned to combat hair-splitting innovations that ruin the integrity of the Presocratic periodization (pp. 115–17, 140, etc.). Cf. Lange 1866, 3–4, whose position on the "Preplatonics," "and especially simple materialism," both of which are viewed as revolting against Greek theology ("*es tritt daher jede consequente Philosophie . . . in einen Kampf mit der Theologie seiner Zeit*"), is fundamentally the one Nietzsche will adopt. Cf. further Joël 1903, 3 (the opening sentence of his study), speaking about standard "textbook" wisdom on the periodization of "Presocratic philosophy." Goethe (Diels 1901, viii n. 2), Hölderlin, Hegel, and Schleiermacher all knew Heraclitus inside out; Hegel once even boasted, "There is no sentence of Heraclitus that I haven't taken up [viz., assimilated] in my logic" (cit. by Bernays 1885 [1850] 1:37 n. 2; by Joël 1905, 294; and by countless others). And there were scholarly treatments of Heraclitus and others available, among them those by Heinrich Ritter (1829), Eduard Zeller (1844, rev. 1850), Bernays (1848, 1850, 1854), F. Lasalle (1858; 2 vols.), and Alois Patins (1879). Indeed, Bernays points out that J. M. Gesner had laid the groundwork for his own study some sixty years before Schleiermacher (ibid., 39). See generally, Hölscher 1979; Borsche 1985; and Behler 1997, 520.

Diels' interest in the Presocratics dates back at least to 1880, to an essay entitled "On Leucippus and Democritus"; in it he announced his intention to collect the Presocratic fragments in 1883 (see Diels 1903, vi; but see Burkert [forthcoming] on the correspondence between Diels, Usener, and Zeller in which the idea for the collection was already being discussed in 1880). Diels' *Doxographi Graeci* (1879), a study of ancient historiography of Greek philosophy, was inspired by his teacher Hermann Usener, who moreover gave Nietzsche's published work on Diogenes Laertius a good press (see Stroux 1925, 33–34, citing Usener; Wilamowitz 1928, 129; Mansfeld 1986, 48–49). But Nietzsche's systematic treatments of the Presocratics were not published until 1896 ("Philosophy in the Tragic Age of the Greeks"), 1903 ("We Philologists"), and 1913 (the lectures on "The Preplatonic Philosophers"); and it is doubtful that the existence, let alone contents, of these can have been widely known prior to 1895. (Elisabeth Förster-Nietzsche's biography of her brother, in the first volume from 1895, includes a few extracts of the *philologica* down to 1869 as well as a partial list of their contents; vol. 2.1 [1897] covers later developments down to 1880. Letters from the Bonn-Leipzig-Basel years were sporadically published, the largest collection known to me being the letters from Nietzsche to Ritschl (in *Die neue Rundschau*, 1904 [Wachsmuth 1904]). His other writings preserve only hints about philosophy before Socrates and Plato, and (as we saw) not all of these hints point in the same direction. In sum, Diels' edition of the Presocratics, or one very like it, would have appeared around the time it did even if Nietzsche had never existed. One has to place its appearance in the context of the nineteenth-century collections of fragments, of which Karl Marx's intention to produce an edition of *Democritea* (announced in his dissertation on Democritus and Epicurus in 1841), like Nietzsche's own, is but a symptom (Burkert [forthcoming]; cf. Most 1998). Nietzsche may have given a further impetus and even helped to color the new spate of research after the turn of the century. But if so, then Oehler had every reason to want to control the reception of Nietzsche, by giving the refractory evidence of the latter's philological writings, once they were to appear in print, an appropriate spin. In short, the burst of activity around this period is best seen not as a newly discovered interest sparked by Nietzsche, but either as a continuation in the evolution of the field or, in a few cases at least, as an attempt to align Nietzsche's imagined meanings with an understanding of the Presocratics. In a word, any influence Nietzsche may have had in the field of Presocratic philosophy will have consisted in a misprision and a reduction of the views variously on offer in his published and unpublished writings.

For one example, see Diels 1901, ix, 24, n. to fr. 102, interpolating the thought of "beyond good and evil" into the Greek. This is a purely fortuitous guess, possibly helped along by what might look like Goethe's Nietzscheanism *avant la lettre* (see Hölscher 1979, 160; or *BT* §8: "'an eternal sea, changeful strife, a glowing life,'" which is quoted from Goethe's *Faust*), that is anyway contradicted by Nietzsche's early lecture and by Heraclitus; see "PP," 278: "What is Heraclitean is, on the contrary, the idea that to god everything appears good, while to mankind much appears bad"; further, *KSA*, 12:7[4] (1887), quoted in n. 114 below. On the other hand, the traits of Nietzsche's archaic vision that color his own view of the Presocratics are inherited from classicism's own insights into the archaic age (see below).

61. Most 1995, 108. That is, outside of classical studies. Within them, it was Diels' monumental collection, nearly sold out by December of 1904 (Ehlers 1992, 2:351; cit. by Burkert forthcoming) and already in its fourth edition in 1922, that had "sown the seeds" for a revival of interest in Presocratic thought and culture (Most, 1995, 95).

62. As is Joël's, who makes no bones about this. His archaic period is an example of "archaic romanticism" (*archaische Romantik*)—so the title of the appendix to the second edition of *Der Ursprung der Naturphilosophie* (1906). Similarly, Bäumler 1929, 31–35, 46–47, in Joël's wake.

63. Strictly, one should speak of Nietzsche's views about the *Preplatonic* philosophers. "Preplatonic" is his favored term, both in the lectures on "The Preplatonic Philosophers" (see "PP," §1:214, for a defense of this choice over the term "Presocratics": "Socrates is the last of this series" of "unmixed types") and in "Philosophy in the Tragic Age of the Greeks": the series runs from "Thales to Socrates" ("PTG," §1:808); "with Plato something entirely new begins," whence the term "Preplatonic philosophers," designating "a homogeneous society [of philosophers]" (§2:809).

64. Letter to Rohde of 16 June 1869. A year earlier, Nietzsche describes his expertise as lying in the "sources and methods of literary history," especially as concerns "Hesiod, Plato, Theognis, the elegiac poets, Democritus, Epicurus, Diogenes Laertius, Stobaeus, Suidas [today known as "the Suda"], Athenaeus" (letter to Zarncke, 15 April 1868). His research and publications bear this out. See Behler 1997, who rightly underscores the dazzling and often postclassical breadth of Nietzsche's interests.

65. Two papyrus finds, published in 1891 and 1925, are now generally accepted as vindicating Nietzsche's thesis. See now O'Sullivan 1992; further Vogt 1962, 110; Pöschl 1979, 145 n. 18; Henrichs 1984, 227 n. 48.

66. *KGW*, 2.1:337. Are the sophists classical or Presocratic? They seem to be both. Cf. *WP*, 428: "The Greek culture of the Sophists . . . belongs to the culture of the Periclean age as necessarily as Plato does *not*: it has predecessors in Heraclitus, in Democritus, in the scientific types of the old philosophy," etc.

67. *KGW*, 2.1:337.

68. See *BAW*, 3:319–31, on the prerequisites to literary historical study (discussed in chap. 2 above), and, for example, 3:330 ("c"): one must assess "the present way of valuing and conducting history." In Nietzsche's studies, the methodological problems of reconstruction are drawn out to exasperating aporetic lengths so as to illuminate this very point of reference in the present.

69. *BAW*, 3:15 (from a sketch of an introduction to the Theognis study [1864]).

70. "HCP," 254; cf. p. 256 on the "vacuum" through which one must "leap" to address the Homeric question today.

71. *KSA*, 7:16[39].

72. Cf. Cancik 1995a, 40, on this typological figure in "We Philologists."

73. Bernhardy 1832, 39, calls the modern world a *Spätling*, a latecomer to the same "stock [*Stamm*]" as the ancients. On the nineteenth-century sense of its own epigonality, see *UM*, II (n. 83 below) and Landfester 1979, esp. 159.

74. *BT* §14 and *KSA*, 1:545 on the "anti-Dionysian" "Socratism" operating "even prior to Socrates."

75. See Porter 1995b, 2000.

76. Cf. *WP*, 419 (1885), on the desire for "the *Greek* world": "But what happiness there is already in this will to spirituality, to ghostliness almost! . . . One wants to go back, . . . from the formulas to the Forms," etc.

77. "*Degeneracy* is lurking behind *every* great appearance; the beginning of the end is to be found in every moment" ("WPh," 5[146]; emphases in original). A similar ambivalence and even tragic mourning in Homer is felt in the Romantic tradition; see Schlegel 1958– , 6:27 (and later, Hegel).

78. *Ersann*. Nietzsche's invention explicitly contradicts Müller 1825, 110 (cited in chap. 1, n. 154 above), who argued in more general terms against a similar kind of "concoction [*Ersonnenes*]."

79. "For he no doubt had around him auditors of both races!" (*D*, 189), although *Gattungen* here is closer to "species" or "kind" than to *Geschlecht* ("race"). But cf. earlier: "From the point of view of those who had to suffer the terrible iron oppression of these adventurous *Gewaltmenschen*, or had heard of it from their forefathers, it appeared *evil*," which suggests the existence of a division already at the time of the "bronze/heroic" age. The contemporaneity of these two "ages" is, moreover, affirmed elsewhere in Nietzsche's notes. See nn. 84, 85 below.

80. In the *Daybreak* passage, Nietzsche further confuses/conflates the three ages through a reference to "the terrible *iron* (!) oppression of these *Gewaltmenschen*" of the heroic age (see previous note).

81. This is surely behind the meaning of "genealogy" itself, which Nietzsche calls "grey" and patiently documentary, but by which he means to single out that which is most unattractive about "the moral past"—and present—"of mankind" (*GM*, Pref., 7). See n. 83 below.

82. This is true in a more literal sense as well. On the parallels between the personae of "Homer" and "Hesiod" as mythical fictions in antiquity, along the lines of the essay "Homer and Classical Philology," see *BAW*, 5:197 (Hesiod is the changing product of an "aesthetic judgment" in antiquity), 220–23, 275—notes in which Nietzsche worked out to his satisfaction the problems of Hesiod and Homer simultaneously (and identically).

83. Indeed, Hesiod's invention of the past is an emblem for modern historical culture and its "inborn grey-hairedness," its sense of epigonality (*UM*, II:5, 8). "To

us, the latecomers [*Spätgekommenen*], the last pale offspring of mightier and happier races," Hesiod's "prophesy" appears only all too accurate, too *prophetic*, and the nineteenth century appears only to be its crushing fulfillment. For Hesiod foresaw, in a dark apocalyptic vision, "that men would one day be born already grey-haired and that as soon as he saw that sign Zeus would eradicate this race. Historical culture is indeed a kind of inborn grey-hairedness, and those who bear its mark from childhood must instinctively believe in the *old age of mankind*" (*UM*, II:8).

84. "HCP," 414–15 n. 37. In the same note, Nietzsche explains the logical identity of the gods just named: they are all manifestations of a single *Grundidee* that renders their chronological distinction irrelevant. Cf. "PP," 225: "The contradiction of the Homeric, nobly [*ritterlich*] heroic world and that of the oppressed peasantry in Hesiod has frequently been noticed: these are in any case not two sequential periods of time [lit., "temporal moods"]; the one does not develop out of the other. Both groups share in common the main substance of the wisdom collections [viz., the maxims inherited from a time before Homer and retailed in Hesiod]."

85. See *KSA*, 7:16[27]. "The world of the *Works* [*and Days*]," viz., "the iron age of the present," "is in fact originally identical with the heroic age." Its predecessor is the age of the "Titans."

86. See Lamberton 1988, 116–20, for an exposition of the problem and some of the proposed solutions; and now Most 1997.

87. To be compared is the parallel treatments of Hesiod's *Theogony* by Müller 1925 (see chap. 4 above) and Welcker 1857–63, 1:232–34, 726–28 (containing ideas about Hesiod's creative projection of a past).

88. "HC," 791.

89. Letter to Rohde of 22 July 1872.

90. Pöschl 1979, 150, writes that "Nietzsche showed"—"with historical accuracy"—"how the Olympian divine world of joy developed out of the original Titanic divine world of terror, and that is the *communis opinio*." Whether or not any of this is true, Nietzsche credits Welcker as a precedent, while Rohde would add Schömann and Preller to the list; see Nietzsche's letter to Rohde (cit. previous note): "Welcker has most explicitly spoken about what is pre-Homeric in the Titanomachy in *Mythologie* [sic] I, 262"; Rohde, *Afterphilologie*, in Gründer 1969, 81; cf. Welcker 1857–63, 1:261–91, a section on the Titans entitled "The Myth is Pre-Homeric"; and see discussion in chapter 4 above, nn. 166, 168. K. O. Müller and Welcker (and others) argued for the comparatively late origins of the Olympian deities (these are "new, ideal, reposing on themselves," of whom "Apollo is the clearest example," Welcker 1857–63, 1:243; cf. Müller 1825, 241). Hesiod's *Theogony* provided all the evidence one needed for this claim (Welcker, 1857–63, 1:237). The Titans represent "the idea of a prehistorical period [*Vorzeit*], in which everything was larger and more violent" (ibid., 1:789). They are "frightful" (Müller, 1825, 374) and irrational (ibid., 118). They represent, at least to Hesiod, "the *Urwesen* of nature" (ibid., 373), which points to "a dark, unfathomable *Urgrund*, a First [Ground], in which resided the ker-

nel of all subsequent spiritual and material existence, but which itself was conceived as still completely indefinite, undifferentiated"—namely, "Chaos" (G. F. Schömann, *Des Aeschylus' Gefesselter Prometheus* [1844], 35; cited in Welcker, 1857–63, 297 n. 4), etc. As old as classicism itself, this "new" and superficially anticlassical orthodoxy— and fascination—reverberated even in popular nonclassical literature, for instance in Lange 1866, 4, where Nietzsche could see confirmed how in the main it was traditional local divinities, not the "poeticized" Olympian deities, who were revered by the Greeks: "It was not the resplendent statues by famous artists that captivated the praying masses, but the old, venerable, and misshapenly carved statues hallowed by tradition." The nineteenth-century conception (see Schlesier 1994, 21–32), which goes back to the previous century, is in its outlines identical to Nietzsche's. (See, e.g., Karl Philipp Moritz's *Götterlehre* [1791] 1981, 2:617, 623: "The dark, the earthly, and the deep is the mother of the heavenly, the high, and the luminous," all of which is but "a beautiful dream"; see also Rehm 1951, 118–19.) We have to look elsewhere for the differences.

91. Cf. Welcker 1857–63, 1:233, on "the ideal impulse of our nature, which conjured up the pure, ideal gods," citing Kant and Schiller by way of confirmation: "Schiller even liked to state . . . that art tore mankind out of a state of wildness for the first time. . . . " See Pfeiffer 1960, 173–74, on Welcker's classicism; see previous note; and cf. Rehm 1951, 139, on the *"je sais bien . . . "* logic of classicism: "The exponents of classicism knew very well that art is the joyful transfiguration of the horror of existence. . . . They wanted to believe [in this ideal]—from time to time against their better knowledge." Indeed, the shadows of *Göttertrauer* darkening the bright vision of classicism, which for Rehm are motivated by a vague presentiment of mortality, should be connected to the symptoms just mentioned and reinterpreted as a reflex of a deeper, unwanted knowing on the part of the exponents of classicism, along the lines suggested in chapter 4 above, and in the last two sections of the present chapter—namely, as an expression of the darker aspects of modernity itself. The thematics of death in Winckelmann, exposed by Potts 1994, belong here as well.

92. Hence the simulated threat of *BT* §10: in Aeschylus' *Prometheus*, "the former age of the Titans is once more recovered from Tartarus and brought to the light."

93. Life is, in other words, pitted against itself, cruelty against cruelty, and horror against horror: "The cruelty of victory won is the culmination of life's jubilation" and the horrible defense against horror ("HC," 785).

94. The essay was conceived during the time of the final drafting of *The Birth of Tragedy*; see *KSA*, 7:16[18]–16[46] (summer 1871–spring 1872), and, for example, 16[44], where both projects (as well as, inter alia, a section on "Rhythm" and another on "Philosophy") are imagined to comprise elements of a larger project entitled *The Rebirth of Greece out of the Renewal of the German Spirit*. The paradoxes of "Homer's Contest" are thus lodged at the heart of this larger project, which I take to be consubstantial with everything discussed in the present study. Elsewhere, the notion of the Greek contest is invoked as a calming, classical principle of "measure" ("PP," 272;

cf. ibid., p. 261). What is more, Nietzsche seems unable to decide whether to place justice (viz., "measure," "invisible harmony") or a terrifying injustice at the heart of reality (ibid., 276, 278). Cf. *KSA*, 7:16[15] ("5"): "The poet overcomes the struggle for existence by *idealizing it* [that is, the struggle] *as a free contest*. Here, existence, over which the contest is waged, is an existence [lived out] in praise, in fame" (emphasis added). At issue, in other words, is the purely *symbolic* nature of the contest, which can be read in two ways: either as masking and concealing an underlying cruelty or (what may amount to the same thing) as romanticizing cruelty in all of its manifestations. The consequences of this latter alternative will be developed in the final section below.

95. Remarkably, the first two entries ("WPh," 5[78], [81]) appear in the closest proximity to each other, and indeed on the very same ms. page (in Mette's numeration U, II, 8, p. 162, as Hildegard Cancik-Lindemaier has kindly confirmed *per litt.*). The claims about naïveté and deceptiveness appear in a single note (ibid., 5[70]; cf. 5[115]), as do the claims about cruelty and flexibility ("SWB," 6[12]). The claim about transfigurative powers is contiguous to another about the Greeks' "childish character" ("WPh," 5[84–85]). The remaining quotations are from "SWB," 6[12].

96. *TI*, X:4. As Nietzsche comments, "No one is likely to take a Lobeck seriously for a moment," except those who did. Lobeck's study, *Aglaophamos sive de theologiae mysticae Graecorum causis* (1826), formed part of Nietzsche's secondary readings in the study of Greek religion (cf. "ECP," 410). Further, cf. (e.g.) Ehrenberg 1935, 95–96: "Greek heroism was childish . . . because it extravagantly expended itself . . . in the name of real and unreal values. But the childishness of the Greek man had something heroic about it . . . ; it filled the whole of life with serenity and naturalness and [nonetheless] could rise to the highest heights of serious thought," etc.

97. "SWB," 6[12].

98. "*Unhistorisch*," "WPh," 5[70]; cf. *UM*, II:9, for a similar mirror-effect: "That celebrated little nation of a *not so distant past*—I mean these same Greeks—during the period of their greatest strength kept a tenacious hold on their *unhistorical* sense" (emphases added), whereby the relative proximity of the Greeks reflects, sotto voce, our own ahistoricity. But of course the contradiction of this claim is expected, and it comes in "WPh," 5[36]: the Greeks show a "purity of historical sense"—unless ahistoricalness is this purity.

99. Marquard 1973, 117, discussing the parallel debates in the philosophy of history at the time. Further, Hölscher 1965, 29, on Wilamowitz; and Horstmann 1978, 55, on Wolf.

100. Cf. "WPh," 3[12–13].

101. *HA*, I:262 (1876); emphasis added. Cf. "WPh," 5[146], 78 (1875), on the effects of the "early, panhellenic Homer": "*er verflachte.*" But note how leveling (*verflachen*, "becoming shallow," also "declining intellectually") is lauded elsewhere as a Greek character trait, one that, moreover, typifies the Greeks from Homer to the

end of the second sophistic in later antiquity (*HA*, II:221). As will be seen momentarily (p. 251 below), *Verflachen* is an attribute of modern classicism as well.

102. See chapter 1 above, on "Homer and Classical Philology." Wilamowitz's complaint (in Gründer 1969, 37) that Nietzsche was completely "unfamiliar" with the Homeric question illustrates—in the most charitable reading of this remark—the difficulty of assessing the various stances assumed by Nietzsche.

103. Cf. *KSA*, 7:16[24]; "ECP," 413. In *KSA*, 16[26] the same practices (the ascetic "purification of the ["terrible"] will") are described as an aesthetic (Apollinian) illusion, whereby the will is "transformed into nobler impulses." See n. 115 below.

104. This point is also noted by Cancik 1995a, 100 ("all of his polemics notwithstanding . . . "). The quotation is from "ECP," 370.

105. "PTG," 822: Anaximander; p. 826: Schopenhauer (similarly, "PP," 281; contrast Schopenhauer *W*, 2.2:§46, where Heraclitus is adduced as an example of dark pessimism); p. 830: "harmony" (cf. "PP," 274: "'most beautiful harmony'"); p. 831: "aesthetic."

106. "PTG," 836.

107. "PTG," 807.

108. "PTG," 813: "What drove [Thales] to this ["generalization," "'Everything is water'"] was a metaphysical article of faith which originates in a mystical intuition and which we meet in all philosophies, including the ever renewed attempts to express it [that is, this intuition] in a better way: namely, the proposition, 'Everything is One.'"

109. "In this way, the equivalence, in Heraclitus, of *activity* [*Wirken*] and knowledge, and accordingly [the concept of] a living, moving One [*hen kinoumenon*], stands in a most pointed contrast to the Eleatics, who in allowing *being* and knowledge to coincide were able to construct at best a 'standing, fixed' One [*hen hestos*]. And these two ways of conceiving the One, as fixed or as moving, govern the history of human thought, both Greek and post-Greek" (Bernays 1885, 1:99; cf. ibid., 40–41). Bernays's final generalization is no more drastic than Nietzsche's in the previous note, above. Needless to say, Aristotle's distinction between the monism of the pluralists and that of the Eleatics (whom he calls *henizontes*, or "unifiers") is only superficially similar to Nietzsche's claims. On Bernays generally, see now Glucker and Laks, 1996.

110. See Hölscher 1979, 161 (where the classicism of Heraclitean thought finally supervenes on its *Sturm und Drang* qualities; cf. ibid., 160). Nietzsche names Goethe in the first sentence of "PTG" as a favored model, and cites him freely thereafter.

111. Schleiermacher's view was propagated by H. Ritter in 1829; see Zeller 1856–68, 1:127; and Borsche 1985, 62–63.

112. "PTG," 852, 813, 807. Cf. 806: "Questions about the beginnings of philosophy are entirely meaningless, for in all beginnings what you find is the uncooked, the unformed, the empty, and the ugly, and in all things only the higher levels are

significant." Cf. Schömann's identical language cited in n. 90 above. See further *KSA*, 7:19[62] (1872/73), characterizing Heraclitus' philosophy as a "poetry beyond the limits of experience, an extension of the *mythical instinct* [*Trieb*]." Cf. Zeller 1856–68, 1:463–70, emphasizing the ultimate unity and harmony of Heraclitean reality; that Heraclitus is thereby emblematic of the classical ideal of Greek philosophy and culture as a whole is evident from ibid., 99, 106, 109, etc., where the language of reconciled opposites, applied to the spiritual life of Greece itself, anticipates Heraclitus' system. Perhaps this ought to put in a different light Nietzsche's citation, as it were, of *Zeller's* (!) claim that for Heraclitus "every single thing *becomes* what it is [*jedes einzelne Ding ist, oder* wird *vielmehr, das, was es ist*] only through the ceaseless occurrence of opposites, between which it itself [that is, the thing in question] stands in the middle," like a golden mean (Zeller, ibid., 464–65, citing Greek testimonia that show, by contrast, how much of this is Zeller's own contribution to the picture of Heraclitus that Zeller is seeking to draw).

113. "PTG," 831; "PP," 278, 280, 281, the latter recalling *BT* §24, and likewise borrowed from Bernays' controversial reading of fr. 52 DK (Bernays 1885, 1:58) in the light of a Homeric metaphor for *Apollo*; see also Borsche 1985, 73–76; and for qualifications, Bollack 1996.

114. "PP," 215 (emphasis added). The closing sentences of this lecture give the tenor of both of Nietzsche's treatments of Heraclitus: "At bottom, Heraclitus is the opposite of a pessimist. On the other hand, he is no optimist: for he does not deny the existence of suffering and irrationality. . . . But he soothes himself [*beruhigt sich*] with [the thought of] an eternal cosmic 'destiny' and calls it 'reason,' because it oversees everything; this is genuinely Greek. There is a 'harmony' [in the fate of the universe]" ("PP," 281–82). Similarly, *KSA*, 12:7[4], 259 (1887), on the "moral interpretations" of Plato's predecessors' metaphysics: whereas "in Anaximander the perishing of all things" is viewed "as a punishment for their emancipation from pure being," "in Heraclitus," by contrast, "the regularity of appearances testifies to the morally just character of the whole of becoming."

115. As did, apparently, Pythagoras, who cast his vote with Apollo and the cult of the Muses (Müller 1825, 383). On Heraclitus, see "PP," 265: "*Er betrachtet den dionysischen . . . Kult . . . ganz feindselig und mißverständlich*"; and *KSA*, 7:19[61] (1872/73): "Heraclitus in his hatred for the Dionysian element, also against Pythagoras and polymathy. He is an Apollinian product." Similarly, ibid., 7[56] (1870/71). On Heraclitus' Apollinianism, see "PP," passim, but especially p. 272: "eternal becoming" is both "terrifying and uncanny," most comparable to the feeling of somebody "in the middle of the ocean, or in an earthquake, watching everything move. It took an astonishing degree of strength to translate this effect into its opposite, that of the sublime and of blissful wonderment." (For the classicizing sea-metaphor, cf. pp. 259–60 below; cf. also "PP," 267 for a similar, as it were Apollinian/Dionysian, tension.) This makes a contrast with *BT* §24, where Heraclitus is said to exhibit Dionysian (not Apollinian) tendencies, but then Nietzsche's views of antiquity are, as

I have been arguing, anything but consistent across his works—which ought (as I have also been arguing) to cause us to be wary of any attempt to locate his "conception" of antiquity.

116. *KSA*, 7:3[76]. Cf. "HCP," 251, critiquing the false assurances of "modern man" that the classical ideal, and Greece itself, have been "overcome" (a critique that would apply to a later generation of classicists as well; see below). Cf. Nietzsche's critiques of "the reigning view about the Greeks" and about the Preplatonic philosophers in particular, namely that they were "clear, sober, harmonic practitioners" of philosophy or, conversely, that they were "only aesthetically minded, indulging in artistic enthusiasms of all kinds"—these are what "the unlearned phantast" today imagines his Greeks to have been, but not Nietzsche ("PP," 211; "PTG," 805). The astonishing paradox of these criticisms is that Nietzsche's Presocratics are a mixture of both sets of traits in purer, but no less criticizable, form.

117. "PTG," 856: "[He] made a leap, closed his eyes, and said . . . " (said of Anaxagoras' claim concerning the infinity of substances). Cf. 822–23: Heraclitus "denied being in general [*leugnete überhaupt das Sein*]," on the promptings of his "aesthetic" imagination of reality (p. 833). The phrase is lifted from Zeller 1856–58, 1:458: "*Während . . . Parmenides das Werden geläugnet hatte, . . . läugnet Heraklit umgekehrt das Sein*"; this mutual relativization is implicit in Nietzsche's account, which embroiders freely upon Zeller (among others).

118. See *TI*, III:2, for the later critique, which is hard to square with the view that, "like Heraclitus, Nietzsche believed that 'all is one'" (Hershbell and Nimis 1979, 23, where a few pages later (p. 28) the *TI* passage is cited as evidence for the claim). Cf. *WP*, 412, for further criticisms of Heraclitus.

119. *KSA*, 7:3[74].

120. For a reading of Nietzsche's archaic period not as a (counter-)myth but as a "historical epoch" that doubles as a "historical model," see Cancik 1995a, 48–49. Cf. ibid., 48, for a list of evident deficiencies in Nietzsche's archaic period, so conceived, to which should be added the sheer lack of consistency in Nietzsche's depiction of it. In any case, this doubling is a typical trait of classicism. See below.

121. Humboldt 1969d, 92 (III:188). Humboldt speaks of *Menschenstamm* rather than *Rasse*. I am aware that to render his thought in terms of "racial" purity may seem a confusion governed by hindsight, a "foregone conclusion" of sorts (see Bernstein 1994). On the other hand, I am not convinced that the sense of ethnic belonging found here excludes the idea of racial identity or even biological identity. *Stamm*, after all, can mean "race" in addition to "stem, stock, breed, clan, tribe," etc. Compare Humboldt's language in the passage quoted: "Wir sehen auf sie [sc., die Griechen], wie auf einen aus edlerem und reinerem Stoffe geformten Menschenstamm, auf die Jahrhunderte ihrer Blüthe, wie auf eine Zeit zurück, in welcher die noch frischer aus der Werkstatt der Schöpfungskräfte hervorgegangene Natur die Verwandtschaft mit ihnen noch unvermischter erhalten hatte." Accordingly, when I speak of "racial" purity here and below I intend the loosely knit views of classicist

ideology that amount to a kind of "racialism," and which no doubt contributed to making the global and pernicious expressions of "racism" more thinkable later on, but which nonetheless remain distinct from these developed forms of prejudice.

122. Winckelmann 1972, 158.

123. Winckelmann 1995, 149, 151.

124. Cf. Winckelmann 1972, 150, explicitly claiming indeterminacy (*Unbezeichnung*) as a distinctive feature of ideal beauty, and—interestingly—as analogous to the "Epicurean" indifference to particulars. It is as if Winckelmann were here fusing a piece of Epicurean-like logic (sketching out a kind of prolepsis, or "general concept," of beauty) with an attested element of Epicurean psychology (tranquility as a source of pleasure; see n. 150 below). The attribution of indeterminacy as a feature of beauty is, however, uniquely Winckelmann's, not found in Epicurus—or in Bellori or Lomazo for that matter (see in Panofsky 1993, 122–39, pace Panofsky, ibid., 117, n. 261; though cf. Plato, *Symposium* 210a–212b, where the pressure to idealize beyond the particular is intense to the point of vagueness, if not indeterminacy). Is Winckelmann registering something, nonetheless, about the reality of Greek art? Remarking on the variability of the kouros-type, an ideal, freestanding male statue-form from the Greek archaic period, Stewart 1997, 67, makes a nice point: "Clearly, no single example was felt to be definitive." Not only was the ideal embodied in the kouros "far from universally manifest"; its very lack of determinacy suggests "that men felt considerable anxiety about whether [this ideal of *kosmos*, or decorum] existed at all, or if it did, what it consisted of" (ibid., 68). Needless to say, Winckelmann's anxiety will have been differently motivated, though formally tied to the same problematic of representing an ideal of manhood and beauty.

125. Barkan 1991, 72.

126. Compare Humboldt's remarks, without even a hint of apology: "By 'ancients' I mean exclusively the Greeks, and by 'Greeks' often exclusively the Athenians," Humboldt would remark, speaking for an entire generation. And less abashedly: "Insofar as 'ancient' means 'ideal,' the Romans partake of this only insofar as it is impossible to distinguish them from the Greeks" (Humboldt 1969a, 9 [I:265], 1969c, 66 [VII:610]). On the persistence of this prejudice, and for a recent attempt to challenge it, see Feeney 1997.

127. Humboldt to Schiller, 16 November 1795; Humboldt 1969d, 95 (III:191).

128. Humboldt 1903–36, 1:411–29 ("Pindar" [1795]).

129. Humboldt 1969a, 22 (I:279); emphasis added; cf. id. 1969d, 92 (III:188), quoted in n. 121 above.

130. Humboldt (1969b, 25 [III:136]) could write, "Greece, feelings of melancholy," with a delicious ambiguity (cf. id. 1969d, 93 [I:189], on modern "mourning" and depression at the thought of Greece; and below, on the melancholy exhibited by the Greeks themselves). On Winckelmann's own "dark" views in this respect, see Zeller 1955, 226; and more generally, Rehm 1951.

131. Humboldt 1969b, 43–45 (III:152–154); and id. 1969d, 94 (III:190).

132. "The Greeks are like the genius, *simple, simplex*: they are for that reason immortal teachers. Their institutions, their products, bear the impress of the simple, so that one often marvels at how unique they are in this regard. To our astonishment they show themselves to be as *deep* as they are simple" ("ECP," 437; emphasis in original).

133. Cf. *WP*, 419 (1885).

134. See Elias 1997 [1939], 1:89–131; and Lepenies 1998 [1969], 76–141, and passim. For the qualification, see Eley 1996. The speculation about posturing is my own and would obviously need to be examined further.

135. That the idea of flight from social reality had currency by Nietzsche's time is plain from "WPh," 3[13], [16] (*"Flight from reality* to the ancients: isn't the conception of antiquity thereby falsified?"); see chapter 4 n. 133 above. Elias' description of the eighteenth-century *Bilderbürgertum* mentality (previous note) has a nearly verbatim echo in Reinhardt 1966, 343, where, however, the subject is philology at the end of the next century: "If the *fin de siècle* is readily depicted as pessimistic, overrefined, feeble, aestheticizing, decadent, one shouldn't forget that ultimately in it, too, there was an escape available—in productivity." When Reinhardt goes on in the next breath to say, "How differently did the adept behave towards what is classical about the 'fine sciences' [viz., the liberal arts] in the age of Goethe!" he shows how much in the grip of a wishful ideal he is. The history of mentalities is indeed a history of misunderstandings and fantasies. Such misunderstandings may well have a structural function, insofar as they are part of "the more insidious process of ideological structuration" (Eley 1996, 41) that goes into a culture's self-definition, beyond the reach of conscious manipulation.

136. Humboldt 1960–81, 1:388 (II:12). Cf. his remarks on the "necessary" fiction of classical antiquity, cited on p. 193 above.

137. Nisbet 1985, 6; cf. Hatfield 1964, 12; and Martin 1996, 145 (the operative verb in all three cases being "suppresses").

138. In Nisbet 1985, 42; trans. mod.; German text as in Pfotenhauer et al. 1995, 30. Compare the sequel: "The physical pain [*Der Schmerz des Cörpers*] and spiritual greatness [*die Grösse der Seele*] are diffused *with equal intensity* throughout his entire frame [*durch den gantzen Bau der Figur*], and held, as it were, in balance" (emphasis added).

139. Winckelmann 1972 [1764], 166–67: "Laocoön is a picture of the most deeply felt pain," etc.; that picture is juxtaposed with Niobe's "indescribable . . . terror before death," with Philoctetes' agonies, with the madness and despair of Ajax, and with the vengeful anger of Medea (ibid.).

140. Winckelmann 1995, 165.

141. Again, Guido Reni's painting of the archangel Michael in Rome (in Nisbet 1985, 44) evokes a quiet grandeur that is meaningless without the contrasting narra-

tive background of violent and wrothful vengeance (which is left, Winckelmann observes, to an implication for the viewer). On the dynamic tensions within Winckelmann's ideal, see Baeumer 1973; Potts 1994.

142. The translation of "despite [Laocoön's] most violent torments" (Nisbet), standard for *bey dem heftigsten Leiden* (thus, too, Silk and Stern 1981, 5, as well as the translations by Hatfield 1964, 11, and by Elfriede Heyer and Roger C. Norton [La Salle, 1987] 33), suppresses the coefficiency of pain and serenity. Serenity is born literally "in the midst of" torment and is unthinkable in the latter's absence.

143. See Rehm 1951, 147, with n. 63 for examples of melancholy culled from Winckelmann's descriptions of classical Greeks.

144. Humboldt 1969b, 44 (III:153); emphasis added.

145. The painting discussed (in Nisbet 1985, 44–45) is the Sistine Madonna, which is marked by Winckelmann with traits of "serenity," "nobility," "sublimity," and "ecstasy [*Entzückung*]," though to be sure no pain.

146. In Winckelmann's account of Laocoön in *Thoughts on Imitation*, the "frame" (*Figur*) through which pain and spiritual greatness are diffused (see n. 138 above) is not equivalent to Laocoön's body; it is the artistic form that organizes the pain of a body and the greatness of a soul into a supersensuous, unified, and balanced totality. The body thus becomes a "figure." But this ideal is prefigured by a division between the *Unter-Leib* and the suprasensible face.

147. In Nisbet 1985, 43. Cf. ibid.: "The artist put him in a position [literally, "an action" (*eine Aktion*)] as close to the state of rest as was compatible with his agony."

148. The first of these images is from a 1759 description of Apollo Belvedere (Winckelmann 1847, 2:324); the second is from his *Geschichte der Kunst* (Winckelmann 1972, 152; cf. p. 162).

149. To be sure, the allusion is to Schopenhauer, *W*, 1.2, §63 (cf. *BT* §1), which is not to say that Schopenhauer did not know Winckelmann too (cf. Löhneysen 1987). The conceit may just be generically classical (cf. Goethe's poem "Auf dem See"). But underlying everything else are Epicurean, or rather atomistic, allusions (Lucretius, *On the Nature of Things*, bk. 2.1–2; cf. Bornmann 1984, 180 with n. 13; Rehm 1951; ; Zeller 1955, 226–35; Hatfield 1964, 12–13). Cf. further *BAW*, 3:327 (1867/68), where Democritus' ethics are described, after Cicero (*De finibus* 5.8), as capable of producing a "feeling of security" and "the sea-like calm of the soul."

150. Winckelmann 1972, 161; cf. p. 150. For the argument, see Zeller 1955, 226–35, who insists, more so than Rehm 1951, on the specifically Epicurean hue of the Winckelmannian ideal. To their arguments should be added two further considerations: Winckelmann's appeal to Epicurus and (implicitly) to his theory of the *prolēpsis*, or general notion or concept, of beauty (see n. 124 above); and a seeming allusion (Winckelmann 1972, 158) to the process by which such notions are formed, as it were through the precession of simulacra ([*die*] *von Gott ausfließenden und zu Gott führenden Schönheit*); the language closely echoes Epicurus' own attested account of the formation of the concept of God (see Long and Sedley 1987, 1:141–42).

151. As in *GS*, 370; or in *NCW*, 6; cf. *BGE*, 7; and *BT*, "Attempt," 1: "The Epicureans' resolve *against* pessimism—a mere precaution of the afflicted?"; cf. ibid., 4. Friedrich Albert Lange had similarly contrasted the "harmless serenity [*Heiterkeit*]" of Epicurus with the sublime imaginative flights of Lucretius (Lange 1866, 37), and Nietzsche in his *Democritea* concurs (see chap. 2 n. 5 above).

152. "DW," 560; *KSA*, 11:35[73] (1885), where Epicurean divinity, freed from anxiety and pain, is equated with the Overman, "the transfigurer of existence," and with Dionysus; similarly, *KSA*, 10:7[21] (1883).

153. Letter to Fuchs, end of August 1888.

154. Cf. *GS*, 96: "[The truly engaged speaker] is at the height of his passions when he resists the flood of his emotions and virtually derides it; only then does his spirit emerge fully from its hiding place—a logical, mocking, playful, and yet awesome spirit"; and, e.g., *HA*, I:221. See further next note.

155. "We presuppose the Dionysian understanding"; "the wisdom of Dionysus is [of the two] the more intimately familiar form for us"; "the Apollinian is *hard for us to understand*" (*KSA*, 7:9[10], [92]). We might recall that what Nietzsche resists in Euripides and in Plato's rhapsode *Ion* in *The Birth of Tragedy* is the way in which they are given over to unrestrained pathos and emotionality: "Here [in the *Ion*] we no longer remark anything of the epic absorption in mere appearance, or of the dispassionate coolness of the true actor. . . . Euripides is the actor whose heart beats, whose hair stands on end" (*BT* §12). For the anachronistic appeal of Dionysian pathos, see chapters 3, 4 above; this chapter, n. 163 below and Porter 2000.

156. See n. 145 above; Zeller 1955, 226, on the recurrent terms of Winckelmann's own aesthetic vocabulary, *Rührung, Wollust, Entzückung, außer sich, glückselig*. Dionysian "sensuality" (*Wollust*), "rapture" (*Verzückung*), "ecstasy" (*Entzückung*), exorbitation (*ausser sich* [*sein*]), etc. (*BT* §§2, 7, 8, 17), are no different from this.

157. *WP*, 799.

158. See Winckelmann, in Nisbet 1985, 43: "In the case of Laocoön, his pain, if depicted in isolation, would have been *parenthyrsus*," that is, excessively and falsely Bacchic ("too fiery and wild"; trans. mod.). *Parenthyrsus* is a literary-critical term transmitted by the author of *On the Sublime* (3.5). Winckelmann's aesthetic is consciously Longinian, and its prerequisites are both pathos and grandeur (two key elements of the sublime). See Baeumer 1973, esp. pp. 63, 67. Baeumer's attempt to correlate this contrast with two types of ideal beauty in Winckelmann, exemplified by Bacchus and Apollo, is to my mind unconvincing.

159. In Winckelmann's reception, this proximity will be lost, and the contrast will be strongly enforced (as in Humboldt 1960–81 1:304–8 [I:342–45]).

160. Schelling 1856–61, 2.3:512; cit. in Rehm 1951, 162. Whether Nietzsche knew Schelling directly is another question (see Baeumer 1976, 186). Nietzsche's knowledge of Schelling's philosophy of religion may have been filtered through the philological tradition. See "ECP," 410, where Schelling's influence on Creuzer is named.

161. Feuerbach 1855, for example, 256–57. Cf. ibid., 264, where he defends a female observer of the Belvedere Apollo, whose gushing enthusiasms Feuerbach calls a "genuinely ancient" and not a "romantically modern" response to the statue; the observer is a figure for the feminized (viz., Winckelmann's) response to a statue whose spiritual authenticity Feuerbach defends: the work may be a late Roman copy, but it displays an "unfalsified Greek spirit," and the ecstatic response to the work is "a de facto proof" of this authenticity (cf. ibid., 366). See also n. 124 in chapter 3 above.

162. See Rehm 1951, 162, and passim.

163. See Joël 1905, 305, 314 (on Friedrich Schlegel), 331, and passim (on the Romantic heritage in Nietzsche). Joël's point is not just that Nietzsche is a continuator of the Romantic view of Greece, but, more devastatingly, that he is a continuator of their peculiar form of anachronism: for all his "Graecomania," "I can scarcely find a passage that justifies his study of the Greeks from the [historical] particularity of the Greeks" (ibid., p. 280). Never was a truer statement made. Joël knows enough to cite Schlegel's *mot* about discovering oneself in the Greeks (p. 193 above): "They were [for Nietzsche] merely the glittering medium of his self-understanding" (ibid., 314–15). Nobody else can have been much fooled either. See further Bäumler 1929, 34–35: "But what do [Nietzsche's] Greeks have to do with a phenomenon that everywhere betrays its origins in a modern, musically intoxicated soul? . . . With his refined psychology and his rational conception of myth, Nietzsche made no specific contribution to the illumination of Greek religion and art. The Dionysian-Apollinian contrast, conceived as it is here, is a general one, hardly specifically Greek, and is everywhere so used today." See further Andler 1920–31, 2: 219–74 on Nietzsche's "sources" in *The Birth of Tragedy* (the Schlegels, A. Feuerbach, Creuzer, K. O. Müller, Welcker, Bachofen, Franz Liszt); and Baeumer 1976 (e.g., p. 188: "The many-sided Dionysian tradition ends with Bachofen, and with him the connection is established with Nietzsche's alleged discovery of the Dionysian and the Apollinian"). That Nietzsche's Dionysus is not Greek goes without saying, but cf. ibid., 165 n. 2. See further Porter 1999, 171–72. Hence, too, Nietzsche's identification of Germanness with Dionysus merely makes (more) explicit the grounds of the earlier fascination. Needless to say (but it needs nonetheless to be said), all this goes strongly against the arguments that champion Nietzsche's insights into the authentic Greek character, of the sort mentioned in n. 7 above. For all his exoticism, Dionysus was consistently figured as arriving in Greece from the north, both prior to and after Nietzsche. Cf. Ernst Samter, *Die Religion der Griechen*, 2d ed., 1925 [1914], 30–31: "Dionysus came from the north, from Thrace, to Greece. The adoration of the northern [*nordisch*] god diverged greatly from the style of divine worship in Greece," cit. in Schlesier 1994, 214–15; and see ibid. on this "Germanization of Dionysus" at the turn of the twentieth century, a tendency that was anyway built into the Dorian myth (as in the case of K. O. Müller; cf. the first sentence of the introduction to Müller 1844 [1:1, and generally ibid., pp. 1–17]). Cf. further Karl Blind in Schliemann 1884, 355,

357–60 (tracing the identification—the "Teutonic kinship of the Thrakians"—back to Fischart and Voss in the previous century, and wondering rhetorically, "Do not these martial, musical, Bacchic, and philosophical traits point strongly to the Teutonic stock?"); Ehrenberg 1935, 93–94: "Was the contest form [*das Agonale*]," characteristic of the Greeks and preeminently of the Dorians, "thereby 'Nordic'?"; Ehrenberg's own answer is equivocal.

164. *HA*, I:221.

165. Feuerbach 1855, 5–9; here, p. 9. Of course, this overinvestment was what gave Winckelmann his following in the previous generation.

166. See, for example, Moritz's *Götterlehre* (1791) and its depiction of the Titanic struggles of the gods: "Power [*Macht*] is insurgent against power—one of the sublimest objects that the visual arts ever made use of" (Moritz 1981, 2:621).

167. For an argument that the Dionysian metaphysics of *The Birth of Tragedy* is in fact a further *Apollinian* illusion, see Porter, 2000.

168. "WPh," 5[146], p. 79; Nietzsche's emphasis. Cf. ibid., 5[118]: "The panhellenic Homer derives pleasure from the frivolity of the gods; but it is astonishing how he can turn around and restore dignity to them. This enormous capacity for lifting themselves up [*dieses ungeheure Sich-Aufschwingen*] is, however, [characteristically] Greek." The capacity is anything but a sign of *Tatenlust*: it is simply the capacity for denial, dressed up as its opposite (while Nietzsche's account repeats the denial it describes). This gesture is patented by classicism. Cf. Humboldt's advice that we understand our relationship to the Greeks by analogy with the way in which they understood their relationship to the gods:

> The gods wore human shapes, like them, and were formed from human stuff. The same passions, pleasure, and pain, stirred their breasts; also the effort and hardship of life were not strange to them; hatred and persecution ran mightily through the halls of the domiciles of the gods. . . . No differently do we find in Greece all the unevennesses of life: not only the afflictions that befall individuals and nations, but also the powerful passions, excesses, and even crudenesses of unbridled human nature. But as all those darker colors were melted and dissolved by the singular brilliance of cloudless Olympus, so too was there something in the Greeks that doesn't let their spirits ever actually sink, that wipes away the hardness of earthly existence, that transforms the frothing-over of energy into a luxurious game, and that mitigates the iron pressure of fate, rendering it a gentle seriousness. (Humboldt 1969d, 93–94 [III:189–90])

169. "WPh," 5[146].

170. *HA*, II:220. Cf. *GM*, II:23, on similar "expedients." The earlier note speaks only of what is "human," prior to Nietzsche's discovery of the later formula for the same ("all too human"). Cf. further "WPh," 5[36], on the way in which the Greeks manage to "ennoble jealousy," and below, on Prometheus.

171. Collected in Jaeger 1931. The conference is a virtual fulfillment of Nietz-

sche's statement of the need for just such a convocation (letter to Rohde of 18 June 1872); its location in Naumburg, the home of Nietzsche and of Schulpforte, the preparatory school of the greatest living philologist and his greatest nemesis, has a telling ambiguity to it as well. Schadewaldt 1931 frequently evokes the spirit of Nietzsche, against Wilamowitz, without naming either. Nor is his endorsement of Nietzsche unqualified. In the face of a classical object, be it Sophocles or the Parthenon, "our eye is seized and led round by a liberating power, which I would like to call the power of the surface. Because no swirling compulsion expects us to dip into tortuous depths and no alluring magic of the unfathomable nears us in an all-too-human way, *we remain who we are in the face of that form, which is entirely itself*" (ibid., 15–16; emphasis added). It may be that Schadewaldt cannot endorse Nietzsche fully because Nietzsche's Apollinian Dionysianism is in itself so contradictory, but Schadewaldt's tautologies here are stunning and above all defensive: they are meant at least in part to ward off an unwarranted transport of classicism into "the realm of general aesthetic theory" (ibid., 17), and thus in a direction away from its original historicity. Schadewaldt's careful revision of Nietzsche would merit closer study.

172. Humanist gymnasial teachers around the turn of the century often enlisted Nietzsche in their cause (see Cancik 1987), but this they could do only on a highly selective reading of him. The Third Humanism has its grass roots in this movement, as did the Third Reich's appropriation of Nietzsche for its own purposes. On Jaeger's rehabilitation of Nietzsche as a humanist forebear (his 1919 *Antrittsvorlesung* at Basel needs to be reread in this light too), see Landfester 1995, 18–19, n. 24.

173. Reinhardt 1966, 345, 344.

174. Nor was Reinhardt's relationship to humanism entirely one of ease or free of conflict; see Hölscher 1995, 78.

175. Humboldt 1903–36, 1:411 ("Pindar"), where, however, "historical" factors amount to ethnological speculations no firmer than those advanced by K. O. Müller (see below); ibid., 8:134–35 (introduction to his translation of the *Agamemnon*); and Humboldt 1969a, 11–12 (I:267), insisting that the distinctive character of the poetry of the Greeks came from its cultural settings ("symposia, festivals, sacrifices"), and so their poetry forever "bore the mark of its historical, not really aesthetic, origins." Humboldt's desires for an authenticated and ideal antiquity are a constant in his career. His early cowerings before Wolf's philological rigor are well known (see Stadler 1959, 57; and Humboldt's letter to Wolf from 1794, cited in n. 107 of chapter 4 above). Here, in the case of the *Agamemnon*, Humboldt may be sensing the intimidating presence of Gottfried Hermann breathing over his shoulder (Hermann provided the text, a brief apparatus, and a control on the translation). Humboldt's later view of history reimports these ambivalences into the nature of historical truth itself; see "Über die Aufgabe des Geschichtsschreibers" (1821), in Humboldt 1960–81, 1:585–606; translated as "On the Historian's Task," in *History and Theory*, 6.1 (1967), 57–71.

176. Opinions on Winckelmann's historicist impulses vary. See Pfeiffer 1960,

172; Silk and Stern 1981, 11; Mansfeld 1985, 195 n. 89; Himmelmann 1985; Potts 1994, 8 (who puts the problem well). Interestingly, Winckelmann depreciates the bulk of the ancient reports on Greek art as "merely historical" at the conclusion of his *Geschichte der Kunst* (1972, 394).

177. Wolf's and Boeckh's positions on hermeneutical understanding were touched on in the previous chapter. Boeckh, too, reckons philology to be a *Humanitätsstudium* (Boeckh 1874, 14). See also ibid., 114, where "feeling" precedes and confirms historical analysis: "Once one recognizes [a given] historical connection" in a poem by Pindar—that is, once one has already had a long familiarity (*sich eingelebt*) with the poet (p. 112)—"the poem comes together in a perfect unity and gains in color and force"; needless to say, the premise of this humanistic hermeneutics is of the unrivaled "nobility" of Greco-Roman antiquity as a paradigm and ideal of "humanity" (pp. 25, 256–57). Nietzsche replicates the assumptions of this kind in his "Encyclopedia," but adds another, namely that such understanding "possibly" rests on an "unconscious construction of parallels [*unbewußtes Parallelisieren*]" ("ECP," 373). Nietzsche's entire pedagogical program as worked out in the lectures is designed to secure such an unconscious parallelism. The redundancy of this program (its replication of the inevitable) is its irony. See p. 183 above.

178. "HCP," 252.

179. See Schadewaldt 1931, who puts his finger on this problem with a subtle reproval of the historicists' denial of their hidden classicism, while he simultaneously attempts to reclaim a certain historicity for classicism: "The boundaries [of classicism] comprehend the aesthetic realm, but they also run past this into the depths of human existence as a whole and then lose themselves in the broad realm of historical life in its concrete reality" (1951, 15). Further, Hölscher 1965, 70: "In the intellectual world of the *Gründerzeit* [of the Bismarckian era], positivism and idealism enter into a marriage unforeseen by anyone." See also Grafton 1991, 23–46 on the parallel "interpretive schizophrenia" (p. 37) found among Renaissance humanists.

180. Significantly, Humboldt sided with Goethe against the Romantics; see Humboldt 1969c, 71–72 (VII:615–16); Hatfield 1964, 203. See Stadler 1959, 68, on the Sturm und Drang features of the later Humboldt, with attempted nuances. I concur with Hölscher 1965, 69, where classicism and romanticism are said to share essential features that contradict their conventional contrast (e.g., a "conception of antiquity as an age of naïveté and perfection separated from our own world, and in whose simplicity and grandeur the affected and narrow-minded present has to renew and heal itself," etc.). When Humboldt in his *Agamemnon* preface speaks about the "horrible grandeur," "passion," and "fearfulness" of the play (Humboldt 1903–36, 8:122), is he resorting to a German typology or is he describing objective features of the drama? One might as well ask whether melancholy is a possible trait of Greek psychology. Its identification is tricky, and as such comes late (see S. H. Butcher, "The Melancholy of the Greeks," in id., *Some Aspects of the Greek Genius* (London, 1891); and Helmut Flashar, *Melancholie und Melancholiker in den medi-*

zinischen Theorien der Antike (Berlin 1966); Theophrastus calls Heraclitus a "melancholic" (DL 9.6), and Nietzsche reasons that Democritus must be reckoned one too, like all philosophers (citing the Aristotelian work *Problems*; *BAW*, 4:85)—that is, when Democritus isn't laughing at mankind's woes. But irrespective of such questions, Humboldt's difficulties arise when he tries to account for the totality of these disparate traits by way of idealist solutions (as discussed in the foregoing chapter).

181. Müller is often portrayed as though he were a historicist, but his historical fantasies aside (Pfeiffer 1976, 187), he often puts one in mind of Humboldt. Compare the following: "What do we finally want from history? . . . I believe that the knowledge of antiquity *elevates* us and *humanizes* us for no better reason than that it puts before our eyes a foreign humanity [*Menschheit*] in its whole, sound, and fully perfected [*in sich vollendeten*] existence" (Müller 1825, 207; emphasis added). Müller is equally capable of Winckelmannian insights, for instance when he describes the "simplicity" and "quiet grandeur" of Doric architecture (Müller 1844, 3:253). Cf., further, K. O. Müller, reacting to Welcker's assumption of the editorship of Rheinisches Museum in 1831: the journal "will now have a warmer feeling for the totality of the study of antiquity than it did under Niebuhr" (cit. by Gossman 1983, 74).

182. Mansfeld 1986, 45. See Pfeiffer 1961, 18–19, for the more conventional view.

183. Cf. "WPh," 3[4].

184. Theodor Mommsen, *Römische Geschichte* (1854–56), Leipzig; here, 3:301 (emphasis added).

185. See Landfester 1988; Momigliano 1994, 151, on Droysen's Prussianization of Macedon; and ibid., 154, on Droysen's residual classicism.

186. Theodor Mommsen, *Juristische Schriften*, 3 vols. (Berlin, 1905–7), 3:513; cit. in Landfester 1979, 168.

187. Pfeiffer 1976, 182 (pinpointing Bursian 1883 as the culprit for the *Sach-* and *Sprachphilologie* contrast); id. 1960, 172, where the opposition between humanism and historicism is called "in multiple ways a mirage." Ibid., 173, for the justification of *humanitas* nonetheless; and id. 1976, 190 (the final paragraph of this work): "In the middle of the nineteenth century there was a definite break. No longer was humanism to be the driving force," and "the forces of historicism and realism" took over. Opting for a historicizing humanism, Pfeiffer reaffirms rather than heals the antagonisms of the tradition. Nietzsche knows this traditional idiom and ridicules it as well: "*Wort-* und *Sach-philologie*—a stupid conflict" ("WPh," 8, 5[106] [1875]; similarly, *BAW*, 5:476 ("*Nachbericht*" to p. 288, l. 9 [1869]).

188. Wilamowitz, 1972, 6:79. He had already stated in 1897 that the antiquity sponsored by classicism and made by it into "an absolutely binding model [*Vorbild*] for art and life" was a "delusion" (1926, 2:11–12). Cf. further his claim from 1900: "The historical view has replaced the aesthetic view" (cit. in Paulsen 1919–21, 2:742).

189. Wilamowitz to Schadewaldt, June 1931, reproduced in Calder 1975, 455.

190. Wilamowitz 1921, 1; similarly id. 1913b, 105 (1892). See Pfeiffer 1960, 172–73, on the epithet's vicissitudes.

191. "Vorwort" to Wilamowitz 1880.

192. See Wilamowitz 1921, 1: "The goal is the pure, pleasurable [almost, "cheering": *beglückende*] perception of the object of understanding in its truth and beauty. Because life, which we are struggling to understand, is a unity, so too is our discipline a unity." The invocation of Boeckh's name alongside Hermann's in the "Vorwort" cited in the previous note might be thought to signal a reconciliation of the two strands of philology, historicism and classicism; in fact, the "Vorwort" is merely reaffirming the historicist aspirations of classicism (see pp. 266–68 and n. 179 above).

193. He complains about Bergk, for instance, that "every individual object detains him, which is why his history of Greek literature falls apart into unconnected pieces" (Wilamowitz 1921, 63).

194. See Schadewaldt 1931 (sotto voce); Pfeiffer 1961, 19–20; and 1960 [1931–32], 269–76; Horstmann 1978, 56; Landfester 1979; Momigliano 1980; Calder 1981, 43; Mansfeld 1985 ("inner conflict," p. 187); and 1986; Henrichs 1995, 453. See further the documentation provided by Calder 1981.

195. Nietzsche's point, exactly (*BT* §12). Aeschylus is the gifted unconscious artist, Euripides the struggling rationalist and no longer classical, for both Nietzsche and Wilamowitz (who, interestingly, is echoing A. W. Schlegel, as it were against his own better judgment; see Wilamowitz in Gründer 1969, 48). On the conventional nature of this judgment and its classicist bias, see Behler 1986, passim, and (e.g.) 365.

196. In Gründer 1969, 32 and 37 (Winckelmann and Schiller); 51 (the tragedians); 134 ("eternal beauty"). These early declarations of classicism are curiously passed over in the literature (Hölscher 1965, 14, is an exception).

197. See Wilamowitz in Gründer 1969, 48. See further Rohde's defense in Gründer 1969, 89, 92, 94, attempting to show that Nietzsche is not quite on the lunatic fringe as Wilamowitz declares him to be; Rohde appeals to Welcker and Müller as predecessors. Nietzsche could be critical of both figures, whether in "ECP" (see chap. 4 above) or in later notes (e.g., "WPh," 5[114], attacking both philologists); but then, he could be critical of everybody.

198. Beyond the two unexpected points of convergence mentioned in chapters 3 and 4 above (on the evolution of Greek rhythm and of Greek religion), further shared traits are cultural elitism, philology by personality, methodological irrationalism (intuitionism, bordering on mysticism), powerful interests in Greek irrationalism, and philhellenism. See further Landfester 1979, Momigliano 1980; Mansfeld 1985, 1986; Canfora 1995, 65; Gigante 1997, 320. There are also uncanny and haunting echoes, as when Wilamowitz 1913b, 104, starts off a paragraph "*Und wir Philologen?*" (a common refrain, in fact: cf. id., 1891, 2, 3, 4; id., 1895, 1:257).

199. In Gustav Droysen, *Johann Gustav Droysen* (Leipzig, 1910), 1:89; cit. by Reinhardt 1966, 342. Droysen goes on to add that "the age of philology is over": it must cede to historical study. See Pfeiffer 1961, 19; id. 1976, 188–90.

200. Ernst Curtius, *Gesammelte Abhandlungen*, vol. 2 (Berlin, 1894), "Vorwort," in which he invokes the great tradition of Boeckh, Welcker, and K. O. Müller, from whom "I have learned to grasp all aspects of classical antiquity as an indivisible unity." But cf. Bérard (1894, 9), writing in the same year: "The generous philhellenism of 1820 is no longer in fashion. But one can say that the sentiment has not greatly changed: the poet's dream has remained our own, *o! ubi campi, / Spercheosque et virginibus bacchata Lacaenis / Taygeta!*, and the reality often appears to us only through this dream. We can only conceive of Greece as the country of heroes and gods. Under porticos of white marble, in front of a temple with noble lines, among the crowd of immortal statues, we imagine a people as divine as its gods," etc.

201. Lloyd-Jones 1976, 13 (= id. 1982, 178). Cf. Pfeiffer 1960, 173, reaffirming the organic totality of classical studies in a Boeckhian vein.

202. Wilamowitz 1926, 2:12 [1897]: "A hundred years of historical research has swept aside [the "delusion" of classicism], even if the uninstructed go on arguing for and against classicism." That humanism was very much alive in the Wilhelmian era school systems at exactly this time was undeniable; see Cancik 1987, esp. 71.

203. Wilamowitz 1891, 2–4; id., 1895, 2:257–58; 1913b [1891], 2–3; id. [1892], 105, 109, 111–12; 1926 [1908], 2:245, revising the 1900 claim: "The tradition is dead," not the ideal; hence, "our job is to bring the past back to life" (cf. also 1921, 1). The list, which flows from both his academic and his more popularly aimed writings, goes on and on, as Robert Fowler reminds me (*per litt.*). A nicely compressed example, which takes the prize, and which I owe to R. F., is the following: "Only once one is rid of classicism can one clearly recognize for the first time what is truly classical and therefore incomparable and eternal" (Wilamowitz 1929, 203).

204. See the closing comment by Stephen Owen in Ziolkowski 1990, 78: "Questioning ["words honestly and bravely . . . by the very procedures of philology"], we come to a level that is more fundamental than the last, but at which the criteria of validation that philology uses to stabilize its questioning are no longer adequate." This is part of "the peculiar experience of not being able to come securely home to the word." Similarly, Reinhardt 1966, 335: "Why not rather speak in terms of grandness, certainty, beauty? . . . Because every discipline, and so too classical philology, not only has to know about its limits, but also needs an atmosphere around its limits; and this [atmosphere] is not created through enthusiasm alone, but at times also through a questionableness [*ein Fragwürdiges*] that attaches to it [that is, the discipline itself]." Nietzsche's philology, as we have seen, is driven by this concern with the questionableness of philology and its limits—but in a less polite and more questionable form.

205. I decided upon the phrase "open secret" before discovering that Schadewaldt had used it himself in a slightly different sense (Schadewaldt 1931, 15). It is likely that Schadewaldt is in turn paying homage to Hugo von Hoffmannsthal, who two years earlier had described "the spirit of classical antiquity" as a *"numen"* that is "so large that no single temple can comprehend it, although several are dedicated to

it"; at the same time this spirit is "an intellectual world pregnant with life within ourselves—our true inner Orient, our open, incorruptible secret" (1928, 101; Schadewaldt's essay originally appeared in the same journal, *Die Antike*, in 1930). This divul-
gence of "our true inner Orient" is as questionable as some of the open forms of
racial imagery to be discussed in a moment.

206. Schadewaldt 1931, 21; cf. Reinhardt 1966, 344, on "the noble continuation
of the old ideal in up to date historical garb," where Ernst Curtius is rightly named
as an example of what Reinhardt wrongly takes to be an exceptional tendency.

207. In Gründer 1969, 74. Rohde's language and his metaphors are strikingly
reminiscent of Nietzsche's from around this same time and shortly afterward (Cf.
"HCP," 267, *BT* §§3, 20, and "WPh," 7[1], cit. p. 210 above). See Wilamowitz's preface to his *Griechisches Lesebuch I*, 12th ed. (Berlin, 1929), iv, for a de facto refutation.

208. See Pfeiffer's penetrating comment (1960, 172): "Nietzsche . . . ruthlessly
held the mirror up to philology, wherein its face, otherwise so full of dignity, is evilly
distorted." The present tense betrays the actuality of Nietzsche's revelation. Wilamowitz's intuitionism is a hidden constant in his own philology. See his letter to a
friend, Bormann, from 1869, in which Wilamowitz affirms the value of the "intuitive" as opposed to the "historical" method: "It is just this [former] approach that
comprehends the essence of the thing and—if it is successful—brings out from
within through intuition far more perfect results than we, who only believe what we
know, can bring into it from without" (in Calder 1970, 156). As Calder, who discovered this letter, says, "The decisive question, never posed, is why approval of Bormann in 1869 was not extended to Nietzsche in 1872" (Calder 1983b, 116). One factor, surely, is the one I just mentioned: Nietzsche is a grotesque reflection of
philology's uncomfortable but necessary flirtation with the irrational dimensions of
"intuition" (compare the opening sentence of *The Birth of Tragedy*)—its "leap of
faith," whenever confronted with the spectacle (or specter) of antiquity.

209. "We must also admit to ourselves that we are in the end always dependent
on the shaping powers of the imagination . . . , for the tradition offers up only ruins
that do not join into a whole. The tradition is dead: our task is to resuscitate the life
of the past. We know that shades speak only once they have drunk their fill of blood,
and the spirits we summon demand the blood of our hearts. We give it gladly. But if
they give answer, then something of us has entered into them, something strange
that has to come back out again, something that has to come out again for the sake of
truth." So Wilamowitz 1926, 2:245 (cf. id., 1891, 2, and 1895, 1:257), inspired by,
and possibly offering quiet homage to, the ghost of Nietzsche (and, incidentally, reiterating Rohde's point and some of his language from *Afterphilologie* just quoted). Cf.
HA, II:126: "It is only if we bestow our soul upon [the works of earlier times] that
they can continue to live: it is only *our* blood that constrains them to speak to *us*. A
truly 'historical' rendition would be ghostly speech before ghosts." What is most
uncanny about this coincidence is not Wilamowitz's reanimation of Nietzsche's
ghost, but Nietzsche's seemingly proleptic allusion to *Wilamowitz*. As "a truly 'his-

torical' rendition" suggests, Nietzsche probably had Wilamowitz's charge of ahis-
toricism from 1872 in mind when he wrote the later passage. But Winckelmann's
closing image in his *Geschichte der Kunst* (1972, 393) of "people who want to get to
know ghosts and believe they see them, where there is in fact nothing," an erotically
charged metaphor for the modern recuperation of the classical past, is also worth
bearing in mind; as is Ritschl's talk about "enlivening and animating the dead matter"
of antiquity—"with the penetrating Idea" (1866–79, 5:3 [1833]).

210. "In these [Dionysian] festivals nature reveals an as it were sentimental trait"
that evokes in the celebrants a "yearning lamentation for an irretrievable loss" (*BT*
§2; trans. mod.). Cf. §§8, 19, 21, naming the contemporary sources of this sentimentality. See also Silk and Stern 1981, 164: "Nietzsche's Olympians (like 'the
Apolline' in general) are in essence no more 'rational' than his Dionysus." Cf. Wilamowitz, who in his memoirs holds (albeit by way of self-justification) that it is
Apollo, not Dionysus, who is the ecstatic god: "Apollo, not Dionysus, inspires the
seer and the Sibyl to clairvoyant madness, and it is the flute's music, not the god's
cithara, that awakens ecstasy and that is supreme in his Delphic cult" (Wilamowitz
1929, 130).

211. Cf. "WPh," 5[20], where the goal is *"unabashedly to bring to light the unreason
in human affairs"* generally (Nietzsche's emphasis); cf. ibid., 5[30].

212. "SWB," 6[1].

213. Cf. *BT* §23 (addressing the needs of the present): "Only a horizon defined
by myths completes and unifies a whole cultural movement."

214. Welcker 1857–63, 2:274.

215. The association of Dionysus and the "Titan's nature" is anticipated by
Creuzer 1836–43, 4:117 (cf. 4:196).

216. Obtaining a satisfactory representation (in the end, a woodcutting by
Leopold Rau) cost Nietzsche precious months and a publication date of 1872 instead
of 1871 for *The Birth of Tragedy*. See Brandt 1991 for documentation of this episode.

217. *GM*, I:11; I:5. Rawson (1969, 30) greatly underestimates such continuities:
"Nor does any stage in his winding intellectual journey ever bring him back to
Sparta; neither the doctrine of superman, nor . . . the Dionysiac element." The
reverse is in fact true.

218. See Römer 1985; Reibnitz 1992, 246–49, with bibliography; and now Cancik 1995a, 122–33.

219. Curtius' personal devotion to Müller is well known; see Christ 1996, 132.
The essay "Der Wettkampf" was first published in Curtius's *Göttinger Festreden*
(1864); some of its central tenets are developed in the first volume of his *Griechische
Geschichte* (1857–67). See further Janz 1978–79, 1:498–99; and Rohde to Nietzsche,
22 April 1871, where Curtius' collection is cited as an instance of deluded "cheerful"
classicism. Nietzsche and his friends took no prisoners. Nietzsche may well have
arrived at an agonistic view of culture independently of Curtius, no doubt inspired by

Schopenhauer's existentialism, although the idea of culture as a struggle is surely in the air. See *BAW*, 3:324 (1867/68): "What else is history if not the struggle [*Kampf*] among endlessly different and countless interests for their existence?"; and cf. *BAW*, 2:434 (quoting from Mundt 1856) on the "struggle for existence" in society, with a critical reference to socialism and communism.

220. See Gutha-Thakurta 1995, 66 (discussing Orientalist perceptions of India): "The context was provided by the persisting European obsession with the biblical origins of history, and the resulting theory of all nations of the world springing from a single land. For the belief was then strongly rooted among antiquarians and classical scholars, whether their preference was for the Egyptians or for the Hebrews as the oldest nation. [In this way,] Europe began to locate its own distant lineage and prehistory" in the various cradles of civilization. I owe this to Sally Humphreys.

221. Curtius 1875, 136, 138–41. See, for example, p. 138 on the Greeks as "state-builders": "They were and remain, in art and science, the lawgivers until today," a trait that "left them with no repose [*Ruhe*]." It would be a mistake to read this last trait as an anti-Winckelmannian touch; see below. This fantasy later appealed to Alfred Bäumler, who located Nietzsche's deepest contribution to the world not in his Dionysian mythology but in his "discovery of the *agon* ["contest"]" as something tied to the brutal reality of the will to power ("*diese Tatseite des Nietzeschen Wesens*"; 1929, 37). Further developments of this tendency include Carl Schmitt's *Der Begriff des Politischen* (1932).

222. Ibid., 144.

223. Ibid.

224. Ibid., 143–45.

225. See Žižek 1997, 102–4, on the binding effect of such ideological postures, especially when they take the form of a "dematerialization" of one's commitments, as here: "The dematerialization, however, only strengthens its hold."

226. For one assessment of Curtius' obsession with (in his own words) "the national character of the Germans" and of his fascination first with the Prussian monarchy and later with Bismarck, see Christ 1996, 25–27, 123–43; and see ibid., 131 n. 42, citing Bismarck's encouraging response to Curtius (letter of 4 December 1869). Christ fails to discuss the essay "Der Wettkampf" with its Aryanism, and his criticisms of Müller (pp. 19–20) are limited to the latter's "one-sidedly idealizing approach."

227. Pace Janni 1968. Cf. Müller to C. O. M. Elvers, beginning of December 1830 (in Kern 1936, 130; trans. Gossman 1983, 79, n. 142): "If only the wretched half-knowledge and liberal way of reasoning had not taken hold of every one in Germany too. When I hear the philistines holding forth in the *Zivilklub* and I imagine these people taking part in elections and assemblies—God preserve our old governments. Constitutional wisdom seems to me a great folly."

228. See generally Rawson 1969, and now Christ 1996. This divided view of

social "antagonism" has a particular history in German culture, and it is productive of divided fantasies about individuals and the state, as in Nietzsche's later writings (Porter 1998, 167) and in Hegel's early *Schrift über die Reichsverfassung* (1801).

229. Wolf 1869, 2:817; further defenses (and exclusions—Asia and Africa) follow on the next pages. The achievements of the Hebrews in prose are "merely natural, scarcely on the level of genuine art," and the Near East remains alien to "European tastes" up until the point when it is finally "Hellenized." Even then, the region remains intractable: the only unity it can produce is that of "a very heterogeneous whole"(!) (ibid., 818–19); cf. also id., 1831, 33–34; and the troubled defense of these exclusions by Ritschl, 1866–79, 5:4–5. Wolf's opposition offers a complete confirmation of Elias' observation that, in contrast to the early French concept of "civilization," which is processual, dynamic, and open-ended, the German concept of "culture," which takes shape in the eighteenth century, "marks off," it "lays stress on national differences, on the peculiarities of groups," and thus gives expression to anxieties about identity at home (Elias 1997, 1:91–92, 113). Most treatments of the history of philology from within the discipline pass over these issues. See Bernhardy 1832, 19–20, celebrating Wolf's foundational achievement, but without batting an eyelash at the exclusions it entailed. Brief exceptions are Flashar 1979, 24; Gossman 1983, 22 n. 41 (on Jacob Burckhardt); and Cancik 1995a, 135. More generally, Said 1978 (where, however, Wolf and Humboldt receive only a bare mention) and Bernal 1987 (see n. 241 below). It would be interesting to consider what impact if any Wolf's dim view of Hebrew literature may have had upon his likely adoption, in his analysis of the Homeric texts, of J. G. Eichhorn's methods for reconstructing the biblical texts (on which, see Grafton 1981; and cf. Momigliano 1980, 347).

230. "*Unser Alterthum ist, als ein Ganzes gedacht, gleichsam eine in sich geschlossene Welt,*" etc. (Wolf, ibid., 2:892).

231. Müller 1844, 3:4. The reality of Dorian colonizations abroad has to be suppressed to achieve some of this contrast, as Müller's earliest critics were quick to note.

232. See chapter 4 above.

233. Wolf 1869, 2 (*Darstellung*):877; cf. ibid., 802. See also Balibar, "Racism and Nationalism," in Balibar and Wallerstein 1991, esp. 56–61, 63–64.

234. Humboldt 1960–81, 5:215. Pace Poliakov 1987, 115.

235. Humboldt 1969d, 92 (III:188); for the full passage, see n. 121 above. Cf. further Humboldt to Welcker in Humboldt 1859, 79, 102. Sweet 1978–80, 2:208, cites another letter by Humboldt, but not that to Goethe, this time from 1816 (to his wife, Caroline, herself an outspoken anti-Semite): "I like the Jews *en masse; en détail,* I very carefully avoid them." Poliakov 1987, 115, surprisingly overlooks such evidence; but not so Arendt 1968, 30.

236. "ECP," 390.

237. See, for example, "HC," 785, on the pre-Homeric features of Greece, which surprisingly turn out not to be "specifically Hellenic: in them [that is, in its

pre-Homericness], Greece comes into contact with India and with the Orient generally."

238. As in 1809, when he interceded on behalf of the Prussian Jewry. See "Über den Entwurf zu einer neuen Konstitution für die Juden," in Humboldt 1960–81, 4:95–112 (X:97–115). Emanicpation was, however, a conflicted business, hovering between assimilationism and expediency. See further Arendt 1968, 28–35; Berding 1988, 25–31.

239. Humboldt's ambivalence toward Jews and his anti-Semitic prejudices (which go beyond mere assimilationism) are discussed by his biographer Sweet 1978–80, 2:74, 207–8. See Potts 1994, 160–62, for a balanced discussion of Winckelmann.

240. See Römer 1985, covering developments in linguistic philosophy down to 1945. On the origins and vicissitudes of what has been called "modern anti-Semitism," see Berding 1988. If by this Berding means something like racial as opposed to religious anti-Semitism, the conventional distinction (see ibid., 42, 85–86), in what follows I am speaking of the complex of factors that come together at the end of the eighteenth century and that make possible remarks like the one by Humboldt just quoted (viz., insistence on racial purity, exclusionary demarcations—some subtler than others—in a disciplinary object of study, national identifications, classicist-humanist ideology, and so on). Revulsion at Christian strictures at this time in no way precludes Christian-sounding hostility to Jews, any more than it precludes the displacement of religiosity onto another spiritual, if paganistic, level (namely, the worship of Greece itself). Another well-known exception is Theodor Mommsen's and J. G. Droysen's open opponency to Heinrich von Treitschke, a prominent historian and publicist, and a determined Biskmarckian, who in 1879 in a Berlin academic journal ventilated the popular view that "the Jews are our misfortune!" But neither did this prevent Mommsen from promoting the German *Machtstaat* through his philology (see Berding 1988, 114–115) or from publishing views about the superiority of the "Indo-Germanic" races (see Welcker 1857–63, 1:117 n. 2). See further Momigliano 1980, passim, and esp. 347, for an incisive portrait of Wilamowitz, who in this respect, too, follows the humanist paradigm: "Wilamowitz wanted to close off the Greeks, to isolate them in an ideal sphere. . . . But it was understood that the Jews remained Jews and the Greeks Greeks" (citing *Der Glaube der Hellenen* [1931–32] 2:323); and see Canfora 1995, 61–89, for further documentation. Compare Wilamowitz's Jewish pupil Paul Maas in his study on Greek meter: "The many Semitic proper names of the Bible could be given only an arbitrary quantitative value [in Greek transliteration], and this must have helped to blunt people's feeling for quantity," the original and pure Greek rhythmic sensibility (Maas 1962, 14). Not even the mitigating qualifications at the end of the same section in Maas' study can erase the effect of this beginning, which places the degeneracy of classical linguistic culture squarely within the familiar matrix of a Nietzschean genealogy (see *KSA*, 7:3[86] quoted on p. 280). Finally, see Hermann Diels to Eduard Zeller, letter of 20 January 1906 (in Ehlers 1992, 2:370); and Diels to Usener, 17 November 1892 (ibid., 1:436).

The first of these letters associates a Nietzschean student movement against Catholics and Protestants with Zionism: "*dahinter steckt natürlich auch wieder Zion!*" Tarring Nietzsche and Jewish-mindedness with the same brush is a not uncommon reaction to Nietzsche at this time, in part due to his complicated and (evidently) objectionable politics of anti-anti-Semitism (see Porter 1998, 171–72 n. 36), by no means the only stance he successfully deployed. The "naturalness" of Diels' assumption and its easy communicability, however, are remarkable. It is likewise astonishing to note how easily the Müllerian myth of racial purity (which does not in itself constitute anti-Semitism) can be reaffirmed in more recent scholarship. For one example, see Otto Regenbogen, "Griechische Gegenwart," in *Kleine Schriften*, ed. Franz Dirlmeier (Munich, 1961), 525–26, repeating all the clichés, including the ethos of the contest; likewise, Ehrenberg 1935 (e.g., 87, 93, 95–96). A related carryover is the celebration of what Müller and others call *Tatenlust*, the image of pure, unalloyed, virtually primordial "activity"; see Fränkel 1976 [1st ed., 1962], 88, 91, 93, on "Homeric man" (Porter 1998, 171 n. 35).

241. Here I would single out Bernal 1987, whose treatment, while laudable in some respects, is all too monolithic and schematic. His contrasts are too starkly drawn, and he seems to forget that what he calls the "ancient model" is itself an imaginary construction (a point also made by Assmann 1997, 13), and not free by any means of the mirage of purity that hovers over the so-called Aryanist model. In a word, Bernal has no notion of the ways in which disavowal is a factor in ideological illusions. For a critique of Bernal, see Blok 1995, who tends, however, to tar Bernal's arguments with the brush of his own and Müller's confusions, fancifulness, or sloppiness (see ibid., p. 711). The only viable argument in Bernal, the general case against the racialized philology in the eighteenth and nineteenth centuries (cf. ibid., 720 [citing Momigliano], 722–23) and its connections with nationalist sentiments (a missing ingredient in the article), still stands. Nor is it either convincing or true to claim that "Müller himself was not interested in race but rather in religion" (ibid., 723). See nn. 240 and 265.

242. *KSA*, 7:3[86]; cf. ibid., 3[73] ("III"), [76].

243. See *GM*, III:26, where Nietzsche lunges at the "latest speculators in idealism, the anti-Semites, who today roll their eyes in a Christian-Aryan-bourgeois manner"; and see Porter 1998, 169 n. 32.

244. *Dolon* and congeners: Hesiod, *Theogony*, vv. 540, 550, 560, 562; Pandora: *ibid.*, vv. 570–611; "sufferings and sorrow": passim. The essays and drafts preparatory to *The Birth of Tragedy* follow Hesiod. In "Socrates and Greek Tragedy," Nietzsche has Aeschylus enhance the "truly typical image of the Greek, the Odysseus-figure, into the magnificent, crafty and noble (*listig-edlen*) Prometheus-character" (*KSA*, 1:534). Cf. "DW," 565 (= 593) for a less happy account of Prometheus than that given by *BT*; and *KSA*, 7:38[3] (1874): "What would have happened if Prometheus at Macone hadn't been crafty [*listig*]!" Elsewhere, guilt is more readily admitted to lie within reach of Greek conceptuality: see "ECP," 413: "The concept of *guilt*. Whence

the expiatory festivals. Main content of the mysteries." In other words, here, at least, guilt is a central feature of the religious mentality that produces Dionysianism, as a kind of utopic compensation (cf. *KGW*, 2.2:370–71). A further set of notes (*KGW*, 2.2: 347–72), stemming from lectures on the *Certamen* that Nietzsche delivered five times between 1869 and 1873 and then a final time in 1876, are equally telling. Here we find all the missing elements. Prometheus' theft of fire is called "the main deception [*Hauptbetrug*]," one that reflects a "feeling of guilt" on the part of mankind. Probing further, Nietzsche deduces that the feeling felt is "twofold": it consists both in a "consciousness of guilt" and in a "consciousness of higher culture"; and "Prometheus arose out of" this divided feeling, as its mythical expression—or else its deflection (365; cf. 366, 368). In a word, guilt and its disavowal lie at the origins of culture. Curiously enough, Nietzsche takes elements of the myth to be "neither Hellenic nor Indogermanic [but] *Boeotian* Heliconian," viz., indigenous (Nietzsche's emphasis). For later parallels, see *GM*, II:23 (p. 264 above); *GS*, 300.

245. Cf. *GS*, 135, 300.

246. "Apollo wants to grant repose to individuals precisely by drawing boundaries between them," and yet "the Titanic impulse to become, as it were, the Atlas for all [*sic*] individuals, carrying them on a broad back, higher and higher, farther and farther, is what the Promethean and the Dionysian have in common" (*BT* §9); cf. §1 ("Now the slave is a free man" and the "barriers . . . between man and man are broken"). Cf. further "GrS," 767, where the essentialness of slavery to culture is stated to be a "truth" that is "the vulture that gnaws at the liver of the Promethean patron of culture. The misery of toiling mankind has to be increased to make possible the production of the world of art by a small number of Olympian individuals." There is no pretense to universalist concessions here.

247. *BT* §4.

248. *KSA*, 7:7[18] (1870/71). The essay "The Greek State," which grew out of an earlier draft of *BT*, realizes these implications and generalizes them for Greek culture as a whole.

249. *KSA*, 7:38[1–7] (late 1874). There, Prometheus makes a gift of life to mankind, namely "the very old Pandora," who seems to represent "history and memory," viz., these things in the form of myth, and ultimately the myth of Greek culture itself; mankind is revived, as is Zeus ("out of a *fable* of the myth")—"fabulous [*fabelhafte*] Greece seduces one to life"—and Prometheus (presumably it is he, but it could be Zeus) later ejaculates, "Ah, unlucky me! I've become a myth!" These Kafkaesque notes sketch a stunning Moebius-strip paradox. They seem to have been intended as a skeleton to a future play. A very early obsession (see n. 42 above), Prometheus in this form strikingly anticipates *GS*, 300.

250. For a sweeping study of this myth in Europe, see Poliakov 1987, and within the tradition of nineteenth-century comparative philology, see further Oliender 1989.

251. Goethe's "Promethean poem . . . in its basic idea is the veritable hymn of impiety" (*BT* §9).

252. Nietzsche's interpretation of Prometheus returns to the aesthetics of denial of the *Goethezeit*: disguised as a lament on the death of beauty (Nietzsche's "twilight of the [Olympian] gods"), the myth symbolizes an anxious reassertion of the classical ideal in the face of its patent falsehood; see Rehm 1951, 146–48, on Stolberg, Schiller, and others and their Promethean ideology. Nietzsche brings out these anxieties in a different, and more objectionable, form. Curtius (1875) calls his privileged Aryan race the *Japetiden* (sons of Iapetos). This etymology was a standard component of the Aryan myth, and not only in Germany; see Poliakov 1987, 272, and passim. It is also found in Welcker (1857–63, 1:754).

253. See Hoffmannstahl in n. 205 above.

254. Welcker is keen not to credit the supposition that the "Semites" are the "*Ur-fathers of the Greeks*" (1857–63, 1:760–61); cf. ibid., 117: "The Aryan *Stamm* in its spirit and endowments does not rank below that of the Semites."

255. "WPh," 5[198] ("The [Greek] coasts [were] trimmed with a Semitic strip"; "much Mongolian material in the fantastic portions of the *Odyssey*"); cf. ibid., 2[5], "doubting" linguistic arguments about "nationality": "Where could there ever have existed autochthonous races!" On Nietzsche's dialogue with contemporary racist sources, of which Curtius 1857–63, 1:117 (denying the Phoenician presence in Greece) is surely one typical instance, see Cancik 1995a, 122–33; and id. 1997.

256. "WPh," 5[114]; "PTG," 807.

257. See *GM*, I:8–9, 16; *A*, 24; Porter 1998, 171 n. 36.

258. See "WPh," 6[27], where the Persian wars are called a "national disaster" precisely because they *unleashed* nationalist, patriotic feelings that culminated in "the spiritual rule of Athens."

259. Silk and Stern 1981, 356–57, hint at the right problem but from the wrong direction: "More interesting [than Nietzsche's distasteful Aryanism] is the question how Nietzsche got himself landed with a set of concepts so much closer to a Judaeo-Christian than a Greek view of life" in *BT* §9. Cf. also "GrS," 771–72, on the self-destructive frenzy of Greek contest culture: "So overloaded is this instinct among the Greeks that it continually starts to rage against itself afresh and clamps its teeth into its own flesh. This bloody jealousy from city to city, from party to party, this murderous desire for those little wars, . . . whither does this *naive barbarity* of the Greek state point, whence does it receive its pardon before the tribunal of eternal justice?" (emphasis added). The metaphor of self-laceration is an allusion to the Schopenhauerian agonies of individuation and their delusive appearances (cf. ibid., 765: *Wahnbilder*) but also to Nietzsche's critique of the same (see Porter 2000).

260. Wilamowitz does not even comment on the question in his pamphlets against *The Birth of Tragedy*, although he brushes past this very passage from §9 (in Gründer 1969, 33). The reason may not lie far off: he follows the Aryanist paradigm himself, in all probability in the wake of Welcker. See ibid., 133 (*Zweites Stück*): "This artistic tendency is again only a pure expression of the Greek spirit, which, in place of the formless natural powers that it brought with itself from its Aryan homeland,

created for itself ethical, i.e., humanely feeling, beings for gods; that is, instead of the fetishes of the Semites, or the *monstra* of India and Egypt, the Greek spirit endowed images of supernatural beings with divinity only by means of a humanity that was elevated to eternal beauty." Kaufmann tries to whisk away the problem with a terse note to his translation of the passage: "After his emancipation from Wagner, Nietzsche came to consider the terms 'Aryan' and 'Semitic' more problematic." Silk and Stern 1981, 356, find "this whole racial vocabulary . . . too obvious to need emphasizing." More nuanced is Reibnitz 1991, 249. Harshly critical of Nietzsche's "approval" of "the racist theories of his time" is Cancik 1995a (here, 63; *BT* §9, is discussed on pp. 63, 128, and 135); and id. 1997. My own view is closer to that of Behler 1997, 526–29.

261. Most recently by Reibnitz 1992. Wilamowitz (in Gründer 1969, 33 n. 6) was the first to perceive the importance of Müller for *The Birth of Tragedy*. See also Andler 1920–31, 2:244–53; and Henrichs 1986, 394. One feature that has not been sufficiently stressed is the communication within the antagonism between Dionysus and Apollo that structures both Müller's and Nietzsche's accounts. Cf. Müller's "Eleusinian" article from 1840: "The worship of the *chthonic gods* [explicitly identified with Dionysus] stands opposed to that of the *Olympian* [identified with Apollo] in a way found in no other religion, *even though much points to an original unity and totality in which the one [kind] essentially belonged to the other*. The bulk of the history of the religious belief of the Greek nation rests on the unity, the separate developments, the predominance of the one or the other element, and the influences that are thereby exercised by the one element upon its opposite" (Müller 1847–48, 2:288–91; here 288–89; first two emphases Müller's). Now compare Nietzsche: "These two different tendencies run parallel to each other, for the most part openly at variance; and they continually incite each other to new and more powerful births, which perpetuate an antagonism [*Kampf*], only superficially reconciled by the common term 'art'; till eventually, by a metaphysical miracle of the Hellenic 'will,' they appear coupled with each other" in tragedy (*BT* §1). On a closer look, this "antagonism" in both Müller and Nietzsche proves not merely to exist between the two impulses, but to be built into their essential (and problematic) oneness, and ultimately to be internal to each element. See next note; and more generally, Porter 2000.

262. Cf. *KSA*, 7:16[22]: "The contest unfetters the individual; and it simultaneously restrains him according to eternal laws." See "GrS," 771 (n. 259 above).

263. Cf. *KSA*, 7:16[20]: "The gloomy atmosphere of the Boeotian peasant [is] to be used in the characterization of the pre-Homeric [world]." In other words, or so it would seem, Nietzsche will draw on the depressive mentality of Hesiod (the Boeotian peasant) to account for the pre-Homeric dimension (its *invention*). Cf. Theognis' fantasy of pure racial lineage, a more wishful but no less "gloomy" and pessimistic projection.

264. Müller 1844, 2:309 (emphases added). Compare the following: "Wir werden, um dieses Gegensatzes willen, den Cultus des Apollon einen dualistischen nennen, der die Gottheit, *nicht als das ganze Sein erfüllend, sondern als im Widerstreit wirk-*

end . . . wobei stets ein Theil der Wesenwelt als dunkel und unrein zurückgestellt wird" (ibid.; emphases added). This dualism is deeply imprinted in the nature of Müller's vision of Greece. It corresponds to a Dionysian/Apollinian contrast that in Müller assumes different forms: in the contrast between dark, moody, and mystery-worshipping Minyans and the classical Dorians (who cannot ever fully repress a strain of darkness within themselves); in the framework of his history of religion, which divides neatly along dark, melancholic, morbid Chthonic and cheerful and life-affirming Olympian lines (coordinated with a contrast between Dionysus and Apollo), but which ultimately confesses to the insolubility of the two poles (see previous note); and here, in the "dualism" of Apollo. Cf. *BT* §1: Apollo's "eye *must* be 'sunlike,' as befits his origin; even when it is angry and distempered it is still hallowed by beautiful illusion," viz., the illusion of Apollo's cheerful purity. Again, denial is written into this image, which is calqued on Müller's and others' visions of Olympian serenity.

265. We might say that for Müller classicism and questions of race stand in a relationship of fatal antagonism. This is true in a very obvious way. The classical ideal is literally distributed over both "tribes": Dorians (Sparta) represent the purest form of Greek ethnicity, but Ionians (Athens), whom Müller ambivalently admires, represent the decline of *Doriertum* (in this zero-sum scenario) and another set of virtues (see Müller 1844, 2:194–99). Finally, while Olympian and chthonic deities are currently seen to exhibit functions that are not neatly polarized let alone systematic and that can frequently overlap (see Schlesier 1994, 32, 175–76), what Müller's account reflects is not this highly complex Greek religious reality but a resistance to any such view of it from within the then reigning classicizing paradigm.

266. Curtius 1875, 136. This topos is repeated in milder form in Ehrenberg 1935: contest culture was the source of Greek flourishing and decay (e.g., p. 78).

267. Ibid., 137. To be sure, the dangers and frailty of power and of flourishing were acknowledged in antiquity (e.g., in Herodotus' moral history and in Greek popular morality), but the contradictions of Curtius' theory in terms of literally "restless" contest energies (cf. ibid., 138) are distinctively modern (and bound up, for example, with the aesthetics of classicism and its contradictions). Cf. H. G. Wells' remark from 1894: "In the case of every other predominant animal the world has ever seen, we repeat, the hour of its complete ascendancy has been the beginning of its decline"; or Francis Galton's view from the 1860s and '70s that "the struggle for existence seems to me to spoil and not improve our breed" (cit. in Pick 1989, 158, 192). See Pick, passim, on this well-documented nineteenth-century anxiety.

268. "HC," 785.

269. Ibid. Contest culture is a defense against this kind of nausea: "The nobler culture takes its first victory crown from the altar of the expiation of murder" (ibid.), just as it is a defense against (its own) cruelty: "If we take the contest away from Greek life, we immediately glimpse into that pre-Homeric abyss of a horrifying fierceness of hatred and of pleasure in destruction" (p. 791).

270. A similar picture of archaic insecurity and guilt was canonically drawn by E. R. Dodds' *The Greeks and the Irrational* (1951).

271. Cf. "WPh," 5[146]; p. 178: "The agonistic principle [and practice] is at the same time a danger to every development; it overstimulates the drive to create.—The best-case scenario of development [occurs] when several geniuses keep one another in check." This thought is presented in the context of another about the "degeneracy" lurking behind every expression of power (n. 77 above).

272. See Porter 1999.

273. See above on the Presocratics and, for example, "PP," 281 ("At bottom, [Heraclitus] is the opposite of a pessimist"), or compare *EH*, V, "The Birth of Tragedy," 1: "Precisely tragedy is proof that the Greeks were *no* pessimists," a claim that any careful reading of *The Birth of Tragedy* will bear out (and as has long been acknowledged). Achilles "longs for a continuation of life," and the effect of tragedy is to "reverse" the wisdom of Silenus, not to confirm it (*BT* §3, passim). See, for example, Pöschl 1979, 149, contrasting Burckhardt's pessimism with Nietzsche's optimism. Nietzsche plays with the positionalities of pessimism and optimism, ultimately rejecting both (see Porter, 2000). On Boeckh, see next note.

274. See Wolf 1869, 2:819–20 (*Darstellung*): "The first of these peoples [viz., the Greeks] was also the first on earth for whom the impulse [*Trieb*] to cultivate itself in manifold ways arose out of its innermost intellectual and emotional needs, and for whom a well-ordered sphere of arts and sciences resulted from their passionate inclination to hurry [*forteilen*] from one object to another," thereby "lifting human life to a selfless employment of its higher potencies [*Kräfte*]." The presence of "passionate" in this classicizing context should no longer cause surprise, while the distracted tempo of the search conceals the anxiety we have been discussing. Cf. Humboldt 1969d, 111 (III:206) on the distracted, nearly absent-minded Greeks: "The Greek was inspired by yearning. His intentional and mundane doings [*Treiben*] were often quite scattered and fragmented, but from that same yearning burst forth, along the way and unbidden, heavenly and enchanting blossoms." "Restlessness" is recognized by Nietzsche to be a characteristically modern trait; see *HA*, I:221 (n. 282 below) and "OF," 745: today's scholar "looks for consolation in hasty, ceaseless activity, under the cover of which he seeks to conceal himself *from himself*" (emphasis added). The occurrence of restless activity is virtually coded in the tradition in which Nietzsche operates. On the nineteenth-century thematics of energy and dissipation, see (e.g.) Rabinbach 1982; Most 1989; and Pick 1989. Jacob Burckhardt's recognition that the inadequacies of the Greek gods reflect the gods (and so too the Greeks') *own* felt inadequacies (*Griechische Kulturgeschichte*; cit. by Rehm 1951, 178) is a restatement of eighteenth-century classicizing thought (see Rehm 1951, 176, with 356 n. 125; and the discussion of Humboldt in chap. 4 above). One surprising link in the chain was doubtless August Boeckh, who could hold in 1817 that "the Greeks, amid the luster of art and the blossoming of freedom, were unhappier than most people believe" (Boeckh 1886, 1:710). See Momigliano 1994, 48–49, on Burckhardt and Boeckh.

Momigliano fails, however, to connect up this strand of thinking with the darker moods of the earlier classicism, let alone with those of Ernst Curtius' "serene" classicism (ibid.). Boeckh's remark, which concludes the first volume of his massive study, shows how a pessimistic view of ancient society is scarcely in itself a reliable index of modern pessimism. If the Greeks "bore the seed of their decline within themselves," this merely goes to show how "the formation of larger state entities in constitutional monarchies, wherein the passions of individuals are allowed less scope," have made possible greater constitutional stability, security, peacefulness, etc., all of which now "appears [to us] as a substantial progress in the development of civilized [*gebildet*] humankind" (ibid., 710–11).

275. See, for example, Humboldt 1969b. I hope to discuss this elsewhere.

276. Humboldt endorses the same model as Müller (Greeks at their purest are Dorians), and he runs into the same contradictions. Humboldt's Pindar is typically Dorian: in addition to his classicizing traits (the "tranquility, cheerfulness, and radiating sublimity" of his poetry), he betrays signs of an "awkward gravity," austerely religious and "almost Hebraic" "seriousness, dignity, and awe," "reverence for heroes of the distant past," "bitterness," and "harshness," undeniable "appetite for riches," and he also knows *Knabenliebe* (Humboldt [1795] 1903–36, 1:422; 415). Schlegel is their common predecessor (*Von den Schulen der griechischen Poesie* [1794], e.g., "The Dorians were so to speak the older, purer, most representative [*nationalste*] Greek race [*Stamm*]"; Schlegel 1958–, 1:8), but so is Winckelmann (see next note).

277. See Humboldt 1969d, 73 (III:171), on the competitiveness that, deeply rooted in Greece, leads to its ruin; further, Humboldt 1903–36, 1:417–18 ("Pindar"). Winckelmann's aesthetic ideal not only combines austerity and purity (Dorian traits) with sensuousness and gracefulness (Athenian traits); it is itself grounded in, and constrained by, the Greek ethic of competition, of which Spartan manhood is just one example. See Potts 1994, 5: "Conflict becomes the condition of [the] existence" of "an ideally free self." For a convincing elaboration of this question, see Raimund Fridrich, *Etappen der europäischen Rezeption von Johann Joachim Winckelmann: Vom Geniekult zum Aesthetizismus* (ms. in progress).

278. See Goethe's letter to Eckermann of 3 May 1827, in which he casts a longing glance at Paris, the site of vibrant intellectual activity, in contrast to the situation at home, where the absence of this activity is to be blamed on the "state of culture of our nation [*Nation*] and the great difficulties we all experience as we try to help each other in our isolated ways." Paris, on the other hand, is a place "where the preeminent minds of a whole empire [*Reich*] meet in one spot and reciprocally enrich and enhance one another in daily intercourse, struggle, and contest [*Kampf und Wetteifer*]." The passage is cited in Elias 1997, 1:122, as an expression of the felt cultural inferiority of Germany in the nineteenth century. The fantasy of culture as a productive contest here plainly springs from a sense of deficiency at home, and that is its attraction later on as well.

279. *KSA*, 7:3[74].

280. "HCP," 251–52.

281. "At the same time [that we rediscover Greece] we have the feeling that the birth of a tragic age simply means a return to itself of the German spirit, a blessed self-discovery."

282. *HA*, I:221: "Since [Voltaire's] time the modern spirit, with its restlessness, its hatred for bounds and moderation, has come to dominate in every domain, at first let loose by the fever of revolution and then, when assailed by fear and *horror of itself*, again laying constraints upon itself—but the constraints of logic, no longer those of artistic moderation. It is true that for a time this unfettering enables us to enjoy the poetry of all peoples, all that has grown up in hidden places, the primitive, wild-blooming, strangely beautiful and gigantically irregular. . . . But for how much longer?" (emphasis added).

283. *"Die griechische [Cultur] ist als Urbild zu kennzeichnen und zu zeigen, wie alle Cultur auf Vorstellungen ruht, die hinfällig sind"* ("WPh," 5[157]). This is perhaps Nietzsche's most devastating—and consistent—insight (or else claim). Culture is the transmission of delusions (*Wahnvorstellungen*); "consequently, every *new production of a culture* [is achieved] through strong paradigmatic natures," namely, individual personalities, *"in whom the delusions are produced anew"* (*KSA*, 7:5[106–7] [1870–71]; emphasis added). Cf. further ibid., 5[25]: "How does instinct manifest itself in the form of consciousness? In delusions [*Wahnvorstellungen*]. Even knowledge of their nature fails to negate their effectiveness. Yet such knowledge does give rise to a tormented condition: the only cure lies in the illusory appearances [*Schein*] of art. . . . The 'ideal' is one such delusion." In other words, the only cure for one delusion is—another delusion. Similarly, from two years later, *KSA*, 7:19[43] ("Life needs illusions"); ibid. [64] (the progress of culture is dependent upon illusion). For the later writings, see Porter 1999.

284. "WPh," 5[200].

Works Cited

I. A. WORKS BY NIETZSCHE IN GERMAN AND ABBREVIATIONS

KGW, KSA: The definitive edition of Nietzsche's published writings from 1867 onward and of his unpublished notebooks from 1852 to 1858 and from 1869 to 1889 is the monumental *Werke: Kritische Gesamtausgabe (KGW)*, edited by Georgio Colli and Mazzino Montinari (Berlin, 1967–). Citations to texts found in both editions will be to *Sämtliche Werke: Kritische Studienausgabe (KSA)*, edited by Colli and Montinari (Berlin, 1988), equivalent in all but pagination to *KGW*. The Colli-Montinari manuscript numeration will be given after volume numbers (e.g., *KSA*, 7, 7[156]), with page numbers and years appended when greater precision is needed. Publication of the juvenilia in the *Kritische Gesamtausgabe* is underway. *KGW* is cited in this study wherever new editions of the *philologica* are available. Until *KGW* has been completed, the following editions must be consulted (abbreviations as given in *KSA*, 14:21):

GA: Großoktavausgabe. = Nietzsche's Werke. 1899–1913. 2d ed. Leipzig. 19 vols. Edited by F. Koegel. (1st ed. 1895–97. Edited by F. Koegel. Leipzig). Referred to mainly for its editorial remarks, occasionally for an alternate transcription of the mss. Vols. 17–19 (1910–13) contain the first edition of Nietzsche's *philologica*.

BAW: Friedrich Nietzsche, *Historisch-kritische Gesamtausgabe. Werke.* 5 vols. Edited by Joachim Mette et al. Berlin, 1933–43. This remains the best source for much of the earliest philological and philosophical material (*Democritea*, "On Schopenhauer," the preparatory notes and drafts of the early publications, etc.). The edition was never completed. Mette manuscript signatures (e.g., "P I 15") are occasionally given for convenience of reference.

The following editions and abbreviations are also used:

BAB: Historisch-kritische Gesamtausgabe. Briefe. 1933–43. 4 vols. Edited by Joachim Mette et al. Berlin.

KGB: Briefwechsel. Kritische Gesamtausgabe. 1975–. Edited by Georgio Colli and Mazzino Montinari. Berlin.

KSA: Sämtliche Werke. Kritische Studienausgabe in 15 Einzelbänden. 1988. 2d, corrected ed. Edited by Georgio Colli and Mazzino Montinari. Berlin.

KSB: Sämtliche Briefe. Kritische Studienausgabe in 8 Bänden. 1986. Edited by Georgio Colli and Mazzino Montinari. Berlin.

MusA: Gesammelte Werke. 1920–29. Edited by Richard Oehler, Max Oehler, Friedrich Chr. Wurzbach. 33 vols. Munich.

B. TRANSLATIONS

Beyond Good and Evil: Prelude to a Philosophy of the Future. Translated by Walter Kaufmann. New York, 1966.

The Birth of Tragedy and The Case of Wagner. Translated by Walter Kaufmann. New York, 1967.

Daybreak: Thoughts on the Prejudices of Morality. Translated by R. J. Hollingdale. Cambridge, 1982.

Ecce Homo: How One Becomes What One Is. Translated by R. J. Hollingdale. London, 1979.

The Gay Science: With a Prelude in Rhymes and an Appendix of Songs. Translated by Walter Kaufmann. New York, 1974.

Human, All Too Human: A Book for Free Spirits. Translated by R. J. Hollingdale. Cambridge, 1996.

On the Genealogy of Morals: A Polemic. Translated by Walter Kaufmann. New York, 1967.

"On Truth and Lying in an Extra-Moral Sense." Translated by Carole Blair. In Gilman et al. 1989, 246–57.

Thus Spoke Zarathustra: A Book for All and None. Translated by Walter Kaufmann. New York, 1966.

Twilight of the Idols and The Anti-Christ. Translated by R. J. Hollingdale. London, 1968.

Untimely Meditations. Translated by R. J. Hollingdale, with an introduction by J. P. Stern. Cambridge, 1983.

The Will to Power. Translated by Walter Kaufmann and R. J. Hollingdale. Edited by Walter Kaufmann. New York, 1968.

For a complete list of abbreviations, see "Abbreviations" in the front matter.

II. OTHER WORKS CITED

Adorno, Theodor W. 1982. *Negative Dialektik.* Frankfurt am Main.

Allen, W. Sidney. 1973. *Accent and Rhythm. Prosodic Features of Latin and Greek: A Study in Theory and Reconstruction.* Cambridge.

———. 1987. *Vox Graeca: A Guide to the Pronunciation of Classical Greek.* 3d ed. Cambridge.

Andler, Charles. 1920–31. *Nietzsche, sa vie et sa pensée.* 6 vols. Paris.

Arendt, Hannah. 1968. *Antisemitism.* Part 1 of *The Origins of Totalitarianism.* New York.

Arnold, Matthew. 1996. *Culture and Anarchy.* Edited by J. Dover Wilson. Cambridge.

Asmis, Elizabeth. 1984. *Epicurus' Scientific Method.* Ithaca, N.Y.

Assmann, Jan. 1997. *Moses the Egyptian: The Memory of Egypt in Western Monotheism.* Cambridge, Mass.

Bakhtin, M. M. 1981. *The Dialogic Imagination: Four Essays.* Edited by Michael Holquist. Translated by Caryl Emerson and Michael Holquist. Austin.

Balibar, Etienne, and Immanuel Wallerstein. 1991. *Race, Nation, Class: Ambiguous Identities.* Translated by Chris Turner. London.

Barkan, Leonard. 1991. "Rome's Other Population." *Raritan* 11, no. 2 (fall): 66–81.

Barker, Andrew. 1978a. "Music and Perception: A Study in Aristoxenus." *Journal of Hellenic Studies* 98: 9–16.

———. 1978b. "*Hoi kaloumenoi harmonikoi*: The Predecessors of Aristoxenus." *Proceedings of the Cambridge Philological Society* n.s., 24: 1–21.

———. 1984. "Aristoxenus' Theorems and the Foundations of Harmonic Science." *Ancient Philosophy* 4: 23–63.

———, ed. 1989. *Greek Musical Writings, Volume II: Harmonic and Acoustic Theory.* Cambridge.

Barnes, Jonathan. 1982 [1979]. *The Presocratic Philosophers.* Rev. ed. London.

———. 1986. "Nietzsche and Diogenes Laertius." *Nietzsche-Studien* 15: 16–40.

Barthes, Roland. 1968. *Writing Degree Zero.* Translated by Annette Lavers and Colin Smith. New York.

Baeumer, Max. 1973. "Winckelmanns Formulierung der klassischen Schönheit." *Monatshefte* 65, no. 1: 61–75.

———. 1976. "Nietzsche and the Tradition of the Dionysian." In O'Flaherty et al. 1976, 165–89.

Bäumler, Alfred. 1929. *Bachofen und Nietzsche.* Zürich.

Behler, Ernst. 1986. "A. W. Schlegel and the Nineteenth-Century *Damnatio* of Euripides." *Greek, Roman and Byzantine Studies* 27: 335–67.

———. 1997. "Nietzsche und die Antike." Review of Cancik 1995a. *Nietzsche-Studien* 26: 514–28 (English version in *International Journal of the Classical Tradition* 4, no. 3 [winter, 1998]: 417–33).

Bérard, Victor. 1894. *De l'origine des cultes arcadiens: Essai de méthode en mythologie grecque.* Paris.

Berding, Helmut. 1988. *Moderner Antisemitismus in Deutschland.* Frankfurt am Main.

Bergk, Theodor. 1845. "Ueber die Kritik in Theognis." *Rheinisches Museum* N. F. 3: 206–33, 396–433.

Bernal, Martin. 1987. *Black Athena: The Afroasiatic Roots of Classical Civilization.* Vol. 1: *The Fabrication of Ancient Greece 1785–1985.* New Brunswick.

Bernays, Jacob. 1885. *Gesammelte Abhandlungen.* 2 vols. Edited by H. Usener. Berlin.

Bernhardy, Gottfried. 1832. *Grundlinien zur Encyklopädie der Philologie.* Halle.

Bernstein, Michael André. 1994. *Foregone Conclusions: Against Apocalyptic History.* Berkeley, Calif.

Billeter, Gustav. 1911. *Die Anschauungen vom Wesen des Griechentums.* Leipzig.

Blok, Josine H. 1996. "Proof and Persuasion in *Black Athena*: The Case of K. O. Müller." *Journal of the History of Ideas* 57, no. 4: 705–24.

Blunck, Richard. 1953. *Friedrich Nietzsche.* Vol. 1: *Kindheit und Jugend.* Munich.

Boeckh, August. 1858–74. *Gesammelte kleine Schriften.* 7 vols. Edited by Ferdinand Ascherson, Ernst Bratuscheck, and Paul Eichholtz. Leipzig.

———. 1877. *Encyklopädie und Methodologie der philologischen Wissenschaften.* Edited by Ernst Bratuscheck. Leipzig.

———. 1886 [1st ed., 1817]. *Die Staatshaushaltung der Athener.* 3d ed. Edited by Max Fränkel. 2 vols. Berlin.

Bollack, Jean. 1996. "Un homme d'un autre monde." In *Jacob Bernays: Un philologue juif.* Edited by John Glucker and André Laks, 135–225. Villeneuve d'Asq (Nord).

Bornmann, Fritz. 1984. "Nietzsches Epikur." *Nietzsche-Studien* 13: 177–88.

———. 1989. "Nietzsches metrische Studien." *Nietzsche-Studien* 18: 472–89.

Borsche, Tilman. 1985. "Nietzsches Erfindung der Vorsokratiker." In *Nietzsche und die philosophische Tradition.* Edited by Josef Simon, 1:62–87. Würzburg.

Borsche, Tilman, Frederico Gerratana, and Aldo Venturelli, eds. 1994. *"Centauren-Geburten": Wissenschaft, Kunst und Philosophie beim jungen Nietzsche.* Monographien und Texte zur Nietzsche-Forschung. Vol. 27. Berlin.

Brandt, Richard. 1991. "Die Titelvignette von Nietzsches *Geburt der Tragödie aus dem Geiste der Musik.*" *Nietzsche-Studien* 20: 314–28.

Bravo, Benedetto. 1968. *Philologie, histoire, philosophie de l'histoire: Étude sur J. G. Droysen, historien de l'antiquité.* Breslau.

Burkert, Walter. 1959. "*Stoicheion*: Eine semasiologische Studie." *Philologus* 103, no. 3–4: 167–97.

———. forthcoming. "Diels' Vorsokratiker: Rückschau und Ausblick." In *Entretiens Fondation Hardt.* Geneva.

Bursian, Conrad. 1883. *Geschichte der classischen Philologie in Deutschland von den Anfängen bis zur Gegenwart.* 2 vols. Munich.

Bury, J. B. 1900. *A History of Greece to the Death of Alexander the Great.* London.

Cage, John. 1961. *Silence: Lectures and Writings.* Middletown, Conn.

Caizzi, Fernanda Decleva. 1984. "Pirrone e Democrito: Gli Atomi: Un 'Mito'?" *Elenchos* 5: 5–23.

Calder, William M., III. 1970. "Three Unpublished Letters of Ulrich von Wilamowitz-Moellendorff." *Greek, Roman and Byzantine Studies* 11, no. 2: 139–66.

———. 1975. "Ulrich von Wilamowitz-Moellendorff to Wolfgang Schadewaldt on the Classic." *Greek, Roman and Byzantine Studies* 16, no. 4: 451–57.

————. 1981. "Ulrich von Wilamowitz-Moellendorff: An Unpublished Latin Autobiography." *Antike und Abendland* 27: 34–51.

————. 1983a. "The Wilamowitz-Nietzsche Struggle: New Documents and a Reappraisal." *Nietzsche-Studien* 12: 214–54.

————. 1983b. Rev. of Silk and Stern 1981. In *Classical and Modern Literature: A Quarterly*. 3: 113–16.

Calder, William M., III, Hellmut Flashar, and Theodor Lindken, eds. 1985. *Wilamowitz nach 50 Jahren*. Darmstadt.

Campbell, David A. 1967. *Greek Lyric Poetry: A Selection of Early Greek Lyric, Elegiac and Iambic Poetry*. London.

Cancik, Hubert. 1987. "Der Einfluß Friedrich Nietzsches auf Berliner Schulkritiker der wilhelminischen Aera." *Der Altsprachliche Unterrricht* 30, no. 3: 55–74.

————. 1994. "'Philologie als Beruf': Zu Formengeschichte, Thema und Tradition der unvollendeten vierten *Unzeitgemäßen* Friedrich Nietzsches." In Borsche et al. 1994.

————. 1995a. *Nietzsches Antike: Vorlesung*. Stuttgart.

———— (with Hildegard Cancik-Lindemaier and Roswitha Wollkopf). 1995b. "Der Einfluss Friedrich Nietzsches auf klassische Philologen in Deutschland bis 1945: Philologen am Nietzsche-Archiv (I)." In Flashar, ed., 381–402.

————. 1997. "Mongols, Semites, and the Pure-Bred Greeks: Nietzsche's Handling of the Racial Doctrines of His Time." In Golomb 1997, 55–75.

————. 1998. *Antik-Modern: Beiträge zur römischen und deutschen Kulturgeschichte*. Edited by Richard Faber, Barbara von Reibnitz, and Jörg Rüpke. Stuttgart.

Cancik, Hubert, and Helmuth Schneider, eds. 1996– . *Der neue Pauly: Enzyklopädie der Antike*. Stuttgart.

Canfora, Luciano. 1995. *Politische Philologie: Altertumswissenschaften und moderne Staatsideologien*. Translated by Volker Breidecker, Ulrich Hausmann, and Barbara Hufer. Stuttgart.

Chatman, Seymour. 1965. *A Theory of Meter*. Janua linguarum. Series minor. 36. The Hague.

Christ, Karl. 1996. *Griechische Geschichte und Wissenschaftsgeschichte. Mit 7 Tafeln*. Stuttgart. (= Historia Einzelschriften 106.)

Cole, Thomas. 1990 [1967]. *Democritus and the Sources of Greek Anthropology*. Atlanta, Ga.

Comotti, Giovanni. 1989. *Music in Greek and Roman Culture*. Translated by Rosaria V. Munson. Baltimore, Md.

Conway, Daniel W., and Rudolf Rehn, eds. 1992. *Nietzsche und die antike Philosophie*. Bochumer Altertumswissenschaftliches Colloquium, vol. 11. Trier.

Crawford, Claudia. 1988. *The Beginnings of Nietzsche's Theory of Language*. Monographien und Texte zur Nietzsche-Forschung, vol. 19. Berlin.

Creuzer, Georg Friedrich. 1973 [1836–43 (1st ed., 1810–12)]. *Symbolik und*

Mythologie der alten Völker, besonders der Griechen. 4 vols. 3d ed. Leipzig. (Reprint, New York, 1973.)

Curtius, Ernst. 1875. "Der Wettkampf." In *Alterthum und Gegenwart: Gesammelte Reden und Vorträge,* 1:132–47. Berlin.

Deleuze, Gilles. 1983. *Nietzsche and Philosophy.* Translated by Hugh Tomlinson. New York. (French original: 1962.)

Devine, A. M., and Laurence D. Stephens. 1994. *The Prosody of Greek Speech.* New York.

Diels, Hermann. 1901. *Herakleitos von Ephesos. Griechisch und Deutsch.* Berlin.

———. 1902. "Wissenschaft und Romantik. Rektoratsrede 23. Januar 1902." In *Sitzungsberichte der Königlich Preussischen Akademie der Wissenschaften zu Berlin* 4: 25–43.

———. 1903. *Die Fragmente der Vorsokratiker. Griechisch und Deutsch.* Berlin.

———. 1905. "Aristotelica." *Hermes* 40: 300–316.

———. 1951–52. *Die Fragmente der Vorsokratiker, Griechisch und Deutsch.* Edited by Walther Kranz. 6th ed. 3 vols. Berlin.

Ducat, Philippe, trans. 1990. *Friedrich Nietzsche: Sur Démocrite.* Translated by Philippe Ducat. Postface by Jean-Luc Nancy. Paris.

Dühring, Eugen. 1865. *Der Werth des Lebens: Eine Philosophische Betrachtung.* Breslau.

Dumont, Jean-Paul. 1990. "*Ouden Mallon* chez Platon." In *Le Scepticisme Antique: Perspectives historiques et systématiques. Actes du Colloque international sur le scepticisme antique, Université de Lausanne, 1–3 juin 1988,* edited by André-Jean Voelke, 29–40. Geneva.

Ehlers, Dietrich, ed. 1992. *Hermann Diels–Hermann Usener–Eduard Zeller, Briefwechesel.* Berlin.

Ehrenberg, Victor. 1935. "Das Agonale." In Victor Ehrenberg, *Ost und West: Studien zur geschichtlichen Problematik der Antike,* 63–96. Brünn.

Eley, Geoff. 1996. "Modernity at the Limit: Rethinking German Exceptionalism before 1914." *New Formations* 28 (spring): 21–45.

Elias, Norbert. 1997 [1939]. *Über den Prozeß der Zivilisation: Soziogenetische und psychogenetische Untersuchungen.* 2 vols. Frankfurt am Main.

Farrar, Cynthia. 1988. *The Origins of Democratic Thinking: The Invention of Politics in Classical Athens.* Cambridge.

Feeney, Denis. 1998. *Literature and Religion at Rome: Cultures, Contexts, and Beliefs.* Cambridge.

Ferrari, Gian Arturo. 1981. "La scrittura invisibile." *Aut-Aut* 184–85: 95–110.

Feuerbach, Anselm. 1855 [1st ed., 1833]. *Der vaticanische Apollo: Eine Reihe archäologisch-ästhetischer Betrachtungen.* 2d ed. Stuttgart.

Figl, Johann. 1984. "Hermeneutische Voraussetzungen der philologischen Kritik: Zur wissenschaftsphilosophischen Grundproblematik im Denken des jungen Nietzsche." *Nietzsche-Studien* 13: 111–28.

Flashar, Hellmut. 1979. "Die methodisch-hermeneutischen Ansätze von Friedrich

August Wolf und Friedrich Ast—Traditionelle und neue Begründungen." In Flashar et al. 1979, 21–31.

———, ed. (with Sabine Vogt), 1995. *Altertumswissenschaft in den 20er Jahren : Neue Fragen und Impulse*. Stuttgart.

Flashar, Hellmut, Karlfried Gründer, and Axel Horstmann, eds. 1979. *Philologie und Hermeneutik im 19. Jahrhundert: Zur Geschichte und Methodologie der Geisteswissenschaften*. Göttingen.

Förster-Nietzsche, Elisabeth. 1895–1904. *Das Leben Friedrich Nietzsche's*. 2 vols. Leipzig.

Fortlage, Carl. 1847. *Das musikalische System der Griechen in seiner Urgestalt aus den Tonlectern des Alypius zum ersten Male entwickelt*. Leipzig.

Foucault, Michel. 1977. *Language, Counter-Memory, Practice: Selected Essays and Interviews*. Edited by Donald F. Bouchard. Translated by Donald F. Bouchard and Sherry Simon. Ithaca, N.Y.

Fränkel, Hermann. 1976. *Dichtung und Philosophie des frühen Griechentums: Eine Geschichte der griechischen Epik, Lyrik und Prosa bis zur Mitte des fünften Jahrhunderts*. 3d ed. Munich.

Fritz, Kurt von. 1938. *Philosophie und sprachlicher Ausdruck bei Demokrit, Plato und Aristoteles*. New York.

Fuhrmann, Manfred. 1959. "Friedrich August Wolf." *Deutsche Vierteljahrsschrift für Literaturwissenschaft und Geistesgeschichte* 33, no. 2: 187–236.

Furley, David. 1967. *Two Studies in the Greek Atomists*. Princeton.

———. 1987. *The Greek Cosmologists*. Vol. 1: *The Formation of the Atomic Theory and Its Earliest Critics*. Cambridge.

Gigante, Marcello. 1984a. "Demokrit und Nietzsche." In *Praktika tou 1 Diethnous Synedriou gia ton Demokrito, Xanthe 6–9 oktobriou 1983*. (Proceedings of the First International Congress on Democritus' Xanthi, 6–9 October 1983), 345–57. Xanthi.

———. 1984b. "Friedrich Nietzsche e l'*Academicorum Index Herculanensis*." *Cronache Ercolanesi* 14.

———. 1986. "Friedrich Nietzsche e i Papiri Ercolanesi." *Cronache Ercolanesi* 16: 93–94.

———. 1994. "Friedrich Nietzsche und Diogenes Laertius." In Borsche et al. 1994, 3–16.

———. 1997. "Nietzsche e la filologia classica." *Studia slavistica et humanistica in honorem Nullo Minissi*, 310–322. Katowice.

Gigante, Marcello, and Giovanni Indelli. 1980. "Democrito nei papiri ercolanesi di Filodemo." *Democrito e l'atomismo antico: Atti del Convegno Internazionale, Catania, 18–21 Aprile 1979* [Catania], 458–59.

Gilman, Sander L., Carole Blair, and David J. Parent, eds. and trans. 1989. *Friedrich Nietzsche on Rhetoric and Language*. New York.

Glucker, John, and André Laks. 1996. *Jacob Bernays: Un philologue juif*. Villeneuve d'Ascq (Nord). (= Cahiers de philologie. Vol. 16.)

Goethe, Johann Wolfgang von. 1948–54. *Gedenkausgabe der Werke, Briefe und Gespräche, 28. August 1949.* 27 vols. Edited by Ernst Beutler. Zürich.

Golomb, Jacob, ed. 1997. *Nietzsche and Jewish Culture.* London.

Gossman, Lionel. 1983. *Orpheus Philologus: Bachofen versus Mommsen on the Study of Antiquity.* Transactions of the American Philosophical Society. Vol. 73, part 5.

Gourgouris, Stathis. 1996. *Dream Nation: Enlightenment, Colonization, and the Institution of Modern Greece.* Stanford.

Grafton, Anthony. 1981. "*Prolegomena* to Friedrich August Wolf." *Journal of the Warburg and Courtault Institutes* 44: 101–29.

———.1983. "Polyhistor into *Philolog*: Notes on the Transformation of German Classical Scholarship, 1780–1850." *History of the Universities* 3: 159–92.

———. 1990. *Forgers and Critics: Creativity and Duplicity in Western Scholarship.* Princeton.

———. 1991. *Defenders of the Text: The Traditions of Scholarship in an Age of Science, 1450–1800.* Cambridge, Mass.

Gründer, Karlfried. 1969. *Der Streit um Nietzsches "Geburt der Tragödie": Die Schriften von E. Rohde, R. Wagner, U. v. Wilamowitz-Möllendorff.* Hildesheim.

Gutha-Thakurta, Tapati. 1995. "Recovering the Nation's Art." In *Texts of Power: Emerging Disciplines in Colonial Bengal,* edited by Partha Chatterjee, 63–92. Minneapolis, Minn.

Guthrie, W. K. C. 1965. *A History of Greek Philosophy.* Vol. 2: *The Presocratic Tradition from Parmenides to Democritus.* Cambridge.

Gutzwiller, Hans. 1951. "Friedrich Nietzsches Lehrtätigkeit am Basler Pädagogium 1869–1876." *Basler Zeitschrift für Geschichte und Altertumskunde* 50: 148–224.

Halliwell, Stephen. 1986. *Aristotle's Poetics.* London.

Hartmann, Eduard von. 1869. *Philosophie des Unbewussten: Versuch einer Weltanschauung.* Berlin.

Hatfield, Henry. 1964. *Aesthetic Paganism in German Literature: From Winckelmann to the Death of Goethe.* Cambridge, Mass.

Hayman, Ronald. 1980. *Nietzsche: A Critical Life.* Harmondsworth.

Hazard, Paul. 1968 [1935]. *Crise de la conscience européene, 1680–1715.* Paris.

Henrichs, Albert. 1984. "Loss of Self, Suffering, Violence: The Modern View of Dionysus from Nietzsche to Girard." *Harvard Studies in Classical Philology* 88: 205–40.

———. 1985. "'Der Glaube der Hellenen': Religionsgeschichte als Glabensbekenntnis und Kulturkritik." In Calder et al. 1985, 263–305.

———. 1995. "Philologie und Wissenschaftsgeschichte: Zur Krise eines Selbstverständnisses." In Flashar, ed. 1995, 423–57.

Hermann, Gottfried. 1826. *Ueber Herrn Professor Böckhs Behandlung der griechischen Inschriften.* Leipzig.

———. 1827–77. *Opuscula.* 8 vols. in 7. Leipzig.

Hershbell, Jackson P., and Stephen A. Nimis. 1979. "Nietzsche and Heraclitus." *Nietzsche-Studien* 8: 17–38.

Himmelmann, Nikolaus. 1985. *Ideale Nacktheit.* Opladen.

———. 1990. *Ideale Nacktheit in der griechischen Kunst.* Jahrbuch des Deutschen Archäologischen Instituts. Ergänzungsheft 26. Berlin.

Hoffmannstahl, Hugo von. 1928. "Vermächtnis der Antike: Rede anlässlich eines Festes von Freunden des humanistischen Gymnasiums gehalten." *Die Antike* 4, no. 2: 99–102.

Hölscher, Uvo. 1965. *Die Chance des Unbehagens: Drei Essais zur Situation der klassischen Studien.* Göttingen.

———. 1979. "Die Wiedergewinnung des antiken Bodens: Nietzsches Rückgriff auf Heraklit." *Neue Hefte für Philosophie* 15/16: 156–82.

———. 1995. "Strömungen der deutschen Gräzistik in den zwanziger Jahren." In Flashar, ed. 1995, 65–85.

Horstmann, Axel. 1978. "Die 'klassische Philologie' zwischen Humanismus und Historismus: Friedrich August Wolf und die Begründung der modernen Altertumswissenschaft." *Berichte zur Wissenschafts-Geschichte* 1: 51–70.

Howald, Ernst. 1920. *Friedrich Nietzsche und die klassische Philologie.* Gotha.

Hübner, Emil. 1889 [1st ed., 1876]. *Bibliographie der klassischen Alterthumswissenschaft. Grundriss zu Vorlesungen über die Geschichte und Encyclopädie der klassischen Philologie.* Berlin.

Humboldt, Wilhelm von. 1841. *Briefe an F. A. Wolf.* In *Wilhelm von Humboldt's Gesammelte Werke,* edited by Karl Heinrich Brandes, 5:1–316. 7 vols. Berlin.

———. 1859. *Wilhelm von Humboldts Briefe an F. G. Welcker.* Edited by R. Haym. Berlin.

———. 1903–36. *Wilhelm von Humboldts Gesammelte Schriften.* Edited by Albert Leitzmann et al. Published by the Königlich Preussischen Akademie der Wissenschaften. 17 vols. Berlin. [= "*Akademie* ed."]

———. 1960–81. *Werke in Fünf Bänden.* Edited by Andreas Flitner and Klaus Giel. Darmstadt. (Appended parenthetical references are to the *Akademie* edition = Humboldt 1903–36.)

———. 1969a. "Über das Studium des Alterthums, und des griechischen Insbesondre" (1793). In Humboldt 1960–81, 2:1–24.

———. 1969b. "Latium und Hellas oder Betrachtungen über das classische Alterthum" (1806/7). In Humboldt 1960–81, 2:25–64.

———. 1969c. "Über den Charakter der Griechen, die idealische und historische Ansicht Desselben" (1807). In Humboldt 1960–81, 2:65–72.

———. 1969d. "Geschichte des Verfalls und Unterganges der griechischen Freistaaten" (1807). In Humboldt 1960–81, 2:73–124.

Jaeger, Werner, ed. 1931. *Das Problem des Klassischen und die Antike: Acht Vorträge gehalten auf der Fachtagung der klassischen Altertumswissenschaft zu Naumburg 1930.* Leipzig.

Janko, Richard. 1990. "The *Iliad* and Its Editors: Dictation and Redaction." *Classical Antiquity* 9.2: 326–34.

———. 1991. "*Philodemus'* On Poems *and Aristotle's* On Poets." *Cronache Ercolanesi* 21: 5–64.

Janni, Pietro. 1968. "Romanticismo e mito della 'Doricità': Karl Otfried Müller." *Studi Germanici* 6, n.s. no. 3: 13–43.

Janz, Curt Paul. 1974. "Friedrich Nietzsches Akademische Lehrtätigkeit in Basel 1869–1879." *Nietzsche-Studien* 3: 192–203.

———. 1978–79. *Friedrich Nietzsche: Biographie in drei Bänden.* 3 vols. Munich. (v. 1 = Blunck 1953).

Jebb, R. C. 1887. *Homer: An Introduction to the Iliad and the Odyssey.* 2d ed. Glasgow.

Joël, Karl. 1903. *Der Ursprung der Naturphilosophie aus dem Geist der Mystik.* Programm zur Rektoratsfeier der Universität Basel. Basel.

———. 1905. *Nietzsche und die Romantik.* Leipzig.

———. 1906. *Der Ursprung der Naturphilosophie aus dem Geist der Mystik. Mit Anhang: Archaische Romantik.* Jena.

Judet de la Combe, Pierre. 1993. "Eigentliche oder symbolische Namen: Die Streitfrage der griechischen Mythologie in Leipzig und Paris zu Beginn des 19. Jahrhunderts." In *Von der Elbe bis an die Seine: Kulturtransfer zwischen Sachsen und Frankreich im 18. und 19. Jahrhundert,* edited by Michel Espagne and Matthias Middell, 314–29. Leipzig.

Kaufmann, Walter. 1974 [1950]. *Nietzsche: Philosopher, Psychologist, Antichrist.* 4th ed. Princeton, N.J.

Kern, Otto, ed. 1936. *Aus dem amtlichen und wissenschaftlichen Briefwechsel von Carl Otfried Müller: Ausgewählte Stücke mit Erläuterungen.* Göttingen.

Kirk, G. S., J. E. Raven, and M. Schofield. 1983. *The Presocratic Philosophers: A Critical History with a Selection of Texts.* 2d ed. Cambridge.

Koselleck, Reinhart. 1985. *Futures Past: On the Semantics of Historical Time.* Translated by Keith Tribe. Cambridge, Mass.

Lamberton, Robert. 1988. *Hesiod.* New Haven, Conn.

Lamberton, Robert, and John J. Keaney, eds. 1992. *Homer's Ancient Readers: The Hermeneutics of Greek Epic's Earliest Exegetes.* Princeton, N.J.

Landfester, Manfred. 1979. "Ulrich von Wilamowitz-Moellendorff und die hermeneutische Tradition des 19. Jahrhunderts." In Flashar et al. 1979, 156–80.

———. 1988. *Humanismus und Gesellschaft im 19. Jahrhundert: Untersuchungen zur politischen und gesellschaftlichen Bedeutung der humanistischen Bildung in Deutschland.* Darmstadt.

———. 1995. "Die Naumburger Tagung 'Das Problem des Klassischen und die

Antike' (1930). Der Klassikbegriff Werner Jaegers: Seine Voraussestzung und seine Wirkung." In Flashar, ed. 1995, 11–40.

Lange, Friedrich Albert. 1866. *Geschichte des Materialismus und Kritik seiner Bedeutung in der Gegenwart.* Iserlohn.

———. 1974 [1873–75]. *Geschichte des Materialismus und Kritik seiner Bedeutung in der Gegenwart.* 2d ed. 2 vols. Frankfurt.

Langerbeck, Hermann. 1935. *Doxis Epirhysmiē: Studien zu Demokrits Ethik und Erkenntnislehre.* Berlin.

Latacz, Joachim. 1996/97. "Der neue Ameis-Hentze: Projektskizze und Erreichter Abstand." *Würzburger Jahrbücher für die Altertumswissenschaft* 21: 7–23.

Lea, F. A. 1957. *The Tragic Philosopher: A Study of Friedrich Nietzsche.* London.

Lepenies, Wolf. 1998 [1969]. *Melancholie und Gesellschaft.* Frankfurt am Main.

Lloyd, G. E. R. 1990. *Demystifying Mentalities.* Cambridge.

Lloyd-Jones, Hugh. 1976. "Nietzsche and the Study of the Ancient World." In O'Flaherty et al., 1–15.

———. 1982. *Blood for the Ghosts: Classical Influences in the Nineteenth and Twentieth Centuries.* London.

Löhneysen, Wolfgang Frhr. von. 1987. "Der Apoll von Belvedere: Kunst als Grund philosophischer Gedanken." In *Schopenhauer im Denken der Gegenwart: 23 Beiträge zu seiner Aktualität,* edited by Volker Spierling, 97–121. Munich.

Long, A. A. 1971. "*Aisthesis, Prolepsis* and Linguistic Theory in Epicurus." *Bulletin of the Institute of Classical Studies* 18: 114–33.

———. 1978. "Timon of Phlius: Pyrrhonist and Satirist." *Proceedings of the Cambridge Philosophical Society* n.s. 24: 68–91.

Long, A. A., and David Sedley. 1987. *The Hellenistic Philosophers.* 2 vols. Cambridge.

Lucretius. 1910. *On the Nature of Things.* Translated by Cyril Bailey. Oxford.

Luria, Salomo. 1970. *Democritea.* Leningrad.

Maas, Ernst. 1880. "De biographis graecis quaestiones selectae." In *Philologische Untersuchungen,* vol. 3. Berlin.

Maas, Paul. 1962. *Greek Metre.* Translated by Hugh Lloyd-Jones. Oxford. (*Griechische Metrik* [1923]. In *Einleitung in die Altertumswissenschaft,* edited by Alfred Gercke and Eduard Norden, 1.7:1–32. Berlin.)

Mannoni, Octave. 1969. *Clefs pour l'imaginaire, ou l'autre scène.* Paris.

Mansfeld, Jaap. 1985. "Wilamowitz' Ciceronian Philosophy." In Calder et al. 1985, 178–221.

———. 1986. "The Wilamowitz-Nietzsche Struggle: Another New Document and Some Further Comments." *Nietzsche-Studien* 15: 41–58.

———. 1994. *Prolegomena: Questions to be Settled before the Study of an Author, or a Text.* Leiden.

Marquard, Odo. 1973. *Schwierigkeiten mit der Geschichtsphilosophie.* Frankfurt am Main.

Martin, Nicholas. 1996. *Nietzsche and Schiller: Untimely Aesthetics.* Oxford.

Mejer, Jörgen. 1978. *Diogenes Laertius and His Hellenistic Background*. Hermes Einzelschriften, Vol. 40. Wiesbaden.

Melsen, Andreas Gerardus Maria van. 1952. *From Atomos to Atom: The History of the Concept Atom*. Translated by Henry J. Koren. Pittsburgh, Pa.

Menze, Clemens. 1965. *Wilhelm von Humboldts Lehre und Bild vom Menschen*. Ratingen bei Düsseldorf.

Momigliano, A. D. 1980. "Premesse per una Discussione su Wilamowitz." In *Sesto Contributo alla Storia degli Studi Classici e del Mondo Antico* 1: 337–49.

———. 1984. "K. O. Müller's *Prolegomena zu einer Wissenschaftlichen Mythologie* and the Meaning of 'Myth.'" In *Settimo Contributo alla Storia degli Studi Classici e del Mondo Antico*, 271–86. Rome.

———. 1994. *Studies on Modern Scholarship*. Edited by G. W. Bowersock and T. J. Cornell. Berkeley, Calif.

Moritz, Karl Philipp. 1981. *Werke*. Edited by Horst Günther. 3 vols. Frankfurt am Main.

Most, Glenn W. 1989. "Zur Archäologie der Archaik." *Antike und Abendland* 35: 1–23.

———. 1995. "*Polemos pantōn patēr*: Die Vorsokratiker in der Forschung der zwanziger Jahre." In Flashar, 1995, 87–114.

———. 1997. "Hesiod's Myth of the Five (or Three or Four) Myths of the Ages." *Proceedings of the Cambridge Philological Society* n. s. 43: 104–27.

———. 1998. "*A la recherche du texte perdu*: On Collecting Philosophical Fragments." In *Fragmentsammlungen philosophischer Texte der Antike / Le raccolte dei frammenti di filosofi antichi. Atti del Seminario Internazionale, Ascona 22–27 Settembre 1996*, edited by W. Burkert, L. Gemelli Marciano, E. Matelli, and L. Orelli, 1–15. Göttingen.

Müller, Karl Otfried. 1825. *Prolegomena zu einer wissenschaftlichen Mythologie*. Göttingen. (Reprint, Darmstadt, 1970.)

———. 1844 [1st ed., 1824]. *Geschichte Hellenischer Stämme und Städte*. Edited by F. W. Schneidewin. Vols. 2 and 3: *Die Dorier*. 2d ed. Breslau.

———. 1847–48. *Karl Otfried Müller's Kleine deutsche Schriften über Religion, Kunst, Sprache und Literatur, Leben und Geschichte des Alterthums*. Edited by Eduard Müller. 2 vols. Breslau.

———. 1875–76 [1841]. *Geschichte der griechischen Literatur bis auf das Zeitalter Alexanders. Nach der Handschrift des Verfassers herausgegeben von Dr. Eduard Müller*, 3d ed. Edited by Emil Heitz. 2 vols. Stuttgart.

Mullach, Friedrich Wilhelm August. 1843. *Democriti Abderitae operum fragmenta*. Berlin.

———. 1860–81. *Fragmenta philosophorum graecorum*. 3 vols. Vol. I [1860]: *Poeseos philosophicae caeterorumque ante Socratem philosophorum quae supersunt*. Paris.

Mundt, Theodor. 1856 [1st ed. 1844]. *Die Geschichte der Gesellschaft in ihren neueren Entwickelungen und Problemen*. Leipzig.

Nancy, Jean-Luc. 1973. "La Thèse de Nietzsche sur la téléologie (I)." In *Nietzsche aujourd'hui?* 1:57–89. Paris.

Natorp, Paul. 1893. *Die Ethika des Demokritos.* Marburg.

Negri, Antimo, ed. 1985. *Friedrich Nietzsche: Teognide di Megara.* Rome.

Niehues-Pröbsting, Heinrich. 1980. "Der 'Kurze Weg': Nietzsches 'Cynismus.'" *Archiv für Begriffsgeschichte* 24, no. 1: 103–22.

———. 1983. "Anekodote als philosophiegeschichtliches Medium." *Nietzsche-Studien* 12: 255–86.

———. 1996. "The Modern Reception of Cynicism: Diogenes in the Enlightenment." In *The Cynics: The Cynic Movement in Antiquity and Its Legacy,* edited by R. Bracht Branham and Marie-Odile Goulet-Cazé, 329–65. Berkeley, Calif.

Nietzsche Aujourd'hui? Exposés [par] Pierre Boudot [et al.]. Table ronde [par] Sylviane Agacinski [et al.] Interventions [par] S. Allen [et al.]. 2 vols. 1973. Paris.

Nisbet, H. B., ed. 1985. *German Aesthetic and Literary Criticism: Winckelmann, Lessing, Hamann, Herder, Schiller, Goethe.* Cambridge, U.K.

Oehler, Richard. 1904. *Friedrich Nietzsche und die Vorsokratiker.* Leipzig.

O'Flaherty, James C., Timothy F. Sellner, and Robert M. Helm, eds. 1976. *Studies in Nietzsche and the Classical Tradition.* Chapel Hill, N.C.

Olender, Maurice. 1989. *Les langues du Paradis. Aryens et Sémites: un couple providentiel.* Paris.

O'Sullivan, Neil. 1992. *Alcidamas, Aristophanes and the Beginnings of Greek Stylistic Theory.* Hermes Einzelschriften. Vol. 60. Stuttgart.

Panofsky, Erwin. 1993 [1924]. *Idea: Ein Beitrag zur Begriffsgeschichte der älteren Kunstheorie.* Berlin.

Parry, Adam, ed. 1971. *The Making of Homeric Verse: The Collected Papers of Milman Parry.* Oxford.

Pattison, Mark. 1889. *Essays by the Late Mark Pattison.* Edited by Henry Nettleship. 2 vols. Oxford.

Paulsen, Friedrich. 1906. *Das deutsche Bildungswesen in seiner geschichtlichen Entwickelung.* Leipzig.

———. 1919–21. *Geschichte des gelehrten Unterrichts auf den deutschen Schulen und Universitäten vom Ausgang des Mittelalters bis zur Gegenwart.* 3d ed. 2 vols. Leipzig.

Pearson, Lionel, ed. 1990. *Aristoxenus Elementa Rhythmica: The Fragment of Book II and the Additional Evidence for Aristoxenean Rhythmic Theory.* Oxford.

Pfeiffer, Rudolf. 1960. *Ausgewählte Schriften: Aufsätze und Vorträge zur griechischen Dichtung und zum Humanismus.* Edited by Winfried Bühler. Munich.

———. 1961. *Philologia Perennis: Festrede gehalten in der öffentlichen Sitzung der Bayerischen Akademie der Wissenschaften in München am 3. Dezember 1960.* Munich.

———. 1968. *History of Classical Scholarship from the Beginnings to the End of the Hellenistic Age.* Oxford.

———. 1976. *History of Classical Scholarship from 1300 to 1850.* Oxford.

Pflug, Günther. 1979. "Methodik und Hermeneutik bei Karl Otfried Müller." In Flashar et al. 1979, 122–40.

Pfotenhauer, Helmut, Markus Bernhauer, and Norbert Miller (with Thomas Franke), eds. 1995. *Frühklassizismus. Position und Opposition: Winckelmann, Mengs, Heinse.* Frankfurt am Main.

Pick, Daniel. 1989. *Faces of Degeneration: A European Disorder, c. 1848–c. 1918.* Cambridge.

Poliakov, Léon. 1987. *Le Mythe Aryen: Essai sur les sources du racisme et des nationalismes.* Rev. ed. Brussels.

Pollitt, J. J. 1986. *Art in the Hellenistic Age.* Cambridge.

Porter, James I. 1986. "Saussure and Derrida on the Figure of the Voice." *Modern Language Notes* 101, no. 4: 871–94.

———. 1989. "Philodemus on Material Difference." *Cronache Ercolanesi* 19: 149–78.

———. 1992a. "Nietzsche's Atoms." In Conway and Rehn 1992, 47–90.

———. 1992b. "Hermeneutic Lines and Circles: Aristarchus and Crates on the Exegesis of Homer." In Lamberton and Keaney, 67–114. Princeton, N.J.

———. 1993. "The Seductions of Gorgias." *Classical Antiquity* 12, no. 2: 267–99.

———. 1994. "Nietzsche's Rhetoric: Theory and Strategy." *Philosophy and Rhetoric* 27, no. 3: 218–244.

———. 1995a. "Content and Form: The History of an Evasion." In *Philodemus and Poetry: Poetic Theory and Practice in Lucretius, Philodemus, and Horace.* Edited by Dirk Obbink, 97–147. New York.

———. 1995b. "The Invention of Dionysus and the Platonic Midwife: Nietzsche's *Birth of Tragedy.*" *Journal of the History of Philosophy* 33, no. 3: 467–97.

———. 1998. "Unconscious Agency in Nietzsche." *Nietzsche-Studien* 27: 153–95.

———. 1999. "Nietzsche et les charmes de la métaphysique: 'La logique du sentiment.'" *Revue germanique internationale* 11 ("*Nietzsche moraliste*"): 157–72.

———. 2000. *The Invention of Dionysus: An Essay on "The Birth of Tragedy."* Stanford.

———. forthcoming. "Des sons qu'on ne peut entendre: Cicéron, les kritikoi et la tradition du sublime dans la critique littéraire." In *La Polémique entre écoles philosophiques à Rome au Ier s. av. n. è.: Cicéron et Philodème de Gadara*, edited by Clara Auvray-Assayas and Daniel Delattre (Paris).

Pöschl, Viktor. 1979. "Nietzsche und die klassische Philologie." In Flashar et al. 1979, 141–55.

Potts, Alex. 1994. *Flesh and the Ideal: Winckelmann and the Origins of Art History.* New Haven.

Preller, Ludwig. 1837. *Demeter und Persephone: Ein Cyclus mythologischer Untersuchungen.* Hamburg.

Rabinbach, Anson. 1982. "The Body without Fatigue in Nineteenth Century Utopia." In *Political Symbolism in Modern Europe: Essays in Honor of George L.*

Mosse, edited by Seymour Drescher, David Sabean, and Allan Sharlin. New Brunswick, N.J.

Rawson, Elizabeth. 1969. *The Spartan Tradition in European Thought*. Oxford.

Regenbogen, Otto. 1961. *Kleine Schriften*. Edited by Franz Dirlmeier. Munich.

Rehm, Walther. 1951. *Götterstille und Göttertrauer: Aufsätze zur deutsch-antiken Begegnung*. Munich.

Reibnitz, Barbara von. 1992. *Ein Kommentar zu Friedrich Nietzsche, "Die Geburt der Tragödie aus dem Geiste der Musik": Kap. 1–12*. Stuttgart.

Reinhardt, Karl. 1966. *Vermächtnis der Antike: Gesammelte Essays zur Philosophie und Geschichtsschreibung*. Edited by Carl Becker. 2d ed. Göttingen.

Ribbeck, Otto. 1879–81. *Friedrich Wilhelm Ritschl: Ein Beitrag zur Geschichte der Philologie*. Leipzig. 2 vols.

Ritschl, Friedrich Wilhelm. 1866–79. *Opuscula philologica*. 5 vols. Edited by Otto Ribbeck and Curt Wachsmuth. Leipzig.

Ritter, Heinrich. 1829–34. *Geschichte der Philosophie alter Zeit*. 4 vols. Hamburg.

Rodi, Frithjof. 1979. "'Erkenntnis des Erkannten': August Boeckhs Grundformel der hermeneutischen Wissenschaften." In Flashar et al. 1979, 68–83.

Römer, Ruth. 1985. *Sprachwissenschaft und Rassenideologie in Deutschland*. Munich.

Rose, Valentin. 1854. *De Aristotelis librorum ordine et auctoritate commentatio*. Berlin.

———. 1863. *Aristoteles pseudepigraphus*. Leipzig.

Rosenmeyer, Patricia. 1991. "Simonides' Danae Fragment Reconsidered." *Arethusa* 24, no. 1: 5–29.

Rosenmeyer, Thomas G. 1957. "Hesiod and Historiography (*Erga* 106–201)." *Hermes* 85: 257–85.

Rossbach, August. 1854. *Griechische Rhythmik*. Leipzig. (= vol. 1 of Rossbach and Westphal, 1854–65.)

Rossbach, A., and R. Westphal. 1854–65. *Metrik der griechischen Dramatiker und Lyriker nebst den begleitenden musischen Künsten*. 2 vols in 3. Leipzig.

———. 1867–68. *Metrik der Griechen im Vereine mit den übrigen musischen Künsten*. 2d ed. 2 vols. Vol. 1 (1867) = Westphal 1867, 2:1–323 = Westphal 1865 (rev.). Leipzig.

Said, Edward W. 1978. *Orientalism*. New York.

Salaquarda, Jörg. 1978. "Nietzsche und Lange." *Nietzsche-Studien* 7: 236–60.

———. 1979. "Der Standpunkt des Ideals bei Lange und Nietzsche." *Istituto Universitario Orientale. Annali. Studi Tedeschi* 22: 133–60.

Schadewalt, Wolfgang. 1931. "Begriff und Wesen der antiken Klassik." In Jaeger 1931, 15–32.

Schelling, Friedrich Wilhelm Joseph von. 1856–61. *Friedrich Wilhelm Joseph von Schellings Sämmtliche Werke*. 14 vols. Stuttgart.

Schelsky, Helmut. 1963. *Einsamkeit und Freiheit: Idee und Gestalt der deutschen Universität und ihrer Reformen*. Reinbek bei Hamburg.

Schiller, Friedrich. 1943– . *Schillers Werke. Nationalausgabe.* Edited by Julius Petersen, Gerhard Fricke, et al. 43 vols. Weimar.

Schlechta, Karl. 1948. *Der junge Nietzsche und das klassische Altertum.* Mainz.

Schlechta, Karl, and Anni Anders. 1962. *Friedrich Nietzsche: Von den verborgenen Anfängen seines Philosophierens.* Stuttgart.

Schlegel, Friedrich. 1958– . *Kritische Friedrich-Schlegel-Ausgabe.* Edited by Ernst Behler, with Jean-Jacques Anstett and Hans Eichner. 35 vols. Paderborn.

Schlesier, Renate. 1994. *Kulte, Mythen und Gelehrte: Anthropologie der Antike seit 1800.* Frankfurt am Main.

Schliemann, Heinrich. 1884. *Troja: Results of the Latest Researches and Discoveries on the Site of Homer's Troy . . . in the Year 1882.* New York. (Reprint, 1976.)

Schmidt, Johann Hermann Heinrich. 1868. *Die Eurhythmie in den Chorgesängen der Griechen. Allgemeine Gesetze zur Fortführung und Berichtigung der Rossbach-West- phalschen Annahmen. Text und Schemata sämmtlicher Chorika des Aeschylus. Schemata sämmtlicher Pindarischer Epinikien.* Leipzig.

Schopenhauer, Arthur. 1977. *Zürcher Ausgabe: Werke in zehn Bände.* Edited by Angelika Hubscher, Claudia Schmolders, Fritz Senn, and Gerd Haffmans. Zurich. (*Die Welt als Wille und Vorstellung* = vols. 1–4.)

———. 1989. *Sämtliche Werke.* Edited by Wolfgang Frhr. Von Löhneysen. 5 vols. Darmstadt. Rpt. of 2d ed., 1968. (*Parerga und Paralipomena: Kleine philosophische Schriften* = vols. 4 and 5.)

Sedley, David. 1976. "Epicurus and the Mathematicians of Cyzicus." *Cronache Ercolanesi* 6: 23–54.

———. 1982. "Two Conceptions of Vacuum." *Phronesis* 27: 175–93.

———. 1983. "Epicurus' Refutation of Determinism." In *SYZETESIS: Studi sull'epicureismo greco e romano offerti a Marcello Gigante,* 1:11–51. 2 vols. Naples.

———. 1988. "Epicurean Anti-reductionism." In *Matter and Metaphysics: Fourth Symposium Hellenisticum.* Edited by Jonathan Barnes and Mario Mignucci, 297–327. Naples. (= *Elenchos* 14)

Selden, Daniel L. 1990. "Classics and Contemporary Criticism." *Arion* 3d ser. 1, no. 1: 155–78.

Silk, M. S., and J. P. Stern. 1981. *Nietzsche on Tragedy.* Cambridge.

Smyth, Herbert Weir. 1900. *Greek Melic Poets.* London.

Stack, George J. 1983. *Lange and Nietzsche.* Monographien und Texte zur Nietzsche- Forschung. Vol. 10. Berlin.

Staden, Heinrich von. 1989. *Herophilus: The Art of Medicine in Early Alexandria: Edi- tion, Translation, and Essays.* Cambridge.

Stadler, Peter Bruno. 1959. *Wilhelm von Humboldts Bild der Antike.* Zürich.

Stanford, W. B. 1967. *The Sound of Greek: Studies in the Greek Theory and Practice of Euphony.* Berkeley, Calif.

Stewart, Andrew. 1997. *Art, Desire, and the Body in Ancient Greece*. Cambridge.

Stroux, Johannes. 1925. *Nietzsches Professur in Basel*. Jena.

Sweet, Paul R. 1978–80. *Wilhelm von Humboldt: A Biography*. 2 vols. Columbus, Ohio.

Timpanaro, Sebastiano. 1981. Introduction to Giorgio Pasquali, *Preistoria della poesia romana*. Florence.

Turner, R. Stephen. 1980. "The Prussian Universities and the Concept of Research." *Internationales Archiv für Sozialgeschichte der deutschen Literatur* 5: 68–93.

———. 1983. "Historicism, *Kritik*, and the Prussian Professoriate, 1790 to 1840." In *Philololgie und Hermeneutik im 19. Jahrhundert II/Philologie et herméneutique au 19ème siècle II*, edited by Mayotte Bollack, Heinz Wismann, and Theodor Lindken, 450–89. Göttingen.

Usener, Hermann, ed. 1887. *Epicurea*. Leipzig.

Vaihinger, Hans. 1911. *Die Philosophie des als ob. System der theoretischen, praktischen und religiösen Fiktionen der Menschheit auf Grund eines idealistischen Positivismus. Mit einem Anhang über Kant und Nietzsche*. Berlin.

Vernant, Jean-Pierre. 1980. *Mythe et pensée chez les Grecs: Études de psychologie historique*. 2 vols. Paris.

Vlastos, Gregory. 1945–46. "Ethics and Physics in Democritus." *Philosophical Review* 54: 578–92; 55: 53–64.

Vogt, Ernst. 1962. "Nietzsche und der Wettkampf Homers." *Antike und Abendland* 11: 103–14.

Volkmann, Richard. 1874. *Geschichte und Kritik der Wolfschen Prolegomena zu Homer: Ein Beitrag zur Geschichte der Homerischen Frage*. Leipzig.

———. 1887. *Nachträge zur Geschichte und Kritik der Wolf'schen Prolegomena zu Homer. Zweiter Teil*. Jauer.

Wachsmuth, Curt. 1904. "Briefwechsel zwischen Friedrich Ritschl und Friedrich Nietzsche." Edited by Carl Wachsmuth. *Die neue Rundschau*. 1:257–76, 474–501.

Wagner, Richard. 1871–83. *Gesammelte Schriften und Dichtungen*. 10 vols. Leipzig.

Welcker, Friedrich Gottlieb. 1826. *Theognidis reliquiae*. Frankfurt am Main.

———. 1857–63. *Griechische Götterlehre*. 3 vols. Göttingen.

West, M. L. 1982. *Greek Metre*. Oxford.

———. 1987. *Introduction to Greek Metre*. Oxford.

———. 1992. *Ancient Greek Music*. Oxford.

Westphal, Rudolf. 1861. *Die Fragmente und die Lehrsätze der griechischen Rhythmiker. Supplement zur griechischen Rhythmik von A. Rossbach*. Leipzig.

———. 1863. *Harmonik und Melopöie der Griechen*. Leipzig.

———. 1865. *Allgemeine griechische Metrik*. Leipzig. (= vol. 2.2 of Rossbach and Westphal 1864–65.)

———. 1867. *Griechische Rhythmik und Harmonik nebst der Geschichte der Drei Musischen Disciplinen*. 2d ed. 2 vols. Leipzig.

Whitman, James. 1986. "Nietzsche in the Magisterial Tradition of German Classical Philology." *Journal of the History of Ideas* 47: 453–68.

Wilamowitz-Moellendorff, Ulrich von. 1880. *Aus Kydathen: Mit einer Tafel.* In Philologische Untersuchungen, edited by Adolph Kiessling and Ulrich v. Wilamowitz-Moellendorff, vol. 1. Berlin.

———. 1886. *Isyllos von Epidaurus.* Philologische Untersuchungen, vol. 9. Berlin.

———. 1891. *Euripides, Hippolytus: Griechisch und Deutsch.* Berlin.

———. 1895. *Euripides, Herakles.* 2d ed. 2 vols. Berlin.

———. 1913a. *Sappho und Simonides: Untersuchungen über griechische Lyriker.* Berlin.

———. 1913b. *Reden und Vorträge.* 3d ed. Berlin.

———. 1921. *Geschichte der Philologie.* (= *Einleitung in die Altertumswissenschaft*, 3d ed. Vol. 1, 1927.) Leipzig.

———. 1925–26. *Reden und Vorträge.* 4th ed. 2 vols. Berlin.

———. 1929 [1st ed., 1928]. *Erinnerungen, 1848–1914.* 2d ed. Leipzig.

———. 1962–71. *Kleine Schriften.* 5 vols. in 6. Berlin.

Will, Edouard. 1956. *Doriens et Ioniens. Essai sur la valeur du critère ethnique appliqué à l'étude de l'histoire et de la civilisation grecques.* Paris.

Winckelmann, J. J. *Werke.* 1847. 2 vols. Stuttgart.

———. 1972. *Geschichte der Kunst des Altertums.* Darmstadt. (Rpt. of 1934 Phaidon ed. [Vienna].)

———. 1985 [1755]. "Thoughts on the Imitation of the Painting and Sculpture of the Greeks." In Nisbet 1985, 32–54.

———. 1995. "Apollo-Beschreibungen." In Pfotenhauer et al. 1995, 149–66.

Wismann, Heinz. 1973. "Nietzsche et la philologie." In *Nietzsche aujourd'hui?* 2:325–44. Paris.

———. 1979. "*Atomos Idea.*" *Neue Hefte für Philosophie* 15/16: 34–52.

Wolf, Friedrich August. 1794–95. *Homeri et Homeridarum opera et reliquiae: Ex veterum criticorum notationibus optimorumque exemplarium fide recensuit Frid. Aug. Wolfius.* 4 vols. in 3. Halle.

———. 1795. *Prolegomena ad Homerum, sive, De operum Homericorum prisca et genuina forma variisque mutationibus et probabili ratione emendandi.* Vol. 1. Halle. [= Wolf 1794–95, vol. 1].

———. 1831a. *Friedrich August Wolf's Encyclopädie der Philologie. Nach dessen Vorlesungen im Winterhalbjahre von 1798–1799.* Edited by S. M. Stockmann. Leipzig.

———. 1831b. *Friedrich August Wolfs Vorlesung über die Encyclopädie der Alterthumswissenschaft.* Edited by J. D. Gürtler. Leipzig. (= vol. 1 of *Fr. Aug. Wolfs Vorlesungen über der Alterthumswissenschaft.* 5 vols. Edited by J. D. Gürtler. Leipzig, 1831–1835.)

———. 1835. *Fr. Aug. Wolf über Erziehung, Schule, Universität ("Consilia Scholastica").* Edited by Wilhelm Körte. Quedlinburg.

———. 1869. *Kleine Schriften in lateinischer und deutscher Sprache.* 2 vols. Edited by G. Bernhardy. Halle.

————. 1884. *Prolegomena ad Homerum, sive, De operum Homericorum prisca et genuina forma variisque mutationibus et probabili ratione emendandi.* Vol. 1. 3d. ed. Edited by Rudolf Peppmüller. Halle. (Reprint, Hildesheim, 1963.)

————. 1985. *Prolegomena to Homer. 1795.* Translated by Anthony Grafton, Glenn W. Most, and James E. G. Zetzel. Princeton, N.J.

Zeller, Eduard. 1856–68 [1st ed. 1844–52]. *Die Philosophie der Griechen in ihrer geschichtlichen Entwicklung.* 2d ed. 3 vols. in 5. Tübingen.

Zeller, Hans. 1955. *Winckelmanns Beschreibung des Apollo im Belvedere.* Zurich.

Ziolkowski, Jan, ed. 1990. *On Philology.* University Park, Tex. (= *Comparative Literature Studies* 27, no. 1 [1990].)

Žižek, Slavoj. 1989. *The Sublime Object of Ideology.* London.

————. 1997. *The Plague of Fantasies.* London.

————. 1999. *The Ticklish Subject: The Absent Centre of Political Ontology.* London.

Zuckerman, Elliott. 1974. "Nietzsche and Music: *The Birth of Tragedy* and *Nietzsche Contra Wagner.*" *Symposium* 28, no. 1 (spring): 17–30.

Index